"It's a very good book, a great read."—*Dallas Morning News*

"By mixing enjoyable gossip about the stars' personal lives and behind-the-scenes maneuverings with a shrewd look at the film world's often unsavory industrial underpinnings, Friedrich gives us a much clearer understanding of Hollywood's reciprocal relationships with American reality.... The book's title is apt: with its tough humor, profound cynicism and unerring nose for corruption and hypocrisy, *City of Nets* offers a distinctly Brechtian vision of Hollywood."
—Wendy Smith, *Village Voice*

"Chockablock with wonderful Hollywood anecdotes...Friedrich relishes the irony of encounters between men of genius and the vulgar chiefs of the movie business."—*Washington Post Book World*

"Intelligent, superbly written and thoroughly enjoyable."
—*Kirkus Reviews*

"Rambles through its 10 years scattering the best and the juiciest anecdotes...the ride is fun and the driver is a smart guy with a sense of humor."—*Wall Street Journal*

"Superlative...this requiem for a florid city swathed in greed and perpetual heat."—*Boston Herald*

"The mythology of Hollywood is just as important as the essential history, but we rarely encounter both in the same volume. Otto Friedrich's compelling book is rich with legends as well as crucial information....enormously enlightening."—Nora Sayre

CITY
OF NETS

A Portrait of Hollywood in the 1940's

OTTO FRIEDRICH

PERENNIAL LIBRARY

Harper & Row, Publishers, New York
Cambridge, Philadelphia, San Francisco, Washington
London, Mexico City, São Paulo, Singapore, Sydney

Photo Credits

Facing page 1, Nathanael West, Bettmann Archive. Atlanta ablaze, New York Public Library Picture Collection./page 30, Rubinstein performing, Culver Pictures Inc. Walt Disney's *Fantasia,* Culver Pictures Inc. Stokowski conducting, Gjon Mili, *Life* Magazine © 1948 Time Inc./page 60, Willie Bioff, UPI/Bettmann Newsphotos./page 104, Bob Hope, Wide World. Hedy Lamarr, Culver Pictures Inc./page 140, Errol Flynn and Betty Hansen, Wide World. Rita Hayworth, New York Public Library Picture Collection. Margarita Cansino, Culver Pictures Inc. Anti-Mexican rioting, Julian Robinson, *Los Angeles Times,* Courtesy of Life Picture Service./page 176, Boris Karloff as Frankenstein, Wide World. Charlie Chaplin and Oona O'Neill, Bettmann Archive. Chaplin on trial, Wide World./page 214, Herbert K. Sorrell, UPI/Bettmann Newsphotos. Leftist strike, Culver Pictures Inc. Bogart and Bacall, Wide World./page 256, Bugsy Siegel, Wide World. Bugsy Siegel and George Raft, Brown Bros./page 290, Dalton Trumbo, UPI/Bettmann Newsphotos. Bertolt Brecht, UPI/Bettmann Newsphotos. Jack Warner and J. Parnell Thomas, Martha Holmes, *Life* Magazine, © 1947 Time Inc./page 338, Louis B. Mayer and Lorena Danker, UPI/Bettmann Newsphotos./page 374, Bob Mitchum, Wide World Ingrid Bergman in *Bells of St. Mary's,* Culver Pictures Inc. Ingrid Bergman in *Stromboli,* Culver Pictures Inc./page 414, Gloria Swanson, Culver Pictures Inc.

Grateful acknowledgment is made for permission to reprint:

Excerpts from *Ingrid Bergman: My Story* by Ingrid Bergman and Alan Burgess. Copyright © 1980 by Ingrid Bergman and Alan Burgess. Reprinted by permission of Delacorte Press and International Creative Management, Inc.

Quotes from *Front and Center* by John Houseman. Copyright © 1979 by John Houseman. Reprinted by permission of Simon & Schuster, Inc.

Quotes from Bertolt Brecht's poems from *Bertolt Brecht Poems 1913–1956.* Copyright © 1976 by Eyre Methuen Ltd. Reprinted by permission of the publisher, Methuen, Inc. by arrangement with Suhrkamp Verlag, Frankfurt. All rights reserved.

First PERENNIAL LIBRARY edition published 1987.

Designer: C. Linda Dingler
Copy editor: Marjorie Horvitz
Index by Olive Holmes for Edindex

Library of Congress Cataloging-in-Publication Data

Friedrich, Otto, 1929–
   City of nets : a portrait of Hollywood in the 1940's.

   "Perennial Library."
   Bibliography: p.
   Includes index.
   1. Hollywood (Los Angeles, Calif.)—Social life and customs. 2. Hollywood (Los Angeles, Calif.)—History. 3. Los Angeles (Calif.)—Social life and customs. 4. Los Angeles (Calif.)—History. I. Title.
F869.H74F75   1987   979.4'94   86-45098
ISBN 0-06-091439-4 (pbk.)

87 88 89 90 91 MPC 10 9 8 7 6 5 4 3 2 1

To Liesel and Molly

People of the same trade seldom meet together, even for merriment and diversion, but the conversation ends in a conspiracy against the public. . . .
—ADAM SMITH

Every morning, to earn my bread,
I go to the market where lies are bought.
Hopefully
I take up my place among the sellers.
—BERTOLT BRECHT

It is not unusual in human beings who have witnessed the sack of a city or the falling to pieces of a people to desire to set down what they have witnessed for the benefit of unknown heirs or of generations infinitely remote; or, if you please, just to get the sight out of their heads. Someone has said that the death of a mouse from cancer is the whole sack of Rome by the Goths.
—FORD MADOX FORD

CONTENTS

A page of photographs introduces each chapter

FOREWORD

In 1939, the year of *Gone With the Wind*, of *Ninotchka*, of *Wuthering Heights* and *The Wizard of Oz*, the leading moviemakers of Hollywood could with some justification regard themselves as conquering heroes. The assorted film studios, which really produced nothing but a series of flickering images, had by now become the nation's eleventh-largest industry. They created some four hundred new movies every year, attracted more than fifty million Americans to the theater every week, and grossed nearly $700 million annually. Just a decade later, Hollywood was in a shambles, its biggest studios losing money, its celebrities embroiled in charges of Communist influence, its audiences turning to television. And a community that had once taken in newcomers as diverse as William Faulkner, Alfred Hitchcock, and Thomas Mann now drove away anyone who disturbed its conventions or aroused its fears—away with Charlie Chaplin, Ingrid Bergman, Orson Welles.

This is the story, then, of a great empire built out of dreams of glamour, dreams of beauty, wealth, and success, and of that empire's sudden decline and fall. It is a social and cultural history of Hollywood during the decade of upheaval from the start of World War II to the start of the Korean War. Some marvelous movies were created during these years: *Citizen Kane*, for example, *The Maltese Falcon*, *Double Indemnity*, *All About Eve*. And not only movies; Mann's *Doctor Faustus* was written here, and so was Brecht's *Galileo*, Stravinsky's *Rake's Progress*. And then, scarcely ten years after David Selznick had triumphantly opened *Gone With the Wind*, he was walking along a deserted street at dawn and saying to a companion, "Hollywood's like Egypt. Full of crumbling pyramids. It'll never come back. It'll just keep on crumbling until finally the wind blows the last studio prop across the sands."

Hollywood has survived, of course, but everything has changed since the decay of the great studios. Filmmaking is taught in universities now, and the white-haired survivors of the golden age are cajoled into telling their stories to young interviewers with tape recorders. Is this book then just another exercise in nostalgia? No, I would like to try something quite different, starting with an unorthodox new rule: No more interviews. Surely there is no one of any importance in Hollywood, dead or alive, who has not been interrogated over and over again. And in no other field of history, not in Hitler's Berlin or in Roosevelt's Washington, have so many interviews grown into so many ghost-

written autobiographies. These works include not only major figures like
Chaplin or DeMille but even such ephemeral talents as Jackie Cooper and
Veronica Lake. In other cases—Barbara Leaming's *Orson Welles,* for example,
or Mel Gussow's life of Darryl F. Zanuck—a favored biographer has been
granted such extensive interviews that the result is just as authoritative, for
better or for worse, as an autobiography. All in all, just about everybody has
spoken.

What is needed now, I think, is not more tape-recorded interrogations
but rather a new effort to synthesize what has already been said, to combine,
to interpret, to analyze, to understand. I have read about five hundred books
on Hollywood, ranging from scholarly studies of the Holocaust in films to
exhaustive analyses of Raymond Chandler's screenplays to the lubricious
memoirs of Hedy Lamarr, which she has formally denied writing, dictating,
or confessing. The most remarkable aspect of all these books is how isolated
from one another they all are.

Survivors of the 1940's freely recall that Paramount writers generally
talked only to other Paramount writers, and that a $500-per-week writer
would not be welcome at a party given by a $1,500-per-week writer. As this
self-segregation of the 1940's becomes ossified in the memoirs of the 1970's
and 1980's, it seems astonishing that Billy Wilder, say, and Igor Stravinsky—
and, yes, the future President Ronald Reagan—were hardly aware of each
other's existence. "The only way to avoid Hollywood," Stravinsky once remarked, "is to live there."

Hollywood really is an imaginary city that exists in the mind of anyone
who has, in his mind, lived there. My Hollywood is different from your
Hollywood, just as it is different from Rex Reed's Hollywood or Aljean Harmetz's Hollywood, not because they know more about Hollywood than you or
I do but because they are different from us, just as we are different from each
other.

We are different in time, for one thing. I lived in the Hollywood of the
1940's when I was a student outside Boston and went to the movies two or
three times a week. I loved Ingrid Bergman above all others, but I also loved
such half-forgotten people as Betty Hutton and Ida Lupino, even Diana Lynn.
I know and care much less about the 1950's and 1960's because I spent those
years raising five children, too poor to go to movies.

No matter when one lives in Hollywood, one brings one's own mental
furniture along. In the 1940's, I cared passionately about sports. That's why
tears came to my eyes at the death of Ronald Reagan as George Gipp. The war
was very important too, and so was Hollywood's version of it—Robert Taylor
defending Bataan, Humphrey Bogart steaming across the North Atlantic,
Errol Flynn conquering Burma, all that. Like Reagan himself, I still feel a
tightening of the throat at seeing the death of the Gipper, but I really don't
care very much about football any more, and I dislike military heroics.

So the Hollywood that I have been inhabiting once again for the last few
years is not only different from anyone else's Hollywood but different even

from the Hollywood that I myself inhabited when I was young. Bertolt Brecht, whom I had never heard of when I admired George Gipp, now seems a far more interesting character than many big stars like, say, Cary Grant or Betty Grable. So Brecht plays a fairly large part in my re-creation of Hollywood in the 1940's, while Grant and Miss Grable play almost none. It is astonishing to me, in fact, how a book of this large size could leave out so much about so many celebrities. There is very little here about Jimmy Stewart, for example, or Tyrone Power, or Spencer Tracy. These are all commendable people, but I find that actors seem to me less interesting than writers, gangsters, musicians, tycoons, and sex goddesses. And since Hollywood produced about five thousand movies during the 1940's, one can pick and choose what to write about. Indeed, one must.

There remains a basic question about the mountain of Hollywood's reminiscences: Are they true? Well, perhaps partly true. Remember that Hollywood people lived and still live in a world of fantasy, and they are accustomed to making things up, to fibbing and exaggerating, and to believing all their own fibs and exaggerations. Remember, too, that they all had press agents who made things up, and that fan-magazine writers made things up, and that ghostwriters still make things up, and that the celebrities who sign these concoctions no longer remember very well what really happened long ago. In a few cases, I have offered several contradictory versions of some much-told tale. If the late Jack Warner and the late Darryl Zanuck both claimed to be the one who found William Faulkner working at home in Mississippi rather than at home in Beverly Hills, for example, who am I to decide which one was right? And if all this is true of the printed word, must it not be equally true of the improvised interview?

But if all the details in this book have already been published somewhere or other, then what is new in this portrait of Hollywood in the 1940's? Why, the portrait itself. If you already know a lot about Rita Hayworth, you may not know a great deal about Arnold Schoenberg, or vice versa, and if you know a lot about both of them, you may not know a great deal about Bugsy Siegel, or the aircraft industry, or Herbert K. Sorrell. And even if you know a lot about President Reagan, you may not know a great deal about how he got to be what he is today. Or how, in many ways, we ourselves got to be what we are. This is a portrait of a special place in a special time—an imaginary city, as I have suggested—and yet it was the dream factory of the 1940's that created much of what Americans today regard as reality.

CITY OF NETS

Fire: Nathanael West (*right*) imagined a painted "Burning of Los Angeles." David Selznick set Atlanta ablaze in *Gone With the Wind*.

I

WELCOME

(1939)

To THE CHAMBER OF HORRORS, says the sign. The arrow points off toward the right, where a corridor of darkness leads to the glowing irons of the Inquisition, but what the arrow actually announces is a nearby tableau entitled "The Great Presidents."* George Washington stands proudly aloof in his Continental blue uniform, Lincoln sits reflective, and the others display various attitudes of official interest. Teddy Roosevelt, McKinley, Truman, Eisenhower, Kennedy, Hoover, Coolidge—the creators of the Hollywood Waxworks Museum have odd ideas about which Presidents are great. Franklin Delano Roosevelt is not here, but a special spotlight on the right bathes Richard Nixon in a sepulchral glow. He looks embalmed.

In the foreground, at the center of this presidential assembly, propped up at a speaker's rostrum ornamented with the White House seal, stands the exemplar of Hollywood and of all southern California, the winsome cowboy with the rueful grin. Ronald Reagan's waxen face (waxworks nowadays are actually made of noninflammable vinyl plastisol) wears an expression of amiable bewilderment. He has been outfitted in a dark blue suit, a white shirt with a collar that looks somewhat too large for him, and a rather muddy striped tie. Life may seem difficult, but the plastic Ronald Reagan stands monumental behind the presidential seal, staring bravely out into the darkness.

"Welcome to Madame Tussaud's Hollywood Wax Museum," says the recorded voice across the aisle, emerging from a murky tableau of Queen Victoria and Madame Tussaud herself. Since this is Hollywood, though, the nearby corridor is lined with niches devoted to the movie industry's official gods and goddesses. Here is Tyrone Power, as the young matador in *Blood and Sand,* about to stab an onrushing bull. Here is Clark Gable in evening dress, looking knowingly at Carole Lombard, and Charlie Chaplin in the ruins of a tuxedo, looking imploringly at Mary Pickford, and Rudolph Valentino in the robes of *The Sheik,* looking soulfully into thin air. The image of the desert seems to inspire in southern California a sense partly of recognition and partly of yearning. Here is a luscious mannequin of Hedy Lamarr as Tondelayo in

---

* The sources for all facts and quotations in this book may be found at the end, in the Notes section.

White Cargo, lolling in a tent on an implausible white fur rug. She wears a pink orchid over one ear and several strings of brown wooden beads around her neck, and then nothing else down to her flowery pink skirt.

No city west of Boston has a more intensely commercial sense of its own past, and yet that sense keeps becoming blurred and distorted in Hollywood. Not only do the decades vaguely intermingle, so that Harold Lloyd dissolves into the young Woody Allen, but the various forms of entertainment also merge. Any pilgrim arriving in the movie capital is shown the newest shrines of television and rock music, as though they were all the same. The Hollywood Waxworks Museum understands. Just beyond the rather feral figure of the young Shirley Temple, in white lace, the visitor confronts "An Evening with Elvis Presley." In the half-darkness, the strains of "Hello, Dolly" fade into those of "Love Me Tender," and the king of country singers can be observed entertaining Dean Martin, Farrah Fawcett, Flip Wilson, Sammy Davis, Frank Sinatra, and Elizabeth Taylor. Behind this incongruous gathering stands a mysterious row of six costumed footmen, all in eighteenth-century wigs, all holding up candelabra to illuminate Presley's *soirée.*

The waxworks commentary on Hollywood seems at times to go beyond the frontiers of incongruity into the realms of chaos. It is possible to smile at the juxtaposition of Charlton Heston bearing the sacred tablets down from Sinai and a panoramic re-creation of Da Vinci's *Last Supper,* but why is Anthony Quinn standing next to Charles de Gaulle? And why, in this central group, which is dominated by the Beatles but also includes Sophia Loren, Amelia Earhart, and Thomas Alva Edison—why should the figure between Paul McCartney and Jeanette MacDonald be that of Joseph Stalin? One reason may be that there used to be a tableau of the Allied leaders at Yalta, created perhaps for some other waxworks museum somewhere else, and then, according to the portly Mexican who takes tickets at the door, there was a fire here a few years ago, and things have been moved around a bit. Things are always being moved around a bit in Hollywood. "False fronts!" Nicholas Schenck once cried during a guided tour of the outdoor sets at Metro-Gold-wyn-Mayer, which Schenck, as president of Loew's, Inc., theoretically ruled, owned, commanded. "False fronts! Nothing behind them. They are like Hollywood people."

Outside the waxworks museum, which sprouts between Jack's Pipe Shop and the Snow White Coffee Shop, the California sun beats down on the peculiar black sidewalks of Hollywood Boulevard. Relentless sun, the image of fire and destruction. The sidewalks are not entirely black, for the local authorities have embedded in every other panel a gold-edged metal star filled with crushed pink stone. Within each star, they have inscribed one golden name. There are no explanations or definitions of these multitudinous names (more than 1,775 in all). Since they are all here, they must all be famous. As one strolls westward along Hollywood Boulevard, one treads on a remarkably diverse cast of characters: Charles Chaplin, Ken Maynard, Ilka Chase, Richard Barthelmess, Joseph Schenck, Lee Strasberg, Ingrid Bergman, Red Skelton, Robert Merrill, Eddie Cantor, Marie Wilson, Bing Crosby, Milton Berle, Vivien Leigh, Ray Charles, Elvis Presley, Kirsten Flagstad, Bessie Love, Jascha Heifetz, Judy Canova. . . .

The black sidewalks of Hollywood Boulevard lead eventually to Grauman's Chinese Theater, a large pagoda with a scarlet roof supported by prancing dragons. Next to the entrance stand two fierce beasts, about seven feet high, which Grauman's alleges to be "heaven dogs" of the Ming dynasty. "Half lion and half dog these sacred sentinels stood guard for many centuries at a Ming tomb in China," the sign says. "These massive monsters surnamed the dogs of Foo or Buddha combined leonine ferocity with dog-like devotion and served to terrify the transgressors and inspire the righteous." Officially, this strange palace is now Mann's Chinese Theaters, for an entrepreneur named Teddy Mann bought the establishment in the late 1970's and opened two adjoining theaters in the wings that flank the central courtyard; but to the flocks of tourists who come to marvel, Grauman's remains Grauman's. The tourists gather here to gape at the famous footprints and handprints embedded in the concrete panels of Grauman's courtyard.

> To Sid Grauman   Thanks   Rita Hayworth
> To Sid   A great guy   Henry Fonda   July 2 '42
> To Sid   My greatest thrill   Jeanne Crain   October 7 1949
> To Sid   His fan   Charles Boyer   July 24 '42
> To Sid   Sincere thanks   Gene Tierney   June 24 '46
> Thank you Sid   Jimmy Stewart   Fri. 13 Feb. 1948
> For Mr. Grauman   All happiness   Judy Garland   10-10-39

A showman is what the yellowing newspaper clippings call people like Sid Grauman. Born in Indianapolis, he got his start by selling San Francisco newspapers for one dollar each in remote Alaskan mining camps during the Klondike gold rush of 1896, and yet he attributed his theatrical successes to "the big boss upstairs." "God does my shows," he said.

Grauman brought luxury to the showing of movies. He spent a million dollars to build the Metropolitan Theater in Los Angeles, but that was modest compared to his Egyptian Theater, which opened in 1922 with live tableaux dramatizing the coming attractions. It was here that Grauman invented the "Hollywood premiere," with spotlights sweeping the skies, and eager crowds assembled behind tasseled ropes to watch the stars arriving in their limousines.

Grauman loved practical jokes, and many of them seemed to involve wax dummies. He once filled his dimly lighted room at the Ambassador Hotel with seventy-five mannequins, then persuaded Marcus Loew, the original Loew of Loew's, Inc., that these were fellow theater-owners whom he had assembled to hear an authoritative account of M-G-M's forthcoming features. Loew apparently improvised an impassioned spiel for the seventy-five attentive dummies. On another occasion, Grauman telephoned **Charlie Chaplin and** said he

had found a murdered woman in his hotel room. He begged Chaplin to help
him. Chaplin hurried to the Ambassador and found Grauman crouched over
a bloodstained figure in his bed. Grauman pleaded for help in avoiding a
scandal. Chaplin nervously insisted that the police must be called. Grauman
finally brought Chaplin closer, to see the ketchup smeared on the dummy in
the bed. Grauman's obituary in *Variety* a generation later did not record Chaplin's reaction, but it did say that "among his intimate friends, he was known
as a great gagger." Grauman died of heart failure in the spring of 1950, died a
bachelor, aged seventy-one, and the only people at his deathbed were his
doctor, his secretary for the past twenty-one years, and the publicity chief of
20th Century–Fox.

Long before Grauman or Mary Pickford or the Gish sisters came to live
here, there were mostly barley fields and orange groves. An Ohioan named
Horace Henderson Wilcox, who had been lamed by typhoid fever in childhood
but made a fortune in Kansas real estate, began hopefully mapping out ave-
nues and boulevards through these barley fields in 1887. His homesick wife,
Daeida, named the prospective settlement after the country place of some
friends back in the east: Hollywood. The Wilcoxes were pious. They forbade
any saloons in Hollywood; they offered free land to any church built in their
barley fields.

Oil was discovered in 1892 near Glendale Boulevard, just a few miles to
the south, but Hollywood remained an obscure rural tract until it was bought
in 1903 by a syndicate headed by General Moses Hazeltine Sherman, who had
made millions in railroads, and Harry Chandler, the future publisher of the
Los Angeles Times. This syndicate managed to get the vacant fields incorporated as an independent municipality. It built a rickety trolley line to the
south and called it the Los Angeles–Pacific Railroad, erected the thirty-three-
room, Spanish-style Hollywood Hotel on unpaved Hollywood Boulevard, and
started a campaign to sell building lots by posting hundreds of signs that said
SOLD. Was this the first Hollywood lie? The original deception? The Hollywood town authorities tried to maintain the Wilcoxes' moral tone. Various
edicts by the board of trustees in the early 1900's forbade all sales of liquor,
all bowling or billiards on Sundays, and the driving of herds of more than two
thousand sheep, goats, or hogs through the streets.

Back east, winter storms over the Great Lakes inspired the Selig Studio
of Chicago to abandon its filming of *The Count of Monte Cristo,* and to send
the star, Francis Boggs, off to California in search of a sunnier location. Boggs
found it at Laguna Beach, well to the south of Los Angeles, and finished the
filming there in 1907. Indeed, he found the climate so pleasant that he
returned to Los Angeles the following winter and converted a Chinese laundry
at Eighth and Olive streets into California's first movie studio. The first
complete film shot there was called *In the Sultan's Power.*

Other fledgling filmmakers soon followed, not to stodgy Hollywood but to
Edendale, a few miles to the east, or to the beach at Santa Monica. It was all
rather pristine and primeval. Cops and robbers chased each other through the

streets, and directors improvised their stories as they went along (one of them, Charles K. French, shot 185 films for the Bison Company in a little more than eight months). The official histories explain this first flowering as a happy combination of sunshine, open spaces, and diverse settings: the Sahara, the Alps, and the South Seas could all be simulated within Los Angeles' city limits. And the sun kept shining, all year round.

Many of these pioneers had another good reason for moving west—to escape the law. The moving-picture process had not invented itself, after all. It originated, more or less, in a whimsical wager by Leland Stanford, the railroad tycoon, who in 1872 bet $25,000 that a galloping horse lifted all four feet off the ground at once. Stanford then hired the photographer Eadweard Muybridge to prove him right. Muybridge did so by installing a series of twelve cameras next to a racetrack and filming a classic sequence of a horse in full gallop. In the course of winning Stanford's bet, Muybridge almost invented the movies.

That, however, was left to the restless mind of Thomas Alva Edison, who devised a method of filming movement not with Muybridge's row of cameras but with one camera that could take a series of pictures on fifty feet of continuously running film. Edison, for reasons of his own, photographed a laboratory assistant named Fred Ott in the process of sneezing, and then showed this sequence of moving pictures inside a cabinet called a Kinetoscope. It was one of the big hits of the Chicago World's Fair of 1893. Other inventors were working along similar lines. In France, the Lumière brothers demonstrated in 1895 that a series of pictures of a railroad train puffing its way out of a station could be projected onto a large screen at a rate of sixteen frames per second. Interesting, if enough people wanted to see a train puffing its way out of a station. Or, for that matter, Fred Ott sneezing.

In 1903, an Edison Company cameraman named Edwin S. Porter created a completely different kind of motion picture. Instead of simply filming an event, he created events to be filmed. *The Life of an American Fireman* recorded the rescue of a woman and her child from a burning building. *The Great Train Robbery* recorded exactly what its title promised. These dramas could be shown on sheets hung up in empty stores, and thousands of people were willing to pay a nickel to see them. They were especially popular among immigrants who knew little English. Edison tried to preserve his control over this lucrative process by creating the Motion Pictures Patents Company in 1909, and then licensing others to exploit his discoveries.

Little did he know the ingenuity of the founders of Hollywood. The "Trust," as Edison's company came to be known, kept filing lawsuits in New York against all would-be pirates, but who could track down and enjoin all the violators of New York court orders in obscure suburbs of Los Angeles? Movies could be shot in a few days, and production companies could be dissolved and recreated almost as quickly. "The whole industry . . . is built on phony accounting," David O. Selznick once remarked. And if every other evasion failed, the Mexican border was only about a hundred miles away.

Years before Bertolt Brecht ever came to Hollywood, he had something like this in mind when he wrote the opening of *The Rise and Fall of the City of Mahagonny*. Somewhere in an America of Brecht's own imagining, a battered truck carrying three fugitives from justice broke down and sputtered to a halt "in a desolate region." "We can't go on," said Fatty, the bookkeeper. "But we've got to keep going," said Trinity Moses. "But ahead of us is only the desert," said Fatty. "You know, gold is being discovered up the coast," said Moses. "But that coastline is a long one," said Fatty. "Very well, if we can't go farther up, we'll stay down here . . ." said the Widow Begbick. "Let us found a city here and call it 'Mahagonny,' which means 'city of nets.' "

> It should be like a net,
> Stretched out for edible birds.
> Everywhere there is toil and trouble
> But here we'll have fun. . . .
> Gin and whiskey,
> Girls and boys. . . .
> And the big typhoons don't come as far as here.

If Brecht's vision of an unknown future was prophetic, so was that of the Hollywood Board of Trustees. In 1910, it officially banned all movie theaters, of which it then had none. That same year, however, the town of Hollywood was jurisdictionally swallowed up by Los Angeles, which saw no particular virtue in restricting the newcomers' enterprises.

•   •   •

Thornton Wilder, ordinarily a friendly soul with a rather jaunty manner, was going out to dinner with some old friends in Hollywood one evening when he suddenly began to describe a vision of utter devastation. "You know, one day someone is going to approach this area and it will be entirely desert," the playwright told his friends, Helen Hayes and her husband, Charles Mac-Arthur. "There will be nothing left standing, stone upon stone. . . . God never meant man to live here. Man has come and invaded a desert, and he has tortured this desert into giving up sustenance and growth to him, and he has defeated and perverted the purpose of God. And this is going to be destroyed."

The prospect of cataclysm is one of Los Angeles' oldest traditions. The threat lies in the earth itself, in the sweet-smelling tar that still oozes up out of the La Brea pits, the hungry graveyard for generations of goats and deer, and also the saber-toothed tigers that pursued them to their death. The skeletons of a hundred lions have been unearthed here, and more than fifteen hundred wolves, and one human being, a woman who is believed to have been twenty-five or thirty years old when her skull was mysteriously smashed in about nine thousand years ago.

The first Spanish explorers, led by Don Gaspar de Portolá, riding westward in the summer of 1769 along what is now Wilshire Boulevard, took awed note of "some large marshes of a certain substance like pitch . . . boiling and bubbling," and wondered whether that hellish swamp was the cause or the consequence of the half-dozen earthquakes that had shaken the area during the previous two days. Don Gaspar rode on, and another two years passed before Franciscan missionaries returned to found the San Gabriel Mission, and then, a decade later, El Pueblo de Nuestra Señora la Reina de los Angeles de Porciuncula, the Town of the Queen of Angels.

The city that now numbers more than ten million inhabitants is built atop the San Andreas fault, and when one of the eight-lane freeways cracks open, the traffic simply streams on. Earthquakes are commonplace, and so are the landslides that carry $500,000 hillside homes crashing down into Topanga or Mandeville canyon. But if the trembling and splitting of the insubstantial earth seems fundamental to southern California's half-suppressed sense of fear, there is something even more primal in the sense of desert, aridity, desiccation, burning heat, and hence fire. The very life of the city derives from a thin vein of water, built with vast expense and corruption across the desert from the Rockies. And in the mountains that surround Los Angeles, every autumn brings drought and fire. In 1961, the brushfires blazed out of control and destroyed 460 homes, then worth more than $25 million, in the Bel Air region; in 1976, nearly 168,000 acres throughout the state went up in smoke; in 1978, another 200 homes were destroyed near Malibu. In November of 1980, winds of up to 100 miles an hour drove fires all across the hillsides, fire in Carbon Canyon, fire around Lake Elsinore, fire in Bradbury, near Duarte, fire in Sunland, in the Verdugo Hills. In the streets of downtown Los Angeles, people could smell the odor of charred chaparral and scrub oak and sumac. In the summer of 1983, fire even swept through the Paramount Studios and destroyed the half-century-old "New York Street" set that had provided scenes for *Going My Way* and *Chinatown* and, of all things, *The Day of the Locust*.

The droning voices on the car radio brought constant reports of fire in the mountains as Maria Wyeth sped aimlessly along the freeways in Joan Didion's *Play It as It Lays*. The news was both a sign of larger disaster and a sign of nothing at all. "The day's slide and flood news was followed by a report of a small earth tremor centered near Joshua Tree . . ." Maria noted as she sat in a rented room, preparing herself for divorce and abortion, "and, of corollary interest, an interview with a Pentecostal minister who had received prophecy that eight million people would perish by earthquake on a Friday afternoon in March."

Miss Didion ascribed both the fires and the hysteria partly to the Santa Ana, a hot wind that comes whistling down from the northeast, "blowing up sandstorms out along Route 66, drying the hills and the nerves to the flash point." The Santa Ana brings dread and violence, she wrote in *Slouching Towards Bethlehem*, because "the city burning is Los Angeles' deepest image of itself. . . . At the time of the 1965 Watts riots what struck the imagination most indelibly were the fires. For days one could drive the Harbor Freeway and see the city on fire, just as we had always known it would be in the end. Los Angeles weather is the weather of catastrophe, of apocalypse. . . ."

Nathanael West had seen the same prophecy in fire. Tod Hackett, the central character in *The Day of the Locust,* kept planning and sketching an epic painting to be entitled "The Burning of Los Angeles." "He was going to show the city burning at high noon, so that the flames would have to compete with the desert sun and thereby appear less fearful, more like bright flags flying from roofs and windows than a terrible holocaust. He wanted the city to have quite a gala air as it burned, to appear almost gay. And the people who set it on fire would be a holiday crowd."

West was thirty-five, scarcely more than a year from his absurd death in an automobile crash, when *The Day of the Locust* burst forth and then disappeared in the spring of 1939. He had hoped that its success would free him from the drudgery of Hollywood scriptwriting, but despite the praises of Scott Fitzgerald, Edmund Wilson, and Dashiell Hammett, the novel sold exactly 1,464 copies. That brought West's earnings from four novels over the course of nearly a decade to a total of $1,280, less than a month's pay at his weekly rate of $350 at RKO, which promptly put him back to work writing a remake of *Tom Brown at Culver.* "Thank God for the movies," West wrote to Bennett Cerf, publisher of *The Day of the Locust.*

Like most writers of his time, West was familiar with failure and financial ruin. His father, a somewhat diffident building contractor, sank into bankruptcy during the late 1920's while West was in Paris savoring the pungencies of the surrealists. Back in New York, West could support himself only by working as a night clerk in a hotel partly owned by relatives. That was hardly the role in which he had imagined himself. Born Nathan Weinstein, the young West had repeatedly experimented with new identities, acquired the nicknames "Pep" and "Trapper." He forged a high school transcript to enter Tufts, transferred to Brown with the transcript of a different Nathan Weinstein, then began signing himself Nathan von Wallenstein Weinstein. "He loved custom-tailored clothes . . . first editions and expensive restaurants," his college friend and future brother-in-law S. J. Perelman wrote in *The Last Laugh.* "He fancied himself a Nimrod and fisherman, largely, I often suspected, because of the colorful gear they entailed. . . . For a brief interval, he even owned a red Stutz Bearcat, until it burst into flames and foundered in a West Virginia gorge."

Perelman, who first went to Hollywood to write the scripts for the Marx Brothers' *Monkey Business* and *Horse Feathers,* described the movie capital as "a dreary industrial town controlled by hoodlums of enormous wealth," but he was capable of making marvelous fun of it. "The violet hush of twilight was descending over Los Angeles as my hostess, Violet Hush, and I . . . headed toward Hollywood," he wrote in *Strictly from Hunger.* "In the distance a glow from huge piles of burning motion-picture scripts lit up the sky. The crisp tang of frying writers and directors whetted my appetite. How good it was to be alive. . . ." West's description was more bleak. "This place is just like Asbury Park, New Jersey," he wrote to Josephine Herbst. "The same stucco houses, women in pajamas, delicatessen stores, etc. There is nothing to do except tennis, golf or the movies. . . . All the writers sit in cells in a row and the minute a typewriter stops someone pokes his head in the door to see if you are thinking. Otherwise, it's like the hotel business."

West came to Hollywood in 1933 because Darryl Zanuck's new Twentieth Century Pictures had paid him four thousand dollars for the movie rights to his novel *Miss Lonelyhearts.* This was the era when producers frightened by the advent of talking pictures offered contracts to almost any playwright or novelist or newspaperman who gave any evidence of knowing how to write sharp dialogue. And they all came—William Faulkner, Robert Sherwood, Aldous Huxley, Dorothy Parker, even Maurice Maeterlinck. . . . Twentieth Century proceeded, of course, to turn West's brilliant and bitter satire into what it called a "comedy-melodrama" entitled *Advice to the Lovelorn.* West himself never worked on the project but got himself a job as a junior writer at Columbia. His first assignment, *Beauty Parlor,* was never produced; neither was his next one, *Return to the Soil.*

West worked hard, did as he was told, and seemed not to mind the triviality of his assignments. From the start, he was more interested in exploring the peripheries of Hollywood. He told friends of his encounters with gamblers, lesbians, dwarfs. He began writing a short story about three Eskimos who had been brought to Hollywood to star in an adventure movie and were stranded there after its failure. As the narrator from the studio's publicity department remarked, "It was about Eskimos, and who cares about Eskimos?"

Hollywood jobs were as transitory as Hollywood itself. During a long siege of unemployment, made worse by sickness, West lived in a shabby apartment hotel off Hollywood Boulevard called the Pa-Va-Sed, tenanted by a raffish assortment of vaudeville comics, stuntmen, and part-time prostitutes. He began frequenting the city's Mexican underworld, going to cockfights at Pismo Beach. He began imagining all these figures as the characters in a novel that he planned to call "The Cheated." He told a friend about a newspaper story, perhaps imaginary, of a yacht named *The Wanderer,* which had sailed for the South Seas with a strange assortment of passengers: movie cowboys, a huge lesbian, and, once again, a family of Eskimos.

These were the outcasts who eventually peopled *The Day of the Locust.* There was no Jean Harlow or Rita Hayworth in West's Hollywood, only Faye Greener, with her "long, swordlike legs," whose invitation "wasn't to pleasure but to struggle, hard and sharp, closer to murder than to love." In her one movie role, as a dancing girl in a Damascus seraglio, she "had only one line to speak, 'Oh, Mr. Smith!' and spoke it badly." In this Hollywood, there was no Gary Cooper either, only Earl Shoop, the inarticulate cowboy who survived by poaching game in the hills while he vaguely hoped for a job as a movie extra. And instead of the Zanucks and Selznicks, West introduced Honest Abe Kusich, the dwarf bookmaker, complete with black shirt, yellow tie, and Tyrolean hat. And, of course, the Gingos, a family of Eskimos.

The Hollywood that attracted these outcasts remained always beyond their grasp, rich and tantalizing. West insisted on demonstrating that their city of dreams was really nothing more than "the final dumping ground," a "Sargasso of the imagination." Searching for Faye, who had found a bit part in a movie about Waterloo, Tod Hackett got lost in the back lots and wandered through a tangle of briers past the skeleton of a zeppelin, an adobe fort, a Dutch windmill, a Trojan horse, and "a flight of baroque palace stairs that started in a bed of weeds and ended against the branches of an oak." By following a red glare in the sky, Tod eventually found his way to the new set that was being built for the battle of Waterloo, but just as he reached the slopes of an artificial Mont St. Jean, the whole set collapsed under the charging cuirassiers. "Nails screamed with agony as they pulled out of joists. . . . Lath and scantling snapped as though they were brittle bones. The whole hill folded like an enormous umbrella and covered Napoleon's army with painted cloth."

Theater people have traditionally taken delight in the artifices of their calling, fondly citing Shakespeare's reflections on the world as a stage and all the men and women merely players, but West saw the artificialities of Hollywood as part of a sinister California pattern that eventually became clear only in our time, when San Clemente and Pacific Palisades emerged on the national political landscape. It was a pattern partly of physical extremes, of burning deserts and alkali flats, but also of the spiritual extremes that West derided as the Church of Christ Physical, where "holiness was attained through the constant use of chest weights and spring grips," the Tabernacle of the Third Coming, where a woman in man's clothing preached the "crusade against salt," and the Temple Moderne, where the initiates taught "brain-breathing, the secret of the Aztecs."

The pattern of California extremism became manifest in an atmosphere of rancor and disappointment and ultimately violence. West saw this spirit in the swarms of middle-class migrants who had retired to southern California in the hope of finding some kind of pleasure before they died. They were the people who waited restlessly at a movie premiere at Grauman's—or Kahn's Persian Palace Theatre, as West called it—and who finally burst into mindless rioting. "Until they reached the line," West wrote, "they looked diffident, almost furtive, but the moment they had become part of it, they turned arrogant and pugnacious. . . . All their lives they had slaved at some kind of dull, heavy labor, behind desks and counters . . . saving their pennies and dreaming of the leisure that would be theirs when they had enough. . . . Where else should they go but California, the land of sunshine and oranges? Once there, they discover that sunshine isn't enough. They get tired of oranges, even of avocado pears and passion fruit. Nothing happens. They don't know what to do with their time. . . . They have been cheated and betrayed. They have slaved and saved for nothing."

There was a Gary Cooper in West's Hollywood after all, but only as an unseen figure rumored to be somewhere nearby. Two women caught in the milling mob tried to figure out how the chaos began. "The first thing I knew," said one, "there was a rush and I was in the middle."

"Yeah," said the other. "Somebody hollered, 'Here comes Gary Cooper,' and then wham!"

"That ain't it," said a man in a cloth cap and sweater. "This is a riot you're in."

"Yeah," said another woman. "A pervert attacked a child."

"I come from St. Louis," said the first woman, "and we had one of them pervert fellows in our neighborhood once. He ripped up a girl with a pair of scissors."

"He must have been crazy," said the man in the cap. "What kind of fun is that?"

Everybody laughed. They were enjoying themselves. Rioting was something to pass the time, and as Tod Hackett was swept along by the crowds, he imagined them all as the arsonists of his painting, imagined working on the painting itself, "modelling the tongues of fire so that they licked even more avidly at a corinthian column that held up the palmleaf roof of a nutburger stand."

This city of the inferno, both cruel and grotesque, was somewhat different from the Hollywood that had bewitched the American imagination, and the reviews of West's book were respectful but unenthusiastic. Clifton Fadiman wrote in *The New Yorker* that it had "all the fascination of a nice bit of phosphorescent decay." To Scott Fitzgerald, West wrote: "So far the box score stands: Good reviews—fifteen percent, bad reviews—twenty-five percent, brutal personal attacks—sixty percent." In June, just a month after publication, Bennett Cerf informed West that the sales for the latest two weeks numbered exactly twenty-two copies. He added that the "outlook is pretty hopeless." Cerf was sadly disappointed. "By God," he declared, "if I ever publish another Hollywood book, it will have to be 'My 39 ways of making love,' by Hedy Lamarr."

•   •   •

Hedy Lamarr. Hedwig Kiesler was her real name, Hedwig Kiesler Mandl by marriage, aged twenty-five or thereabouts, a recent immigrant from Vienna. What was there about Hedy Lamarr that should make a sedentary New York publisher like Bennett Cerf, thinking about Hollywood in 1939, start to glow when he thought of her and her thirty-nine ways of making love?

Probably it was the rumors surrounding *Ecstasy,* in which she had been photographed, from a discreet distance, darting through some trees and going for a swim in the nude. When *Ecstasy* was first imported into the United States in the fall of 1934, it was immediately seized by the customs authorities. An official committee, including Mrs. Henry Morgenthau, wife of the Secretary of the Treasury, viewed the film and professed itself shocked not by the nude swimming but by a subsequent scene in which the camera focused on Hedy Lamarr's face while a man supposedly made love to her. "I was not sure what my reactions would be, so . . . I just closed my eyes," Miss Lamarr later recalled.* " 'Nein, nein,' the director yelled. 'A passionate expression on the face.' He threw his hands up and slapped them against his sides. He mumbled about the stupidity of youth. He looked around and found a safety pin on a table. He picked it up, bent it almost straight, and approached. 'You will lie here,' he said. 'I will be underneath, out of camera range. When I prick you a little on your backside, you will bring your elbows together and you will *react!*' I shrugged. . . ."

The customs authorities demanded that this scene be expunged; the distributors refused, so *Ecstasy* was not only banned but literally burned. The distributors imported another copy, and managed to get it past customs, but then a federal jury in New York declared that it was "indecent . . . and would tend to corrupt morals." Various legal appeals permitted showings in Boston, Washington, and Los Angeles. The litigation and publicity rumbled along in New York until a censored version was officially approved in 1940.

By then, of course, Hedy Lamarr was famous, both as a beauty and as a fugitive. Her husband, Fritz Mandl, a munitions manufacturer and a secret financial backer of the Austrian Nazis, was reputed to have spent more than $300,000 buying up and destroying copies of *Ecstasy.* He also kept its heroine under close supervision in his palace in Vienna. According to her disputed memoirs, she disguised herself as her own maid and fled to Paris. The subsequent gossip in Hollywood, according to Errol Flynn, was that the beautiful prisoner had persuaded Mandl to let her wear all the family jewels at a dinner for the Nazi Prince Ernst von Stahremberg, then pleaded a headache and disappeared. When Flynn asked her at a party to tell the details of her departure from her husband, she answered only, "That son of a bitch!"

Frau Mandl's flight in the summer of 1937 led her to London, and there to the hotel of Louis B. Mayer, the chief of M-G-M, and thence to the S.S. *Normandie,* bound for New York. Mayer just happened to be traveling on the same boat; the actress presented herself as a governess to a violin prodigy named Grisha Goluboff; by the time the boat docked in New York, she had acquired M-G-M contracts for both the violinist and herself (at five hundred dollars a week), and a new name as well. When a *Daily News* reporter went to the pier to interview "The Ecstasy Lady, brunette Hedy Kiesler," she said, "My name is Hedy Lamarr. Please call me that." Mayer had apparently named her after Barbara La Marr, a great beauty he had admired in the 1920's, who had succumbed to drugs and alcohol. After Mayer shipped his newest acquisition to Hollywood and signed her up for English lessons, however, he didn't know what to do with her. It was apparently Charles Boyer who encountered her at a party and then persuaded the producer Walter Wanger to borrow her, for a fee of fifteen hundred dollars a week to Mayer, as his leading lady in *Algiers.*

---

* *Ecstasy and Me: My Life as a Woman,* was signed and copyrighted by Hedy Lamarr in 1966, but she later filed suit, trying unsuccessfully to prevent its publication. Although the book was apparently based on taped interviews, her suit contended that the work produced by Leo Guild and Sy Rice was "fictional, false, vulgar, scandalous, libelous, and obscene."

"Come with me to the Casbah." The most famous line in *Algiers* is—like Humphrey Bogart's "Play it again, Sam," in *Casablanca*—not actually in the movie at all.* Boyer, as the fugitive jewel thief Pépé le Moko, could hardly invite the roving Hedy Lamarr to the Casbah, since he himself was already trapped within its walls. The police wanted Hedy to lure him out, and so he was duly enticed, caught, killed. Despite the glib absurdity of the story, the reviewers were very much impress d. "Best of all," said *Time*, "is the smoldering, velvet-voiced, hazel-eyed, Viennese Actress Hedy Kiesler (Hollywood name: Hedy Lamarr)."

•   •   •

This, then, was probably what made Bennett Cerf's wrinkled jowls tingle when he wrote to Nathanael West. These were some of the essential elements of the imagined Hollywood of 1939: imagined romance, imagined sex, vaguely foreign and thus vaguely unreal, and thus permissible. There were, of course, other kinds of unreality also being manufactured and merchandised in Hollywood. The previous year's Academy Awards had been presented to Spencer Tracy as the heroic priest in *Boys Town* and Bette Davis as the Dixie prima donna in *Jezebel*, but Louis B. Mayer's great favorites were the pseudo-family comedies featuring Mickey Rooney as Andy Hardy, fourteen of which were churned out between 1937 and 1943. Once, to demonstrate how Andy should pray for his sick mother, Mayer fell heavily to his knees, clasped his hands together, and looked up toward heaven. "Dear God," he begged, almost in tears, "please don't let my mom die, because she's the best mom in the world. Thank you, God." When Mayer compared such scenes with other movies of the time, his judgments were forthright. "Any good Hardy picture," he said, "made $500,000 more than *Ninotchka* made."

That was the most remarkable thing about Hollywood in 1939: how successful it was. While the rest of the country wallowed along through the remnants of the Depression, Hollywood kept making more and more money. Several major studios went bankrupt and had to be "reorganized," but the movie industry as a whole flourished. Perhaps it was because movies were still a novelty, and still cheap (and some, of course, were good), or perhaps because they offered people an escape from their troubles. "When the spirit of the people is lower than at any other time, during this Depression," President Roosevelt said of Shirley Temple, "it is a splendid thing that for just fifteen cents an American can go to a movie and look at the smiling face of a baby. . . ." Perhaps, on the other hand, Hollywood's success was based on the cruder fact that it required no expensive ingredients like coal or steel, that its largely nonunionized employees could be not only dismissed on a producer's whim but made to take pay cuts for the good of the studio. Or perhaps it was simply because the studios had gradually established what amounted to an

---

* The *Algiers* script was officially credited to John Howard Lawson, the Communist playwright who eventually became the leader of the famous Hollywood Ten, but his script was never used. Producer Walter Wanger decided instead simply to translate the script for Julien Duvivier's original French version, *Pépé le Moko*, which had starred Jean Gabin.

illegal cartel, controlling both their actors and writers at one end of the process and their distributors and exhibitors at the other end. They couldn't lose.

In 1939, there were more movie theaters (15,115) than banks (14,952), and the number of theaters per capita was about twice as high as it is today. More than fifty million Americans went to the movies every single week of the year. There were about four hundred new movies per year to watch. The box office receipts that poured into Hollywood (into New York, actually, for it was always New York that quietly ruled and controlled Hollywood) totaled $673,045,000. The movies were the nation's fourteenth-biggest business in terms of volume ($406,855,095), the eleventh-biggest in terms of assets ($529,950,444), bigger than office machines, bigger than the supermarket chains.

The creation of fantasy made the creators rich. Though Hollywood was not among the ten biggest American industries, it ranked second in the percentage of sales and profits that it awarded to its own executives. It even paid its grumbling writers remarkably well. If Nathanael West's $350 per week seemed small, it nonetheless compared very favorably to the average newspaper reporter's wages of about $50. Scott Fitzgerald was making $1,000 during his last years of ruin, while Ben Hecht once got a contract guaranteeing him $15,000 a week. The highest-paid stars, like Bing Crosby and Claudette Colbert, earned more than $400,000 per year. Shorter contracts were even more lucrative. Douglas Fairbanks once received a stunning $37,000 per week, Walter Huston an even more stunning $40,000.

But the lords of creation were those studio executives who could still remember their boyhoods as penniless immigrants from Eastern Europe, and who, having defeated Thomas Edison's "Trust," formed a trust of their own, and, as lords, paid themselves accordingly. Samuel Goldwyn, born Shmuel Gelbfisz, a former glove salesman from Lodz; Joseph Schenck, of Rybinsk, Russia, the founder and chairman of 20th Century–Fox, and his younger brother, Nick, president of Loew's, Inc.; Lewis Selznick, born Zeleznik, a jewelry dealer from Kiev; "Uncle Carl" Laemmle, the founder of Universal, a clothing store manager from Laupheim, Germany; Adolph Zukor, the head of Paramount, a furrier from Ricse, Hungary—these were the legendary rulers of Hollywood. And those who were not themselves penniless immigrants were generally the sons of penniless immigrants: the ruthless Cohn brothers, sons of a German tailor, founders of Columbia; the Warner brothers, all four of them, sons of a Polish cobbler. Benjamin Warner taught his sons, among other things, to save shoe nails and to store them between their lips while they worked. Many years later, Jack Warner recalled a time when Ann Sheridan was showing a young actor around the Warner Bros. lot and encountered an elderly man walking slowly with his head bowed. Occasionally, he bent down, picked up an object, and popped it into his mouth. "Who's that man and what's he doing?" the actor asked Miss Sheridan. "Doing what comes naturally," she said. "He's picking up nails. His name is Harry Warner, and he happens to be president of the company."

The legend of the ignorant immigrants becoming plutocrats is partly fiction. Leo Rosten demonstrated in his detailed study of *Hollywood, The Movie Colony* (1941) that just as 80 percent of Hollywood actors earned less than $15,000 per year, nearly 60 percent of the 120 leading Hollywood executives had graduated from college and less than 5 percent came from Russia and Poland. Still, the confirmation of all legends, the richest and most powerful of all the semiliterate monarchs, was Louis B. Mayer, who was born in Minsk, probably in 1885, and was probably named Lazar. He himself did not know for sure.

He spent his boyhood as a ragpicker in New Brunswick, Canada. He was twenty-two when he bought a former burlesque theater in Haverhill, Massachusetts, for a down payment of six hundred dollars and began exhibiting a French film of the Oberammergau Passion Play. Though he stood only five feet seven*, he had powerful shoulders and a fierce temper. He attacked and knocked down Charlie Chaplin for speaking disrespectfully of his own ex-wife; he knocked down Erich von Stroheim for saying that all women were whores. In 1937, as president of Metro-Goldwyn-Mayer, he received a salary and bonuses totaling $1,300,000, which made him the highest-paid man in the United States. He was to retain that ambiguous honor for the next nine years, and when he was finally overthrown in 1951, M-G-M declared that over the course of his twenty-seven years in power, he had "received over $20,000,000 in compensation." It was part of the folklore at M-G-M that the studio commissary had to serve at lunch every day, in honor of Mayer's long-dead mother, chicken soup with real pieces of chicken in it, at thirty-five cents a bowl.

One of the most remarkable aspects of these buccaneers was how little they understood either their business or their audience. "Less brains are necessary in the motion picture industry than in any other," Lewis Selznick once testified to a startled congressional committee. He cited an occasion when he had made $105,000 on a $1,000 investment within ten weeks. Selznick eventually went bankrupt, so his testimony is not infallible, but the whole history of Hollywood is a chronicle of misjudgments and miscalculations interspersed among the more celebrated successes. The studio tycoons seemed to have no idea, for example, that the cartel by which they had made themselves rich was vulnerable to a federal antitrust suit, or that the suit originally filed by the Justice Department in 1938 would ultimately devastate their empire. They also had no idea of what technology would mean to them and their fortunes. They had stumbled into the use of sound almost by accident, and they were reluctantly beginning to experiment with color; they completely

---

* A Napoleonic lack of height was common among Hollywood tycoons. With only small exaggeration, Philip French wrote in *The Movie Moguls:* "One could have swung a scythe five and a half feet off the ground at a gathering of movie moguls without endangering any lives; several would scarcely have heard the swish."

ignored the fact that television broadcasts were already emanating from New York, Philadelphia, Chicago, and San Francisco, and that tens of thousands of people were marveling at this novelty at the 1939 World's Fair in Flushing Meadow, New York.

The lords of Hollywood persuaded themselves that they had some mysterious insight into the American public, and that this insight both explained and justified their riches, their courtiers, their palaces and racehorses. They imagined themselves, with the help of their publicity men, as great showmen, daring gamblers willing to stake fortunes on hunches, and when they were eventually dethroned, as most of them eventually were, they seemed surprised, baffled, hurt. Even in their heyday, however, they were continually being surprised. Louis B. Mayer, for example, saw little future for any actor with the protruding ears of Clark Gable; he opposed one of Gable's first great triumphs, *Mutiny on the Bounty,* because he thought the public would never approve of a rebel as a hero. He even rejected a proposal to help finance Mickey Mouse, on the ground that, as he told Walt Disney, "every woman is frightened of a mouse."

Mayer did not read scripts or scenarios, much less books, so when some story had to be officially considered, it was acted out for him by a kind of minnesinger named Kate Corbaley, who was paid to tell him stories just as his mother had done years earlier in New Brunswick. One afternoon in May of 1936, Miss Corbaley told Mayer a new story about a tempestuous southern girl named Scarlett O'Hara, and Louis B. Mayer sagely nodded his million-dollar-a-year head and said, "Let's ask Irving."

A summons was issued for Irving Thalberg, the frail and sickly production chief, who was mainly responsible for Mayer's success at M-G-M. Thalberg had started in New York as a twenty-five-dollar-per-week secretary in the offices of Carl Laemmle. He soon became Laemmle's chief adjutant at Universal, but when he declined an invitation to marry Laemmle's eager daughter, Rosabelle, the slighted father made Thalberg's life so disagreeable that he found himself a new job as vice-president in the fledgling operations of Louis B. Mayer, who offered him six hundred dollars a week and stock options and no marriage proposals. In fact, Mayer warned his twenty-three-year-old protégé that he didn't want a son-in-law with a weak heart. "If a romance developed between you and either of my girls . . ." he said. "I can't allow it to happen."

While Thalberg lived, he was Hollywood's supreme wunderkind, the producer who not only kept raking in money but turned out those self-important M-G-M epics like *The Barretts of Wimpole Street* and *The Good Earth,* and the *Romeo and Juliet* that featured Thalberg's wife, Norma Shearer. "I, more than any single person in Hollywood, have my finger on the pulse of America," Thalberg once said. "I know what people will do and what they won't do." After his death at thirty-six, he became Hollywood's lost hero, its martyr. When Scott Fitzgerald returned to work at M-G-M for the last time in 1939, he recreated the vanished Thalberg as Monroe Stahr in his unfinished novel,

The Last Tycoon. Recalling a rare encounter in the M-G-M commissary back in 1927, Fitzgerald included almost verbatim in his novel something that Thalberg had told him about the essence of authority: A road has to be built over a mountain, and surveyors arrive with plans for several possible routes. "You say, 'Well, I think we will put the road there'. . . and you know in your secret heart that you have no reason for putting the road there rather than in several other different courses, but you're the only person that knows that you don't know why you're doing it and you've got to stick to that and you've got to pretend that you know and that you did it for specific reasons, even though you're utterly assailed by doubts."

Thalberg was the Hollywood executive who said of Warner Bros.' first talking film, *The Jazz Singer,* that "talking pictures are just a passing fad." And his sense for "the pulse of America" was well expressed when he dismissed an assistant's protests about a scenario that called for a love scene in Paris to be played against a background of a moonlit ocean. The assistant brought him maps and photographs to demonstrate that Paris is nowhere near any ocean. "We can't cater to a handful of people who know Paris," said Thalberg, refusing to make any change in the script. So now, in the last year of his life, when Mayer called him in to hear Kate Corbaley tell once again the story of a southern girl named Scarlett O'Hara, Irving Thalberg quickly became restless.

"Forget it, Louis," said the Last Tycoon. "No Civil War picture ever made a nickel."

"Well, that's it," said Mayer. "Irving knows what's right."

•   •   •

Mayer and Thalberg were not Hollywood's only experts on the pulse of America. As soon as the agent Annie Laurie Williams learned that M-G-M was rejecting *Gone With the Wind,* she hurried to Grand Central station and pressed a set of the unpublished galleys on a California-bound producer, Mervyn LeRoy. His wife, Doris, began to read the galleys on the train, and by the time she reached Los Angeles she was determined to persuade her uncle, Jack Warner, that this would be a great part for his main star, Bette Davis. Warner read a synopsis and agreed to make an offer. "I've just bought a book which has a marvelous part for you," he said to Miss Davis, lying. "It's called *Gone With the Wind.*"

"I'll bet that's a pip," said Miss Davis as she departed for England.

RKO's Pandro Berman also read the novel and turned it down; so did David O. Selznick; so did a lot of others. Darryl Zanuck offered $35,000, but Miss Williams hoped to get $65,000. One of Selznick's aides then sent a synopsis to John Hay Whitney, the chairman and chief investor in Selznick's new production company, and Whitney wanted to buy it. That was how, for $50,000, the story rejected by Louis B. Mayer came to be bought by his son-in-law. (Or so goes the generally accepted version. Zanuck's account was less respectable. He claimed that he had bid $40,000, had been topped by a

$45,000 bid from Adolph Zukor of Paramount, had increased his own bid to $55,000, and that Mayer had then proposed a little conspiracy. "To end the bidding, at the suggestion of L. B. Mayer, we met in Thalberg's bungalow, the heads of the studios, about five," Zanuck said. "The lawyer for the producers presided. Someone suggested, let's put our names on slips of paper and put them in a hat and draw one slip out and whosoever's name is on the slip will purchase it—whatever the price. The lawyer churned the slips around. . . . The first paper he touched had Selznick's signature on it. That's how he got *Gone With the Wind*. I remember Thalberg smiling like hell because Metro didn't get it.")

The Selznicks were an extraordinary tribe. The father, Lewis, the former jewelry dealer from Kiev, persuaded his three sons that they were heirs to a kingdom. He read aloud to them from *David Copperfield* and *Little Lord Fauntleroy* and *A Tale of Two Cities*. When young David Selznick went to Columbia University, he went with an allowance of $750 per week, which, in the 1920's, was a substantial sum. "Spend it all," said Lewis Selznick. "Give it away. Throw it away." In the course of amassing his millions in Hollywood, Lewis managed to make many enemies, and when he couldn't pay a debt of a mere three thousand dollars, they forced him into bankruptcy. He never found another job during the ten years before his death in 1933. His sons were appalled. The oldest, Myron, a perpetually angry alcoholic, became the first and most ferocious of Hollywood's big agents. Among the clients for whom he extorted revenge from the studios were Gary Cooper, Henry Fonda, Boris Karloff, Laurence Olivier, George Raft, Merle Oberon, Carole Lombard, Helen Hayes, Lily Pons, and on and on and on.

The youngest son, Howard, who sometimes referred to himself as "the third brother," was a quiet youth, apparently the victim of slight brain damage at birth, and largely ignored by his family. "How is it you always leave after the main course?" his mother once asked him at dinner . "Where do you go?"

"I go to see my wife," Howard answered, according to his sister-in-law, Irene Mayer Selznick.

"What wife? What do you mean?" his mother demanded.

"I've been married for two years," said Howard. With his brothers' help, Howard was eventually established in a Hollywood flower shop called Forget Me Not. The shop almost inevitably failed.

Then there was David, fat, bumptious, impossible David. Paramount's chief of production, Benjamin P. Schulberg, described him as "the most arrogant young man I've ever known," and then hired him as an assistant. Selznick was twenty-six when he applied for work at M-G-M. The application went promptly to Louis B. Mayer, who decreed that no son of Lewis Selznick would ever work at M-G-M. Selznick immediately applied to Mayer's own boss, Nicholas Schenck, president of Loew's, Inc. Schenck, perhaps maliciously, hired him. Selznick immediately began sending out memoranda in all directions. Yet every night, when the young executive returned home, his father would put him to bed. "Regardless of the hour . . ." Irene Selznick recalled, "Pop would read with his ear cocked for David's return, whereupon he would descend to cover David up, stretched out on the couch in his study, instantly asleep. After an hour or two Pop would lead his comatose boy gently to his bed and undress him."

Louis B. Mayer warned his younger daughter against Selznick. "Keep away from that schnook," he said. "He'll be a bum just like his old man." But Irene Mayer was fascinated by Selznick's energy and enthusiasm. After all the usual sparring, the children of the rival producers decided to get married. (Some skeptics naturally jeered. "Someone had to marry Irene Mayer," according to a cruel ditty by the screenwriters Charles MacArthur and Charles Lederer, "someone had to have the guts to lay her . . .") Louis B. Mayer professed to be pleased by the marriage, but he kept insisting on delay. "You cannot do this to me, Mr. Mayer," Selznick finally said. "I cannot wait any longer. You're a man. What kind of hell do you think I go through?"

Mayer was shocked, scandalized, outraged at such a suggestion of sex. When the wedding finally took place, there was almost a public quarrel between Mayer and his daughter. "I marched down the aisle on his arm," she later said, "still pleading with him, as he shushed me, all in full view of the guests. By the time I got to the altar, I had dried my tears, but I looked wan and grave."

Having fought with all his rivals at M-G-M, and at Paramount, and at RKO, David Selznick established his own independent production company. His first film was a story that his father had once read to him, *Little Lord Fauntleroy.*

But throughout the late 1930s, his grand obsession was the filming of *Gone With the Wind,* a project for which he had neither the cast nor the capital. He knew from the start that he wanted Clark Gable to play Rhett Butler, though he considered such possibilities as Gary Cooper, Errol Flynn, Ronald Colman, and even Basil Rathbone. But Gable was owned by M-G-M, which never loaned him out to other studios. Louis B. Mayer was willing to break a rule for his fractious son-in-law, but the terms were murderous. Not only would Selznick have to pay Gable's regular salary of $7,000 per week, but Mayer would put up $1,250,000 as half the financing of the film and would then take world distribution rights plus half the total profits. And Gable wasn't free to start work for two years. That gave Selznick two years to keep revising the script (the original version, by Sidney Howard, was just an agenda for rewrite teams that included Scott Fitzgerald, John Van Druten, and Ben Hecht, the last of these at fifteen thousand dollars for one week's work). It also gave him two years to milk publicity from his own inability to find the perfect Scarlett O'Hara.

The interminable "search," orchestrated by a former Hearst police reporter named Russell Birdwell, featured all the major stars of the day. Joan Crawford, Katharine Hepburn, Bette Davis campaigned fiercely for the part, and the gossip columns chronicled each rise and fall in their prospects. Paulette Goddard nearly won, but various ladies' clubs noisily protested that she was not really married to her supposed husband, Charlie Chaplin. Though she claimed they had been married in Singapore harbor by the captain of an Oriental cruise ship, the lack of any wedding certificate drove Selznick back into his customary state of indecision. Meanwhile, his adjutants wandered across the countryside, interviewing various high school prom queens and other local talents. One girl in crinolines, quite possibly acting on instructions from Birdwell, had herself shipped to Selznick's home in a large packing crate. All in all, fourteen hundred "discoveries" were formally interviewed, and ninety of them were actually tested before a movie camera. The tests totaled 162,000 feet of film, amounting to more than twenty-four hours' running time, all of it worthless. The cost of the famous search was estimated at $100,000, and its value as publicity was priceless.

As the beginning of 1939 drew near, however, some actual work had to be started. The designers had already drawn their plans for the construction of Tara, and Twelve Oaks, and the Atlanta Bazaar, but before the building could begin, some space had to be cleared on the cluttered back lot of Selznick's studio. This studio, set among slatternly bars and apartment houses on Washington Boulevard, had been operated at various times by Sam Goldwyn, Pathé, and Joseph Kennedy's RKO. Its forty acres had served as both English countryside and African jungle. Sets of all kinds were built and then abandoned: a village from *The Last of the Mohicans,* a street from *Little Lord Fauntleroy,* even the giant gateway that once guarded the entry to the domain of King Kong. Eventually, these dilapidated ruins would have to be dismantled, but William Cameron Menzies, who had been hired to design the sets for *Gone With the Wind,* conceived an inspired idea. Why not put a few false fronts on the relics, enough to make them look like an approximation of Atlanta, and then set the whole tumbledown mess on fire?

Cautious M-G-M executives argued that it would be cheaper and simpler to work with models, and local fire officials worried that the conflagration might easily break out of control, but Selznick was adamant. Let it all burn, like the original Atlanta, like London, like Rome. He assigned the technical problems to Lee Zavitz, a special-effects man known as an explosives expert, and Zavitz rigged up an elaborate network of pipes throughout the assembled buildings. Zavitz built his conduits at three levels—on the ground, at the second story, and along the roofs. Throughout this network, he installed two different kinds of pipes that ran alongside each other, with sprinklers at fixed intervals. One set of pipes contained a highly flammable mixture of 80 percent oil distillate and 20 percent rock gas; the other contained water and a fire-extinguishing solution. All of these pipes, designed to make the fires burn more fiercely or to wet them down, led to a kind of keyboard console, where a row of push buttons could regulate the flames in various parts of the holocaust. It was an arsonist's dream. Selznick insisted on operating the console himself.

Though the night of December 10, 1938, was cold, Selznick was determined to make a party of the great fire. He had built an observation platform for his guests. His widowed mother, Florence, was there, wrapped in a shawl, but Myron Selznick was delayed at a dinner party. Selznick waited for more than a hour, and so did twenty-five officers from the Los Angeles Police Department, and fifty firemen, and two hundred studio employees pressed into service as volunteers to man the five-thousand-gallon water tanks. So did three white-suited doubles for Clark Gable, ready to rescue three different Scarletts on three different buckboard wagons. So did seven different camera crews trained to use the new and unpredictable Technicolor process; there would, after all, be no way of correcting mistakes.

When nervous aides finally persuaded the nervous Selznick that he could wait no longer, he started pushing buttons. Suddenly the night was on fire. Selznick pushed a button, and one of the sets from *The Garden of Allah* exploded into flames; he pushed a button and the great gateway from *King Kong* collapsed in ruins. Only now did Selznick's publicity man, Russell Birdwell, telephone the Los Angeles newspapers with anonymous tips that the whole lot was on fire, and when skeptical editors looked out their windows, they could see the sky reddening miles away.

"Burn, baby, burn," was a cry heard only thirty years later, in Watts, and one can only imagine what reverberated inside the head of David O. Selznick as he pushed the buttons that spread the flames through the sham buildings of Atlanta. Burn, Atlanta! Burn, Hollywood, and all of southern California! Burn, Louis B. Mayer, and all the bankers and lawyers and deal-makers! Burn!

The flames were beginning to die down, according to legend, when Myron Selznick finally arrived, half drunk as usual, with some of his dinner guests, among them a relatively obscure young English actress named Vivien Leigh. She had just come to Hollywood because she was following her lover, Laurence Olivier, who had signed to play Heathcliff in Sam Goldwyn's production of *Wuthering Heights*. When drunk, Myron Selznick often addressed his younger brother as "Genius." Sometimes, they got into fistfights. "Hello, Genius," Myron Selznick said now. "I want you to meet your Scarlett O'Hara."

"I took one look," David later declared in a ghostwritten account that sealed the legend, "and knew that she was right."

•   •   •

God never meant man to live here, as Thornton Wilder said, but man had tortured the desert into giving him sustenance. Wilder was only slightly exaggerating the ugly history of Los Angeles' long struggle to provide itself with water. The region was not totally a desert, of course, for the original pueblo was built alongside the Los Angeles River, which meanders southward out of the San Gabriel Mountains to debouch in what is now Long Beach. This river was dammed and used for irrigation in the early nineteenth century, but it was never considered capable of supporting a city of more than 250,000 people. By the turn of the century, the population had already passed

150,000 and was growing rapidly. "The time has come," Water Commissioner William Mulholland declared in 1904, after a survey of the river, "when we shall have to supplement its flow from some other source."

Mulholland was a tall, rawboned Dubliner, a former seaman and lumberjack, who had wandered into Los Angeles in 1877 and found himself a job as a laborer on a pipe-building project alongside the Los Angeles River, which he later recalled as "a beautiful, limpid stream with willows on its banks." Mulholland was a man of large and irresistible vision. The "other source" that he discovered for Los Angeles water was the Owens River Valley, some 250 miles to the northeast, fed from the snows of the High Sierras. President Theodore Roosevelt had already brought the federal government into the field of large-scale reclamation, using the sale of western lands to finance irrigation, and the officials who arrived to buy up water rights in the Owens Valley told the ranchers that they were planning an irrigation project for the valley. By the time the ranchers realized their mistake, their betrayal, Mulholland had floated a $1.5 million bond issue and embarked on his great aqueduct from the Owens Valley to Los Angeles. It was an engineering marvel that extended 233 miles across the Mojave Desert; it had 142 separate tunnels and twelve miles of inverted steel siphons and three large reservoirs, the largest of which could store more than nineteen million gallons of water. "There it is!" said Mulholland when he opened the spillway to the San Fernando Reservoir in 1913. "Take it!"

The new aqueduct could supply a city of two million people, Mulholland figured, and Los Angeles would not reach that size for many years, so the water commissioner used the surplus water to begin irrigating the arid San Fernando Valley just north of the city. Annexed by Los Angeles, it grew green at the expense of the Owens Valley ranchers, whose fertile lands were now doomed to revert to desert. The ranchers fought back with lawsuits and even gunfire. They temporarily seized part of the aqueduct, and even blew it up in 1927. Their protests were futile. Their last outcry was a Los Angeles newspaper advertisement that said: "We, the farming communities of the Owens Valley, being about to die, salute you. . . ." The newspaper ad seemed appropriate enough, for General Harrison Gray Otis, publisher of the Los Angeles Times, was one of the oligarchs who had anticipated Mulholland's benificence in the San Fernando Valley by buying up large tracts of land there. His syndicate paid $3 million for 62,000 acres, which duly became worth about $120 million. Among the other foresighted land-buyers were the railroad magnates E. H. Harriman and Henry Huntington. They also did very well for themselves.

Robert Towne apparently drew inspiration from these half-buried scandals when he wrote the screenplay for Chinatown, for the millionaire land speculator played by John Huston boasted happily that there were only two choices: "Either you bring the water to L.A., or you bring L.A. to the water."

"Why are you doing it?" asked the detective played by Jack Nicholson. "How much better can you eat? What can you buy that you can't already afford?"

"The future, Mr. Goetz, the future!" cried Huston.

The future of Los Angeles had seemed assured by Mulholland's foresight, but the two million people to be served by his aqueduct were already in sight by the early 1920's, and the population was growing by 100,000 a year. Mulholland began planning for yet another aqueduct, this time to reach still farther east and drain water from the Colorado River. Mulholland was not to see the completion of his last great scheme. One of his lesser projects, the St. Francis Dam in the Santa Clara Valley, suddenly gave way on March 12, 1928, and sent a wall of water cascading down on the homes of Mexican citrus workers. Some 385 people drowned, and 1,240 homes were destroyed. Mulholland, by now seventy-two, acknowledged full responsibility for the disaster and resigned, saying unhappily that he "envied the dead." Seven years later, he suffered a severe stroke and died in his sleep.

By then, the New Deal was in full flower, and the harnessing of the Colorado River was one of its major projects. Just two months after Mulholland's death, President Roosevelt voyaged out into the desert southeast of the former Mormon outpost of Las Vegas and dedicated what he called "a twentieth century marvel," then known as Boulder Dam, originally and now again Hoover Dam. It was indeed a marvel, 726 feet high, built out of 6.5 million tons of concrete, but it was built at a cost. Temperatures in the desert climbed as high as 140 degrees, and when some of the laborers attempted a strike against the brutal working conditions and the four-dollar daily wage, the strike was broken by force. Only after the dam was built did the government fine the builders $100,000 for 70,000 violations of the eight-hour-day law. All in all, some 110 workmen died from various accidents during the two years of construction. "They died to make the desert bloom," reads a plaque in their honor. The builders—a Western consortium that included Bechtel, Kaiser, and Morrison-Knudsen, who called themselves the Six Companies, after the group that ruled San Francisco's Chinatown—made a profit of more than ten million dollars.

The aqueduct from the Colorado to Los Angeles was hardly less a marvel. Construction had begun in 1932, and some thirty thousand workmen labored on it throughout the Depression. When the $220 million project was finished in the fall of 1939, a network of canals, tunnels, pumping plants, and reservoirs could carry nearly one billion gallons of water a day nearly three hundred miles across the desert from the Colorado River to Los Angeles. "It is a dream of empire coming true before our eyes," said W. P. Whitsett, chairman of the Metropolitan Water District.

• • •

Hollywood was not particularly interested in water in the fall of 1939, or in the Los Angeles megalopolis that the new water would make possible. Hollywood was largely preoccupied, as always, with itself, with making movies and making money. As a whole, the industry invested $170 million to make 530 feature pictures that year, among them some of the most popular movies ever made. This was the year in which Greta Garbo did not win an Academy

Award for starring in *Ninotchka,* and Judy Garland did not win one for *The Wizard of Oz.* Neither did Laurence Olivier for *Wuthering Heights,* nor John Wayne for *Stagecoach,* nor Jimmy Stewart for *Mr. Smith Goes to Washington,* not to mention *Destry Rides Again.* This was the year in which a million people crowded into Atlanta—still alive despite the ashes to which David Selznick had reduced it—for the ceremonial opening of *Gone With the Wind.* Confederate flags flew everywhere, and hawkers peddled Rhett caramels and Melanie molasses and Tara pecans, and when Vivien Leigh heard a military school band bleating "Dixie," she said, "Oh, they're playing the song from our picture."

There was a grand unreality about all the festivity, this celebration of defeat in a war long finished, as though nobody could understand that a much larger struggle had already begun. That September, a group of Selznick's technicians had been carrying out one of their last tasks, filming the title itself —*Gone With the Wind*—pulling the camera along on a dolly so that each word could be framed separately, when Fred Williams, the head grip, turned on his radio and heard that Britain had declared war on Nazi Germany.

•   •   •

War had been inevitable ever since German Foreign Minister Joachim von Ribbentrop had flown to Moscow the previous week to sign the Hitler-Stalin nonaggression treaty. Hollywood's small but noisy troop of Communists, like Communists everywhere, insisted up to the last minute that what was happening could not be happening. On the night before the Hitler-Stalin treaty was proclaimed, someone asked Herbert Biberman, a writer-director who was acting as chairman of yet another anti-Fascist meeting, about the rumors that such a treaty was impending. Biberman, later to become one of the Hollywood Ten, pounded on the table and denounced the rumors as "Fascist propaganda." That was perfectly appropriate, for Earl Browder, secretary of the U.S. Communist Party, had recently told a gathering in Virginia that "there is as much chance of agreement as of Earl Browder being elected president of the Chamber of Commerce."

"The day after the pact," said Bonnie Clair Smith, who worked at the Hollywood Anti-Nazi League, "you never saw anything like what hit the League's office. The phones didn't stop, the telegrams of withdrawal poured in." Charles Glenn, who wrote a Hollywood column for the *People's Daily World,* recalled that Browder suddenly couldn't be found. "The known Reds were in hiding," he said, "afraid to stick their heads out of doors because the Old Country Jews, the ones who had fled Hitler, would have torn them apart." They soon reappeared, of course, but with a difference. "Before the pact," recalled the writer Philip Dunne, "every other word out of Biberman's mouth spoke of collective security. All of a sudden he added the modifying phrase, 'collective security for peace, not war.' "

Not everyone thought in purely ideological terms. The day after the signing of the Hitler-Stalin pact, Louella Parsons wrote in her column for

August 25: "With war imminent, Hollywood yesterday realized how many of its important stars are still in Europe. Tyrone Power and Annabella . . . Charles Boyer . . . Robert Montgomery . . . Maureen O'Sullivan . . . Bob Hope." Hope and his wife, Dolores, had just arrived in Paris and were scheduled to return to New York on the *Queen Mary* in mid-September, but when they heard rumors that the ship's August 30 sailing might be its last voyage as a civilian vessel, they scrambled back across the English Channel to get aboard.

In France itself, Arthur Rubinstein was spending the season at Deauville with his young children when he noticed that all his neighbors suddenly began leaving, and the streets of the resort were deserted. In the south, though, the rich gathered as usual to watch the fireworks explode in the sky at the annual charity ball for the Petits Lits Blancs at the Palm Beach Casino in Cannes. It was the last day of August, the last day of peace before Hitler invaded Poland. Pola Negri, the star of Ernst Lubitsch's *Madame Du Barry*, who had spent all too much of the 1930's making films in Berlin, recalled later that she was drinking champagne and watching the fireworks at the Cannes casino when a sudden gust of wind sent a dance program flying across the lawn, and the nearby trees began to shudder and sway. "We scurried for shelter," she said, "catching muddied silver heels in spattered silken hems, trampling bruised and battered flowers. Trellised walls crumbled around us, and what had been a rich spectacle was quickly transformed into a pathetic ruin."

"The blackouts made Paris fantastically beautiful . . ." said Salka Viertel, the Polish actress who wrote several of Greta Garbo's notable films of the 1930's. "With Alfred and Lisl Polgar I walked through the Palais Royal flooded with moonlight. We were overcome by a great nostalgia. . . ." M-G-M had sent Mrs. Viertel to France that summer to plan the script of *Madame Curie,* a project for which Scott Fitzgerald had produced one of his last scripts and then been fired again. She had hoped also to visit her mother in Poland, but now M-G-M insisted that she return to Hollywood and even applied some pressure to find her a small cabin on the *Île de France,* sailing from Le Havre on September 1. From the port, Mrs. Viertel tried to send her mother an explanatory cable. *"Pologne?"* the cable clerk asked. *"Les Allemands sont en Pologne, Madame. C'est la guerre."* She clambered aboard the *Île de France,* and the lifeboat drills now acquired an ominous significance. "I put on my life jacket and went to my assigned place," she recalled, "where . . . I was welcomed by Gregor Piatigorsky, the cello virtuoso, who, with his wife and small child, was returning to California. In the same lifeboat would be Nathan Milstein, the famous violinist, and his American wife. . . ."

Aboard the *Queen Mary,* by now at sea, the news bulletins caused a certain amount of panic. Dolores Hope awakened her husband to tell him that France and Britain had declared war. "You ought to see what's going on up in the salon," she said. "People are sobbing. One woman stopped me and said that there are German submarines waiting for orders to sink this boat. They've issued blackout instructions and people are crying—and scared."

Hope responded in his characteristic way. He went to see the captain and arranged to give a special show for the passengers, then started writing himself some new material.

"Thanks for the memory," he sang that night,
"Some folks slept on the floor,
Some in the corridor;
But I was more exclusive,
My room had 'Gentlemen' above the door,
Ah! Thank you so much."

Ingrid Bergman, after the triumph of *Intermezzo,* her first American film for Selznick, had just returned to her family in Stockholm that August. She started a new film in Swedish and celebrated her twenty-fourth birthday, happy that she could once again enjoy "eating everything I want." The idea of war could hardly be more remote. She was "just sewing up the hems of the new curtains for the living room when I heard over the radio that Germany had invaded Poland." Her husband insisted that she take their year-old daughter, Pia, and return to America, and since she was half German on her mother's side, she went from Sweden to Nazi Berlin, then sailed from Genoa.

Whether Sweden was safe—whether any place was safe—depended on one's point of view. Bertolt Brecht, who had fled from Germany in 1933, wandered along the whole circuit of sanctuaries from Prague to Paris before ending in Denmark, where, as a lifelong survivor, he decided in the summer of 1939 to flee to Stockholm. Thomas Mann, by contrast, arrived in Stockholm that August as a Nobel Prize laureate scheduled to address a PEN conference on September 1. On hearing of Hitler's invasion, Mann promptly canceled his speech and flew to London to catch the next sailing of the United States Lines' *Washington.*

And there in London, dying of the cancer that was eating a hole through the side of his face, lay Sigmund Freud, who had foreseen everything and nothing. The incurable wound in his face had begun to give off an appalling stench. When his pet chow was brought to visit him, she cowered in a far corner of the room. The day the war began, Freud lay on a couch in his garden and listened stoically as the radio announced an air raid, then announced that it had been a false alarm. The last book he was able to read was Balzac's *La Peau de Chagrin,* which he described as "just the book for me—it deals with starvation." A hearty voice on the radio proclaimed that this was to be the last of wars. Freud's doctor, Max Schur, asked the dying man whether he could believe that. "Anyhow, it is my last war," said Freud.

Igor Stravinsky, too, was surrounded by death. He spent most of that summer of 1939 confined to a tuberculosis sanitarium at Sancellemoz, France. His daughter Mika had died there in the fall of 1938 and his wife, Catherine, the following spring. That June, his mother died. "For the third time in half a year, I heard the Requiem service chanted for one of my own family," he said, "and for the third time walked through the fields to the cemetery of

Saint-Geneviève-de-Bois, in Montlhéry, which is on the road to Orléans, and dropped a handful of dirt in an open grave. And once again I was able to go on only by composing. . . ." He was composing, miraculously, the gay and charming Symphony in C. He was also organizing the reflections that he had agreed to deliver as the Charles Eliot Norton lecturer at Harvard in September. To him, the invasion of Poland was yet another assault. "Igor is in a terrible state of nerves," his friend Vera Sudeikina wrote in her diary. She had rescued him from the sanitarium, brought him to Paris, and installed him at Nadia Boulanger's country home until the sailing of the S.S. *Manhattan.* "He takes a dozen suitcases—for only two weeks!" Miss Sudeikina marveled. ". . . We have had an alarm every night, and already the stores are advertising 'pajama styles for the basement,' which is very French."

In Hollywood, these events all seemed far away, as indeed they were. Aldous Huxley had just been assigned to write an M-G-M screenplay for *Pride and Prejudice,* and his wife, Maria, stayed up late by herself to hear Neville Chamberlain go before Parliament to call for war. "I heard Chamberlain here in the middle of the night as he addressed you in London . . ." she wrote to Edward Sackville-West. "It still seems unbelievable. Certainly unimaginable." Just a month earlier, she had given her husband a birthday party, and Orson Welles had come, and Lillian Gish and Helen Hayes, and Paulette Goddard had brought an eight-pound birthday cake inscribed *Mon Coeur,* and Charlie Chaplin "gave an exquisite performance, among other things a dance he is going to do with a balloon."

The origins of *The Great Dictator,* like many of Chaplin's creations, are somewhat obscure. Chaplin himself credited Alexander Korda with having suggested in 1937 that he "should do a Hitler story based on mistaken identity," but he added that he "did not think too much of the idea then." (Some years later, a pudgy and walrus-mustached writer named Konrad Bercovicci sued Chaplin for more than six million dollars, claiming that he had suggested not only the basic idea of Chaplin as Hitler but even such details as "a ballet dance with a globe." When the suit finally came to trial in New York, Bercovicci testified that he and Chaplin had discussed his five-page outline for several hours but that Chaplin was worried "because the State Department says we cannot ridicule the heads of two states with which we are at peace." Chaplin in turn testified that he had never seen Bercovicci's outline, and the two then settled out of court for a payment of $95,000 to Bercovicci.)

Chaplin's political doubts and misgivings about *The Great Dictator* seem strange today, but they apparently caused him a lot of anxiety during his preparations in the summer of 1939. "United Artists . . . had been advised by the Hays Office that I would run into censorship troubles," Chaplin wrote rather vaguely in his memoirs. "Also the English office was very concerned about an anti-Hitler picture and doubted whether it could be shown in Britain." When Hitler actually invaded Poland that September, Chaplin was even more worried, not about official objections now but about how audiences would react to a slapstick comedy about the aggressor. Having already spent more than $500,000 before any filming began, Chaplin stopped all work for a week of conferences and soul-searching, then, with even more secrecy than usual, decided to go ahead. What he had started as a comedy would end with his impassioned appeal for brotherhood: "The clouds are lifting! The sun is breaking through!"

Less rhetorical men confronted the simple question of enlisting. When David Niven finished filming *Raffles* on September 1, he told one of the film's writers, Scott Fitzgerald, that he was returning to London to join the armed forces. Fitzgerald declared that he wanted to go too. "I missed out last time," he said. "I left it too late. I didn't join up until 1917—I never got to go overseas." Fitzgerald "became very maudlin," Niven recalled, "with his mind firmly focused on Agincourt and white chargers." Shortly thereafter, Fitzgerald was once again fired. "It always happens," he told Niven as he returned to work on *The Last Tycoon*. (He was to die of a heart attack the following year.)

On Sunday morning, September 3, Niven was sleeping aboard a yacht that Douglas Fairbanks, Jr., had chartered to cruise off Catalina Island; so were Laurence Olivier and Vivien Leigh, and a number of other English in colonial exile. They woke to hear on the radio that Britain had delivered an ultimatum, and that Germany had rejected it, and that the two nations were at war. Fairbanks raised a glass to toast victory. Olivier drank that toast and then proceeded to get wildly drunk. "Smashed as a hoot owl," as Mrs. Fairbanks later put it, he rowed himself to another yacht, climbed aboard, and began bellowing to anyone who would listen, "This is the end! You are finished, all of you! Finished! You are relics! Enjoy your last moments! You're done for! Doomed!" Then, shivering in his swimming trunks, he staggered back aboard the dinghy, rowed to the next yacht, and repeated his jeremiad.

Niven went off to war by himself. Fairbanks gave him a farewell party that featured many of the stars of Hollywood's English colony—Ronald Colman, Cary Grant, Basil Rathbone—who were generally inclined to remain in Hollywood. That was not, of course, shameful. Indeed, any Hollywood celebrities who asked the British Embassy what they should do were generally told to stay where they were and go on with their work. That was what Hollywood wanted too. David Selznick summed up the studios' view splendidly when he asked what would happen if Laurence Olivier and George Sanders abandoned his new production of *Rebecca*. "We would be in a fine pickle if they walked out in the middle," he said. "Not so much of a pickle as Poland, I grant you, but still a pickle."

So Hollywood remained at peace. When Salka Viertel returned to California, she was struck by the prevailing air of complacent prosperity, by the supermarkets heaped with food, and by "the unconcerned sunbathers on the beach, their hairless bodies glistening and brown . . ." And when the renowned Mrs. Basil Rathbone decided to give a gala dinner in honor of Arthur Rubinstein, Leopold Stokowski, and the heroic people of Poland, she had the walls of her sixty-foot-long dining hall decorated with a three-foot cellophane frieze that displayed the notes of Chopin's "Polonaise Militaire." The total effect, according to one contemporary chronicler, was "something pyrotechnic, exotic, ingenious and rare."

Rubinstein (*left*) was performing Brahms when the Japanese hit Pearl Harbor.

Walt Disney's *Fantasia* transformed Stravinsky's *Rite of Spring* into a battle of dinosaurs. Stravinsky hated it and hated Stokowski's conducting of his score (*above*).

2
INGATHERINGS

(1940)

Arnold Schoenberg was one of the first Hollywood immigrants of a new kind, the refugees from political disaster. In the beginning, there had been the ragpickers and song-pushers, the Mayers and Warners and Cohns, who had arrived hungry and proceeded to gorge themselves on whatever they could find. Then came the cosmopolitans, the actors and directors who had already achieved success in Berlin or London—a Greta Garbo or an Ernst Lubitsch —who then signed handsome contracts to come to Hollywood to work for the Mayers and Warners and Cohns. Arnold Schoenberg, the distinguished composer of *Verklärte Nacht* and *Pierrot Lunaire,* the inventor of the twelve-tone "serial" system which he had believed would "guarantee the supremacy of German music for the next hundred years," reached the age of nearly sixty without ever having the slightest intention of going anywhere near Los Angeles.

Proud of his lifetime appointment as professor at the Berlin Academy of Music, Schoenberg realized during the very first year of the Nazi regime that his lifetime appointment was worthless. On vacation in France that summer of 1933, he received word that it would be dangerous for him to return to Berlin at all. Schoenberg was shocked, outraged. Though he had been raised a Catholic, and then converted to Lutheranism in his youth, he went to the main synagogue in Paris and asked to be converted again, this time to Judaism. Then, with his wife and daughter, he set sail into exile. Only one obscure reporter met his ship in New York; he recalled many years later that "he was a lion—a lion—there is no other way to describe it." The League of Composers arranged a Schoenberg concert in Town Hall, and the audience dutifully applauded even the dissonances that arose from the pianist's accompanying the singer in the wrong clef. When it came to finding a job, however, there was nothing available except at the Malkin Conservatory, a small institution in Boston, where not a single student registered for the composition course that Schoenberg offered. New England's winter weather also proved dangerous for his chronic asthma. He had to find a haven in some warmer place. His publisher, Carl Engel of G. Schirmer, wrote letters to various universities to propose a series of lectures. Of the forty-seven colleges approached, only twenty-two answered, and none made a definite offer. Engel was reduced to soliciting charitable contributions for the exile, even a place to stay.

Schoenberg was saved by the continuous competition between UCLA and USC. When USC invited him to lecture in September of 1935, UCLA countered by offering him a professorship. And so, at sixty, small, frail, bald, and gruff-tempered—"his eyes were protuberant and explosive, and the whole force of the man was in them," Stravinsky once wrote—Schoenberg finally established himself in the unlikely sanctuary of Los Angeles, which was in the process of becoming, without ever realizing it, the music capital of the world. Schoenberg had long been bitter about the general failure to acclaim his thorny creations, and now he was more bitter than ever. His UCLA students, he wrote to Hermann Scherchen, had "such an inadequate grounding that my work is as much a waste of time as if Einstein were having to teach mathematics at a secondary school." In perhaps twenty years, he wrote to another colleague, "there will certainly be . . . a chapter in the musical history of Los Angeles: 'What Schoenberg has achieved in Los Angeles . . .' Frankly, I am very disappointed not to find the interest of the society in my doing, not to find appreciated what I am doing in favor of the future state of musical culture in this city. . . ."

What Schoenberg was doing, amid constant interruptions, was to keep on creating music, notably the second suite for strings, the fourth quartet, the violin concerto, a setting of "Kol Nidre," the second chamber symphony. On the death of George Gershwin, with whom Schoenberg liked to play tennis, the exile acclaimed his younger and more successful friend as a comrade. "An artist to me is like an apple tree," Schoenberg said of both Gershwin and himself. "When his time comes, whether he wants it or not, he bursts into bloom and starts to produce apples. And as an apple tree neither knows nor asks about the value experts of the market will attribute to its product, so a real composer does not ask whether his product will please the experts. . . ."

Irving Thalberg, the young chief of production at M-G-M, considered himself both an expert of the market and a man of refined taste, and he listened, as many people did in those days, to the weekly radio broadcasts of the New York Philharmonic. In one of its occasional departures from Beethoven and Brahms, the orchestra performed *Verklärte Nacht,* the almost morbidly luscious nocturne that Schoenberg had written nearly a half century earlier. Thalberg was impressed. This was the kind of music he wanted for his newest production, Pearl Buck's best-selling drama of China, *The Good Earth.*

When Thalberg's inquiries informed him that the composer was living right in Los Angeles, a humble professor at UCLA, he wanted him summoned. Important executives always need intermediaries on such occasions, and since Schoenberg had no agent or business manager, Thalberg invoked a mutual acquaintance, Salka Viertel. Thalberg knew Mrs. Viertel as the writer of several Garbo films, among them *Queen Christina* and *Conquest,* but she was also the sister of Eduard Steuermann, an eminent pianist and advocate of Schoenberg's music.

"How much would they pay?" Schoenberg asked Mrs. Viertel when she told him of Thalberg's desire to hire him for *The Good Earth*.

"About twenty-five thousand dollars, I suppose," she answered.

Schoenberg, who was earning less than one fifth of that sum for a year's teaching, agreed to be interviewed. Mrs. Viertel had to arrange the protocol. An M-G-M car was assigned to bring Schoenberg to the M-G-M studio. An appointment was made for 3 P.M., and Thalberg promised not to keep the composer waiting. (Schoenberg once became furious at Jascha Heifetz for sending a note that said, "You are expected at two o'clock." "Russian peasant!" cried Schoenberg. "In Vienna, an invitation from Franz Josef would read, 'We request the *honor* of your *presence.*' ") By 3:30 P.M., when Schoenberg had not appeared, Thalberg began to get irritated. Secretaries started telephoning. They soon discovered that the composer had wandered by mistake into a guided tour of the studio. He seemed to regard the tour as a perfectly appropriate gesture by Thalberg, an invitation to see whether M-G-M was a studio for which he would like to compose music.

Brought finally to Thalberg's imperial office, Schoenberg took a seat in front of the producer's desk. He kept both hands clasped on the handle of an umbrella, which he refused to give up. Thalberg began explaining his idea.

"Last Sunday, when I heard the lovely music you have written—"

"I don't write 'lovely' music," Schoenberg interrupted.

Thalberg looked puzzled for a moment, then smiled politely and started again. *The Good Earth* was the story of China, he said, so he wanted music that sounded distantly Oriental. Chinese themes. Since Paul Muni and the other characters were supposed to be peasants, there was not much dialogue but lots of action. There was a scene, for example, in which swarms of locusts invaded the fields and ate all the grain. That would require music of a special kind . . .

Mrs. Viertel tried translating all this into German, but Schoenberg stopped her. He said he understood perfectly. And now he would have to explain the problem of music in films. It was generally terrible, he told Thalberg; dull, meaningless. Furthermore, the producers didn't seem to understand that the dialogue also suffered from a certain monotony. He would work on *The Good Earth,* he said, only if he was given complete control of all sound, the dialogue as well as the music.

"What do you mean by complete control?" Thalberg asked in wonderment.

"I mean that I would have to work with the actors," Schoenberg said. "They would have to speak in the same pitch and key as I compose it in. It would be similar to *Pierrot Lunaire,* but of course less difficult."

Schoenberg turned to Mrs. Viertel and asked her if she could remember and recite any of the *Sprechstimme* from *Pierrot Lunaire*. She could and did, valiantly starting to wail and quaver, *"Der Mond, den Mann mit augen trinkt . . ."*

"Well, Mr. Schoenberg," Thalberg managed to say, "the director and I have different ideas, and they may contradict yours. You see, the director wants to handle the actors himself."

"He could do that," Schoenberg said grandly, "after they had studied their lines with me."

Thalberg, who was not accustomed to being patronized, particularly by threadbare professors, could not help being impressed by Schoenberg's self-assurance. He gave the composer a copy of the *Good Earth* screenplay and asked him to read it and think about it. After he had ushered Schoenberg to the door, he could only say to Mrs. Viertel, "This is a remarkable man."

Thalberg assumed, of course, that nobody could decline an M-G-M assignment. "He'll write the music on my terms, you'll see," he said. On the contrary, Schoenberg changed the terms. He had his wife call up Mrs. Viertel the next day to say that not only did he insist on complete control of dialogue as well as music, but the price would have to be doubled, to $50,000. "When I related this to Thalberg," Mrs. Viertel recalled, "he shrugged and said that meanwhile the Chinese technical adviser had brought some folk songs which had inspired the head of the sound department to write some very lovely music."

Schoenberg seemed to think that he had narrowly escaped from Thalberg. "I almost agreed to write music for a film," he wrote to Alma Mahler Werfel, "but fortunately asked $50,000, which, likewise fortunately, was much too much, for it would have been the end of me. . . ."

●   ●   ●

Hollywood's big musical event of 1940—drowning out all the routine M-G-M musical comedies and even the first pairing of Bing Crosby and Bob Hope, in the engaging *Road to Singapore*—was Walt Disney's grandiose venture into culture, *Fantasia*. Disney was then at the height of his success. Not only had his Mickey Mouse become a figure of worldwide renown, followed by such epigoni as Donald Duck and Goofy, but Disney had gambled heavily and triumphantly on the idea of a full-length animated film. The result, *Snow White and the Seven Dwarfs*, appeared in 1937 and eventually grossed eight million dollars, a titanic sum for a film made during the Depression. Once Dopey, Sneezy, and the other dwarfs had become in their turn international celebrities, Disney began building himself a three-million-dollar studio in Burbank. Like the Disney worlds of the future, it was to be a self-contained empire, with its own streets and electric system and telephone exchange, its own sun decks and gymnasium and volleyball courts. Disney's film projects of that period were equally ambitious, full-length versions of *Pinocchio* and *Bambi*.

Disney felt a little unhappy, though, about the overshadowing of his original hero, Mickey Mouse. Somewhere, he got the idea of reviving Mickey's fortunes by starring him in a two-reel version of an old fairy tale, "The Sorcerer's Apprentice," which had been set to music by the late Paul Dukas. Disney saw all kinds of possibilities in this comedy of an overworked apprentice misappropriating his master's magical powers in an effort to get the cleaning chores done, then being overwhelmed by an ungovernable army of household implements, all relentlessly determined to work. Disney casually mentioned his idea to Leopold Stokowski at a dinner party, according to one version, and the tempestuous conductor of the Philadelphia Orchestra eagerly offered to conduct the Dukas score. According to Stokowski's own version, Disney approached him in a restaurant and asked him to help on the project.

Stokowski came to the Disney studio and was enchanted. He toyed with the sound-mixing equipment and pronounced the possibilities "the ultimate in conducting." He recorded the Dukas score—at considerable expense, rather more than the frugal Disney wanted to invest in music for a short— then began suggesting how the movie might be expanded with other pieces that he might perform and Disney might illustrate. His own overblown orchestration of Bach's organ toccata in D minor, for example. Now it was Disney who was enchanted. He and Stokowski puzzled over how to convert Bach's improvisations into moving images. One passage inspired Disney to say that he saw orange. "Oh, no, I see it as purple," said Stokowski.

As the two of them labored on toward what the studio called only "The Concert Feature," Stokowski kept suggesting yet more pieces. What about Wagner's "Ride of the Valkyries"? Perhaps Rachmaninoff could be persuaded to play his second piano concerto, though Stokowski warned that he might refuse because "he's very peculiar, a very nice man, but a very strange one." If Rachmaninoff balked, said Stokowski, they could ask Vladimir Horowitz, whom the conductor described as "marvelous." One of Disney's lieutenants objected that Horowitz was not well enough known. "I don't know anything about music," said Disney, "but I have heard of Rachmaninoff for a long time."

Stokowski suggested a Debussy prelude, "Les Sons et les Parfums Tournent dans l'Air du Soir," and he had a special reason. "I have always wanted to put perfume in theaters, have wanted to do it for years," he said. Disney seemed enthusiastic. "Get a good flower smell," he said. "There you've got something. . . . You could get them to name a special perfume for this— create a perfume—you could get writeups in the papers. . . . It's a hot idea."

Out of such conferences, "The Concert Feature" evolved. One of the first selections was Mussorgsky's "Night on Bald Mountain," for Disney believed that he could "build a beautiful thing based on the devil's orchestra [with] a lot of these little devils playing instruments with one big devil conducting." That eventually led to Schubert's "Ave Maria," presented as a torchlight procession in the wake of the Mussorgsky, which prompted the critic Richard Schickel to observe that in Disney's fancies "nothing is sacred, not even the sacred." Ponchielli's "Dance of the Hours" became a ballet for prancing elephants, alligators, and ostriches, and Beethoven's "Pastoral" Symphony turned into a frolic for fauns, nymphs, centaurs, "centaurettes," and other inhabitants of Disney's Mount Olympus. When Disney saw the final version of what his animators had done to the "Pastoral" Symphony, he was impressed. "Gee, this'll *make* Beethoven," he said.

Disney had wanted from the beginning to include some sort of legend of the creation, volcanoes and tidal waves and lumbering dinosaurs. He assigned his research assistants to discover some appropriate music, but all they could offer him was Hadyn's *Creation,* which somehow didn't seem sufficiently epic. Disney presented the problem to Stokowski, and Stokowski offered a bold solution.

"Why don't we do the *Sacre?"* he said.

"Socker?" Disney asked. "What's that?"

"Sacre de Printemps—Rite of Spring, by Stravinsky," said Stokowski. He told Disney about the famous ballet, which Stravinsky had originally conceived as "a scene of pagan ritual in which a chosen sacrificial virgin danced herself to death," and which the riotous audience at the Paris premiere of 1913 had turned into one of the delicious uproars of its time. And if Stravinsky's work wasn't actually about dinosaurs, well, *caveat emptor.*

Igor Stravinsky was the only composer being featured in "The Concert Feature" who was actually alive and might have some opinions on the subject, so the Disney studio sent a message to France, offering to pay the composer $5,000 for the legal right to use *Le Sacre* in the planned film. The offer, Stravinsky later recalled with some bitterness, was "accompanied by a gentle warning that if permission were withheld the music would be used anyway," since the prerevolutionary Russian copyrights no longer protected it. The offer of $5,000 was certainly modest, since the production cost of *Fantasia* was $2,280,000, but Stravinsky had other things on his mind—his struggle with tuberculosis, the death of his wife and daughter, the threat of imminent war —so he took the money and signed the contract.

By this time, Disney was so involved in *Fantasia* that if his adjutants had not been able to produce the creation music that he wanted, he probably would have tried to write it himself. He summoned paleontologists like Chester Stock of Cal Tech for expert advice on protozoic life and sent his technicians to the Mount Wilson Observatory to study the shapes of nebulae. "A herd of pet iguanas and a baby alligator wriggled over the Burbank lot, while animators studied their lizardy movements . . . " according to a rather feverish cover story on *Fantasia* in *Time.* "The Disney zoo contained eusthenopterons, brachiosaurs, brontosaurs, plesiosaurs, mesosaurs, diplodocuses, triceratopses, pterodactyls, trachodons, struthiomimuses, stegosaurs . . . and enough plain run-of-the-Jurassic dinosaurs to people a planet. Studio cameras groaned under the burden of the whole story of evolution."

Stravinsky had made occasional forays to distant America during the 1930's, reaching as far as Los Angeles in 1935, meeting Charlie Chaplin, and even then he "thought of living somewhere in the hideous but lively Los Angeles conurbation . . . for reasons of health primarily, but also because Los Angeles seemed the best place in America for me to begin my new life." That December of 1939, during the Christmas break at Harvard, Stravinsky returned to Hollywood to see what Disney had done with *Le Sacre.* The studio provided him and his friend George Balanchine with a private showing of *Fantasia.* "I remember someone offering me a score," Stravinsky recalled later, "and when I said I had my own, the someone saying, 'But it is all changed.' It was indeed. The instrumentation had been improved by such stunts as having the horns play their glissandi an octave higher in the *Danse de la Terre*. The order of pieces had been shuffled, too, and the most difficult of them eliminated."

Stravinsky seemed to realize his helplessness and stifled his grievances. When he published his account of the scene nearly twenty years later, Disney expressed benign surprise. Disney's recollection, according to an associate, was that Stravinsky had come to the studio and seen the original sketches for the *Fantasia* version of *Le Sacre*, had been "excited" over the film's possibilities, had even observed that "the concept of the world's creation and prehistoric life were what he 'really' had in mind when he wrote *Le Sacre*," and that he had agreed to "certain cuts and arrangements" of his music. When Stravinsky saw the final film, according to the Disney version, he "emerged from the projection room visibly moved." Furthermore, said Disney, "we paid him $10,000, not $5,000." Stravinsky denied all this, except the statement that he had been "moved" by the showing. He declared that Stokowski's performance of his music had been "execrable," and that Disney's illustrations were "an unresisting imbecility." That he should ever have said anything different was "highly improbable—though, of course, I should hope I was polite."

The week after this revelation, Stravinsky cabled money from the Beverly Wilshire Hotel to Vera Sudeikina, whom he had described to the U.S. ambassador to France as "my best friend," so that she could come to America. They were married in March of 1940, and after establishing themselves in Los Angeles, they went to Mexico in July so that they could reenter the U.S. on the Russian quota and apply for citizenship. "I remember that one of the immigration officials asked me whether I wished to change my name," Stravinsky wrote later. "It was the most unexpected question I had ever heard, and I laughed, whereupon the official said, 'Well, most of them do.' " The Stravinskys lived first on South Swall Drive in Beverly Hills, and then, after a two-month stay at the Chateau Marmont, moved into a pleasantly terraced one-story house behind a white picket fence at 1260 North Wetherly Drive. It was "an American transposition" of his European habitat, according to the Polish composer Alexandre Tansman. "Two pianos, one a grand, the other a half-muted upright, occupy a good half of [the workroom]," Tansman wrote. "The work desk is encumbered by a quantity of odd objects: multicolored pencils, inks, erasers, clef makers, chronometers. . . . The drawers contain manuscripts, business papers, documents, his correspondence, everything arranged in irreproachable order. . . . On the walls pictures and drawings by his son Theodore, by Picasso, Fernand Léger, and Eugène Berman . . . together with a framed extract of a contemporary newspaper containing a very bad criticism of a new work by 'Herr Ludwig van Beethoven.' "

Unlike Schoenberg, Stravinsky was almost accustomed to exile—no one ever gets completely accustomed to it—and these Hollywood years, the sixties of his own life, proved extremely fruitful. He finished here the marvelous

Symphony in C, begun in Paris while his first wife was dying. One passage in the last movement, he later observed, "might not have occurred to me before I had known the neon glitter of Los Angeles' boulevards from a speeding automobile." Here he wrote the Sonata for Two Pianos and the Symphony in Three Movements and the mysteriously powerful *Mass*. Yet Stravinsky was always tempted—also unlike Schoenberg—to gather in some of the money that seemed to lie scattered all around him.

"I wonder if you'd like to do a little ballet with me," said George Balanchine on the telephone, long distance, "a polka, perhaps."

"For whom?" said Stravinsky.

"For some elephants," said Balanchine.

A pause.

"How old?" said Stravinsky.

"Very young," said Balanchine.

Another pause.

"All right," said Stravinsky. "If they are very young elephants, I will do it."

Thus was born "Circus Polka," which was actually performed in 1942 by a troupe of fifty elephants of the Ringling Brothers Circus. Then there was the "Ebony Concerto," commissioned by the jazz clarinetist Woody Herman. And "The Star-Spangled Banner," which Stravinsky arranged for chorus and orchestra in 1941 and later conducted in Boston, where, as he recalled, "I stood with my back to the orchestra and conducted the audience, who were supposed to sing but didn't. . . . Just before the second concert, a police commissioner appeared in my dressing room and informed me of a Massachusetts law forbidding any 'tampering' with national property. He said that policemen had already been instructed to remove my arrangement from the music stands. . . . I do not know if my version has been performed since."

But it was the movies that provided the great temptation, the movies that constantly promised riches if only the terms could be negotiated. Stravinsky was not an amateur in these matters. According to one account of a meeting with Sam Goldwyn, the producer acknowledged that the composer's fee was $25,000, and then the conversation "went something like this":

GOLDWYN: "Well, you have to have an arranger."

STRAVINSKY: "What's an arranger?"

GOLDWYN: "An arranger! Why that's a man who has to arrange your music, who has to fit it to the instruments."

STRAVINSKY: "Oh."

GOLDWYN: "Sure, that'll cost you $6,000. And it'll have to come off your $20,000."

STRAVINSKY: "I thought it was $25,000."

GOLDWYN: "Well, whatever it was."

Stravinsky thereupon stood up, according to this account, stuffed his black cigarette holder into his pocket, jammed his hat onto his head, and walked out. So there was no deal. In fact, Stravinsky never actually wrote the music for a single Hollywood film. But some of his gyrations and maneuvers were worthy of his new surroundings. He composed, for example, some hunting music for Orson Welles's version of *Jane Eyre*, and when the contractual negotiations came to nothing, he frugally used the same music to fulfill a commission from the Boston Symphony Orchestra for an Ode to the memory of Serge Koussevitzky's wife. The recycled piece suggested, Stravinsky explained, Mrs. Koussevitzky's love of outdoor concerts. Then there were negotiations for Stravinsky to write incidental music for a film on the Nazi occupation of Norway, *The Commandoes Strike at Dawn*. Stravinsky hastily began arranging a collection of Norwegian folk tunes that his wife had picked up in a secondhand bookstore in Los Angeles. When, once again, the negotiations faded, the Boston Symphony performed what Stravinsky had stoically turned into a piece he called "Four Norwegian Moods."

Perhaps the most astonishing example of Stravinsky's accommodation to the ways of Hollywood was his accommodation to that same Walt Disney whose transformation of *Le Sacre* he considered "an unresisting imbecility." On October 23, 1940, two of Disney's aides—not even Disney himself— came to call on Stravinsky to discuss an animated version of his musical folk tale *Renard,* and a week later he sold them an option on not only *Renard* but *The Firebird* as well.

No matter how venal Stravinsky became, though, Hollywood always managed to surprise him. "They want my name, not my music," he said. "I was even offered $100,000 to pad a film with music, and when I refused, was told that I could receive the same money if I were willing to allow someone else to compose the music in my name." Recalling that offer reminded Stravinsky of Schoenberg's encounter with Thalberg. Twenty years had passed by now, and both antagonists were dead, and their meeting had acquired encrustations of legend. "The great composer, who earned almost nothing from his compositions, was invited to supply music for *The Good Earth*, at a fee that must have seemed like Croesus' fortune to him, but with impossible artistic conditions attached," Stravinsky said. "He refused, saying, 'You kill me to keep me from starving to death.' "

• • •

It was natural enough for the movie producers to treat major composers like hired servants, since they treated everyone that way. Most of the composers they dealt with were already on the payroll, and everyone acted accordingly. Dimitri Tiomkin, for example, was a native of St. Petersburg, just like Stravinsky; he played the piano and composed ballet music, just like Stravinsky. But he came to Hollywood in 1929 and began producing what ultimately became a total of more than 160 film scores. (It was Tiomkin who, on winning an Academy Award in 1954 for *The High and the Mighty*, gave thanks for help not to the usual array of agents and producers but to Beethoven, Brahms, and Wagner, the composers he had so often found so helpful.) David Selznick summoned Tiomkin to his studio one day and asked him to become the seventh composer to try writing the music for *Duel in the Sun* (1947). He wanted, he said, eleven main themes: a Spanish theme, a ranch theme, a love theme, an orgasm theme—

"Orgasm?" Tiomkin said. "How do you score an orgasm?"

"Try," said Selznick. "I want a really good *shtump.*"

Tiomkin labored for weeks on his eleven themes, then assembled an orchestra and played them for Selznick. Selznick was pleased. Tiomkin labored for weeks more to produce a complete score. It included forty-one drummers and a chorus of one hundred. Selznick kept worrying. He asked Tiomkin to whistle the love theme for him. Tiomkin whistled.

"Fine, fine," said Selznick. "Now the orgasm theme."

Tiomkin whistled. Selznick shook his head somberly.

"That isn't it," Selznick said. "That's just not an orgasm."

Tiomkin went away and worked some more. He combined the sighing of cellos and a brassy stirring of trombones, all in the rhythm of what he later described as a handsaw cutting through wood. Once again, he was summoned to Selznick's studio, once again the orchestra assembled, and this time Selznick ordered Tiomkin's music played during a screening of a stormy love scene between Gregory Peck and Jennifer Jones (whom Selznick was to marry three years later). Everything seemed to go splendidly until the orgasm theme, which Selznick wanted to have repeated, and then repeated again.

"You're going to hate me for this, but it won't do," he finally said to Tiomkin. "It's too beautiful."

"Mr. Selznick, what is troubling you?" Tiomkin protested. "What don't you like about it?"

"I like it, but it isn't orgasm music," Selznick said. "It's not *shtump*. It's not the way I fuck."

"Mr. Selznick, you fuck your way, I fuck my way," cried Tiomkin. "To me, *that* is fucking music."

On this one occasion, Selznick relented, and Tiomkin had it his way. More often, the producers simply decreed that the traditions of the factory were the law, that whatever they decreed must be obeyed. Hanns Eisler, a Berlin radical who had written the music for a number of Bertolt Brecht's plays, was astonished, on his first visit to Hollywood in 1935, to see the system at work. "Every factory has five or six music specialists who . . . have to keep punctually to their office hours," he later wrote. "Number one is a specialist in military music, number two in sentimental love songs, number three is a better trained composer for symphonic music . . . number four is a specialist in Viennese operetta, number five is for jazz. So if music is required for a film, then every composer has to work on a certain section, according to his specialty. The composers have no idea of what is happening in the rest of the film."

André Previn, who was working for $250 a week at M-G-M in those days, was a bit less indignant about the system, but his recollections were no less tart. He recalled that one of M-G-M's top officials had complained about some musical passage in a biblical epic, and he had not been mollified when the composer explained that it was "nothing but a minor chord." From the producer's office came an announcement that remained for years on the bulletin board of the M-G-M music department: "From this date forward, no M-G-M score will contain a minor chord."

Music, major and minor, had been an essential element in movies from the beginning, for even the earliest silent films were shipped out with suggested programs for the hired pianist to thump at in the darkness of the neighborhood theater. When sound came, and Hollywood began buying all the writers it felt it needed, it bought all the composers too. George Gershwin was hired to write the score for *The Goldwyn Follies,* and Aaron Copland for *Of Mice and Men,* Darius Milhaud for *The Private Affairs of Bel-Ami,* Virgil Thomson for *Louisiana Story.* In Europe, too, the new art of film exerted a magnetic attraction on all kinds of composers: Prokofiev and Shostakovich, Honegger and Vaughan Williams and Poulenc.

The Hollywood authorities bought anyone they wanted, but, like David Selznick, they all had definite ideas of what they wanted done. Their idea of a truly distinguished musician was Erich Wolfgang Korngold, who had been earnestly composing since the age of six. While still an adolescent, he saw his operas performed at the Vienna State Opera and praised by Mahler, Strauss, and Puccini. In Hollywood, where he arrived in 1934, his first assignment from Warner Bros. was to doctor Mendelssohn's music for Max Reinhardt's version of *A Midsummer Night's Dream.* From there, it was only a short move to *Captain Blood* and *The Adventures of Robin Hood.*

Korngold's scores were lush and melodious imitations of Brahms, not to say Rachmaninoff. So were those of his most successful colleagues, like Max Steiner, another Viennese, whose works extended from *King Kong* to *Gone With the Wind* to *Casablanca,* or Franz Waxman, a Pole, who orchestrated Friedrich Holländer's songs for *The Blue Angel,* achieved his first Hollywood success with *The Bride of Frankenstein,* and eventually composed the theme performed on each of the five hundred–odd television installments of *Peyton Place.*

These were the stars, who succeeded from time to time in having their background music performed and recorded as symphonic suites, but when the M-G-M factory reached its height in the mid-1940's, it had about fifteen films in production on any given day. Its music department, Hollywood's largest, boasted twenty full-time composers on the payroll, as well as twenty-five arranger-orchestrators and forty copyists. "The music department," said André Previn, "was no more nor less important than the Department of Fake Lawns." Previn's first success for M-G-M had been to write some jazzy variations on "Three Blind Mice" for José Iturbi to "improvise" in a film called *Holiday in Mexico,* to demonstrate, as was generally required in such films, that classical musicians were not snobs. M-G-M's hired composers couldn't afford to be snobs either. "We shaped up at the Music Department each day like truckers waiting to see who had tomatoes to be driven to Chicago or furniture for Delaware," Previn recalled. "We never knew who might need what. If some composer was in trouble with a prize-fight film that had to be finished immediately, we might all be rushed over to that set to pitch in for a few days."

For the true professionals—and Hollywood had the standard proportion of experts, mediocrities, and incompetents—writing for film was an extremely exacting craft. Each piece of music had to accompany not just a specific scene but a specific piece of film. Hence the click track. The standard film moved through a projector at a rate of 24 frames per second, or 1,440 frames per minute. A click track consisted of holes punched into the sound track that ran along the edge of the film. A composer could either write for a click track or somebody else would have to do it for him. So in Max Steiner's score for *Since You Went Away,* for example, at the point marked "The Kiss," where the violins played a series of sweet high quarter-note chords while an arpeggio swept up from below, the score was marked not only "measure 44" but "5/53" on the click track. The conductor listening through earphones knew exactly what was expected of him.

When these musicians went home at the end of a day's work, they wanted very much to play a different kind of music. Leonard Slatkin, the conductor of the St. Louis Symphony Orchestra, grew up in Hollywood and recalled that his father, Felix Slatkin, a violinist who worked at 20th Century–Fox, and his mother, Eleanor Aller, a cellist who worked at Warner Bros., met at the Hollywood Bowl and eventually founded the Hollywood Quartet. "They would come home at 5 o'clock and play music all night," said Slatkin. "They knew everybody, and you never could tell who might drop in, anybody from Schoenberg to Sinatra."

These Hollywood musical encounters could reach a rather exalted level. Stravinsky had already gone to bed one night in July of 1942 when he heard a noise on the steps leading to his front door. He went to investigate and found himself confronting a tall and austere-looking man who apologized in Russian for the lateness of his visit but said he wanted to bring Stravinsky a jar of honey and to invite him to dinner. He promised that music would not be mentioned. Stravinsky naturally recognized his nocturnal visitor as the unmistakable Sergei Rachmaninoff, and accepted. If no music was discussed— it seems hard to believe—that was hardly the case when Vladimir Horowitz came to visit Rachmaninoff's home shortly before the composer's death in 1943. The two master pianists spent the evening—imagine the scene!—playing four-hand duets.

The superb RCA Victor recordings of Beethoven's "Archduke" Trio and the Schubert B-flat came about largely because Arthur Rubinstein, Jascha Heifetz, and Emanuel Feuermann were all neighbors. "After those recordings . . ." Rubinstein recalled later, "the three of us, joined by other musicians, spent glorious days and nights playing chamber music." Some of these occasions, though, were less distinguished. Oscar Levant, who had been studying desultorily with Schoenberg, wrote a piano concerto that Schoenberg thought might interest Otto Klemperer, another Berlin refugee, who had become the conductor of the Los Angeles Philharmonic. When they all met at one of Salka Viertel's parties, Schoenberg urged Levant to perform his new work. "This was the opportunity that would have meant so much to me," Levant confessed, "but my unpredictability and my quixotic impulse to undo myself resolved into a bad joke. I sat at the piano and played and sang 'When Irish Eyes are Smiling,' and to this day I am perplexed by my own behavior. . . . To top it off, I asked Klemperer if he liked Beethoven."

Ben Hecht played the violin with amateur gusto, so he decided to organize what he called the Ben Hecht Symphonietta, which was to meet for concerts every Thursday night in Hecht's hilltop home. He recruited a peculiar variety of talents. Charles MacArthur played the clarinet, and Harpo Marx the harp, but only in A major. George Antheil, the composer, was supposed to keep order of a sort on the piano. Groucho Marx wanted to join in, but the others decided that he was ineligible since the only instrument he could play was the mandolin, which the others considered beneath the dignity of the Ben Hecht Symphonietta. It was all partly a joke, but all chamber music players take their obsession seriously.

On the night of the first rehearsal, in an upstairs room of Hecht's house, the musicians had just started to play when someone began a loud banging on the door of their rehearsal room. The door suddenly flew open, and Groucho Marx appeared on the threshold.

"Quiet, please!" he shouted, then disappeared again, slamming the door behind him.

The assembled musicians looked at one another with some embarrassment. "Groucho's jealous," Harpo Marx explained. Hecht thought he had heard strange sounds downstairs, but the musicians all decided to ignore the interruption and let Groucho go his own way. They started playing again. Once again, there came a banging on the door. Once again, Groucho Marx appeared.

"Quiet, you lousy amateurs!" he shouted.

When the musicians still ignored him, Groucho turned and stamped down the stairs. Yet again, the musicians turned to their instruments. Then came a resounding orchestral flourish from below. It was the overture to *Tannhäuser*.

"Thunderstruck," Antheil recalled, "we all crawled down the stairway to look. There was Groucho, directing with great batlike gestures, the Los Angeles Symphony Orchestra. At least one hundred men had been squeezed into the living room. Groucho had hired them because (as he later explained) he had been hurt at our not taking him into our symphonietta. We took him in."

●   ●   ●

The rise of Hitler brought America some of its best filmmakers, just as it brought some of its best composers, teachers, nuclear physicists, and everything else. America welcomed them, for the most part, with variations of apathy and dismay. Samuel Wilder, born in a Galician town not far from Krakow and nicknamed Billy because of his mother's enthusiasm for Buffalo Bill's Wild West shows, got to Hollywood early in 1934 through a series of misunderstandings. In Paris, he had written a jazzy story entitled "Pam-Pam," about a runaway girl who took refuge in an abandoned Broadway theater. He sent it to a friend from Berlin named Joe May, who had become a producer at Columbia. The studio offered Wilder a one-way ticket to Hollywood and a six-month contract at $150 per week, and only then discovered that its latest acquisition could hardly speak English.

"Pam-Pam" never got filmed, nor did the other scenarios that Wilder kept frantically churning out. By Christmas of 1935, he was living in a basement anteroom outside the women's toilets in the Chateau Marmont. "This Christmas of 1935," Wilder said later, "when I could not sleep, when women were coming in and peeing and looking at me funny, when I . . . knew that war was on the way for Europe, suddenly I wasn't sure if I fitted in around here in Hollywood. I had the feeling I was not in the right country and I didn't know if there was a right country for me. Right here was the low point of my life."

Wilder was still only twenty-nine, an ebullient youth with curly red hair and the courage of desperation. Erich Pommer, the former UFA producer in Berlin now under contract at RKO, bet Wilder fifty dollars at a party that he wouldn't dare jump into the swimming pool with all his clothes on. Wilder promptly earned himself fifty dollars. Eventually, he found a job at Paramount, at $250 a week, as a foot soldier in the studio's army of 100-odd contract writers. They were required by their contracts to turn in at least eleven pages of copy every Thursday. It was more or less assumed that nobody could write a movie script by himself. Paramount assigned the unruly young Wilder to the most implausible of partners, a wealthy New Yorker and Harvard Law School graduate named Charles Brackett, fourteen years his senior. Together, they were supposed to rewrite for Ernst Lubitsch a creaky Alfred Savoir play entitled *La Huitième Femme du Barbe-Bleu.*

Bluebeard—Gary Cooper in pursuit of Claudette Colbert—was a solid success. Then came *Midnight* and the triumphant *Ninotchka.* And *Hold Back the Dawn,* in which Billy Wilder, having finally become an American citizen in 1939, wrote a sad little comedy about the refugees who were trapped in Tijuana, waiting for U.S. visas that never came. Wilder's hero, who had arrived jaunty and confident, was finally reduced to lolling on his dirty hotel bed and addressing a bitter monologue to a cockroach. "Where you going?" he snarled at the cockroach, in the manner of an immigration official. "Let's see your papers."

On the set one morning, Wilder was dismayed to hear that the scene had been cut. Charles Boyer, the star, a onetime classical actor who now lived mainly by his toupee, his corset, and his heroic image of himself, didn't like it. Wilder went to Lucey's restaurant, found Boyer having breakfast, and started to protest. "I could not speak such lines," said Boyer. "One does not talk to cockroaches. You wish to make me look *stupide?*" Wilder tried to explain the scene, but Boyer was not interested. "I don't wish to have these discussions while I am at the table," he said. "Go away, Mr. Wilder, you disturb me." Angry and helpless, Billy Wilder returned to his office, pounded on his desk, and shouted, "I'll kill him! I'll kill him!" He vowed that he would become a director, the man who gave the orders.

Fritz Lang, by contrast, was already a famous director before he ever left Germany. Almost too much so. Joseph Goebbels, newly installed as Minister of Propaganda and Public Enlightenment, had summoned Lang to his office to tell him that Adolf Hitler was a great admirer of his film *Metropolis*. He wanted Lang to take charge of all film production under the Third Reich. Lang reminded Goebbels that he was partly Jewish. Goebbels said that could be overlooked. Lang asked for twenty-four hours to consider the offer, then fled under an assumed name on the night train to Paris.

David Selznick, who was then still at M-G-M, brought Lang to Hollywood under a personal contract, but could find nothing for the creator of *M* and *Dr. Mabuse* to do. Lang studied English, refusing to speak or write a word of German. He read comic strips. He learned that his wife, Thea von Harbou, who had written several of his most successful films, wanted to stay in Germany, join the Nazi Party, and get a divorce. He spent two months in Arizona, studying the Navajo Indians and photographing their sand paintings.

When David Selznick finally quit his father-in-law's empire to form an independent production company, he left the unemployed Fritz Lang behind. M-G-M duly informed the celebrated immigrant that his contract would not be renewed. "You can't do this to me, I am the first director of Europe," Lang protested to Eddie Mannix, M-G-M's general manager. Mannix apparently took pity on Lang. According to one account, he asked Lang what he would like to do, and Lang said he had found in the story department an interesting outline for a film about a lynching (eventually called *Fury*). According to another version, Mannix simply handed him Norman Krasna's outline of a lynching story and told him to film it. In yet another version, Krasna told his idea to Joseph Mankiewicz—this idea, based on a recent lynching of two kidnappers in California, was that an accidental photograph of the lynch mob could bring the ringleaders to justice—and Mankiewicz sold the idea to M-G-M, with himself as producer. Once the idea was sold, Krasna said he had no recollection of what his story had been. Mankiewicz had to pay Krasna $25,000 for the screen rights to the idea, which subsequently won Krasna an Academy Award, and then write the scenario himself. And then he, Mankiewicz, supposedly asked that Lang be assigned to direct it.

"Joe was much impressed by the Great German Director and his monocle, long cigarette holder, etc.," said Mankiewicz's ex-wife, Elizabeth Young. Others were less impressed. Joseph Ruttenberg, the cameraman who actually shot the film, described Lang as a "mean, ornery German, arrogant and domineering." Perhaps Lang really was all that, or perhaps, badly frightened, he was trying to play the role he thought was expected of him, or perhaps he was simply engrossed in his work. He seemed to be unaware that Hollywood film crews generally took a break for lunch. After several days of Lang's ignoring such details—"German production methods," Mankiewicz remarked, "meant that you never called 'lunch' and that you had your secretary bring you a pill and a glass of brandy on the set"—Spencer Tracy spoke up for the crew.

"What about some lunch?" he asked Lang.

"It is I who will decide when lunch is called, Mr. Tracy," Lang said.

"Oh," said Tracy. He smeared a hand through the makeup on his face, walked off the set, and called out, "Lunch!"

Everything kept getting worse. The lynch scenes had to be shot at night. Rain poured down. Lang insisted on reshooting and reshooting again. At one point, during a scene in which the lynch mob set fire to the jail, Lang insisted on throwing a smoke pot himself and managed to hit one of his actors in the head. According to Mankiewicz, the film crew planned to stage an accident in which a heavy spotlight would fall on Lang and kill him. He claimed that he dissuaded them.

The crisis ended like many Hollywood crises. Lang did his shooting, refused to let anything be changed, and was fired. Mankiewicz edited what Lang had created, and almost everyone at the studio was amazed when *Fury* proved to be a great success. After the premiere, Mankiewicz encountered Lang and Marlene Dietrich at the Brown Derby restaurant and held out his hand. Lang refused to shake it. "You have ruined my picture," he said.

Lang did not return to M-G-M for more than twenty years (Louis B. Mayer hated the whole idea of a film about a lynching from the beginning), but the success of *Fury* demonstrated that a German director could shoot Hollywood action, and so it led to other things. By 1940, Darryl Zanuck had Lang working on *The Return of Frank James,* a sequel to the previous year's big hit about Jesse James, and from that he proceeded immediately to *Western Union.* "The Western," said Lang, who had filmed the epic version of *Die Nibelungen* back in 1924, "is not only the history of this country, it is what the Saga of the Nibelungen is for the European."

• • •

It is remarkable that none of these gifted refugees from Hitler made much of an effort to create films opposing Nazism. One reason was simply fear. Every refugee carried fear in his suitcase—far more than he ever remembered in later years—fear of unemployment and ostracism, of hunger, of disgrace, fear even of retribution from the evil regime he had fled. "Be very careful," Schoenberg wrote to his son-in-law, Felix Greissle, on his arrival in New York. "Here they go in for much more politeness than we do. Above all, one never makes a scene; one never contradicts. . . . Everything must be said amiably, smiling, always with a smile. . . . Something very important: Don't say anything you don't have to say about your experiences of the last few weeks. Especially not to newspapermen or to people who might pass it on to them. You know the Nazis take revenge on relatives and friends still in their power. So be very reserved and don't get mixed up in politics."

More important, though, was that Hollywood itself had no desire to oppose Nazism. A variety of liberal and leftist worthies had joined in 1936 to found the Anti-Nazi League (Dorothy Parker and Oscar Hammerstein were the chief organizers, and Donald Ogden Stewart the chairman), which engaged in speechmaking and fund-raising and attempted a boycott of German goods. Unfortunately, this lasted only until the Hitler-Stalin pact, when the group suddenly changed its name to the Hollywood League for Democratic Action and supported a policy of neutrality. On the other hand, Harry Cohn, the *Duce* of Columbia Pictures, had made a 1933 documentary entitled *Mussolini Speaks*, had gone to Rome to receive a medal for his efforts, and had been so impressed by Mussolini that he not only kept an autographed photograph of the dictator on his office wall but had the office itself rebuilt in the Mussolini style—his own desk raised on a platform so that he could survey visitors as they approached, with the lights in their eyes.

These were all personal idiosyncrasies. Hollywood as a whole made movies only for profit, and it earned about one third of its income from abroad. The studios didn't want to offend anyone, neither Fascists nor anti-Fascists. And the studios' monopolistic domination of all production and distribution meant that there were virtually no independent filmmakers able to produce anything that might offend anyone, neither Fascists nor anti-Fascists nor anyone else. (Besides, who was really anti-Fascist anyway? The English and French who acquiesced so tamely in Hitler's Austrian Anschluss and stood by while the Nazis helped Franco conquer Spain?)

Hollywood's political timidity toward Nazism was also a consequence, however, of its feelings about Jewishness and anti-Semitism. Schoenberg was not the only one who would advise a relative to "be very reserved and don't get mixed up in politics." Anti-Semitism in America in 1940 was widespread and strong, far more so than is now remembered or acknowledged. Jews were totally excluded from many executive jobs and from many of the best places to live. There were quotas limiting Jews in many universities, clubs, corporations. Ordinary Americans did not often act violently against Jews—certainly less so than against blacks, Mexicans, Chinese—but they generally regarded them as an alien people, avaricious, scheming, and dishonest. "What they [the Jews] seem to resent," Raymond Chandler wrote to his English publisher in a fairly typical expression of the common view, "is the feeling that the Jew is a distinct racial type, that you can pick him out by his face, by the tone-quality of his voice, and far too often by his manners. In short, the Jews are to some extent still foreigners. . . . I've lived in a Jewish neighborhood, and I've watched one become Jewish, and it was pretty awful." Such statements may seem surprising today, but the most surprising thing is that Chandler was writing in this vein as late as 1950, five years after the liberation of Auschwitz, and that he was writing to deny any suggestion that he might be considered anti-Semitic. "After all I dealt with dozens and dozens of Jews in Hollywood," he declared, "and was never accused by any of them of any such feeling."

Most Jews of that time had been taught to shrug and accept. Sigmund Freud had been twelve when his father told him how an arrogant gentile had knocked his new fur cap into the muddy gutter and shouted: "Jew! Get off the pavement!" "And what did you do?" asked young Sigmund. "I stepped into the gutter and picked up my cap," said Jakob Freud. In America, though—as in many areas of Germany—Jews clung to the belief in assimilation, the belief that if one behaved just like everyone else, then one would be considered to *be* just like everyone else, a good American. In Hollywood, stars assumed neutral names like Fairbanks or Howard or Shaw; actresses underwent plastic surgery; some made a point of going to Christian churches or donating money to Christian charities. This was not so much a denial of Jewishness—though it was also that—as an effort to make Jewishness appear insignificant, too unimportant to be criticized, or even noticed.

That defense provided protection part of the time, but every failure, when it inevitably occurred, illustrated the failure of the whole illusion, and therefore had to be denied, an aberration. The Bel Air Country Club did not accept Jews as members; they could play golf as guests, but they could not join the club. So a number of Jews started a country club of their own, Hillcrest, inspiring Groucho Marx's famous remark that any club that would let him in was not a club he wanted to join. These were small conflicts and small defeats, but always defeats. The wife of a famous screenwriter remembered that the Santa Monica beach club had a chart on its wall naming such members as Louis B. Mayer, but when a friend put her up for membership, she was puzzled by the application form. "This old man handed me a paper for me to fill out, and it said, 'Religious affiliation,' and I said, 'What does that mean?' I really didn't know what it meant. So he said, 'It means, are you Jewish or not?' I said, 'I'm Jewish.' He reached for the paper to take it back. I said, 'Oh, no, I want the pleasure of tearing this up myself.' As I was tearing it up, I said to the old man, 'How come you have a lot of Jewish people there on your chart as members?' He said, 'Well, they got in before we made this rule.'"

Scott Fitzgerald apparently thought that his employers at M-G-M would be impressed by his friendship with the famous Ernest Hemingway, and that Hemingway would be impressed at meeting the rulers of Hollywood's biggest studio, so he brought his friend for a visit to the offices of Louis B. Mayer. First, though, he introduced Hemingway to one of Mayer's chief producers, a small and cherubic figure named Bernie Hyman. "You're doing pretty well for a Heeb," Hemingway said by way of a jocular greeting. There is no record of what the celebrated novelist said on being ushered into the vast white-on-white office of Louis B. Mayer, but the studio president soon called for his private police. "If this man isn't out of my office in five minutes, it's your job," said Mayer. Hemingway retired to a bar across the street, the Retake

Room, and proceeded to tell everyone how he had stood up to the president of M-G-M.

This was the same Mayer, however, who worried about what the Hitler government would think of one of his new movies, *Three Comrades*, which was based on Erich Maria Remarque's novel set in Weimar Germany. The script, written by Fitzgerald (and rewritten, to Fitzgerald's great dismay, by the producer, Joseph Mankiewicz), blurred the identity of the various factions fighting in the streets, but it was clear enough that the Nazis were Nazis. Mayer invited an official from the German consulate in Los Angeles to a private screening. The German official came, saw, and disapproved.

Mayer apparently was quite willing to make changes. Mankiewicz, however, refused. Joseph I. Breen, the head of Hollywood's self-censoring Production Code Administration (the Hays Office), offered what he considered a solution: Let the rioters be clearly identified as Communists. Mayer ordered that the changes be made. Mankiewicz threatened to resign, and to explain his reasons to the *New York Times*. Mayer shrugged and decided to leave the movie alone. "M-G-M kept on releasing its films in Nazi Germany until Hitler finally threw them out," Mankiewicz recalled. "In fact, one producer was in charge of taking anyone's name off a picture's credits if it sounded Jewish." As late as 1941, Mayer called in the director William Wyler to complain that the early rushes of *Mrs. Miniver* showed an anti-German bias. One scene, in particular, portrayed a downed German pilot as a Nazi fanatic.

"We're not at war with anybody," Mayer explained. "This picture just shows these [English] people having a hard time, and it's very sympathetic to them, but it's not directed against the Germans."

"Mr. Mayer, you know what's going on, don't you?" Wyler protested.

"This is a big corporation," Mayer said. "I'm responsible to my stockholders. We have theaters all over the world, including a couple in Berlin. We don't make hate pictures. We don't hate anybody. We're not at war."

It was only after Pearl Harbor, when Hitler actually did declare war on the United States, that Mayer again summoned Wyler and grandly permitted him to portray the downed German pilot as he saw fit. "You just go ahead," Mayer said. "You do it the way you wanted."

Warners had a much better record. "Warner Brothers had guts," Mankiewicz recalled. "They hated the Nazis more than they cared for the German grosses." Warners also had a special reason for being anti-Nazi: the studio's Berlin representative, Joe Kauffman, was beaten up in a random attack by Nazi toughs and died of his injuries. Warners closed down its Berlin office.

It also began working, apparently at the urging of FBI director J. Edgar Hoover, on a movie called *Confessions of a Nazi Spy*, in which Edward G. Robinson played an FBI agent named Leon Turrou, who had infiltrated the Germans' underworld of propaganda and espionage in America. In retrospect, it seems a rather modest sort of exposé, but the German Embassy made its customary protests and threats. And Hollywood was impressed by all threats. "Look, Jack, a lot of us are still booking pictures in Germany, and taking money out of there," Jack Warner later quoted "one studio owner" as telling him. "We're not at war with Germany, and you're going to hurt some of our own people." Warner quoted himself responding with high-minded indignation: "Hurt what? Their pocketbooks? Listen, these murdering bastards killed our own man in Germany because he wouldn't heil Hitler. The Silver Shirts and the Bundists and all the rest of these hoods are marching in Los Angeles right now. There are high school kids with swastikas on their sleeves a few blocks from our studio. Is that what you want in exchange for some crummy film royalties out of Germany?"

Self-dramatization apparently came naturally to Warner, and though *Confessions of a Nazi Spy* was hardly a landmark in cinema history, it did create a stir when it was released in 1939, the first openly anti-Nazi film that Hollywood had produced.* Not only did the German government lodge complaints with the State Department but the German-American Bund filed a suit for $500,000 in damages. Anonymous letters threatened the lives of Jack Warner, production chief Hal Wallis, producer Robert Lord, and Edward G. Robinson. This was the kind of agitation that made other producers nervous. Even Charlie Chaplin kept worrying about hostile reactions to *The Great Dictator*. When his film finally appeared in 1940, however, Americans were becoming quite accustomed to jeers about Hitler and his absurd mustache, his supposed name of Shicklgruber, his supposed career as a paperhanger. The New York premiere of *The Great Dictator* was a huge success.

The Hollywood Production Code still insisted, however, that the movie industry must not urge American involvement in the war. So when Walter Wanger (né Feuchtwanger) and Alfred Hitchcock decided to film Vincent Sheean's *Personal History,* they managed to concoct a rattling good tale of Nazi espionage without ever saying that the spies were Germans. Actually, Hitchcock was less interested in politics than in the wonderful sets that Wanger let him build: a $200,000 model of a public square in Amsterdam, a huge pipeline from the Colorado River so that the square could be filmed in drenching rain, a 600-by-125-foot copy of London's Waterloo Station (filled with five hundred extras in handsome summer costumes). But Wanger kept demanding that the script, now called *Foreign Correspondent* and far removed from Sheean's memoirs, be revised to include the latest war news—the Nazi invasion of the Low Countries, the fall of France. And though the story was supposed to take place in the fall of 1939, the reports of an impending battle of Britain inspired Hitchcock to call in Ben Hecht to write a stirring ending. "Hello, America," the foreign correspondent, Joel McCrea, began his wildly implausible broadcast from London. No sooner had he started than bombs exploded outside, the electricity failed, and McCrea had to improvise. "It feels as if the lights are all out everywhere—except in America," he declared, as "The Star-Spangled Banner" began sounding in the background. "Keep those lights burning!

---

* By comparison, Warners' 1937 *Life of Emile Zola* never mentioned the fact that Captain Dreyfus, the victim of French anti-Semitism, whom Zola helped to liberate from prison, was a Jew.

Cover them with steel, ring them with guns! Build a canopy of battleships and bombing planes around them! Hello, America! Hang on to your lights! They're the only lights in the world. . . ."

Such flights of rhetoric helped to spread reports that Hitchcock remained in America at the behest of the British authorities. One might suppose that these authorities, threatened with a major military catastrophe, had better uses for their energies, but the British tradition of obliquely effective propaganda and sabotage prepared one to believe anything. If the Korda family legends can be believed, Sir Alex (somewhat mysteriously knighted in 1942) produced *That Hamilton Woman* at the direct suggestion of Winston Churchill —who, according to the romantic account of Korda's nephew Michael, may even have written Nelson's long speech warning that Napoleon would have to be fought to the death. More important, Korda supposedly carried out a request from Churchill to use his corporate offices in New York and Los Angeles for the benefit of British intelligence. "These offices would exist for their own sake as a moneymaking enterprise of Alex Korda's," Michael Korda wrote, "but they would also serve as 'cover' for British agents working in what was then neutral America. American isolationists had made it difficult for British intelligence operatives to work freely in the United States, but a movie company offered unparalleled opportunities. . . ."

American isolationists were not guileless innocents either, of course. They represented, to some extent, all those unpleasant American characteristics of xenophobia, anglophobia, anti-Semitism, and a general hostility toward anything eastern and cosmopolitan. To some extent, too, they were the creatures of Nazi Germany's official propaganda and unofficial manipulation. But they also represented simply the traditional American desire to avoid getting involved in European quarrels. They kept reminding anyone who would listen that George Washington—or was it Thomas Jefferson?—had warned all Americans against foreign entanglements.

Senator Burton Wheeler, a Democrat from Montana and a prominent member of the America First Committee, accused the movie industry of conspiring with the Roosevelt administration to conduct "a violent propaganda campaign intending to incite the American people to the point where they will become involved in this war." Another isolationist senator, Gerald Nye of North Dakota, shared Wheeler's suspicion that Hollywood wanted "to rouse war fever in America and plunge the nation to her destruction." Nye also offered an explanation. "In each of these companies," he said in a speech, "there are a number of production directors, many of whom have come from Russia, Hungary, Germany, and the Balkan countries. . . . They are interested in foreign causes." Out in the countryside, Charles Lindbergh was more explicit in describing the Jews as the "principal war agitators." "Their greatest danger to this country," he said before a crowd of eight thousand in Des Moines in September of 1941, "lies in their large ownership and influence in our motion pictures, our press, our radio, and our government."

Nye introduced a resolution calling for an official investigation of "pro-war" propaganda. The Senate voted its approval, and so a Senate Subcommittee on War Propaganda duly began investigating forty-eight allegedly pro-war movies. These ranged from Warners' *Confessions of a Nazi Spy* and *Sergeant York* (which was to win Gary Cooper an Academy Award) to ten *March of Time* newsreels. Hollywood's producers reacted with indignant denials and even hired Wendell Willkie to represent their interests, but by the time the subcommittee hearings under Senator D. Worth Clark of Idaho finally opened, in September of 1941, American policy toward the Axis was generally acknowledged to be an issue larger than anything that might be suggested in Hollywood.

More ambiguous and more ominous than the fretting of the isolationists was the announcement by Congressman Martin Dies of Texas, founding father* of the House Un-American Activities Committee, that Hollywood should be investigated as a "hotbed of Communism." Dies had made his first raid on Hollywood in 1938, but his indictment was so sweeping that he was widely ridiculed for accusing even Shirley Temple, then ten years old, of aiding the forces of subversion. Dies shifted to an attack on the WPA's Federal Theatre Project, and Congress backed him up by voting in June of 1939 to cut off all the project's funds. That triumph revived Dies's interest in investigating Hollywood. He announced early in 1940 that "forty-two or forty-three prominent members of the Hollywood film colony either were full-fledged members of the Communist Party or active sympathizers and fellow travelers." Though he cited no names, he suggested that "Communist influence was responsible for the subtle but very effective propaganda which appeared in such films as *Juarez, Blockade,* and *Fury.*" He also offered an explanation for Communist influence in Hollywood: "Most of the producers are Jews."

Dies kept announcing throughout the summer of 1940 that he would soon hold hearings in Hollywood, but the man who saw real opportunity in this prospect was Buron Fitts, who had been the Los Angeles district attorney since 1928 and now faced a difficult election campaign. Fitts persuaded a former Communist named John L. Leech, who had been executive secretary of the party's Los Angeles branch before he was expelled in 1937, to tell a grand jury all about communism in Hollywood. Leech's testimony was then artfully leaked to the press, which duly reported that Leech's naming of names had involved Humphrey Bogart, James Cagney, Fredric March, Melvyn Douglas, Franchot Tone, and a dozen others.

Congressman Dies, annoyed at seeing a local prosecutor take over his investigation, hurried to Los Angeles and announced that he wanted to inter-

---

* Though Dies was the first chairman, true fatherhood of the committee might better be attributed to Samuel Dickstein, congressman for Manhattan's Lower East Side, who began in 1934 to campaign for congressional investigation of pro-Nazi propaganda and subversion. While Dies was more interested in strikes in Detroit, Dickstein demanded "a standing committee of this House known as the Committee on Un-American Activities, which should watch every subversive group in this country." The two joined forces, but when Congress approved the plan in 1938, Dies became chairman. Dickstein, perhaps because he was too abrasive, perhaps because he was a Jew, failed even to win a seat on his committee. Thus was its future course charted.

rogate everyone involved. Hollywood reacted in a way that probably seemed forthright at the time but looks worse in retrospect. Paramount's Y. Frank Freeman, who was then also president of the Association of Motion Picture Producers, led a Hollywood delegation to Dies's hotel room and declared that the moviemakers would not "yield to anyone in their true Americanism." The studios, he said, would "welcome a complete and impartial investigation," and if such an investigation unearthed anyone who "brought discredit upon this industry," then, by God, "there will be no attempt to protect those individuals."

Hollywood's progressives made more of a fuss. There were protest meetings. "The people want democracy—real democracy, Mr. Dies," cried Dorothy Parker at a meeting in Philharmonic Hall, "and they look to Hollywood to give it to them because they don't get it any more in their newspapers. And that's why you're out here, Mr. Dies—that's why you want to destroy the Hollywood progressive organizations—because you've got to control this medium if you want to bring fascism to this country." But all Dies really wanted, he kept saying, was to ask a few questions. The stars whom he wanted to question, including Cagney, Bogart, and March, proved quite willing to talk. They "were very frank and submitted their books and records for our inspection," Dies said afterward. As a result of his investigation, he could add that they "are not or never have been Communist sympathizers."

Hollywood was content. It had been cleared, exonerated. And since publicity was always the main purpose of these maneuvers, Dies was content too. He went darting off to investigate the TVA and the WPA. If Communist influence in Hollywood could not be made to seem a national peril in 1940, that was because the time was not yet right.

•　　•　　•

None of these political problems really played a very large part in the Hollywood of 1940. There was another war in Europe, but Europe was far away. There were criticisms in Washington, but Washington was also far away. Hollywood still shared the belief of Calvin Coolidge that the chief business of America was business, and the business of the big movie studios was to churn out whatever the box offices in Dallas or Indianapolis seemed to want. "Hollywood made 350 pictures last year," said Walter Wanger, a producer who was thought to be intellectual because he had once gone to Dartmouth. "Fewer than ten of these pictures departed from the usual Westerns, romances, and boy-meets-girl story." When it came time for that year's Academy Awards, by which Hollywood somehow managed to define itself, Selznick's *Rebecca* (Hitchcock's *Rebecca,* Olivier's *Rebecca,* Daphne Du Maurier's *Rebecca*) won the honors as the best movie. Jimmy Stewart was cited as the best actor for his role in *The Philadelphia Story* and Ginger Rogers as the best actress for *Kitty Foyle.*

•　　•　　•

When President Ronald Reagan played *his* favorite movie of 1940 in the aqua-and-white family theater in the East Wing of the White House not too long ago, he chose neither *Rebecca* nor *The Philadelphia Story* but *Knute Rockne —All American.*

Reagan had arrived in Hollywood at the age of twenty-six, an ambitious sports broadcaster from Iowa, and soon found that Warners' promise of a contract meant nothing but a series of thoroughly second-rate movies: *Love Is on the Air, Submarine D-1, Cowboy from Brooklyn, Hollywood Hotel.* Reagan later declared that everyone came to Hollywood with "the desire to see a certain story become a picture," and that the story he yearned to see on the screen was the life of Knute Rockne. Perhaps it was the influence of his alcoholic father, Jack Reagan, who had never been to Notre Dame but who worshiped the football coach from afar. (When the film was finally finished, Reagan had to arrange for his father to attend the triumphant premiere in South Bend, and to worry over the father's night-long carousing.) "Being brand-new in Hollywood," Reagan said later, "I explored my idea openly, questioning all who would hold still about whom to see, whether simply to do a treatment, or try to write a script. . . ."

Reagan claimed that his only ambition for himself was to play the part of George Gipp, the accidental hero. Scott Fitzgerald once wrote that he used to put himself to sleep by reliving a perpetual fantasy: "Once upon a time (I tell myself) they needed a quarterback at Princeton, and they had nobody and were in despair. The head coach noticed me kicking and passing on the side of the field, and he cried: 'Who is *that* man . . . ? Bring him to me.' " Reagan cherished exactly the same fantasy about the Gipp he wanted to play: "As a freshman walking across the practice field, he had picked up a bouncing football and kicked it back toward the varsity players who were calling for it. He kicked it clear over the fence. . . ."

After all his careless chattering, Reagan was startled to read in *Variety* that Warners had decided to do the story of Rockne. Pat O'Brien, Reagan's own choice for the title role, had already signed up. Reagan implied in his autobiography that his casual talk had inspired someone to steal his idea, and that he didn't even mind. ("The truth is, it had never occurred to me that one got money for story ideas: I just wanted them to make the picture so I could play Gipp.") Ten men had already been tested for the part of Rockne's great star, as Reagan told the story, but he rushed to the producer's office to claim the role for himself. The producer felt that the slender young actor was too frail for such a heroic part, but Reagan hurried back to his apartment to find some photographs of himself all decked out in the shoulder pads of his own football days at Eureka College. Then came a screen test, and, as Reagan laconically noted, "I got the part."

It is easy to be cynical about *Knute Rockne.* Even on its original appearance, Bosley Crowther of the *New York Times* cited the Gipp scenes as "largely sentimental and on the mock-heroic side." And now when it flickers onto the late-night television screen, the archaic qualities of Robert Buckner's script seem almost comic. At Warner Bros. in 1940, the message of the day echoed Emma Lazarus's poem on the Statue of Liberty. In one of the very first scenes, Rockne's father was shown telling his friends in Norway that he was going to America because it was the land of equal opportunity, and his son would be just as good as the son of a king. Once in America, the Rocknes were shown demonstrating the traditional virtues of hard work, thrift, and acquiescence. Those were not enough to achieve true Americanism, however. When the young Knute arrived home late for supper, with his nose slightly bloodied on the football field, his immigrant father started to scold him in Norwegian, and the unrepentant boy parried his father by telling him to "talk American." Hollywood believed in the "melting pot." The Warner brothers could all remember their father, the cobbler from Poland, and young Ronald Reagan could remember the struggles of old Jack.

The message of *Knute Rockne* was not only that immigrants (and refugees) could make good by working hard but that they and all other Americans could best succeed by being tough. As a student at Notre Dame, the young Rockne became the protégé of a chemistry professor, played by the unmistakably German Albert Basserman, a famous Berlin actor who reached the United States in 1939 without knowing more than a few words of English. Torn between the German voice sternly urging a career as a science teacher and the roar of the crowds cheering the Fighting Irish, Rockne did not hesitate long. And as a coach, he constantly emphasized drill, discipline, self-sacrifice for the good of the team. Summoned before a congressional committee investigating the violence of college football, Rockne counterattacked by warning the fluttering congressmen that the greatest problem facing America was that it was "getting *soft!*" That was Hollywood's pronouncement on the eve of war.

Sentimental, yes, simplistic, yes, old-fashioned and perhaps almost fascistic. But to any boy who first saw it in the darkness of some town auditorium, *Knute Rockne* was an absolutely thrilling movie. When Pat O'Brien told his battered players at halftime how the dying Gipp had said to "tell them to go out there with all they got and win just one for the Gipper," and when the players then charged back onto the field and slashed a proud West Point team to pieces—nobody, at least nobody in a small-town auditorium in 1940, could watch those scenes without choking. Nobody except Ronald Reagan at the sneak preview in Pasadena. "When I read Gipp's death scene," he recalled, "I had a lump in my throat so big I couldn't talk. I can get the same lump just thinking the scene, but suddenly there I was on the screen playing the scene, and I was as unmoved as if I had a cold in the nose. It was a terrible letdown and I went home thinking I was a failure. . . ."

Ah, but it is all different now. Reclining in the darkness in the East Wing of the White House, the septuagenarian President can watch his younger self charging into history. He remembers it all, remembers and believes. In the darkness, the President can still feel moved.

●　　●　　●

The refugees kept coming. The fall of France in the summer of 1940 put to flight a whole covey of Parisian filmmakers—René Clair, Max Ophuls, Julien Duvivier, and Jean Renoir, who even brought along Antoine de Saint-Exupéry so he could finish his new novel, *Vol de Nuit*, in Hollywood. It also drove into a new exile those anti-Nazi Germans who had previously taken refuge west of the Rhine.

Thomas Mann's white-bearded and quixotic older brother Heinrich, for example, had established himself in Nice to work on a historical novel about France's King Henry IV. A vociferous anti-Nazi, he prided himself on being president of a nebulous leftist organization called the German Popular Front Abroad. His personal life was equally unworldly. When war broke out in 1939, one of his first acts had been to go to the city hall and marry his mistress, Nelly Kroeger, a half-crazy Berlin barmaid who had already made one drunken attempt at suicide. "By marrying her, I can help her get well," Heinrich wrote to his dismayed younger brother in America. Now that the Germans had swept into Paris, both Heinrich and Nelly Mann had to flee further, and flight became more difficult every day. The eminent novelist Lion Feuchtwanger, for instance, was interned by the French as an enemy alien in 1939, then released under British pressure, then interned again in May of 1940. A newspaper photograph of the sickly Feuchtwanger staring out from behind barbed wire prompted his American publisher to protest to President Roosevelt, who indulgently asked the State Department to provide whatever help seemed appropriate.

Franz Werfel, an exile who happened to be Czech by birth, was living near Toulon when the French government fled Paris, and he, too, began one of those typical refugee flights from anywhere to anywhere. He and his wife, Alma, the celebrated Alma Mahler, who was eleven years his senior, drove first to Marseilles, vainly sought exit visas, then wandered circuitously to Bordeaux, where the French government itself had taken refuge from the invading Germans. "Get away from here, Bordeaux is hell!" an old friend warned them, so they set off again for Biarritz, trying to reach the Spanish border, which they had no permission to cross. Alma, who had made a sort of career out of marrying first Gustav Mahler and then Walter Gropius and now Werfel, mourned the inevitable loss of her various suitcases, stuffed with Mahler scores and other mementos. She consoled herself with Benedictine. The Werfels finally reached Lourdes, in the unoccupied zone, where they were trapped in one sleazy hotel room for week after week while they tried anew to get exit papers. Werfel promised the spirit of the local saint, Bernadette Soubirous, that if he ever escaped from this nightmare, he would write a book in her honor.

Roosevelt's request for assistance to Feuchtwanger inspired the U.S. vice-consul in Marseilles to organize a virtual kidnapping of the imprisoned novelist. The consulate then turned the whole problem over to a gallant young Quaker named Varian Fry, who represented the fledgling Emergency Rescue Committee. Fry had undertaken the mission of getting a whole flock of eminent German refugees across the Spanish border (he was ultimately to rescue nearly two thousand of them). It was not a heavily guarded border, but still, the troupe that Fry herded onto a night train to the frontier town of Cerbère that September was not young. It consisted of the fugitive Feuchtwanger; his wife, Marta, who had been freed from the internment camp at Gurs; Heinrich Mann, nearly seventy, and his alcoholic wife, Nelly; their nephew Golo Mann, Thomas's son; and the Werfels, Franz beginning to brood about the message of Bernadette, and Alma fretting about the music scores that had magically reappeared from Bordeaux.

Now they had to climb the Pyrenees. "It was sheer slippery terrain that we crawled up, bounded by precipices," Alma Werfel said later. "Mountain goats could hardly have kept their footing on the glassy shimmering slate. If you skidded, there was nothing but thistles to hold on to." When they finally reached the mountaintop border, they were stopped by "a dull-faced Catalan soldier" and turned over to a French police officer. "I was wearing old sandals and lugging a bag that contained the rest of our money, my jewels and the score of Bruckner's Third. . ." Mrs. Werfel said. "After the march in the broiling sun we felt utterly wretched."

Money and cigarettes began to change hands, and the tottering exiles were allowed to clamber over the iron chains that marked the frontier of Spain. Once over that frontier, they flew to Lisbon. There, a Greek steamer, the *Nea Hellas,* one of the last ships still making regular voyages to New York, was ready to set sail.

Heinrich Mann contemplated his future in America with little enthusiasm. "He stayed in his cabin as he was sick," Mrs. Werfel wrote in her diary. "He was also feeling angry with the world. When his nephew went to see him he was in bed. He was drawing women with large breasts; sometimes just the latter." Thomas Mann was waiting at the dock to greet his older brother on his arrival in mid-October of 1940. He also helped arrange a job of sorts in Hollywood. The medium for these arrangements was the European Film Fund, which had been created in 1939 by Ernst Lubitsch, Salka Viertel, and the agent Paul Kohner, to find some kind of work for the fugitives from Hitler. After some arm twisting by Kohner—that was his job, after all—Warner Bros. and M-G-M both agreed to pay at least a hundred dollars a week to such shocked, helpless, and basically useless exiles as Alfred Döblin, the author of the novel *Berlin Alexanderplatz,* and Walter Mehring, a founder of Dada poetry in Berlin.

And so it was that while Thomas Mann's novels about Joseph the Provider were selling tens of thousands of copies, enabling him to build himself a new house on San Remo Drive in Pacific Palisades, his older brother went to work for $125 a week as a scriptwriter at Warner Bros. Heinrich Mann was given very little to do since, among other things, he spoke very little English, but like all the rest of Warners' scriptwriters, he was expected to appear at the office every morning at nine. Perhaps a few of the writers in adjoining cubicles recognized the white-bearded old German as the author of the novel on which Josef von Sternberg had once based that harrowing chronicle of a man's degradation *The Blue Angel*. To Thomas Mann, Pacific Palisades seemed a paradise. "I have what I wanted," he wrote, "—the light; the dry, always refreshing warmth; the spaciousness . . . the holm oak, eucalyptus, cedar, and palm vegetation; the walks by the ocean. . . ." Heinrich Mann saw little of that. He wrote of "loneliness and ingratitude."

Werfel was more fortunate. His most recent novel, *Embezzled Heaven*, had been a Book-of-the-Month Club choice and a best-seller, so he and Alma moved right into a handsome house on Los Tilos Road, off Highland Avenue, and began entertaining their musical friends: Schoenberg and Stravinsky, always separately, and Klemperer, Bruno Walter, and Erich Korngold ("We rejoiced whenever he sat down at the piano," Alma said). And since Werfel had made a vow to Saint Bernadette, he now began carrying out that pledge. "He wrote the new novel in a state of rapture, without tiring once," according to Mrs. Werfel. "He brought me each finished chapter and often said, 'I'm sure this can't interest anybody.' Just the same, he kept writing with joy. At the end he said it had been like taking dictation. We celebrated the completion of the first draft like a great holiday."

The Song of Bernadette was a smashing success, as befitted a novel written "with joy." The Book-of-the-Month Club chose it early in 1942, the regular edition sold 350,000 copies, 20th Century–Fox bought it for $100,000, and it became one of the most successful movies of 1943. Jennifer Jones played the soulful peasant girl with all the soulfulness she could command, which was quite a lot, and won herself an Academy Award as the best actress of the year. (Stravinsky hovered at the outer edge of this triumph too, for Werfel asked him to write the background score, but the negotiations, as usual, came to nothing. The piece that Stravinsky actually did write for Bernadette's vision of the Virgin eventually became, with the usual Stravinskian practicality, the Andante of his Symphony in Three Movements.)

Perhaps, though, the transformation of a mystic vision into a commercial triumph can be dangerous. At a Hollywood dinner party during the success of *Bernadette*, Werfel regaled the other guests with stories of his flight across France, the same flight that had brought him to the grotto of Bernadette at Lourdes. He told of a little Jew named Jacobowsky and of an anti-Semitic Polish colonel, who had fallen in together during their flight from the Nazis, and of how they had gradually acquired a mutual respect and even a grudging affection. The host, Max Reinhardt, insisted that Werfel must write this story as a play. When Werfel expressed misgivings about his unfamiliarity with Broadway, another one of the guests, S. N. Behrman, was urged into service as a collaborator. As often happens, Werfel and Behrman started with great enthusiasm, then began arguing, and finally reached the point of no longer speaking to each other. Werfel sequestered himself in a hotel in Santa Barbara to do rewrite after rewrite.

And life with Alma had its own difficulties. Benedictine was by now an important part of her diet. She "has the bosom of a pouter pigeon," Stravinsky's friend Robert Craft wrote maliciously in his diary, "and the voice of a barracks bugle in one of her first husband's symphonies." Behrman was no less malicious. He described a dinner at the Schoenbergs' at which Mrs. Werfel relentlessly analyzed the comparative merits of her various husbands and lovers. "She went on and on," Behrman recalled, "till she came to Werfel; she included him in her list as if he weren't there. Finally, looking straight at her husband, she made a grand summation: 'But,' she said, 'the most interesting personality I have known—*was Mahler*.'" Then, as a last twist, there was a man who reappeared out of the Werfels' past, who had occupied an adjoining room at their hotel in Lourdes, and who now went to court to claim that Werfel had stolen his life story, that he was Jacobowsky. . . .

Werfel suffered his first major heart attack in September of 1943. "He was running a fever and fighting for breath," Mrs. Werfel recorded. "The doctors gave him injections, but in his agony he kept crying, 'Morphine! Morphine!'" He recovered and wrote a poem about his encounter with Death, who ended by speaking "two words only:/'Not Today.'"

Jacobowsky and the Colonel finally opened on Broadway in the spring of 1945, to rave reviews. Werfel hated the final version and never saw it on stage. He was working on a futuristic novel, *Star of the Unborn,* and shortly after writing the last page that August, he collapsed. "He lay on the floor in front of his desk, a smile on his face, his hands limp, unclenched," Mrs. Werfel wrote. "I screamed—screamed as loud as I could scream. The butler came running. . . ."

The funeral was, of course, a great Hollywood event. Not on the scale of the funeral of Rudolph Valentino, or even Harry Cohn, but still, within the large refugee community, a great event. Lotte Lehmann sang Schubert lieder. Bruno Walter, who lived next door to the Werfels, accompanied her on the organ. Werfel himself was decked out in what his wife said had been his own wish, a tuxedo and a new silk shirt, with, mysteriously, a spare silk shirt and several handkerchiefs tucked away inside the coffin. But Alma herself was not there. "'I never come to these things,' this grand woman had said," according to Thomas Mann, who added that her remark "affected me as so comic that I did not know whether the heaving of my chest before the coffin came from laughing or sobbing."

Bruno Walter's organ playing went on and on, while everyone waited for the Franciscan abbot Georg Moenius to deliver his commemorative address. "At the last moment, Alma had insisted on seeing the manuscript," Mann said, "and was giving it a vigorous going-over." Stravinsky was there too, of course, waiting like all the rest. He had admired Werfel as a man of "acute musical judgment," a rare compliment from so caustic a judge as Stravinsky, but when he came to write of the funeral in his memoirs, the thing he remembered most vividly about the occasion was that it had "confronted me for the first time in thirty-three years with the angry, tortured, burning face of Arnold Schoenberg."

Willie Bioff ran the stagehands' union, with the help of the mob.

3

TREACHERY

(1941)

Money attracts deals—and dealers, men with a talent for various combinations of lures and threats and deceptions. As money kept flowing into Hollywood, and all of Los Angeles, the whole place increasingly acquired the seductive glitter of the City of Nets, where, as in *Mahagonny*, everything was permitted. Raymond Chandler's emblematic detective, Philip Marlowe, observed and hated the change. "I used to like this town," he remarked as he drove westward along Sunset Boulevard with a scrumptious model named Dolores (in *The Little Sister*). "A long time ago. There were trees along Wilshire Boulevard. . . . Los Angeles was just a big dry sunny place with ugly homes and no style. . . . Now we've got the big money, the sharp shooters, the percentage workers, the fast-dollar boys, the hoodlums out of New York and Chicago. . . . We've got the flashy restaurants and night clubs they run, and the hotels and apartment houses they own, and the grifters and con men and female bandits that live in them. The . . . riffraff of a big hardboiled city with no more personality than a paper cup."

Hardly anyone could fit Marlowe's indictment better than Willie Bioff—alias William Berg, alias Henry Martin, Harry Martin, and Mr. Bronson—a jowly, blubbery figure from Chicago who had great plans for Hollywood. "I want from the movie industry two million dollars," Bioff said to Nicholas Schenck, president of Loew's, Inc., and thus ruler of M-G-M. "Schenck threw up his hands and raved," Bioff recalled. "I told him if he didn't get the others together we would close every theater in the country." Schenck got the others together, and they negotiated an annual tribute to Bioff.

Schenck went to Bioff's room at the Waldorf-Astoria Hotel in New York with fifty thousand dollars in cash wrapped up in a paper bundle, Schenck testified at Bioff's trial for racketeering in October of 1941. He laid the bundle of money on the bed. Bioff handed the bundle to George Browne, president of the International Alliance of Theatrical Stage Employees (IATSE) and a vice-president of the American Federation of Labor (AFL), and told him to count it. While Browne counted, Schenck stood by the window, smoking and looking thoughtfully out over Manhattan. As he stood and smoked, another visitor arrived, Sidney Kent, president of 20th Century–Fox. He, too, had a paper-wrapped bundle that he placed on the bed. Bioff told Browne to count that as well. Kent's bundle also contained fifty thousand dollars.

That was the way Willie Bioff did business in Hollywood. "I've found out that dickering with these picture producers goes about the same all the time," he observed. "You get into a room with them, and they start yelling and hollering about how they're being held up and robbed. That goes on and on. Me, I'm a busy man and don't get too much sleep. After a while it dies down, and the quiet wakes me up, and I say, 'All right, gentlemen, do we get the money?' "

His real name was Morris Bioff, according to the testimony of his sister, two brothers, and a second cousin, who all said that not only Morris preferred to be called William but so did his older brother Peter, who joined the navy during World War I and was never heard from again. When the prosecutors cited to Bioff the 1916 naturalization papers of his father, Louis, born Lazar Bioffsky, they asked him to sort out the listed children, and he said, "Morris is me."

Brought from Russia at the age of five ("Don't let nobody hand you the bunk that I wasn't born in Chicago," he told one reporter. "There's been talk that I'm a foreigner"), Bioff quit school in the third grade and lived mainly on the streets of Chicago's West Side. He was a newsboy. He worked in an icehouse. He ran errands for various local hoodlums. "I got wise to the trick of stealing hams from Swift's warehouse back of the yards," he said. "Some weeks I wouldn't have nothing but hams to eat except maybe apples that I would sneeze from peddlers' carts in South Halsted Street."

Bioff was arrested a few times, but only one charge counted. A prostitute named Bernice Thomas, working in a brothel on South Halsted Street, serviced thirteen men one day and gave Bioff twenty-nine dollars as his share of her earnings. He was convicted in 1922 on a charge of pandering, sentenced to six months in jail and a fine of three hundred dollars. He served eight days, then was released on an appeal, and the case somehow went into a kind of official limbo. "I made mistakes as a boy," Bioff cried when the charges resurfaced two decades later. He blamed the new publicity on "plutocrats in Hollywood who are attacking me because I am fighting for the little fellows in the picture studios."

As an obscure noncom in the ragged armies trying to maintain the empire of the imprisoned Al Capone, Bioff was maneuvering unsuccessfully to organize the kosher butchers of Chicago when he happened to meet George Browne, the hard-drinking business agent for Local 2 of the Stagehands Union. ("Is it true," a reporter later asked Bioff, "that Browne drank 100 bottles of beer a day?" Bioff pretended to be shocked.) Times were hard. Franklin D. Roosevelt had just been elected President on his promises of a new deal, but 250 members of Browne's local were unemployed, and the rest had recently been forced to take a wage cut. The union was running a soup kitchen to keep its workers going. Bioff talked Browne into hiring him as an assistant at thirty dollars per week, then offered his new boss a proposal. Why not ask the candidates running in the next local elections to contribute to

Browne's soup kitchen in the hope of winning the union members' votes? Bioff's idea promptly earned some handsome donations for the soup kitchen. Then he had another idea. "Let's put the clout on the Balabans," he said to Browne.

John and Barney Balaban (the latter was eventually to become president of Paramount) ran a chain of movie theaters in Chicago and had succeeded in forcing their employees to take a 20 percent wage cut. It was supposed to be temporary, until a specified date. When that date came and went without any changes, Browne demanded that the old pay scales be restored. The Balabans complained of hard times and offered Browne $150 a week for his soup kitchen if he would forget about any restoration of the old wages. Browne reported this offer to his friend Bioff, and Bioff thought he could strike a better bargain.

Bioff began grandly. He demanded fifty thousand dollars. The Balabans pleaded poverty, misery, the ruin of their business. That evening, all the Balaban theaters began to be plagued by a series of accidents in the projection rooms. The projectors ran film upside down, or showed the pictures out of sync with the sound, or put different parts of the film in the wrong order. Customers began demanding their money back. The Balabans, richly aware that Browne's union controlled what was shown in all their theaters, agreed to pay Bioff twenty thousand dollars.

Bioff was triumphant. He and Browne went to an expensive nightclub and ordered champagne. The operator of this nightclub, Nick Circella, naturally wondered how two such unimpressive characters had managed to acquire such impressive amounts of cash. Circella told some of his friends about Browne's mysterious riches, and the friends took Browne for a ride in one of their cars. When they returned from the ride, they knew all they needed to know. Browne and Bioff were thereupon summoned to the home of Frank Nitti, one of Al Capone's chief lieutenants and heirs, known as "The Enforcer." Also in attendance was a visitor from New York, Louis Lepke Buchalter, the head of an organization later known as Murder Inc. The end of prohibition meant that the underworld had to find new ways of making money. Buchalter, too, had begun investigating the possibilities of profit in the film projectionists' power over the movie theaters.

Nitti saw opportunities on a grand scale. In June of 1934, in Louisville, Kentucky, IATSE would hold its national convention. Fat, amiable, alcoholic George Browne had foolishly put himself forward for president in 1932 and been defeated. "Well, you'll run again and you'll win," Nitti supposedly told him now. "Louis [Buchalter] here will talk to Lucky [Luciano] and the eastern outfits will vote for you." And of all the money that could be made from all this, Nitti told Browne, Nitti and his associates would take half (a little later, Nitti raised his share to two thirds). Nick Circella, the sometime restaurateur, would join Browne's staff to keep watch on all the accounts.

So it was that George Browne was elected head of the labor union known as IATSE. And so it was that Willie Bioff, newly appointed as Browne's international representative, summoned the Chicago Exhibitors Association and told its representatives that they would henceforth need two union projectionists in each theater.

"My God! That will close up all my shows," said Jack Miller, labor representative for the theater owners.

"If that will kill grandma, then grandma must die," said Bioff, according to his subsequent testimony. "Miller said that two men in each booth would cost about $500,000 a year. So I said, 'Well, why don't you make a deal?' And we finally agreed on $60,000."

There were more such deals to be made in both New York and Hollywood, so Browne and Bioff began traveling. In New York, they quickly won $150,000 from the theater owners. In Hollywood, where IATSE had been crippled by a strike in 1932, Browne and Bioff coolly announced to the badly divided locals that they, Browne and Bioff, were now in charge of the twelve thousand assorted members, and that they would soon get all these members a 10 percent raise. Then back to New York, where Bioff first made his demand for two million dollars then took Schenck aside and told him, "Maybe two million is a little too much. I've decided I'll take a million." After what Bioff called "yelling and screaming," they all agreed that the four major studios (M-G-M, Warners, Fox, and Paramount) would each pay $50,000, and the minor studios $25,000. Then back to Hollywood, where Bioff told his members that they would have to pay the union 2 percent of their wages for a war fund, in case of strikes. Of that war fund, which totaled about $1.5 million per year, two thirds apparently went to Nitti and his friends in Chicago, the rest to Browne and Bioff. There were a few stirrings of protest, but Browne and Bioff sent some burly assistants to deal with them. Besides, times were hard and jobs scarce.

There actually was one short strike in the spring of 1937, called not by Bioff but by a loose coalition of painters, plumbers, grips, draftsmen, and others who had named themselves the Federated Motion Picture Crafts. Bioff did not approve of such independent maneuvers. "There was disorder, fisticuffing, free-for-all fights," reported Florabel Muir of the *New York Daily News*. "At the height of the trouble a group of strange outlanders arrived in town. Some of these men told around that they came from Chicago. Bioff . . . testified under oath . . . a few months later that all stories of the importation of Chicago gunmen to smash the F.M.P.C. strike were lies. My testimony on this point is not hearsay. I saw these fellows in action. They all drove Lincoln-Zephyr cars and obtained gun permits from the Los Angeles police. The F.M.P.C. people heard of their arrival and immediately sent to the port of San Pedro for C.I.O. longshoremen to protect them. The longies, tough mugs all, came trooping up to Hollywood eager for battle, scorning guns, brandishing only gnarled fists. . . . Four of the Lincoln-Zephyrs filled with gunmen were attacked and rolled over bottom-side up. I saw one major engagement between the longies and the invaders near the Pico Boulevard gate of the Twentieth Century–Fox studio in which fists proved a far more potent weapon than guns. . . ."

Willie Bioff, however, had a still more powerful weapon: the IATSE union card that he issued to anyone who wanted to walk through the picket lines. He issued thousands of them, and in about ten days the strike fizzled out. A few days after that, Bioff received a check for $100,000 from Joseph Schenck, who happened to be not only the chairman of 20th Century–Fox but also the president of the Motion Picture Producers Association. Why Schenck paid this $100,000 to Bioff has never really been explained, though there have been many explanations. Schenck first claimed that it was just a friendly loan, but when the matter ended in court, he declared that Bioff had extorted the money from him as the price of labor peace. Others claimed it was a bribe by the producers to keep the union docile. Schenck's charge of extortion played well in the newspapers, which savored the image of union racketeers preying on respectable businessmen. But bribery and extortion can turn out to be much the same thing. Money is paid in exchange for a service; both sides agree on the price and the service; the only question is who is corrupting whom; perhaps both, perhaps neither.

The antithesis of union racketeers versus respectable businessmen also depends on antithetical images of personality and class. Bioff and Schenck were not exactly opposites. Schenck, too, was an impoverished immigrant from Russia, where his father had sold vodka to riverboats plying the Volga. As boys in New York, he and his younger brother, Nick, had gone to work in a drugstore, a good sort of place for a wide variety of deals. They soon bought the store, then invested in a dance hall across the Hudson, then added a Ferris wheel, then bought all of Palisades Park. Their partner in that last maneuver was a nickelodeon operator named Marcus Loew, who urged them to join in buying some theaters in Hoboken. From there to the presidency of Fox was just another series of deals.

Bioff may not have been the Schencks' third brother, but his version of the $100,000 check made it sound as though they were all members of some sort of family. Bioff actually provided two versions, both fantastically complicated. One story, quite implausible, was that he wanted to invest some of his money in an alfalfa farm, and feared that a large cash payment might look suspicious, and thought that if Schenck loaned him the money, which he would soon repay . . . and so on. Bioff's other story, which sounded a little better but was never publicly investigated, claimed that the studios were raising a fund to lobby for their interests, and that Nick Schenck had asked Bioff to act as a conduit to carry money to his brother Joe. "The motion picture industry is being sandbagged in different parts of the country through legislation," Bioff quoted Nick Schenck as telling him.

The charge that it was all bribery came from a gaunt C.I.O. organizer named Jeff Kibre, who officially represented an organization called the Motion

Picture Technicians Committee and who was subsequently accused of being a Communist. Kibre filed a complaint with the National Labor Relations Board charging that Schenck's $100,000 had been paid "to balk collective bargaining." Kibre's complaint said that Bioff, "while purporting to act as an official representative of the head of the union," was actually in the pay of the producers. This charge was later endorsed by a Chicago tax court, where Judge John W. Kern found that the studios "knowingly and willingly paid over the funds and in a sense lent encouragement and participated with full knowledge of the facts in the activities of Browne and Bioff." Dealing with Browne and Bioff, according to one affidavit, saved the studios an estimated fifteen million dollars. The NLRB duly ordered an election to see who should represent the studio workers. Schenck and Bioff held a strategy meeting, according to subsequent testimony by a IATSE official, and Bioff said IATSE must win the election, and Schenck said, "You're damned right it must. You've got to win."

Bioff did win. After all the threats and shouts, his IATSE received 4,460 votes in that 1939 election while the CIO's United Studio Technicians Guild got 1,967. But like any tragic hero, Bioff appeared unaware of the forces gathering to ruin him. He began planning still greater triumphs. Why should the union limit itself to mere stagehands and electricians? Why not take over the actors, collect a share of the fortunes paid to the stars, become a friend and protector to the pretty girls? Bioff saw his opportunity when a quarrel broke out between the Associated Actors and Artists of America and some officials of its subsidiary, the American Federation of Actors. Bioff's IATSE immediately took in the dissidents by granting the AFA a union charter and promising all of IATSE's muscular support. "We had about 20 percent of Hollywood when we got in trouble," Bioff later said. "If we hadn't got loused up, we'd have had 50 percent. I had Hollywood dancing to my tune."

Many of the actors were rather tempted by Bioff's overtures. Although a few big stars made big money, the vast majority of actors got very little. Their median income in 1939 was $4,700, and many of them were unemployed. Bioff's success in getting the stagehands a 10 percent raise sounded impressive in those Depression days (those who were impressed didn't realize that Bioff's contract also reduced overtime pay and thus saved the studios a lot of money). Bioff encountered strong resistance, however, from the president of the Screen Actors Guild, Robert Montgomery, who asked the union's board for $5,000 to hire a detective agency to investigate Bioff's background. If the board didn't provide the money, Montgomery declared, he would pay it out of his own salary. The detectives hired by the Guild soon discovered—and the Guild publicized—two embarrassing facts. One was Bioff's failure to serve his sentence for pandering; the other was the charge that he had taken a $100,000 bribe from Joe Schenck.

The Internal Revenue Service was already investigating Schenck, and Schenck urged Bioff to "be out of the way." In fact, according to Bioff's later testimony, Schenck paid for Bioff to take his wife, Laurie, on the S.S. *Normandie* on a cruise to Rio de Janeiro and then to spend two months touring London, Paris, and the Low Countries. Bioff's extended vacation served no real purpose. When he returned, he was indicted in January of 1940 for evading nearly $85,000 in taxes in 1936 and 1937. Schenck was indicted the following June for tax frauds of more than $400,000, and for perjury in his explanations of why he had paid $100,000 to Bioff.

Only after Bioff was indicted did the Illinois authorities bestir themselves and ask that he be shipped home to finish serving the eighteen-year-old sentence for pandering. Bioff resisted extradition. "I would call my plight persecution," he said. "Maybe I have been doing too much for the working man. The money interests want to see me out of the picture. So do the CIO and the Communists." None of these writhings saved Bioff from being shipped back to Chicago to serve out his term in Bridewell prison from April to September of 1940. Released then, and departing in a rented car to return to Hollywood, he handed reporters a typewritten statement declaring: "I have paid my pound of flesh to society."

The federal prosecutors artfully brought Schenck to trial first, in March of 1941. The producer tried to defend himself by marshaling an array of character witnesses—Charlie Chaplin, Chico and Harpo Marx, Irving Berlin —but he declined to testify himself. He was duly convicted and sentenced to three years in prison. A few weeks later, after contemplating the various possibilities, Schenck said to his prosecutors: "I'll talk, gentlemen. I don't want to spend three years in jail."

So then Bioff was brought to trial in October, not only for tax evasion but also for racketeering and conspiracy. He was charged with extorting $550,000 from the four big studios. With characteristic *élan,* he admitted to having taken more than twice that much, but always at the producers' request. The testimony was rich and colorful. "Now look, I'll tell you why I'm here," Bioff had said, according to Nick Schenck. "I want you to know that I'm the boss—I elected Mr. Browne." Schenck said he protested against Bioff's financial demands, but Bioff told him, "Stop this nonsense. It will cost you a lot more if you don't do it." Schenck said the meeting was "terrifying." He further testified that Bioff blamed Louis B. Mayer for the official investigation of his affairs, and he threatened revenge. "There is not room for both of us in this world, and I will be the one who stays here," Schenck quoted Bioff as warning. "Mr. Mayer was terribly scared," Schenck added.

Bioff described his encounters in more amiable terms. "He don't eat no lunch, he eats an apple," he said of Nick Schenck. "I had an apple with him." Bioff told his bizarre tale about borrowing money from Joe Schenck to buy an alfalfa farm, and then he was convicted and sentenced to ten years in prison. His nominal boss, the pitiful George Browne, who did not testify at all, was sentenced to eight. Once Bioff had been consigned to Alcatraz, he decided in 1943 that he wanted to testify more fully about his activities. He told for the first time of the fortune he had been forced to pay to Frank Nitti and Nitti's associates in Chicago. Delighted federal prosecutors duly indicted Nitti and five of his peculiarly named lieutenants: Paul "The Waiter" de Lucia, Phil "The Squire" D'Andrea, Charles "Cherry Nose" Gioe, Louis "Little New York" Campagna, and Frank "The Immune" Maritone. On the day the indictments were handed down, a drunken man clutching a bottle was seen reeling alongside some railroad tracks at Riverside, near Chicago. Several people called out to him, jeering. The drunken man pulled out a pistol and fired wildly at them. Then he put the gun to his own head and pulled the trigger. That was the end of Frank Nitti, "The Enforcer."

Bioff was a star witness against Nitti's friends. He admitted under cross-examination that he had "lied and lied and lied" in his previous court appearances, but he declared that the outbreak of war had greatly affected him. It was solely to join the fight against the Axis, he said, that he had petitioned for his release from prison. The assorted gangsters whom he accused were duly convicted and sentenced to ten years each. Bioff and Browne were paroled after three years of their sentences. Joe Schenck served four months and five days, then received a presidential pardon.

On emerging from prison, Willie Bioff disappeared from sight, or at least from public view. He called himself Bill Nelson and moved to Phoenix. He bought a small house just outside city limits and planted a flowering hedge of lantana and plumbago. He told neighbors that he was a retired businessman, but it was said later that he dabbled in diamonds, or in cattle brokerage, or that he occasionally did some work for old friends in the Las Vegas casinos, or that he acted as an FBI informant. One day in November of 1955, he waved goodbye to his wife, walked out to his Ford pickup truck, and started the engine. The explosion flung his body about twenty-five feet from the wreckage of the truck. "He was so good and kind . . ." his wife said later. "He didn't have an enemy in the world." The murder has never been solved.

Joe Schenck spent his last years in a state sometimes called "confused," at his penthouse suite atop a Beverly Hills hotel, and there he died of a heart attack in 1961. Many friends and associates praised him as one of Hollywood's founding fathers, and Anita Loos eulogized him by saying, "One of the best Christians I've ever known was a Jew." He left an estate of $3.5 million.

•   •   •

At a meeting of the Motion Picture Producers Association, one day in 1941, Louis B. Mayer worked himself into a rage about a novel that had just been published by the son of another one of the producers.

"God damn it, B.P., why didn't you stop him?" demanded Mayer, whose patriarchal authority was such that he refused to allow his own daughters to go to college because their morals might be corrupted there. "How could you allow this? It's your fault."

"Louis, how can I stop him?" retorted Ben Schulberg, the longtime chief of production at Paramount. "It's a free country."

"Well, I don't care," Mayer grumbled. "You should have stopped him, and I think it's an outrage, and he ought to be deported."

"Deported? Where?" Schulberg laughed. "He was one of the few kids who came out of this place. Where are we going to deport him to? Catalina? Lake Helena? Louis, where do you send him?"

"I don't care where you send him," said Louis B. Mayer of Minsk, "but deport him."

What Makes Sammy Run?, the novel that had just been published by the twenty-seven-year-old Budd (originally Seymour) Schulberg, was not a very distinguished work. Its hero, Sammy Glick, was a crude caricature of the Jew as betrayer.* From his boyhood in the East Side ghetto to his apogee as a producer in Hollywood, Sammy Glick lied and cheated, stole ideas, plagiarized stories, double-crossed everyone he knew—not just because it was in his interest, as one former Washington official said of a recent secretary of state, but because it was in his nature. Schulberg kept explaining that nature in terms of social Darwinism. Sammy had been rocked in "his cradle of hate, malnutrition, prejudice, suspicions, amorality, the anarchy of the poor." So he grew into a creature trained only for combat. "I saw Sammy Glick on a battlefield where every soldier was his own cause, his own army and his own flag," said Schulberg's narrator, Al Mannheim. Perhaps anticipating the inevitable charge of anti-Semitism, Schulberg made his preachy narrator a Jew as well, so that in one of his sermons about Sammy's swindling of yet another Jew, Mannheim could urge, "as a last resort, the need of Jews to help each other in self-defense."

" 'Don't pull that Jewish crapola on me,' Sammy said. 'What the hell did the Jews ever do for me?—except maybe get my head cracked open for me when I was a kid. . . .'

" 'Jews,' he said bitterly and absently.

" 'Jews,' he said, like a storm trooper."

Jewish anti-Semitism, Jewish self-hatred, is the standard accusation applied to such an outburst, and it comes easily to accusers who did not experience the gentile anti-Semitism of the 1930's, or the desperation of the victims' efforts to escape it. But if Sammy Glick was a caricature, he nonetheless achieved the durability of such older paradigms as Sinclair Lewis's George Babbitt or Ring Lardner's Jack Keefe. This was partly because of an element of truth at the heart of the caricature and partly because of the richly ornamented detail surrounding the portrait. When Mannheim went to visit Sammy in his new house in upper Beverly Hills, Sammy insisted on turning on the floodlights that illuminated the garden. "I've got my own barbecue pit and my own badminton court," he proudly announced. "And have I got flowers! Do you realize you're looking at twelve hundred dollars' worth of hibiscus plants?" A bit later, when Sammy's boasting made Mannheim feel "as if I

---

*Samuel Goldwyn, after reading the galleys, telephoned Schulberg and reputedly offered him $200,000 not to publish the book, "because you are double-crossing the Jews."

were watching *The Phantom of the Opera* or any other horror picture," he could not resist setting a trap. " 'Sammy,' I said quietly, 'how does it feel? How does it feel to have everything?' He began to smile. It became a smirk, a leer. 'It makes me feel kinda . . .' And then it came blurting out of nowhere —'patriotic.' "

Hollywood was accustomed to such barbs from visiting English novelists, but what made *Sammy* so wounding was that Schulberg had grown up in Hollywood and had known it from the inside all his life. He and his best friend, Maurice Rapf, the son of M-G-M producer Harry Rapf, spent their boyhood playing hide-and-go-seek on the stage sets of "their" studios, watching the creation of *The Merry Widow* and *Ben Hur.* The young Schulberg had been petted and kissed by Mary Pickford and Clara Bow. His mother, Adeline, built the first house on Malibu Beach and spent her time trying to elevate the cultural tastes of Sylvia Thalberg, Rosabelle Laemmle, and the Mayer girls. So Schulberg was intensely pleased when Dorothy Parker praised him by saying, "I never thought anyone could put Hollywood—the true shittiness of it—between covers." For that was indeed what he had done.

The element that Dorothy Parker thought so characteristic of Hollywood appeared most noxiously in its labor union struggles, which Schulberg, almost alone among the novelists of the subject, explored in considerable detail. But that Hollywood struggle can only be understood within the framework of Los Angeles as a whole, which had been for more than half a century the capital of the open shop, and thus of the open labor market, and thus of low wages. Indeed, Los Angeles' officially organized resistance to unions was one of the major reasons why it overtook San Francisco as the great metropolis of California. San Francisco in the late nineteenth century boasted not only a great natural harbor and a rich agricultural hinterland but an established base of commerce and industry and even a cultural heritage of sorts; Los Angeles had relatively nothing.

The arrival of the Southern Pacific Railroad in 1883 started a great real estate boom in Los Angeles. The fare from Kansas City dropped to as low as one dollar, and land sales to the immigrants from the Middle West soared to thirteen million dollars a month. When the boom collapsed at the end of the decade, the city's entrepreneurs faced disaster. General Harrison Gray Otis of the *Los Angeles Times* decided that he had no alternative but to cut all his employees' wages by 20 percent. The unionized printers objected; Otis refused to negotiate; the printers went out on strike in August of 1890; Otis began importing strikebreakers from Kansas. Otis continued publishing, and as the depression of 1893 began ruining both farmers and bankers, Otis became the vociferous champion of economic growth based on low labor costs. "Los Angeles wants no dudes, loafers, and paupers," the *Times* declared, "people who have no means and trust to luck, cheap politicians, failures, bummers, scrubs, impecunious clerks. . . . We need workers! Hustlers!"

The midwesterners who had been lured to California by promises of cheap houses and sunshine were now trapped there in their little houses. Otis helped organize the Los Angeles Merchants and Manufacturers Association, generally known as M & M, which not only opposed unions but threatened and even cut off bank credit to any business that hired union labor. The unions, in turn, organized strikes; the merchants broke them, often with violence. During the whole period of 1890–1910, Los Angeles wages averaged 20 to 30 percent lower than those in San Francisco. And business flowed in. One October night in 1910, a bomb exploded in the main plant of the *Times,* and twenty employees were killed. "O you anarchic scum," Otis declared in his newspaper, "you cowardly murderers, you leeches upon honest labor, you midnight assassins, you whose hands are dripping with the innocent blood of your victims. . . ." Otis hired the William J. Burns detective agency to catch the bombers, and when the detectives produced two Irish toughs, who confessed, on the eve of a hotly contested mayoralty election, Otis stood triumphant. And more business kept flowing in. Among the newcomers were those buccaneers who founded the movie industry.

In the prosperous 1920's, when it seemed easy for anyone to make money, there was little thought of labor unions in Hollywood, but even then, Louis B. Mayer had an interesting idea. As host at a dinner party in his house, Mayer was entertaining himself by playing solitaire, but he also eavesdropped on two of his guests talking about the need for an organization that would include all elements of the industry and would act for the common good. "Why don't you get together, then, and try it out?" said Mayer. They did, but it was Mayer's invitation that summoned thirty-six notables to a private dinner at the Biltmore Hotel, where Mayer explained the idea of a Hollywood organization that would make it unnecessary for anyone to organize any unions. And so was born, in 1927, the Academy of Motion Picture Arts and Sciences. It included producers, directors, writers, actors, technicians, anyone who "contributed in a distinguished way to the Arts and Sciences of Motion Picture Production." The distinguished contributors promptly began giving each other prizes, Academy Awards—to Emil Jannings for *The Way of All Flesh* and Janet Gaynor for *Seventh Heaven,* and to Paramount for *Wings,* best picture of the year.

This convivial system seemed to work admirably until 1931, when a spokesman for the producers blighted an Academy Awards dinner by announcing that because of hard times, all wages would have to be cut by 10 to 25 percent. Paramount and Universal had already imposed 25 percent reductions on people earning more than $150 per week. The Academy's directors made a fuss about the general cut, though, and the producers postponed their maneuver. Until March 8, 1933. Then, in the midst of the financial collapse that President Roosevelt ended by the temporary shutdown called a "bank holiday," the movie producers couldn't meet their payrolls. Three days later, appropriately enough, Hollywood trembled and shook from the thrusts of a major earthquake.

The studios were all determined now to cut their payrolls by 50 percent, regardless of any previous contracts or agreements, and Mayer took the lead by summoning his employees to a pay-cut meeting in the Thalberg Projection Room. He kept his victims waiting for twenty minutes before making his entrance. "His face [was] stubbled and his eyes red, as if his nights had been as sleepless as his days were unshaven," M-G-M story editor Sam Marx recalled. "He began with a soft utterance: 'My friends . . .' Then he broke down. Stricken, he held out his hands, supplicating, bereft of words."

Lionel Barrymore knew a cue when he saw one. "Don't worry, L.B.," he said huskily. "We're with you."

A Hungarian scriptwriter named Ernest Vajda ventured to disagree. "I read the company statements, Mr. Mayer," he said. "I know our films are doing well. Maybe these other companies must do this, but this company should not. Let us wait. There's no reason to cut our pay at this time."

Barrymore recognized another cue.

"Mr. Vajda," he said, "is like a man on his way to the guillotine, waiting to stop for a manicure."

Dutiful laughter and applause rippled through the Thalberg Projection Room. But would all the M-G-M employees who had contracts allow Mayer to renege on those contracts?

May Robson, who had been a star for Vitagraph back in 1916, rose to her feet and said, "As the oldest person in the room, I will take the cut." A now-forgotten child actor echoed her: "As the youngest person in the room, I will take the cut." Mayer beamed paternally at his employees and asked if they would all vote to accept lower pay until "this terrible emergency is over," and they all shouted their approval. As Mayer left the meeting, Marx heard him gloat to one of his lieutenants, Benny Thau,* "How did I do?"

The technicians were the only workers who had a union contract, so they didn't have to take the cut. Their union, IATSE, was not strong in its pregangster days, however. When the inevitable conflict broke out, between M-G-M and a crew of sound men, the studio called in strikebreakers, and when IATSE pulled out all of the six thousand members it then represented, the other studios hired still more strikebreakers. "We expect to keep on the job every man and woman who wants to be," said Mayer.

The most unorganized of all the studio employees were the writers. They liked to think of themselves as creative and independent. They were also the most vulnerable to competition from every young newspaperman or novelist who yearned to become a success in Hollywood. The producers hired these neophytes as "junior writers," the literary equivalent of starlets, at thirty-five dollars per week, or less, or assigned them to write scripts on speculation.

---

*Thau was sometimes described as an M-G-M executive without portfolio. When someone asked Herman Mankiewicz exactly what Thau did, Mankiewicz replied that it was his function to watch from the window of the third floor of the Thalberg Building and to report any appearance of the north wind.

One studio, Republic, achieved a certain notoriety for firing all its writers the day before Thanksgiving so that they could be rehired on Friday without being paid for the holiday. Other than Louis B. Mayer's Academy, the writers had no organization except the Writers Club, which occupied a pleasant house with a fireplace and a billiard room on Sunset Boulevard. Though it had been officially connected with the Authors League of America since 1920, it was a social club and nothing more.

Early in 1933, even before the general wage cut, ten writers met at the Hollywood Knickerbocker Hotel to talk about reorganizing their lives. They were easterners, for the most part, liberal to leftist in politics, and with some record of accomplishment on the New York stage. John Howard Lawson had achieved a considerable reputation in 1925 with his play *Processional.* Samson Raphaelson had written in that same year *The Jazz Singer,* on which the first sound movie had been based. Among the others were Edwin Justus Mayer, Lester Cole, and John Bright. They decided not only that a new writers' organization should be founded but that it should be allied with the Dramatists Guild in New York, so that if the predictable conflicts reached the point of a strike, the writers' organization would cover the whole field of dramatic writing.

The studios' wage cuts provided a powerful inducement to the writers to start a union, and in April of 1933, they founded the Screen Writers Guild. A total of 173 charter members paid one hundred dollars each. John Howard Lawson was elected president. He was not then a Communist, but he publicly announced a year later that he had joined the party. Such things were not secret in those days. "As for myself," Lawson wrote in *New Theatre* magazine, "I do not hesitate to say that it is my aim to present the Communist position and to do so in the most specific manner."

Lawson's politics were not of critical importance, since the producers made it perfectly clear that they would not recognize the SWG as a union or negotiate with it under any circumstances. The movie industry was not an industry, the studios argued, and its writers were not employees. Since the new National Recovery Act forbade this line of argument, however, there now began the long and ugly process of forcing the producers to come to terms. The whole thrust of the New Deal supported the writers, and so did the rulings of the National Labor Relations Board, but the producers fought back with every weapon they could find. They threatened, they delayed, they cajoled, they delayed some more, they sued, they appealed, they even sent Nicholas Schenck to Hyde Park with a large donation for President Roosevelt, and then they delayed some more.

In 1936, the period central to *What Makes Sammy Run?,* the two sides clashed over the issue of the Screen Writers Guild joining forces with the Dramatists Guild in New York. The producers, who still didn't recognize the SWG, raised shrill cries of warning that the writers were trying to subject Hollywood to the domination of New York Communists. And since the Guild was asking all its members not to sign any contracts extending beyond May of 1938, so that they would then be legally free to go on strike, every writer was subject to all the pressure that the producers could apply, which was considerable. "If those guys set up a picket line and try to shut down my studio," cried Darryl Zanuck, "I'll mount a machine gun on the roof and mow them down."

The Guild called a meeting on May 2, 1936, for a vote on the alliance with New York. Shortly before that meeting, a half-dozen well-established screenwriters, to whom the studios had offered new contracts as writer-producers, announced that they were forming an opposition movement to fight the Guild leadership and the alliance with New York. In Schulberg's version, one of these half dozen was naturally Sammy Glick. "I'm catching the express now, baby," he told Mannheim. "I'm getting off at my station in one stop."

On the day before the Guild vote, the new producers summoned all their employees to a series of meetings in each studio. At M-G-M, for example, Thalberg arrived with Eddie Mannix, the ex-bouncer who now served as general manager. "The scene," said Schulberg's friend Maurice Rapf, "was similar to one you might find in Tammany, or even in the gangster movies—the hard guy and the so-called Little Czar, whom everybody loves." Thalberg was now just as tough as Mannix, according to Rapf. "What he said, in effect, was 'You've all gotten a great deal out of this industry. It's been good to you and what you're proposing to do is to give it away and turn it over to outside interests, and we are not going to tolerate it. . . . We have a lot to protect here, and we are going to protect it with everything we've got.'"

When the meeting was finally held, the Guild leaders, rather surprisingly, tried to compromise. They proposed to enlarge the executive board to take in several of the conservative dissidents. The dissidents announced their agreement, and as Schulberg's narrator put it, "Suddenly everybody was loving everybody else."

But that was only a tactical move. Three days after the Guild meeting, the dissident members resigned from the Guild board and announced that they were forming a rival group called Screen Playwrights. The studios looked on the new organization with warm favor and increased their pressure on anyone who remained with the Guild. Within a week, 125 writers had abandoned the Guild and joined the Screen Playwrights. "You've got to resign from that union," Zanuck told one of his writers, Milton Sperling. "Look at all I've done for you." Sperling sensed that a blacklist was already beginning to grow. "More of a graylist, really," he said, "a hesitation about hiring. It was emotional rather than institutional." Dalton Trumbo heard much the same from Harry Cohn. "You will hear a lot of talk about there being no blacklist in this town," Cohn said. "But now there *is* a blacklist and you are definitely on it, and you have your chance of signing or staying out of the business."

The studios' strategy was extremely successful. The Guild had claimed nearly a thousand members at the time of its May meeting. By the end of that summer, the number had shrunk to about a hundred. Only ninety-two appeared at the organization's last meeting, in a grimy office building on North Cherokee, just off Hollywood Boulevard, to hear Guild President Ernest Pascal announce the union's death. "There's no point in going on," said Pascal. "We can't even pay the rent."

Schulberg's version of the story ended about there. The blacklist drove his narrator, Al Mannheim, back to New York. He returned only much later to observe Sammy Glick becoming the head of his studio, and marrying the chairman's beautiful daughter, who forecast Sammy's future by defiantly committing adultery on her wedding night.

Schulberg published a short story entitled "What Makes Sammy Run?" in *Liberty* magazine in 1937, but when he told his colleagues in the Communist Party that he planned to expand the story into a novel, they disapproved. "The reaction . . . was not favorable," Schulberg later testified before the House Un-American Activities Committee. "The feeling was that this was a destructive idea; that . . . it was much too individualistic; that it didn't begin to show what were called the progressive forces in Hollywood." Another screenwriter named Richard Collins urged Schulberg to confer with John Howard Lawson and submit an outline of his plans. "I decided I would have to get away from this if I was ever to be a writer," Schulberg testified. "I decided to leave the group, cut myself off, pay no more dues, listen to no more advice . . . to go away from the Party, from Hollywood, and try to write a book, which is what I did." Schulberg went to Vermont in 1939 and wrote his novel and returned to Hollywood the following year to find both Louis B. Mayer and the Communist Party mad at him. Though he felt that he had quit the party, he did go to a meeting with Lawson, who sharply criticized him, and then to another meeting with the party's cultural commissar, V. J. Jerome, who criticized him some more. "I remember being told that my entire attitude was wrong," Schulberg testified, "that I was wrong about writing; wrong about this book; wrong about the Party."

What remains most interesting is not the squirming of either the Hollywood establishment or the Hollywood Communists but the ending of the story itself. For the Guild did not die after it announced its own death in the summer of 1936. Meetings continued to be held in the homes of the most active members, among them Dorothy Parker, Lillian Hellman, Samson Raphaelson, Dashiell Hammett, Donald Ogden Stewart, John Howard Lawson, and Nathanael West. Early in 1937, the producers signed a tentative agreement with their protégés, the Screen Playwrights, to take effect in case the Supreme Court upheld the Wagner Act of 1935, which guaranteed the rights of workers to form unions. A week after the Court did uphold the Wagner Act, in the spring of 1937, the Guild reemerged from underground and petitioned the National Labor Relations Board for the right to represent all screenwriters. The revived Guild claimed four hundred members, but the producers claimed they now had a binding contract with the Screen Playwrights. The

NLRB held extensive hearings and then ruled in June of 1938 that Hollywood was indeed an industry, that its writers were indeed employees, and that they had a right to vote on a union to represent them. In the voting held later that June, the reborn Guild defeated the crumbling Screen Playwrights by a majority of more than four to one. The next month, the federal government applied still stronger pressure on the studios by filing an antitrust suit against Loew's, Warners, Paramount, Fox, Columbia, Universal, United Artists, and RKO.

Now the studios had no choice but to negotiate with the hated Guild, but still they stalled. They said they wouldn't negotiate with any Communists. All Communists on the Guild side withdrew. In 1940, the producers finally agreed to a six-month contract, which included a minimum wage of fifty dollars per week, but when that expired, they balked at any renewal. Delegates from both sides met for dinner at the Brown Derby in May of 1941 and then settled down for a bargaining session. Mendel Silberberg, an attorney for the producers, warned that international events might overtake them all. "This country might go to war, the studios might be closed," Silberberg said.

Sheridan Gibney, who was now the Guild president, acknowledged the political uncertainties and asked that the producers accept a provisional agreement: recognition of the Guild as representative of the writers, an 85 percent Guild shop, and a minimum wage of $120 per week. After eight years of bargaining, of threats and lawsuits and claims of Communist subversion, eight years of defeats by the courts and the Administration and the votes of the employees, this basic proposal for a minimum wage of $120 per week struck Harry Warner, the president of Warner Bros., as an absolute outrage. He rose to his feet and turned to his colleagues and rhetorically asked, "Is that all they want?"

"We think, under the circumstances, it's fair," Gibney replied.

"That's all they want! They want blood!" Warner bellowed. "They want to take my goddamn studio. My brothers built this studio. I came here from Europe. My father—" Then he turned and started shouting at the Guild delegation. "That's all you want, you goddamn Communist bastards! You dirty sons of bitches! All you'll get from me is shit!"

"And he let out a stream of obscenities I wouldn't dare repeat," according to Dore Schary, who was present as one of the Guild representatives, "calling us all sorts of wild names and screaming. Well, we were stunned. We didn't even get angry, because we were watching a man who was obviously getting blown out of his head." The other producers were also somewhat taken aback by Warner's frenzy. Two of them, Y. Frank Freeman of Paramount and Eddie Mannix of M-G-M, got to their feet and each took one of Warner's arms, and then they all lurched toward the doorway. "They kind of carried him out," Schary recalled, "and he was still screaming, 'And furthermore, you dirty commies,' and they took him out to the parking lot, and there was an absolutely dead silence."

The Guild delegates sat in wonderment for a while, and then the producers returned, without Harry Warner. "Gentlemen, we regret that Mr. Warner cannot rejoin us," Silberberg said. "He wasn't feeling well. But we've discussed your proposal, and we find it acceptable. You have your contract."

• • •

Dashiel Hammett knew the corruption of the labor wars in his bones. He had been a Pinkerton detective in the days when corporate managements hired Pinkerton agents to break strikes and break unions. "I was just doing a job, and if our clients were rotten it didn't concern me," he said later. "They hired us to break up a union strike, so we went out there to do that."

Hammett had become a Pinkerton agent almost by accident. The son of an unsuccessful Maryland farmer, he dropped out of school at fourteen and worked as a stevedore, a stockbrokerage clerk, a cannery laborer, a railroad freight agent. "Usually, I was fired," he said of these brief jobs. In 1915, he answered what he later described as "an enigmatic want-ad," which called for varied experience and a willingness to travel but didn't specify what the work involved. So Hammett applied and was hired, at the age of twenty-one, at a starting salary of twenty-one dollars per month, in the Baltimore office of Pinkerton's National Detective Agency. Its symbol was an all-seeing eye; its slogan, "We never sleep."

Hammett apparently enjoyed disguise and deception and the pursuit of suspected thieves, forgers, murderers. He carried a gun and sometimes used it. "It is held by the agency that the ends being for the accomplishment of justice, they justify the means used," Allan Pinkerton had written in the handbook he provided for his agents. The quarry, of course, took a similar view of the pursuers. Hammett carried to the end of his life a long knife scar on his leg and a deep indentation on his skull. "He was shadowing someone," his wife, Josephine, later recalled, "but what he didn't know was that he was not shadowing one, he was shadowing two, and the second one came up behind him and dropped a brick on his head."

As part of "the accomplishment of justice," the Pinkerton agency sent young Hammett to combat the efforts of the Industrial Workers of the World (IWW) to organize the Anaconda copper miners in Montana. Hammett posed as an enthusiastic supporter of the IWW and got himself confined in a hospital so that he could cajole information out of a suspected radical lying sick in a neighboring bed. Though such treachery apparently did not trouble his conscience at the time, it came to haunt him later. Not long after he met Lillian Hellman, who was then a discontented twenty-four-year-old scriptreader at M-G-M, and the discontented wife of the screenwriter Arthur Kober, Hammett told her that an officer of Anaconda "had offered him $5,000 to kill Frank Little, the labor union organizer." Hammett apparently told the company that murder was not part of his job, so other arrangements were made. A lynch mob seized Little and three other union men and did them to death.

Hammett "was to repeat that bribe offer so many times," Miss Hellman later wrote in *Scoundrel Time*, "that I came to believe . . . that it was a kind of key to his life. He had given a man the right to think he would murder." That idea seems to have shocked Hammett, but a man who would masquerade as a hospital patient in order to extract information from a patient in a neighboring bed was presumably the kind of man to whom a corporate official might feel he could entrust any kind of mission.

Miss Hellman's admiring memoirs of Hammett, with whom she carried on an intermittent but hectic liaison for more than thirty years, have helped to create the legend that this former gunman was a proud stoic living by some intensely chivalric code of honor. Hammett himself presumably knew better. An inveterate philanderer, afflicted more than once by gonorrhea, he was sued for $35,000 on one occasion by a minor Hollywood actress named Elise de Vianne, who claimed that he had "forced his sexual attentions" upon her. That may have been little more than a nuisance suit, but it sounds rather like rape. A Los Angeles judge awarded Miss de Vianne $2,500 in damages. An inveterate gambler and a profligate too, Hammett not only squandered Hollywood earnings of $100,000 a year but ran up absurdly large bills for hotel suites and rented limousines, then evaded payment and left his unfortunate creditors to pursue him in the courts. There was an inherent dishonesty in all this, but Miss Hellman eulogized Hammett at his funeral by saying, "He never lied. He never faked." She herself coolly billed his estate for forty thousand dollars that she said she had loaned him, and she used his debts as part of her successful suit to gain control of his copyrights.

The screenwriter Nunnally Johnson offered an explanation for Hammett's behavior by recalling that he had been deathly ill from tuberculosis since his army service in World War I. The illness had forced him to retire after three years with the Pinkertons, and that in turn led him to start writing. "Here was a man who had no expectation of being alive much beyond Thursday," Johnson said, "—which is why he spent himself and his money with such recklessness." Perhaps. But after writing all of his five novels in six years, Hammett wasted much of his last thirty years, the Hellman years, on drunken quarrels. He blamed his drinking on illness too, but once claimed that it derived from his painful sense of the differences between what people said and what they meant. A detective would appreciate those differences.

When Hammett's third and best novel, *The Maltese Falcon*, appeared in 1930, Warner Bros. paid his publisher, Knopf, $8,500 for all movie rights. That certified, to the rest of Hollywood, Hammett's commercial value. "We have an opportunity to secure Dashiell Hammett . . ." young David O. Selznick wrote in a memo to his boss at Paramount, B. P. Schulberg. "Hammett is unspoiled as to money . . . I have tentatively discussed the following: Four weeks at $300 weekly." So Hammett went to Hollywood, that summer of 1930, and Paramount assigned him to try to concoct a gangster movie for one of its new stars, Gary Cooper. Hammett did produce a story, which was eventually filmed as *City Streets,* pairing Cooper with Schulberg's mistress, Sylvia Sydney.

The Maltese Falcon, meanwhile, was destined for strange metamorphoses. This had been Hammett's first effort to break away from the routine pursuits of the anonymous Continental (Pinkerton) operative. His new hero, Sam Spade, was in business for himself; he was perfectly willing to take criminals as his clients; he was having an affair with his partner's wife; he liked to believe that he belonged to nobody. Hammett later claimed that his hero "had no original. . . . He is a dream man in the sense that he is what most of the detectives I worked with would like to have been . . . a hard and shifty fellow, able to take care of himself in any situation, able to get the best of anybody." If Sam Spade was a dream man, though, his identity was hardly accidental; everyone who knew Hammett in his detective days knew him not by his middle name, Dashiell, but by his first name, Sam.

The Maltese Falcon was also Hammett's first attempt to break away from the mindless violence of the "action" stories he had published in *Black Mask* magazine, to create a drama of primarily psychological tension. The climactic scene occurred when Spade and the beautiful Brigid O'Shaughnessy and the bloated Casper Gutman and the twittering Joel Cairo all sat confined in one room and tried to outwit each other to get possession of the jeweled statue of the Maltese falcon. It was another variation on Hammett's favorite situation, the detective attempting to provoke the criminals into fighting and betraying each other, though the actual violence all occurred offstage. Hammett suggested richer possibilities when he portrayed Spade trying to persuade Gutman to pin a murder charge on his own bodyguard, Wilmer. "But that's ridiculous," Gutman protested. "I feel towards Wilmer just exactly as if he were my own son. I really do. But if I even for a moment thought of doing what you propose . . ."

In a Hollywood that paid people a weekly wage to rewrite *A Farewell to Arms* and *Miss Lonelyhearts,* that hired Salka Viertel to "adapt" *Anna Karenina,* nothing, obviously, could be left alone. Warners assigned *The Maltese Falcon* not to Hammett but to three of its regular employees, Maude Fulton, Lucien Hubbard, and Brown Holmes. And since it was unthinkable for the hero to denounce the heroine as a murderess and then turn her over to the police ("I'll be sorry as hell—I'll have some rotten nights—but that'll pass," Spade had said to Brigid), the trio of rewriters ended by suggesting that Spade would win a fine new job in the district attorney's office, that Brigid would get out of prison soon, and that she and Spade would finally be reunited. Warners assigned the role of Spade to Ricardo Cortez (né Jacob Krantz), who was trying to become the successor to Rudolph Valentino and played several of his scenes with Brigid in a silk lounging robe. Brigid was Bebe Daniels, who was known mainly as a comedienne. The whole thing was renamed "Woman of the World," then "Dangerous Female," and it inevitably failed.

In 1936, Warners tried again. One of the three rewriters, Brown

Holmes, was assigned once again to claw at the bones of Hammett's novel. This time, Spade turned into a lawyer named Ted Shayne. He ended by marrying his secretary. Casper Gutman became a woman. The black figure of the falcon turned into a jeweled French horn. This version, too, received several new titles: "Men on Her Mind," then "Hard Luck Dame," then, finally, and most ludicrous of all, "Satan Met a Lady." Spade/Shayne was played by Warren Williams, and Brigid O'Shaughnessy (renamed Valerie Purvis) by Bette Davis, who called this farrago "one of the worst turkeys I ever made."

And in 1941, Warners tried yet again. This time, though, as so often happened with Hollywood's great successes, there occurred a series of happy accidents. The driving force behind them was John Huston. Having been a semiprofessional boxer, a Mexican cavalryman, a painter of sorts, and finally a screenwriter of considerable promise (*Juarez, Dr. Ehrlich's Magic Bullet, High Sierra*), Huston had reached the age of thirty-five and wanted to strike toward the center of Hollywood power. His agent, Paul Kohner, had artfully inserted a clause into his screenwriting contract that committed Warners to letting him choose one picture to direct himself. "I selected Dashiell Hammett's *The Maltese Falcon*," Huston rather laconically recalled in his memoirs. "It had been filmed twice before but never successfully. Blanke and Wallis [his producers] were surprised at my wanting to remake a two-time failure, but the fact was that *Falcon* had never really been put on screen." Allen Rivkin's recollection is more vivid: "Johnny . . . asked me to work with him as screenwriter on a new version of *Falcon*, telling me, 'Christ, Al, the book has never been done right.' "

Jack Warner grudgingly approved the idea of a second remake if Huston could produce a satisfactory script. "You and I—we'll do the screenplay," Huston said to Rivkin, who shared his office and his secretary at Warners. "But first, before we do that—let's get it broken down. You know, have the secretary recopy the book, only setting it up in shots, scenes, and dialogue. Then we'll know where we are. Okay, kid?" So the anonymous secretary dutifully converted Hammett's novel, without substantial change, into a preliminary script for Huston. As a matter of company procedure (or perhaps secretarial ambition?), this preliminary version went not only to departmental headquarters but to Jack Warner himself. Warner was delighted. "You've got my okay, Johnny," he told Huston. "It's a great script." "Goddamnedest thing happened, kid," Huston reported to Rivkin. "Warner said he wants me to shoot it, and I start next Monday."

The next accident involved the casting of Warner's biggest gangster star, George Raft, as Sam Spade. Raft had grown up in the slums of New York's Ninth Avenue, and he remained a lifelong friend of various Hell's Kitchen gangsters, so much so that these professional gunmen imitated the styles that Raft created for them. The white tie on black shirt was a Raft trademark, as was the nonchalant flipping of a coin (actually suggested by Howard Hawks when he hired Raft to co-star in *Scarface*). Al Capone himself asked Raft why he kept flipping the coin, and Raft casually said, "Just a little theatrical touch." But for all his seeming authority, Raft not only had no talent as an actor but had no sense of his own public identity. He refused to play the gangster in Sidney Kingsley's *Dead End* (1937) unless he was allowed to warn the Dead End kids that crime did not pay. So the part went to a young actor named Humphrey Bogart. Raft also refused to play the fugitive hero in Huston's latest script, *High Sierra* (1941), because the fugitive got shot at the end, and Raft didn't want to play men who got shot. He had other objections as well. "Too many words, Irving," he said to an intermediary. "Too many words."

Warners turned to some of its other eminent gangsters. Paul Muni, who had been Raft's boss in *Scarface,* rejected the role because Raft had rejected it; so did Edward G. Robinson; so did John Garfield. Bogart said only, "Where the hell's the script and when do I start?" It was his first starring role.

Now Raft didn't want to play Sam Spade either. He said that *The Maltese Falcon* was "not an important picture." His chief reason seems to have been that Huston was a novice director, but his agent, Myron Selznick, was also skeptical, and Raft's contract said he didn't have to perform in any remakes. "I didn't know much so I listened to guys who were supposed to know something," Raft later explained. "It was a low-budget picture." Jack Warner broke the news to Huston: "Guess you'll have to settle for Bogie." There were other complications of the same sort. Huston wanted Geraldine Fitzgerald to play Brigid O'Shaughnessy, but Warners insisted on Mary Astor.

Sidney Greenstreet as Gutman was one of Huston's inspirations. At a waddling 285 pounds and sixty-one years of age, Greenstreet had never made a movie, but Huston had seen him playing butlers on Broadway and insisted on signing him up. Peter Lorre, a witty and cultivated refugee from Berlin, had become an exemplar of loathsome perversions when Fritz Lang cast him as the compulsive child-murderer in *M,* so he brought a cringing malevolence to the role of Joel Cairo. And for good luck, Walter Huston, the young director's famous father, agreed to play the bit part of the dying ship captain who staggered into Spade's office with the crudely wrapped package containing the legendary falcon. It was, in short, a spectacularly talented cast. And then there was Huston himself. "As a rule," he recalled later, "at the end of the day everyone goes home, each to his separate domicile. But we were all having such a good time on *Falcon* that, night after night after shooting, Bogie, Peter Lorre, Mary Astor and I would go over to the Lakeside Country Club. We'd have a few drinks, then a buffet supper, and stay on till midnight. We all thought we were doing something good, but no one had any idea that *The Maltese Falcon* would be a great success."

Much of that success can be credited, if only by default, to Huston himself. Just as he relied heavily on Hammett's original novel for his screenplay, he relied heavily on Arthur Edeson's quasi-documentary photography for the bleak, dark, claustrophobic quality that came to be known as *film noir*. Some experts ascribe the flowering of *film noir* during the early 1940's to some of the German refugees—Lang, Wilder, Preminger, Siodmak—who brought with them memories of the style that had been developed at the UFA studios in Berlin. Others suggest that it was simply a matter of economics. At Warners, a studio so frugal that some of its employees called it "San Quentin," shooting a film in moody darkness and rain tended to disguise the cheapness of the sets. These elements all suited the young Huston on his first assignment, for, as Charles Higham has written, "the film's most striking feature is its insolent casualness, its deliberate lack of flourish."

Huston also had the wit to sense in Bogart an actor on the verge of triumph and to focus on him in scene after scene. For if the script was a faithful translation of Hammett's novel, it was Bogart who made the movie not only different from the novel but substantially better. When we imagine Spade, a half century after Hammett created him, we don't see anything like the figure that Hammett described: "Samuel Spade's jaw was long and bony, his chin a jutting v under the more flexible v of his mouth. . . . His yellow-gray eyes were horizontal . . . He looked rather pleasantly like a blond Satan." Nor do we hear the voice that might have come from such a "Satan." We see, hear, recognize, and know the somewhat wrinkled and battered figure of Humphrey Bogart. *The Maltese Falcon* was the movie in which he created the persona that not only made him famous for the rest of his life but gradually became his own permanent identity.

Bogart had not been born for any such fate. His father, Dr. Belmont DeForest Bogart, was a prosperous physician in New York; his mother, Maude Humphrey, was a suffragette, a magazine illustrator who prided herself on having studied in Paris with Whistler. Humphrey, their firstborn, arrived on Christmas Day of 1899. ("I never had a birthday of my own to celebrate," he later complained.) There were two younger sisters, one who suffered a mental breakdown and another who died of peritonitis. Young Humphrey went to Trinity, a starchy Episcopalian school on New York's Upper West Side, then to Andover, which was supposed to prepare him for Yale and a life of upper-middle-class respectability. He flunked five of seven subjects, however, flunked Bible, French, English, chemistry, and geometry. The headmaster wrote sternly to Dr. Bogart that he was "forced to advise you . . . that it becomes necessary for us to require his withdrawal from the school."

Dr. Bogart was shocked. It was 1918, though, so Humphrey enlisted in the navy, served a few months on a troop transport, then emerged into a New York where, for a handsome young man, nothing was very serious and anything was possible. A school friend named Bill Brady had a father who dabbled in theatrical productions and agreed to hire Bogart as an office boy. Office boys traditionally became understudies, and understudies eventually won bit parts. The morning after Humphrey's Broadway debut, his mother woke him up to read him Alexander Woollcott's review: "The young man . . . was what might mercifully be described as inadequate." Even then, though, he had admirers. "My first impression of Humphrey Bogart," Louise Brooks wrote of meeting him in 1924, "was of a slim boy with charming manners, who was unusually quiet for an actor. His handsome face was made extraordinary by a most beautiful mouth. It was very full, rosy, and perfectly modeled. . . ."

Such views enabled Bogart to keep finding roles throughout the 1920's. It has been reported, but never proved, that he appeared on stage in a blue blazer and actually said, "Tennis, anyone?" He was beginning, though, to acquire a label as an aging juvenile. Then he got a chance to audition for a wildly unlikely role, the fugitive gangster in Robert Sherwood's *The Petrified Forest*. Leslie Howard, who was not only the star but the coproducer, quickly decided that Bogart would be perfect as the psychopathic Duke Mantee, and when the play opened in 1935, the theater critics warmly endorsed Howard's judgment. Warners bought the play, hired Howard to star in it, took an option on Bogart, and then assigned the part of Duke Mantee to Edward G. Robinson. Bogart unhappily telegraphed this news to Howard in Scotland. Howard telegraphed Warners that he would not play the hero unless Bogart played the gangster. Warners gave in and summoned the young man to Hollywood.

On late-night television, Bogart's famous performance as the swaggering Duke Mantee seems almost preposterous. His two-day growth of stubble is supposed to make him look sinister but succeeds largely in making him look disreputable. His voice is supposed to be a guttural snarl but it fluctuates between an affected drawl and bombastic shouting. In short, Bogart looks and sounds like a nice young man trying very hard to appear tough and terrifying. In its day, the pretense was a great success. Richard Watts of the *New York Herald Tribune* was reasonably typical in declaring that Bogart "provides a brilliant picture of a subnormal, bewildered and sentimental killer." Perhaps American audiences of the mid-1930's, when more than one third of the work force could not find jobs of any sort, liked to imagine that they were frightened by imitations of gangsters.

So Humphrey Bogart, who had failed in his destined course toward Yale, became a gangster. "Over the years," Louise Brooks recalled, "Bogey practiced all kinds of lip gymnastics, accompanied by nasal tones, snarls, lisps and slurs." He snarled and lisped through a whole string of superficial roles: *San Quentin. Dead End. The Roaring Twenties.* He got $650 a week, and toward the end of most movies, he got shot, snarling. American audiences were fascinated by the gangsters who had suddenly emerged from the dark slums into the sunshine of political power during Prohibition, but nobody was quite sure how gangsters really talked, or even what they looked like. The gangsters themselves, ignorant ghetto boys like Louis Buchalter or farmhands like Clyde Barrow, didn't themselves know how they were supposed to behave. So Hollywood taught them. Just as George Raft, recollecting his boyhood as a dance hall gigolo, taught them how to dress, so Humphrey Bogart (and Jimmy Cagney too) taught them how to snarl. "His voice was the elaborately casual voice of the tough guy in pictures," Raymond Chandler's Philip Marlowe remarked of a gunman in *The Big Sleep*. "Pictures have made them all like that."

The Hays Office, which Hollywood established as a system of self-censorship after various scandals of the 1920's, insisted that movie gangsters must die before the pictures ended. Crime does not pay. Unlike George Raft, who didn't want to be shot, the best of the gangster actors quickly realized that violent death had been the fate of Macbeth and Hamlet. Did Edward G. Robinson ever declaim a more famous line than his question in the snows of *Little Caesar:* "Mother of God, is this the end for Rico?" But Bogart must have instinctively realized, as he was shot down over and over again during the late 1930's, growling his defiant last words each time with that throaty gangster accent he had invented for himself, that he was going nowhere. Every role was just another job, every snarling death just another snarling death, until, in *High Sierra*, he saw his first chance at playing a fugitive convict who could become a romantic hero. Ida Lupino loved him, and when he inevitably died at the end, the audiences did not relish his death, as they traditionally relished the shootings of gangsters; they felt saddened. And when Bogart came to New York to churn up some publicity for the film, he was surprised—Warners was even more surprised—to find himself mobbed by his new fans.

Bogart was having terrible troubles during these years with his third wife, Mayo Methot. She drank heavily, and as she drank, she first began accusing him of flirtation, vanity, and various other sins, and then she began smashing things. "I like a jealous wife . . ." Bogart told an interviewer. "And I like a good fight. So does Mayo. We have some first-rate battles." Warring husbands and wives often give each other cues, and one of Mayo's most ominous signals was the song, "Embraceable You." She was singing it one night when Bogart returned home from a drying-out session at the Finlandia Baths on Sunset Boulevard, and that was her only warning before she lunged at him with a butcher knife. Bogart ducked and ran, but she stabbed him in the back. He fell to the floor and passed out, woke to hear someone calling for a doctor, passed out again, woke to hear a doctor say, "It's not so bad. Only the tip went in. He's a lucky man."

Bogart often spent all night drinking, then appeared at the studio fully ready to work. His portrayal of Sam Spade embodied all that. It was the portrait of a man who had been up all night, a man with both a hangover and a determination to get a day's work done, a man whose wife had stabbed him in the back and might do so again. Yet Bogart's Spade had another characteristic lacking in Hammett's original creation, and that was humor. When Hammett's Spade roughed up the young gunman, Wilmer, he was just being tough. When Bogart roughed up Elisha Cook, he was being not only tough but perilously funny, mocking and humiliating a man who yearned to kill him. It was a great scene.

Humor combined with a kind of willed toughness made Bogart immensely sympathetic, and real in a way that his gangsters had never been. It was, of course, a reality based on layers of deception. "Don't be too sure I'm as crooked as I'm supposed to be," Spade told Brigid toward the end. So Humphrey Bogart of Andover, who had gained a temporary success playing gangsters, achieved his huge triumph and spent the rest of his life playing pseudo gangsters, enforcers of the higher law of their own creation.

Up to the very end, the authorities at Warners couldn't seem to understand that *The Maltese Falcon* was a marvelous title. Having changed it to "Dangerous Female" and "Men on Her Mind" and "Satan Met a Lady," and having failed every time, they now wanted, even at the last preview, to change it to "The Gent from Frisco." It was apparently Hal Wallis, the production chief, who persuaded all the nervous improvers to desist. So *The Maltese Falcon,* finally, was a smashing success.

And what financial rewards did Dashiell Hammett, the creator, derive from this success? Nothing whatever, for when Warner Bros. had bought the movie rights to his novel eleven years earlier, for $8,500, the studio had bought all movie rights forevermore. A few years later, in fact, when Hammett sold ABC Radio the right to produce a series called *The Adventures of Sam Spade,* Warners filed suit claiming, in the spring of 1948, that the studio owned the name of Sam Spade as well as all related "scenes, language, story, dialogue, plot, characters, and other materials" of *The Maltese Falcon.* It took three years of judgments and appeals before Hammett won the right to his own hero, and by that time the whole show had been forced off the airwaves on the ground that Hammett was a "subversive."

• • •

Despite Hollywood's three versions of its favorite legend about itself, its stars were not born but rather cultivated, like Candide's garden. The studios put their employees in role after role and watched to see what happened. While a complex character like Bogart's transformed itself into something rich and strange, Ronald Reagan seemed to remain perpetually the same, cheerful and friendly. Though Reagan had won considerable attention and praise in *Knute Rockne,* that was only the fourth of his six pictures in 1940. Warners promptly loaned him out to M-G-M for *Tugboat Annie Sails Again,* then put him to work with Errol Flynn in *Santa Fe Trail.* As 1941 started, he went back to M-G-M for *The Bad Man,* then returned to Warners for *Million Dollar Baby.* By now a successful journeyman and a member of the board of the Screen Actors Guild, he was earning one thousand dollars a week, a princely salary during the last years of the Depression for a modestly talented actor just turning thirty, but not very much by Hollywood standards. Claudette Colbert, Bing Crosby, and Irene Dunne each made more than eight times that much. Reagan was generally considered pleasant and hard-working, useful, not much more.

The year 1941 was important to Reagan. It began, almost exactly a year after his marriage to Jane Wyman, with the birth of their first child, Maureen, on January 4. Three months later, Reagan's alcoholic father, who had been such a troublesome hero, died of heart failure. The routine films rolled on: *Nine Lives Are Not Enough* (Reagan recalled his role as a brash reporter: "You could always count on me to rush into a room, grab a phone and yell, 'Give me the city desk—I've got a story that will crack this town wide open' ");* *International Squadron* (Reagan as an American stunt pilot in Warners' version of the RAF: "Our 'Spitfire' was a doctored-up Ryan monoplane that didn't even have retractable gear"). But then came *Kings Row*, which Reagan recalled as a "slightly sordid but moving yarn," which "made me a motion picture star."

Warners had spent fifty thousand dollars to buy this ponderous best-seller, without quite knowing what it was doing. The author, Henry Bellamann, a Vassar professor of music who had turned to writing novels in his fifties, was one of the many disciples of Balzac: *Kings Row* fell about halfway between *Winesburg, Ohio* and *Peyton Place*. Here, there, and everywhere, the disciples of Balzac were determined to demonstrate that the tranquil surface of small-town life covered a roiling inferno of fraud, corruption, treachery, hypocrisy, class warfare, and ill-suppressed sex of all varieties: adultery, sadism, homosexuality, incest. And philistinism, of the kind that could not appreciate Bellamann's florid opening sentence: "Spring came late in the year 1890, so it came more violently, and the fullness of its burgeoning heightened the seasonal disturbance that made unquiet in the blood."

Of such burgeoning and unquiet are best-sellers made, but when Warners bought the novel and turned it over to one of the studio's favorite writers, Casey Robinson, he judged the whole project hopeless. The Hays Office would never allow it. He cabled this verdict from Hong Kong, where he had docked briefly on a vacation cruise through the Far East. Hal Wallis, the prospective producer, cabled back to ask Robinson to read the novel again. Robinson was not easily persuaded. "While sailing between Manila and Bali," Wallis recalled, "he finally tossed the book into the sea, thinking that I was crazy to have bought so downbeat a property." Nothing, perhaps, could so quickly change a writer's mind about a difficult challenge as the sight of that challenge disappearing into the ocean. "As he saw the book floating on the waves," Wallis said, "he suddenly realized how he could lick the subject: make it the story of an idealistic young doctor challenged by the realities of a cruel and horrifying world."

Wallis was naturally delighted at the prospect of small-town sex turning into the saga of an idealistic doctor. He began hiring. He hired Sam Wood, recently acclaimed for *Kitty Foyle,* as his director; and William Cameron

---

*In an interview with Reagan's wife, Jane Wyman, Rex Reed quoted her as telling him, "For ten years, I was the wisecracking lady reporter who stormed the city desk snapping, 'Stop the presses, I've got a story that will break this town wide open.' "

Menzies, the real creator of much of *Gone With the Wind,* as art director; and Erich Korngold as the composer of moody music; and the celebrated James Wong Howe as cameraman. Then came the usual casting problems. Wallis wanted Henry Fonda or Tyrone Power as the idealistic doctor, Parris Mitchell, but Darryl Zanuck at Fox owned them both, and owned their idealistic images as well, and declined to rent them to Warners. The nymphomaniac Cassie Tower presented interesting possibilities. Wallis offered the part to Ida Lupino, but she was busy making *Ladies in Retirement* for Columbia. Bette Davis hungered to play Cassie, but Wallis was afraid that she would dominate the picture. Drake McHugh, the hero's amiably pleasure-loving friend, was a secondary role destined for one of Warners' contract players—Dennis Morgan, or Jack Carson, or perhaps Eddie Albert. Robert Preston and Franchot Tone were also considered. Or maybe Ronnie Reagan. Why not Reagan?

Joseph I. Breen, a professional Catholic who headed the Hays Office, and who had not yet seen a page of the script that Casey Robinson was writing, interrupted all this planning by forbidding the entire project. In a lengthy memo to Wallis, he began by complaining of "illicit relations" between various characters, and "much loose sex everywhere." And there was a "sadistic characterization" of a doctor, that villain who was to amputate Drake McHugh's legs. "Any suggestion of sex, madness, syphilis, illegal operations, incest, sadism, all must go," Breen declared. "If this picture is made . . . decent people everywhere will condemn you and Hollywood."

Jack Warner, Wallis, and Robinson all had to go to Breen's office and argue with a hypocrisy worthy of characters in *Kings Row,* or even in some novel by Balzac himself. They were not just trying to make money, much less to earn the condemnation of decent people everywhere, but rather, in Wallis's words, to "illustrate how a doctor could relieve the internal destruction of a stricken community." Breen, said Wallis, "was impressed." If Warners agreed to take out all references to nymphomania and incest—and no mercy killings, and no nude swimming either—then maybe approval could be granted. Robinson wrote a new version; Breen rejected it; Robinson wrote a third version; Breen rejected it; Robinson wrote a fourth version; Breen reluctantly approved. "In the long run I felt it was all to the good," Wallis declared with the stoicism of the continually censored. "Too much grimness might have wrecked its chances at the box office."

There was one scene that managed to survive all this moral improvement. That was the scene in which Drake McHugh, having been swindled out of his inheritance by the local bankers, having been rejected as unworthy to marry the daughter of the town's preeminent doctor, had to get a job at the railway station, suffered an accident that crushed his legs, and woke to find that the doctor who had rejected him as a suitor for his daughter had now amputated both his legs. Randy Monaghan, Drake's current girl, was trying to nurse him. "It was then that the dreadful sound came from the upper room," Bellamann wrote. "Randy knew even in that terrifying instant that she would never forget the sound of Drake's voice. It was a hoarse scream—almost a yell in which there was horror, and pain, and something worse—sheer animal terror. She tore up the narrow staircase and flung the door open. . . . Drake's eyes were rolling and his face worked violently as if the very bone structure had been shattered. Randy saw with a sick horror that his hands were groping frantically under the blankets. She almost leapt across the room and seized his hands. . . .

" 'Randy!'

" 'Yes, I'm here, Drake. I'm here with you . . .'

"*Randy*—where—where's the rest of me?' "

Ronald Reagan, having finally been chosen to play the part, saw something important in that scene of symbolic castration, in all the implications of the question itself. "No single line in my career has been so effective in explaining to me what an actor's life must be," he said in the ghostwritten autobiography that he produced twenty-five years later. He made Drake's question the title of the book. At the time, however, Reagan saw that scene primarily as a chance to make his mark. Wallis had by now hired a rather remarkable cast. Though Robert Cummings was barely adequate as the young doctor, he was surrounded by experts. His mother was Maria Ouspenskaya, and his mentor was Claude Rains, and the mentor's lustful daughter was Betty Field. There was even Judith Anderson as the wife to the wicked doctor, Charles Coburn, and Ann Sheridan was captivating as Randy Monaghan. Against this array of talent, Reagan had only the one great scene, the one great opportunity.

"I felt I had neither the experience nor the talent to fake it," Reagan recalled. "I simply had to find out how it really felt. . . . I rehearsed the scene before mirrors, in corners of the studio, while driving home, in the men's rooms of restaurants, before selected friends. At night I would wake up staring at the ceiling and automatically mutter the line before I went back to sleep. I consulted physicians and psychiatrists; I even talked to people who were so disabled, trying to brew in myself the caldron of emotions a man must feel who wakes up one sunny morning to find half of himself gone."

After all this self-rehearsal, there inevitably came a day when the scene had to be played out. The night before, Reagan lay in bed and worried. He couldn't sleep. He came to the studio looking pale and haggard—which was, of course, exactly the way he was supposed to look—and approached the set where the scene would have to take place.

"I found the prop men had arranged a neat deception," he recalled. "Under the patchwork quilt, they had cut a hole in the mattress and put a supporting box beneath. I stared at it for a minute. Then, obeying an overpowering impulse, I climbed into the rig." Reagan seems to have undergone some strange emotional crisis there in that bed. He simply lay, "contemplating my torso and the smooth undisturbed flat of the covers where my legs should have been." Ten minutes passed. Twenty. "Gradually," Reagan said, "the affair began to terrify me. In some weird way, I felt something terrible had happened to my body." By now, the camera crew had gathered around. They didn't seem to know what to do. Somebody lit the lights. Reagan lay there in a kind of trance. The director, Sam Wood, finally approached the prostrate actor and bent over him.

"Want to shoot it?" he murmured.

"No rehearsal?" Reagan asked, just as though he hadn't been rehearsing brilliantly for the past hour.

"God rest his soul—fine director that he was, he just turned to the crew and said, 'Let's make it.' There were cries of 'Lights!' and 'Quiet, please!' I lay back and closed my eyes, as tense as a fiddle-string. I heard Sam's low voice call, 'Action!' There was the sharp *clack* which signaled the beginning of the scene. I opened my eyes dazedly, looked around, slowly let my gaze travel downward. I can't describe even now my feeling as I tried to reach for where my legs should be. 'Randy!' I screamed. Ann Sheridan (bless her), playing Randy, burst through the door. She wasn't in the shot and normally wouldn't have been on hand until we turned the camera around to get her entrance, but she knew it was one of those scenes where a fellow actor needed all the help he could get and at that moment, in my mind, she was Randy answering my call. I asked the question—the words that had been haunting me for so many weeks—'Where's the rest of me?' "

One take was enough. "It was a good scene," Reagan said with some satisfaction. It was good enough, in fact, to lift him out of the ranks of pleasant young men and make him a star. Warners realized that and promptly renegotiated his contract to triple his pay to three thousand dollars per week. By the time *Kings Row* was released in February of 1942, however, the war had just begun and Reagan was subject to call-up by the army. The stardom that he seemed to have won had to be postponed, and he was never able to capture it again.

•   •   •

"As in some grotesque fable," one of *Time*'s nameless writers wrote in March of 1941 about a new movie called *Citizen Kane*, "it appeared last week that Hollywood was about to turn upon and destroy its greatest creation." That judgment has withstood quite well the passage of nearly half a century. If it is possible to single out any movie as Hollywood's "greatest creation," then the best choice is probably *Citizen Kane*. Even now, squeezed into television and repeatedly interrupted by commercials, it still shows immense confidence, high spirits, vitality. It was hardly a Hollywood creation, though, but rather the creation of Orson Welles, who didn't want to come to Hollywood at all when he was invited there late in 1938, after the wild success of his radio version of H. G. Wells's *War of the Worlds*. George J. Schaefer, whom Nelson Rockefeller had just helped to install as the new president of the foundering RKO studio, made Welles an irresistible offer: $100,000 to produce, direct, write, and star in one movie per year, with total autonomy for himself and the whole theater company that he had organized in New York, the Mercury Theatre. Welles was then twenty-three.

The saga of *Citizen Kane* is by now one of Hollywood's most beloved legends—a somewhat more intellectual version of *A Star Is Born*—and scholars of the cinema have analyzed not only cameraman Gregg Toland's striking use of 24 mm wide-angle lenses, stopped down to achieve deep focus, but even the sources for the libretto for the fake opera, *Salammbo,* briefly and badly sung by Kane's second wife (a text that was excerpted, as a sort of private joke, from Racine's *Phèdre:* "Ah, cruel! tu m'as trop entendue!"). At the time of Welles's spectacular arrival, though, Hollywood keenly resented the celebrated newcomer, particularly when he took a tour of RKO and called it "the biggest electric train a boy ever had." A popular Hollywood ditty by a minor actor named Jean Hersholt ridiculed the fact that "Little Orphan Annie's come to our house to play," and when Welles invited Hollywood's notables to his own house for a party, almost nobody came. Welles nonetheless set up his command post in the virtually bankrupt hulk of RKO and began experimenting. He worked on a film of Joseph Conrad's *Heart of Darkness*—what a movie *that* would have made!—then on a thriller by C. Day Lewis called *The Smiler with a Knife,* which was vaguely based on the life of the British Fascist leader Oswald Mosley and involved a pro-Axis putsch in Mexico. There was even talk of his filming a life of Christ.

By a series of turns of fate, Welles soon joined forces with Herman J. Mankiewicz, a onetime *New Yorker* theater critic who had served as the Pied Piper leading many of the Algonquin writers to Hollywood. ("Millions are to be grabbed out here, and your only competition is idiots," Mankiewicz had announced in a famous telegram to Ben Hecht back in 1926.) Mankiewicz was so dedicated to his own wit that he would sacrifice a job for a joke, as he did when he actually dared to remark, after Harry Cohn had declared to his assembled sycophants at Columbia that he could always foretell the future success of a movie by whether it caused a tremor in his own rear end: "Imagine! The whole world wired to Harry Cohn's ass!"* Mankiewicz was also a dedicated gambler, who borrowed in order to gamble and lied in order to borrow and drank in order to lie. Drinking got him fired from several good jobs (as producer of the Marx Brothers' *Night at the Opera,* for example), but it was gambling that brought his final downfall at M-G-M. He had not only begged Louis B. Mayer for a thirty-thousand-dollar advance on his new con-

---

* As though to test this same capacity in his lieutenants, Cohn installed in Columbia's executive dining room a chair that looked like all the others but gave a shock when an unsuspecting victim sat in it. Frank Capra once came in after a hard day's work and unthinkingly sat in the chair, which promptly gave him a shock. "Oh, shit," Capra said wearily, without moving. "That stupid son of a bitch Cohn and his goddamn chair." Then Capra got up and tore the chair to pieces. Cohn subsequently had the electric chair repaired and restored to use. He gave it up only after one of his victims suffered a mild heart attack.

tract but sworn to give up gambling ("A compliment from Mayer," he once said of his patron, "is like having Nathan Leopold tell you that you're lovable"), and then he looked up from the poker game that he had organized in the M-G-M dining room and found himself confronting the implacable eye of his employer. Fired the next day, and more or less blackballed among the major studios, Mankiewicz left his wife to deal with his gambling debts and started driving back to New York with another writer, who skidded off the road and smashed up the car. That was how Herman Mankiewicz, jobless, penniless, hung over, and imprisoned in a plaster cast from hip to ankle, received a visit from Orson Welles, who charitably offered him five hundred dollars a week to convert tales like *Rip Van Winkle* into radio scripts. It was only a matter of time before they began talking about movie possibilities. Mankiewicz had wanted for years to write a story that he called *American*. It was about William Randolph Hearst.

Hearst was one of the liberals' bogeymen of that era, a man whose control of a large newspaper empire devoted to reactionary politics and cheap crime seemed to make him a demagogue of towering menace. The fact that his newspapers generally lost money and had very limited power did not deter his detractors from worrying about the potentialities of his sinister influence. Mankiewicz knew all the newspaper gossip, of course, but he also knew his subject firsthand. Hearst had enjoyed his company, and so had Marion Davies, the charming and funny actress whose relationship to Hearst was conventionally disguised as mere friendship. "One last thing to remember [is that] writers are always selling somebody out," Joan Didion once observed. And so Mankiewicz proceeded to include in his cruel portrait of Charles Foster Kane the portrait of an untalented and alcoholic young protégée who liked to spend her time, as did Miss Davies, on jigsaw puzzles.

Welles was pleased with Mankiewicz's script, but he also thought it somewhat wordy and slow-moving. He was accustomed to making substantial revisions himself, even on Shakespeare, and now he cut out whole scenes, whole subplots. He wrote in others that derived from his own instincts— Kane's disastrous attempts to make his new wife an opera singer, for example. The megalomaniac Charles Foster Kane was, after all, to be at least partly Orson Welles. Yes, and as both writers kept revising each other's drafts, Mankiewicz also had views of Welles that he wanted to include. Kane's great furniture-smashing tantrum, for example, was a reenactment of one of Welles's own explosions.

Once they had created their marvelous script, of course, they had to fight over who should get the credit. Welles's RKO contract specifically said that "the screenplay for each picture shall be written by Mr. Orson Welles," and Welles probably thought that an old drunk like Mankiewicz should be content with his five hundred dollars a week for collaborative ghostwriting. But Mankiewicz knew that *Citizen Kane* was an accomplishment that made up for all the wasted years of hack work and drunken jokes. It made him unhappy to hear Welles quoted in Louella Parsons's column, before the question of screen credits was officially settled, as saying, "So I wrote *Citizen Kane*." So Mankiewicz went to the Screen Writers Guild and declared that he was the original author. Welles later claimed that he planned on a joint credit all along, but Mankiewicz claimed that Welles offered him a bonus of ten thousand dollars if he would let Welles take full credit. Since Mankiewicz was chronically in debt, he asked Ben Hecht what he should do about this proposal, and Hecht gave him a characteristic answer: "Take the ten grand and double-cross the son of a bitch." The Screen Writers Guild eventually decreed a joint credit, with Mankiewicz's name first.

Welles, who prided himself on his skill as a practicing magician, engaged in some extraordinary legerdemain to get *Citizen Kane* on film at all. Schaefer had granted him creative autonomy, but only subject to RKO approval of each script and budget, and there was considerable question whether a nearly bankrupt studio would approve a thinly disguised attack on one of the nation's most powerful newspaper publishers. Welles thought up the remarkable expedient of shooting repeated "tests," which needed no official approval, until the accumulated "tests" represented such a large portion of the prospective movie that Welles was able to bluff Schaefer into approving what was almost a *fait accompli*. It may be, as some say, that RKO knew perfectly well what Welles was doing, but his bluff was a kind of prank, typical of the youthful exuberance that pervades *Citizen Kane*.

Welles relied just as much on bluff in winning the approval of Hearst's elephantine movie columnist, Louella Parsons. It is almost impossible now to realize the power once exercised by Mrs. Parsons, and her rival, Hedda Hopper, but in the 1940's, these two vain and ignorant women tyrannized Hollywood. Mrs. Parsons (née Ottinger) was already a twice-divorced woman* of twenty-nine when she first came to Chicago in 1910, got herself a job on the *Tribune,* and began spending her nights writing movie scenarios. She more or less invented the idea of a movie gossip column in the *Chicago Record-Herald,* then moved to the *New York Morning Telegraph,* then, in 1924, went to cover Hollywood for Hearst. There is a popular legend that Mrs. Parsons owed her job to the death of Thomas Ince, a successful director whom Hearst had just hired to take charge of his Cosmopolitan Films. Ince died suddenly aboard Hearst's yacht, the *Oneida,* and although the official cause of death was angina, some gossips claimed that Hearst had shot him after discovering him in flagrante delicto with Marion Davies. According to an even more colorful version, Hearst had discovered Miss Davies with Charlie Chaplin, began shooting wildly, and killed Ince by mistake. In either case, Mrs. Par-

* She achieved happiness of a sort with her third husband, Dr. Harry "Docky" Martin, a urologist, for whom she found work as a "technical adviser" on various films and then as a $30,000-per-year part-time staff physician at 20th Century–Fox. Martin was such a heavy drinker that he often passed out at parties. When somebody once tried to lift him off the floor, according to one much-told tale, Mrs. Parsons said, "Oh, let him rest. He has to operate in the morning."

sons was said to have been aboard the yacht and to have kept Hearst's secret. Unfortunately for this story, Ince seems actually to have died of too much food and liquor, and Mrs. Parsons seems to have been in New York at the time. Her chief appeal to Hearst was her gushing enthusiasm for the movies, and specifically for all movies featuring Marion Davies.

What Mrs. Parsons now asked Welles, on behalf of her thirty million readers, was whether his new movie dealt with William Randolph Hearst. Why, of course not, said Welles. It was entirely a work of fiction. Perhaps because Welles was feeding her a five-course lunch in his dressing room, which had belonged to Gloria Swanson and was still lined with red satin, or perhaps because he was young and handsome, Mrs. Parsons believed him. And so it was not until the official press screening in New York in early January of 1940 that Hedda Hopper first saw *Citizen Kane* and said to Welles, "You can't get away with this." Said Welles: "I will." When Hearst read Mrs. Hopper's column, he hastily asked Mrs. Parsons what was going on, and she rushed to a special screening with two lawyers. Then she began telephoning. She telephoned Schaefer, and Rockefeller, and every member of the RKO board of directors, and Will Hays, and Louis B. Mayer, and Darryl Zanuck— anybody she could think of. She said, among other things, "Mr. Hearst says if you boys want private lives, I'll give you private lives."

Citizen Kane was scheduled to open on February 14, 1941, at Radio City Music Hall in Rockefeller Center (the Rockefellers owned a large share of RKO). Then the theater abruptly canceled the opening. Schaefer called Nelson Rockefeller to find out the reason and learned some details of Mrs. Parsons's threats of retribution. "Rockefeller told me," Schaefer recalled later, "that Louella Parsons . . . had asked him, 'How would you like to have [Hearst's] *American Weekly* run a double-page spread on John D. Rockefeller?' " And then, suddenly, Schaefer had trouble booking *Citizen Kane* anywhere at all. And there was more. Hearst photographers began following Welles through the streets, hoping to catch some moment of indiscretion. Inquiries to his draft board persistently raised the question of why he was not in the army. Hedda Hopper predicted darkly that "the refugee situation would be looked into," which seemed to threaten a general investigation by the Hearst newspapers and the American Legion and other patriotic organizations into the question of why so many Hollywood studios employed so many foreigners, particularly those of leftist sympathies. "Nor are private lives to be overlooked," Mrs. Hopper warned.*

Then came the most extraordinary proposal of all. Nicholas Schenck, the head of Loew's, invited Schaefer to New York and made him an offer. He was

---

* In the midst of all this, on the day of the San Francisco opening, Welles met Hearst for the first time, an accidental encounter in the elevator of the Fairmont Hotel. Welles said later that he was unable to resist introducing himself as the son of Hearst's old friend Richard Welles. Then he invited Hearst to the premiere. Hearst said not a word and stalked off the elevator when it reached his floor. Welles impudently called after him: "Charles Foster Kane would have *accepted.*"

making this offer, he said, on behalf of Louis B. Mayer, who considered himself not only a friend of Hearst's but also the patriarch of the movie business. Mayer proposed to pay RKO $842,000 in cash if Schaefer would destroy the negative and all the prints of *Citizen Kane*. Since the film had cost $686,000, Mayer's offer represented a fairly handsome profit on a movie that Schaefer was having trouble in booking anywhere. Schaefer, to his credit, refused. Schaefer, to his credit, didn't even mention this irresistible offer to his own board of directors, for he feared that the directors might order him to accept it. Schaefer, to his credit, responded to the M-G-M bribe by threatening a conspiracy suit against all the major theater chains: Fox, Paramount, Loew's. This was the crisis that roused *Time* and other journals to protest. And since the theater chains were just as terrified of conspiracy suits as they were of Hearst boycotts, they relented enough to provide a few showings for *Citizen Kane*, which, in the final accounting, just barely broke even.

And then, in one of those executive whirlwinds, a major RKO stockholder named Floyd Odlum, a Texas entrepreneur of nebulous ambitions, bought enough additional shares from David Sarnoff to give him control of the whole studio, and that was the end of Schaefer. And two weeks after Schaefer was evicted, Orson Welles was also evicted, given a few hours' notice to move out (the Mercury Theatre's space was needed for a Tarzan film crew). One of the contributing reasons for this upheaval was a widespread rumor, apparently sponsored by Louis B. Mayer, that Schaefer couldn't get good bookings for RKO films because he was anti-Semitic.

•   •   •

It is difficult to maintain a sense of perspective. The year 1941—the year in which Hollywood granted its Academy Award not to *Citizen Kane*, nor to *The Maltese Falcon*, nor even to *King's Row*, but to *How Green Was My Valley* —was the year in which Adolf Hitler betrayed his ally Stalin and sent more than 150 *Wehrmacht* divisions plunging eastward on a front that reached from the Baltic to the Black Sea. Yet the epic overview often fails to see what is really happening. In *Mother Courage*, written in exile in Denmark in 1938, Bertolt Brecht had demonstrated brilliantly that all the grand strategies of the Thirty Years' War could be reduced to one woman wheeling her wagonload of supplies in the wake of whichever army needed food. "Christians, awake! The winter's gone!" she sang. "The snows depart, the dead sleep on . . ."

Brecht himself, who remembered this as "the dark time [when] we went changing countries more often than our shoes," had fled from Berlin to Prague to Austria to France to Denmark and found refuge at last in a whitewashed and thatch-roofed farmhouse on the island of Langeland. He liked to imagine it as an outpost of anti-Nazi resistance. "Fled under a thatched Danish roof,/ My friends, I follow your struggles," he wrote. "Here I send you—from time to time—/Verses raked up through bloody visions." Yet here in exile, between 1937 and 1940, he wrote three of his greatest plays, *Mother Courage, The*

Good Woman of Setzuan, and *Galileo.* (Andrea: "Unhappy is the land that breeds no hero." Galileo: "No, Andrea: Unhappy is the land that needs a hero.")

Brecht never wanted to leave the periphery of Germany, never felt at ease in any land that did not speak German, but some combination of shrewdness, instinct, and luck kept him in flight. In March of 1939, just a few months before the war began, he applied for an American visa, and since the American authorities were in no hurry to process such applications, Brecht moved in April from Denmark to the slightly safer sanctuary of Stockholm. A year later, on April 9, 1940, the Nazis marched into Denmark and attacked Norway; on April 17, Brecht sailed for Finland and once again "took up the exile's trade: hoping." Brecht considered himself a Marxist, but he had no intention of establishing himself in the Soviet Union. Too many of his friends had disappeared in the recent purges. But other friends, in both Hollywood and New York, were actively working to bring him to America. Fritz Lang solicited funds to keep Brecht going, and Erwin Piscator persuaded Alvin S. Johnson of the New School for Social Research to appoint the exile as a lecturer in literature. That enabled Brecht to reapply for an American visa. "Curiously, I examine the map of the continent," he wrote. "High up in Lapland,/Toward the Arctic Ocean,/I still see a small door."

Brecht was trying to arrange not only his own flight, not only the flight of his wife and two small children, but also that of two women who served, as women did all through his life, as his secretaries, collaborators, assistants, mistresses. One was a Danish actress named Ruth Berlau, who had left her husband to follow Brecht; the other was a Berliner named Margarete Steffin, who had already lost one lung and was deathly ill with tuberculosis. In December of 1940, the Brechts got visas to Mexico, but Miss Steffin was barred on medical grounds. Brecht stayed on in Helsinki—one of his rare acts of altruism—to keep his tribe together. Not until the following May did the U.S. authorities grant visas to the whole ménage, and even then, Miss Steffin was granted only a visitor's visa, as a secretary to Brecht's wife, Helene Weigel. The next day, they all boarded a train for Moscow, where Miss Steffin soon collapsed and had to be hospitalized. Altruism could go only so far. After making arrangements for Miss Steffin to follow him as soon as she recovered, Brecht led the rest of his flock aboard the trans-Siberian railroad to catch a small Swedish freighter, the S.S. *Annie Johnson,* which was to sail from Vladivostok on June 14. Before he even got there, he received a telegram announcing that Miss Steffin had died. And while the *Annie Johnson* was wallowing across the Pacific, he learned of Hitler's attack on Russia.

Marta Feuchtwanger, the wife of the novelist, who had escaped over the Pyrenees just the year before, went to meet the Brechts at San Pedro harbor and drove them to an apartment that the director William Dieterle had rented for them at 1954 Argyle Avenue in Hollywood. Argyle Avenue. Hollywood. There was a time when such exotic American names had rollicked in Brecht's imagination. "Oh, moon of Alabama,/We now must say goodbye . . ." the chorus of whores had crooned in *Mahagonny,* and the whole opera was full of such geographical evocations. When a hurricane threatened Mahagonny, Brecht relished the announcements from the radio: "Zerstört ist Pensacola! Zerstört ist Pensacola!"

But to the Brecht of the 1920's, the America of the Jazz Age had been a wildly hedonistic fantasy, a land of boxing, gangsters, and perpetual movement. When he had actually visited New York briefly in 1935, to direct his adaptation of Maxim Gorky's *Mother,* he had quarreled with everyone involved, and now that he had been forced to flee to Hollywood, he regarded everything around him with loathing. "I get the impression of having been removed from my age," he wrote in his diary. "This is Tahiti in metropolitan form. . . . I have the feeling of being like Francis of Assisi in an aquarium, Lenin at the Prater (or the Oktoberfest), or a chrysanthemum in a coal mine." Nothing could please him. The opulent fruits of California impressed him as having "neither smell nor taste." The pretty little houses on which Californians prided themselves were still worse—"additions built onto the garages." In fact, prettiness itself was an affront. "Cheap prettiness," said the exile, "depraves everything."

"On thinking about Hell," Brecht wrote, "I gather/My brother Shelley found it was a place/Much like the city of London. I/Who live in Los Angeles and not in London/Find, on thinking about Hell, that it must be/Still more like Los Angeles./In Hell too/There are, I've no doubt, these luxuriant gardens/With flowers as big as trees, which of course wither/Unhesitantly if not nourished with very expensive water . . . /And endless processions of cars/ Lighter than their own shadows, faster than/Mad thoughts, gleaming vehicles in which/Jolly-looking people come from nowhere and are nowhere bound./ And houses, built for happy people, therefore standing empty/Even when lived in. . . ."

Despite all these laments, Brecht was as determined to conquer Hollywood as he had once been determined to conquer Berlin. It was just a matter of concocting a few ideas, and movie ideas had been part of Brecht's life for years. As early as 1921, he had written scenarios for various silent films, and when *The Threepenny Opera* became a great theatrical hit in 1928, he demanded an opportunity to take part in G. W. Pabst's film version. *The Threepenny Opera* was a masterpiece of treachery and betrayal, in which the police and the underworld not only cooperated but virtually merged, yet no drama of deception could have outdone Brecht's own maneuvering. Having become a doctrinaire Marxist since the original creation of the play, he now demanded the right to rewrite his own work, and when Pabst rejected his attempts to convert a cynical melodrama into a didactic attack on capitalism, Brecht sued, claiming an artist's right to control his own creation—and quite ignoring the fact that John Gay had created the whole play some years earlier. When the courts proved unsympathetic to Brecht's claims, he wrote a chronical entitled *The Threepenny Trial,* excoriating them as well.

Controversy was, of course, Brecht's lifeblood. When he finally wrote a movie that was actually produced—not before the producers went bankrupt, and the successors declared that shooting could continue only if everyone worked without salary—the Weimar Republic's official censors banned it early in 1932 out of fear that it would cause riotous demonstrations by Nazi storm troopers. *Kuhle Wampe,* named after a district of Berlin, was about the suicide of an unemployed youth, and the censor complained that "your film has the tendency to present the suicide as typical, as something not just appropriate to this or that (morbidly inclined) individual but rather as the fate of an entire class!" Brecht was delighted. "The sharp-witted censor . . ." he remarked, "went much deeper in understanding our artistic intentions than our friendliest critics did."

In Hollywood, now, there were no censors, no storm troopers, no interest in controversy or politics of any sort. This was the place dominated by Louis B. Mayer, and Mayer liked Andy Hardy movies. Brecht remained Brecht. He read in a copy of *Life* that an Ohio farmer named Frank Engels had been selected, together with his wife and three children, as the state's "most typical farm family," and that the Engelses had been hired to spend a week living their typical family lives in a model home at the Ohio State Fair. Brecht thought it would be interesting to imagine what would happen if Ohio's typical family should start quarreling bitterly on the night before the state fair opened, and then smashed up the model home that had been prepared for them.

And then there was bread, *Brot.* The tastelessness of what emerged from the American assembly lines seemed to the exile from Berlin to symbolize everything that was lacking in American society. Back in the 1920's, Brecht had started an adaptation of *The Pit,* Frank Norris's epic novel about the extravagances of the Chicago wheat exchange, but what interested Brecht was not the wheat exchange as such but the corrupting process that separated the growing wheat from the final loaf. As in his *Saint Joan of the Stockyards,* he wanted to pit the soulless entrepreneur, Joe Fleischhacker, against the humble creator, the baker, and to dramatize the creator's triumph over the merchants. After a long talk with a German-American writer named Ferdinand Reyher, Brecht wrote in his *Arbeitsjournal:* "I tell Reyher the plan for *Joe Fleischhacker in Chicago,* and in a couple of hours we develop a film story, *The Bread King Learns Bread Baking.* There is no real bread in the States, and I really like to eat bread; my main meal is at night, and it is bread with butter. R thinks the Americans have always been nomads, and nomads understand nothing about eating." The idea of these two nomad writers was that Joe Fleischhacker, the villainous millionaire, should find happiness in munching bread baked by a poor farmer's wife. When he tried to buy her recipe, waving his checkbook as a weapon, he was told that good bread required not only good flour but "one day of good work; one world of good neighbors; a heart of good will; and a good appetite."

Brecht finished this peculiar scenario on a Saturday night in October of

1941, and he was so pleased with himself that he hurried over to M-G-M the following Tuesday to present his creation to Max Reinhardt's son, Gottfried, who was then working as an assistant to one of the studio's leading producers, Bernie Hyman. "For an hour and a half," Reinhardt recalled, "Brecht fascinated me in his unalloyed Augsburg dialect with a film story about the production, distribution, and enjoyment of bread. . . . He had the right man but the wrong place, and he had no illusions when I said as he left that I would try my best to sell the story." Reinhardt apparently did make some effort to interest M-G-M in Brecht's idea, but the results were predictable. Brecht's scenario, Reinhardt later observed, "had as much chance of being sold to M-G-M as 'Gone with the Wind' had of being played at the Berliner Ensemble."

But Brecht did have illusions. He registered his idea about bread at the Screen Writers Guild to protect his claims on it. And his journal records at the end of 1941 a frantic assortment of movie projects: a biography of the labor leader Samuel Gompers, which William Dieterle hoped to direct; an adaptation of Arthur Schnitzler's comedy *Reigen,* which was supposed to interest Charles Boyer; a lost work known as *Days of Fire.* The journal even contains lists of Brechtian titles: *Refugees Both, The Senator's Conscience, The Traitor,* and, most self-defeating of all, *Boy Meets Girl, So What?* None of these was ever finished, much less sold or produced.

"Again and again . . ." Brecht wrote bitterly, "seeking a living, I am told:/Show us what you're made of/Lay it on the table!/Deliver the goods!/Say something to inspire us! Tell us of your own greatness!/Divine our secret desires!/Show us the way out/Make yourself useful!/Deliver the goods!" Then one night, he sat up late with Salka Viertel, talking about the pain of flight and exile. Mrs. Viertel told him her own sense of guilt at having failed to get her family out of Poland. The next morning, she found a poem that Brecht had stuck under her door.

> I know of course: it's simply luck
> That I've survived so many friends. But last night in a dream
> I heard those friends say of me: "Survival of the fittest"
> And I hated myself.

•   •   •

By arriving on one of the last ships to cross the Pacific before Pearl Harbor, Brecht managed to miss the social event of the year for Hollywood's refugees, the celebration of Heinrich Mann's seventieth birthday. Actually, the Mann brothers missed it too, for on Heinrich's birthday in March, Thomas was scheduled to receive an honorary doctorate from the University of California at Berkeley, and after that he had to go on a lecture tour. Since nothing could disturb Thomas Mann's schedule of awards and speeches, and since Heinrich's birthday could not be celebrated without the presence of his famous younger brother, who was also supporting him, Heinrich had to wait until the end of April.

Salka Viertel, who was acting as the hostess, in her house on Mabery Road in Santa Monica, needed all that time to handle the diplomatic negotiations among the factious refugees. Heinrich Mann's alcoholic wife, Nelly, was feuding with Alma Werfel and opposed invitations to anyone who was particularly friendly with the Werfels. There had been times of political conflict, in fact, when the Mann brothers themselves didn't speak to one another. The Feuchtwangers finally succeeded in arranging a general truce, and Mrs. Viertel provided a table for forty-five, with candles and flowers and a good German menu that started with good German soup. There were three German servants on hand to do all the work, but many refugees who weren't worthy of an invitation volunteered for the kitchen so that they could catch a glimpse of the distinguished exiles who represented what Mrs. Viertel proudly called "the true Fatherland": the Manns, the Feuchtwangers, the Werfels, Alfred Döblin, Walter Mehring, Alfred Neumann, Bruno Frank, Ludwig Marcuse. "At the open door to the pantry," Mrs. Viertel noted when the speechmaking began, "the 'back entrance' guests were listening, crowding each other, and wiping their tears."

After the soup, when the roast beef was supposed to arrive, one of the servants pointed out to Mrs. Viertel that Thomas Mann had risen to his feet and put on his spectacles and taken a thick manuscript out of an inner pocket of his tuxedo. The roast beef had to wait. "It was a magnificent tribute to the older brother," Mrs. Viertel said, "an acknowledgment of Heinrich's prophetic political wisdom, his far-sighted warnings to their unhappy country, and a superb evaluation of his literary stature." Everyone was deeply impressed. Glasses were raised to toast Heinrich Mann's good health. But then Heinrich, too, arose. And put on his spectacles. And took out of his pocket a thick manuscript. And began to read. "First he thanked me for the evening," Mrs. Viertel said, "then, turning to his brother, paid him high praise for his continuous fight against fascism. To that he added a meticulous literary analysis of Thomas Mann's *oeuvre* in its relevance to the Third Reich."

The roast beef was ruined by now, but the eminent refugees all ate, and Salka Viertel was impressed and moved, as she watched her famous guests devour her chocolate cake. Even when Nelly Mann screamed with drunken laughter as her red dress split open, Mrs. Viertel focused her thoughts on higher things. She told Bruno Frank how touched she had been by the Mann brothers' tributes to each other.

"Yes," said Frank. "They write and read such ceremonial evaluations of each other every ten years."

• • •

One of the pleasant traditions of the 1940's was the Sunday afternoon broadcasts by the New York Philharmonic. The concerts began at 3 P.M., which, of course, was noon in Hollywood, so everyone of refined sensibility made it a practice, after a leisurely breakfast, to turn on the radio. Many of them remembered for years afterward that on December 7, 1941, Arthur Rubinstein played the Brahms Concerto in B-flat.

At Bob Hope's home on Navajo Street in North Hollywood, the sensibilities were divided. Dolores Hope, who had recently met Rubinstein, retreated to her sitting room to listen to the concert. Hope lolled in bed in the adjoining room and listened to the pro football game from the Polo Grounds in New York, and fretted about an article in that morning's *Los Angeles Times,* which reported all too publicly that his gross income for that year would be nearly $600,000. The game was suddenly interrupted.

"Dolores!" Hope shouted. She came to the door.

"What happened?"

"The Japs bombed Pearl Harbor."

Rubinstein himself recalled hearing the news just after the intermission. "I was about to take the steps leading to the platform when I heard an outcry of horror from several stagehands and from [Artur] Rodzinski himself, who arrived gesticulating dramatically. 'Japan has attacked the United States in Honolulu. . . .' We were all thunderstruck, but the concert had to go on. Rodzinski was charged with announcing the dreadful news to the public. On my way to the piano he said to me, 'You must first play "The Star-Spangled Banner."' We found the audience in a great state of agitation but 'The Star-Spangled Banner' restored order; everyone stood at stiff attention but then settled down quietly to listen to the Brahms concerto, which we played with special fervor. With the last note, the audience ran to the door, and the orchestra, Artur, and I went to listen to the radio."

Not everyone was so genteel. Lana Turner, for example, was immensely proud of having just bought her first house, a large cottage on a hilltop in Westwood, which she regarded as "a lush, green community with attractive white Moderne-style houses . . . nestled in the curves and dips of hills amid the eucalyptus and cypress trees." In keeping with all that, she had bought a white piano and started giving parties. On this particular Sunday, the party started in the early afternoon. The guests included Frank Sinatra, Tommy Dorsey, Buddy Rich, and "two of my favorite girl friends, Linda Darnell and Susan Hayward." When Miss Turner's mother arrived late in the evening, she was surprised at all the hilarity. "You mean you haven't heard?" she cried. "Turn on the radio, for heaven's sake!"

The news on the radio caught many people in strangely incongruous places. Sam Wood, the director, was high in the Sierra Nevada mountains, trying to finish filming a scene in *For Whom the Bell Tolls,* in which Fascist planes bomb a guerrilla camp; the radio broadcasts that flickered through the static told him that all aircraft were grounded. Alan Ladd, stricken with pneumonia in the midst of filming his first great hit, *This Gun for Hire,* was still confined to a hospital bed when he heard the news. It was alleged by an imaginative gossip reporter that he leaped up from his bed and shouted, "I've got to get out of here, they'll be needing guys like me!"

John Houseman and Pare Lorentz were returning aboard the Santa Fe Super Chief from New York, where they had been interviewing actors for their prospective film, "Name, Age, and Occupation," about auto workers on the Detroit assembly lines, a film that was never made. They heard the news from Honolulu in the lurching club car, where, in Houseman's words, they clustered around "the train's only working radio, drinking bourbon as we listened through the night to the mounting list of disasters."

Maxine Andrews was in Cincinnati to sing with her sisters Patti and LaVerne, the Andrews Sisters ("Don't sit under the apple tree/With anyone else but me. . ."), and she liked walking to the theater to see people standing in line to get tickets. "This Sunday, I walked over and there were no lines," she recalled. "I thought, Now, this is funny. I walked onto the stage, which was very dark. The doorman and the stagehands were sitting around the radio. They had just one light on. They were talking about Pearl Harbor being bombed. I asked the doorman, 'Where is Pearl Harbor?' "

Mary Astor was in love with a publicity man who also gave flying lessons, so she had signed on to learn flying, and the two of them were returning that Sunday from the resort of La Quinta. "As we came in for a landing at Grand Central Airport," she recalled, "an odd sight greeted us: not a single plane was on the field; none was even in sight. A colored boy came with a step to help us down from the plane; he was babbling something about the Japanese attacking Pearl Harbor, and telling us to get our plane off the field and into a hangar."

Gene Tierney and Henry Fonda were filming a comedy called *Rings on Her Fingers* on the beaches of Catalina Island. The cameras had just been set up when an assistant director came running down the beach, shouting the news of the attack and adding that everyone would have to return to the mainland immediately. "We wrapped up at once and were soon sailing toward San Pedro," Miss Tierney said. "The radio reports of the Japanese attack . . . led to wild speculation aboard our boat. Some of the cast thought that they might hit the California coast next. For all anyone knew, the waters we were now churning through might have been mined."

This mixture of fear, rumor, and a sudden sense of vulnerability was the dominant emotion in Los Angeles that Sunday. If the Japanese had dared to launch a surprise attack against the strong defenses of Pearl Harbor, how could they fail to strike next against feebly defended Los Angeles? Two thirds of the nation's aircraft production came from southern California, and just north of Los Angeles, the Douglas, Lockheed, North American, and Vultee plants offered obvious targets. It so happened that four thousand antiaircraft troops had arrived from Camp Haan that weekend for maneuvers in the Los Angeles area, so they were immediately assigned to guard the aircraft plants.

Antiaircraft artillery and high-angle machine guns soon surrounded the factories.

None too soon. That Monday, the Fourth Interceptor Command in San
Francisco announced that two formations of "many planes," believed to have
come from Japanese aircraft carriers, had flown over San Francisco and then
headed south. All military installations along the coast were ordered blacked
out. Guileless reporters asked why the Japanese planes had not attacked anything, and why no American planes had taken off to attack the attackers. The
military authorities responded with bluster. "Why bombs were not dropped, I
do not know," said Lieutenant General John L. DeWitt, chief of the Western
Defense Command. "It might have been better if some bombs had dropped to
awaken this city. Death and destruction are likely to come at any moment."

The following night, the phantom Japanese planes were reported over
Los Angeles, and all radio stations were ordered off the air, all planes
grounded. The Eleventh Naval District decreed a blackout from Los Angeles
harbor across an area fifteen miles inland. All street lights, advertising signs,
and oil refinery lights were turned off. Police stopped cars and forced them to
cut their headlights and rely on dimmers. Nobody apparently had any authority to order lights off in stores and private homes, though, so the blackout was
at best partial. The authorities broadcast appeals, however, to everyone to
keep lights to a minimum. Outdoor Christmas trees nonetheless glittered
brightly in both Hollywood and downtown Los Angeles.

Los Angeles dreaded not only phantom Japanese bombers but phantom
Japanese saboteurs. Its "Little Tokyo," just north of the main business district, was the center of the nation's largest Japanese-American community,
about fifty thousand people, of whom roughly one third were native Japanese,
the rest Japanese-American nisei. Within two hours of the news from Honolulu—hardly time for Rubinstein to finish his Brahms concerto—the first
arrests began. Police greeted the municipal ferry as it docked at San Pedro,
rounded up everyone who looked Japanese, and herded them into a wire
enclosure at the Sixth Street pier. The Paramount studio's baseball team was
in the third inning of a game against the L.A. Nippons when the news from
Pearl Harbor began. "FBI men allowed the game to finish," The Hollywood
Reporter said, gloating over Paramount's 6–3 victory, "then rounded up the
Jap contingent."

The authorities kept announcing that it was not a general roundup, that
the FBI had been carefully investigating each case, seeking only potential saboteurs. "Less than 1,000 Japanese nationals will be affected," U.S.
Attorney General Francis Biddle told a press conference that Monday, December 8. "Procedures are being established to provide a fair hearing for all."
Actually, the number of Japanese arrested came to 1,370 within four days and
2,192 by mid-February. A delegation from the Japanese-American Citizens
League went to call on Mayor Fletcher Bowron at City Hall to assure him of
their patriotism. "Treat us like Americans," said the league's spokesman,

Fred Tayama. "Give us a chance to prove our loyalty." Bowron smiled politely, but by then most of the main stores in Little Tokyo had closed, and they stayed closed. In Hollywood, people complained that the gardeners had all disappeared.

So Hollywood began going to war. The army moved into Walt Disney's new studio in Burbank with hardly more than a by-your-leave, and established a searchlight battery to guard the adjoining Lockheed plant. And at Warner Bros., also in Burbank, some people began fretting that the Japanese bombers that would inevitably fly overhead in search of the Lockheed plant might bomb the movie studio by mistake. The Warners authorities decided to build a bomb shelter to protect the executive talent. "I vaguely remember," said Jack Warner, "sitting in this rough underground haven playing checkers with Jesse Lasky, Mervyn LeRoy, and others, and expecting to have the game broken up any moment by Japanese bombs."

Stoic acceptance was not sufficient, though, for a man who had once tried out vaudeville routines with Sid Grauman. "I thought the situation called for a sense of humor, even if I had to stretch it a bit," said Warner. "I went to our painting shop and had an enormous sign made for the roof of one of our sound stages. It had a twenty-foot arrow painted toward Burbank and the lettering read: LOCKHEED THAT-A-WAY."

In the natural course of events, Donald Douglas, president of Douglas, asked Warners technicians to camouflage his aircraft plant in Santa Monica, and they did the job so well that Robert Gross, president of Lockheed, asked Warner for the same protective coloring for his plant. He added dryly that it might include an arrow and a sign saying: WARNER BROS.—THAT-A-WAY. After finishing the camouflage job for Lockheed, Warner ordered his preposterous sign removed and sheepishly admitted that "this gag does not seem so funny in retrospect."

Hollywood at war: Bob Hope (*left*) took his gags wherever the GI's were stationed; Hedy Lamarr (*below*) welcomed them at the Hollywood Canteen.

4

AMERICANISM

(1942)

Jimmy Stewart quietly began putting on weight so that he could meet the army's physical requirements, and then he enlisted as a private (he soon became a bomber pilot and eventually a lieutenant colonel). Robert Montgomery joined the navy and ultimately commanded a destroyer at the invasion of Normandy. Tyrone Power abandoned both his wife and his male lover to join the marines; he became a transport pilot in the South Pacific. William Holden joined the army as Private William F. Beedle, Jr. Henry Fonda, who was thirty-seven years old and had three children, waited only until the final shooting on *The Ox-Bow Incident* and then enlisted as a sailor. He got as far as boot camp in San Diego, where the shore patrol picked him up and sent him back to Los Angeles. "Why?" Fonda still bristled at the memory forty years later. "Because Darryl F. Fuck-it-all Zanuck had pull in Washington and demanded, 'I want Henry Fonda for a picture I'm planning. It's for the war effort and I need him.' And he had enough weight to swing it."

Zanuck, who was thirty-nine himself, also had enough weight to get a commission as a colonel in the Army Signal Corps so that he could, as Otto Preminger sardonically put it, "photograph the war." Zanuck spent his last weeks at Fox firing off a whole broadside of patriotic films—*To the Shores of Tripoli, Secret Agent of Japan, Immortal Sergeant, Crash Dive, Tonight We Raid Calais*—and when he went off to war, he donated his entire string of twenty Argentine polo ponies to West Point. Colonel Zanuck's mogul style remained unique. Sent to London to coordinate training films, he took up residence at Claridge's and duly accompanied a team of British commandos on a real night raid on Calais (actually, it was Saint-Valery). Sent to North Africa to produce a documentary, he took to carrying not only a .45 automatic but a tommy gun, and when he saw a German plane flying overhead, he began firing wildly. "I probably did no damage," he acknowledged, "yet there was always the chance that a lucky shot might strike a vital spot."

Each celebrity's call to colors was a major event in his studio's publicity department, and in the fan magazines that fed at the studio publicity trough. Ronald Reagan, despite his poor eyesight, had long been a lieutenant in the cavalry reserve, so he was summoned early in 1942 to report to Fort March in San Francisco. "It's Jane's war now," began an account by Cynthia Miller in *Modern Screen*. This story was entitled "So Long, Button-Nose," which was apparently Reagan's nickname for his wife, Jane Wyman. The story reported that she had "seen Ronnie's sick face bent over a picture of the small swollen bodies of children starved to death in Poland. 'This,' said the war-hating Reagan, 'would make it a pleasure to kill.' That night he'd stood a little longer beside the crib of Button-Nose the Second, who'd inherited both the nose and the name from her mother. She'd known Ronnie would go, that he'd probably have enlisted after Pearl Harbor if he hadn't been a member of the Cavalry Reserve." And so on.

By October of 1942, some 2,700 Hollywood people—12 percent of the total number employed in the movie business—had joined the armed forces. But it was impractical and unrealistic for the celebrities to pretend that they were just ordinary citizens eager to do their patriotic duty. As a grizzled navy petty officer said to Fonda when he volunteered for service as a gunner's mate, "You know what the fuckin' gunners' mates do in this man's fuckin' Navy? They get killed! . . . You're too smart to be some fuckin' gunner's mate." The stars' value to the war effort obviously lay not in becoming cannon fodder but in exploiting their stardom, in making propaganda films, entertaining the troops, selling war bonds.

Women were especially good at that, selling war bonds. Hedy Lamarr offered to kiss any man who would buy $25,000 worth of bonds. She once sold more than $17 million worth of government paper in a single day. Lana Turner's price for the promise of a kiss was $50,000, and she recalled that she "kept that promise hundreds of times," adding that she "appeared in so many cities that they're all blurred together in my mind." Dorothy Lamour was perhaps the most successful of all. The people who kept track of such things estimated that she once sold $30 million worth of bonds in four days, and ended with a total of $350 million, with and without kisses.

It was all very organized. Treasury Secretary Henry Morgenthau chose M-G-M's publicity director, Howard Dietz, to promote the sale of bonds, state by state. Dietz sent his plans to Clark Gable, who had been asked to head the actors' division of the Hollywood Victory Committee. Among those plans was a proposal that the bond drive in Indiana be launched that January by one of the state's most popular citizens, Carole Lombard, who was also Mrs. Gable. Dietz warned her and all his other recruits to avoid airplanes, which he considered unreliable and dangerous, so Miss Lombard set off by train, selling bonds at various stops en route to Indianapolis. Gable had to stay behind to start work with Lana Turner on *Somewhere I'll Find You*. Miss Lombard left in Gable's bed a pneumatic blond dummy, as a substitute for Miss Turner, with a note that said, "So you won't be lonely." Gable chortled at her ribaldry. ("I'm really nuts about him," Miss Lombard had once said to Garson Kanin. "And it isn't all that great-lover crap because if you want to know the truth, I've had better.") He spent three days building a male dummy, expectantly erect, to welcome her home.

Miss Lombard sold two million dollars' worth of bonds, then couldn't wait for the train on which she already had a ticket and a reservation. On the night of January 16, she boarded a TWA DC-3 bound for home. A few minutes after takeoff from Las Vegas, the plane somehow strayed off course. Beacons that might have warned the pilot had been blacked out because of the continuing anxiety about Japanese bombers. The plane smashed into a cliff near the top of Potosi Mountain. The first reports to reach Hollywood said only that the plane was missing, but somehow everyone knew what had happened. M-G-M publicity agents mobilized, chartered planes, organized searches. A dazed Gable asked to join the search parties but was persuaded to wait in Las Vegas. It was Eddie Mannix, the studio's general manager, who accompanied the stretcher-bearing mules up into the snow-covered mountains and retrieved the charred and decapitated corpse of Carole Lombard.

Gable was distraught for months. "Why Ma?" he kept asking. (He and his wife had called each other Ma and Pa.) He bought a motorcycle and drove wildly through the canyons north of Hollywood. He refused to speak to anyone, or else talked compulsively about his dead wife. Of the many diamond pieces he had given her, only one mangled fragment was found at the site of the crash, and he wore that around his neck. But there was now a war on, and the army was keenly aware of the promotional value of Clark Gable. On January 23, 1942, at a time when the Japanese were conquering the Philippines and advancing through much of Southeast Asia, a telegram from Lieutenant General H. H. Arnold, chief of staff of the Army Air Forces, informed Gable that "we have a specific and highly important assignment for you," and announced that an aide would soon arrive in California to "discuss my plans with you." The only thing more remarkable than General Arnold's devoting any effort at such a time to recruit a movie star was that M-G-M intercepted his message and repressed it. "Wire to Gable received but not giving it to him as do not think it advisable to discuss with him at present time," Howard Strickling of the M-G-M publicity department cabled back to Washington.

The movie studio's goal, apparently, was to keep Gable at work before the cameras as long as possible (*Somewhere I'll Find You* did get made), but Gable could hardly work at all. He brooded. He drank. Joan Crawford invited him to dinner and listened to him talk about his dead wife until three in the morning. "One night," she recalled, "I said, 'Clark, you have got to stop this drinking, you've got to.' He started to cry, and said, 'I know I must.' " So Gable went to the air force recruiting office that August and enlisted as a private. But an M-G-M cameraman named Andrew McIntyre enlisted at the same time and never left the star's side, and when the two of them were shipped to Miami Beach for training, an Army officer remarked, "Gable is the only private in the history of the Army who had his own orderly." On his first day in camp, in Miami Beach, Gable was asked if he would mind if photographers took pictures of him shaving off his famous mustache. "I'll probably be cooler anyway," he was quoted as saying. Within two months, he was commissioned a lieutenant and sent with McIntyre to Colorado to make a training film about "the day-to-day activities of a typical heavy bombardment group."

•   •   •

Los Angeles was a major point of departure for young servicemen bound for combat in the Pacific, and they all wanted to see the sights before they left. The main sight was Hollywood, and Hollywood naturally wanted to oblige. It wanted to be patriotic; it also wanted its patriotism richly publicized. John Garfield was apparently the man who conceived the brilliant idea of organizing the Hollywood Canteen, where the boys could meet all the glittering stars, and the stars could play at being the girl next door. Garfield also had the no less brilliant idea of recruiting the tireless Bette Davis as president. She found and leased a former livery stable at 1451 Cahuenga Boulevard, just off Sunset, and then dragooned studio workmen into volunteering to paint the walls, install the lights, and turn this refurbished barn into the social center of Hollywood.

Miss Davis also went to her agents at MCA and persuaded the firm's reclusive president, Jules Stein, to push a few buttons. As a start, he proposed a gala opening night in October, with seats at $100 in the surrounding bleachers. "The canteen made $10,000 that night from the bleacher seats," Miss Davis recalled. "It seemed thousands of men entered the canteen. . . . I had to crawl through a window to get inside." But that was only the beginning of Jules Stein's button-pushing. Lo, Harry Cohn of Columbia suddenly felt inspired to donate to the canteen the $6,500 in proceeds from the premiere of *Talk of the Town* (Ronald Colman, Jean Arthur, Cary Grant). Stein even persuaded Warners, which happened to be Miss Davis's studio, to make a movie entitled *Hollywood Canteen* and to donate a share of the proceeds to the operation of the canteen.

Bette Davis worked the phone. She called, for example, Hedy Lamarr.

"Sure . . . but what can I do?" asked Hedy Lamarr, according to her own account.

"We need help in the kitchen," said Bette Davis, perhaps not without malice. But then she became more expansive. "You can sign autographs and dance with the boys. And there are a hundred other things. You'll see when you get there."

Hedy Lamarr remembered herself as being docile. "I couldn't cook. I was a mess in the kitchen. I would wash dishes gladly. . . . This was my adopted land and it had been good to me." She recalled later that she went to work two nights every week in the kitchen of the canteen, which "was always hot, noisy, and swinging." Her chief memory of the place was that the canteen was "where I met my third husband."

He was John Loder, who was wearing a tweed suit with a pipe in the breast pocket as he dried stacks of dishes. The canteen was like that—a social center for even those celebrated stars who often had nowhere to go in the evening, but also a social obligation for those same stars, who knew that their celebrity depended on imagery. Betty Grable, too, met her future husband, Harry James, while he was conducting the orchestra there.

Gene Tierney considered it perfectly natural that someone should call her "to remind me that I had not appeared at the Hollywood Canteen lately to entertain the GIs." She "felt guilty about that," even though she was pregnant and suffering "spells of being tired," so she promised to appear the following night. Miss Tierney was a somewhat unusual figure in Hollywood, a girl of considerable beauty but without either great talent or that animal ambition that vivified a Joan Crawford or a Barbara Stanwyck. Her beauty itself was slightly waxen, like that of a debutante, which was natural enough since her father was a prosperous New York insurance broker, and she had gone to Miss Porter's and made her debut at the Fairfield Country Club. Her father actually filched much of her Hollywood income (he was her trustee until she was twenty-one), but the whole family nonetheless disapproved profoundly of her marrying Oleg Cassini, a rather sleek-looking costume designer at Paramount, who posed as an aristocrat because his mother had once been a Russian countess. After Pearl Harbor, Cassini joined the coast guard, then somehow transferred to the cavalry. That took him to Fort Riley, Kansas, and thus took Gene Tierney there too.

Just before she left Hollywood, though, and just after her appearance at the Hollywood Canteen, she came down with German measles. She postponed her trip a few days until the red spots were gone, then joined the migration of women to army camps. "My first room was in the post guest house, where the walls were made of beaverboard and you could hear everything that went on in the rooms on either side. . ." she said later. "After a week you had to look for housing. . . . I rented a dumpy little place that I soon discovered was inhabited by mice. . . ."

Her daughter was born prematurely, weighed two and a half pounds, and had to have eleven blood transfusions. She was named Daria. When she was about a year old, it became clear that her sight and hearing were impaired, and that there were even worse prospects. It was only beginning to be known in those days that German measles in early pregnancy could seriously damage an unborn child. "I would not, could not, accept the idea that Daria was retarded or had brain damage," Miss Tierney recalled.

The Cassinis struggled on for a time, then agreed on a divorce and consigned their hopelessly retarded daughter to a school in Pennsylvania. Then, at a tennis party on a Sunday afternoon in Los Angeles, Miss Tierney was approached by a young woman who smiled and said they had met at the Hollywood Canteen.

"Did you happen to catch the German measles after that night?" she inquired. Miss Tierney was too startled to answer. "I probably shouldn't tell you this," the woman went on. She had been in the women's branch of the Marine Corps, she said, and her whole camp had been swept by an epidemic of rubella. "I broke quarantine to come to the canteen to meet the stars," she said, smiling cheerily. "Everyone told me I shouldn't, but I just had to go. And you were my favorite."

Miss Tierney stood silent for a moment, then turned and walked away. "After that," she recalled, "I didn't care if I was ever again anyone's favorite actress." She was already beginning to crumble, and the crumbling would lead her to a mental institution, to attempted suicide, to a sense of nothingness and despair. Her lost child, Daria, she wrote in her memoirs, was a war baby, born in 1943. "Daria was my war effort."

•   •   •

These were individual episodes, but there remained always a collective Hollywood, an array of low-lying buildings and streets and people on the northern edge of Los Angeles, a community that was partly an industry, partly a technology, partly a style and a quality of mind, partly a negation of all those things, partly just a hunger for money and success. The war was good for Hollywood. It brought in big grosses, big profits. Hollywood expected as much. One of its first reactions to Pearl Harbor had been a race to register movie titles that might attract audiences to the box office: *Yellow Peril, Spy Smashers, Wings over the Pacific, V for Victory.* . . . (The songwriters were more imaginative, for it took very little time to churn out such novelties as "Goodbye, Momma, I'm Off to Yokohama" or "Slap the Jap Right Off the Map" or "To Be Specific, It's Our Pacific" or "When Those Little Yellow Bellies Meet the Cohens and the Kellys.")

There were problems, though, with film scripts suddenly outdated. What could M-G-M do with an Eleanor Powell musical entitled *I'll Take Manila* when the city was actually being threatened by the Japanese army? At Warners, the *Maltese Falcon* gang—Huston, Bogart, and the rest—was in the midst of filming *Across the Pacific,* which was supposed to be about a struggle to thwart an unthinkable Japanese plot to bomb Pearl Harbor. That was hastily changed to an unthinkable plot to bomb the Panama Canal. More complicated was the fact that Huston was suddenly called to duty as a lieutenant in the Signal Corps. As a going-away prank, he decided to leave Warners a movie that was not only unfinished but virtually unfinishable. He filmed Bogart tied to a chair in a house filled with Japanese guards. "I . . . installed about three 'times as many Japanese soldiers as were needed to keep him prisoner," Huston recalled with satisfaction. "There were guards at every window brandishing machine guns. I made it so that there was no way in God's green world that Bogart could logically escape. I shot the scene, then called Jack Warner, and said, 'Jack, I'm on my way. I'm in the army. Bogie will know how to get out.' " Bogie didn't know, and neither did anyone else. Warner's assigned the mess to one of its more reliable professionals, Vincent Sherman, and he or some nameless underling had to concoct an escape. "His impossible solution," Huston gloated, "was to have one of the Japanese soldiers in the room go berserk. Bogie escaped in the confusion, with the comment, 'I'm not easily trapped, you know!' "

The material demands of the burgeoning war effort caused far greater problems. The windows that heroes used to leap through had been made of sugar, which was now rationed. The chairs that they smashed over each other's heads had been made of balsa wood from the Philippines, now under attack by the Japanese. Harmlessly breakable whiskey bottles suitable for barroom brawls had been made of resin, and that, too, was now needed for military production. Film itself was made of cellulose, which was required for explosives (and for the metastasizing production of official military training and propaganda movies). The amount of film available to Hollywood was cut by about 25 percent. Even the flow of money—Hollywood's lifeblood—was restricted. The War Production Board issued a decree on May 6 limiting the use of new materials for stage sets to $5,000 per picture. James F. Byrnes, the Director of Economic Stabilization, even ordered that all salaries be held to $25,000 as of January 1, 1943 (Louis B. Mayer's salary for the previous year was reported to be $949,766), but Congress soon canceled that unseemly gesture of austerity.

The restrictions had some unexpectedly beneficial results. The assembly-line production of trashy B pictures, required for the double features that had become standard during the Depression, had to be curtailed, and a Gallup poll showed that 71 percent of the supposedly insatiable viewers approved of the curtailment. Overall, Hollywood's output decreased from 533 pictures in 1942 to 377 in 1945. Because of the shortage of film, directors could no longer shoot dozens of takes of each scene, so they devoted more time and effort to rehearsals before filming. And because of the tackiness of sets that relied on painted canvas to substitute for scarce metals and lumber, they began exploring the possibilities of moving out of the sound stages into the real world. Alfred Hitchcock even took the daring step of filming *Shadow of a Doubt* entirely on location.

One shortage was unique: the lack of Japanese villains who could sneer at a captive Bogart or gibber and gesticulate on the bridge of an imperial battleship as the forces of retribution started dropping bombs. All starring parts were played by Caucasians, of course (wasn't Peter Lorre perfectly credible as John Marquand's Mr. Moto, after all, and hadn't Paul Muni and Luise Rainer been admirable as Chinese peasants in *The Good Earth?*), so the only problem was to round up some non-Japanese Orientals to play the secondary Japanese villains. Thus a former beer salesman named Richard Loo* and a poet named H. T. Tshiang suddenly found themselves making around a thousand dollars per week in *The Purple Heart.* "The leading Oriental villains (if we exclude J. Carroll Naish) were Sen Yung, Chester Gan and Philip Ahn," as Richard Lingeman wrote in his witty history of this period, *Don't You Know There's a War On?* "Gan specialized in portraying stolid brutal Japs. Sen Yung was the treacherous, English-speaking Japanese, whose mastery of American slang he turned back on Americans in such films as *Across the Pacific* and *God Is My Co-Pilot* ('OK, you Yankee Doodle Dandy, come and get us . . .'). Philip Ahn, a Korean, was perhaps the most sought-after villain of

---

* Loo, who was born in Hawaii, had actually been making films as early as Frank Capra's *Bitter Tea of General Yen* (1933), and he lived on to become a *Kung Fu* television star, but when he died in 1983 at the age of eighty, the obituaries all featured his World War II villainy. "He was known as the man who died to make a living," said his daughter, Beverly Jane Loo, a New York publishing executive. "He was always either stabbing himself or committing hara kiri."

all, with his nasal flat voice and his mask-like face that looked as if it had been carved out of India rubber. Ahn eventually tired of his type-casting and refused any more Japanese roles, saying he wanted to play romantic Chinese leads. . . . There were no romantic Chinese leads."

•   •   •

The reason for the absence of Japanese villains in Hollywood was that the federal government suspected everyone of Japanese ancestry of being a potential saboteur, and banished all the victims of its suspicion to a newly created network of ten concentration camps in what the army called the Zone of the Interior. This move did not come, surprisingly enough, in the first outburst of hysteria that followed Pearl Harbor. On the contrary, the prevailing attitude in the earliest days of the war seemed to be one of restraint and common sense. There was considerable anger against Tokyo, but the powerful and conservative *Los Angeles Times* reminded its readers in an editorial published on December 8, 1941, that most of the 110,000 Japanese-Americans living on the West Coast were "good Americans." Two days later, the *Times* published an editorial against war hysteria under the headline: "Let's Not Get Rattled."

This admirable advice was destined to be overwhelmed. The press itself began baying. A former sportswriter named Henry McLemore wrote in his syndicated column for the Hearst newspapers that all Japanese should be rousted out of California and shipped to the interior. "I don't mean a nice part of the interior, either," he said. "Herd 'em up, pack 'em off and give them the inside room in the badlands. Let 'em be pinched, hurt, hungry and dead up against it. . . . Personally, I hate the Japanese. And that goes for all of them."

This may seem merely an eructation typical of the Hearst press, but it was soon repeated in the Mandarin preachings of Walter Lippmann. After acknowledging that there had not been a single case of Japanese sabotage on the West Coast—indeed, there never was a single such case throughout the war—Lippmann wrote on February 20, that this meant nothing. "From what we know about the fifth column in Europe, this is not, as some have liked to think, a sign that there is nothing to be feared," he declared. "It is a sign that the blow is well organized and that it is held back until it can be struck with maximum effect." Japanese invaders might soon turn the whole Pacific coast into a battlefield, said Lippmann, and "nobody's constitutional rights include the right to reside and do business on a battlefield." The novelist and screenwriter James M. Cain, who had been a colleague of Lippmann's on the old *New York World,* and who now served with Cecil B. DeMille as a helmeted air raid warden in the Hollywood Hills Air Raid Defense Unit, felt a similar sense of alarm. "I'm not given to easy suspicion about people," he said in a postwar interview, "but . . . there was a general feeling that the Japanese were doing a lot of spying, that getting them all bunched together in one place and keeping them there for the duration was not such a terribly bad idea."

This was largely racism. Though there were laws restricting "enemy aliens," so that potential subversives like Bertolt Brecht had to obey a curfew and stay home after 8 P.M., all special curbs on California's 58,000 Italian and 23,000 German aliens were dropped by the end of 1942. San Francisco's Italian-American mayor, Angelo J. Rossi, testified before a congressional committee that "the activities of Japanese saboteurs" convinced him that "every Japanese alien should be removed from this community," whereas "evacuation of Axis aliens, other than Japanese, should be avoided." Nobody even suggested any moves against native-born citizens of German or Italian ancestry, like Mayor Rossi, and yet Rossi declared that even "Japanese who are American citizens should be subjected to . . . all-encompassing investigation." A minor Hollywood actor named Leo Carillo, who claimed that his Mexican origins made him aware of discrimination against minorities, now cabled Santa Monica Congressman Leland M. Ford to call for action: "Why wait until [the Japanese] pull something before we act . . . ? Let's get them off the coast into the interior." Congressman Ford read this into the *Congressional Record,* then made a similar demand on the floor of the House and in a letter to FBI Director J. Edgar Hoover: "All Japanese, whether citizens or not, [should] be placed in inland concentration camps." California's Senator Hiram Johnson, acting on behalf of all legislators from the West Coast, sent President Roosevelt a letter demanding "immediate evacuation of all persons of Japanese lineage."

The Japanese who were now to be imprisoned had originally been welcomed to California as an alternative preferable to the despised Chinese. In 1869, when the Chinese laborers who built the railroads and tilled the fields represented about 10 percent of the state's population, the first Japanese to arrive from their long-secluded empire were described in the *San Francisco Chronicle* as "gentlemen of refinement and culture," who had brought along wives, children, and new business. As late as 1890, there were only two thousand Japanese in the continental United States. About thirty thousand of them had been brought to Hawaii as contract laborers on the sugar plantations, however, and after Congress passed the Chinese Exclusion Act of 1882, the Japanese began moving from Hawaii to California. Dennis Kearney, the Irish immigrant who had led the demagogic opposition against the Chinese, now launched a new campaign against the Japanese, "another breed of Asiatic slaves . . . men who know no morals but vice."

Federal law at that time limited U.S. citizenship to "free white persons" or "persons of African descent," and when Theodore Roosevelt asked Congress in 1905 to permit Japanese immigrants to become citizens, the legislators refused. Liberals shared in this opposition. "We cannot make a homogeneous population out of a people who do not blend with the Caucasian race," Woodrow Wilson said during his 1912 presidential campaign. The following year, anti-Japanese lobbyists succeeded in getting the California legislature to forbid Japanese immigrants to buy any more land. (Though the diligent Japanese occupied only 1 percent of California's arable land, they produced 10 percent of its crops.) Finally came the Immigration Restriction Act of 1924, which imposed ethnic quotas to favor the British and other Northern Europeans at the expense of Russian Jews, Italians, Greeks. Only one people received an immigration quota of zero: the Japanese.

The FBI and military intelligence agents had begun investigating the entire Japanese-American community as early as 1932, and by the time of Pearl Harbor they had accumulated voluminous files on both aliens and native-born citizens whom they considered potentially subversive. These included not only civic leaders but also "opinion-molders" like schoolteachers and journalists, as well as any fisherman with a ship-to-shore radio. "Two FBI men in fedora hats and trench coats—like out of a thirties movie— knocked on [the] door, and when they left, Papa was between them . . ." said Jeanne Wakatsuki Houston, who was seven at the time, one of ten children of a fisherman in Santa Monica. "He was suddenly a man with no rights who looked exactly like the enemy. But he still had dignity, and he would not let those deputies push him out the door. He led them."

The pressure for a mass evacuation kept building. There were sporadic incidents of Japanese being beaten or stoned. A nisei was stabbed to death on a Los Angeles street. The Dies Committee on Un-American Activities issued a report citing various (false) reports of Japanese wrongdoing. The *Los Angeles Times* abandoned its appeals to reason and declared that "the rigors of war demand proper detention of Japanese and their immediate removal from the most acute danger spots." Both Governor Culbert Olson and Los Angeles Mayor Fletcher Bowron called for the evacuation of the Japanese. Perhaps the most influential Californian to press for a mass evacuation, though, was the state's ambitious Republican attorney general, Earl Warren, who was already making plans to challenge the Democratic governor in that year's election (he did and won). Allowing Japanese to remain in California "may well be the Achilles heel of the entire civilian defense effort," Warren declared in late January. "Unless something is done it may bring about a repetition of Pearl Harbor." Less than a week later, Warren called a meeting of California law enforcement officials, and they passed a resolution demanding that "all alien Japanese be forthwith evacuated from all areas in the state of California." Like Walter Lippmann, Warren managed to convince himself that the complete lack of any Japanese sabotage was no reason to trust Japanese protestations of loyalty. On the contrary, he called the tranquillity "ominous." Of this lack of criminal behavior, the future chief justice of the Supreme Court declared: "It looks very much to me as though it is a studied effort not to have any until the zero hour arrives."

California's other chief source of anti-Japanese pressure was General DeWitt, head of the Western Defense Command, who had declared after Pearl Harbor that "Death and destruction are likely to come at any moment." It is easy to deride DeWitt's apocalyptic view of California's future, but he must have felt keenly both his responsibility for defending the vulnerable California coast and the gross inadequacy of the forces with which he was supposed to carry out that responsibility. DeWitt was then sixty-two, slender, bespectacled, a professional, son of a general, a commissioned officer since the age of eighteen, and he knew the whole coast was wide open.

In late December, a Japanese submarine sank the tanker *Emidio* off Eureka, killing five of its crewmen. The freighters *Larry Doheny, Agiworld,* and *H. M. Storey* were fired upon almost within sight of shore. One Japanese submarine, the I-17, even surfaced just north of Santa Barbara and fired more than a dozen six-inch shells at a cluster of oil tanks. (The salvo did very little damage, except to the social life of William Randolph Hearst, who nervously shut down his nearby castle in San Simeon and fled with Marion Davies and assorted retainers to a more secluded chateau at Wyntoon, 250 miles north of San Francisco.) DeWitt was deeply alarmed by these assaults. He reported, with considerable exaggeration, that "substantially every ship leaving a West Coast port was attacked by an enemy submarine."

DeWitt was no Caesar, just a professional army officer confronted by dangers larger and more mysterious than anything in his experience. And to such officers, the news from the Philippines was in some ways worse than the shock of Pearl Harbor. The Japanese attack on the Philippines was not a hit-and-run raid but a well-planned invasion, and General Douglas MacArthur had been forced to flee, humiliated. And the triumphant Japanese proved ruthless. Corregidor. Bataan. These were names that had a powerful effect on army officers assigned to decide the fate of Japanese fishermen in Los Angeles. "The Japanese race is an enemy race," DeWitt declared, "and while many second- and third-generation Japanese born on United States soil . . . have become 'Americanized,' the racial strains are undiluted." German and Italian immigrants had been largely assimilated, and any individual suspects could be investigated, DeWitt argued, but the Japanese could be neither differentiated nor trusted. Even a year later, in testifying before a House committee in San Francisco, DeWitt summed up his judgment when he said, "A Jap is a Jap."

DeWitt's views were fully endorsed—indeed, encouraged—by his superiors in Washington, Secretary of War Henry Stimson and his deputy, John McCloy. Attorney General Francis Biddle raised a few legal objections to imprisoning U.S. citizens without trial, but he did not object very forcefully. And so, when President Roosevelt decided to take action on February 19, his Executive Order 9066 gave General DeWitt the authority to expel as many Japanese as he chose from the entire area under his command. DeWitt promptly ordered all of them, aliens and citizens alike, to move themselves eastward from the coast. Since many of the victims had no idea where to go or how to get there, however, he suspended his order until some emergency camps could be built. Finally, in April of 1942, he decreed the compulsory evacuation of more than 100,000 Japanese who lived within two hundred miles of the coast to sixteen "assembly centers"—sports stadiums, fairgrounds, tent cities. They were ordered to bring only what they could carry aboard their buses: bedding, extra clothes, the children's toys.

Just as Hollywood had been mildly surprised at the disappearance of its gardeners, it now looked the other way as still more of its inhabitants vanished. "One day the Japanese were there, and the next day they'd simply disappeared," according to one witness, Anne Relph, who was an elementary school pupil in North Hollywood at the time of Pearl Harbor. "I can remember going to a friend's home and seeing that suddenly her bedroom was just filled with beautiful toys, and I said, 'Where did you get those?' She said, 'Macimo (or whatever her name was) gave them to me last night before she went to the internment camp.' A lot of the Japanese children had done this, given their toys away to friends rather than have them confiscated." Children could give away toys, but their parents had a more difficult time dealing with the people who began eyeing their possessions. Jeanne Wakatsuki Houston watched a dealer offer her mother fifteen dollars for a twelve-place dinner set of blue and white porcelain that had been brought from Japan. The mother told the dealer that it was worth at least two hundred dollars. The man thought for a moment and then said he might be able to pay $17.50. "She reached into the red velvet case, took out a dinner plate and hurled it at the floor right in front of his feet," Mrs. Houston wrote.

"The man leaped back shouting, 'Hey! Hey, don't do that! Those are valuable dishes!'

"Mama took out another dinner plate and hurled it at the floor, then another and another, never moving, never opening her mouth, just quivering and glaring at the retreating dealer, with tears streaming down her cheeks. He finally turned and scuttled out the door. . . . She stood there smashing cups and bowls and platters until the whole set lay in scattered blue and white fragments across the wooden floor."

"My dad had just purchased a 1941 Packard—he had probably bought it for fourteen hundred dollars, and he had to sell it for seven hundred dollars," said Norman Mineta, a Democratic congressman who was ten at the time of Pearl Harbor. "There were other people who had businesses and grocery stores. What do you do with a grocery store? In thirty days? A lot of them just padlocked their businesses and had to walk away from them. They lost thousands and millions of dollars totally."

Mineta and the rest of his family were assigned to a hastily built barracks in the Santa Anita Racetrack, which ultimately held a total of nearly nineteen thousand bewildered Japanese refugees. "In a room about the size of this [his congressional office] there were six of us . . . from May until October of 1942. From Santa Anita we went to a camp at Hart Mountain, Wyoming. These camps were all barbed wire, guard towers, searchlights. . . . In the summer these places were extremely hot and in the winter extremely cold. They put them in isolated spots so that even if you jumped the fence and got away, you'd still be twenty miles from any community. . . . They were concentration camps. There's no question about it."

"Concentration camp" is a term that arouses emotional reactions, and the barbed wire and the searchlights and the crying children all sound distant echoes of the Nazi Holocaust, but this was not the Holocaust, just the army carrying out orders with the standard proportion of army inefficiency and incompetence. It was all very unpleasant. Nobody tried to beat or starve the prisoners—on the contrary, the army mess hall slopped out rations with a prodigality that shocked the frugal Japanese—but life in a row of tar-paper barracks was undeniably harsh. Mrs. Houston's mother, who had smashed all her cherished dinner plates, was appalled to find herself standing in line for a chance to use one of twelve unseparated toilets in a communal latrine. Another aging lady of similar sensibilities had brought with her a large carton originally designed to hold boxes of Oxydol soap. By sliding this over her head, she could retain an absurd modicum of privacy. The old lady graciously offered to loan her Oxydol carton to Mrs. Houston's mother, and Mrs. Houston's mother gratefully accepted.

The scene of this exchange was a remote and windswept place called Manzanar, the first of the Japanese relocation camps. When Mrs. Houston arrived in late afternoon after a day-long bus trip from Los Angeles, the first thing that impressed her was "a yellow swirl across a blurred, reddish setting sun. The bus was being pelted by what sounded like splattering rain. It wasn't rain. This was my first look at something I would soon know very well, a billowing flurry of dust and sand churned up by the wind through Owens Valley." Owens Valley, that garden spot of the past, that fertile ranchland from which the authorities of Los Angeles had siphoned off all the water, until it turned into a parched wasteland, a wilderness, a place fit only for the Japanese.

● ● ●

While Pearl Harbor was a disaster for some, it was a boon for Hollywood and a bonanza for the nearby aircraft plants. The two fledgling industries had grown up together in Los Angeles, but the aircraft builders had had a considerably harder time of it. At the end of the 1930's, when the movie business was the nation's fourteenth largest (and the largest of all in Los Angeles), aircraft manufacturing still ranked only forty-first.

Though Glenn Martin had started making planes in Los Angeles as early as 1916, the demand for aircraft in World War I prompted him to move east, where more skilled labor was available. Donald Douglas, who had worked for Martin, moved back to the non-union West in 1922 and made friends with Harry Chandler of the *Times,* who wrote him a check for fifteen hundred dollars and helped him open a small plant in Santa Monica. A. P. Giannini of the Bank of Italy (which changed its name to the Bank of America only after Mussolini attacked Abyssinia in 1936) was also willing to finance airplane builders, just as he enjoyed financing movie studios. But many of these operations were small and primitive (Howard Hughes began by leasing one corner of a Lockheed hangar). The manufacturers bought most of their engines and instruments in the East. "It was sheer tin-bending," said one veteran who lived on into the huge growth of the city's aerospace industry.

Pearl Harbor naturally brought convulsive upheavals in all the industries that could provide weapons. Detroit's automobile assembly lines simply shut down and began converting to the manufacture of tanks and artillery. The highly individualistic airplane builders of Los Angeles, who ran their competing firms a bit like Hollywood studios, could hardly believe President Roosevelt's announcement that their industry would have to produce 50,000 warplanes in 1942, ten times the targets for 1939. But when they were threatened with the prospect of a "czar" imposed by Washington, they hastily organized an Aircraft War Production Council and began sharing their resources. In one week early in 1942, for example, Vultee solved a shortage of step nuts by getting 1,000 of them from Lockheed; Douglas, in turn, got 1,000 needed cotter pins from Vultee. When Northrup's hydro press broke down that same week, it borrowed the use of North American's press, while North American acquired sixteen engine mount forges from Consolidated. The industry produced a record 47,000 planes that year, 86,000 the year after, and more than 100,000 the year after that.

Through no foresight of the Los Angeles authorities, the manpower for this tremendous surge in production was providentially available: the despised Okies from the dust bowl, who had poured into California during the Depression despite all of California's stern efforts to keep them out. Even with the Okies finally at work, and with thousands of women emerging from kitchens to enter factories, still more help was needed, and the high pay in the Los Angeles area lured in swarms. All told, 780,000 new immigrants came to southern California from 1940 to 1944. And though the movies had long been Los Angeles' biggest industry, that ended in 1940, for government spending fed not only the aircraft plants but shipbuilding, rubber goods, chemicals, nonferrous metals. From being the nation's seventh-largest manufacturing center in 1939, Los Angeles during the war became second only to Detroit.

•   •   •

One of the few Americans who seemed to ignore the first news from Pearl Harbor was Howard Hughes. The tall, gaunt Texan had been working compulsively at his office all that Saturday night, heard the bulletins on the radio Sunday morning, and went right on working. He was working on a twin-engine plane known as the D-2, which he hoped to sell to Washington as a medium bomber; he was working on a pressurized airliner that would be able to fly in the stratosphere and was known only as "the Buck Rogers ship"; he was also trying to run an airline that he had acquired the year before, which was called Transcontinental and Western Air and would soon be renamed Trans World Airlines.

When Hughes first came to Hollywood in 1925 and rented a room at the Ambassador Hotel for himself and his new wife, Ella, he was twenty years old and vaguely on the lookout for movie projects to finance. He had abandoned his lackadaisical studies at Rice the year before, when his father had suddenly died and left him heir to the Hughes Tool Company and an estate conservatively estimated, for tax purposes, at $871,518. His first movie, entitled *Swell*

Hogan, was so bad that it was never released. *Everybody's Acting* made him a small profit, and *Two Arabian Knights* did fairly well, and then Hughes embarked on the movie he really wanted to make, an epic of the fighter pilots of World War I. The director, Marshall Neilan, thought up a splendid title, *Hell's Angels,* but he and Hughes soon quarreled, so Hughes took over the direction himself.

He was now twenty-two, and he had a lot of money. He spent more than $500,000 to buy eighty-seven vintage Spads and Fokkers and Sopwith Camels, the largest private air force in the world. Then he began waging his private war—over Mines Field, now the site of Los Angeles International Airport—and suffering private casualties. Three stunt pilots were killed in crashes during the months of filming *Hell's Angels.* Hughes himself tried out an obsolete Thomas Morse scout plane and lost control as it went into a spin. He was pulled unconscious from the wreckage and had to undergo complicated surgery to repair a crushed cheekbone.

For one big scene, the shooting down of a German Gotha bomber, Hughes insisted that the pilot put the plane into a real spin, and then bail out if necessary. But the scene also required a technician who would crouch in the rear of the fuselage and set off a series of smoke bombs as the doomed plane was supposedly hit by machine-gun bullets. Then he, too, could bail out as the plane went into its spin. Several pilots refused the assignment, but Hughes paid a substantial bonus to one willing daredevil, Al Wilson, and then hired as his assistant an eager mechanic named Phil Jones. When the plane went into its spin, only the pilot bailed out, but the crash of the Gotha made a great scene.*

Hughes was nearly finished, after two years of filming and more than two million dollars in expenses, when he rather belatedly realized, as other Hollywood executives were just as belatedly realizing, that all silent films had been doomed ever since *The Jazz Singer* had opened two years earlier. Hughes characteristically determined to begin all over again. He hired a scriptwriter to start providing *Hell's Angels* with some dialogue, and he even decided that he had to eliminate his star, Greta Nissen, who could not play the English heroine without a thick, Norwegian accent. While reshooting around his missing heroine, Hughes tested dozens of replacements. When the inevitable agent, Arthur Landau, inevitably appeared with an eighteen-year-old blonde named Harlean Carpenter, Howard Hughes looked at the screen test of the future Jean Harlow and inevitably said, "In my opinion, she's nix." Perhaps

---

* As often happened throughout Hughes's career, the mysterious accidents during *Hell's Angels* inspired a lot of rumors. Lester Cole, a prominent screenwriter who later went to prison as one of the Hollywood Ten, wrote in his memoirs, *Hollywood Red,* that the mechanic had not been given a parachute because the plane was supposed to pull out of its dive. The pilot took along a spare parachute and gave it to the mechanic at the last minute, Cole said, but the mechanic was too terrified to use it. "The pilot tried to put it on him when the plane was in a spin, a second plane photographing it all," Cole wrote. "Desperate at three thousand feet, the pilot leaped to safety, unable to help the frozen-with-fright mechanic, who crashed with the plane in flames. (What a scene *that* would have made!)"

just as inevitably, though, Hughes let the agent talk him into hiring his young client for $250 a week.

Hughes's overall costs on *Hell's Angels* eventually reached a towering $3.8 million, a record for extravagance at that time, and although the film achieved a considerable success, it could never earn back Hughes's investment. There was a pattern here. Partly, it was an idiosyncratic psychological pattern, which Hughes's admirers liked to call "perfectionism," but which actually started with Hughes's eagerness to confront, all by himself, a series of challenges beyond his experience or ability. Then, after repeated refusals to take any advice from anyone, there came a number of predictable mistakes, miscalculations, failures, and then a desperate effort to correct those mistakes, or rather not to correct them but to deny them, to obliterate them.

Such spectacles of self-indulgence were familiar enough in Hollywood. Though Hughes was no immigrant from Eastern Europe, his inherited wealth gave him the same sense of infallibility that acquired wealth gave to a Louis B. Mayer or a Jack Warner. Theoretically, according to the economic laws proclaimed by Adam Smith, the bungling misjudgments of the average millionaire should end in ruin, thus enabling the system to correct itself, but millionaires have generally found it more convenient to suspend Smith's laws by bribery and monopoly. Just as it was monopoly that persuaded the Mayers and Warners and the rest that they were great showmen with an instinctive understanding of what the American people wanted, so it was the Hughes Tool Company's control of an indispensable oil drilling bit that enabled Howard Hughes to imagine himself one of the kings of Hollywood. No matter what he did, no matter how much money he wasted, the Hughes drilling bit would always pay his bills, would always protect him from harm.

Having conquered Hollywood at the age of twenty-five, Hughes went on to make five more movies within a year, notably *Scarface* and *The Front Page* (for which he rejected two still-obscure young actors named James Cagney and Clark Gable), but Hughes's passion now was to fly. It was not a new passion. He had been a schoolboy of sixteen when he first learned to pilot a rickety plane, but this had become the age of Lindbergh, whose solo flight to Paris had redefined the nature of heroism. Hughes acquired a Boeing pursuit plane and began streamlining it (that was originally the sole purpose of the Hughes Aircraft Company). He won his first trophy in Miami in 1934 for flying the Boeing at 185 miles an hour, then built a plane of his own called the H-1 and piloted it to speed records of 339, 351, and 355 mph. In 1937, he flew from Los Angeles to Newark at an average of 332 mph, a coast-to-coast record of seven hours, twenty-eight minutes. The following year, he cut Lindbergh's flight time to Paris by half, and then flew on to set a round-the-world record of three days, nineteen hours, seventeen minutes.

He was a national hero, a second Lindbergh, and since his ignored wife, Ella, had gone back home to Houston during the filming of *Hell's Angels,* he was now regarded as one of the nation's "most eligible bachelors." It was an honorific that made him a regal figure in Hollywood. No photographic record of that period would be complete without a picture of the tall, scarred, and inarticulate millionaire ambling into some neon-lit nightclub, outfitted in Hollywood's black-tie uniform and displaying a beautiful blonde on his elbow. No matter how late Hughes telephoned, no matter how imperiously he demanded that some starlet prepare herself for his arrival, there is no record of anyone ever rejecting his invitations.

On the other hand, there is ample testimony to his fumbling and tongue-tied helplessness as a courtier. Darryl Zanuck recalled that Hughes once said he would like to meet Norma Shearer, so Zanuck invited the two of them, along with an appropriate smattering of Hollywood celebrities, to his estate in Palm Springs. When Hughes met the object of his desire, he said, "I'm very pleased to meet you"—and left. Lana Turner recalled that Hughes was "likable enough but not especially stimulating." Hughes once got as far as announcing his "preference for oral sex," but Miss Turner reported that she "wasn't interested." "That didn't seem to bother him . . ." she added. "He'd come to my house just to sit and talk to my mother." Hughes also kept company with Ava Gardner for a time, but he could not reconcile himself to her independent ways. When his spies reported that she had gone dancing after midnight at the Mocambo, he summoned her to his place in Beverly Hills for a scolding. She swore at him. He slapped her face. She reached for the nearest object, a brass bell, and knocked him cold.

Hughes apparently suffered an affliction known as ejaculatory impotence, which rather surprised Bette Davis, who had taken him quite seriously. So much so, in fact, that her husband, Harmon Nelson, who spent his evenings as a bandleader in the Blossom Room of the Hollywood Roosevelt Hotel, became suspicious. Nelson hired a detective to wire the bedroom, and then, as required by the primitive technology of the day, established himself in a sound truck parked in a nearby canyon. After listening for a while to his wife and Hughes struggling to achieve some sort of climax, Nelson went running down the hill to his home, burst into the bedroom, and threatened to make his recordings public. Hughes swung wildly at the cuckold but missed. Miss Davis went into hysterics. Nelson finally decided to salvage his honor by blackmailing Hughes for seventy thousand dollars, and Hughes, terrified by the threatened disclosure of his sexual problems, paid the money. Bette Davis, the only one in the triangle who showed any sense of honor at all, insisted on repaying Hughes every cent.

So Hughes went on with his highly publicized romances. Gene Tierney, who was eighteen when Hughes was thirty-five, found, like Lana Turner, that dates with the millionaire often included her mother. And some grand gestures. "Before our first date, he sent me flowers," she recalled. "Not just flowers, but a roomful of gardenias. My mother looked around the small, modest apartment we had rented in Westwood and said it smelled like a funeral home." Hughes liked to take his girls and their mothers out flying. He once flew Miss Tierney and her mother to lunch in Tijuana, where he had reserved an entire restaurant and a band for the three of them. "He did not make conversation easily," Miss Tierney observed, and he spoke ardently only of airplanes, "all the while quoting weights and measures and ratios that were just so much confetti to me."

Despite his incoherence, Hughes had a basic attraction. "Money is sexy and he certainly had a blinding overabundance of cash appeal," according to another pigeon, Joan Fontaine, who reported that Hughes proposed marriage to her after one casual meeting. But Gene Tierney was accustomed to mon-eyed people, and she liked Hughes because of what she considered "a soft, boyish, clear-eyed quality about him." She remembered, too, that when Hughes somehow heard of her infant daughter's mental retardation, he flew a prominent specialist to see the child and unquestioningly paid the doctor's outrageous bill of fifteen thousand dollars for one day's useless services.

This aspect of Hughes seemed to die in the worst of his plane crashes, in Beverly Hills, when he suffered nine broken ribs, a broken nose, a fractured skull, a collapsed left lung, and third-degree burns over much of his body. After he emerged from the hospital, Miss Tierney recalled, "the eyes had turned beady, the face had tightened. Rather than adding character, the scars only aged him. . . ." At some point in this series of crashes, Hughes also began suffering a major hearing loss, though it was typical that one of his glamorous friends, Veronica Lake, insisted it was all a charade. "Howard, for some reason, pretended he was deaf," she said. "I suppose he found it advan-tageous in business dealings, a technique to keep others off their guard while he took in everything they said."

The disastrous crash in Beverly Hills was the first flight of the XF-11, in which Hughes had invested more than six million dollars of his own money. Originally, it had been the D-2, a five-man bomber designed to fly at 450 miles per hour. The D-2 was a commonplace project, though, compared to the vast flying boat that was taking shape in the mind of Henry J. Kaiser. Kaiser and Hughes were both such public heroes that the War Production Board authorized the payment of eighteen million dollars for this inherently absurd project. And so Hughes began designing and building the plane that was officially named the Hercules; some irreverent employees began calling it the Spruce Goose. Designed to carry 700 passengers or a load of 60 tons, the first prototype of the gigantic flying boat stood 30 feet high and had a wingspan of 340 feet, longer than a football field. Its tail alone was 100 feet high, almost as tall as a ten-story building. And it was made entirely of wood. The only trouble was that the war was long over before Hughes was able to take his prototype out for its first flight.

These were not Hughes's only aircraft projects. He owned the patent on a device that could speed the loading of machine guns on B-17 bombers, and the 90,000 that he produced were eventually used on 90 percent of all U.S. bombers. And he made airplane parts: 6,370 fuselages for other manufactur-ers' planes, 5,576 aircraft wings, 14,766 landing gear struts. His plants also manufactured nearly one million artillery shells. But though he eventually acquired a forty-million-dollar contract to manufacture his D-2—a contract that he won after some subsequently disputed entertainment of President Roosevelt's son Elliott and several other entertainable air force officers— Hughes never managed to build and deliver, before the war came to an end in 1945, one single warplane.

He had other things on his mind. One of them was a movie that he had been puttering around with since 1939. It was called *Billy the Kid,* and it had been written by Ben Hecht, who had learned about Howard Hughes while writing *Scarface* a decade earlier. Hecht insisted that he be paid one thousand dollars in cash every day, promptly at 6 P.M. "In that way," he wrote later, "I stood to lose only a day's labor if Mr. Hughes turned out to be insolvent." Hughes did not turn out to be insolvent, only neurotic. When two scowling gunmen from Chicago came to interrogate Hecht about whether they should grill Hughes on the moral niceties of *Scarface,* Hecht said Hughes was completely innocent. "He's got nothing to do with anything," said Hecht. "He's the sucker with the money."

Then came the usual search for unknown performers. Hughes eventually signed up a baby-faced actor named Jack Buetel at $75 a week to play Billy the Kid (what ever became of Jack Buetel?). He also signed up a few experienced professionals, Walter Huston and Thomas Mitchell—and Howard Hawks as director—and then he indulged himself in the more gratifying task of hunting a heroine. He and his cronies spent hours looking through heaps of photographs of ambitious girls, and in due time he paused over a picture of a buxom creature who was earning $27.50 a week as a receptionist in a chiropodist's office.

"Give this Jane Russell a test," Hughes said as he went on thumbing through the photographs. The job of taking off the chiropodist's patients' shoes and dipping their feet into pails of warm water had actually taken only about a week of Miss Russell's young life. Newly out of high school, she had also spent some time at the Max Reinhardt School, though she never actually met Reinhardt, and then she had some pictures taken by a photographer, who hung one up on the wall of his studio. There it was seen by one of those agents who made a practice of collecting such pictures and showing them to men like Howard Hughes. So Hughes had her summoned and given a screen test and then signed up for $150 a week. Hughes was not at all certain that he wanted to use her as his heroine, but he had long made it a practice to sign up girls at small salaries and then keep them on call indefinitely. At about the same time that he acquired Miss Russell, for example, he bought from Warners the contract of a beautiful fifteen-year-old named Faith Domergue. After four years of waiting for something to happen, Miss Domergue finally threw a tantrum. "All right, you pick the story you want to do," said Hughes. When Miss Domergue selected an antique melodrama called *Vendetta,* Hughes ordered another one of his victims, Preston Sturges, to start filming it. (What ever became of Faith Domergue?)

Something about Jane Russell spoke to Howard Hughes. She had no talent, and she wasn't even very good-looking, but Hughes decided that she had commercial possibilities. He sent Howard Hawks out to Arizona to start filming *Billy the Kid.* Theoretically, Hawks was in charge of the production—Hughes had promised him that—but Hughes could never abide by his own rules. After midnight one day in 1940, he telephoned Russell Birdwell, the press agent, and ordered him to come immediately to Hughes's headquarters on Romaine Street. Hughes himself ran through all the rushes on the projector and then demanded to know what Birdwell thought.

"Excellent," said the uncomprehending Birdwell.

Hughes ran through the rushes all over again.

"I think the rushes are brilliant," Birdwell tried again. "Of course, they are rough. . . ."

"Didn't you notice anything?" asked Hughes.

"Notice something?" Birdwell echoed.

"No clouds," said Hughes. "Why go all the way to Arizona to make a picture unless you get some beautiful cloud effects? The whole purpose of going on location is to get scenery you cannot achieve in a Hollywood studio. The damn screen looks naked. Naked."

Birdwell suggested that there might not be any clouds in Arizona at that particular moment, and that it would be a waste of time to keep the whole company waiting for them to appear. Hughes sent him home, spent the rest of the night rerunning the rushes of *Billy the Kid,* then telephoned Hawks in the morning. "Howard, you're turning out one hell of a movie," Hughes said, according to Birdwell's account. "In fact, the project is so promising that I want to up the budget from $400,000 and give you $1 million to work with. And, Howard, I would like you to get some clouds in the sky, even if you have to wait a little while."

Hawks may have been paranoid, or he may just have been sensitive to Hollywood language, or he may just have wanted to escape from Howard Hughes. "Look, Howard," he said. "I've been offered a new picture with Gary Cooper called *Sergeant York,* and I can't take it until I get *Kid* out of the way. I have an idea. You apparently don't like what I'm doing out here, so why don't you take over on this picture? Then you can do what you want, and I can do what I want." It was Marshall Neilan and *Hell's Angels* all over again. Howard Hughes was being challenged once again to take the controls. How could he refuse?

Hughes's first act was not to fly to the scene but rather to demand that the entire cast and crew, some 250 people, abandon all work at the site nearly 100 miles beyond Flagstaff, Arizona, and return to Los Angeles for consultations. When filming resumed under Hughes's direction, it resumed at Hughes's own bizarre pace. Often he appeared only late at night and then insisted on filming all night long. Sometimes he demanded thirty retakes of a simple scene, sometimes none at all. While Hughes dawdled, M-G-M stole his title and hastily produced its own *Billy the Kid,* starring Robert Taylor. Hughes called up Louis B. Mayer to protest.

Mayer was not stricken by remorse. Hughes had to change to a new title: *The Outlaw.*

If Hughes could not coerce Mayer, he could at least torment his own employees, and so, during one of those all-night filming sessions, there occurred the famous scene of the Jane Russell brassiere. The heroine was supposed to be undergoing torture by Indians, supposed to be tied by the wrists between two trees, supposed to be writhing in pain. Hughes, playing director, insisted on having the scene shot over and over. It eventually became clear that he was having trouble in satisfying his own fantasy of what a girl strung up between two trees should look like. "This is really just a very simple engineering problem," he said as he called for a drawing board, paper, and pencil. The legend is that Hughes regarded the Russell bosom as a challenge to his skill in aeronautical design, that he quickly sketched a plan for a new brassiere, and that a wardrobe mistress immediately stitched together something that would fulfill Hughes's fantasies. The legend defies plausibility, if only because of Hughes's continuing inability to design airplanes that functioned properly. The only plausible element, indeed, was Hughes's morbid insistence that his employees spend their evening hours watching him direct other employees in taking pictures of a girl strung up between two trees. As for what actually happened, Miss Russell herself is the best witness: "When I went into the dressing room and tried it [the new bra] on, I found it uncomfortable and ridiculous. Obviously he wanted today's seamless bra, which didn't exist then. . . . So I put on my own bra, covered the seams with tissue, pulled the straps over to the side, put on my blouse and started out. . . . Everybody behind the camera stared, and Howard finally nodded okay, and filming proceeded."

The Outlaw was complete rubbish, of course, but that hardly bothered anyone. To Hughes, and to Birdwell, its trashiness was simply another challenge. The first step was to produce a photograph that would serve as the one great publicity picture. "What would you charge," Birdwell asked a Beverly Hills photographer named George Harrell, "to photograph a girl [who] will sit, stand, roll around, dance, smile, sing, laugh, and cry? All you will do is shoot. I am after one, perhaps two, great photographs." Harrell suggested two hundred dollars. Birdwell was horrified. "Perhaps you didn't understand me," he said. "This must be a master photograph." They finally settled on $2,500. Miss Russell duly arrived at the Harrell studio and spent an afternoon lounging around in a haystack, provided by Birdwell, and sucking thoughtfully on a stalk of hay. The result went to *Life* magazine, and from *Life* to U.S. Army camps all over the world. Jane Russell was famous.

As for the awful movie, *The Outlaw,* that was another problem to be solved by the appropriate promotion. Hughes hired the Geary Theater in San Francisco for his premiere and then plastered the city with posters of Miss Russell lolling in her haystack. Anticipating some still-imaginary opposition, Hughes's poster announced: "*The Outlaw*—the picture that couldn't be stopped." Hughes himself piloted a planeload of fifty Hollywood correspondents up to the premiere, but his guests' reactions ranged from nervous embarrassment to open ridicule. *Time* called the movie "a strong candidate for the flopperoo of all time."

The only solution, obviously, was to play the censorship game. Birdwell called up the San Francisco police department and demanded that *The Outlaw* be suppressed as an outrage to public morals. The police department showed no interest. Birdwell telephoned clergymen, parent-teacher groups, women's organizations, urging them to join in a public outcry against his employer. The forces of virtue remained apathetic. Birdwell wrote and planted in a San Francisco newspaper an article entitled "What Time Does Reel Six Go On?" It implied that unspeakable depravities occurred during reel six of *The Outlaw* and that armies of insiders who knew the secret were storming the theater to witness the orgy, although, as Birdwell later admitted, "there was nothing in reel six that you couldn't have seen in reel five, four, or seven."

Finally, Birdwell had discovered the right method. The rituals of moral protest began, the police bestirred themselves, arrests were made, lawyers were hired, censorship was decried, civil liberties were proclaimed, and attendance records were broken. At that very moment, at the edge of triumph, Howard Hughes withdrew his ludicrous film from circulation. He offered no explanation, simply took it back and locked it up in a special airtight room that he had built for that purpose at his headquarters on Romaine Street.

•   •   •

The greatest playwright within a thousand miles of Hollywood could not find work in the world's movie capital. In a small house on Twenty-fifth Street in Santa Monica, Bertolt Brecht set up his typewriter on a small table in the small bedroom, which had pink doors. For this house, he paid $48.50 per month in rent. Having reached America largely on funds solicited by Fritz Lang, he now lived entirely on a $120 monthly dole from the European Film Fund organized by Charlotte Dieterle and Liesl Frank. Brecht's wife, Helene Weigel, bought the necessary furniture and the clothing for the two children from Salvation Army and Goodwill stores. A German refugee doctor sent no bills for treating Brecht's tubercular daughter, Barbara. As an "enemy alien," provided with an alien identity card numbered 7624464, Brecht was not allowed outside his home after 8 P.M., and not allowed to travel more than five miles from that home without special permission. "I can't recall a single breath of fresh air in all these months," he wrote in his journal. "It's as if I was sitting a kilometer deep under the ground, unwashed, unshaven, waiting to hear the result of the battle for Smolensk."

He referred to Hollywood as "the world center of the narcotics trade," but he kept trying to write for the movies. He showed William Dieterle a screen treatment entitled "The Business Affairs of Mr. Julius Caesar." He drafted a scenario entitled "Rich Man's Friend," roughly based on an episode in the life of his fellow exile Peter Lorre. He wrote a story about the founder of the Red Cross, "The Malady of Monsieur Dunant." Then there was an outline on Walter Reed's struggle against malaria, "The Fly," and notes for various projects with titles like "Horoscope," "The Traitor," "The Mexican."

Brecht worked with Elisabeth Bergner's husband, Paul Czinner, on an idea that Miss Bergner had given him, about a girl who became a political radical while under the influence of hypnosis. Brecht later claimed that Billy Wilder had heard about his scenario and sold the idea to some producer for $35,000. (Wilder not long ago dismissed the charge: "I met him two or three times at parties during the war. That's all I can tell you.") Brecht engaged in the traditional writer's revenge of crying "J'accuse." "When I was robbed in Los Angeles, the city/ Of merchandisable dreams," he wrote, "I noticed/ How I kept the theft, performed,/ By a refugee like me, a reader/ Of all my poems,/ Secret, as though I feared/ My shame might become known,/ Let's say, in the animal world."

It was Fritz Lang, once again, who came to Brecht's rescue, by opening up the possibility of a film about a spectacular killing in Europe. On May 27, 1942, two Czech guerrillas whom the British had parachuted into Nazi-occupied Czechoslovakia ambushed the green Mercedes carrying Reinhard Heydrich, deputy chief of the Gestapo and organizer of the still-secret "final solution." Their grenade shattered his spine. The next day, while Heydrich lay dying, and the Nazi police began rounding up hostages, Brecht and Lang went walking along the beach at Santa Monica, like the walrus and the carpenter, wondering if the manhunt for the assassin of Heydrich the Hangman would make a good movie.

It obviously would. Working together, in German, Lang and Brecht soon produced a one-hundred-page treatment, which Lang then sold to an independent producer, another refugee, named Arnold Pressburger. The penniless Brecht got a beggarly advance of $250, which filled him with hope for the future. Would $3,000 be too much to ask for the finished script? Brecht asked. Not at all, said Lang, who grandly promised him $5,000 for the script plus $3,000 more for any necessary revisions. Brecht felt prosperous enough to move into a slightly larger house in Santa Monica, one block away, which cost $12.50 per month more in rent.

Lang was not a real movie writer, and neither, as he well knew, was Brecht, so Lang hired as a collaborator a professional named John Wexley. He paid a stiff price, $1,500 per week, for Wexley had written some very successful screenplays, notably *Angels with Dirty Faces* and *Confessions of a Nazi Spy*. Lang may also have promised Wexley full script credit (subsequent accounts contradict each other), but Brecht accepted him simply as a colleague. He described him as "very leftist and decent." And so they began their doomed collaboration. Pressburger had rented some space in the Charlie Chaplin studio, and when the work stretched on after the alien curfew of 8 P.M., they would meet at Brecht's house. The collaboration was doomed not only because

Brecht and Wexley had very different ideas about the film—Brecht's title, "Trust the People," implied the kind of *Lehrstück* that he wanted to write, complete with choruses and montages of headlines—but also because Brecht regarded all collaboration as an ideologically inspired mating of his genius and his colleagues' suggestions for the fulfillment of that genius. He was nettled that Wexley addressed him as "Bert," when even his own wife called him "Brecht," but he wrote of Wexley's efforts in his journals, "I correct his work."

Wexley naturally viewed the situation quite differently. He saw himself as the skilled professional summoned west from his Bucks County farm to create a viable screenplay out of the jotted notes of two gifted refugees who could hardly speak English. And as he dictated his own work to a secretary, he made sure that each page bore his name. When the two writers argued, as they inevitably did, they often ended by including in the script both Brecht's Berlinisms and Wexley's Hollywoodisms. Their joint creation eventually reached about three hundred pages, roughly twice the standard size. Then Lang's own anxieties intervened. He took Wexley aside and told him that what he wanted to make was "a Hollywood picture." That injunction, that concept, was presumably something that the two of them could understand, not Brecht. One of the most interesting elements, though, was Lang's objection to scenes in which Brecht showed Nazis mistreating Jews, even scenes in which Jews were seen wearing the Star of David. The question that Lang kept raising, according to Brecht, was whether or not "the public will accept this." What he meant by the "the public," of course, was the authorities in both Hollywood and Washington, who decided what it was that the public would accept. In both places, it was more or less official policy that the Jews were incidental to the larger struggle between freedom and dictatorship. So here was Lang, a Jew, warning Brecht, a Gentile, that their movie about Nazism must not show Jews being persecuted as Jews. And this in 1942, when the four gigantic gas chambers at Auschwitz were in the process of being built.

Once the three-hundred-page script was finished, Lang adopted the predictable expedient of paying off Brecht, thanking him for his services, promising him that all would be well, and then telling Wexley to cut the script in half. The next time Brecht saw Wexley, he described him as looking like a "living bad conscience." And when he was invited to watch the actual filming, the first scene he saw was one in which the heroine argued with her aunt about the décolletage of her wedding dress, a scene that he thought had been cut out. In general, he thought he had been "able to remove the main stupidities from the story. Now they're all back in." And of course his title, "Trust the People," never had a chance. Neither did some other possibilities he had considered: "Never Surrender," "Unconquered," "Silent City." Instead, Lang and Pressburger solicited suggestions from their office staff—an idea that Brecht should have approved as an example of collective creativity—and some nameless secretary won the hundred-dollar prize by proposing the title that the film eventually acquired: *Hangmen Also Die*.

For Brecht, who still felt that Lang's successful film contained some mutilated fragments of his ideas, there remained one last degradation: Wexley received the sole credit as the author of the screenplay. Brecht formally appealed to the Screen Writers Guild, since, as he put it, "credit for the film would possibly put me in a position to get a film job if the water gets up to my neck." The Guild, which had struggled for years for the right to adjudicate such disputes (as many as a hundred per year), followed a basic rule, that a writer who had contributed one quarter of the final script deserved a share of the credit. But when the union's three examiners investigated this case, Wexley produced pages and pages of the final script that he had dictated, with his own name at the top of each page, whereas Brecht could provide only a memorandum on all the meetings that had produced the script. Lang testified on Brecht's behalf, citing many passages that "only Brecht could have written." And Brecht could hardly have asked for a court more in accordance with his own ideology, a court organized by the union of his fellow writers, but that court ruled exactly as the author of *Mahagonny* might have anticipated. It voted to give the full screen credit to Wexley, and not because he had written the whole script but because Brecht was a German, who would someday go back to Germany, whereas Wexley would remain in America, and therefore the screen credit, the lifeblood of the Hollywood writer, was more important to Wexley, the American, than to the refugee from the Nazism that was the basic subject of the movie.

• • •

Like Detroit, Hollywood was by now producing war movies on an assembly line. It requisitioned Ronald Reagan back from the Army training-film center known as Fort Roach to star in Irving Berlin's *This Is the Army*. It saluted American pilots in *Air Force* and *Destination Tokyo*, and Marines in *Guadalcanal Diary*, and merchant seamen in *Action in the North Atlantic*, and army nurses in *So Proudly We Hail*. Some of these films made a dogged pretense at realism, like *Wake Island*, in which William Bendix and Robert Preston fought gallantly against overwhelming hordes of Japanese. Some were shamelessly sentimental, like *Mrs. Miniver*, in which the beautiful Greer Garson seemed to save the entire British army from Dunkirk. Some were primarily thrillers, like Hitchcock's *Saboteur*, with that unforgettable finale of the villain dangling by his sleeve from the hand of the Statue of Liberty—and then the sleeve starting to tear. Even the movies that were purely escapist, like *You Were Never Lovelier*, in which Fred Astaire found his new dancing partner in Rita Hayworth, or *Reap the Wild Wind*, in which John Wayne, Paulette Goddard, and Hedda Hopper were all upstaged by a giant squid— even these were escapes from the war, and the war remained in the anxieties of everyone who watched them.

Hollywood's shrewder producers knew that the most successful war films would play on those emotions without addressing them too literally. Let war, like so many other difficult realities, be symbolic, an outpouring of patriotism without too much actual gore. It was Warner Bros. that perhaps best understood the possibilities, understood, for example, the new value in the story of an aged vaudevillian who had once sung the cock's crow of combat in an earlier time, not against Hitler but simply "Over There."

George M. Cohan, who knew all too well that he was dying of bladder cancer, had been trying for several years to interest some studio in his life story. Samuel Goldwyn was willing to explore the idea and offered it to Fred Astaire, but Astaire declined. Cohan tried negotiating at Paramount, without success. His aura as the composer of "Over There" and "Yankee Doodle Dandy" and "Give My Regards to Broadway" was also the aura of an anachronism, and that quality of outdated rhetoric extended into politics. Cohan had strongly supported the theatrical producers during the Actors Equity strike of 1919, and his Irish-American jingoism was not entirely free of anti-Semitism.

Everything that made the Cohan story a problem in Hollywood, however, made it a solution to the problems of James Cagney, who was best known for his gangster roles but had once been a song-and-dance man. Cagney was also an ambitious stalwart of the Screen Actors Guild (he became its president in the autumn of 1942), and when various official bodies began "investigating" Hollywood, a former Communist Party official named John L. Leech falsely identified Cagney and various others as fellow conspirators. Harry Warner was appropriately indignant, not at the slandering of his star but at the star himself. "He told me in no uncertain terms," said Cagney's brother William, who by then was managing most of the actor's affairs, "that if my brother didn't clean his skirts of this charge, he was going to destroy him."

William Cagney apparently thought the solution would be to win the approval of Martin Dies, so he went to see the visiting congressman at the Biltmore Hotel in downtown Los Angeles. Dies listened with interest but wanted to know why Jimmy Cagney himself had not come. William Cagney said his brother was vacationing on Martha's Vineyard. Dies was not satisfied. "Well, where I come from," he said, "somebody calls you a sonofabitch and you do nothing about it, you're a sonofabitch." Dies demanded that the actor return to California immediately for "a clean bill of health." William Cagney telephoned Martha's Vineyard to urge his brother to comply. Jimmy Cagney agreed in principle, but the famous tough guy was terrified of flying and had never boarded a plane in his whole life. "To his credit," William Cagney said later, "Jimmy got on the plane, which is probably the hardest thing he ever did." Cagney not only flew to California but testified about his political beliefs for about fifteen minutes behind the closed doors of the Dies committee, then emerged with Dies's approval.

William Cagney was still worried. "We're going to have to make the goddamndest picture that's ever been made," he said to his brother after the encounter with Dies. "I think it's the Cohan story." There followed then the usual Hollywood controversies and confusions. Jack Warner and his production chief, Hal Wallis, both claimed later that it had been their idea to film the Cohan story, and that Cagney was their choice as the star. "Cagney refused to make the picture," said Wallis, who had never gotten on well with the actor. Wallis hoped to change Cagney's mind by assigning the project to Robert Buckner, an amiable ex-journalist who had done well for the studio with such scripts as *Jezebel* and *Knute Rockne*. Buckner had never seen Cohan on stage, but he went to visit the dying man at his Fifth Avenue apartment, and the two began going out for long walks together. Cohan approved of him, Buckner said, partly because of "the fact that I am a gentile." Cohan sang some of his old songs, even attempted a dance step from time to time, and Buckner soon concocted a saga of heroic dimensions. Wallis was pleased with Buckner's effort and sent it to Cagney to impress him. "I got the impression I had made a dent in Jimmy's armor," he said.

Cagney's impression was the exact opposite. He said he read the script "with incredulity. There wasn't a single laugh in it." Cagney acknowledged, however, that his brother "wanted to do the Cohan story as a 100 percent American experience principally to remove the taint that apparently still attached itself to my reputation—a reputation now scarred by my so-called radical activities in the thirties when I was a strong Roosevelt liberal." Cagney's solution, he said, was to announce that he would play Cohan only if the script was turned over to the Epstein brothers, whom he regarded as "two very bright lads." These two, Julius and Phil Epstein, were identical twins, both quite bald even in their youth, who modestly toiled away for anyone who would pay them. It was said, in fact, that Budd Schulberg used the two of them as the model for Julian Blumberg, the talented but timorous writer whose scripts were all plagiarized by Sammy Glick. The Epsteins so disliked Buckner's flag-waving script that they declined the job, but William Cagney pursued them until they agreed to rewrite it. Buckner complained bitterly, of course, and so did Cohan, but it was the Epsteins who wrote that saccharine deathbed scene for Cohan's father (Walter Huston). And it was they who solved the problem of Cohan's first wife, a fellow vaudevillian named Ethel Levey, who was preparing to sue everyone involved (and eventually did, without success), by combining her and the second Mrs. Cohan into an idealized creature named Mary ("And it was Mary, Mary, long before the fashions changed . . ."), enchantingly played by the seventeen-year-old Joan Leslie.*

It was Buckner, though, who conceived the flashback structure that

---

* Miss Leslie was actually sixteen at the start of the filming and celebrated her seventeenth birthday on the set. Jack Warner, who professed a paternal interest in her career, had a new car wheeled across the set to be presented to her. "Enjoy it," he said as he handed her the keys. After the photographers had recorded this tender scene, Warner departed, the keys were taken back, and the car was wheeled away. Miss Leslie never saw it again.

began with an almost godlike President Roosevelt, nameless and filmed only from behind, presenting the aging Cohan with a medal and thus enabling him to tell his inspiring story, and thus making that story an allegory of innocent America catapulted once more into the sordid conflicts of Europe. But it was Cagney, of course, who carried the whole movie. Twice, he sprained an ankle as he struggled to master that oddly stiff-legged way in which Cohan danced, but his strutting performance of "Yankee Doodle Dandy" is still marvelous. "A proud and feverish characterization," as one critic put it. And even the scene in which Cagney sits at the piano and dabbles at the theme that will eventually become "Over There"—even that is strangely moving, strange because it is so obvious and so mawkish, but perhaps we were all mawkish in 1942. Cagney naturally won an Academy Award, and when he accepted the statue, he had the wit to say, "Don't forget to say that it was a good part, too."

There had been many liberties taken, however, and Warners worried about Cohan's approval. The studio shipped a projector and a screen in that April of 1942 to the firehouse in Monroe, New York, and there both Cohan and his second wife, Agnes, sat in their wheelchairs and watched. The cancer-ridden Cohan had to be escorted from the room several times to relieve himself, but when it was all over, Agnes Cohan was so captivated by Cagney's impersonation that she said to Cohan, "Oh, George, you were fine. And I always *knew* I was 'Mary' to you."

Warners had planned to stage the gala premiere on July 4 (Cohan really was, as Cagney sang, "a real live nephew of my Uncle Sam, born on the fourth of July"), but Cohan was so sick that the studio advanced the premiere to May 29, and the opening-night audience bought six million dollars in war bonds. "As our soldiers and sailors depart to fight on the seven seas and five continents . . ." Howard Barnes wrote in the *New York Herald Tribune,* "what could be more timely than to have recalled for us the career of America's lustiest flag-waver?"

●   ●   ●

It was typical of Warners to assign *Yankee Doodle Dandy* to a tall and rather handsome Hungarian director who had never mastered more than the rudiments of English. Michael Curtiz had been born Mihaly Kertész, and his background was very Hungarian. The son of either a wealthy architect or a poor carpenter, depending on which press release could be believed, he either was or was not a strongman (or perhaps an acrobat) with a touring circus, then served in the Austrian artillery (or cavalry) in World War I, then organized Hungary's first film studio. Harry Warner heard praises of a Curtiz film made in Germany, *Moon of Israel,* so he signed him up and brought him to America in 1927. One of the legends is that Curtiz was gratified to see flags and fireworks welcoming him to New York. "All this for me?" he asked. "Sorry, Mike," said Warner, "it's the fourth of July."

If Curtiz knew little about America, he was a phenomenally hard worker, and he had a certain talent for whipping up scenes of action, crowds, battles. He helped make a star out of Errol Flynn in *Captain Blood* (1935), and then went on to make *The Charge of the Light Brigade* (1936), *Robin Hood* (1938), and six other Flynn epics. It was in *The Charge of the Light Brigade* that Curtiz delivered his famous command for a herd of riderless horses by shouting, "Bring on the empty horses!" David Niven, who made that the title of his Hollywood memoirs, wrote that he and Flynn both doubled up guffawing at Curtiz's order. Their laughter did not please the director. "You lousy bums," Curtiz shouted, "you and your stinking language . . . You think I know fuck nothing . . . well, let me tell you—I know *fuck all!*"

And there was more. Hal Wallis insisted that Curtiz once described Bette Davis as "the flea in the ointment and a no good sexless son of a bitch." Less belligerent was his request to an actress to "sit a little bit more feminine." Or "Watch me, I'll give you the cue a feet before." And to a pair of lovers: "Come a little closer together apart." And to an assistant returning from an unsuccessful errand: "Next time I send some fool for something I go myself."

Not until 1940 did Curtiz belatedly go back to New York to visit some of the scenes that had appeared in his movies—Broadway, Times Square, Madison Square Garden. He had dinner at Jack Dempsey's restaurant and then wandered around to look at pictures on the walls and eavesdrop on conversations at the bar. "It is not the way I pictured it," he told a reporter from the *Herald-Tribune*. "I thought it would be more intimate and filled with literati."

None of this innocence really mattered very much, for Curtiz kept laboring away at whatever outpouring of patriotism Warners assigned him. *Yankee Doodle Dandy* came to seem almost pacifist compared to Curtiz's bugle-blowing version of Irving Berlin's *This Is the Army*. But Curtiz could also do comedies or thrillers or whatever anyone wanted—he eventually made seventy-four pictures for Warners, ranging from *Angels with Dirty Faces* to *Life with Father* —and when the exhibitors polled by *Film Daily* named Curtiz the top director of the 1942–43 season, one of the main reasons was that he had somehow concocted, out of an unlikely script and an unwilling cast, the most romantic wartime romance ever filmed.

●   ●   ●

Out of somewhere in the jungle of the story-buying process had come an unproduced play entitled *Everybody Comes to Rick's,* by two unknown dramatists named Murray Burnett and Joan Alison. "Just before war broke out in Europe," according to Hal Wallis, "they had visited a nightclub in the south of France, called La Belle Aurore, a gathering place for raffish expatriates, where a black pianist played the blues." The two of them had turned this scene into a melodrama about "Rick Blaine, a tough American running a nightclub in Casablanca; Sam, his black piano player; Captain Louis Renault, the French prefect of police; and Ilsa Lund, Rick's former girlfriend, involved with a Czech underground leader named Victor Laszlo. . . ."

Several studios had rejected this tale (indeed, when someone tried the experiment of resubmitting an outline of the story to all the major studios a few years ago, they all rejected it all over again), but Jack Warner decided to buy it, for a princely twenty thousand dollars,* because he thought it might make another *Algiers,* with Hedy Lamarr again, and George Raft as Rick. Raft showed the same judgment he had shown on *The Maltese Falcon:* he refused the part.† Warners had a lot of contract players to keep busy, however, and so the studio executives began considering new possibilities. Dennis Morgan might play Rick, and Ann Sheridan could be Ilsa. And Ronald Reagan, who had just co-starred with Miss Sheridan in *Kings Row* and had not yet gone off to war, could play the part of the Czech underground leader, Victor Laszlo.

Wallis called in the Epstein twins to write a script, and then turned back to the question of casting. The man he wanted for Rick, he finally decided, was Humphrey Bogart, but Bogart was irritated at playing another role that had been rejected by Raft. Besides, Warners had promised to loan Bogart to Columbia for a picture called *Sahara,* in exchange for Harry Cohn's promise to provide Cary Grant to Warners for *Arsenic and Old Lace,* and now Cohn kept switching the starting dates for *Sahara.*

Wallis also encountered problems in signing up the heroine, Ingrid Bergman. She had made a deep impression on him as the pianist in *Intermezzo,* her first American movie—who could have seen her in *Intermezzo* and not been deeply impressed?—but she was under personal contract to the most possessive of owners, David Selznick, and what she really wanted was a chance to play Maria in *For Whom the Bell Tolls.*

Her relationship with Selznick had begun almost by accident. A Swedish elevator boy who worked at 230 Park Avenue in New York, the offices of Selznick's New York representative, Kay Brown, told Miss Brown one day that his parents had been overwhelmed by a new Swedish movie called *Intermezzo,* and by its twenty-one-year-old heroine. Kay Brown dutifully went to a screening and dutifully reported to her boss that this young actress was "the beginning and end of all things wonderful." Selznick was accustomed to her effusions (she was the one who had vainly urged him to buy *Gone With the Wind*). He told her to buy the story, not the actress; she bought both.

Selznick was perhaps the only man in America who could have greeted the radiant young Ingrid Bergman on her arrival in Hollywood by saying, "God! Take your shoes off." She told him that it wouldn't do any good, since

---

* The standard Warners contract required the authors to transfer to the studio all rights "of every kind and character whatsoever, whether or not now known or contemplated, for all purposes whatsoever." Despite this, Burnett, now in his seventies, began suing Warners in 1983 in an effort to regain control of his characters, but his pleas have repeatedly been rejected.

† Raft eventually became so dissatisfied with the parts being offered him at Warners that he asked for an end to his contract. Jack Warner, who was sick of Raft's grumbling, agreed to pay him off. "What do you say we settle for ten thousand dollars?" Warner offered. Raft, according to Hollywood legend, promptly took out his checkbook and wrote Warner a check for $10,000. "I was never very good with money," Raft later explained.

she was five feet eight inches tall, with or without shoes. Selznick sighed and started the customary assertions of authority. "You realize your name's impossible," he said. Nobody could pronounce Ingrid, and Bergman sounded too German.* "There's obviously trouble with Germany coming up, and we don't want anyone to think we've hired a German actress." Selznick thought that "Berriman" might make a better name. Or, although her married name of Lindstrom wouldn't do, perhaps "Lindbergh" might capitalize on the popularity of the aviator. (Selznick seemed not to realize, or not to care, that Lindbergh was now prominent in the isolationist America First movement.) "Maybe you could take that name?" Selznick asked.

Miss Bergman resisted all this. She said that her name was Ingrid Bergman, and that anyone who couldn't pronounce it would have to learn. Selznick ruminated on that for a while—he had invited her to stay in his home, but this midnight supper was his first appearance there since her arrival—and then he made a new pronouncement: "Well, we'll discuss that in the morning. Now what about your makeup, because your eyebrows are too thick, and your teeth are no good, and there are lots of other things. I'll take you to the makeup department in the morning and we'll see what they can do. . . ."

Miss Bergman's response was exemplary. She quit. "I'd rather not do the movie," she told Selznick as he kept munching. "We'll say no more about it. No trouble of any kind. We'll just forget it. I'll take the next train and go back home." Selznick was impressed, or amused, or something. He decided to turn Miss Bergman's intransigence into a promotion of his own. "You are going to be the first 'natural' actress," he told her. "Nothing about you is going to be touched. Nothing altered." Actually, Selznick was overwhelmingly busy with *Gone With the Wind,* and so the remake of *Intermezzo* remained relatively free from his interference, and it did very well. "What star," asked a young English movie critic named Graham Greene, "has made her entrance with a *highlight gleaming on her nose-tip?* The gleam is typical of a performance which doesn't give the effect of acting at all but of living—without make-up. . . ."

Miss Bergman went cheerfully back to Sweden after *Intermezzo,* then returned to Hollywood with the start of the war, and found that Selznick had nothing for her to do. The producer had gone into a complicated kind of funk, convinced that nothing could match his triumph in *Gone With the Wind* (plus *Rebecca* in 1940). He could not bring himself to make another movie. He gambled and drank. Hemming and hawing over various projects, he lived on the stars whom he had made his personal properties, renting them out to various studios at considerable profit. He owned not only Ingrid Bergman but Vivien Leigh and Joan Fontaine and even Alfred Hitchcock. "I couldn't understand what there was to be proud of in getting a sum many times these people's salaries and not sharing with them," Mrs. Selznick later observed.

---

* Actually, Selznick had wired Miss Brown earlier that Miss Bergman's name would have to be changed because it had a "somewhat unattractive and even Semitic sound."

"It was not nice money, not our kind. . . ." Selznick knew better. Like his brother Myron—not to mention his father-in-law, Louis B. Mayer—he knew that all successful Hollywood people lived on other people. When one of his protégés complained that Myron took only 10 percent while David took everything, David just shrugged.

He rented Ingrid Bergman to Columbia to make *Adam Had Four Sons,* a flop, and to M-G-M to make *Rage in Heaven,* a modest success, written by Christopher Isherwood, and then to M-G-M again for its clumsy version of *Dr. Jekyll and Mr. Hyde.* Not an incandescent career, so far, and yet the appeal of the young Ingrid Bergman was irresistible. "She was," said Hal Wallis, looking back on the preparations for *Casablanca,* "the only actress with the luminous quality, the warmth and tenderness for the role." Jack Warner worried about what he would have to do to get her away from Selznick. He summoned the Epsteins, who had not yet written the script, and told them to go and persuade Selznick that they had written a superlative story for her. "We said we didn't know what to say," Julius Epstein recalled later, "but Warner told us to make up something, anything, just bring back Bergman. Phil and I were ushered into Selznick's office, and Selznick was eating a bowl of soup. I got things started by saying it was a romantic melodrama with a sinister atmosphere. Dark lighting and a lot of smoke . . . crooks, refugees pouring in, a mysterious man who runs a nightclub. I said, 'Oh, hell, it's a lot of junk like "Algiers." ' Selznick slapped the desk top and said, 'That's all I need to know, you've got Bergman.' "

The stars were by no means the only problems. Wallis wanted a woman —specifically Lena Horne, or Hazel Scott, or perhaps Ella Fitzgerald—as the singer in Rick's place. Nothing came of that. The Warners executives finally chose Dooley Wilson, who couldn't sing or play the piano, so they determined to give him lessons, then decided that they preferred him as he was. They also found that he was owned by Paramount and on loan to M-G-M, and they had to buy him for $3,500 a week, which was $375 more than they were paying Ingrid Bergman.

Everybody suddenly became absurdly expensive. For the trivial part of a waiter in Rick's Café, Warners had to increase S. Z. Sakall's pay to $1,750 a week. Peter Lorre, who was owned by Warners but on loan to Universal, had to be retrieved at a cost of $2,750 per week. Sidney Greenstreet, who, since *The Maltese Falcon,* had become almost mandatory in any scene of international intrigue, demanded and got $3,750 per week for a minor part as the owner of the Blue Parrot Café. Claude Rains, a free lance, got $4,000 to play the Vichy police chief. And for Conrad Veidt, as the evil Major Strasser, M-G-M had to be paid $5,000 a week, almost twice the cost of Ingrid Bergman.

And there was still no script. The Epsteins had suddenly been called to Washington to work on a war project, which eventually became Frank Capra's series, *Why We Fight,* and so Warners called in Howard Koch to finish *Casa-*

blanca. Koch was an amiable and conscientious writer with some impressive credits. As a novice playwright, he had gone to work for Orson Welles's Mercury Theatre and written the sensational radio script for the Martian invasion in H. G. Wells's *War of the Worlds.* In Hollywood, he had written *The Sea Hawk* for Errol Flynn, *The Letter* for Bette Davis, and *Sergeant York* for Gary Cooper—and now this. "I had inherited from the Epsteins excellent material, some in sequence, some not," Koch recalled, "which I assumed contained what was useful from the original play [which seems to mean that Koch never read it]. However, there was still much work to be done."

Even though *Casablanca* had never been considered a major production, all those actors' contracts created considerable pressure. As soon as Koch finished a few pages, the studio had them mimeographed and sent to various departments—the designers, the costumers, and, of course, the actors. When Koch was about halfway through, and Curtiz had already started shooting, Koch was surprised to receive from the mimeograph machine several pages of script that he had never seen before. Unknown to him, the Epsteins had returned from Washington and been reassigned to the project. Producer Wallis also called in his old friend Casey Robinson to strengthen Paul Henreid's role as Laszlo, and Henreid later recalled that Albert Maltz worked on the film but got no screen credit. Koch, an ardent liberal, gave a political twist to the portrait of Vichyite authority, but it was Curtiz who somehow assembled all the pages coming from all directions and continued shooting. When Koch protested that some of the new episodes were illogical, Curtiz retorted: "Don't worry what's logical. I make it go so fast no one notices."

The expensive cast was even more unhappy. Ingrid Bergman fretted over the fact that nobody seemed to know how the movie was going to end. Would she stay with Bogart or fly away with Henreid? If nobody could tell her that, which of the two was she supposed to be really in love with? "Just play it, well . . . in-between," Curtiz told her. "It was ridiculous," Miss Bergman said later. "Just awful. . . . Every day we were shooting off the cuff. Every day they were handing out the dialogue and we were trying to make some sense of it. No one knew where the picture was going."

Bogart seemed to be angry all the time. He not only disliked the script but he was getting frequent telephone calls from his wife, Mayo, who accused him of courting Ingrid Bergman and threatened to kill him. It was this ill-suppressed rage that provided the sting to his performance, provided the sarcastic contempt in some of the lines he made famous, like "I came to Casablanca for the waters." Claude Rains, as the Vichyite police official, played the victim perfectly: "The waters? What waters? We're in the desert." And Bogart: "I was misinformed."

It may be, in fact, that the unhappiness of the whole cast was what made *Casablanca* such a triumph. Ingrid Bergman's uncertainty about which of the two heroes she was supposed to love was not a problem, as she thought, but the essential point in the character she was playing. And her anxiety about the possibility of playing Maria in *For Whom the Bell Tolls*—which had just been assigned to, of all, people, Vera Zorina—helped give her portrayal of Ilsa a marvelously distraught quality. As for Paul Henreid, who complained bitterly that no Resistance leader would wander around Vichyite Casablanca in a white suit, he succeeded precisely because of the slightly pretentious unworldliness implicit in that white suit. Even Max Steiner, assigned to compose the score, was unhappy. He hated "As Time Goes By."

In this state of general havoc, the word spread on the *Casablanca* set that the grand ruin known as John Barrymore had just died, and this apparently inspired Peter Lorre to think of a lugubrious prank. Barrymore had spent much of his last year lounging around in the home of Errol Flynn, one of the few people who could put up with his drunken misbehavior, and Lorre thought it would be amusing to bribe the funeral home into letting him install the corpse in Flynn's house.

"I know he's shooting and gets home late," Lorre said to Henreid, Bogart, and two others, according to Henreid's account of the affair, "and we arrange it [the body] in that chair in the living room he always used to sit in, then we hide and watch Flynn's face. Is that or isn't it fantastic?"

Henreid said they all laughed—"uncontrollable laughter"—and chipped in to provide the two hundred dollars that Lorre estimated he needed to pay bribes at the funeral home. Henreid said that he paid his share but backed out of actually taking part in the expedition. He said Lorre giggled as he reported the details. Flynn "came in, threw his hat and coat on a chair and walked across the room, past Barrymore's chair to the bar. He nodded at Barrymore and took about three steps, then froze. That moment was fantastic! There was a terrible silence, then he said, 'Oh my God!' and he hurried back and touched Barrymore, then jumped. Barrymore was ice cold. 'I think in that second, he realized what was happening,' Lorre said, 'and he shouted, "All right, you bastards, come on out." ' Lorre said that Flynn offered his visitors a drink, 'but wouldn't help us take the body back.' "

Casablanca came to its end in about the same spirit. There was such indecision about the ending that the authorities finally decided to shoot both possibilities. "They were going to shoot two endings," Miss Bergman said, "because they couldn't work out whether I should fly off by airplane with my husband or stay with Humphrey Bogart. So the first ending we shot was that I say good-bye to Humphrey Bogart and fly off with Paul Henreid. . . . And everybody said, 'Hold it! That's it! We don't have to shoot the other ending.' "

Even that ending, with Bogart and Rains walking off into the night, needed a closing line. One version was that Bogart would say, "Louis, I might have known you'd mix your patriotism with a little larceny." Wallis claimed that he was the one who thought of something better: "Louis, I think this is the beginning of a beautiful friendship." And even then, they didn't know what they had achieved. At a sneak preview in Huntington Park, the audience seemed mildly pleased, but several viewers handed in cards that said the ending seemed unclear. Would Bogart and Rains be arrested? Wallis ordered a new closing scene written, in which Bogart and Rains escaped from Casablanca on a freighter. And somebody in the publicity department said a new title should be found, because Casablanca sounded like a brand of beer.

On November 8, an Anglo-American armada landed all along the North African coast, seized Tangiers, Oran—and Casablanca. Jack Warner was ecstatic: headlines about Casablanca, publicity for his new movie. And when Roosevelt and Churchill met there in January, Warner wanted a new ending shot to include the Casablanca conference. Somebody managed to dissuade him, probably for the wrong reasons. Perhaps it cost too much, and besides, the movie had been out for two months. Who today remembers anything about the Casablanca conference? Casablanca is where Humphrey Bogart ran Rick's Café, and where the ineffably beautiful Ingrid Bergman leaned on the piano and said, "Play it, Sam."

Conflicts: Sex symbol Errol Flynn (*left*) turned his back on Betty Hansen, who accused him of having raped her. The glamorous Rita Hayworth (*below*) of *Cover Girl* was a very anglicized version of Margarita Cansino (*bottom right*). And U.S. sailors led anti-Mexican rioting (*bottom left*).

5
PREJUDICE
(1943)

Just after dark, on a June evening slightly chilled by fog, a score of taxis loaded with U.S. Navy men poured into Broadway in downtown Los Angeles. The doors burst open and disgorged a swarm of sailors armed with clubs and weighted ropes. A crowd of bystanders cheered them on as they crashed into the Orpheum Theater and marched down the aisles, shouting for any Mexicans to stand up and fight. In the balcony, they found several victims, including a seventeen-year-old boy named Enrico Herrera, who was sitting with a girl. The sailors dragged them all downstairs into the street. Out there, the waiting crowd formed a ring, shouting and cheering as the sailors mauled the Mexicans, stripped off their clothes, and beat them bloody. Herrera's jaw was broken. Only then did the Los Angeles police move in and arrest Herrera and carry him off to a police station. His mother found him there three hours later, still naked and still bleeding.

There was more. Four Mexicans emerging from a pool hall at Twelfth and Central were ordered into police cars. When one of them asked why he was being arrested, a policeman hit him three times on the head with a nightstick, then kicked him in the face as he lay on the sidewalk. "Police had difficulty loading his body into the vehicle because he was one-legged and wore a wooden limb," according to a bystander named Al Waxman. "Maybe the officer didn't know he was attacking a cripple." At the next corner, Waxman saw a Mexican woman, who was carrying a baby, protest against the arrest of her fifteen-year-old son. "He did nothing," she cried. "She was struck across the jaw with a night-stick," Waxman said, "and almost dropped the . . . baby that was clinging in her arms."

And more. A seaman named Donald Jackson, twenty, was attacked by four Mexican youths, who blackjacked him and slashed him across the abdomen. A band of servicemen dragged a black man off a streetcar and gouged out his eye with a knife. A policeman named C. D. Medley stopped to help a Mexican lying in the street—a decoy. A carload of Mexicans deliberately ran down the policeman and broke his back. The man who had been lying on the pavement scrambled into their car, and they all drove off.

These were the *pachuco* or zoot suit riots that roiled downtown Los Angeles throughout the first week of June 1943. They are largely forgotten now, partly because much worse rioting broke out between blacks and whites in Detroit two weeks later. Thirty-four people died there, and about seven hundred were injured, before the national guard restored order. To anyone who is young enough to think that American race riots involve gangs of black marauders attacking frightened whites, let it be recalled that in the race riots of the 1940's (Harlem and St. Louis suffered major outbreaks too), blacks fled for their lives from pursuing gangs of whites. In Los Angeles, though, where there were still very few blacks, just beginning to immigrate to work in the arms factories and to occupy the abandoned tenements of Little Tokyo, the victims were the Mexicans, and the attackers were the United States armed forces.

The irony was that Los Angeles prided itself on the Spanish heritage implicit in its very name, and on the few blocks around Olvera Street that the *Los Angeles Times* liked to call "a bit of old Mexico." As for the Mexicans who actually lived in Los Angeles, about 250,000 of them, roughly one tenth of the city's population, they were largely degraded or ignored. More than half the city's substandard housing was occupied by Mexicans, and the area known as Mexican Town, in an unincorporated section of the county, didn't even have paved streets. It was not clear whether Mexicans were legally white or colored, but schools were unofficially segregated, and so were many public swimming pools. Chicanos and blacks were allowed to swim only on Wednesdays, the day before the pools were cleaned and refilled.

That was because the Mexicans, like many oppressed people, bore the additional curse of appearing to be sexually threatening. Nathanael West caught the image perfectly in *The Day of the Locust,* when a Mexican named Miguel not only moved into Faye Greener's garage but brought along his fighting cocks. When the Hollywood director, Claude Estee, came to see the cockfight, he stayed to watch Fay dancing erotically with the Mexican. "He held her very tight," West wrote, with a certain gloating, "one of his legs thrust between hers, and they swayed together in long spirals that broke rhythmically at the top of each curve into a dip. All the buttons on her lounging pajamas were open. . . ."

The reality was much less glamorous. The reality was rats and police nightsticks. One of the ways the young Mexicans defended themselves was to form neighborhood gangs—the White Fence Gang, Alpine Street, El Hoyo. Another was to wear the strange costumes known as "drapes," which the newspapers took to calling zoot suits. They had immensely long jackets and immensely wide trouser legs, pegged at the ankle, and often a key chain dangled from the vest almost to the ground. Zoot suits were ugly, impractical, even absurd, but they announced as loudly as any costume could that the wearer was a defiant rebel, and sexy too. Respectable society reacted accordingly. When a gang of sailors attacked some zoot-suited Mexicans in Venice that May, the police, as usual, arrested the Mexicans. And though Judge Arthur Guerin dismissed the charges for lack of evidence, he warned the victims that "their antics might get them into serious difficulties unless they changed their attitudes."

The police attitude was best expressed in a report by Captain Ed Duran Ayres, head of the so-called Foreign Relations Bureau of the Los Angeles police department, which suggested that Chicanos were inherently criminal. According to a bitter summation by Rodolfo Acuña of California State University, "Ayres stated that Chicanos were Indians, that Indians were Orientals, and that Orientals had an utter disregard for life." As Ayres himself put it, Caucasians fought with their fists, "but this Mexican element considers all that to be a sign of weakness, and all he knows and feels is a desire to use a knife . . . In other words, his desire is to kill." This police report urged that all Chicanos over the age of eighteen be compelled to get jobs or join the armed forces. In actual fact, though the Los Angeles press spread the image of idle zoot-suiters shirking the national war effort, the Chicanos who formed one tenth of the city's population not only joined the armed forces in droves but suffered one fifth of the combat casualties. But when Sergeant Macario García, who had won a Congressional Medal of Honor, tried to buy a cup of coffee at a "white" restaurant in Richmond, California, the owner chased him out with a baseball bat.

Against that background, the specific origins of the 1943 riots hardly matter. In fact, nobody really knows exactly how they started. The neon-lit streets of downtown Los Angeles were fairly rough. Sailors on leave assumed that Mexican girls could be had for the asking; Mexican boys defended their territory. It is silly, of course, to assume that all the Chicanos were innocent victims. There were plenty of muggings and robberies of young sailors who meant nobody any harm. One of these ruckuses occurred on the night of June 3, when a band of eleven sailors apparently tried to pick up some Mexican girls on a slummy stretch of North Main Street. The sailors later said they had been attacked for no reason by a gang of about thirty Mexicans. One of the sailors was badly injured, the others bruised and bloodied. The police roamed around the neighborhood but found nobody to arrest.

The next night, June 4, about two hundred sailors from the naval Armory in Chavez Ravine hired a fleet of about twenty taxis and cruised along Whittier Boulevard, on the east side of Los Angeles. Every time they spotted a young Mexican in a zoot suit, they piled out of their taxis and beat him up. They were determined, according to the *New York Times*'s typically jingoistic account of the raid, "to accommodate any of the zoot-suiters who thought Uncle Sam's fighting men were not just that." As in a czarist pogrom, the police pretended to be helpless. They did arrest nine sailors but soon released them without any charges filed. A nameless petty officer who seemed to be unofficially in command of the sailors declared that there was more violence to come. "We're out to do what the police have failed to do," he said. The next night, he added, "the sailors may have the Marines along." The Los Angeles press was thrilled. SAILOR TASK FORCE HITS L.A. ZOOTERS, cried the headline in Hearst's *Herald & Express*.

The next night, just as the petty officer had predicted, soldiers and marines joined the marauding sailors. They marched through the streets four abreast, stopping anyone wearing a zoot suit, beating some, threatening others. The only people arrested were twenty-seven Chicanos, who were booked "on suspicion" of various offenses. The press warned of savage Mexican retaliations. ZOOT SUIT CHIEFS GIRDING FOR WAR ON NAVY, cried the *Daily News.* But it was the navy that kept attacking, abetted by the police. On the night of June 6, a half-dozen carloads of sailors cruised down Brooklyn Avenue, caught and beat up eight Mexicans, smashed up a bar on Indiana Street, attacked eleven more Mexicans on Carmelita Street. The police followed in the sailors' wake, arresting their victims. That night, they jailed forty-four Mexicans, all badly beaten.

The press kept warning of Mexican revenge. ZOOTERS PLANNING TO ATTACK MORE SERVICEMEN, said another headline in the *Daily News,* adding that the Chicanos "would jab broken bottlenecks in the faces of their victims." ZOOTERS THREATEN L.A. POLICE, said the *Herald & Express,* which claimed that an anonymous telephone call to police headquarters had said, "We're meeting 500 strong tonight and we're going to kill every cop we see." Such stories served mainly to attract crowds of would-be spectators to downtown Los Angeles on the night of June 7, when a mob of several thousand soldiers, sailors, and civilians rampaged through Main Street and Broadway.

This was the night they broke the jaw of young Enrico Herrera, but he was only one of countless victims. The sailors broke into several theaters— the Rialto, the Tower, Loew's, the Roxy, the Cameo—demanded that the lights be turned on, and then attacked any Chicanos they could find. They invaded bars, tore apart the stools, and used them as clubs. Mexicans were the main victims, but blacks and Filipinos were also attacked and stripped of their clothes. There was a peculiar sexual element in all this, as though the wearing of zoot suits was a sexual affront that had to be sexually punished— and this by young men in sailor suits. "So our guys wear tight bottoms on their pants and those bums wear wide bottoms," complained one battered twelve-year-old Chicano in a hospital. "Who the hell they fighting, Japs or us?"

The Los Angeles police did what they conceived to be their duty. They jailed six hundred Chicano youths as a "preventive" measure. And the navy finally did what it conceived to be its duty. It declared all of downtown Los Angeles off limits to all sailors. But Rear Admiral D. W. Bagley, commander of the district, insisted that the sailors had only acted in "self-defense against the rowdy element." And when the Mexican government protested to Washington and asked for damages for injuries to Mexican citizens, Mayor Fletcher Bowron insisted that "there is no question of racial prejudice involved." He appointed a committee to "study the problem." He also ordered the police to stop using "cream-puff techniques."

Other authorities applied similar wisdom. The Los Angeles City Council voted to make it a crime to wear a zoot suit, punishable by thirty days in jail. And Senator Jack Tenney of the California state legislature announced that he was investigating "a possible connection between the activities of the juvenile gangsters and Axis agents."

• • •

The anti-Mexican riots of 1943 were embarrassing to Washington because President Roosevelt took a personal interest in what he called his Good Neighbor Policy toward Latin America. This policy was partly an attempt to recruit the Latin Americans into the still perilous struggle against the Fascist states that many South Americans regarded as home: Italy, Germany, and, to some extent, Spain. Just that April, Roosevelt had journeyed to Mexico to visit President Avila Camacho and to salute him as an ally. "Our two countries," Roosevelt said, "owe their independence to the fact that your ancestors and mine held the same truths to be worth fighting for and dying for. Hidalgo and Juárez were men of the same stamp as Washington and Jefferson."

The riots were hardly less embarrassing to Hollywood, which had been trying to replace its lost revenues from Europe, once nearly a third of its income, by increasing its sales in Latin America. Hence the appearance, in some otherwise innocuous musical, of Xavier Cugat and his rumba band. Hence the implausible stardom of Carmen Miranda, with her swirling skirts and fruit-topped hats, in *Down Argentine Way* (1943). Hence the equally implausible phenomenon of José Iturbi, a Spanish pianist of limited talent, who usually played himself and performed such trifles as "Clair de Lune," occasionally adding an outburst of boogie-woogie.

Washington was eager to help. The State Department sponsored a South American tour by Walt Disney, which resulted in a concoction titled *Saludos Amigos* (1943). Nelson Rockefeller, who had long taken a proprietary interest in Latin America, now held the post of Coordinator of Inter-American Affairs, so he was especially cooperative. He gave Darryl Zanuck forty thousand dollars of Washington money to reshoot some of the more unlikely sections of *Down Argentine Way*, which audiences down that way had greeted with jeers. Rockefeller had also been a sponsor of Orson Welles at RKO, and now he hoped to recruit Welles to the Latin American campaign. As it happened, Welles was already shooting a story called "My Friend Bonito," a tale of a Mexican boy raising a bull for the *corrida*, which was a segment of a four-part film to be called *It's All True*. Rockefeller and John Hay Whitney, who was acting as one of his deputies, urged Welles to reshape his project and start by filming the carnival in Rio. Rockefeller offered a guarantee of $300,000 against any losses. "It will be a polyglot movie," Welles announced as he flew south (leaving a rough version of *The Magnificent Ambersons* to be edited and botched by other hands), "by which I mean we are designing it to be completely understandable, no matter what the language of the audience. Some of it will be silent, part will be in color."

The only movie of 1943 that dealt seriously with Mexicans was *The Ox-Bow Incident,* based on Walter van Tilburg Clark's novel about a lynching. But it dealt with the racial aspect of the lynching by never mentioning that the victim, played by Anthony Quinn, was a Mexican. (And Quinn, in an autobiography filled with self-pity over the hardships of being a Mexican in Hollywood, never mentioned this oddity either.) It was Henry Fonda, apparently, who persuaded Darryl Zanuck to film *The Ox-Bow Incident* as a vehicle for his yearning to do good deeds. When the two men subsequently fought about future projects, and when Fonda said he wanted to do more pictures like *The Grapes of Wrath* and *The Ox-Bow Incident,* Zanuck hauled out an account book on all his films. "Read this," Zanuck said. "See how well *The Ox-Bow Incident* did." Fonda looked at the account book, saw all the figures on the page in red ink, and charged out of Zanuck's office, slamming doors behind him.

● ● ●

Hollywood's final verdict on Latins was its transformation of a young Spanish dancer named Margarita Carmen Dolores Cansino into the greatest romantic star of this decade, a transformation that could take place only after she had dyed her hair red and changed her name to Rita Hayworth.

That had been approximately the maiden name of her mother, Volga Haworth, a showgirl in the Ziegfeld Follies, who had fallen in love with a dancer from Madrid named Eduardo Cansino. The Cansinos liked to proclaim a family tree that was rooted back in the Middle Ages, when they were Sephardic Jews. Their fifteenth-century progenitor, Isaac Cansino, bowed to the threats of the Inquisition, converted to Christianity, and bequeathed to his descendants the accursed brand of the Marranos.

Young Margarita, born in New York and educated at P.S. 79 in Jackson Heights, Queens (she never did get beyond the first year of high school), knew nothing of that. She was chubby and shy, and she liked to dance. Indeed, she had no choice. "They had me dancing almost as soon as I could walk," she said. "They" were her father, who toured the vaudeville circuit with his sister Elisa, and her uncle Angel, to whose dance classes in Carnegie Hall she was sent at the age of four. Eduardo eventually wanted to retire from the stage, so he moved his family to Los Angeles in 1930. He worked as a choreographer at Warners and opened his own little dance studio on the second floor of a building at the corner of Sunset and Vine. His sister Elisa returned to Spain and had children and grew fat. But when the Depression began crushing little operations like Cansino's dance studio, he found that he had to go back on stage, found that he had to train a new partner, found that there was no prospect better than his own daughter, Margarita, who was then a blossoming thirteen. The first time he saw the effect she had on an audience at the Carthay Circle Theater, it was a revelation. "All of a sudden I woke up to the fact that my baby was no longer a baby," he said. This revelation filled him with proud anticipation, not about her future but about his own. "Here was a girl, my own daughter, with whom I could build a whole new dance act."

There were legal problems. California law required that thirteen-year-old dancers go through elaborate procedures of pretending to do homework to make up for lost schooling. More important, the law forbade them to dance in any place where liquor was sold, which eliminated most of the places that were interested in hiring Spanish dancers. Cansino followed the obvious course and took his daughter across the Mexican border to the Foreign Club Café de Luxe in Tijuana. "Between shows," said one of Cansino's friends, "Eduardo locked his buxom daughter in the dressing room to keep her out of harm's way, as he saw it, while he and Volga spent their time and money gambling."

One of Cansino's pupils was a rumba dancer named Grace Pioggi, a protégée of Joseph Schenck, who, in addition to being a founder of 20th Century–Fox and a friend of Willie Bioff, was also the head of the Agua Caliente Jockey Club. It took only a few phone calls for the Cansinos to make an appearance at the Jockey Club, which called itself "A Dreamland in Old Mexico eighteen miles below San Diego." Hollywood producers came here to gamble and sometimes paused to observe the girls onstage, like Margarita Cansino. "I first saw her around 1933," said Max Arno, who was then the casting director at Warners. "This very young, beautiful girl came down the steps of a very high staircase, moving to the music like some marvelous big cat. . . . I did nothing about her then because she was still immature, but about a year later we made a photographic test of her at Warners, just a head close-up—turn this way, turn that, smile, no dialogue. She didn't say much and we thought she couldn't talk English. In the end we decided not to sign her because of certain hair problems she had."

The "hair problems" were that her thick, dark, curly locks, which she parted in the middle, sprouted very low on her forehead and made her look not only very Hispanic but somewhat primitive. She was also quite inarticulate: shy, timid, nervous. She danced, though, with a marvelous sensuality that she seemed to take for granted, leaving it to others to explain. "Where most dancers move from the hips down Hayworth moves from the knees up, her shoulders drawn back, projecting her breast cage forward in the most enticing manner, only acceptable in the young and very beautiful," explained Jack Cole, the choreographer who started working with her in *Cover Girl* (1944), then staged *Tonight and Every Night* (1945) and ultimately *Gilda* (1946). "To see her in that moment's hesitation [her entrance] is to experience a sense of joy pure and simple."

Middle-aged men were always trying to take care of Margarita Cansino. One of the first of these, back in the 1930's, was Winfield Sheehan, another friend of Joe Schenck's, and vice-president in charge of production at the Fox Film Corporation. After watching the Cansinos dance at Agua Caliente, Sheehan duly introduced his new discovery to Louella Parsons, who found her "painfully shy . . . her voice so low it could hardly be heard . . . hardly the material of which a great star could be made." Sheehan brusquely announced: "I've signed her to a contract." It was a modest little contract that promised two hundred dollars a week (Sheehan originally offered seventy-five dollars) plus daily diction and drama classes. Cansino himself signed the document, since Margarita was still only fifteen.

Sheehan shortened her name to Rita and began casting her as an earthy Latin. She did a Spanish dance of sorts in a disaster titled *Dante's Inferno*. She did another one in *Under the Pampas Moon* and yet another in *Human Cargo*. Sometimes she was more exotic, as in *Charlie Chan in Egypt*, in which, much like Faye Greener in *The Day of the Locust*, she had three lines, one of which was "Yes, Effendi." Allan Dwan, who directed *Human Cargo* (1936), saw the potential. "She was very nervous, terribly emotional," Dwan said, "and when she got frustrated battling with the dramatic expressions required in some of her scenes she'd be inclined to burst into tears. . . . She was probably just an innocent little virgin, but on the screen she's always a woman. She looks as if she had the knowledge of everything when in fact she didn't know a damn thing."

After five small parts, Sheehan announced that Rita Cansino would star in the title role of Helen Hunt Jackson's popular romance, *Ramona*, but then Fox merged with Twentieth Century, and in came Darryl Zanuck, thirty-three-year-old boy wonder, who asserted his new authority in the usual ways. Out went Winfield Sheehan, out went *Ramona*, out went Rita Cansino, fired. "I vowed I would show those people they'd made a terrible mistake," she said later. She free-lanced for a while, but that only led her to routine roles at poverty-row studios like Grand National (*Trouble in Texas*), Crescent (*Old Louisiana*), and Republic (*Hit the Saddle*).

Then along came another middle-aged mentor who wanted to take care of her. This was Edward C. Judson, a suave and portly "man about town," though of uncertain financial resources. He had been a moderately successful car salesman, and he now received a small retainer from a Texas oil promoter who wanted Los Angeles contacts. There was occasional talk of criminal connections. Judson met Sheehan just as the film tests for *Ramona* were being screened. Judson was so impressed by Rita Cansino that he asked Sheehan to introduce him to her. Judson was rather fat and getting bald, but he was also kind and solicitous, part Pygmalion and part Svengali. He asked Eduardo Cansino's permission to take Rita out on her first date. Cansino was suspicious, his wife openly hostile. Judson was not only Cansino's age, fortyish, but even had the same first name. Judson was persuasive, however. He began taking Rita to Ciro's and the Trocadero to show her off, and he also told her what to wear and how to wear it. Rita was impressed. When Judson proposed marriage, she accepted. They drove to Las Vegas for the ceremony in one of those roadside wedding emporia. She was eighteen, he was forty. Her parents were appalled.

But Judson, alone among the people around Rita Cansino, including Rita herself, knew what needed to be done and how to do it. He started by negotiating a new studio contract for her. If the best place that he could find was Columbia, which was just beginning to swallow up the other poverty-row studios along Gower Street, then let it be Columbia. Harry Cohn, who still kept a portrait of Mussolini in his office, grudgingly agreed to pay $250 a week, declared that the name of Rita Cansino would have to be changed, and then turned away to more important matters. And so, taking her mother's maiden name, Rita Cansino became Rita Hayworth. But that was just the beginning. Judson knew, and perhaps Harry Cohn also knew, that the possibilities of a Spanish dancer were limited. She had to be changed into something else.

There was the hair problem. Judson went to Helen Hunt, the chief hair stylist at Columbia, and said, "Tell me what we can do about Rita." Miss Hunt suggested dying her black hair a gentle auburn, but the main problem was the low hairline. Miss Hunt recommended an electrolysist, and Rita agreed to begin the slow and painful process of having each hair removed, one at a time, and killing every single follicle on her forehead. Judson himself paid ten dollars for each treatment, and it took two years. "Eddie went to the top jewelry shops and borrowed jewelry for Rita," Miss Hunt recalled, "and even evening gowns—he took her to the finest restaurants—saw that she was seated in a good view." To make sure that these events became known to the world—not to mention her employers at Columbia Pictures—Judson hired a press agent at seventy-five dollars a week.

Since all these maneuvers cost money that Judson did not possess, he had the temerity to demand a financial accounting from Eduardo Cansino of the money that Rita had earned as a minor, money that Eduardo had long since spent and now had to repay under threat of litigation. The Cansinos' loathing for Judson became a passion. But at their daughter's little house in Brentwood, Judson still couldn't afford to buy any furniture. On the bare floor of the living room, he kept an electric train set for Rita to play with when she got bored. And it was only after she married him that she learned he had been married twice before.

The complex process of creating a movie star, which the nervous and inarticulate Rita Hayworth passionately wanted to be, had now begun. Harry Cohn put her in five forgotten pictures in 1937, five more in 1938, and then Judson decided to gamble on a chance at bigger things. Rita spent five hundred dollars to buy the perfect gray-and-silver dress in which to go to the Trocadero and sit near the table occupied by Harry Cohn and Howard Hawks, who were casting Columbia's big picture of 1939, *Only Angels Have Wings*. "I had a few uncomfortable moments thinking of my extravagance," she supposedly said to some writer at *Photoplay*. "But when I saw myself in the mirror I felt reassured. I had never looked like that before." Everything worked out just as Judson planned. Rita got the part, the film was a hit, and Harry Cohn renewed her contract, though he insisted that the fifty-dollar-a-week raise go not to her but to a dramatic coach, Gertrude Vogler.

The next step in the process was the traditional lucky break: Ann Sheridan got tired of playing the same sketchy roles, so she walked out of a Warners film that was almost ready for shooting, *The Strawberry Blonde*. Jack Warner called in the director, Raoul Walsh, and said, "Irish, we're up against it. The film's ready to go. Who can we get at this stage?" Walsh later claimed that his answer was instantaneous: "The most beautiful girl in pictures, Rita Hayworth." And so she acquired not only a starring role in a major production, with Jimmy Cagney as her co-star and James Wong Howe as her photographer, but also the last element in her anglicization: flowing red hair.

Having then become the complete Anglo, she was able to compete for one of the big roles of 1941, that of Doña Sol, the femme fatale in Fox's *Blood and Sand*—able to compete not as a Latin, who would never have been considered worthy of such an important part, but as a Latin pretending to be an Anglo pretending to be a Latin. Darryl Zanuck, who had fired her a few years earlier, tested dozens of actresses for the role, including Gene Tierney and Dorothy Lamour, and then acquiesced in the inevitable. He not only had to hire back the girl he had fired, he had to pay five times her normal salary to Harry Cohn for the privilege of making her a major star. And she was sensational. Zanuck didn't even bother with the traditional sneak previews in little California suburbs. "No preview," he decreed, according to Rouben Mamoulian, the director. "It's the greatest film I've ever seen. Ship it."

Once Miss Hayworth had become a star as an actress, she could reenter the role of a dancer on a completely different level, not as a sexy Latin but as the whirlwind partner of Fred Astaire. *You'll Never Get Rich* inspired *Time* magazine to put her on its cover in late 1941 and to describe her as "the best partner [Astaire] ever had." It added that she was personally "easygoing and sometimes inert," but that "before the camera, she is bright as a dollar." Everyone wanted to see more of her, so Cohn loaned her to Fox for a turn-of-the-century turn called *My Gal Sal,* then for a pastiche titled *Tales of Manhattan.* Then he brought her back to Columbia to pair her with Astaire again in *You Were Never Lovelier,* and then came *Cover Girl.*

It was apparently Harry Cohn's idea, and, as usual, he stole it. Robert Taplinger, publicity man for Warners, had suggested to his own bosses the idea of doing a musical about a magazine cover girl—nothing more than that —and Warners rejected it, so he tried it on Cohn, and Cohn grabbed it. Actually, Cohn's real role was a kind of inspired delegation of authority. He hired as producer Arthur Schwartz, a successful songwriter who had never produced a single film, and Schwartz managed to sign up Jerome Kern to write the music. He also managed, over Cohn's strenuous opposition, to hire as co-star and choreographer the young and relatively unknown Gene Kelly, who had just achieved his first big success on Broadway as the star of *Pal Joey.* As for the script, Virginia Van Upp concocted a fairly familiar confection out of half a dozen other writers' preliminary drafts: Kelly runs a little nightclub in Brooklyn, and when some Broadway producers come to inspect his variety show, it is Miss Hayworth whom they lead off to the Great White Way, but it is Kelly whom she really loves, and so on.

Cover Girl was an immense success, perhaps the greatest of all the Hayworth musicals of the early 1940's. To have seen it in 1943, in the midst of the hushed audience in some neighborhood theater, was to fall hopelessly in love with Rita Hayworth. There could never be anyone more beautiful, more romantic, more glamorous. But late-night television, which keeps alive all these nostalgic memories, which keeps the Alzheimer's victim Rita Hayworth a perpetual beauty of twenty-five, is a treacherous guardian of one's own memories. Not only does it show *Blood and Sand* as a creaky travesty of romantic melodrama, but it also shows Miss Hayworth as a creaky travesty of the femme fatale. By this time, she had learned to speak like a graduate of an elocution class, and her heavily rouged cheeks and long red fingernails implied not passion so much as long hours at the makeup mirror.

Cover Girl, which also appears on television from time to time, is in some ways worse, for it demanded much more of its star. Miss Van Upp's script, which was considered above average at the time, rejoiced in its comic-strip characters: a stage-door guardian called "Pops," a bespectacled comic called "Genius," a suavely white-haired publisher who suavely said, "She wants luxury, beautiful things." "How do *you* know?" snarled Kelly. "Doesn't every girl?" said the suave producer, and that, implicitly, was that. Well, it was 1943, a simpler time, and nothing dates *Cover Girl* more than the production number for the title song, in which Miss Hayworth, outfitted in flowing draperies that billow about in mysterious breezes, dances up and down a vast circular ramp while an orchestra plays romantic arpeggios and the camera admires various models posing on the covers of all the great magazines that no longer exist: *Liberty, Woman's Home Companion, Look, The American, Coronet, Collier's.* . . . Memento mori!

The purpose of the script, though, was to put Miss Hayworth on display not only as a beauty but as a talented actress. She was given a scene that required her to portray unhappiness by getting drunk. She was decked out in white boots and a feathered hat to sing a song with a British accent (which she doggedly practiced with the visiting Gracie Fields). On television, nearly half a century later, these demonstrations only demonstrate her limitations. She couldn't act at all, her face was a frozen mask of makeup, her speech stilted and lifeless. Her singing, we now know, was always dubbed in by someone else (in this case, Martha Mears).

Yet there was still one element that made up for everything else. When Rita Hayworth danced, she became transformed. *Cover Girl* gave her many dances but none better than "Make Way for Tomorrow," in which she and Kelly and Phil Silvers went romping through the streets in an orgy of high spirits. When Rita Hayworth danced, the waxen makeup disappeared, the acting lessons, the elocution lessons, the self-consciousness, all the attempts to become something other than what she was—all that disappeared. She became not only supremely sensual but supremely happy in her own sensuality. She could do anything. The spectacle was electrifying then, and it still is.

She had another reason for her obvious happiness in *Cover Girl,* particularly in the scene in which she was supposed to marry a Broadway producer (she didn't, of course, for no Broadway producer ever got the girl in any self-respecting Hollywood musical). "She looked very lovely sitting there in her wedding dress while the crew were setting up," said Lee Bowman, who played the doomed producer. "Rita sat there with her hands in her lap, her eyes very big and a lovely big pussy smile on her face. When any of us asked, 'What is it, Rita?' she'd just shake her head and say, 'Mmm, I've got a secret.' Wouldn't say anything else. The first we knew what it was came when somebody brought us the papers with the headlines." What the headlines said, to everyone's amazement, was that Rita Hayworth had got married that day to Orson Welles.

The marriage to Judson was long behind her, of course. Having married Margarita Cansino and created Rita Hayworth, Judson had created something beyond his own capacities. He demonstrated that all too well at the time of the breakup, in 1942, when he demanded that his departing wife pay him thirty thousand dollars for his time and services in creating her. She refused, but her testimony in defense of her refusal tended to demonstrate (if, as Hollywood generally believed, everybody was to be judged by his value in the marketplace) that he was right. "I was never permitted to make any decisions," she said. "He robbed everything of excitement." She admitted, though, that "running my career was his only concern, and he gave it everything he had, and his efforts paid off."

Harry Cohn, who suffered from a hopeless infatuation with Miss Hayworth, an infatuation that he expressed by browbeating her, eavesdropping on her, insulting her, and generally harassing her, did not enjoy this kind of publicity about her private life. It was Cohn, the penny-pinching tyrant of Columbia, who paid off Judson's claim of thirty thousand dollars. Perhaps Cohn hoped for some kind of reward. He got none. Miss Hayworth began going out on the town, and she was quickly picked up by Victor Mature, a sleepy-eyed actor of sorts who had made a reputation for himself by flexing his muscles in various crime dramas. When Mature joined the coast guard and was shipped to a base in Connecticut, Miss Hayworth followed him there; Harry Cohn forbade her to go; she went anyway. She wore a ring that Mature had given her.

Love is eternal as long as it lasts. At a dinner party given by Joseph Cotten, Miss Hayworth met the legendary Orson Welles, by now twenty-eight, who was not only the creator and star of *Citizen Kane* but also six feet four inches tall and quite attractive, endowed with an interesting face that he himself described as that of "a rather depraved baby." Jean Cocteau spoke of him more elaborately as "a kind of giant with the look of a child, a tree filled with birds and shadows, a dog that has broken its chain and lies down in the flower beds. . . ." And that sonorous voice that had recited on the radio every week: "Who knows what evil lurks in the hearts of men? The Shadow knows!" That voice, said Micheál MacLiammóir, reckoning back to the day when the sixteen-year-old Welles first appeared at Dublin's Gate Theatre in search of a job, "bloomed and boomed its way through the dusty air . . . as though it would crush down the little Georgian walls and rip up the floor."

Welles asked Miss Hayworth out to dinner, and she accepted. And Welles, like every self-conscious intellectual, tried to impress her with what passed for erudition—books, paintings, famous people. She, who had never gone beyond the ninth grade, was appropriately impressed. He gave her books to read, and she struggled with them, trying to play a wholly new role. But there was already aflame in Welles a self-destructive folly that would devour both his marriage and his career.

The trip to the Rio carnival the year before had been orgiastic, a swirl of dancing and drinking and magic tricks from nightclub to nightclub, and even one episode of furniture being flung out of a hotel window. But Welles had discovered, in an old copy of *Time,* a wonderful way of telling his story: Four penniless fishermen had sailed a log raft nearly two thousand miles from the hump of Brazil to Rio, inspired by God, they said, to tell the government of the people's suffering. Welles promptly signed up these overnight heroes and made plans to film their leader, a wiry little man known as Jacaré, the alligator, sailing the raft into Rio at the height of the carnival. During the filming of this scene, there was suddenly a convulsion in the waters, and then a shark erupted from the waves, locked in combat with a giant octopus. The filmmakers' raft tipped over, and while most of the crew made their way to safety, Jacaré, the alligator, disappeared in the foam. A week later, the shark was caught and cut open. Its innards were found to contain Jacaré's head, along with various pieces of the octopus. Welles suddenly became very unpopular in Brazil, and several members of his film crew were afraid to be seen on the streets of Rio, but Welles insisted that the filming go on. Indeed, he shot a preposterous 400,000 feet of color film on the Brazilian segment of the project. Back at RKO, however, Rockefeller sold all his stock, leaving the studio in the control of the entrepreneur Floyd Odlum, who had no interest whatever in the wild installments of film being sent back from Welles's crew in Rio de Janeiro. *It's All True* was never finished; some of the film was never even developed; some began to deteriorate so much by the late 1950's, when RKO was taken over by Desilu, and then Desilu by Paramount, that it was dumped unseen into the Pacific Ocean.

But in 1943, Welles's South American adventures seemed like just another manifestation of his eccentric genius, and perhaps what Rita Hayworth loved best in him was the playfulness in this eccentricity. Ever since his childhood, Welles had delighted in performing magic tricks, and now that there was a war on, he performed a magic show for servicemen in a large tent installed on Cahuenga Boulevard. When he married Rita Hayworth, he entertained the soldiers, night after night, by putting her in a box and sawing her in half. Any magician who would put Rita Hayworth in a box and saw her in half was clearly no ordinary magician.

● ● ●

Of the Hollywood figures who actually put on uniforms, many did go and fight, of course, but a substantial number devoted their war years to doing what they had always done, making movies. Although these films were conceived as propaganda, some of them achieved considerable distinction. Major Frank Capra, head of an outfit called the 834th Photo Signal Detachment, was summoned to the office of the chief of staff, General George Marshall, and told to make a series of documentaries "that will explain to our boys in the Army *why* we are fighting." Inspired by Leni Riefenstahl's *Triumph of the Will,* which he regarded as a "lethal . . . psychological weapon aimed at destroying the will to resist," Capra produced *Why We Fight,* a highly successful series of seven one-hour documentaries on the origins of the war.

Major William Wyler directed for Capra's series a documentary on *The Negro Soldier,* then went to England and began flying bombing runs over Germany to supervise the shooting of his remarkable film about one Flying Fortress, *Memphis Belle.* Lieutenant John Huston's orders were somewhat less exalted. He was told to go and shoot a documentary on the defense of Alaska. His *Report from the Aleutians* was to be followed, in 1943, by his celebrated documentary on the Italian campaign, *The Battle of San Pietro,* and then by his even more celebrated study of the army's psychiatric casualties, *Let There Be Light,* which the army, in its wisdom, decided to suppress.

Jack Warner, by contrast, responded to the call to service by saying that he wanted to start out as a general. He added that he would be happy to telephone the White House to get President Roosevelt's approval. Persuaded to settle for the rank of lieutenant colonel, and assigned to a public relations post in Los Angeles, Warner proceeded to the studio tailoring shop to get himself outfitted for his new role. Though his military duties never called him far from his office in Burbank, he let it be known that he liked to be addressed as "Colonel" while he produced films like *Winning Your Wings* and *Rear Gunner.* On the day that a full colonel came to the studio to discuss future film projects, though, when Jack Warner graciously welcomed his visitor by shaking his hand, and the visiting colonel said, "You should have saluted me" —that was the day Jack Warner resigned his commission.

Before that unfortunate encounter with military protocol, Warner had already organized his two major contributions to the war effort. One was to become a major embarrassment, the other a source of pride. The embarrassment originated, according to Warner's own account, with an invitation from President Roosevelt to lunch at the White House. (Warner insisted, in another version, on bringing along his own silverware, to the dismay of Mrs. Roosevelt.) The President apparently told Warner that he wanted him to make a movie of *Mission to Moscow,* Ambassador Joseph Davies's glowing account of his recent diplomatic service in Russia. "Jack, this picture *must* be made, and I am asking you to make it," Warner quoted the President as saying. "I'll do it," Warner answered. "You have my word." "We simply can't lose Russia at this stage . . ." Roosevelt supposedly went on. "We have to keep Stalin fighting—and your picture can make a case for him with the American people."

White House officials later denied that any such meeting ever occurred, and so did Ambassador Davies, but Warner presumably had some kind of high-level Washington encouragement to undertake the project. He assigned it to Howard Koch, the chief writer of *Casablanca,* and to Mike Curtiz, who had directed that and almost everything else, and Davies himself oversaw the political perspectives. ("There is no man in the world I would trust more fully than Joe Stalin . . ." Davies said at a Warners lunch shortly before the movie was released.) The result of all this patriotic endeavor was a disaster. William

Randolph Hearst personally denounced Warner for showing only "the Communist side," and so did such anti-Stalinist liberals as John Dewey and Robert La Follette, who called it a "whitewash." * Warner felt aggrieved. "There are some controversial subjects that are so explosive . . . that it doesn't pay for anyone to be a hero or a martyr," he complained. "You're a dead pigeon either way. Unless, of course, you do it under orders from the President of the United States. Even then, you're just as dead."

Warner's other big project contained no such booby traps. *This Is the Army* was a star-spangled affair derived from a show that the young immigrant Irving Berlin had written about the desolate Long Island camp where he had been stationed in World War I, *Yip Yip Yaphank.* Soon after Pearl Harbor, Berlin began writing an updated version, reserving a place for himself to don his old doughboy uniform and sing, "Oh, how I hate to get up in the morning." Warner paid nearly two million dollars to army charities for the film rights, and the army provided 350 servicemen, all on army salaries, as the cast. One of them was Lieutenant Ronald Reagan.

Reagan had managed to remain in the cavalry reserve ever since his college days, even though his eyesight was so poor that when he was called to duty one doctor said, "If we sent you overseas, you'd shoot a general." A second doctor said, "Yes, and you'd miss him." The army could find some use for almost anyone in those days, however, so Reagan was assigned to the staff at Fort Mason, in San Francisco, as a liaison officer responsible for the loading of convoys. And as a cavalryman, he still wore spurs. "I'm sure many people . . . have forgotten that spurs are a regulation part of the uniform for mounted troops," Reagan happily recalled. The cavalry had other uses for the young lieutenant besides the wearing of spurs. It sent him back to Hollywood to appear at a fund-raising rally for the USO. His commanding officer, who was an admirer of Jeanette MacDonald, even got Lieutenant Reagan to make some telephone calls so that Miss MacDonald would come to Fort Mason to sing the national anthem as part of the fort's observation of I Am an American Day. And finally Reagan was sent back to Hollywood to help make training films, an assignment that his commander proudly described as "putting a square peg in a square hole."

The Army Air Corps had taken over the nine-acre Hal Roach studio on Washington Boulevard in Culver City, and the First Motion Picture Unit now operated in what was unofficially known as Fort Roach. Since air corps regulations said that only a flying officer could command a post, the thirteen hundred assorted moviemakers at Fort Roach were put under the command of Paul Mantz, Hollywood's preeminent stunt pilot. Fort Roach made training films and documentaries; it trained combat camera units; it produced combat film segments for commercial newsreels; it even made films simulating flight over a city to be bombed, so that a pilot assigned to raid Hamburg or Yokohama

---

* In her witty book *Running Time,* Nora Sayre captured the essential quality of *Mission to Moscow* by observing that "in no other film have I seen so many spinning globes. . . . Again and again, world leaders pensively twirl the spheres while asserting that peace (or war) is possible."

could acquire some idea of what his target would look like from his cockpit. The one thing that Fort Roach didn't do, or didn't do very well, was to preserve the rituals of army ceremony.

Lieutenant Reagan apparently had to be taught that. On his first day overseeing basic training, according to one account, he disapproved of the haphazard way the men marched, so he began drilling them.

"We aren't going to do this, Ronnie," one of the men rebuked him.

"What do you mean?" asked the nonplussed Lieutenant Reagan.

"You're an actor, and a lot of us are producers and directors. Right?"

"Right."

"And after the war you're going to be an actor again and we're going to be producers and directors. Right?"

"Right."

"So knock off with the marching around."

Reagan was always a quick study. In his own account of those days, he portrayed himself not as a parade ground martinet but as an outspoken critic of such a martinet. "I was standing at the corner of a studio street," Reagan said, "when they came swinging by, four abreast, our ex-cadet shouting orders like a true drillmaster. I shouldn't have done it, but on the other hand we should have been making pictures, not playing soldiers. When the column was just about halfway past me, so that my voice was audible to most of the men but not to their commander, I said, 'Splendid body of men—with half this many I could conquer M-G-M.' The ranks dissolved . . ."

There was equally little reverence for military protocol at the old Paramount studio in Long Island City, which was Fort Roach East. Its Company B was a company in which, when the red-faced sergeant shouted names at roll call, the Cheever who said "Here!" was John Cheever, the Laurents was Arthur, the Saroyan was William, and the Shaw was Irwin. It was also a company in which PFC Carl Laemmle, Jr., heir to the founder of Universal Pictures, would start his weekend leave by taking a limousine to a Manhattan bank that was being kept open solely in order to provide him with whatever money he might need that weekend.

Gottfried Reinhardt, who had been a fledgling producer at M-G-M, was a sergeant in Company B, so he had to go to the major's office to get the telephone call from his father. Max Reinhardt was seventy years old now, and fat, and almost accustomed to living at the brink of disaster, but he was still determined to produce *La Belle Hélène* if he could just find somebody willing to provide the last twenty thousand dollars needed for a Broadway production of an Offenbach operetta in the year of Stalingrad. Max Reinhardt had gone to Fire Island to brood. It was late September of 1943, and after most of the summer cottages had been locked up, Reinhardt liked to walk along the windswept beach with his Scottish terrier, Mickey.

Wandering there, perhaps daydreaming, Reinhardt suddenly became aware of a wild barking and lunging at the end of the leash. He and his little terrier had encountered a solitary boxer, and the Scottie refused to concede an inch to the bigger dog. He yapped and growled and scurried in and out of the old man's legs. The boxer grimly advanced, preparing for the kill.

Alone on the stormy beach, Reinhardt looked around for help and saw nothing, except for a telephone booth standing alone in the wind. He lurched toward it, dragging the frantic terrier after him on its leash. He hauled the terrier into the telephone booth and slammed the folding door shut against the boxer, which sniffed and pawed and barked. Reinhardt may have thought that he had saved his pet, but the terrier was wild with rage. It turned on its aged master inside the closed telephone booth, and began biting whatever it could reach. It bit his shoes, through and through. It bit his legs, his arms, even his sides and chest. As the old man tried to defend himself from the terrier inside the telephone booth, he apparently suffered a stroke. He bit his own tongue, badly. Somehow, after the boxer had loped off down the beach, Reinhardt managed to struggle home, dragging the terrier behind him. "He came home with his face all out of shape," a caretaker later told Gottfried Reinhardt. "And his talk—you couldn't understand a word. In the morning it looked like he was better again. Till I made his bed. He wet it in the night. Me, I'm not staying with this old man any more. I'm quitting."

"When are you coming?" Max Reinhardt asked his son, on the phone in the major's office.

"Tomorrow, just as we said," said Gottfried, who still knew nothing about the crisis.

"When are you coming?" Reinhardt repeated, haltingly, in the slurred voice of a man who must concentrate on the essentials and cannot make those essentials clear. Perhaps he knew that he was never going to recover, that he had just another two months to live.

"Anything wrong?" Gottfried asked.

The answer sounded "muddled," Gottfried wrote later. "Only a single word is clear: 'Come!' It keeps recurring and then the line is dead."

Reinhardt apologized to the major, whom he had known slightly in Hollywood as an irregularly employed screenwriter. "Skip it, sergeant," said the major. "I'm crazy for Kraut dialogue."

•   •   •

Hollywood people who weren't in the army entertained the army. Touring military camps was one of the major productions in this midwar year of 1943. Perhaps it was pure patriotism; perhaps it was partly publicity for all those wartime movies that kept rolling off the assembly lines; perhaps there was even a touch of guilt that all the war movies (and nonwar movies) were making so much money. The armed forces had by now become Hollywood's biggest customer. Never before had there been such a captive audience as the twelve million servicemen, most of them idle and bored. And so, through this new evolution of its traditional monopoly, Hollywood became richer than ever. The least it could do in return was to send some of its celebrities on tours of military bases.

In one reasonably typical week in September of 1943, Judith Anderson was declaiming high drama in Hawaii and Ray Bolger was dancing in the South Pacific, Al Jolson was performing at bases in the Middle East, and so was Larry Adler, the harmonica virtuoso, and so was Jack Benny (but without Eddie Anderson, who regularly played the part of Benny's scapegrace black chauffeur, Rochester, for the U.S. Army of 1943 was a segregated army). The king of all these wandering jongleurs was Bob Hope, not because he was exceptionally talented but because he devoted his whole existence to these tours. He was an odd man for the mission. Originally christened Leslie, the sixth child of a hard-drinking English stonecutter, Hope seemed to have little natural humor and relied heavily on a large team of gagwriters for his weekly radio show. The gags consisted of endless variations on a few crude themes— Hope's nose, his cowardice, his failures in pursuing girls, his rivalry with Bing Crosby—but crowds of lonely soldiers greeted every one of his vaudeville turns with wild applause. They loved Hope for coming to see them, and he loved them for loving him. In Korea, later, in Vietnam, even in Beirut, he would go on spending Christmas with the troops for half a century.

Hope began simply enough as part of a fund-raising show called the Hollywood Victory Caravan. The three-hour production included bigger movie stars than Hope—Cary Grant, Jimmy Cagney, Claudette Colbert, Groucho Marx—but Hope was the master of ceremonies, in charge of keeping everything moving. The tour, which started with a garden party at the White House in April of 1942, was a huge success. Thousands of people waited to greet the stars at Boston's South Station, and thousands more welcomed them to Philadelphia, Cleveland, Detroit, Chicago, Dallas. At the end of the journey, most of the stars wearily headed back to Hollywood, but Hope couldn't stop. He organized a tour of sixty-five military bases in a month. He took with him the main figures on his radio show—an attractive blond singer named Frances Langford, a manic clown with huge mustaches named Jerry Colonna, his bandleader, Skinnay Ennis—and began broadcasting from his travels: New Orleans, Quantico, Mitchell Field.

A friend urged Hope to take his troupe to Alaska, but the military warned that he might get snowed in. "FOUR DISAPPOINTED THESPIANS WITH SONGS AND WITTY SAYINGS ARE ANXIOUS TO TOUR YOUR TERRITORY," Hope wired the commanding general. "PLEASE GIVE US YOUR CONSENT AND LET US TAKE OUR CHANCES WITH THE WEATHER." The general wired back: "YOU LEAVE TUESDAY." In the spring of 1943, Hope took his show to England. "I've just arrived from the States," he announced in his first appearance at a bomber base called Eye Aerodrome. "You know . . . that's where Churchill lives. . . . He doesn't actually live there . . . he just goes back to deliver Mrs. Roosevelt's laundry." Funny? Hope's rudimentary comedy always had some of the quality of the neighborhood fat boy trying to ingratiate himself on the street corner, but none of that mattered now. "We soon discovered," he recalled, "that you had to be pretty lousy to flop in front of these guys—they yelled and screamed and whistled at everything."

Hope became a man possessed. He did three or four shows a day, all across western England, through Wales, in Northern Ireland, then back to London. He made a special effort at hospitals, clowning through ward after ward. "All right, fellas, don't get up," he would say as a greeting to the bedridden. "Did you see our show—or were you sick before?" Dumb jokes like that, and more dumb jokes like that, repeated over and over, and the homesick soldiers kept whistling and cheering. "The most wonderful thing about England right now is Bob Hope," Burgess Meredith wrote to Paulette Goddard. "The boys in camp stand in rain, they crowd into halls so close you can't breathe, just to see him. He is tireless and funny, and full of responsibility, too, although he carries it lightly and gaily." "When the time for recognition of service to the nation in wartime comes to be considered," John Steinbeck cabled from London to the *New York Herald Tribune,* "Bob Hope should be high on the list. . . . He has caught the soldier's imagination. He gets laughter wherever he goes from men who need laughter."

By now, the Allies had invaded North Africa, so Hope flew south to follow them. "We're off on the road to Morocco," he sang at a farewell appearance at Prestwick, Scotland, and then the star of *The Road to Morocco* was actually in Morocco, spieling and spieling. "Hiya, fellow tourists!" he cried in what he himself cited as a typical routine. "Well, I'm very happy to be here [boos]—course *I'm* leaving as soon as I finish the show. But this is a great country, Africa . . . this is Texas with Arabs. . . . And I tried to find a few Lamours over here, but they all wear their sarongs a little higher . . . under their eyes. And, boys, don't ever lift one of those napkins. I did, and . . . what I saw! A B-bag with legs! Anyway, I'm happy to be here. But hey, isn't it hot? Is it true the scorpions take salt tablets?" And so on.

Morocco was by now safely under Allied control, but when the air corps flew Hope to Tunisia, the Germans were still staging nightly raids. "All of a sudden a couple of red tracer bullets came pretty close over our heads," Hope recalled of his effort to escape in a jeep from an attack on Bizerte, "and the MP hollered, 'Get out and get under something.' For the first time in my life, I wished I was a gopher. . . . The MP kept hollering, 'Don't just stand there, Hope! Crawl in here!' I said, 'That's a sewer!' 'Listen, Mac, you're lucky to get in anywhere at this hour! Don't argue!'. . . Have you ever crawled into a North African sewer? If you have there's nothing I can tell you about it. If you haven't. . . ."

The Allies invaded Sicily that July, and within a week, Hope flew to Palermo to do more shows. Once again, the air raid sirens began to sound. "When I heard the drone of JU-88s, I knew we were in for it," Hope said. "The docks, which were naturally the target for the raid, were only about two blocks away. And two blocks isn't very far as the bomb flies. . . . They say when you're drowning your whole life flashes before your eyes. . . . With me, it's the same way with bombing. I thought of my first professional tour in vaudeville. . . . A great big hunk of red-hot flak sailed past my window and the Heinies started dive-bombing. . . . I threw up my dinner. . . ."

Hope did several shows at frontline infantry bases in Sicily, then flew back to Tunisia for another appearance in Bône (Hope did more than two hundred fifty shows in all during this three-month, twenty-thousand-mile tour), and there somebody in the back of the auditorium shouted: "Draft dodger! Why aren't you in uniform?" Stung, hurt, Hope remained the consummate professional. "Don't you know there's a war on?" he shouted back. "A guy could get hurt!"

•   •   •

Billy Wilder, who had once been a kind of ballroom gigolo in Berlin, an *Eintänzer* ready and available to dance with the matrons who came to the regular *thé dansant* at the Eden Hotel, wanted to make a musical, a stunning, spectacular musical. Then he saw Rita Hayworth in *Cover Girl*. "I realized," he told an interviewer, "that no matter how good my musical might be, most people would say it was no *Cover Girl*. This *Double Indemnity* looked like a better chance to set Hollywood back on its heels. And I like to set Hollywood back on its heels."

This *Double Indemnity*, as Wilder called it, was something that derived from an old newspaper story. Back at the dawn of time, back even before Arthur Krock first arrived in Washington to cover the administration of William Howard Taft for the *Louisville Times*, a terrible thing happened at the printing plant in Louisville. There was an ad in the paper for women's underwear, as Krock recounted the episode to a young writer on the *New York World*, and it was supposed to say, "If these sizes are too big, take a tuck in them." But as Krock was reading through that night's first edition, he saw that somebody had changed the first letter in the word "tuck."

Krock ordered the ad changed for the next edition, then summoned the printer and demanded an explanation. The printer couldn't provide one. He couldn't understand how such an embarrassing accident could have happened. Krock remained suspicious. Two days later, he went and interrogated the printer again, in the interrogatory manner that would daunt future presidents and secretaries of state when Krock became Washington bureau chief for the *New York Times*. The printer confessed. "Mr. Krock," he said, trying finally to explain, "you do nothing your whole life but watch for something like that happening, so as to head it off, *and then*, Mr. Krock, you catch yourself watching for chances to do it."

The young writer to whom Krock told this story, James M. Cain, was fascinated by the idea of a young man yearning to commit the one crime he is responsible for preventing, using his specialized knowledge to violate the social contract that assigned him that specialized knowledge. Cain had once been an insurance salesman, and his father had been an insurance executive, so as Krock's story floated around in his mind over the course of many years, it acquired a characteristically Cainian form: insurance fraud. And since Cain's plots generally revolved around lust and murder, the half-remembered tale of the hapless printer in Louisville eventually became the story of an insurance salesman who meets an attractive woman who wants to have her husband insured and then killed. And only the salesman can teach her how to commit the perfect crime against her husband and his own employers.

Cain, who had been living in Hollywood since 1931, writing intermittently and unsuccessfully for various studios, banged out *Double Indemnity* as a magazine serial, hoping that the serial could then be sold as a movie. He was dismayed when several major magazines rejected it. To his publisher, Alfred Knopf, he described it as "a piece of tripe [that] will never go between covers while I live." The Hollywood possibilities seemed somewhat better. Cain's agent, James Geller, had sent a mimeographed typescript to five major studios, and they all said they were interested in the story if the Hays Office would clear it. After all, Cain's first novel, *The Postman Always Rings Twice*, had been a major best-seller in 1934, but the Hays Office had blocked M-G-M's efforts to turn it into a movie. When Geller finally telephoned Cain with the news about *Double Indemnity*, it was as bad as possible. "The Hays Office report on that story just came in," Geller said. "It starts out: Under no circumstances, in no way, shape or form. . . . Want to hear the rest?"

Cain's New York agent eventually sold *Double Indemnity* to *Liberty* for five thousand dollars as an eight-part serial that ran through much of 1936. Like most such things, it appeared and then disappeared, and it was not until 1943 that Cain persuaded Knopf to publish a collection of three of his magazine fictions under the title *Three of a Kind*. Two were "The Embezzler" and "Career in C Major," and the third was the story that Cain had said would "never go between covers while I live." *Three of a Kind* did quite well, received respectable reviews, and began circulating around the Hollywood studios.

Billy Wilder, according to Cain's version of the story, couldn't find his secretary one morning. She wasn't at her desk, and he kept asking where she was. Another secretary finally said, "I think she is still in the ladies' room reading that story."

"What story?" Wilder asked.

At that point, the secretary emerged with the bound galleys of Cain's *Three of a Kind*. Wilder, recognizing the ultimate proof of popular appeal, took the galleys away from her and carried them home. Wilder was still near the beginning of the series of pictures that would establish him as one of the great filmmakers of the 1940's. As a writer for other people, he had reached his peak in *Ninotchka*, and having determined to direct his own stories, he had begun well with *The Major and the Minor*, and now he had just finished *Five Graves to Cairo*, with his preposterously marvelous casting of Erich von Stroheim as Marshal Rommel. (Wilder loved to tell of his first encounter with Stroheim, the son of a Jewish hatmaker, who had somehow managed to convince the world that he was both a Prussian nobleman and an artistic genius. "You were always ten years ahead of your time," said Wilder, obsequiously, to the director of *Greed*. "Twenty, Mr. Wilder, twenty," said Stroheim.)

Wilder had taken a different route: Americanization. Having arrived in Hollywood unable to speak English, less than a decade earlier, Wilder was now an encyclopedia of American slang, baseball statistics, Tin Pan Alley trivia, everything that a refugee from Galicia would consider emblematic of his new homeland. This was a matter not just of factual detail but of style. Billy Wilder saw in southern California things that no Californian could see, things that only an ex-Berliner could consider self-evident.

Paramount bought *Double Indemnity* for Wilder for fifteen thousand dollars, but Wilder's regular collaborator, Charles Brackett, refused to work on the script. He said Cain's story was disgusting. Wilder didn't care. He hoped to get Cain himself to work on the script, but Cain was under contract to Fox, working on a treatment of *Western Union* for Fritz Lang. Then Wilder's producer at Paramount, Joe Sistrom, suggested a relatively obscure detective story writer named Raymond Chandler. Wilder had never heard of him, so Sistrom gave him a copy of Chandler's first novel, *The Big Sleep*, published four years earlier, and Wilder was captivated. Paramount telegraphed Chandler's publisher, Knopf, to find out where he was—and was surprised, of course, to find that he was living right there in West Hollywood, in a little Spanish-style house on Drexel Avenue.

Chandler was a strange and crotchety man, an American by birth but obsessed with the fact that he had learned Latin and Greek at an English public school, Dulwich, and that he had therefore acquired a degree of gentility that he thought nobody in Los Angeles could possibly understand. A former businessman, an executive for the Dabney Oil Syndicate, Chandler was also an alcoholic, disastrously dependent on whiskey, and oddly dependent, too, on a wife eighteen years his senior, whom he had not dared to marry until the death of his disapproving mother. Chandler had been fired by Dabney for alcoholism in 1932, and so he found himself, at the age of forty-four, unemployed and unemployable in the depths of the Depression in southern California. He began eking out a living by producing detective stories, written in the tough manner of Dashiell Hammett but so luxuriantly overdone that S. J. Perelman was ultimately inspired to murderous parody: "From an open window beyond the bed, a roscoe coughed, 'Ka-chow!'. . . A brunette jane was lying there, half out of the mussed covers . . . dead as vaudeville." Still, Chandler doggedly kept writing: *The Big Sleep* (1939) was followed by *Farewell, My Lovely* (1940), *The High Window* (1942), *The Lady in the Lake* (1943).

Summoned to Paramount for a story conference, Chandler had to confess that he didn't know where the studio was. Then came a disastrous encounter with Wilder. Chandler, by now in his fifties, was wearing a tweed jacket with leather-patched elbows, a button-down shirt, and a striped tie, and he smoked a pipe. Wilder was deeply suspicious. Wilder himself wore a baseball cap and waved a riding crop whenever he spoke. Chandler was equally suspicious. He truculently announced that he would have to be paid $150 a week. Sistrom, the producer, said Paramount had expected to pay him $750. In fact, Sistrom felt it his moral duty to call in an agent, H. N. Swanson, to protect Chandler from both Paramount and himself.

Chandler, who had never before written anything for the movies, said it

might take him two or even three weeks to finish a script of *Double Indemnity*.
Wilder, who was accustomed to spending months on such a project, provided
Chandler with one of his own scripts, *Hold Back the Dawn*, as a specimen of
how such things were done, and then awaited the results. Chandler returned
a month later with a script filled with impressive technical instructions like
"DOLLY IN FOR CU." Wilder read the script, while Chandler sat there waiting
for approval, and then threw the manuscript at him. It hit him in the chest
and fell to the floor. "This is shit, Mr. Chandler," said Wilder. Chandler was
speechless. Wilder insisted, then, that they work in the only way Wilder
knew how to work, "We are going to write this picture *together*. We are going
to lock ourselves in this room and write a screenplay. It is going to take us a
long time. You will be on salary even if it takes a year to write this picture."

It was a kind of torture. Wilder respected Chandler's talent but yearned
for some kind of respect in return. Chandler scorned him. Yet Wilder was
the one who knew how to write movies. Working with Wilder, Chandler
wrote to a friend, "was an agonizing experience and has probably shortened
my life." Wilder was no less bitter. "He gave me more aggravation than any
writer I ever worked with," he told an interviewer. Yet they labored together
for months, hating the collaboration, hating each other. They talked, they
argued, they imagined all the various ways to film *Double Indemnity*.

Wilder wanted to follow Cain's novella as closely as possible. Chandler
insisted that this approach wouldn't work. Chandler despised Cain's writing
in general. "James Cain—Faugh," he wrote to Knopf, with a vehemence that
suggested a bit of jealousy. "Everything he touches smells like a billygoat. He
is every kind of writer I detest, a faux naif, a Proust in greasy overalls, a dirty
little boy with a piece of chalk and a board fence and nobody looking." More
specifically, Chandler was convinced that Cain's jazzy dialogue wouldn't work
on the screen. It sounded like "a bad high school play," Chandler argued.
"The dialogue oversaid everything and when spoken sounded quite colorless
and tame." He insisted on this judgment even in a conference with Cain
himself, and Cain, who never seemed to be able to write successfully for the
movies, docilely acquiesced.

So the struggles went on. Chandler puffed on his pipe. Wilder went
often to the bathroom, not to urinate but just to escape from Chandler. In
Wilder's absences, Chandler would take a pint of bourbon from his briefcase
and drink. Finally, Wilder would return to the smoke-filled office and cry out,
"For Chrissakes, Ray, open a window." Chandler became filled with alcoholic
anger at being ordered around. One day, when the sun came pouring through
the venetian blinds, Wilder gave one order too many. "Go and fix that, will
you, Ray?" he said. Chandler got up and walked out of the office, walked out
of Paramount, and went home. Three days later, he turned up in Sistrom's
office and said he wanted to quit the whole project. By this time, he had a
long list of grievances against Wilder, all written out in quiet fury on a series
of pages of legal-sized yellow paper. He demanded, among other things, that
Wilder apologize. Sistrom summoned Wilder to his office, and Wilder came.
Wilder apologized. Sistrom apologized.

But Chandler still had his list of indignities that must cease. According to John Houseman, who was then an assistant producer at Paramount, the indictment and proposed settlement went into considerable detail: "Mr. Wilder was at no time to swish under Mr. Chandler's nose or to point in his direction the thin, leather-handled malacca cane which Mr. Wilder was in the habit of waving around while they worked. Mr. Wilder was not to give Mr. Chandler orders of an arbitrary or personal nature such as 'Ray, will you open that window?' or 'Ray, will you shut that door please?' " Wilder himself remembered a few more of Chandler's grievances: "Mr. Wilder frequently interrupts our work to take phone calls from women. . . . I can't work with a man who wears a hat in the office. I feel he is about to leave momentarily."

And so on. How did they ever continue? Somehow they did, for another six months, with Chandler repeatedly threatening to resign, and Wilder repeatedly cajoling him into continuing, until finally there was a script, which seemed to be a faithful re-creation of the novel but was markedly different. Wilder's direction would make it more different still (but, strangely, more faithful too). In the novel, for example, after Walter Neff, the insurance man, impersonated his victim and then jumped off the train near where the body was to be found, and then Mrs. Dietrichson had to drive him away from the scene, Cain wrote only, "She started up. We passed the factories." In the film, that became the famous scene of the car refusing to start, the engine endlessly going *urrun-urrun-urrun,* until Fred MacMurray leaned over and turned on the ignition, which the panicky Barbara Stanwyck had forgotten to do. "Barbara and I sat in this dummy car," MacMurray said later. "Just a car seat. No dashboard. No ignition key to turn. We faked it, pantomimed it. When I changed places with her and turned the key I remember I was doing it fast and Billy kept saying, 'Make it longer, make it longer,' and finally I yelled, 'For Chrissake Billy, it's not going to hold that long,' and he said, 'Make it longer,' and he was right. It held. It held. . . ."

That was much later, of course. That was after MacMurray, who didn't want to play the part of Walter Neff at all, realized that he had been tricked and manipulated into the best role of his life. That kept happening. Many of the famous talents in Hollywood never seemed to recognize a good idea when it was proposed to them. So Billy Wilder, having bullied and maneuvered Chandler into helping to create a great script, now discovered that nobody wanted to play in it. Paramount's biggest star, Alan Ladd, wouldn't touch it. And then there was the inevitable scene with George Raft. Wilder wanted to send him the script.

"I don't read scripts," said Raft. "Tell it to me."

Wilder told it to him, but Raft couldn't understand what had happened to "the lapel bit." Wilder looked blank. "You know," said Raft, who couldn't bear the idea of playing a villain, "when the guy flashes his lapel, you see his badge, you know he's a detective."

Wilder told him there wasn't any lapel bit in *Double Indemnity,* so Raft turned him down. Perhaps Wilder sighed in relief—"That's when we knew we had a good picture," he said later—for the star he really wanted, he claimed, was MacMurray, somebody amiable and happy-go-lucky and slightly flabby, the all-American salesman, ready to be corrupted. MacMurray was fighting with Paramount about a new contract, and he knew that the studio's production chief, Y. Frank Freeman, disliked Wilder and particularly disliked Wilder's newest project. So MacMurray agreed to Wilder's importuning as a way to torment Freeman, confident that Freeman would forbid him to play such a sordid part, but Freeman consented because he thought *Double Indemnity* would ruin MacMurray's career and thus punish him for arguing about his contract. "I never dreamed it would be the best picture I ever made," MacMurray said.

Barbara Stanwyck, too, was terrified of the best role she ever had. She was afraid, she told Wilder, "to go into an out-and-out cold-blooded killer." Wilder bullied her too. "Well, are you a mouse or an actress?" he demanded. And when he got her to take the part, he insisted on outfitting her in a blond wig because "I wanted her to look as sleazy as possible." Paramount's chief of chiefs, Buddy DeSylva, was dismayed at seeing his star in such a wig. "We hire Barbara Stanwyck and here we get George Washington," he said.

Wilder pressed on. He defied the studio conventions by shooting much of his film on seedy locations around the Los Angeles railroad station. He alone knew what he was doing, and even when he didn't know what he was doing, he knew how to correct his course. He proved that in the ending. Cain's original ending had been a rather absurd demonstration of the villainess turning into an angel of evil, dressed all in scarlet and trying to destroy the corrupted salesman. The Chandler-Wilder script was more practical, and also conformed to the Hays Office rules on crime and punishment: The salesman died in the gas chamber at Folsom. A strong ending, sharp, indisputable. Wilder spent $150,000 to recreate the Folsom death chamber, and he devoted five days to filming the whole scene, and then he decided that the ending was wrong. Too blunt. It lacked subtlety.

Chandler didn't want to rewrite the ending, and Paramount certainly didn't want to throw away $150,000 to restage and refilm that ending, but Wilder insisted. His new scene, one of his very best scenes, went very quietly. MacMurray, wounded and bleeding badly, asked Edward G. Robinson, the insurance investigator who represented a figure of paternal authority, for twenty-four hours to get to the Mexican border. "You'll never make it to the elevator," said Robinson, lighting MacMurray's last cigarette. MacMurray said Robinson had been unable to solve the crime because the murderer had been "too close, right across the desk from you." Robinson said, "Closer than that."

When Wilder went to Grauman's for the Academy Award ceremonies the following spring, he hoped and expected to win an Oscar even though he knew that Paramount had been pushing Leo McCarey's saccharine *Going My Way,* which was in fact voted best picture of the year. When McCarey was also named best director, though, Wilder could not bear it. As McCarey proudly marched down the aisle of Grauman's to receive his award, Wilder stuck out a foot and tripped him.

• • •

It was never completely clear why Vera Zorina was cast in the choice role of Maria in *For Whom the Bell Tolls*. A Norwegian known primarily as a ballerina, she had made some undistinguished appearances in *The Goldwyn Follies* (1938) and *On Your Toes* (1939). Many newspapers reported that Ernest Hemingway had seen Ingrid Bergman in *Intermezzo* and wanted her to play Maria. David Selznick, who owned Miss Bergman's contract, claimed that he himself almost bought the Hemingway novel for her but "was so exhausted after *Gone with the Wind* and *Rebecca* that I simply could not face a job of this size." Selznick said he was determined to get Miss Bergman the part no matter who produced the movie, so he "planted all kinds of newspaper items to the effect that she was the only possible Maria." He also telephoned Miss Bergman on a ski vacation in Sun Valley and asked whether it would be possible for her to have lunch with Hemingway in San Francisco before the novelist departed for China. "Is it possible?" Miss Bergman echoed. "Possible? I am already on my way." She had been skiing in the sun for a week, so her face was very tanned and her nose was peeling from sunburn. Hemingway was awed by her beauty—indeed, he remained somewhat in awe of her for the rest of his life. "You'll get the part, don't worry," he said.

Hemingway had turned over his best-selling novel to Paramount for a sum of money that he called "bloody wonderful"—between $100,000 and $150,000, according to different accounts, more than twice the payment for *Gone With the Wind*—but that did not give him any control over what was done with it. So Paramount, having paid a lot of money for the novel, and a lot more to get Gary Cooper from M-G-M, probably decided to economize by assigning the role of Maria to Vera Zorina, who was under contract to Paramount and needed a part. ("Zorina . . . is a lovely dancer," Hemingway complained to Maxwell Perkins, "but has a face rather like a dachshund.") Sam Wood, the director, later blamed this inept decision on Paramount's DeSylva, while DeSylva blamed it on Wood. In any case, the Paramount authorities sheared off all Miss Zorina's hair—as had happened to Maria in the course of being mauled and gang-raped by the Fascists—and sent her off to Wood's headquarters in the Sierra Nevadas. Then, when they looked at the first three weeks of rushes, they decided that she couldn't play the part.

Ingrid Bergman was in the midst of *Casablanca* during all this. Paul Henreid was impressed by how "sweet and gentle" she was, "a retiring, patient woman, wonderful to work with and an excellent actress, but . . . terribly vulnerable. We wanted to take care of her, to protect her." Henreid was surprised to find her in tears one day, and to learn that it was because she had lost the part of Maria, and to see a different side of Ingrid Bergman. "Those idiots!" she cried, in what Henreid called a "hardened" voice. "What the hell do they know? Picking Vera Zorina of all people. She can't act, Paul. She just can't, and I'm good. I'm really good!" Henreid was present, too, when Miss Bergman got the telephone call that she had been hungering for. "She went to it and said, 'Yes, yes . . .'" then let out a yell I can only compare to that of a tigress who has made a kill, a yell of such joy and triumph that I was stunned. Was this submissive Ingrid? She put down the phone and yelled, 'I got it, Paul! I got it!' "

The day after that phone call, Miss Bergman said farewell to the set of *Casablanca* and drove nearly five hundred miles into the mountains until she found a group of cabins just beyond the Sonora Pass. "Then I see this beautiful man coming down the mountainside toward me," she recalled. "He looked at me, and I looked at him, and I blushed naturally. Then he said, 'Hallo, Maria?' and I blushed again. . . ." Gary Cooper took her to meet Sam Wood and helped her to get installed and then asked if they could rehearse some of their dialogue. She agreed, and so he started right in. "I thought he was still talking to me, because he didn't change his voice," she said. "He didn't become an actor who acted, he was exactly the same. So I kept saying, 'Excuse me, what did you say? I can't understand what you're talking about.' And he said a little reprovingly, 'I'm reading the dialogue, that's the dialogue.' So I blushed again and said, 'Oh, that's the dialogue.' "

Dialogue was one of the things for which Ernest Hemingway had originally become famous, but Hollywood had to improve on everything, so Paramount hired Dudley Nichols to improve on *For Whom the Bell Tolls*. Nichols was both a successful screenwriter (*The Informer*, 1935; *Stagecoach*, 1939; *Manhunt*, 1941) and a dedicated liberal, one of the founders of the Screen Writers Guild and its president during the difficult years, 1937 and 1938. But somehow, by some half-unconscious process of self-neutralization, a novel that had been conceived partly as a eulogy on the death of the Spanish Republic turned into a movie script about politically indeterminate heroes and villains. Hemingway disapproved. He described Nichols's version of the Loyalist guerrillas as something derived from fourth-rate productions of Bizet's *Carmen*. He particularly objected to their wearing red bandannas and demanded that they all wear blacks and grays. "I went all over Dudley Nichols' script and suggested an enormous amount of changes and absolutely necessary alterations, excisions, and additions," Hemingway wrote to Perkins. "In the end he rewrote it and incorporated almost everything I had suggested."

But even then, as usual, things somehow got changed, depoliticized, neutralized. This was largely the work of Sam Wood, who had the authority, far off in those Sierra Nevadas, to shade the script as he pleased. "It is a love story against a brutal background," Wood said. "It would be the same love story if they were on the other side." Wood had originally seemed an ideal director because he was a Hemingway-style man of action (one of his previous successes had been to guide Ronald Reagan through *Kings Row*), and only after the filming was done did it become apparent that Wood's conservatism was turning into an obsession.

Wood was by no means alone in his obsession. In February of 1944, he announced the formation of a militant organization called the Motion Picture Alliance for the Preservation of American Ideals. Among the founders were Clark Gable, Robert Taylor, Gary Cooper, Walt Disney, Roy Brewer, Ginger Rogers, Barbara Stanwyck, John Ford, Irene Dunne, and John Wayne. Wood's announcement was timed to appear the day before a lavish dinner by the Hollywood Free World Association, under the chairmanship of Dudley Nichols, to hear a speech by Henry Wallace. "The American motion picture is, and will continue to be, held by Americans for the American people, in the interests of America, and dedicated to the preservation and continuance of the American scene and the American way of life," Wood proclaimed in his inaugural address.

After that heroic beginning, the organization met every month at the American Legion auditorium on Highland Avenue, conducted its routine business, and then listened to inspiring talks from anti-Communist crusaders like J. B. Matthews, Louis Budenz, and Ralph de Toledano. That might have been harmless enough, but the organization also began quietly lobbying for the House Un-American Activities Committee to come and investigate un-American influence, Communist influence, in Hollywood.

By this time, Wood was carrying a little black notebook in which he jotted down names of Hollywood subversives who would have to be purged. In his family, according to Wood's daughter Jeane, his crusade was known simply as "It." " ' It' invariably transformed Dad into a snarling, unreasoning brute," she said. "We used to leave the dinner table with our guts tangled and churning from the experience." When the House Un-American Activities Committee finally did descend on Hollywood in 1947, Wood was one of the first of the "friendly" witnesses (right after Jack Warner and shortly before Gary Cooper), welcoming its investigation and testifying to his own struggles in the cause. At a meeting of his own MPA one day in 1949, finally, Wood worked himself into a rage at the news that a liberal screenwriter was suing the organization for slander. Shortly after the meeting ended, Wood suffered a heart attack and died. When his will was read, it turned out that he had left his various bequests on one condition. Except for his widow, whom he apparently trusted, no heirs could inherit anything until they filed with the probate court an affidavit swearing that they "are not now, nor have they ever been, Communists."

But all this lay in the future, when Miss Bergman herself would be cast out of Hollywood on grounds of grave moral dereliction. Back on the mountain setting of *For Whom the Bell Tolls,* Wood presided over a rather happy band of Spanish guerrillas, cast as only Hollywood could cast Spanish guerrillas: the Swedish Ingrid Bergman as Maria, the Russian Akim Tamiroff as Pablo, the Greek Katina Paxinou as Pilar, and so on. It was an old rule in Hollywood that all foreign accents sounded the same. Even the authentic mountain landscape was fake, for that matter, not just because it was Californian rather than Spanish but because the California moviemakers decided that their own mountains looked too beautiful, so they started spraying gray paint in all directions. "We even uprooted wildflowers and greenery to prevent the harsh landscape from becoming 'pretty' for the technicolor camera," Wood recalled.

Miss Bergman was enchanted. "It was so primitive and romantic up there among the stars and the high peaks before the winter snows cut off the whole region . . ." she said. "I sat and laughed on the set. Looking at Gary Cooper, it was so wonderful." In her diary, she noted: "What was wrong was that my happiness showed on the screen. I was far too happy to honestly portray Maria's tragic figure."

It was not wrong, though. It was spectacular. During the famous scene in which Cooper and Miss Bergman made love in a sleeping bag, the one in which she said she felt the earth move beneath her, some enterprising reporter felt hot under the collar and decided to check on the temperature in the theater. He found that the temperature rose several degrees every time the scene was shown.

•   •   •

One major Hollywood star who made no effort whatever to take part in the war was Errol Flynn, an Australian by origin, though he became a naturalized American citizen in 1942. "He felt no loyalty to Britain and little to Australia," said his friend David Niven. "He had no intention of being called to the colors." There have even been allegations that Flynn acted as an Axis agent, but most of the evidence portrays simply an irresponsible hedonist, eager to smuggle drugs and to star in that international "high society" where Fascist sympathies were commonplace. "Jew bastard" was Flynn's standard term to describe his boss, Jack Warner. Now, at the age of thirty-three, Flynn had come to the end of his stormy marriage to Lili Damita, an actress.

To Warner Bros., he was the ideal war hero, handsome, muscular, debonair. The studio cast him in *Dive Bomber, Edge of Darkness, Objective Burma.* In the last of these, which proclaimed that U.S. reinforcements would soon save the beleaguered British in a campaign where no Americans actually fought at all, producer Jerry Wald had simply invented an American hero to be played by Flynn. This seemed reasonable enough in a war that was actually filmed on a Santa Anita ranch. Alvah Bessie, a Spanish War veteran who had been assigned to write the scenario, telephoned Wald with an objection: "Look, Jerry, there *are* no American troops in Burma." Wald offered a characteristic answer: "So what? It's only a moving picture." The British, however, were furious. The *London Daily Mirror* published a cartoon showing Flynn in battle costume in a director's chair, and the caption quoted a ghostly Tommy as saying, "Excuse me, Mr. Flynn, but you're sitting on some graves." Flynn was pained. "Why blame the actor?" he protested. "He does not produce the picture or write the screenplay."

Flynn's search for enjoyment consisted of endless drinking and fornicating, plus a certain indulgence in drugs. On the crest of a hill on Mulholland Drive, he designed and built a $125,000 house that embodied all the sensual fantasies of that time and place, from glass cases filled with guns to a cock-fighting arena in the stable to bedrooms outfitted with black silk hangings, sable bed coverings, and two-way mirrors in the walls and ceilings, so that guests could watch the other guests at play. "Strange people wended their way up the hill to Mulholland," Flynn observed. "Among them pimps, sports, bums, down-at-the-heel actors, gamblers, athletes, sightseers, process-servers, phonies, queers, salesmen—everything in the world. . . . They came by day and by night. Invited and uninvited."

Among the many unverifiable legends about Flynn's pleasure dome, there is one that tells of a paunchy Central European diplomat who was determined to investigate the wild rumors of wild orgies. Flynn was elusive, and irritated, but the diplomat kept making hopeful inquiries among Warners executives until finally his cajoling brought him an invitation to dinner on Mulholland Drive. Black tie. When the diplomat descended from his limousine and rang the bell at Flynn's mansion, the door was opened by a young blonde wearing nothing but a small apron and a pair of high-heeled shoes. She smiled. He smiled. She invited him to follow her to what she called "the disrobing room." When he had taken off all his clothes, she said, he should go through the door at the far end of the room to join the other guests. The diplomat was happy to follow her instructions. Stark naked, quivering with excited anticipation, he marched through the door. He thereupon found himself in Flynn's dining room, where everyone else was fully clothed in evening dress.

It was to this palace that Flynn welcomed John Barrymore, not realizing (or perhaps he did realize it) that Barrymore's alcoholic ruin and degradation provided a forecast of his own future. Flynn was impressed by Barrymore's scandalous reputation, and by his intermittent charm, so Barrymore simply moved in and started pouring himself drinks. "Jack thought it was a waste of time to go to the bathroom if there was a window close by," Flynn recalled. "During his visit he took all the varnish off one of my picture windows that overlooked the San Fernando Valley. One day I complained bitterly, 'For God's sake, look at the varnish here. Your piss has eaten away the paint. Can't you do it somewhere else?' . . . He immediately went to the fireplace and let go there. The smell through the room was atrocious. . . ."

When Barrymore died a few months later, his friends took him to the Pierce Brothers Mortuary on Sunset Boulevard and then gathered in a nearby bar called The Cock and Bull. There was much morose drinking and telling of Barrymore stories, according to Flynn. One celebrant who left early was Raoul Walsh, a former actor whose accidental loss of an eye had made him turn into a director. Walsh went from the bar to the funeral home, accompanied by two friends named Bev Allen and Charles Miller, and persuaded the undertakers, for a couple of hundred dollars, that they had to take away the corpse for one last viewing by Barrymore's crippled aunt. Then they took it to Flynn's house and propped it up in his favorite chair. Flynn returned home drunk and lurched into the living room. "The light went on and—my God—I stared into the face of Barrymore!" Flynn reported in his memoirs. "His eyes were closed. He looked puffed, white, bloodless. They hadn't embalmed him yet. I let out a delirious scream . . . ."

But haven't we already heard this same story with quite different details? Yes, all the best Hollywood stories have several contradictory versions. Paul Henreid, in the memoirs written with Julius Fast in 1984, reported that it was Peter Lorre who had spirited Barrymore's corpse into Flynn's living room. Flynn, in his supposedly unassisted memoirs, *My Wicked, Wicked Ways* (1959), described exactly the same event as a prank organized by Raoul Walsh.

Fun, fun, fun—that was the height of it that year for Flynn, until his doorbell rang and two Los Angeles detectives told him that he faced a charge of statutory rape.

"I don't know what you're talking about," Flynn said.

"It concerns a Miss Betty Hansen," one of the detectives said, according to Flynn's account, "—and we are holding you."

"I've never heard of her. Betty Hansen? Who is she?"

Betty Hansen was a girl of seventeen who had come west from Nebraska to visit her sister, and then wandered off into the wilderness of Los Angeles. After worrying for a while, the sister reported her absence to the police and asked them to find her. The police soon discovered her in a Santa Monica hotel. In the course of their questioning about what she had been doing, she said she had gone to a party where she had met Errol Flynn and, as she later testified, "I had an act of intercourse."

This must have impressed any Los Angeles police officer as a matter of supreme insignificance, but according to California law, an "act of intercourse" with a girl less than eighteen years old constituted statutory rape and could be punished by five years in prison, even if the girl was a willing partner. This law was not very vigorously enforced. For some reason, however, the authorities decided to take Betty Hansen's accusation to a grand jury in October of 1942. The grand jury understandably declined to indict Flynn. Instead of abandoning this inconsequential affair, the authorities then decided to investigate further, and so they unearthed the case of Peggy LaRue Satterlee, whose mother had appeared at the sheriff's office the year before and complained that her fifteen-year-old daughter had been seduced by Flynn aboard his yacht, the *Sirocco*. At the time, the sheriff's office had shrugged off the mother's complaint, but now the Satterlee story was resurrected and added to the Hansen story.

As charges of rape, these stories were so absurd that it is hard to imagine why the authorities pursued them. The least plausible explanation was that of District Attorney John Dockweiler, who had been elected just two years earlier in place of Buron Fitts, the heavily subsidized friend of the movie business. "I must let the public know," said Dockweiler, "that all men and women are equal when they come before our courts and that no one can violate the law and escape punishment because of wealth or position." A more interesting explanation—though quite undocumented—appeared in Kenneth Anger's *Hollywood Babylon*. Anger, a onetime child actor and later an "underground" film director, wrote that when Flynn returned home after being bailed out on the original charge, his phone rang. "An unknown voice said:

'Tell Jack I want $10,000,' and hung up. The entire affair might have been dropped then and there, if Jack Warner, Flynn's boss, had returned the extortionist's call." In this version, Flynn was simply a victim of a system in which the movie industry paid off "corrupt Los Angeles politicians" in exchange for protection. "These payoffs had been habitually turned over to the 'bosses,' who would make sure that the police got its take of the cut," Anger wrote. Just before Miss Hansen told her story, he added, "some changes had been made in the chain of command at L.A. City Hall. When Jack Warner had failed to cough up to the new bosses, the first rape charge against Flynn had been brought up as a warning. When that could not be substantiated, the second chippie was pushed forward by the cops to chirp her year-old charges."

Florabel Muir, a reliable reporter who covered Hollywood for the *New York Daily News,* also saw political manipulation in the case, but she was more sympathetic to the authorities. She believed that Warner Bros. was intervening from the beginning and "pulling strings like crazy to keep Flynn from being indicted." When the studio maneuvering succeeded, she added, the embarrassed police complained angrily to Dockweiler, whom she described as "an honest and religious man." Flynn had little choice then but to call in the man whom all Hollywood stars called in when they were threatened with imprisonment: Jerry Giesler. A potbellied and rather courtly attorney with a high-pitched voice, meticulous in his preparations for each case and exhaustive in his questioning, Giesler managed to turn his newest defendant into a kind of folk hero. His basic approach, he said later, was to portray the two young accusers as "not as unversed in the ways of the world as the district attorney's office would have the public believe." An army of reporters savored every word. In a time of worldwide war and devastation, the prosecution of Errol Flynn for fornication with two eager adolescents was treated as a news story of major importance, often worthy of front-page headlines.

Betty Hansen claimed that after meeting Flynn at a party, she had felt sick and wanted to go upstairs to lie down, that Flynn had pursued her and taken advantage of her. Flynn denied everything, so it was up to Giesler to make Miss Hansen's perfectly plausible story sound ludicrous.

Q: When he told you to lie down on the bed, did he tell you what he wanted you to lie down for?

A: No, he did not.

Q: Did you have any thoughts of what he wanted you to lie down for?

A: No. . . .

Q: What did you think was going to happen—just going to take a nap?

A: Yes.

Even when Miss Hansen's story had the horrid ring of truth, Giesler made it sound ludicrous. He insisted on asking every detail of who took off which pieces of clothing, and thus elicited the fact that Flynn had kept his shoes on throughout the episode. And when it was all over, what did Flynn do? He went into the bathroom and doused himself with hair oil. "What else do you recall that happened there?" Giesler prodded. "I think he asked if I ever used it and I said no," the wretched girl testified.

If Betty Hansen's night of romance sounded squalid, Peggy LaRue Satterlee's cruise on Flynn's yacht sounded, in Giesler's own term, "preposterous." She had gone aboard at midnight and repaired to her cabin and taken off most of her clothes. Giesler wanted to know every detail.

Q: So you took your socks off too, and you wear those— What do you call those things? . . . Brassiere?

A: Yes, sir.

Q: Did you take that off?

A: No, sir.

Q: You did not take that off?

A: I mean yes, sir.

Q: Which was it?

A: I took it off.

And so on. Miss Satterlee, who was now a nightclub dancer, claimed that Flynn had entered her cabin and she had protested that "You should not be here, because it is not nice to come in a lady's bedroom when she is in bed." She quoted Flynn, who was already outfitted in striped pajamas, as saying that he just wanted to talk. "He said, 'Let me just get in bed with you and I will not bother you. I just want to talk to you.' " Giesler, perhaps remembering Miss Hansen's testimony, wanted to know about Flynn's shoes. "Did he have anything on his feet?" Miss Satterlee said she "did not notice his feet."

Q: Did you let him get in bed?

A: No, sir.

Q: Did he get in bed?

A: Yes, sir. . . .

Q: Did he say anything at that time before the act of intercourse?

A: Not that I recall. . . .

Q: Did you fight him then?

A: Not very much, no, sir.

Q: Did you fight with him at all?

A: No, sir, I cried.

Giesler made it clear that Miss Satterlee had not only not resisted Flynn's advances but that she had spent all of the next day swimming and chattering and posing for pictures with Flynn aboard the yacht. That evening, she made some remark about the moon shining upon the sea, and Flynn lured her belowdeck, she said, by saying that the moon could best be viewed through a porthole. Giesler pursued every possibility. Had Flynn carried her downstairs? No. Pulled her downstairs? No. Had he taken her arm? "He might have taken hold of my arm on the way down the steps," Miss Satterlee said. Did she know where they were going? Flynn had led the way. Had she followed him? Yes. Why? "Because I wanted to see the moon through the porthole." And so she had looked through the porthole, on the right side of the ship, and then "Mr. Flynn . . . said since he had possession of me once, naturally why wouldn't I let him do it this time?"

Giesler had an exquisite sense of detail.

Q: Did he direct his privates into you?

A: Yes, sir.

Q: How did he do it, do you know?

A: No, sir.

Giesler kept questioning her about her resistance or lack of resistance. "You did not want to protect your honor, did you?" he demanded at one point. The prosecutor objected that the question was "argumentative" but the judge overruled him. "Did you?" Giesler insisted to Miss Satterlee. "After that I did not count my honor," she said, "because I had no honor anyway after he was finished."

All this melodrama, which the press treated with headlines worthy of the fall of France, was just a preliminary hearing, a dress rehearsal. At the end of November, Los Angeles Municipal Court Judge Walters ruled that Flynn should go on trial on three counts of statutory rape. So the crowds stood in line for hours, in January of 1943, for a chance to watch Flynn defend himself in Los Angeles Superior Court. Giesler took pride in getting nine women on the jury—would the same assumptions apply today?—for he was confident in their judgments of Flynn's accusers. He made Betty Hansen tell her implausible story all over again and then insisted on even more details.

Q: Miss Hansen, the act itself lasted, how long, please?

A: About fifty minutes.

Q: About fifty minutes?

A: Yes, that is right.

Q: And during the entire time he was on top of you?

A: That is right.

Q: Did it pain you?

A: Yes, it did.

Q: You did not scream?

A: I did not. . . .

Q: Did it hurt very much?

A: No.

Q: Did you take part in the performance of the act yourself?

A: Explain that some to me, please.

Q: I am asking you if you took part in the performance of the act yourself. Did you respond to him in his performing the act with you?

A: I did.

Peggy LaRue Satterlee was even less plausible as a rape victim, not only because she willingly boarded Flynn's yacht, not only because she was now a nightclub dancer, but because Giesler had discovered from an anonymous telephone tip that she had engaged in some weird antics with a Canadian pilot named Owen Cathcart-Jones, who called her, among other things, Scrumpet and Bitchy Pie. Miss Satterlee had lived with her sister in the Canadian's apartment during the summer of 1941, and she had gone with him to a funeral parlor. Giesler demanded that Cathcart-Jones provide the details.

Q: And she was kind of playing hide-and-seek around the corpses, wasn't she? Do you remember that night?

A: Yes.

Q: Do you remember she showed you—opened it up and showed you—the body of an elderly lady?

A: Yes.

Q: And pulled the sheet down in the mortuary on a Filipino who had been crippled across his center?

A: Yes, I remember that.

Q: And then went back to where they inject the veins of corpses and there looked down at an elderly man lying there, and her head was pushed down against the man's face. Do you remember that?

A: Yes, I remember that.

Could any Los Angeles jury, whether it included nine women and three men or nine men and three women, hear testimony like that and then convict Errol Flynn of rape? Giesler was nothing if not thorough. Having heard Peggy LaRue Satterlee testify that Flynn had led her belowdeck to look at the moon through a porthole on the starboard side of the yacht, he put a federal meteorologist on the stand to testify that the moon by which Miss Satterlee had been seduced was actually shining on the opposite side of the *Sirocco*. There remained then only the testimony of Errol Flynn himself, who took the stand and presumably lied as he denied everything. He swore that he had never had sex with either one of the girls.

Two of the three male jurors wanted to convict Flynn, but what did their views matter? After a day of arguing, the jury announced its verdict: Innocent. A little girl rushed forward and handed Flynn a bouquet of flowers. And Flynn declared, as every exonerated criminal has always declared, "My confidence in American justice is completely justified."

● ● ●

If Bertolt Brecht couldn't get a job in a movie colony filled with successful German refugees, what hope could there be for the greatest film director from Spain? Luis Buñuel, dismissed as a leftist from his minor job in the film department of the Museum of Modern Art in New York, managed to get another job, dubbing movies into Spanish for Warner Bros. Too late. "As a dubbing capital, Hollywood was finished," Buñuel later recalled, "since it was being done in every country where the film was to be shown."

So the creator of the surrealistic classic *Un Chien Andalou* just wandered around, observing the southern California landscape. It naturally fascinated him in ways in which only Buñuel could be fascinated. "One day while I was out driving," he recalled, "I discovered the enormous two-mile-long Los Angeles garbage dump, with everything from orange peels to grand pianos to whole houses. Smoke from the fires rose here and there; and at the bottom of the pit, on a small piece of land raised slightly from the piles of garbage, stood a couple of tiny houses inhabited by real people. Once I saw a young girl, perhaps fourteen or fifteen, emerge from one of the houses, and I fantasized her involved in a love affair in this infernal decor. Man Ray and I wanted to make a film about it, but we couldn't raise the money."

Boris Karloff (*left*) as the Frankenstein monster was a substitute for real horrors. Charlie Chaplin (*below*) had boldly ridiculed Hitler, but moralists made him a villain. Shortly after marrying young Oona O'Neill, he had to stand trial for fathering Joan Barry's daughter (*bottom right*).

6

REUNIONS

(1944)

The Hollywood people who had gone off to war returned home from time to time, and sometimes they lurched into unexpected battles with the Hollywood people who had stayed home. Lieutenant John Huston, back in California on a visit, went to one of David Selznick's parties and encountered Errol Flynn. When Flynn said what Huston called "something wretched" about Olivia de Havilland, Huston snapped at him: "That's a lie! Even if it weren't a lie, only a son of a bitch would repeat it."

Flynn, the movie hero who disdained military service, asked Huston if he wanted to make something of it. Huston said he did. Huston had once been a semiprofessional boxer, but Flynn was also an experienced fighter, and twenty-five pounds heavier. Besides, Huston was half drunk. Flynn led the way to a dark corner of Selznick's garden, and both men took off their coats and started swinging. "I was knocked down almost immediately, landing on the gravel drive on my elbows," Huston later recalled. "I was up right away, and I was down again." When Huston fell, he rolled away from Flynn because he expected Flynn to kick at him in an effort to finish him off, but Flynn, to Huston's surprise, held back. "The fight was conducted strictly according to Queensberry," said Huston, "for which I take my hat off to Errol Flynn."

Unlike the brawls in Hollywood movies, real fights between two strong antagonists do not end in quick knockouts. Flynn's first assaults had broken Huston's nose and opened a cut over his eye, but the lieutenant was in good physical condition, and sobering up by now, and determined to keep fighting. As a veteran of the ring, he knew that the main target was not the enemy's chin but his body, so he kept pounding at Flynn's ribs. Flynn began to clinch and wrestle, to hang on to the smaller man, and they both swore furiously as they fought. "The language . . . although not heated, was about as vile as it could get . . ." Huston said. "And those were the days when 'mother-fucker' was not a term of endearment."

For the better part of an hour, they flailed away at each other, out there in David Selznick's dark garden. When the party finally began to break up, the headlights of the cars emerging from the gravel driveway illuminated the two men still struggling. Selznick, the host, came running out to see what was happening. Half drunk himself, and pugnacious by nature, he assumed that Flynn was the aggressor and tried to join the fight on Huston's side. Then the usual chorus of bystanders managed to separate and restrain the combat-ants, as well as the would-be combatants. Both Flynn and Huston had to go to the hospital, Huston for his broken nose, Flynn for two broken ribs. Flynn later telephoned Huston to ask about his condition. "I said that I had thor-oughly enjoyed the fight," Huston said, "and hoped we'd do it again some time."

•   •   •

The war was clearly drawing to an end. The Allies landed in Normandy that June, and on the Riviera in August; Paris was liberated; General Mac-Arthur staged his melodramatic return to the Philippines. Soldiers were dying every day, but there was nonetheless a sense that the great struggle was ending, and already some of the lucky ones were coming home.

Darryl F. Zanuck inevitably saw to it that he was one of the lucky ones. Actually, he was pushed somewhat. A Senate investigating committee headed by Harry Truman of Missouri, which devoted most of its time to checking reports of waste and corruption in military spending, announced that it wanted to look into the army commissions that had been so easily granted to so many Hollywood notables—Colonel Zanuck, Colonel Capra, Colonel Roach, and the rest. Zanuck, for reasons never fully explained, flew to Wash-ington to see General Marshall, and then announced his resignation.

He returned to 20th Century–Fox and found it somewhat changed. His cofounder, William Goetz, the inept producer whose career was based largely on his marriage to Louis B. Mayer's older daughter, Edith,* had dared to assert his own authority. He had dared to order Zanuck's office repainted. It had always been a lurid shade of green known as "Zanuck green," which the producer applied not only to his office but to his house, his private sauna, his limousines, even his telephone. (Zanuck green turned out, on investigation, to be the shade of green that Zanuck's mother used to paint her fingernails.) Goetz had repainted Zanuck's office blue and decorated it with photographs of baseball players. Zanuck called in the studio painters to restore everything to Zanuck green.

Goetz had also bricked up the back entrance that Zanuck had used for his four o'clock rituals. ("Every day at four o'clock in the afternoon some girl on the lot would visit Zanuck in his office," said Milton Sperling, a young Fox writer who had made a reputation of sorts by concocting those ice-skating epics for Sonja Henie. "The doors would be locked after she went in, no calls were taken, and for the next half hour nothing happened—headquarters shut down. Around the office work came to a halt for the sex siesta. It was an understood thing. . . .")

Zanuck did not reopen the bricked-up back door—perhaps his army life had taught him to be slightly more discreet—but concentrated his fire on the

* When Zanuck walked out of Warners in 1933 and began organizing Twentieth Century Pic-tures, Nicholas Schenck invested $375,000 so that his brother Joe could be a partner, and Louis B. Mayer invested $375,000 so that Goetz could be one too.

"crap" that Goetz had approved. Some of the films in production, Zanuck said in a formal memo, "make me vomit—and will make the public vomit too if we make the mistake of showing them." Goetz tried briefly to defend himself. At one meeting, he accused the five-foot-five-inch Zanuck of bullying him and declared that he refused to be a doormat, but then he fled from the room, near tears. He went to seek counsel from his father-in-law, Louis B. Mayer, who advised him to abandon Fox and offered one million dollars to finance the move. And so it was announced that Goetz was moving to Universal as the head of an autonomous operation named International Films. Zanuck resumed full control at Fox.

Zanuck saw something that Mayer and the Warners never saw—that the war was changing American attitudes and perceptions, and that the sprightly little movies of the 1930's, the B pictures, the cheap Westerns and detective stories, would never again support the Hollywood studios. "The war is not yet over, but it soon will be," Zanuck declared to a meeting of his chief producers and directors on his first day back in command. "And when the boys come home from the battlefields overseas, you will find they have changed. They have learned things in Europe and the Far East. How other people live, for instance. How politics can change lives. . . . Oh, yes, I recognize that there'll always be a market for Betty Grable and Lana Turner and all that tit stuff. But they're coming back with new thoughts, new ideas, new hungers. . . . We've got to start making movies that entertain but at the same time match the new climate of the times. Vital, thinking men's blockbusters. Big-theme films."

Brave words, and basically true, but Zanuck didn't really have the judgment to carry out the mission he was proclaiming. The most important event in this last full year of war, apart from the battlefields on the road to victory, was the first revelation of the incredible things that had been happening in Poland. There had been reports of massacres of Jews ever since 1940, but it was only in the spring of 1944 that the holocaust reached its unimaginable climax in the shipment of nearly half a million Hungarian Jews to Auschwitz, and only in the summer of 1944 that the Soviet army liberated the first of the Polish death camps, Maidanek, and discovered the great heaps of bone and ash that had once been a whole people. Hollywood can hardly be blamed too harshly for failing to grasp what was happening, since President Roosevelt and a lot of other people failed in much the same way. But when one of Zanuck's lieutenants suggested that he should consider making a movie about the Nazi concentration camps, Zanuck briskly scorned the idea. "Any story about Germany or labor slaves appalls me," he declared in a memo to Kenneth MacGowan, the director. "Every picture yet made dealing with occupied countries including [John Steinbeck's] *The Moon Is Down* has laid a magnificent egg with the public. I can imagine no subject less inviting to an audience than the subject of slave labor at this time. . . . Show me how I can make a good story out of the life of Ernest R. Ball, and the great Irish songs he wrote."

Zanuck did produce a film on Ball, *Irish Eyes Are Smiling,* but the project that really captured his imagination, that struck him as a "thinking man's blockbuster," was a biography of one of America's coldest and most unloved presidents, Woodrow Wilson. Zanuck labored long over the script, struggling to convert the complexities of America's relationship to the world into the kind of scenes that his audiences would applaud. As President Wilson bade farewell to a group of departing doughboys, for example, one of them recited the traditional litany that appeared in so many World War II pictures: "Mike yonder's a Bohunk, this guy's Irish, Tex here claims he's just from plain Texas, and my name's Vespucci, Mr. President, but I'm just an American too." The only additional element needed to guarantee the failure of *Wilson* was to assign the title role to an obscure actor who actually resembled the frigid president, Alexander Knox. When Zanuck showed the final print of his patriotic pageant to his dutiful wife, Virginia, she dutifully said, "I'm proud of you." Zanuck was impressed. "I'm kind of proud of myself," he said. "I think it will win the Oscar."

Zanuck characteristically decided to stage the premiere not in Washington, not in Wilson's home town, but in his own, Wahoo, Nebraska. He took there a trainload of his highly paid captives—Betty Grable, Tyrone Power, Joan Fontaine, Gene Tierney—plus the usual contingent of the kept press. To the guests at a civic luncheon, he announced, "If my movies have reflected the spirit of America, the inspiration came from my boyhood days in Nebraska." The Wahoo movie theater was crowded at the premiere that October day in 1944, but the next day it was embarrassingly empty. One of the local citizens had to explain the spirit of America to Zanuck. "The people of Wahoo wouldn't have come to see Woodrow Wilson if he'd rode down Main Street in person," he said, "so why in hell should they pay to see him in a movie?"

Zanuck already had another vital, thinking man's blockbuster on his schedule. Like many self-made executives of his time, he had been mesmerized by the 1940 presidential campaign of Wendell Willkie, and Willkie's loss of the election did not disillusion him. When Willkie wandered around through all the regions of conflict and then produced a hopeful book titled *One World,* Zanuck glowed. He paid $100,000 for the movie rights, assigned the project to one of his favorite writers, Lamar Trotti, and spent nearly a year of his own time working with Trotti on the screenplay. When that was done, he tried to hire Spencer Tracy to play Willkie; Tracy was not interested. He tried to hire John Ford to direct the film; Ford was not interested. "If they aren't successful," he said of his blockbusters, *Wilson* and *One World,* "I'll never make another film without Betty Grable." *Wilson* lost a stunning two million dollars; *One World* was never filmed at all; Betty Grable went on supporting Zanuck's studio.

●　　●　　●

Another one of the unpleasant surprises that Zanuck discovered on his return from the wars was that Bill Goetz had somehow been persuaded to rehire Otto Preminger, a man Zanuck thought he had banished from the studio forever. Preminger was an ambiguous figure, very bright, very ambitious, very assertive, but somehow limited, conventional even in his most belligerent attempts to be unconventional. His father had been attorney general of Austria, a remarkable achievement for a Jew in a profoundly anti-Semitic society, but Preminger abandoned his own legal studies to become an actor on the Viennese stage, to become a director, to become an aide to the great Max Reinhardt and then his successor. He was only twenty-nine when Joe Schenck heard about him and signed him up during one of his talent-hunting tours of Europe. On his arrival, a chauffeured limousine took Preminger to a suite at the Beverly Wilshire, where flowers and champagne awaited him. Schenck welcomed him with a grand party. "Otto, this house will always be open to you," Schenck said. "Any time you want to come to dinner, don't even bother to phone. Just arrive. There will always be a plate for you on my table. As though you were my own son."

Zanuck, who was more directly in charge of things at Fox, told Preminger to spend his first weeks at the studio watching other directors and seeing how films were made. "When you think you're ready, just let me know," Zanuck said. When Preminger duly announced that he felt ready, he was handed a disaster, a stalled film entitled *Under Your Spell*, starring Lawrence Tibbett, a Metropolitan Opera baritone whom Zanuck had decided he should never have hired. Preminger somehow turned this disaster into a modest success. Zanuck was surprised and pleased. Preminger got better assignments, a new contract, a raise, invitations to dinner at Zanuck's palace. (It was perhaps during this phase of his success that Preminger encountered a group of his fellow expatriates, all talking Hungarian. "Come on," he protested, "we're all in America now, so talk German.")

Then Zanuck handed him one of the studio's biggest projects, one of Zanuck's personal productions, *Kidnapped*. Preminger had never heard of the Stevenson novel, had never been to Scotland, didn't want to make the movie. One of Zanuck's aides persuaded him that Zanuck could not be refused, but the first rushes did not look good. Zanuck summoned Preminger to scold him about a scene in which the boy said farewell to his dog. Once Zanuck had approved a script, no director was supposed to make any changes.

"I don't like the cuts you've made in that scene," Zanuck said, according to Preminger. "That's a very touching moment in the script. I am the producer. You have no right to make cuts."

"I didn't make any cuts in that scene," Preminger said.

"Do you mean to tell me I don't know my own script?" Zanuck shouted, turning to a revolving bookcase that contained all the scripts in production.

"Look at it!" Preminger shouted back. "You'll see that I have not cut a word."

"He began to suspect he was mistaken, which made him even wilder," Preminger recalled. "He ordered me out of his office." Zanuck's aide warned Preminger that he could save himself only by an immediate letter of apology to the producer. Preminger refused. Then he began learning for the first time how the Hollywood studios really worked. There were no further summonses to Zanuck's office, nor any invitations to the executive dining room. *Kidnapped* was assigned to someone else, and failed.

Since Preminger had a contract, he simply sat in his office and waited. One day he arrived to find that his name had been removed from the door, and the lock changed. He stayed at home, still being paid, but he wanted to work. He called Joe Schenck, who had told him to consider himself as Schenck's own son. Schenck's secretary said he was busy. Preminger called every day for several weeks, but Schenck was always busy. Preminger hired an agent to get him a job at any other studio, doing anything. Nobody wanted to risk offending Darryl Zanuck.

When Preminger's contract expired, he went to New York and found himself several plays to direct. One of them was Clare Boothe Luce's *Margin for Error,* and as she watched Preminger directing, she said to herself, according to Preminger's friend Willi Frischauer, "There's a Nazi for you." So when the German playing the villainous Nazi consul decided in the midst of rehearsals to return to Germany, Mrs. Luce proposed that Preminger replace him. There was something lugubrious about a Jew playing a Nazi in 1939, but Preminger delighted in his monocle, his saber scar and shaven head. He was such a success that when Fox decided to film the play—now that Zanuck was off at war—the studio asked Preminger to play the same role. Preminger boldly asked Bill Goetz to let him direct the movie, as he had directed the play. Goetz nervously refused. Preminger even more boldly offered to direct the film without pay. He added that if his first week's rushes were not satisfactory, he would accept dismissal and serve only as an actor. Goetz nervously agreed. And that was how, when Zanuck returned from the army, he found Preminger, whom he had exiled from Hollywood, back under contract at Zanuck's own studio.

One of the remarkable qualities about Zanuck, who was a very remarkable man, was that he had great confidence in his own ability to judge things on their merits, and to . . . not admit a mistake but correct a mistake, in his own seigneurial way. He summoned Preminger, whom he had not seen or spoken to for more than five years, to his mansion. A butler led the way to the garden. "Zanuck was sitting in swimming trunks beside his pool," Preminger recalled. "His back was to me. He glanced around briefly and then gave me the back of his head again. He picked up a piece of paper and said: 'I see you are working on a few things. I don't think much of them except for one, *Laura*. I've read it and it isn't bad. You can produce it but as long as I am at Fox you will never direct. Goodbye.' 'Goodbye,' I said to his back and left."

Everything in Preminger's life was a struggle, Preminger against the rest of the world. He worked on *Laura* with three different screenwriters, including the poet Samuel Hoffenstein, and the final script offended Vera Caspary, who had written the original novel. The supervising producer, Bryan Foy, didn't like it either. Foy didn't actually read scripts; he had an assistant named

David who did that. "David read the *Laura* script and says it's lousy," Foy said. Preminger gave a Hollywood answer: "David is making seventy-five dollars a week and I'm making fifteen hundred. He doesn't like it but I do. Maybe you'd better read it yourself." Foy did read it, or pretended to, and announced the next day: "David's right. The script stinks." Preminger asked him to send it to Zanuck for a verdict. "Zanuck hates you," Foy said. "All you need is for him to read this lousy script. He'll fire you."

Laura was all a series of gimmicks, true enough. The beautiful heroine was reported to have been murdered, and the young detective assigned to the case became infatuated with the portrait of the dead girl on the wall of her apartment (and there was that song by David Raskin and Johnny Mercer: "Laura is the face in the misty light . . . the laugh that floats on a summer night . . ."). And then there she was, not dead at all, and now a suspect in the murder of the friend who had been found dead in her apartment. And the demon in this dance of death was the waspish newspaper columnist Waldo Lydecker, who loved Laura not wisely and not well. Preminger always bore a grudge against such people, critics and columnists, so it must have seemed a great idea to have the homicidal villain be one of them, and one with odd sexual proclivities. *Laura* was to become one of the most celebrated examples of that odd and semi-European genre of the mid-1940's subsequently known as *film noir*.

Zanuck read the script, called both Preminger and Foy into his office, heard out Foy's criticisms, and then removed not Preminger but Foy from the project. But several directors declined the script, either because they didn't like it or because they didn't want to get caught in the continuing crossfire between Preminger and Zanuck. Yet the two enemies were already engaged in casting. Zanuck wanted John Hodiak as the young detective; Preminger persuaded him to gamble on a relatively untried newcomer, Dana Andrews. The title role, which was actually of secondary importance, was apparently turned down by Jennifer Jones, and then Zanuck talked a rather reluctant Gene Tierney into taking it. ("I have never felt my own performance was much more than adequate," she said later, with becoming modesty.)

For the essential part of Waldo Lydecker, Preminger was determined to hire Clifton Webb, who had never made a movie but was then playing in Noel Coward's *Blithe Spirit* at the Biltmore Theater in Los Angeles. Zanuck was dubious. His casting director, Rufus LeMaire, claimed that he had seen a test that M-G-M had made of Webb. "He doesn't walk, he flies," LeMaire sneered. Preminger asked to see the test, and LeMaire promised to produce it, but apparently no such test existed. Webb had been under contract to M-G-M for eighteen months without ever going before a camera. Preminger got Zanuck's approval to test Webb himself, but Webb refused to be tested. "My dear boy," he said, according to Preminger, "if your Mr. Zanuck wants to see if I can act let him come to the theater. I don't know your Miss Tierney. . . ." Zanuck was indignant. "I don't want to see him on the stage playing Noel Coward. I want to see him on film playing the part of Waldo

Lydecker." Preminger worked out an odd solution. On his own authority, he took a film crew to the Biltmore and filmed Webb delivering a monologue from *Blithe Spirit*. Then he showed the film to Zanuck, who was still indignant, and Zanuck said, "You're a son of a bitch, but you're right. He's very good."

By this time, Rouben Mamoulian had been signed up to direct *Laura*, and Mamoulian had lots of ideas of his own about sets and costumes and how the actors should act. He also asked Preminger, the producer, not to come near the set. "He said I made him nervous," Preminger recalled. Preminger acquiesced but insisted that the rushes be sent to Zanuck. Zanuck hated them. In the crowded executive dining room at Fox, Zanuck suddenly said to Preminger, "What do you think? Shall I take Mamoulian off the picture?" Preminger's answer was unequivocal: "Yes." So Zanuck finally gave him control of *Laura*, and he made the picture as he pleased, and nobody liked that either. The standard procedure, according to Preminger, was for a rough cut of a finished film to be shown in Zanuck's projection room, with Zanuck and the director in the front row and "a dozen of Zanuck's yes-men" arrayed behind them. "They didn't pay much attention to the picture," Preminger recalled. "They had developed the art of reading the back of Zanuck's neck to perfection. They were able to anticipate whether he liked the film or not and adjusted their reaction accordingly." On this occasion, Zanuck didn't even ask their opinions but just said gruffly to Preminger, "Well, we missed the boat on this one. Be at my office tomorrow at eleven."

As usual, Zanuck had a theory on how the picture should be fixed. He walked up and down his office, chewing his cigar, waving his polo mallet, dictating to a secretary his plan for a new ending. The first half of the film was narrated by Lydecker, the second half by the detective. Zanuck wanted a conclusion narrated by Laura herself. Preminger's reaction was to scowl, as only Preminger could scowl. "If you don't like it, I'll get another director," Zanuck snapped. Preminger professed his willingness to obey orders, if only "to save what I could."

So Zanuck's new ending was reluctantly filmed, and then the whole movie was brought back to Zanuck's projection room. This time, in addition to the yes-men, there was a newcomer sitting in the back of the room, Walter Winchell, accompanied by what Preminger described only as "a young lady." Winchell was an old friend of Zanuck's and also a very powerful Hearst columnist and radio newscaster ("Good evening, Mr. and Mrs. North and South America . . . let's go to press"). Winchell and the girl ignored the back of Zanuck's neck. They enjoyed the movie. They laughed at the right spots. "Zanuck seemed amazed," Preminger recalled. "He turned around several times and looked at them. When the screening was over, Winchell walked up to Zanuck and said in his staccato manner: 'Big time! Big time! Congratulations, Darryl. Except for the ending. I didn't get it. Didn't get it.' "

Once again, Zanuck demonstrated his ability to change course. "Would you like to put your old ending back?" he asked Preminger. "Yes," said Preminger. And so it was done. And it was about then that Clifton Webb, whose ill-suppressed hysteria was essential to the malevolent fascination of *Laura,* suffered a nervous breakdown. He checked himself into a sanitarium in New England. "He came out of it rested and restored," Miss Tierney said, "but the main effect of his analysis was to encourage him to be rude to his mother."

•   •   •

After the emotional triumph of *The Great Dictator,* which also grossed more money than any film that its creator had ever made, Charlie Chaplin floated from one possibility to another. At a dinner with Igor Stravinsky, the composer suggested that they try a collaboration, and Chaplin began improvising. The film would be set in a nightclub. The floor show would be the crucifixion of Christ. Most of the customers ignore it. A group of businessmen at one table go on talking excitedly about a big deal. At another table, a woman says, "I can't understand why people come here. It's depressing." "It's good entertainment," says her husband. "The place was bankrupt until they put on this show. Now they are out of the red." A drunk starts to shout: "Look, they're crucifying him! And nobody cares!" Stravinsky, who was then undergoing some kind of religious crisis—this was the period in which he wrote his great *Mass*—looked appalled. "That's sacrilegious!" he declared. "Is it?" Chaplin protested. "I never intended it to be."

At a lunch with Sir Cedric Hardwicke and Sinclair Lewis, he heard the two of them extol Paul Vincent Carroll's *Shadow and Substance,* in which Hardwicke had recently starred. Lewis said the character of Bridget was a modern Joan of Arc. Chaplin was interested, partly because he was also interested in a would-be actress named Joan Barry. She told him that she had seen the play on Broadway, and she asked to read some of Bridget's scenes from the script that Hardwicke had sent to Chaplin. Chaplin was surprised and impressed by her "excellent reading." He put her under contract at $250 per week and sent her to Max Reinhardt's acting school. He also bought the film rights to *Shadow and Substance* for $25,000 and set to work writing a screenplay. He soon began to have doubts about Miss Barry, however, about both her talent and her stability.

Then Orson Welles came to Chaplin's house one day with a new idea. He wanted to make a series of documentaries, and he was fascinated by the case of a French murderer named Henri Désiré Landru, a respectable Parisian *père de famille* who rented a villa near Rambouillet in 1914 and began advertising for women interested in matrimony. Landru was a bald and black-bearded man of nearly fifty, but throughout the five desperate years of World War I, he recorded in his account books that he had made love, of one sort or another, to 283 lonely and prosperous matrons. He was guillotined in 1922, protesting his innocence to the end, for having murdered ten of them. Welles, who had not yet encountered Rita Hayworth, wondered whether Chaplin would be interested in this misogynistic tale. Chaplin was very much interested—his first break from comedy—and asked to see the script. There wasn't any script yet, Welles said smoothly, just the record of Landru's trial.

"I thought you might like to help with the writing," Welles said. Chaplin was annoyed at such a demeaning offer and immediately rejected it, but a few days later he began to think that the story of Landru would make "a wonderful comedy." He telephoned Welles and bought all rights to the idea for five thousand dollars. "Now I put aside *Shadow and Substance* and began writing *Monsieur Verdoux*," Chaplin said. "I had been working three months on it when Joan Barry blew into Beverly Hills. My butler informed me that she had telephoned. I said that under no circumstances would I see her."

For most of his life up to that point, Chaplin had had the worst of luck with women. He wasn't really interested in them. He regarded them as toys, to be taken to bed and then put aside whenever he had serious work to do. "I must find a woman who understands that creative art absorbs every bit of a man," he once said. "When I am working, I withdraw absolutely from those I love. I have no energy, no love to give them." He also wanted those he loved to be very young, which usually meant that they had suspicious mothers. Late in 1917, at a party in Sam Goldwyn's house on the beach, Chaplin met someone he recalled as "a very silly young girl" named Mildred Harris. She was eighteen and he was twenty-nine. In about a year, she thought she was pregnant, and so they got married. The pregnancy was a false alarm, but then the new Mrs. Chaplin really got pregnant and gave birth to a malformed son, who died in three days. "We were irreconcilably mismated," Chaplin said later, recalling that when he proposed divorce to his young wife, who could rarely be found at home, she said, "All I want is enough money to look after my mother."

Lillita McMurray was six years old when her mother took her to a Hollywood restaurant for a birthday party, spotted Chaplin, and insisted on making introductions. She was twelve when one of her mother's friends introduced her to Chaplin again, and he was sufficiently impressed to cast her as the angel in *The Kid*. Four years later, Chaplin tested her as the dance hall girl in *The Gold Rush,* and with the hard-eyed innocence of an adolescent starlet, she asked Chaplin how he liked the test. "Not bad," he said. ("Marvelous," he had said to one of his aides.) "Goody, goody," said Lillita McMurray. Chaplin signed her to a contract at seventy-five dollars per week. He also changed her name to Lita Grey.

By this time, of course, he was much involved with the girl, and therefore he had to deal with her mother too. One of the mother's brothers, who happened to practice law, threatened to sue Chaplin if he did not marry his protégée, by then pregnant. Chaplin docilely took her and her mother to Mexico and got married. He was thirty-five and Lita sixteen. When they returned to Hollywood, they all moved into Chaplin's new mansion in Beverly Hills. This was a forty-room Spanish stucco place on a six-acre plot just below Pickfair, the famous estate of Mary Pickford and Douglas Fairbanks, Chaplin's partners in the founding of United Artists.

The new marriage was a disaster from the start. Chaplin's mother-in-law not only ran the house but regularly filled it with her friends and relatives. Chaplin spent most of his time at his office. He saw his young wife often enough for her to have two sons, Charles, Jr., and Sydney, but at the end of two years the Chaplins officially separated. Lita and her relatives demanded a big settlement, and so, since Chaplin was notoriously stingy, they filed a fifty-two-page document accusing him of transgressions ranging from spying to temporary desertion to infidelity with "a certain prominent moving picture actress" to demands that the young Lita gratify Chaplin's "degenerate sexual desires . . . too revolting, indecent and immoral to set forth in this complaint . . . the act of sex perversion defined by Section 288a of the Penal Code of California." Those who consulted Section 288a of the code discovered that it forbade oral sex, even between married couples, and threatened punishment of fifteen years in prison. Mrs. Chaplin also demanded half of the star's community property, which she estimated at $16 million (an estimate that apparently inspired the Internal Revenue Service to file a claim for $1,133,000 in back taxes). She also got a court order for temporary alimony of $3,000 a month. Chaplin responded by charging her with "unwomanly, unseemly" behavior and offering to let her have $25 a week. By the time all that was settled, Chaplin had to pay $625,000 for Lita, $200,000 for the children, and $950,000 for the lawyers.

Paulette Goddard, née Marion Levy, didn't have a mother with her when Chaplin first met her aboard Joe Schenck's yacht. She was already twenty-one, already a bit player in Hal Roach's Laurel and Hardy pictures, already married and divorced. Chaplin, by now forty-three and somewhat scarred, was charmed. With good reason. Miss Goddard was not only beautiful but intelligent, good-natured, and funny. Also very ambitious. Chaplin bought up her contract from Roach and starred her in *Modern Times* (1936), which ended with the two of them walking into the sunset, and *The Great Dictator*, which ended with Chaplin preaching the humanitarian virtues at her ("Look up, Hannah! Look up!"). Perhaps she was too ambitious, certainly too ambitious to accept Chaplin's total control of her career. He resented her applying to Selznick for the role of Scarlett O'Hara, and she resented his resentment. "It was inevitable that Paulette and I should separate," Chaplin later said, rather grandly. They agreed on a separation even before he started *The Great Dictator*, and though there was some doubt whether they had ever really been married, on that ship in Singapore Harbor, Miss Goddard went to Mexico in 1942 and got a divorce that ended whatever marriage had existed. (It was stated in connection with this divorce that she had married Chaplin in Canton, China, in 1936.) Miss Goddard never disclosed how much money she received—estimates ran to one million dollars—but she enjoyed joking about it. "I even got the yacht," she remarked.

Maybe Chaplin realized, for the first time, that he had lost someone valuable. He was now fifty-three, not a good age to be divorced for the third time. Perhaps that was why he seemed so vulnerable to the advances of an attractive redhead named Joan Barry. She was a friend, as they say, of J. Paul Getty, the oilman, who was just two years younger than Chaplin. She came

from Mexico to Hollywood with some letters of introduction that led her to
Tim Durant, a tennis-playing friend of Chaplin's, and they all went out to
dinner at Perrino's. "Miss Barry was a big handsome woman of twenty-two,"
Chaplin later recalled, in the peculiar prose of his memoirs, "well built, with
upper regional domes immensely expansive and made alluring by an extremely
low decolleté evening dress. . . ." That first encounter was "an innocuous
evening," Chaplin thought, but then Miss Barry telephoned and asked him to
invite her to lunch. He agreed, taking her first to an auction in Santa Barbara.
She told him that she had quarreled with Getty and was about to return to
New York but would stay in Hollywood if Chaplin wanted her to remain.
Chaplin "reared away in suspicion," he later claimed, and told her "not to
remain on my account." She called a day or two later and said that she was
still in Hollywood, and wondered whether she could see him that evening.
She could. "The days that followed were not unpleasant," Chaplin confessed,
"but there was something queer and not quite normal about them. Without
telephoning she would suddenly show up late at night at my house. . . ."

It was at about that time that Chaplin became interested in *Shadow and
Substance* and bought it for Miss Barry to star in. He seems to have thought
that she was really talented—and maybe she was—but her behavior became
increasingly bizarre. "Barry began driving up in her Cadillac at all hours of
the night, very drunk, and I would have to awaken my chauffeur to drive her
home," Chaplin recalled. "One time she smashed up her car in the driveway
and had to leave it there. . . . Finally she got so obstreperous that when she
called in the small hours I would neither answer the phone nor open the door
to her. Then she began smashing in the windows. Overnight, my existence
became a nightmare."

Chaplin learned that she hadn't been going to her classes at Max Reinhardt's school, and when he confronted her with that discovery, she said she
didn't want to be a movie star after all. She said, according to Chaplin, that if
he gave her five thousand dollars plus the train fare back to New York for
herself and her mother, she would tear up the contract between them. Chaplin agreed, relieved, and off she went.

Chaplin was busy, these days, not only with his movie projects and his
love life but also with politics. One of the big issues for speechmaking at this
particular point in the war was the Soviets' need for the Western allies to
open a second front by invading France. The American Committee for Russian War Relief asked Chaplin to substitute for the ailing Ambassador Davies
at a rally in San Francisco, and Chaplin began his emotional speech by saying,
"Comrades! And I mean comrades!" There was great applause. Chaplin was
quick to add: "I am not a Communist, I am a human being." But he went on
to urge that everyone in the audience of ten thousand send a telegram to
Roosevelt to urge the opening of a second front. This now seems innocuous
enough, but Chaplin claimed that he soon "began to wonder if I had said too
much and had gone too far." He reported that John Garfield told him after the
rally, "You have a lot of courage."

New invitations to speak kept arriving, and Chaplin kept accepting. ("How much was I stimulated by the actor in me and the reaction of a live audience?" he wondered.) A few weeks after his San Francisco speech, he addressed a CIO-sponsored rally in Madison Square Garden over a telephone hookup. He sounded much the way he had at the end of *The Great Dictator*: "Let us aim for victory in the spring. You in the factories, you in the fields, you in uniforms, you citizens of the world, let us work and fight towards that end. . . . Remember the great achievements throughout history have been the conquest of what seemed the impossible."

Then he got an invitation to speak at Carnegie Hall.

"Don't go," said Jack Warner, who had come to play tennis on Chaplin's court.

"Why not?" Chaplin asked.

"Let me tip you off, don't go," Warner mysteriously repeated.

Warner himself later claimed that, as in the making of *Mission to Moscow*, he was acting on a secret request from the White House. In his memoirs, which are perhaps even less reliable than those of Chaplin, he reported that Press Secretary Steve Early called him up and said, "The President wants you to see Chaplin and beg him to stay away from that rally. It could be very damaging to us at this stage if Chaplin lends his name to this movement."

Warner claimed that he told Chaplin that "some very big people in Washington told me to tell you about this," adding his own military judgment that "we're just not ready for a second front, and we don't want to kill a million men now just because Stalin is screaming." Warner further claimed that he had persuaded Chaplin.

"You promise not to go?"

"I promise."

Chaplin acknowledged no such promise. He said he regarded Warner's warnings only as "a challenge," and off he went.

In retrospect, there seems to be a certain element of fantasy and paranoia in all these recollections. The U.S. and Russia had been fighting on the same side for nearly six months by now, and the various organs of public enlightenment continually hymned the glories of the new alliance. The Red Army Chorus performed in New York, department stores sold babushkas, and even hardhearted old Louis B. Mayer produced the saccharine *Song of Russia*. It was in fact U.S. military policy to open a second front as soon as possible, not later than 1943. Dwight Eisenhower had drawn up the plans, and though the British were hesitant, General Marshall and President Roosevelt had endorsed them. So why should anyone object to a movie star urging a second front?

Chaplin insisted that dark forces were at work. Until the very eve of Pearl Harbor, he said, "the Nazis had made inroads into American institutions and organizations; whether these organizations were aware of it or not, they were being used as tools of the Nazis." Even after the U.S. went to war, he believed, the dark forces exercised dark powers. "As a result of my second front speeches my social life in New York gradually receded," he said. "No more was I invited to spend weekends in opulent country houses." Much the same sort of thing apparently happened in Hollywood. "The little tennis house and green lawn where once my father had held a gracious court were practically deserted on Sunday afternoons," his son Charles Chaplin, Jr., recalled. "I think my father must have been the loneliest man in Hollywood those days."

It is quite possible that politics played only a small part in the increasingly widespread dislike of Chaplin, that people were tired of his boundless egotism, his posturing and pretentiousness. Everyone seemed to know that the little tramp would never be seen again, and that Chaplin, having created him, was somehow responsible for killing him, and that the megalomaniac tyrant who danced with the globe in *The Great Dictator* was Hynkel/Hitler but was also Chaplin himself. Chaplin's three film statements from the late 1930's to the late 1940's were remarkably prophetic, remarkably right: *Modern Times, The Great Dictator,* and *Monsieur Verdoux.* Yet there is an old and very understandable tradition of beating the messenger who brings the bad news. That is not pure superstition; perhaps he deserved to be beaten.

Chaplin went to New York to make his second speech in October of 1942. On checking in at the Waldorf-Astoria Hotel, he found several messages saying that Joan Barry had called. "My flesh began to creep," he said later. Miss Barry had been staying at the Waldorf herself but had recently moved to Getty's hotel, the Pierre, and she wanted to see Chaplin. He did not answer her messages. A few nights later, he accidentally encountered her at the Stork Club, and she again asked if she could come to see him. In a misjudgment that seems almost suicidal, Chaplin agreed. He made sure, however, that his friend Tim Durant stayed with them. Miss Barry told Chaplin her latest financial troubles, and he gave her three hundred dollars. Nothing more happened, Chaplin insisted, and that was their only encounter in New York.

With the three hundred dollars that Chaplin had given Miss Barry to alleviate her financial troubles, she followed him back to Hollywood. That was when his butler told him that she was telephoning, and Chaplin said he wouldn't talk to her. Miss Barry bought a gun, drove to Chaplin's house at 1 A.M., broke a window, and clambered into his study. She found Chaplin in his second-floor bedroom and kept him covered with the gun while she harangued him for an hour and a half about her problems. Then she put the gun on a bedside table. Then they had sex. Then she picked up the gun, and they spent the night in separate bedrooms. Then he agreed to give her some more money, and she went away.

A week later, she reappeared at Chaplin's house, and this time he called the police, "something I should have done before." Chaplin had dreaded what the newspapers would make of this saga, but he found that the Beverly Hills police were, as anyone could have told him, "most cooperative." They booked Miss Barry on a charge of vagrancy but said that the charge would not be pressed if Chaplin paid her fare back to New York, and if she went. An emissary from the Chaplin studio paid her one hundred dollars to leave, but she didn't leave. She went out to Chaplin's house again and created what the police called "a disturbance." Chaplin again telephoned for help, and the police reappeared. During these alarums and excursions, Miss Barry took an overdose of barbiturates. The police pumped out her stomach. They kept her in jail for thirty days on the vagrancy charge.

Early in 1943, Miss Barry found that she was pregnant and accused Chaplin of being the father. "Isn't it a fact," Jerry Giesler later asked her in court, "that on June first, 1943, in the yard of Mr. Chaplin's home, when you were alone with him, you accused him of being the father of your unborn child, and didn't you tell him that unless he gave your mother $65,000 and placed $75,000 in trust for the baby, you'd make trouble for him—that the press was on your side, and when they got through with him they would blast him out of the country?" Miss Barry denied making any such threat, but she did file a paternity suit against Chaplin. He denied everything.

Chaplin by now was once again involved with an adolescent girl, and a beauty, Oona O'Neill, the daughter of Eugene O'Neill. She was just seventeen, a debutante with vague theatrical ambitions, out in Hollywood to inspect the scene. Orson Welles, the eternal magician, took her to a nightclub on their first date and read her palm and said, "Within a very short time you will meet and marry Charles Chaplin." Hal Wallis's sister Minna, a Hollywood agent who thought that Miss O'Neill might get the part of Bridget in Chaplin's version of *Shadow and Substance,* invited them both to dinner at her house. Chaplin found Miss O'Neill "of a luminous beauty, with a sequestered charm and a gentleness that was most appealing." They were married that June.

In October, Miss Barry gave birth to a girl she named Carol Ann. Chaplin's lawyer had worked out a deal to pay her $25,000 if she and the baby would submit to blood tests to see whether Chaplin was the father. If they all had the same blood type, that would not prove that he was the father, of course, but a difference would prove that he wasn't. In the midst of these negotiations, Chaplin got a call from Justice Frank Murphy of the Supreme Court, who warned him that some politicians he had met at a dinner party in Washington had spoken of planning "to get Chaplin." More paranoia? In January of 1944, a federal grand jury indicted Chaplin for violating the Mann Act, an antiprostitution law of 1910, which made it a federal crime to transport a woman across a state line for immoral purposes. Every once in a while, not often, the federal authorities invoked this antique statute to harass someone they didn't like. The first black heavyweight champion, Jack Johnson, who married three different white women, was convicted under the Mann Act in 1913, fled the country to avoid imprisonment, but finally served a year in jail for his sins. And now, on February 10, 1944, the federal authorities claimed that Chaplin had violated the Mann Act by paying Joan Barry's railroad fare to New York and then meeting her there.

Five days after Chaplin's indictment, the blood tests on Miss Barry's baby showed that Chaplin couldn't possibly be the father. Miss Barry was type A, her baby was type B, and Chaplin was type O. Chaplin felt exonerated, but the federal indictment did not say that he had fathered Miss Barry's baby; it said that he had transported her across a state line for immoral purposes. Chaplin's friends persuaded him to call in the famous Jerry Giesler, and Giesler fought the case on what he considered the perfectly sensible ground that a man "who could have enjoyed Miss Barry's favors in Los Angeles for as little as twenty-five cents carfare, would [not] pay her fare to New York . . . for immoral purposes."

Chaplin suffered a lot of criticism in the press, which regarded him as vain and arrogant, but he knew how to play his new role. "Chaplin was the best witness I've ever seen in a law court," Giesler said later. "He was effective even when he wasn't being examined . . . but was merely sitting there, lonely and forlorn, at a far end of the counsel table. He is so small that only the tops of his shoes touched the floor. He looked helpless, friendly and wistful, as he sat there with the whole weight of the United States Government against him." The federal indictment was ridiculous, and Giesler won a fairly quick acquittal. "I believe in the American people," Chaplin said, just like Errol Flynn, just like every acquitted criminal. "I have abiding faith in them. In their sense of fair play and justice."

He was to learn better. Chaplin thought that Miss Barry's paternity suit against him had been nullified by the blood tests, certified by three doctors, declaring that he could not be the father of the baby. But the judge ruled that the "ends of justice" would best be served by a "full and fair trial of the issue." Chaplin, perhaps overconfident that a medical decree of his innocence must lead to an acquittal, had abandoned the artful Giesler and entrusted his case to a more ordinary lawyer. Miss Barry entrusted hers to an old-fashioned orator named Joseph Scott. Ignoring the scientific evidence of Chaplin's innocence, Scott proceeded to attack the star as a "master mechanic in the art of seduction," and a "cheap Cockney cad," and a "little runt of a Svengali," and a "gray-headed old buzzard," and a "reptile [who] just looked upon her as so much carrion."

The trial ended with a hung jury, seven to five for acquittal; the second trial, in April of 1944, ended with an eleven-to-one verdict for Miss Barry. Chaplin, who could not have been the father, was ordered to pay $75 per week to support Carol Ann until the age of twenty-one, a tidy sum amounting to $82,000, and he did pay it. He then took Oona, pregnant, to live in Nyack, up the Hudson from New York, while he wrote the screenplay of *Monsieur Verdoux,* about a man who murdered love-hungry women. Miss Barry was eventually committed to a state mental hospital.

•   •   •

One of the cornerstones of the Hollywood studios' monopoly was the standard contract by which they controlled actors, directors, and any other people they considered valuable. The standard contract lasted for seven years, renewable every six months at the wish of the studio, usually with an increase in pay if the studio decided to renew. The studios justified these contracts on the ground that they invested time and money in developing an actor's career, and during the Depression, both the actor and the studio benefited from the security of a long-term contract. It was theoretically possible to free-lance (Charles Boyer, Cary Grant, and a few others insisted on signing for just one picture at a time), but the studios naturally favored their contract players, and few people dared to take the risks of the jungle.

They were frightened people, many of these famous stars, emerging from origins of poverty and conflict, driven onward not by talent or vocation so much as by the simple hunger for what Hollywood could give them: riches, success, fame. (Lana Turner was surprised to realize, on making a count, that she had acquired 698 pairs of shoes.) And among the few who triumphed, and thus acquired a surrounding phalanx of managers, agents, publicists, paid companions, there remained always an element of panic. "They didn't know what they had," as the screenwriter Daniel Fuchs put it in his novel *West of the Rockies,* "what it was in them that accounted for their good fortune. They didn't know how to present it, manipulate it, embellish it, portion it out— since they didn't know what it was or whether in fact they had anything at all."

The standard contract gave the studio not only the right to decide on each renewal but also the right to make all the professional decisions in the actor's life. The studio told him which film he would make next, and who else would be in it, and who would produce and direct it. If the studio had no immediate work for the actor, it could "loan" him out to another studio for any film that the other studio wanted to make, and the loan-out fee went entirely to the studio, which paid the actor his regular salary out of its profits on the loan. If the actor heard of an interesting movie at some other studio and wanted to be loaned out to take a part in it, that, of course, was a decision to be made by the studio that owned him. It might agree, or it might think him too valuable to loan, or it might, for various reasons, want to punish him by refusing. The studio that owned him could also command him to take part in publicity tours, or just about anything else that it wanted him to do. In fact, some studio contracts forbade an actor to leave Los Angeles for any reason without the studio's permission.

In addition to all this, the standard contract contained what was known as the "morals clause." When M-G-M signed up the nineteen-year-old Ava Gardner in 1941, for example, its contract made her promise that she agreed "to conduct herself with due regard to public conventions and morals," and that she would not "do or commit any act or thing that will degrade her in society, or bring her into public hatred, contempt, scorn or ridicule, that will tend to shock, insult, or offend the community or ridicule public morals or decency, or prejudice the producer or the motion picture industry in general." Miss Gardner signed, perhaps with fingers crossed, and so did everybody else.

If an actor objected to the next film assignment, or anything else, his only recourse was to refuse the studio's orders, whereupon the studio was entitled to suspend the actor without pay, indefinitely, or until he agreed to do as he was told. Furthermore, the period of suspension was added to the end of the contract, so that the actor owed the studio not just seven years of his life but seven submissive and obedient years. To any reasonable outsider, this standard contract seemed extremely unfair, and the only thing more remarkable than the contract itself was the labor unions' docile acceptance of it. "As a union contract which gives the employer the right to fire a worker every six months . . . it is unique in trade union history," wrote a sociologist named Hortense Powdermaker in *Hollywood, The Dream Factory* (1950). "Hollywood presents the picture of a 100 percent union community, paying the highest salaries in the country . . . but with the atmosphere of a company town." The standard contract, she added, "smacks more of mediaeval power relationships between lord and serf than of employer and employee in the modern world of industry."

The first rebel to challenge this system in court was Bette Davis. Having won the 1935 Academy Award for *Dangerous,* she didn't like the scripts that Warner Bros. kept sending her. She also wanted her sixteen-hundred-dollar weekly salary doubled. Jack Warner balked, and when the news of the argument leaked out, a producer in London offered Miss Davis a contract to make two movies for him. She accepted and promptly departed for England. Jack Warner pursued her with a charge of breach of contract, and in the fall of 1936, the controversy came before the bewigged legal authorities of London. It was not a very distinguished trial. Jack Warner testified that his company had built Miss Davis "up almost from oblivion to what the company thinks is a very great height." His lawyer, Sir Patrick Hastings, accused Miss Davis of being "a very naughty young lady." But the main legal point was that a contract was a contract, and the London court could only conclude that Miss Davis had freely committed herself to Warner Bros. The decision left her with nothing but a thirty-thousand-dollar legal bill. Jack Warner, to his credit, paid most of it.

Still, holdouts and suspensions were more of a problem at Warners than anywhere else. They were relatively rare at M-G-M and almost unknown at Paramount. Perhaps Warners' problem lay in Jack Warner's fondness for typecasting, or perhaps simply in the feistiness of his repeatedly suspended stars—Bette Davis, Errol Flynn, Jimmy Cagney, Humphrey Bogart, John Garfield. (Warner had similar difficulties with one of his three-hundred-dollar-per-week hirelings, William Faulkner.)

The one star who fought him the hardest was Olivia de Havilland, whom Warner had first seen and admired as Hermia in Max Reinhardt's Hollywood Bowl version of *A Midsummer Night's Dream.* She was eighteen, and according to Warner, she was "a girl with big, soft brown eyes . . . and a fresh young beauty that would soon stir a lot of tired old muscles around the film town." Despite all this, Warner had very little idea what to do with her. Almost by chance, he cast her opposite the unknown Errol Flynn in *Captain Blood* (1935), and when that proved a great success, he cast them both in a variety of sequels.

It was after the friendly intervention of Warner's wife, Ann (Miss de Havilland was nothing if not resourceful), that the actress got permission to play Melanie in *Gone With the Wind.* After that, Warner went right on putting her in second-rate films like *Devotion,* an ill-conceived biography of the Brontë sisters, and *Princess O'Rourke,* the title of which is description enough. There were various explanations for this Hollywood tradition of miscasting. One was that the studios had to produce a good deal of fodder to satisfy their theater chains; another was that they believed a star could carry an inferior film; another was that they sometimes assigned a star to a bad script as a form of discipline; and yet another was that they didn't know the difference between good and bad, and didn't much care.

Whatever the reasons, Warner's assignments exasperated Miss de Havilland, and her exasperation was compounded by the fact that David Selznick was finding much better roles for her beautiful but somewhat less talented younger sister, Joan Fontaine. *Rebecca* had made Miss Fontaine a star, and Hitchcock's *Suspicion* had won her an Academy Award in 1941. While Miss de Havilland was struggling to impersonate Charlotte Brontë in *Devotion,* her sister was starring opposite Orson Welles in the title role of *Jane Eyre.* Miss de Havilland began suffering from a series of headaches, temper tantrums, mysterious swellings in the legs. She refused Warner's latest offering, *The Animal Kingdom,* and so she was suspended.

It was her sixth suspension, and since the periods of suspension kept being added to her contract, she went to her lawyer, Martin Gang, and asked whether there was any way to break the Warner Bros. standard contract. Gang said he had been doing some research on this very question, and he believed that the studio contract violated an old California law against peonage. He urged her to sue for relief, and so she did. Ronald Reagan, oddly enough, later credited this idea not to Gang but to an agent, Lew Wasserman. He said that he and Miss de Havilland and Wasserman were all having lunch together when Wasserman remarked that "Hollywood contracts are always seven years [because] there is a California law that anything beyond seven becomes slavery. . . . It was his opinion that the Hollywood custom of suspending actors . . . and then adding the suspension time to their contracts was illegal. Fiery Olivia rose to this like a trout (a pretty trout) to a fly. She had taken so many suspensions she could grow old and still be on her original seven-year deal. What happened is history. . . ."

What happened was also prophetic. Jack Warner's response to Miss de Havilland's suit was to blacklist her. He did this by notifying every other studio in writing that she was under exclusive contract to Warner Bros., and although she was suing to break that contract, Warners would insist on its rights until the litigation was settled. The obvious result of Warner's letter was that Miss de Havilland remained unemployed and unemployable, and her legal bills were to reach twelve thousand dollars, which Warner did not pay. There were protracted hearings. Warner's attorneys even dragged in Miss de Havilland's private life, asking whether she had declined *The Animal Kingdom* because of an affair. When Gang asked that all this be stricken from the record, the judge refused, observing that "it's nice to have a little romance in the hearing, isn't it?"

In March of 1944, the court ruled in Miss de Havilland's favor. Jack Warner appealed the verdict, and once again wrote to all the other studios, threatening a lawsuit against anyone who hired the rebellious actress. Nobody did. Unable to work, Miss de Havilland decided to spend her time touring military bases in Alaska. Warner, by now vindictive beyond all reason, approached General Hap Arnold, head of the Army Air Forces, and tried to get Miss de Havilland barred from the tour. Arnold quite sensibly declined. In the fall of 1944, Miss de Havilland set off to entertain the troops in New Caledonia, in the South Pacific. She was in Suva, in the Fiji Islands, when she collapsed with viral pneumonia, suffered a fever of 104, coughed blood, shrank to ninety pounds. And it was there that she learned that the California Supreme Court had ruled in her favor. She was free of her contract. She had won. Jack Warner had lost, and by implication, the whole studio system had lost. It was only a crack in that system, but the cracks were spreading.

There was another crack in the system, which would ultimately prove considerably more important—in fact, devastating—but these future effects were still unknown, unanticipated, unfeared, for the crack had been there more than a decade. At issue was whether the big studios, which had started as rebels against Thomas Edison's "Trust," had now formed an illegal trust of their own, monopolizing the business, suppressing competition. They had, of course, but that remained to be proved. And though it was symbolically significant that a Jack Warner could blacklist an Olivia de Havilland, the most important aspect of the monopoly was that the producers controlled their own distribution system. As of 1940, a Justice Department survey of thirty-five major cities showed that Paramount owned thirty-five first-run movie houses, Warner Bros. thirty-five, 20th Century–Fox thirty, RKO twenty-nine, and Loew's (M-G-M) twenty-four. There were also independent chains and individual theaters, but they could buy only what they were offered, and the studios offered only "block booking," that is, one or two popular movies plus a cluster of B pictures, westerns, whatever the studio wanted to sell. The theater owners, moreover, had to buy what they were offered without seeing it. This was how the great showmen made their money.

The long and complicated effort to break up the Hollywood monopoly began in 1933 with an obscure suit in Camden, New Jersey. It was filed by an independent distributor named the Victoria Amusement Company, which had been unable to get the pictures it wanted from Warner Bros., and which charged in Camden Federal Court that Warners was part of "a motion picture trust" that was trying to "impair and destroy" all independents like the Victoria Amusement Company. More than fifty attorneys representing various interested parties descended on Camden to argue the case, and it was finally dropped. Perhaps some money changed hands, perhaps not.

The suit served, however, to interest the Justice Department in whether Hollywood's practices really did violate the Sherman Anti-Trust Act. After a five-year FBI investigation, it decided that they did. In July of 1938, the chief of the department's antitrust division, Thurman Arnold, charged the eight biggest film companies, twenty-four subsidiaries, and 133 individual executives with violating the Sherman Act. Hollywood's first response was to send its figurehead, former Postmaster General Will Hays, to see President Roosevelt and complain that if the Justice Department deprived the studios of their distribution systems, they would be "wrecked at a blow." Roosevelt brushed him aside.

The same conflict was taking place in Congress. Starting in 1935, several bills were introduced to regulate Hollywood, or at least to outlaw block booking and blind selling, and each measure attracted flocks of lobbyists from both sides, not only the studios and the theater owners but also civic and educational organizations. In the spring of 1939, the Senate passed a ban on block booking, but the House delayed.

Thurman Arnold, whom some regarded as a leading light of the New Deal and others as a pretentious publicity-seeker, brought the Justice Department's case to trial before Federal Judge Henry W. Goddard in June of 1940. "If we are to maintain an industrial democracy we must stop the private seizure of power," he warned, "and that is exactly what we have in the film industry." He even suggested that the studio chiefs deserved to face criminal charges, but he added that "it seems a little late to start" a criminal prosecution.

The Hollywood forces responded with various kinds of bombast. The attorney for M-G-M, John W. Davis, the Democratic presidential candidate who had lost to Coolidge in 1924, spoke scornfully of Arnold as a "knight in shining armor" and shook his fist at him. Paramount attorney Thomas D. Thacher wanted it known that his client had "progressed in the extraordinary perfection of its product . . . and in the excellence of conditions surrounding its exhibition." After several days of argument, Arnold surprised many observers by accepting a rather feeble compromise, which ended not only the litigation but also the congressional action. In a consent decree designed to last three years, the government agreed to drop its attempts to separate the studios from the theaters, and the studios agreed to limit block booking to five films, to stop pressuring theaters to take films they didn't want, and to halt any further expansion of their theater ownership.

There it might have ended, but during the three years covered by the consent decree, the studios went right on applying pressure on the theaters. Or so the Justice Department said. So in August of 1944, Justice started all over again. It reactivated its complaint against Paramount and others, charging once again that the Hollywood system was illegal.

●   ●   ●

Thunder and lightning. In the darkness, an old coach creaks and lurches along a mountain road. By a flash of lightning, we see that the antique lettering on the side of the wagon says "Professor Lampini's Chamber of Horrors." Darkness again. In the distance a medieval castle, all turrets and ramparts. The camera abandons the rickety coach and closes in on the castle. We see a warder with a lantern, and we follow him down a long, dark corridor lined with barred cells. Suddenly a long arm flashes out from one of the cells and grasps the warder around the neck. Gurgles and groans. Closeup on a white-bearded man who has seized the struggling warder. And now, at last, the white-bearded man speaks the first words in this grotesque movie: "Where is my chalk? Give me my chalk!"

It is Boris Karloff, the evil Dr. Gustav Niemann, who has been sentenced to fifteen years in this dungeon for having experimented in transplanting human brains. His brother, it soon turns out, once worked for the famous Baron Frankenstein and "learned his secrets," and even though Dr. Niemann has been locked up in this dungeon, he is trying to continue planning future experiments on a blackboard. Hence his rage at the loss of his chalk.

In the adjoining cell, there is a hunchback named Daniel (J. Carroll Naish), who calls Karloff "master" and dreams of being made tall and straight. "If I had Frankenstein's records to guide me," says Karloff, "I could give you a perfect body." Almost on cue, a bolt of lightning strikes the ancient fortress and knocks a big hole in the wall. Dr. Niemann and Daniel totter out through the rubble and find themselves free men. And whom should they encounter in the pelting rain but Professor Lampini, whose peripatetic chamber of horrors is stuck in the mud? A stout shove by Daniel helps get the show back on the road, so Professor Lampini can hardly help giving his rescuers a ride, and telling them a bit about his treasures, notably the coffin that contains the staked skeleton of Count Dracula.

Fascinating, says Dr. Niemann, who is determined to roll on to Reigelburg, where he has some scores to settle with the doctors and bureaucrats who had him locked up. But we're not going to Reigelburg, says Professor Lampini. A long pause. Then, at a nod from Dr. Niemann, Daniel lunges toward Professor Lampini, his hands stretched forward to strangle. "No! No!" cries Professor Lampini. The next morning, we see a clean-shaven Dr. Niemann setting up shop in Reigelburg, pretending to be Professor Lampini, demonstrating such marvels as the staked skeleton of Count Dracula. Rubbish, says Burgomaster Russmann, one of those narrow-minded children of the Enlightenment. That night, Dr. Niemann pulls the stake from the skeleton, and the skeleton quickly turns into the black-caped figure of John Carradine, ready to go hunting. And we haven't yet come near to Frankenstein's ruined castle, where Dr. Niemann will discover the fabulous monster, entombed in ice. Curt Siodmak, another one of those versatile refugees from Berlin, concocted this delectable absurdity, and it was to be called *The House of Frankenstein.*

Absurdity—campy absurdity—was probably the only way Hollywood could deal with horror, because that was the only way it had ever known. Hollywood horror films, no matter how gory or pseudo-gory they were to become, never approached real horror. How could they—nurtured on the remembered images of a Lon Chaney scuttling about in *The Hunchback of Notre Dame* or *The Phantom of the Opera*? If it seems vaguely ironic that *The*

House of Frankenstein appeared in 1944, the year in which the Red Army liberated Maidanek, the first of the horrifying Polish death camps to be captured, perhaps it is only the accidental irony of coincidence. There is certainly a long tradition of critics trying to explicate the inner significance of Hollywood's horror movies. Parker Tyler, for example, suggested that Frankenstein's monster was a phallic symbol, rigid and threatening. But if this seems an excessively psychoanalytic view of a few *schlockmeisters* trying to make a few dollars, Stephen King has offered an interesting counterargument. "These were nightmares for profit, granted," the creator of *Carrie* wrote in *Danse Macabre,* "but nightmares is nightmares, and in the last analysis it is the profit motive that becomes unimportant and the nightmare itself which remains of interest."

It is hard to tell exactly where in the tribal memory the nightmare of the man-made monster originated. Mary Wollstonecraft Shelley said she had gone to bed and could not sleep, and her imagination "possessed and guided me, gifting the successive images that arose in my mind with a vividness far beyond the unusual bounds of reverie." It had been an exciting evening in the villa on the outskirts of Geneva in June of 1816. Lord Byron, busily working away on the third canto of *Childe Harold,* had suggested to his cluster of friends that each should tell a ghost story. He himself told one, which later appeared at the end of his *Mazeppa,* and Shelley told one, but the nineteen-year-old Mary Shelley couldn't think of anything until that night, when her imagination possessed her and made her see a vision.

"I saw—with shut eyes, but acute mental vision—I saw the pale student of unhallowed arts kneeling beside the thing he had put together," Mrs. Shelley later wrote. "I saw the phantasm of a man stretched out, and then, on the working of some powerful engine, show signs of life and stir with an uneasy, half vital motion. Frightful must it be, for supremely frightful would be the effect of any human endeavor to mock the stupendous mechanism of the Creator of the world." Despite these pious objections, Mrs. Shelley went on to report that her vision included the sight of the created man confronting his creator "and looking at him with yellow, watery, but speculative eyes."

Mrs. Shelley's monster was rather intellectual, and after eavesdropping on other intellectuals, it could quote freely from Plutarch's *Lives* or Milton's *Paradise Lost,* but when this saga was presented on the London stage in 1823 as *Presumption; or the Fate of Frankenstein,* the monster had already acquired his modern form; he was bluish in color, and his speech was limited to grunts. And so he remained up through Peggy Webling's *Frankenstein,* which appeared on the London stage in 1927. Carl Laemmle of Universal had wanted to film Mrs. Shelley's *Frankenstein* since the early 1920's. He saw it as a vehicle for Lon Chaney, his star monster, but Chaney apparently considered this Gothic melodrama too horrendous for him. Laemmle then settled on a Hungarian newcomer, Bela Lugosi, who had seemed ripely evil in the recently completed *Dracula.* Outfitted with a wig and covered with a coating of clay, Lugosi tottered around in a series of tests. Carl Laemmle, Jr., newly in command, thought the results ridiculous and canceled his father's whole project. So *Frankenstein* returned to that limbo of stories that somebody or other wanted to do but nobody knew how to do right.

Then along came James Whale, an English theater manager who had achieved a modest success in Hollywood by directing *Waterloo Bridge*. Universal asked him what he would like to do next, and out of about thirty moribund projects that were awaiting someone to harness lightning and bring them to life, Whale chose *Frankenstein*. "I thought it would be amusing," he said later, "to try and make what everybody knows is a physical impossibility believable for sixty minutes." Universal wanted Leslie Howard to play Frankenstein, but Whale insisted on casting a friend of his, Colin Clive. And then there was the question of the monster.

Whale was eating lunch in the Universal cafeteria when he saw a middle-aged man with a remarkable face. He had been born William Pratt, the ninth child in a family largely devoted to the British colonial service, but as a wandering actor in Canada, supporting himself between theatrical jobs by working as a farmhand or truckdriver or whatever he could find, he took for himself a name from somewhere in his mother's family, Karloff, and preceded it with a name of his own invention, Boris.

He had drifted down to California and played a number of bit parts, and he was later to say that success was "simply a matter of being on the right corner at the right time." Karloff's corner was the cafeteria at Universal, where he was eating lunch when an emissary from Whale came and asked him to join the director for a cup of coffee. "He asked me if I would make a test for him tomorrow," Karloff recalled. " 'What for?' I asked. 'For a damned awful monster!' he said. Of course, I was delighted, because it meant another job if I was able to land it."

At forty-four, Karloff was still no more than a journeyman character actor. His top rate was $150 a week, and he had already made thirteen movies that year. Now he stoically consigned his future to Universal's chief makeup man, Jack Pierce. This virtuoso, who was later to create such cosmetic marvels as the Mummy and the Wolf Man, blamed himself for Lugosi's failure as the Frankenstein monster. Before letting Karloff be tested, he spent three weeks experimenting in what a monster should look like. He investigated various aspects of anatomy and surgery. "I discovered there are six ways a surgeon can cut the skull," he said later, "and I figured Dr. Frankenstein, who was not a practicing surgeon, would take the easiest. That is, he would cut the top of the skull straight across like a pot lid, hinge it, pop the brain in, and clamp it tight. That's the reason I decided to make the Monster's head square and flat like a box and dig that big scar across his forehead and have metal clamps hold it together. The two metal studs that stick out the sides of his neck are inlets for electricity—plugs. Don't forget that the Monster is an electronic gadget."

Every aspect of the monster's appearance had to be worried about. "My first problem," Pierce said, "was not to let his eyes be too intelligent, which is why I decided to use the false eyelids that half veil the eyes." These were made of rubber and glued onto Karloff's eyelids, then covered with a layer of wax. Then there was the porous-looking skin, which Pierce built up with layers of cheesecloth, and the coloring, which was supposed to be grayish-white but didn't look right under klieg lights until Pierce used a grayish-green tone. It took the makeup man three and a half hours every morning to apply all his magic to Karloff's face, and nearly as long every evening to wipe it off. And then Karloff had to be dressed in a double-quilted suit with a short-sleeved coat, to make his arms look longer, and propped up with steel struts, to make his legs stay stiff, and shod with huge eighteen-pound boots used by asphalters, to achieve a properly lumbering gait. Thus outfitted, he stood seven and a half feet high and could hardly move. "We shot *Frankenstein* in mid-summer," Karloff recalled. "After an hour's work, I would be sopping wet. I'd have to change into a spare undersuit, often still damp from the previous round. So I felt, most of the time, as if I were wearing a clammy shroud. No doubt it added to the realism."

Realism, of course, was not what made *Frankenstein* a pop classic. Like the original novel from which it so markedly differed, it had the quality of a fable, fabulous both in its exaggerations and in its essential innocence. And Karloff endowed the monster with a kind of guileless charm. In its day, though, it was considered quite shocking. At a preview in Santa Barbara, one woman and her daughter ran screaming from the theater, so Universal edited out the scene in which Karloff accidentally drowned the girl with whom he had been picking flowers. The studio also decided to change the ending, in which Frankenstein and the monster both died in the flames of a burning mill. In the revised version, the aristocratic scientist survived to hear his father propose a toast "to a son of the house of Frankenstein." Carl Laemmle, Sr., also insisted that his son provide an introductory warning about how horrifying the film was, and "if any of you do not care to subject your nerves to such a strain, now's your chance to . . ." And so on.

It was an enormous success, and deservedly so. And coming right after Lugosi's *Dracula,* it inspired Hollywood's imitators to create a whole cycle of horror movies. The first actual sequel was the admirable *Bride of Frankenstein* (1935), in which a frizzy-wigged Elsa Lanchester was brought to life as a companion for the lonely monster—and rejected him. Then, almost inevitably, came *Son of Frankenstein* (1939). But the horror stars were believed to transcend their roles. Universal combined Karloff and Lugosi in its far-fetched version of Poe's *The Black Cat* (1934) and *The Raven* (1935). By the end of the 1930's, though, the endless reworking of the formulas had become rather tiresome. *Dracula* had given birth to *Son of Dracula* (written by Siodmak) and *Dracula's Daughter; The Invisible Man* had led to *The Invisible Woman* (also by Siodmak); *The Mummy* reappeared in *The Mummy's Hand; The Werewolf of London* evolved into *The Wolf Man,* and then came *Frankenstein Meets the Wolf Man* (Siodmak again).

Karloff, who appeared in some of these things, and worse, was always very professional (he was one of the founders of the Screen Actors Guild and took pride in possessing membership card number nine), but he did wonder why all the mad-scientist plots had to be so similar: "A man who gets hold of [an] idea," as he put it, in a quite unconscious analogy to the Hollywood view of the rise of fascism, "where if he can work it out right (some new force, new medicine, or a new way of operating) it will be of enormous value to mankind at large. But he becomes fanatical about it, and the thing goes wrong, and he goes wrong with it. He goes off his head, and reluctantly, in the last act, you have to destroy him. . . ." Perhaps better writers might concoct some new ideas, Karloff suggested to Harry Cohn, who had signed him up for a series of thrillers at Columbia. "He was in an expansive mood," Karloff recalled. "He opened the desk drawer and pulled out a great chart. 'Here,' he said, 'here's your record. We know exactly how much these pictures are going to make. They cost so much. They earn so much. Even if we spent more on them, they wouldn't make a cent more. So why change them?' "

The one man who tried to change this system, early in the 1940's, was Val Lewton, a Russian-born writer of poetry and short stories, whose history of the Cossacks somehow led David Selznick to hire him as a consultant on a projected film version of Gogol's *Taras Bulba*. Nothing ever came of that, but Lewton began earning credentials as an executive. RKO decided in 1942 to make a series of cheap thrillers and put Lewton in charge of them. Then, in typical Hollywood style, Charles Koerner, the head of the studio, met somebody at a party who suggested that he should make a movie called *Cat People*. The next morning, Koerner passed that on to Lewton as an order, and Lewton called together a few friends and said, "I don't know what to do." When *Cat People* was remade in the 1970's, there was much gory clawing to suit the modern sensibility, and that was probably what Koerner wanted from Lewton, but it was not what Lewton was willing to produce. "The only way he would do it," said Jacques Tourneur, who eventually directed the film, "was not to make the blood-and-thunder cheap horror movie that the studio was expecting but something intelligent." The script that Lewton eventually got from DeWitt Bodeen was ominously ambiguous: A fashion designer, played by Simone Simon, thought she was descended from a group of women who could turn themselves into cats, but though the studio eventually insisted on one shot of a real panther crouching for the kill, it remained uncertain at the end exactly what Miss Simon's supernatural powers were.

That was the trademark of Lewton's films: a horrendous title to please the studio and a story that suggested but never demonstrated the implications of the title. Bodeen had written a play about the Brontës, so Lewton commissioned a script loosely based on *Jane Eyre,* which did very nicely under the title I *Walked With a Zombie* (1943). And though *The Leopard Man* (also 1943) implied that a series of murders in New Mexico might have been committed by a runaway leopard, the most frightening scene was one in which a girl was forced by her mother to go and get some groceries after dark, and walked in terror through the empty streets, and managed to carry the groceries home, and only then encountered the horror, of which the audience heard only an animal snarl and saw only a trickle of blood.

If Lewton wanted to be enigmatic, the RKO chiefs decided, he would have to be provided with a moneymaking star, and so they presented him, to his ill-concealed dismay, with Boris Karloff. Lewton hated monster movies, hated all the clichés that his bosses and his audiences loved, and so he cast Karloff in three strangely sadistic films, *The Body Snatchers* and *Isle of the Dead* (1945) and *Bedlam* (1946). This last one, in which Karloff played the cruel warder of the celebrated London insane asylum and ended being walled up alive by his patients, was so grim that the British censors banned its release there for years. In a sense, they were right, for most horror movies have a tendency toward morbidity, and the nearer they get to reality, the more dangerous that tendency becomes.

The classic horror films were not really supposed to be horrible. They were mildly symbolic legends, fairy tales, and so, when Boris Karloff sent John Carradine off to wreak vengeance on his prosecutors in *The House of Frankenstein,* Carradine remained (except when he occasionally turned into a large bat) an elegant figure in evening dress. As he showed his magic ring to Mayor Russmann's beautiful daughter-in-law, she looked admiringly at it and said, "I see glimpses of a strange world where people are dead." Carradine pressed the ring on her, naturally, and then she said, "I see your world more clearly now. I am no longer afraid." And he said, his eyes glittering, "I shall return for you before the dawn."

Who could object? Only her stodgy husband, who had been poking around in the wine cellar for something to offer the distinguished guest, then came upstairs to find his wife embracing the vampire in the garden and departing in the vampire's coach. And then, in a wonderful but unconscious parody of all chase scenes, the husband set out to find help and soon joined forces with some mounted police, and though these horsemen should have been able to catch the vampire's coach in good time, the camera lovingly portrayed an interminable pursuit. Carradine was trying, of course, to return before sunrise to the coffin in Professor Lampini's wagon, filled with the ancestral Transylvanian soil. But the pseudo Lampini (Karloff) wanted to flee from any difficulties with the authorities. And so there followed the extraordinary spectacle of the galloping police somehow unable to overtake the vampire's much slower coach, and the vampire's coach unable to overtake Karloff's still slower circus wagon. Karloff eventually decided to throw out the vampire's coffin, and Carradine then tried to stop his carriage, which promptly fell on its side. As the dawn sky brightened, Carradine crawled toward his coffin, and the first rays of the rising sun turned his outstretched hand into the bones of a skeleton.

And that was just the first half hour of *The House of Frankenstein.* The remarkable thing was that Siodmak, the master of sequels and spin-offs, managed to include here not just a sampling of horror-movie clichés but virtually every cliché that existed. When Karloff and the hunchback duly reached the house of Frankenstein, they found not only the mechanical monster frozen in ice but also a frozen werewolf, left there at the conclusion of Siodmak's *Frankenstein Meets the Wolf Man.* They lit fires and thawed out the Wolf Man, who promptly returned to his "natural" form as an amiable if bewildered-looking young man named Lawrence Talbott (Lon Chaney, Jr.). Karloff's first order of business, though, was to punish the authorities who had incarcerated him, and now that he had lost the services of John Carradine, he reverted to his traditional weapon, the brain transplant. "The monster is put in a glass case where steam will soften his frozen tissues," according to one synopsis of the unsynopsizable, "while Niemann and Daniel capture Strauss and Ullmann, the last remaining witnesses against the doctor. Niemann removes their brains for his fiendish plan of revenge. Ullmann's is to be inserted into the Monster, the Monster's brain into Talbott, and Talbott's into Strauss. . . ."

The one monster left out of this game of musical brains was Daniel, the homicidal hunchback, to whom Karloff had originally promised, before he got so involved in brain transplants, a handsome new body. This was particularly important to the hunchback because he had just fallen in love with a *zaftig* Gypsy girl named Ilonka, and she ignored him because she herself had just fallen in love with the burly Talbott. Talbott morosely confessed to her that he had a problem, which only she could solve by shooting him with a silver bullet when he came in pursuit of her at the next full moon. Quick shot of full moon scudding through clouds, then one of those wonderful sequences in which Jack Pierce's makeup magic made the whiskers sprout and the fangs grow. Lo, the snarling Wolf Man.

Ilonka was a little hesitant about firing her silver bullet, so she was clawed to death before she managed to do her duty. This outraged poor Daniel, who had now lost the main incentive for the new body that Karloff had been too busy to give him. Daniel lugged the girl back to Karloff's laboratory, intending to demonstrate the mad doctor's guilt and then to kill him. This intrusion in the midst of Karloff's effort to reactivate the Frankenstein monster naturally aroused the hostility of the reviving monster, who lurched off his laboratory table, grappled with the frenzied hunchback, and finally flung him out a window. By now, of course, it was time for Siodmak's last cliché: the crowd of villagers marching toward the accursed castle with all their torches ablaze. And so on.

One last question: How could Boris Karloff, the original Frankenstein monster, play the role of the mad scientist bringing the frozen monster back to life? The fact is that Karloff had tired of playing the monster (he did so three times), and so, in *The House of Frankenstein*, he passed on his most famous role to a stunt man named Glenn Strange. Unlike Karloff, Strange was never on the right corner at the right time. He had once been chosen to play Tarzan, but then he was pushed aside by Johnny Weissmuller. Now that he was assigned to imitate Karloff, Jack Pierce again did the makeup, and Pierce could probably have made even Gary Cooper look like the Frankenstein monster. Strange would reenact the role in *House of Dracula* (1945) and in the ultimate degradation, *Abbott and Costello Meet Frankenstein* (1948). But Strange's last major decision was to reject the role of the legendary gillman in *The Creature from the Black Lagoon*, and he worked out his last years as Sam the bartender in the television series *Gunsmoke*.

• • •

The Hays Office objected to the heroine's description of the evening on which she got pregnant, ". . . and then kinda . . . out to a roadhouse somewhere and then you know . . . like that. . . ." It also asked that "all the material set forth on pages 33, 34, 35, 36, and 37, having to do with the pregnancy of the girl, be drastically cut down and the matter entirely rewritten." For good measure, it asked that a clergyman named Upperman be renamed, "because the name has a comedy flavor which is not good when used in connection with a clergyman."

In such circumstances, it was hard to see how Preston Sturges could ever get Hays Office approval for his comedy about a girl named Trudy Kockenlocker, who found herself pregnant with sextuplets by a soldier whose name she could remember only as something like Private Ratskywatsky. Not only was it immoral but it was unpatriotic, and this in 1944, when American troops were fighting their way across northern France. The studio bosses at Paramount had let Sturges make the movie, but they anticipated nothing but trouble. They delayed for more than a year in releasing it at all. But Sturges had a way of getting what he wanted, and of making even the most grievous situations funny. Not cruelly funny—anybody could do that—but charmingly funny.

The premiere of *The Miracle of Morgan's Creek* was, of course, a triumph. James Agee, writing in *Time,* said Sturges's new film was "a little like talking to a nun on a roller coaster." Writing in *The Nation* (Agee was a regular reviewer for both magazines), he said that "the Hays Office has either been hypnotized into a liberality for which it should be thanked, or has been raped in its sleep." The *New York Times* was equally pleased: "A more audacious picture—a more delightfully irreverent one—than this new lot of nonsense at the Paramount has never come slithering madly down the path." And lines began forming outside the theater. *The Miracle of Morgan's Creek,* immoral and unpatriotic as it was, became the biggest commercial hit of 1944, taking in what was then an impressive sum of nine million dollars.

That was the way things generally happened in Preston Sturges movies. The impossible triumphed; the powerful were made ridiculous; penniless idealists became millionaires. This kind of upheaval may have seemed merely the product of a fertile imagination—and Sturges's imagination was certainly that—but much of Sturges's life was a Sturges comedy. His real name was Edmund Preston Biden, that being the name of his father, who worked for a Chicago collection agency and played the banjo and drank too much. His mother, Mary Dempsey Biden, who loathed the banjo, was a woman of considerable charm and considerable imagination. "Anything she said three times she believed fervently," Sturges recalled. "Often twice was enough."

When her son was two, she fled Chicago and took the boy to Europe, where she became a great friend of Isadora Duncan. (It was she who eventually painted the red Chinese shawl that Miss Duncan managed to get caught in the wheel of her Bugatti, and so choked to death.) She also convinced herself that her real name was not Dempsey but Desmond, and then D'Este, and thus she became, in her own mind, an Italian princess. Her mother persuaded the princess to return to Chicago, with her son Preston, the prince, and there she married a quiet stockbroker named Solomon Sturges. Two years later, though, she was off to Europe again, to the Bayreuth of Wagner, where she shared a villa with Isadora Duncan.

Her next husband was a Turk named Vely Bey, whose father had been a physician to the sultan. One day when Mary suffered a rash on her face, her new father-in-law concocted a purple lotion that soon cured it. Mary saw vast possibilities. She thought of a splendid name for her discovery, *Le Secret du Harem*, and she opened the Maison d'Este on the Rue de la Paix. The real D'Este family threatened a lawsuit to stop this absurd usurpation of a famous name, so Mary changed the name of her store to Maison Desti. She put her son Preston, by now fifteen, in charge of operating a new outlet on the *plage* at Deauville.

None of this is of surpassing significance, except that, like the childhood images that keep reappearing in the films of Federico Fellini—the fat woman on the beach or the unattainable angel—such situations of cheerful implausibility came to animate all of Sturges's comedies, and these were among the best and funniest comedies of the early 1940's. After the most haphazard of educations, Sturges joined the Army Air Corps and acquired a passion for flying, but the war ended before he ever got to France. His mother, tired of running the Maison Desti in New York, handed it all over to her son, and he found that he enjoyed inventing new lipsticks and makeups.

He met a girl of twenty, named Estelle Godfrey, who, primarily to escape a mother addicted to drugs, had married a man of sixty-four. Within a few months, she abandoned her husband and married Sturges, bringing with her a trust-fund income of eleven thousand dollars a year. The Sturgeses bought a house in the country, and Preston spent his time inventing things—a new kind of automobile with the engine in the rear, a new photoengraving process, a flying machine that was a hybrid of airplane and helicopter. After four years of this, Estelle suddenly announced to Sturges that she no longer loved him.

Sturges was devastated, contemplated suicide, then tried writing songs—"Oh, Minnie" and "Asia Minor Blues" and "Maybe You'll Be My Baby." Nobody wanted to publish them, so he wrote a play, *The Guinea Pig*, and when nobody wanted to produce it, he produced it himself. It was a moderate success, enough to interest Broadway producers in his next venture. He wrote *Strictly Dishonorable* in nine days, and it soon became, implausibly but inevitably, the smash hit of 1929. His first week's royalty check was fifteen hundred dollars.

On a train to Palm Beach, he met Eleanor Post Hutton, the stepdaughter of Edward F. Hutton, the Wall Street millionaire, and the granddaughter of C. W. Post, the Battle Creek cereal millionaire. She was twenty, and charming; they charmed each other. Arriving in Palm Beach, Sturges went to stay at her family palace. He announced to her father that he wanted to marry her.

"You can't afford to marry a girl like Eleanor," said E. F. Hutton.

"Why not?" said Sturges. "I've got a hit play and an income of fifteen hundred a week."

"For her that's pin money," said E. F. Hutton.

The same kind of dialogue was taking place between Eleanor and her mother. "He even owns a yacht," said Eleanor.

"How large?" asked Marjorie Post Hutton.

"Fifty-two feet," said Eleanor.

"My dear, you mean a *yawl*," said Marjorie Post Hutton.

The headline on the front page of the *New York Times* a month later said: ELEANOR HUTTON ELOPES WITH PLAYWRIGHT; WEDS PRESTON STURGES OVER PARENTS' PROTEST.

It didn't last, of course. Nothing in Sturges's life lasted; that was the essence of Sturges's comedies. Everything was breakable. And there could be no preposterous triumphs until there had been preposterous failures (and vice versa). Sturges was somehow persuaded by a French musician named Maurice Jacquet to rewrite the libretto for a Jacquet operetta named *Silver Swan*, which had already flopped. Sturges not only wasted his time writing a new libretto, he also wasted $64,000 of Eleanor's inheritance to produce it himself. Eleanor loved Sturges, but she was used to being taken care of, not to doing the cooking. She decided she would go to Paris.

Sturges was completely uninterested in movies, but Hollywood offered what it always offered, money. Walter Wanger promised him one thousand dollars a week to adapt *The Big Pond* for Maurice Chevalier. Sturges did it in two weeks, and only then learned that he was supposed to take ten weeks. Carl Laemmle, who had produced the successful film version of *Strictly Dishonorable*, invited Sturges to come and work at Universal at the same one thousand dollars a week. He was supposed to rewrite H. G. Wells's *Invisible Man*, which eight other writers had failed on, as a possible vehicle for Universal's newest star, Boris Karloff. "I like it out here very much," Sturges wrote to a friend in New York, "but it's very God Damned far away from everything. . . . [It] really is like Bridgeport with palm trees, only Bridgeport is greener."

Like the eight previous writers, Sturges wrote an *Invisible Man* script that Universal didn't like, and so he was unceremoniously fired. Sturges didn't much care, for he was already engrossed in a new idea, a film based on the story of Eleanor's grandfather, C. W. Post, founder of the Postum Cereal Company, rancher, inventor, art collector, who mysteriously killed himself at the age of fifty-five. A decade before *Citizen Kane*, Sturges began writing *The Power and the Glory*. Like *Kane*, it would begin with the death of the millionaire. Like *Kane*, it would be told in a series of flashbacks narrated by various people who had known him. And like Orson Welles, Sturges wanted to do the story his own way.

When he was about one third of the way through his screenplay, he met at a party a man who worked as a story editor for Jesse Lasky, one of the founding fathers of Paramount but now an independent producer at Fox. A meeting was arranged. Lasky was interested. He wanted to see a brief "treatment." Sturges refused. He was busy writing a finished script, which he agreed to show Lasky when it was done. Lasky planned to assign the inevitable rewriting to several other writers. Then he got Sturges's script. "I was astonished," he said later. "It was the most perfect script I'd ever seen." They had one brief story conference to discuss changes. "We tried to find something in the script to change, but could not find a word or situation," Lasky said. "Imagine a producer accepting a script from an author and not being able to make ONE CHANGE."

There was only one thing more unheard of than a writer creating all by himself a script that didn't need any changes, and that was a writer demanding a percentage of the gross, and getting it, and an advance of $17,500 against 3.5 percent of the first $500,000 and then escalating up to 7 percent of everything over $1 million. Hollywood was shocked. B. P. Schulberg even wrote a protest in *The Hollywood Reporter,* warning everyone that this was a dangerous precedent.

The Power and the Glory (1933), starring Spencer Tracy as the railroad tycoon, got splendid reviews and did very well commercially in New York, but not in the rest of the country. People said it was depressing. And a few years later, the negative was accidentally destroyed in a studio fire. Again, nothing lasted. But Sturges was now an established Hollywood writer, making $1,500 a week in the worst of the Depression. He worked on Fanny Hurst's *Imitation of Life* (Claudette Colbert) and a Samuel Goldwyn version of Tolstoy's *Resurrection* titled *We Live Again* (Fredric March) and even an M-G-M musical called *Broadway Melody of 1939* (Eleanor Powell). For that, his pay was $2,750 a week, but what he was now determined to do, well before the emergence of a Billy Wilder or a John Huston or a Joe Mankiewicz, was to direct his own screenplays. Paramount kept refusing, so Sturges finally offered the studio one of his scripts for a dollar if he could direct it himself. It was called "The Vagrant," the story of a bum who, through a series of absurdities, became governor of the state. And if his one-dollar offer was not good enough, Sturges made it clear that he would quit.

Paramount's William LeBaron grudgingly agreed to let Sturges hang himself. But he offered a budget of only $325,000, with Brian Donlevy as the star. Donlevy couldn't act very well, but he was diligent. He started his working day by inserting his false teeth; then he squeezed himself into a very tight girdle, then put on platform shoes, and a jacket with padded shoulders, and then a hairpiece. Thus outfitted, he played tough-guy parts. Sturges was still so inexperienced that he didn't know which end of a viewfinder a director was supposed to look into, but he nonetheless brought in his first film on schedule and under budget. Artfully retitled *The Great McGinty,* it earned handsome reviews and handsome profits. Sturges's script, which nobody would buy when he originally wrote it as a sequel to *The Power and the Glory* back in 1933, won him an Academy Award for 1940. For his acceptance speech, Sturges "tried to think of something funny" and finally announced to the audience: "Mr. Sturges was so overcome by the mere possibility of winning an Oscar that he was unable to come here tonight, and asked me to accept it in his stead." Since very few people in the audience knew what

Sturges looked like, his joke was received with total incomprehension, and, as he said, "I walked dismally back to my table."

At Paramount, though, Sturges now could do no wrong. What would he like to work on next? One of the pleasures of success is that past failures can be triumphantly revived. Back in 1931, Sturges had written a little comedy that he called "A Cup of Coffee," about an eager young man who keeps submitting advertising slogans for contests, and who comes to believe, mistakenly, that he has won. ("All his films," André Bazin wrote of Sturges long afterward, "are an exploitation of a misunderstanding.") Paramount happily approved this as Sturges's next project, but by now the making of films was only part of Sturges's hectic life. He was married again, of course, to a sympathetic woman named Louise, but he also clung to the idea of himself as an inventor. He subsidized with more than sixty thousand dollars of his film earnings a small operation in the nearby town of Wilmington, which he had named the Sturges Engineering Company, or, on less solemn occasions, "my machine shop." Its official purpose was to produce a new and improved kind of diesel engine.

More important, Sturges didn't like Hollywood's restaurants. For Paramount writers, the office saloon was Musso and Frank's, just across Hollywood Boulevard. It claimed that its founding in 1919 made it the oldest restaurant in town, but Sturges didn't think much of the food. The Brown Derby on North Vine was famous for looking like a brown derby, and Chasen's, on Beverly Boulevard, was the place to be seen making deals, but Sturges didn't think much of the food there either. He missed New York, and perhaps he even missed Deauville, where, as the fifteen-year-old manager of the Maison Desti, he got free meals at Giro's restaurant in the same building. He now found himself a steeply sloped piece of land at 8225 Sunset Boulevard, across the street from the caravansary called the Garden of Allah, at the intersection of Havenhurst Drive and Marmont Lane. There was a house there that had been turned into a wedding chapel, and Sturges envisioned this as a three-tier restaurant: a street-level drive-in, an informal restaurant above that, and at the top, in the house itself, a very formal dining room, which, in Hollywood terms, meant coat and tie required at all times. In honor of his memories of New York, Sturges called it The Players. He supervised everything, the carpentering and the cooking, and he indulged himself by throwing out anyone he didn't like. The Players cost him $250,000 in its first year and ultimately cost him everything he had.

But these were the years in which everything that Sturges touched flourished. "A Cup of Coffee" turned into the charming *Christmas in July* (showing for the first time that Dick Powell was more than a song-and-dance man). Sturges then directed his third hit of the year, *The Lady Eve,* in which Henry Fonda pursued Barbara Stanwyck in one of the great drunk scenes of all time. In 1941 came *Sullivan's Travels,* in which Sturges demonstrated that he could make even Veronica Lake funny. He also justified his own career in the remarkable scene in which the earnestly liberal movie director, who had been trapped by a series of Sturges twists in a southern penitentiary, watched as his fellow prisoners viewing an animated cartoon were uplifted by the healing force of laughter. And in 1942, *The Palm Beach Story,* in which Sturges explored the interesting question of how far an attractive woman (Claudette Colbert) could travel without any money whatever, and what would happen when her equally penniless husband (Joel McCrea) tried to pursue her. And then *The Miracle of Morgan's Creek.*

One of the many unusual things about Sturges was that he not only was ahead of his time but could recognize his time when it finally caught up with him. Thus *The Miracle of Morgan's Creek,* which seems remarkably attuned to the spirit of 1944, when people were beginning to get a little tired of heroic propaganda, and beginning to realize that a number of propagandized girls did get pregnant by soldiers like Private Ratskywatsky, was actually an idea that dated back to 1937. Sturges's plan then was to write a modern nativity story, about a small-town Virgin Mary who hardly knew how she had become pregnant. Nothing came of it then—Sturges had a whole filing cabinet full of ideas, stories, and even finished screenplays that nothing had come of then— but when Betty Hutton suddenly exploded on Broadway in *Panama Hattie,* which happened to be written by Buddy DeSylva, now the production chief at Paramount, and when Betty Hutton pleaded with Sturges to write a comedy for her, the time for *The Miracle of Morgan's Creek* had obviously arrived.

Even Morgan's Creek itself stood ready and waiting, a small-town set built for some now-forgotten movie. Paramount's accountants urged its demolition, but Sturges persuaded DeSylva that he could make good use of this town. Such *objets trouvés* appealed to some subterranean aspect of Sturges's imagination. He liked to star actors who were not stars—in this case, Eddie Bracken—and to surround them with a kind of repertory company of wonderful character actors whom nobody had ever heard of (Raymond Walburn, for example, the marvelously unctuous corporation president in *Christmas in July,* or Jimmy Conlin, who kept banging out ragtime piano throughout the revels of the Ale & Quail Club in *The Palm Beach Story,* and, of course, William Demarest, who appeared in a half-dozen Sturges movies as the perpetually outraged and uncomprehending representative of authority and respectability).

A movie about an unmarried girl pregnant with sextuplets by Private Ratskywatsky was, of course, impossible. Not only had the Hays Office been established to prevent such things, but there was now a Bureau of Motion Pictures, a subdivision of the Office of War Information, which was assigned to make every Hollywood producer keep in mind one basic question: "Will this picture help win the war?" Officially, Washington disavowed any thought of censorship. "The motion picture must remain free in so far as national security will permit," said President Roosevelt. "I want no censorship of the motion picture." Roosevelt made that resounding promise, however, in the course of appointing a former newspaperman named Lowell Mellett as the chief of the OWI's Bureau of Motion Pictures at the end of 1941.

Like any good bureaucrat, Mellett echoed the decree that the government did not want to censor anything. All he wanted to do was to "review" movie scripts to see that they did not conflict with the national interest. To carry out this mission, he soon acquired a staff of 140 employees and a budget of $1.3 million. And to make the government's view clear, he produced a document entitled *The Government Information Manual for the Motion Picture*. It offered a remarkable series of prescriptions: "At every opportunity, naturally and inconspicuously, show people making small sacrifices for victory—making them voluntarily, cheerfully and because of the people's own sense of responsibility. . . . For example, show people bringing their own sugar when invited out to dinner, carrying their own parcels when shopping, travelling on trains or planes with light luggage, uncomplainingly giving up seats for servicemen or others travelling on war priorities." More generally, the BMP urged moviemakers to remember their responsibilities toward "(1) the Issues of the War: what we are fighting for, the American way of life; (2) the Nature of the Enemy: his ideology, his objectives, his methods; (3) the United Nations and United Peoples: our allies in arms . . ." And so on.

In theory, Hollywood agreed with these idealistic principles, but once the BMP began reading scripts, its suggestions became more than suggestions. It objected to a farm boy enlisting in the army, for example, on the ground that Hollywood should make it clear that agricultural production was important to the war effort. It objected to a movie that showed a sit-down strike, on the ground that all labor-management relations should be portrayed as harmonious. It objected to a movie called *The Revenge of the Zombies* for implying that blacks were inferior; it also objected to all banquets at English manorial estates, which might imply that some of the English ate more than their minimum rations. It objected to all gangster movies.

Hollywood was not legally obliged to carry out the BMP's requests, and when the agency asked to see a rough cut of *The Miracle of Morgan's Creek*, Sturges simply ignored its request. The BMP's Hollywood representative sent off an indignant telegram to headquarters in Washington: "THIS IS THE ONLY STUDIO WHICH HAS EVER REFUSED SPECIFICALLY REQUEST OF THIS NATURE. IT IS ONLY STUDIO NOT FULLY COOPERATING AND IS NOT COOPERATING ONE IOTA." This might have become the first step in a campaign of government pressure against any signs of excessive independence in Hollywood, but the BMP was actually doing its job slightly too well for its own good. In Congress, there were still those who regarded the war as Roosevelt's war, and any war propaganda as Roosevelt propaganda, and next year would be an election year. In May of 1943, the House, ignoring its own appropriations committee, cut the BMP budget from $1.3 million to a mere housekeeping fund of $50,000. Its chief, Lowell Mellett, dutifully resigned and was appointed to the limbo of a special mission to the Middle East.

Ignoring the Washington censors did not save Sturges from the nuisances of political censorship, however. Paramount had its own staff censor, Luigi Luraschi, and he, too, wanted to make sure that Sturges did not sabotage the war effort. At one point, for example, Eddie Bracken's jalopy was supposed to screech to a halt outside Betty Hutton's house, and Luraschi described this as "contrary to the rubber conservation program." He wondered if Sturges could replace the squeal of tires with "possibly a funny toot on the horn." Nor was that all. The Catholic Legion of Decency, which not only rated movies but enforced its ratings with threats of boycotts and picketing, demanded still more alterations as the price of changing its preliminary verdict of C (condemned) to B (morally objectionable). DeSylva acquiesced, and Sturges had to do some reshooting to placate his critics.

While DeSylva dithered over *Miracle* (Paramount's real problem now was that it had a backlog of finished movies awaiting release), Sturges went ahead and filmed a kind of sequel that was even more cynical, even more unpatriotic —indeed, the only real satire of the war effort made during the war—and almost equally funny. Sturges was so pleased with Bracken's performance in *Miracle* that he wrote for him a script entitled "The Little Marine." It was the tale of a pitiful young man, rated 4-F because of hay fever, who pretended to join the Marine Corps, in which his father had been a hero, but who actually worked in a defense plant. Then he met in a bar a band of homecoming marines (headed by Demarest, of course, as the tough sergeant who had served under the young man's heroic father in World War I), and the marines all decided to escort him home and vouch for his heroism in combat. In the patriotically deluded home town, the marine conspirators and their constantly protesting victim encountered all the elements of the contemporary homecoming movies: the cheering crowd, the high school band, the mother in her apron, the beautiful girl—all of them unfortunately devoted to the celebration of a fraud. *Hail the Conquering Hero,* it was called, and DeSylva really disliked it. He insisted on re-editing it himself, but the preview screening of his version was a disaster, so he grudgingly allowed Sturges to spend several weeks re-editing DeSylva's re-editing, bringing the film back to more or less its original form. Released finally in August of 1944, it was Sturges's second big hit of the year. "This riotously funny motion picture," said the *New York Times,* "this superlative small town comedy, is also one of the wisest ever to burst from a big-time studio."

So in four years, Sturges had written and directed seven straight hits. Now his contract was up for renewal, and all he wanted was the right to make more, without any interference from Buddy DeSylva or anyone else. That was the one thing that neither Paramount nor any of the other major studios would grant. "I was very happy here without any contract at all," Sturges declared in his last meeting with DeSylva. "I realize quite well that I cannot make the final cutting decision on a picture because that would make it my property instead of yours. . . . I ask that at the conclusion of each picture, for a period of two weeks I have the right to abrogate my contract—not for the purpose of holding a club over your head, because I love Paramount and do not want to leave, but merely to cause your production head, whoever he may be, to treat me with the courtesy due a grown man of known integrity."

No. That was the answer from DeSylva and Paramount's general manager, Henry Ginsberg. Let Sturges be happy with his handsome salary of $3,250 per week, plus a $30,000 bonus for each film completed, far more than President Roosevelt earned for leading a nation at war. These negotiations took place before either *The Miracle of Morgan's Creek* or *Hail the Conquering Hero* was released. According to the rules of Sturges's comedies, that double triumph should have brought all the studio executives to heel. It didn't. What Sturges failed to realize was that the studio authorities considered it less important to make successful movies—much less good movies—than to maintain their grip on power. To relax that grip would have implied, ultimately, that they themselves were unnecessary.

So Sturges and Paramount parted company. Other studios, of course, wanted to hire him. M-G-M offered six thousand dollars a week, but only under the suffocating control of Louis B. Mayer, and what Sturges wanted most was freedom. After considering all the offers, he made a decision that can only be regarded as suicidal. Trusting the friendship of a man who had often been a guest at The Players, who shared his own enthusiasm for both movies and aviation, and who promised a total independence that he would never actually permit, Sturges decided to form a film production partnership with Howard Hughes. *Time* magazine, in one of the few good examples of its passion for portmanteau words, described it as a *"cinemanschluss."*

Hughes had in fact suffered a kind of breakdown in the late summer of 1944. Under the pressure of various problems connected with his inability to produce airplanes for the war effort, he began dictating repetitious memoranda that spiraled around into nowhere. Thus: "A good letter should be immediately understandable . . . a good letter should be immediately understandable . . . a good letter should be immediately understandable." From this, he moved on to a memorandum entitled "Notes on Notes," which dealt at great length with the punctuation in the latest version of his will: "A dash, or two, shall be used to denote words preceding, or following a quotation. Two dashes shall be used to denote the deletion of words when a group of words are quoted . . ." And so on. Toward the end of that August, Hughes simply disappeared. Not until thirty-odd years later did a former Hughes Aircraft mechanic named Joseph Petrali finally disclose that he and the boss had spent months shuttling around from Las Vegas to Palm Springs to Reno, checking in and out of various hotels under various assumed names.

Hughes recovered, partly, and in his own way, and indeed went on to acquire control of RKO. But now, for a time, he simply let Sturges make one film on his own. It was a very funny picture, entitled *The Sin of Harold Diddlebock*. Then Hughes began telephoning and interfering. That was how Sturges, who yearned for independence, found himself writing a melodrama called *Vendetta* for one of Hughes's protégées, Faith Domergue. That was also how Sturges eventually found himself called on the telephone at seven o'clock one morning in 1946, called on the telephone at the apartment of Frances Ramsden, a young fashion model whom Sturges had insisted on casting as the heroine of *The Sin of Harold Diddlebock,* called on the telephone at seven o'clock in the morning at the apartment of Frances Ramsden and awakened out of bed and told by Hughes that his partner, Hughes, was taking over control of their joint production company, and that he, Preston Sturges, was fired.

Herbert K. Sorrell (*left*) led a leftist strike that ended in street violence and failure (*bottom left*). Bogart and Bacall (*below*), in *To Have and Have Not,* represented romantic fantasy.

7
BREAKDOWNS
(1945)

When David Selznick fell in love, he did so with all the elegance of a wounded elephant trumpeting in the canebrake. Ever since his marriage to Irene Mayer back in 1930, there had periodically been little adulteries—that was almost expected of a Hollywood producer—but Selznick remained true to Irene, in his fashion, and she did to him, in hers. When he threw his clothes on the floor and stamped on them, to demonstrate something or other, she would order him to pick them up and put them away neatly. "If I were married to Irene," her father, Louis B. Mayer, once remarked, "I'd hit her." But while Mrs. Selznick bossed her husband around, she also took care of him and his household, and he needed her for that.

Now, one night in February of 1945, as they lay awake in the darkness, Mrs. Selznick fumbled in a drawer of the night table to get another sleeping pill.

"Why aren't you asleep?" Selznick asked. "What's the matter?"

"Nothing," said Mrs. Selznick. "I was just thinking."

"What are you thinking about?"

"Nothing." There was a pause. Then, Mrs. Selznick later recalled, her voice came welling up "out of nowhere" and saying: "The jig's up."

"What do you mean?" Selznick asked.

"I want out."

"You can't do this to me!" cried Selznick. "My God, explain!"

She really couldn't explain. It was just that after fifteen years of living with Selznick, she was sick of living with Selznick—and that baffled him. So he assumed that the explanation must be the obvious one, that she had heard about his latest affair. He decided to confess yet another self-indulgence, to plead for understanding, sympathy. Mrs. Selznick was surprised, or so she later claimed. She said that she hadn't known and didn't want to know. Selznick kept on explaining and explaining, and none of it did any good.

Phyllis Walker had originally seemed a girl of no great importance. After Selznick first met her in the spring of 1941, he couldn't even remember who she was. In a memo to Kay Brown in his New York office, he confused Phyllis Walker with Phyllis Thaxter, a pleasant-looking and rather tweedy actress he was considering for a movie version of the Broadway hit *Claudia*. Then he added: "Is this the big-eyed girl we saw in the office who had two chil-

dren . . . ? Incidentally, if it is the big-eyed girl I certainly think she is worth
testing no matter when she would be available." A few days later, though,
Selznick was indignant that one of his aides had offered the big-eyed Mrs.
Walker too much money. "Here is a girl who has done nothing, or next to
nothing, and we think of starting her at $200," he scolded. "This isn't bad
enough, but at the end of her contract she gets up to $1,500. . . . I think we
are losing all sense of proportion." An afterthought: "Incidentally, what is the
husband like . . . . ? We ought to preserve his pride."

By September, Selznick had already taken over all professional aspects of
his new protégée's life. He sent a memo to his publicity director saying that
he wanted to "get a new name for Phyllis Walker," that he didn't particularly
care about names but he thought Phyllis Walker "particularly undistinguished," and that he "would appreciate suggestions." A week after that, he
was worrying about the corrupting effects of Hollywood. "I am terribly afraid
the girl is going to get spoiled," he wrote to Kay Brown. "Already she has lost
some of that eager, blushing quality that made her so enchanting when we
first saw her."

She had been born Phyllis Isley, and she was twenty-two when she met
Selznick, who was then thirty-nine. She came from Tulsa, Oklahoma, where
her parents managed a touring theatrical stock company. She was quite pretty,
in an apple-cheeked, chipmunky sort of way, but hardly a great beauty, and
she was almost morbidly shy, insecure, withdrawn. In the make-believe of
acting, she found a kind of release, a way to exist, so she went to Northwestern and then the American Academy of Dramatic Arts in New York. There
she met another student much like herself, shy, lonely, anxious. His name
was Robert Walker, and she married him in 1939 and bore him a son in 1940
and another in 1941, the year she met David Selznick.

The Walkers had recently been living in Greenwich Village, and job-
hunting. Walker found occasional work in radio soap operas. His wife decided
to take a chance and just walk into Selznick's New York office and ask for an
opportunity to try out for Claudia. In the midst of her reading, she nervously
burst into tears. Selznick was charmed. His contract offer broke up the family
for a while, but then Walker also got a lucky break. A part in M-G-M's Bataan
reunited him with his wife in a little house in Pacific Palisades. "All we have
is three beds, a dining-room table and a refrigerator," Walker cheerily told
Hedda Hopper. "We're going to furnish it like we want it."

It had been several years since Selznick had actually produced a film (he
fretted that he could never surpass Gone With the Wind), but he lived well on
his stable of stars. He justified his usurious profits by portraying himself as a
master packager. He cast a newcomer named Gregory Peck in A. J. Cronin's
The Keys of the Kingdom, for example; then instead of making the movie, he
sold the whole project to Fox. He talked of filming Mein Kampf and even tried
to lay claim to the title. But mostly Selznick just kept loaning out his stars,
just as all the other producers did, and his deals were extravagantly profitable.
On one loan of Joan Fontaine, he collected $150,000 and gave her $30,000.

For loaning out Ingrid Bergman, who liked to work as much as possible, Selznick cleared $425,000 in one year alone; she got $60,000. So when Selznick heard that his brother-in-law Bill Goetz was looking for an unknown actress to star in *The Song of Bernadette,* he sent over Phyllis Walker, whom he had decided to rename Jennifer Jones.

"This girl *is* Bernadette," said Henry King, whom 20th Century–Fox had assigned as director. Selznick didn't seem to mind that his discovery would become a star under the aegis of somebody else. He still owned her; he was still working on her. He hired an ex-model named Anita Colby to advise him on how his various actresses should dress and behave, and she had to devote special attention to Mrs. Walker. Miss Colby had to teach her not only what clothes to buy—sending back any wrong choices—but even how to look back into people's eyes when they were speaking to her. But the success of Jennifer Jones in *Bernadette* was probably what inspired Selznick to go back to producing a real movie. He bought a rather sentimental novel about the wartime home front, *Since You Went Away,* by Margaret Buell Wilder, and he decided that he would write the script himself. As he wrote, or rather dictated, and rewrote and redictated, the part for Jennifer Jones, as the older daughter in Claudette Colbert's husbandless household, kept getting larger and larger.

There was also a substantial part for Robert Walker, not only because he was Jennifer Jones's husband but because his recent success in an innocents-in-uniform comedy called *See Here, Private Hargrove* made him almost as big a star as his wife. It was nonetheless important that he was also Jennifer Jones's husband. These complexities were all more than the young Mrs. Walker could bear, particularly the love scenes that Selznick had written for her to play with her husband, and the farewell scene in which he went off to war (from the same railroad station that had once served Selznick for *Gone With the Wind*). Mrs. Walker burst into tears in the middle of that scene and fled to her dressing room. Selznick had to be summoned to the set, and to that dressing room, to quiet her down and lead her back in front of the camera to bid farewell to her husband. Not long afterward, the day after she won the Academy Award for *Bernadette,* she announced that she was suing Walker for divorce.

Walker never recovered. He had always been somewhat unstable, but now he began drinking ferociously, and smashing things, and telling anyone who would listen his accusations against Selznick. "My personal life has been completely wrecked by David Selznick's obsession for my wife," he told another young newcomer, June Allyson. "What can you do to fight such a powerful man? My life has been hell. . . ." M-G-M officials persuaded Walker to go to the Menninger Clinic, where he started getting psychotherapy six days a week. "I hated myself and blamed myself all my life for things I shouldn't have blamed myself for," he later said. "I felt that everybody was against me, hated me. . . ."

In due time, Walker persuaded the clinic to release him, and so he returned to Hollywood and again began drinking heavily. The nurse who kept house for him called his psychiatrist, and the psychiatrist came to give him an injection of sodium amytal. Walker resisted, so various friends were summoned to control him. They held him down while the doctor prepared the injection. "Don't give it to me," Walker pleaded while the friends held him. "I've been drinking. It will kill me. Please don't give me that shot." The doctor knew better, of course. Walker had often been injected with sodium amytal (and a subsequent autopsy declared that this last dose was not in any way abnormal). There, there, this would calm him down, and while the friends held the squirming actor in place, the doctor administered his soothing injection. A few minutes later, Walker collapsed, and in two hours he was dead. At thirty-two. All very sad.

That was in 1951, part of the future, but the breakup of David Selznick's marriage probably went back well into the past, far beyond his encounter with Mrs. Walker, back to the breakup of the marriage of Irene Selznick's father, Louis B. Mayer. As the head of the largest and most successful movie studio, Mayer had long imposed his own social code on much of Hollywood (and, it could be argued, on much of the United States). That social code was one of rigid conformity to the ideals of paternalistic respectability, come what might. Back in 1904, when Mayer first courted Maggie Shenburg, the daughter of the cantor of the Emerald Street Synagogue in Boston, she was pretty and a high school graduate and socially far superior to the semiliterate junk dealer from New Brunswick. Thirty years later, when Louis B. Mayer was one of the highest-paid executives in the United States, his wife had become a self-effacing *hausfrau,* ill at ease outside her own front door in Santa Monica. Success made Mayer increasingly tyrannical over his family as well as his employees (the two tended to merge in his mind). When his two daughters grew old enough to go to college, Mayer forbade it; he didn't want their minds or morals corrupted. But by all accounts, Mayer remained "faithful" to his wife, in the technical meaning of that word, until she had to have a hysterectomy late in 1933.

It was a psychological disaster for the whole family. Mrs. Mayer sank into what was officially termed "involutional melancholia," a postoperative condition that is now routinely treated by hormone therapy. She moped tearfully around the house and complained of vague pains that no doctor could diagnose. Finally she was sent off to a mental institution, the Riggs sanitarium in Stockbridge, Massachusetts. For Mayer, this was both a condemnation and a liberation. He had been told, as doctors often told their victims in those days, that Mrs. Mayer must never again have sex after her operation. He didn't want it anyway. He confessed to a surprisingly large number of people that his knowledge of her hysterectomy made the very idea of sex with her repugnant.

So now that his poor wife was confined in a mental hospital, Mayer felt free, for the first time in his life, to explore all the possibilities. The richest and most powerful man in the world capital of temptation was ready to be tempted. Aides and adjutants arranged parties for him and invited willing girls, but Mayer always seemed to spend his time asking them about their families. One of Mayer's new friends, a Detroit gambler named Lew Wertheimer, said of the would-be adventurer, "He couldn't get laid in a whorehouse!"

Mayer explained to a solicitous assistant that he didn't really want any girl unless he knew her and liked her. On his own, he apparently attempted various fumbling advances toward some of his stars. Both Jeanette MacDonald and Myrna Loy, according to studio gossip, had to make it clear to him that they were not interested. But more girls kept appearing, and getting screen tests, for this was M-G-M's business, after all. One of these newcomers was a twenty-four-year-old Ziegfeld Follies dancer from Texas named Jean Howard. Her screen test went well, so she was taken around to meet various producers. When she met Mayer, he asked her, characteristically, "Do you have a dentist if you have a toothache? Do you know any doctors if you need one?" She said no. Mayer said she should call him if she needed any help of this kind. She smiled. Mayer fell in love.

All that spring of 1934, Mayer pursued his new discovery. He took her to lunch, he asked her about her family, he stared at her, but nothing more. "I'm sure I would have gone to bed with him if he had asked me," Miss Howard later said of her admirer, but she thought of him as "a mental adolescent in perpetuity." And, of course, ugly as a toad. And fifty-two years old. And married. None of this deterred Louis B. Mayer, the lord of M-G-M. His wife duly returned home from Riggs and remembered a promise that he had once made, to take her to Paris. Well, why not? Mayer had heard (mistakenly) that it was easy to obtain a quick and quiet divorce there. So he decided to embark for France, taking along his wife, who would learn there of her destiny, and his girl, who would marry him there, and the girl's best friend, Ethel Borden, whom Mayer was paying to serve as a kind of confidante and intermediary in his awkward courtship. For good measure, Mayer also took along his chief publicity man, Howard Strickling.

The main obstacle to Mayer's plan, an obstacle about which he knew nothing, was that Miss Howard was in love with a young lawyer-agent named Charlie Feldman. They slept together whenever they could arrange it, and shortly before Mayer's great expedition to Paris, they decided to get married. Miss Borden, apparently doing her paid duty to Mayer, urged her friend not to throw away a free trip to Paris, and Feldman reluctantly agreed to postpone the marriage for a month, until Miss Howard's return to New York. Though Mayer knew nothing of this, he thought it a useful precaution to hire a private detective agency to shadow Miss Howard for a while, just to be sure. When the agency sent him its report, however, he simply stuffed it in his pocket, telling himself that it was surely innocuous, and that he would read it later.

On the boat train from Le Havre to Paris, Mayer finally made it fully clear to Miss Howard what he had in mind. He told her, she said later, that Mrs. Mayer had agreed to a divorce, that he wanted to marry Miss Howard, and that he would provide her with a premarital contract that would make her rich. And more. "Do you realize the power you have?" Mayer exulted. "If you make me unhappy, everybody in the M-G-M studio would feel it. But if you make me happy, it will make five thousand people happy too!"

Miss Howard, perhaps a little disingenuously, claimed to be "stunned." She had no intention of marrying her aged suitor, but she didn't feel she could explain everything amid the clatter of the boat train. Better wait until they all got settled at the hotel in Paris, the George V. Just as she was settling in there, Strickling knocked at her door and announced that Mayer wanted to see her immediately. "When we went in," she recalled later, "he was white and shaking, with a large envelope in his hand. . . . It was from a detective agency in Hollywood and told him all about Charlie and me. Suddenly he picked up a bottle of Scotch, poured out a whole glass and gulped it down. He never drank and it made him drunk. He went wild. He roared around the room and then, suddenly, made a move to throw himself out the window. The three of us needed all our strength to hold him back. We got him down on the floor, where he wept and moaned. I went straight back to New York, and Charlie and I were married."

Mrs. Mayer suffered a relapse. She kept weeping. Mayer brought in psychiatrists from London, who didn't provide much help. Mayer vowed he would be faithful once again. He also sent back orders to Hollywood that Charlie Feldman was never again to be allowed on the M-G-M lot.* So they tried to patch things together, Louis and Maggie, but some things can't be patched. There were occasional returns to Riggs, and although Mrs. Mayer spent perhaps two thirds of the next ten years at home, according to her daughter Irene, "she could never quite pick up the threads of her life."

Then began Mayer's decade of hypocrisy. There were timorous nights out, like the occasion on which the manager of a well-known Hollywood establishment asked all her customers to leave because "Mr. Mayer has just called and wishes to come here incognito. He doesn't like to be here with strangers." The man who didn't like to have strangers see him at a brothel remained always the man who insisted that there mustn't be too much kissing in his Andy Hardy pictures, and that Mickey Rooney should get down on his knees to pray for the health of his mother. After the decade of hypocrisy, then, Mayer simply announced to his wife, in the summer of 1944, on the eve of their fortieth wedding anniversary, "I'm leaving." And moved out, first to the San Fernando Valley ranch of his patient publicity man, Strickling, and then into the Beverly Hills house that had once been Marion Davies's bungalow dressing room at M-G-M (it was later hauled across town to make Miss Davies feel at home at Warner Bros., and then finally moved to Benedict Canyon Drive). In his lordly years of power, Mayer had spent a fortune on buying and raising racehorses, and in the autumn of the year of his divorce,

* A doomed decree. Feldman's operations eventually became the powerful Famous Artists Agency.

he invited several friends to watch him gallop around on his training track. The horse reared up and flung him to the ground. He broke his pelvis, and then, in the hospital, he developed pneumonia. It was a hard year.

When Louis B. Mayer abandoned the long effort to pretend that he was contentedly married to the girl of his youth, that made it vaguely all right for all the other restless tycoons to abandon similar pretenses. Harry Cohn, who always moved quickly, had divorced his Rose a couple of years before Mayer finally walked out on Maggie, and Darryl Zanuck remained with his Virginia a couple of years longer, but the principle was the same: The Andy Hardy series was coming to an end. The person who naturally heard that message most clearly was Mayer's own daughter, Irene. Less than a year after her father had said, "I'm leaving," she said, in the darkness, "The jig's up."

Before she decided that the jig was up, though, Irene Selznick insisted that her husband see a psychoanalyst. Selznick's behavior was always erratic, but it seemed to keep getting more bizarre. He drank heavily, dosed himself with Benzedrine, gambled wildly, and quarreled with everyone he knew. The divorce and death of his alcoholic brother, Myron, in March of 1944, struck him a heavy blow. Holed up in the Waldorf in New York, unwilling or unable to see anyone, Selznick told his wife that he was "really scared . . . afraid that he was actually going insane." Mrs. Selznick asked Dorothy Paley, wife of the head of CBS, to recommend a psychoanalyst. Mrs. Paley arranged a meeting with Sandor Rado, one of the pioneers of the psychoanalytic movement in Berlin, who had come to America in 1931 to take charge of the New York Psychoanalytic Institute. Selznick's behavior was characteristic. He couldn't bring himself to go to Dr. Rado's office; he wanted Rado to come to him. Mrs. Selznick finally escorted her husband to the psychoanalyst's office, and the doctor soon told her his verdict. He said Selznick "was having a breakdown." He said Mrs. Selznick should take her husband back to Los Angeles and get him into treatment there. There were few analysts in Los Angeles then, and the only one Rado could vouch for was Dr. May Romm. Mrs. Selznick followed instructions.

It is a little hard now to realize how esoteric and how controversial psychoanalysis still was in the early 1940's. Sigmund Freud had long been established as a pop oracle, an explicator of sex, but not as the creator of a psychiatric system that would solve, as its more ardent supporters believed, many of the fundamental problems of mankind. In America, in particular, psychoanalysis was widely regarded as something foreign, alien, and therefore not quite serious, not quite respectable. American psychiatrists tended to be mechanistic, devoted to the study of rats in mazes. If they had a contemporary hero in the era between the wars, it was probably J. B. Watson, the founder of the movement that he named in his book *Behaviorism,* in which he dismissed "the elaborate nonsense the Freudians have written." Hitler changed all this by uprooting the Freudians from their Central European nests and dispersing them into their golden exile. Freud himself was barely rescued from Nazi-occupied Vienna in 1938, and then only after he signed a statement declaring that he had been well treated (to which he added a sentence that one of his admirers defended as "ironic": "I can heartily recommend the Gestapo to anyone").

The psychoanalysts driven into exile were by no means an army. One authoritative account estimated the total who came to America at not more than about two hundred. Most remained in New York, but one of their favorite oases in the West was Los Angeles, perhaps simply because of the climate that so enchanted Thomas Mann, perhaps because people like Mann lived there. Ernst Simmel, a dedicated Socialist who had been one of the founders of the Berlin Psychoanalytic Institute, received word early in 1933 that the Nazis were coming to get him. He left through a back window and didn't stop running until he reached Los Angeles, where he inevitably founded the Los Angeles Psychoanalytic Study Group. To this he welcomed such Berlin comrades as Otto Fenichel. (Before he left his last way station in Prague, Fenichel reported, someone asked him what was the most pressing question confronting psychoanalytic research, and Fenichel answered: "The question of whether the Nazis come to power in Vienna.") Simmel also welcomed that whole group of sociologists known as the Frankfurt Institute, headed by Max Horkheimer and Theodor Adorno. These Frankfurt exiles cherished the idea of synthesizing Marx and Freud in their critique of modern society, and although they never accomplished anything very substantial, they did their best to serve as an irritant even in southern California. Blessed with foundation grants from the East, they staged little seminars, attended by fellow exiles like Brecht and Feuchtwanger, on various cultural topics, the significance of jazz or the movies.

What attracted the refugee psychoanalysts at least as much as the climate or the émigré atmosphere was, of course, money. Hollywood was full of neurotic people who wanted the meaning of their lives explained to them and who had lots of money to pay for the explanations. At one point in the turbulent life of Judy Garland, for example, when she was in the midst of a floundering affair with Joseph Mankiewicz, he sent her to be treated by Simmel. Just as Simmel was getting started, Miss Garland's mother reported this development to Louis B. Mayer, and Mayer called in Mankiewicz for a scolding, and Mankiewicz quit M-G-M forever. And Miss Garland broke off her therapy.

Artie Shaw, who spent the war years leading a navy band on hectic tours of overseas military bases, was another one of those who felt that he was cracking up; the navy agreed, granting him a medical discharge. "This was in 1944," Shaw recalled, "and at that point I wanted nothing more than to lie down somewhere in a deep hole and have someone shovel enough dirt over me to cover me." Being an avid reader, Shaw duly found his way to psychoanalysis and to Dr. May Romm, who began leading him back through his days as young Arthur Arshawsky of the Bronx. No sooner had he recovered sufficiently to start courting Ava Gardner than he wanted her to join him in consulting Dr. Romm. Miss Gardner dutifully began to prepare herself for analysis, but then Shaw began to worry that his own analysis might cure him of wanting to marry Miss Gardner, so he gallantly abandoned Dr. Romm.

Beyond such contretemps, there was a more serious controversy that tormented the psychoanalysts when they established themselves in Hollywood in the early 1940's. Was Freud's system basically a philosophy, an attempt to explain the world's problems, or was it a medical therapy, a cure for what people now called "mental illness"? The former alternative seemed important in 1945, when the world was trying to comprehend the successive shocks of the Nazi death camps, of the atomic bomb, and then of the epochal war coming to an end. But although Freud's writings provided insights into contemporary disasters, American psychoanalysts showed a certain practicality in arguing that their system was basically nothing more than a medical therapy, that analysts were not theoreticians but simply doctors, certified by MD degrees, who devoted their time to curing the sick.

One unfortunate victim of this practicality was Otto Fenichel, who had come to Los Angeles in 1938 with impressive credentials as one of the leaders of the Berlin Psychoanalytic Institute. Fenichel believed passionately that Marx and Freud both offered answers to the disaster engulfing Europe, but there was very little that one lonely refugee could do. When Fenichel conducted a seminar on literature at Simmel's Psychoanalytic Study Group, one admirer commended the effort with the somewhat ambiguous judgment that it was "one of the last refuges of the avant-garde period of the psychoanalytic movement before it became a commercialized specialty." To keep in touch with his scattered allies, those who believed in the Marxist aspects of psychoanalysis, Fenichel sent out a series of more than one hundred circular letters, or *Rundbriefe*, reporting on who was doing what, and what he thought of their activities. It was a hopeless task. In his last *Rundbriefe*, in July of 1945, Fenichel wrote mournfully that he had recently spoken with several sympathetic colleagues and wondered whether any of them would suggest organizing a conference of politically minded analysts. "Silently I thought that such a wish would be a sign that the *Rundbriefe* still have some meaning . . ." Fenichel observed. "No one suggested a meeting."

The psychoanalysts of Los Angeles didn't want to get involved in politics. They wanted to get established and make money. And in that city of cults, where, as Nathanael West had written, people preached the crusade against salt and the Aztec secret of brain-breathing, the psychoanalysts wanted respectability, medical certification. Freud had argued fervently for the development of "lay analysts" who could spread the faith without years of medical training, but the American psychoanalytic establishment insisted on exactly that training, that respectability. Fenichel had earned his medical degree long ago at the University of Vienna, which didn't count for much in Los Angeles now. So in the summer of 1945, after sending out his last *Rundbriefe*, he decided to start earning new credentials by becoming an intern at Cedars of Lebanon Hospital. He was forty-seven, and fat, and a friend who visited him on night duty noted that he looked out of shape in a tight and ill-fitting white uniform. He complained of exhaustion. He worried about his ability to keep up with new developments in medicine. He talked vaguely of finding another hospital that didn't require night shifts. Within six months, he collapsed and died of a ruptured cerebral aneurism.

But Hollywood found that psychoanalysis was fun. David Selznick enjoyed pouring out his thoughts to Dr. Romm, and that outpouring apparently helped him to get back to work. Then, of course, he began treating Dr. Romm as one of his employees. "He became too busy for Romm," Mrs. Selznick recalled. "He was forty minutes late, if he showed up at all. When he arrived on time, he was often unwakable through the entire session. He recounted these antics as though they were amusing. . . . He misinterpreted her patience as enchantment with him; in fact, he was afraid she was falling in love with him. He rang her doorbell at midnight and, standing outside, demanded to be heard. He found it unreasonable of her to refuse." After nearly a year of this, Dr. Romm decided to cancel Selznick as a patient. Selznick didn't seem to mind. He told his wife that he now "knew more than she did; *he* could analyze *her*."

One predictable outcome of Selznick's involvement with psychoanalysis was that he decided to make a movie about the subject, a movie that would simultaneously dramatize it, explain it, and proselytize for it. Selznick's desire made him vulnerable to the serpentine intrigues of Alfred Hitchcock, one of the few people in Hollywood who could out-Selznick Selznick. Hitchcock persuaded the producer that he had found exactly what was wanted. This was a peculiar novel called *The House of Dr. Edwardes,* originally published in 1927 by a pseudonymous Francis Beeding, a murder mystery that involved witchcraft and satanic cults in a Swiss mental clinic. Hitchcock told Selznick that this story would portray psychoanalysis both as a cure for mental torment and as a means of solving a murder. He also told him, in due time, that he, Hitchcock, had acquired all rights to the novel, available for resale. He even extracted from Selznick a substantial advance for a nonexistent screenplay. Selznick kept snapping at the bait. "I'd like to stress," he said in one of his myriad memos, "that I'm almost desperately anxious to do this . . . psychiatric story with Hitch."

Hitchcock's customary method of devising a movie script was to consult for hours on end with his chosen writer, then send the writer to his typewriter for a day or two, then consult some more. This suited the needs of Ben Hecht, who was also in the throes of psychoanalysis and who liked to talk out a story while he wrote it. Hitchcock, he later observed, "gave off plot turns like a Roman candle." At the end of a month, the two of them had concocted an implausible but dramatic script, to which one of Selznick's secretaries later gave the title *Spellbound.*

It involved a psychoanalyst who had come to take charge of a mental hospital but soon showed himself to be on the verge of a breakdown. He couldn't bear the sight of parallel lines; he couldn't stand whiteness. The marks of a fork drawn across a white tablecloth drove him frantic, and when in a frenzy, he was apt to faint dead away. In such phobias Hitchcock found what he liked to call the MacGuffin.* Then it turned out that the phobia-ridden doctor was only impersonating the doctor who was supposed to take charge of the clinic, and that the real doctor was dead, and that the imperson-ator might have murdered him. But there was another psychiatrist at the clinic, a woman, who would fall in love with the mysterious stranger and solve all his problems. "Just another manhunt story wrapped up in pseudo-psycho-analysis," Hitchcock said with a shrug.

Selznick had grandiose ideas of luring Greta Garbo out of retirement to play the heroine, and when he turned to Ingrid Bergman, whom he already had under contract, she at first refused him. "I won't do this movie," she said. "The heroine is an intellectual woman, and an intellectual woman simply can't fall in love so deeply." Talked out of that odd misjudgment, she made a splendid effort to portray an intellectual woman falling in love with the rather wooden Gregory Peck. It was a struggle, though. Hitchcock wrote for his two stars a series of psychiatric explanations that now sound platitudinous but also sound like Hitchcock's effort to confess and explain his own obscure sense of guilt. "I'm haunted, but I can't see by what," Peck said at one point. "People often feel guilt over something they never did," Miss Bergman reas-sured him. "It usually goes back to their childhood." And so on. "I had the feeling that something ailed him," Peck later said of Hitchcock, "and I could never understand what it might be."

The most striking novelty in *Spellbound* was Hitchcock's attempt to dra-matize Peck's guilt-ridden dreams by hiring Salvador Dali to design them. "I felt that if I was going to have dream sequences, they should be vivid," Hitchcock said. "I didn't think we should resort to the old-fashioned blurry effect they got by putting vaseline around the lens. . . . I used Dali for his draftsmanship. I wanted to convey the dreams with great visual sharpness and clarity, sharper than the film itself. . . . Chirico has the same quality, the long shadows, the infinity of distance, and the converging lines of perspec-tive."

Dali arrived in Hollywood with his customary fanfare, produced more than a hundred sketches and five paintings to be filmed (at a thousand dollars apiece). Eyewitness accounts of the result vary. "It opened with four hundred human eyes glaring down at [Peck] from black velvet drapes," according to Miss Bergman. "Then a pair of pliers fifteen times taller than Peck chased him up the side of a pyramid." The most spectacular effect was a vision of Miss Bergman as a Greek statue, which slowly cracked apart, enabling a

---

* "MacGuffin" was Hitchcock's term for the seemingly irrelevant point on which a whole plot would eventually be found to turn. The writer Angus MacPhail ascribed the term to an encounter between two men traveling on a train to Scotland. One of them asked the other what his oddly wrapped package on the luggage rack might be. "Oh, that's a MacGuffin," said the other. "What's a MacGuffin?" asked the first. "It's a device for trapping lions in the Scottish Highlands," said the second. "But there aren't any lions in the Scottish Highlands," said the first. "Well, then," said the second, "I guess that's no MacGuffin."

stream of ants to pour forth from her face. Selznick hated the whole thing. "The more I look at the dream sequence in *Spellbound*, the worse I feel it to be," he declared in one of his memos. Hitchcock, too, was less than enthusiastic, and so a twenty-minute sequence of Dali nightmares shrank to a few brief visions. The only regrets came from Miss Bergman, who thought the original Dali sequence had "many wonderful things" and "could have been really sensational."

But that was all irrelevant to the basic message of *Spellbound*, which was the basic message that everyone consciously or unconsciously wanted to hear in 1945: It's not your fault; you didn't do it. Skiing over hill and dale—all those parallel lines! all that whiteness!—Peck seemed to be going madder and madder, helped along by the feverish music of Miklos Rozsa,* until he finally fell, and thus relived the forgotten moment in which his younger brother had slid down a snow-covered stairway and impaled himself on a fence. It was all an accident, Miss Bergman assured him, not a killing, not your fault.

But what had happened to the original Dr. Edwardes? In another message for the atomic-bomb year 1945, but as old as *The Cabinet of Dr. Caligari*, not to mention *Frankenstein*, it soon turned out that it was kindly old Dr. Murchison (Leo G. Carroll), another psychiatrist, who had hoped to become head of the clinic, and then had murdered the destroyer of his ambitions. So even though psychoanalysis can almost magically cure us of our ills and our guilt, not all psychoanalysts (or other scientists) can be trusted. Some of these magicians are insane, homicidal. To dispatch the menacing Dr. Murchison, Hitchcock invoked an idea that he had wanted to use for years. Dr. Murchison, who had been threatening Miss Bergman, finally turned the gun on himself, and on the camera, and thus on the audience, and, with one red burst of flame, fired.

Selznick did his best to interfere with Hitchcock's creation, but Hitchcock was too clever for him. "When Selznick came down to the set," Miss Bergman recalled, "the camera suddenly stopped, and Hitchcock said the cameraman couldn't get it going again. 'I don't know what's wrong with it,' he would say. 'They're working on it, they're working on it.' And finally Selznick would leave, and miraculously the camera would start rolling again." Selznick presumably guessed that he was being deceived (other headstrong directors, like John Ford and Howard Hawks, used similar tactics against meddling producers), but he departed without complaint. Emotionally involved as he was in *Spellbound*, he was far more involved in a far more grandiose and far more demented project, *Duel in the Sun*.

When Selznick originally bought the novel by Niven Busch, he assigned it to King Vidor as director and said he wanted nothing more than "an artistic little Western." Soon, however, he was making announcements like "I want to shoot the works on numbers of horsemen, wild horses, cattle, etc." By the

---

* A classically trained Hungarian, Rozsa won an Academy Award for his *Spellbound* music, which he also turned into a briefly popular *Spellbound Concerto*.

time he had spent more than twenty months on various stages of production, he had invested more than five million dollars, more than the cost of *Gone With the Wind*. Selznick not only indulged in a producer's whims, paying Walter Huston forty thousand dollars for four days' work, for example, but he also wrote the script himself, and so indulged in writer's whims, rewriting scenes that had already been shot and insisting that Vidor reshoot them.

The main reason for all this eccentricity was that *Duel in the Sun* was to star Jennifer Jones as a half-caste in love with the evil hero, Gregory Peck. This was counter-typecasting of the most extreme sort, the hyper-respectable Peck as a killer and Saint Bernadette as a slut. The odd thing was that Miss Jones, perhaps precisely because of the demureness of her previous roles, did have a strangely erotic quality, and Selznick took an almost perverse pleasure in bringing it out of her and putting it on display and having it photographed. "It was on the love scenes especially . . ." Selznick said when a dispute later arose over directorial credits, "that I was on the set morning, noon, and night, redirecting the actors, the camera, and even the lighting."

This constant interference, in which Selznick took such pride, eventually infuriated King Vidor, particularly when the whole crew was sweltering on location in the desert near Tucson. At one point, Selznick began shouting at Vidor about something he wanted changed, and Vidor grimly said, "Don't do that, David. I won't have you doing that in front of the company." Selznick apologized, but he could not stop interfering and domineering. Occasionally, he insisted in playing the grandee, as when he took a band of his employees to a seedy gambling house so they could watch him play roulette at 5 A.M. and lose thirty thousand dollars at the wheel. Then back to work in the desert.

In the bombastic climax to the film, when Peck and Miss Jones shot each other but kept crawling toward each other through the sand, Selznick abruptly decided that the doomed lovers didn't look sufficiently doomed, so he stepped forward and sprinkled some more blood on them. Vidor couldn't stand it any more. "You can take this picture and shove it," he said to Selznick, then stalked off the set, climbed into a black limousine, and told the driver to head for Los Angeles. It happened that the desert road stretched eight miles westward without a bend. The whole *Duel* company, including the perspiring Selznick and the blood-spattered Miss Jones, watched in silence as Vidor's black limousine sped toward the horizon, growing smaller and smaller until it disappeared into a distant row of hills. "Well, that's all for today," said Selznick.

The producer eventually hired William Dieterle to come and clean up the odds and ends, and so his "artistic little Western" was finally finished. The critics laughed at it, laughed at Orson Welles's thunderous off screen narration and at Dimitri Tiomkin's *shtump* music, and at Jennifer Jones crawling through the sand and calling out the name of her lover/murderer, "Lewt! Lewt!" Perhaps the cruelest judgment came from Charles Brackett, the writer who had collaborated with Billy Wilder on such elegant screenplays as *Ninotchka,* and who now compared Selznick's new epic to the famous saga of

Billy the Kid, which Howard Hughes had finally exhumed from his vault and released. *Duel in the Sun,* said Brackett, was *"The Outlaw* in bad taste."

Selznick was unnerved, but by Hollywood standards, *Duel in the Sun* was a big hit, Selznick's last. On its first release, pushed along by a two-million-dollar advertising campaign, it made seventeen million dollars, more than three times its production cost. (*Spellbound* did very nicely too, earning more than $7 million on an investment of $1.5 million, plus an Academy Award nomination as the best picture of the year.) But Selznick was still haunted by demons, and so was Jennifer Jones (it was not until 1949 that they finally married). Mrs. Selznick, who had moved to New York and established herself as a theatrical producer, heard that Miss Jones was repeatedly calling her. She refused to take the calls. Miss Jones then pretended to be Dorothy Paley, the wife of the CBS chairman, and said she was calling on a matter of life and death. Mrs. Selznick came to the phone, found that it was Miss Jones calling again, and tried to turn her away. Miss Jones took to waiting outside the theater where Mrs. Selznick was rehearsing a new play.

"There was no ducking it," Mrs. Selznick said of her eventual meeting with her successor. "I told my driver to take us through Central Park. She was distraught about David's unhappiness—he claimed his life was ruined and she blamed herself. She was bad for him. His career was over. He didn't love her, he loved me. . . . She grew hysterical and tried to throw herself out of the car—I only just managed to pull her back. We drove round and round the park. As I quieted her down, I told her David was bad for himself and nothing she did or didn't do could change that. . . ."

●　　●　　●

After a lifetime of failure, Raymond Chandler found the success of his late fifties rather bewildering. For years, he had sat at home and cranked out pulp fiction, and now he was the coauthor of Billy Wilder's *Double Indemnity,* and Paramount paid him a thousand dollars a week, and the Writers Building was well stocked with liquor, and people told funny stories at the writers' table in the studio dining room ("You mean to say she's a nymphomaniac?" somebody asked about some ambitious actress, and Harry Tugend said, "Well, I guess she would be, if they could get her quieted down a little"). Chandler's wife, Cissy, was now seventy-three, and John Houseman noted that "the presence of women—secretaries and extras around the lot—disturbed and excited him." Houseman, just starting out as a producer at Paramount, worked with Chandler on a minor thriller called *The Unseen* and claimed that Chandler regarded the two of them as bound by the tie of having both gone to English public schools, two gentlemen adrift in the horse latitudes.

When Chandler signed a new three-year contract at Paramount and reported for work at the start of January 1945, the studio was in considerable disarray. Buddy DeSylva, the chief of production, had just suffered a heart attack and never returned to the studio; his right-hand man, Bill Dozier, departed for RKO. The official studio boss, Y. Frank Freeman, was primarily a hand-shaker who knew little about making movies, so the surviving executives were going around in circles. In the midst of this, the word spread that Alan Ladd, the studio's biggest star, was due to be drafted in three months and that nobody had prepared any films to entertain Ladd's fans during his imminent absence. General manager Henry Ginsberg, who seemed to be in charge of the confusion, told a meeting of Paramount executives that anyone who could concoct a Ladd movie that could go into production within a month would, as Houseman recalled it, "earn the eternal gratitude of the Studio."

Houseman went to lunch with Chandler that same day at Lucey's restaurant. Chandler complained, he recalled, of being stuck on a book about three homecoming war veterans. The hero, Johnny Morrison, returned to discover that his wife was being unfaithful. They quarreled. Then she was found dead. Chandler didn't know exactly how the story would turn out. He was thinking vaguely of turning it into a screenplay. Houseman hungrily followed Chandler home to his Spanish bungalow on Drexel Avenue, where they found the aged Cissy swathed in pink tarlatan and nursing a broken leg. Houseman sat down right there and read about a hundred pages of *The Blue Dahlia*. He sensed success. Two days later, Paramount bought the story and assigned Houseman and Chandler to work on it. "They are already casting it without a line of screenplay written," Chandler wrote anxiously to a friend. "Why do I get myself into these jams?"

Worse was to come. When Chandler delivered the first sixty pages of script, roughly the first half of the film, Paramount assigned the picture to a veteran director, George Marshall, and told him to start shooting the beginning while Chandler continued working on the script. After a month or so, a script girl pointed out the alarming fact that Marshall was filming faster than Chandler was writing. At that point, the crew had finished sixty-two pages but the writer had produced only another twenty-two.

"Ray's problem with the script . . ." Houseman cheerily recalled, "was a simple one: he had no ending." Alan Ladd, the betrayed war hero, was naturally a prime suspect in his wife's murder, but many other people might have committed the crime, anyone in that swarm of shadowy dealmakers and black marketeers who had flocked to the dead woman's rowdy parties. Houseman said he remained "quite confident" that Chandler would think up some interesting solution to the murder, but when the front office started worrying about the dwindling number of unfilmed pages, the story conferences began. "It was during one of these meetings, early one afternoon," Houseman recalled, "that a man came running down the Studio street, stopping at various windows to shout to the people inside something we could not hear. When he reached us, he shoved his head in and told us that Franklin D. Roosevelt was dead." They all "sat stunned for a while," and then, like everyone else, "said all the obvious things," and then "fell silent and sat there gloomily for a while." But *The Blue Dahlia* still had no ending, so the executives resumed their search for the murderer. "We went through all the tired alternatives," Houseman said, "using them to smother the realities of the world outside, and Ray sat listening, only half there, nodding his head, saying little."

Two days later, Chandler presented himself at Houseman's office and dolefully announced that he would have to withdraw from the whole project. He looked very shaky. He couldn't solve the murder. Ginsberg, the officious studio manager, had summoned Chandler to his office—warning him not to mention this to Houseman—and then offered him a bonus of five thousand dollars if he could deliver the finished script of *The Blue Dahlia* on time. Chandler appeared to be shocked, stricken. It took Houseman a little time to figure out why, and he concluded that there were three reasons. First, since Houseman had always feigned confidence in Chandler's ability to finish the script, Ginsberg's offer of five thousand dollars provided the first disclosure that Paramount was worried, and therefore Chandler's "sense of security was now hopelessly shattered." Second, Chandler had been "insulted" by the offer of additional money to complete an assignment that he had agreed to undertake. Third, Ginsberg's action in making the offer without Houseman's knowledge meant to Chandler that he was being invited "to betray a friend and a fellow Public School man."

This may sound a little too labyrinthine even for Hollywood, but the Paramount administration building was ornamented with Elizabethan timbering and casement windows and quasi-antique hunting prints, so perhaps it was fitting for Chandler and Houseman to sit there and ruminate on the possibilities of an affront to a Public School man. By now, according to Houseman, there were only thirteen pages of script still to be shot, no prospect of an ending, and Ladd due to enter the army in ten days. While Houseman pondered what to do next, Chandler returned to the studio the following day with a remarkable proposition. Although he remained convinced that he could never finish the script while sober, he was just as convinced that he could easily finish it if he stayed drunk. This was a serious matter, for Chandler had only with great difficulty stopped drinking, and his doctor had warned him that he might jeopardize his life if he ever resumed. But for the sake of honor and all that, Chandler now produced a sheet of yellow paper on which he had listed for Houseman his basic requirements:

A. Two Cadillac limousines, to stand day and night outside the house with drivers available for:

    1. Fetching the doctor (Ray's or Cissy's or both).
    2. Taking script pages to and from the studio.
    3. Driving the maid to market.
    4. Contingencies and emergencies.

B. Six secretaries—in three relays of two—to be in constant attendance and readiness, available at all times for dictation, typing and other emergencies.

C. A direct line open at all times to my office by day and the studio switchboard at night.

This bizarre proposal included obvious signs of a writer's neurotic need for attention, and of an alcoholic's desire to camouflage his need for liquor, but Houseman took it all very literally. His own boss, Joe Sistrom, approved the arrangement on the ground that "if the picture closed down we'd all be fired anyway." And so, to get the project under way, Houseman took Chandler to an expensive lunch at Perrino's, where the novelist fortified himself with three double martinis before eating and three double stingers afterward.

For the next week, according to Houseman, Chandler "did not draw one sober breath." Nor did he eat. His doctor came twice a day to give him injections of glucose. He worked intermittently and drank steadily, around the clock. From time to time, he would fall into a light sleep. "He woke in full possession of his faculties," Houseman recalled, "to pick up exactly where he had stopped with whichever of the rotating secretaries happened to be with him. He continued until he felt himself growing drowsy again, then dropped back comfortably into sleep while the girl went into the next room, typed the pages and left them on the table beside him to be reread and corrected when he woke up."

Houseman, who dropped by periodically to see how Chandler was progressing, arrived one morning to find that the murder had been solved. Although Chandler was lying unconscious on his sofa, there were several pages of neatly corrected script lying next to a half-empty glass of bourbon, and these pages provided the answers. It was Dad Newell, the house detective, who had murdered Morrison's unfaithful wife. And now the killer turned on his pursuers: "Cheap, huh? Sure—a cigar and a drink and a couple of dirty bucks—that's all it takes to buy me! That's what *she* thought— Found out a little different, didn't she? Maybe I could get tired of being pushed around by cops—and hotel managers—and ritzy dames in bungalows. . . ." It was not very plausible, but that didn't greatly matter, since there were so many suspects that almost anyone in the cast could have committed the crime. Besides, it was an Alan Ladd movie, and Alan Ladd movies didn't need to be plausible; they just needed to display the handsome star, always the loner, hard but vulnerable, vulnerable but hard. He was, as Chandler tartly observed, and as *Shane* was later to demonstrate, "a small boy's idea of a tough guy."

"The film was finished with four days to spare," Houseman said, to conclude his splendid story, "Alan Ladd went off to the army, and Paramount made a lot of money." One of several problems with this splendid story, however, is that although there were announcements the previous fall that Ladd would soon be drafted, there seems to be no evidence that he actually did return to uniform. Ladd had in fact joined the Army Air Corps early in 1943, had served nearly a year in various promotional and fund-raising assignments, and then had received a medical discharge for a double hernia. The idea that a man with such a record should be threatened by the draft in 1945, when the war was virtually over, is rather hard to believe. When this flaw in the story was pointed out to Houseman, though, he strongly answered that "the facts about *The Blue Dahlia,* as outlined in my book—believe me—are totally correct." On the other hand, Ladd's biographer, Beverly Linet, stated just as firmly that no such redrafting ever took place. What Ladd did do after finishing *The Blue Dahlia* was to go off to his ranch in Hidden Valley while his wife, Sue Carol, a prominent Hollywood agent, bargained with Paramount for a new contract.

Another problem with Houseman's story is that Chandler seems to have had a solution to the murder from the beginning. The killer was not really the house detective, a very marginal character, but the hero's best friend, Buzz Wanchek. Nor was *The Blue Dahlia* a book on which Chandler found himself blocked. On the contrary, he wrote to a friend at the start of 1945 that he was having "a lot of fun" in "writing an original screenplay—a murder mystery, but not entirely that—and if it turns out good enough, I have the right to make a book of it." Chandler's original idea was that Buzz Wanchek (played to perfection by William Bendix) was a hot-tempered man who returned from the war with a serious head injury that left him periodically subject both to bursts of violence and to spells of amnesia. "What I wrote," Chandler said later, "was a story of a man who killed (executed would be a better word) his pal's wife under the stress of a great and legitimate anger, then blanked out and forgot all about it; then with perfect honesty did his best to help the pal get out of a jam, then found himself in a set of circumstances which brought about partial recall."

In a strange way that Chandler himself could hardly have known, his original plot bore remarkable resemblances to the real relationship between Ladd and Bendix. They had met in 1942 in filming a remake of Dashiell Hammett's *The Glass Key*. It was a peculiarly sadomasochistic film, in which the mountainous Bendix, assigned to guard the diminutive Ladd inside a locked basement, kept hitting him and then picking him up and hitting him again, until, ordered to stop, he complained, "Aw, you mean I don't get to smack baby no more?" This was all playacting, of course, except that in the middle of it, Bendix accidentally smashed Ladd on the jaw and knocked him cold. Then, when he realized what had happened, he burst into tears. "My God, what have I done?" he cried.

Ladd, on recovering, was oddly touched by Bendix's concern, and the two became good friends; so did their wives. Bendix, still a newcomer from Broadway, was living in a rented bungalow, and Ladd insisted that he move up in the world, to a house across from Ladd's own place on Cromwell Avenue. So when Ladd came home on leave in 1943 and grumbled to Bendix about the military life, Bendix felt no hesitation about making light of it. "Aw, come on, Laddie, stop griping," said Bendix, who had been rejected for military service because of severe asthma. "You know you're living a plush life down there in San Diego." Ladd didn't seem to mind, but his wife, who devoted her whole life to shining and polishing the image of her husband/ client, bristled. "You're a fine one to talk—considering you're not rushing off to join up," she said. Bendix, the gentle giant, was stunned. "He just got up from his chair," his wife, Tess, recalled, "and walked right out of Alan's house without saying a word."

Bendix retreated to his own house across the street and waited for his friend Ladd to apologize. Ladd thought that Bendix's abrupt departure was an insult to Mrs. Ladd, for which Bendix should apologize. When Ladd did nothing to make amends, Bendix sold his house on Cromwell Avenue and moved away. For months, the two former friends never spoke to each other, and when business brought them together, the reunions were stiff, polite, formal. As on the set of *The Blue Dahlia,* in which, according to Chandler's original idea, Buzz (Bendix) had been so outraged by the misbehavior of the wife of his best friend, Johnny Morrison (Ladd), that he had killed her, and then forgotten about it.

Chandler had prepared for this explosion—a little obviously but quite powerfully—in the very first scene of his script. Ladd and Bendix, newly out of uniform, got off a bus and went into a bar to toast each other farewell. There, a uniformed marine kept putting nickels into the jukebox, and the noise began to drive Bendix wild.

"*Buzz:* How about giving that thing a rest?

"The Marine grins at him and drops the nickel in the juke box.

"*Buzz:* I got a headache.

"*Marine:* Ain't that a pity!

"The juke box starts up again very loud. Buzz moves around it and kicks the cord loose from the wall. The juke box stops dead.

"*Marine* [in a hard voice]: Plug that in again, chum—but quick!

"Buzz picks up the cord and jerks it loose from the juke box, holds it out to the Marine.

"*Buzz:* You plug it in!"

The marine lunged at Buzz, but Morrison stepped in to break it up, not by fighting, interestingly enough, but by flattering and soothing the indignant marine. Only then, when peace was restored, did the bartender scold the returning veterans: "You gents oughta respect the uniform." And only then did Buzz lean over the bar, part some of the hair over his temple, and say, "What do you figure I had on when I got this? There's a plate under there as big as your brains—maybe bigger."

This idea of the friend as murderer seems to have derived from a still earlier fragment that Chandler sketched in his notebooks, in which a man thought his wife had died accidentally and then made friends with her murderer. Perhaps Cissy Chandler contemplated all these fantasies of uxoricide with some misgivings. In any case, Chandler seemed justified in writing to a friend that the original version of *The Blue Dahlia* was "a fairly original idea." Then, apparently, the U.S. Navy objected to the suggestion that wounded veterans capable of both violence and amnesia were being demobilized and sent forth into the civilian world. Such publicity-minded complaints had carried a certain weight during the war, when the authorities not only provided valuable military services to moviemakers but also felt entitled to request civilian support of the war effort, but why the navy should feel entitled to change the plot of a murder mystery in 1945, and why Paramount should feel obliged to obey, remains unexplained. But so it happened. "What the Navy Department did to the story," Chandler wrote to a friend, "was a little like making me change the murderer and hence make a routine whodunit."

Chandler grumblingly accepted whatever the studio authorities did to his work, for he held to the idea that neither the producers nor their films were of any real importance—except, perhaps, as elements in his own books. He found it interesting, for example, that Y. Frank Freeman had built a special dog run at Paramount, where he exercised his prize boxers. In *The Little Sister,* Philip Marlowe went to interrogate someone at a large movie studio and suddenly found himself in a tiled patio where "an elderly and beautifully dressed man was lounging on the marble seat watching three tan-colored boxers root up some tea-rose begonias." The three boxers urinated in turn on the marble bench, and the old man remarked on the fact that they always did so in the same sequence, according to age. Even in his office, he added, they kept to their rules. Marlowe showed some surprise at that, but the old man went on ruminating about his dogs. "Up against the corner of the desk. Do it all the time. Drives my secretaries crazy. Gets into the carpet, they say. What's the matter with women nowadays? Never bothers me. Rather like it."

This was Jules Oppenheimer, who owned the studio and much else besides, who thought that the trouble with the movie business was "too much sex. . . . Wade through it. Stand up to our necks in it. Gets to be like flypaper." But Oppenheimer was not very much interested in what his studio's movies showed. He just ran the business, which mainly consisted, he said, in owning a string of theaters.

"Fifteen hundred theaters is all you need," said Oppenheimer. "A damn sight easier than raising purebred boxers. The motion-picture business is the only business in the world in which you can make all the mistakes there are and still make money."

"Must be the only business in the world where you can have three dogs pee up against your office desk," Marlowe answered.

"You have to have the fifteen hundred theaters," Oppenheimer said.

This was, of course, what the United States Department of Justice was still trying to prove in court.

•   •   •

James M. Cain had wanted to call his first novel "Bar-B-Que." Alfred Knopf quite rightly thought that was a terrible title. Cain suggested "Black Puma" or "The Devil's Checkbook." The publisher disliked those, too, and proposed calling it "For Love or Money." Then Cain thought of a title he really liked: "The Postman Always Rings Twice." Knopf said he still preferred "For Love or Money." Cain got angry. "There is only one rule I know on a title," he wrote to Knopf. "It must sound like the author and not like some sure-fire product of the title factory." He suggested that "For Love or Money" might do very well for a musical comedy or a movie (Universal finally did use that title in 1963, starring Kirk Douglas and Gig Young), or just about anything. He went on to name some more all-purpose titles that sounded typical of the title factory, like "Hold Everything" or "Hell and High Water." Knopf knew when to retreat.

The Postman Always Rings Twice received excellent reviews and became one of the best-sellers of 1934, which may have inspired M-G-M to pay

$25,000 for the movie rights to a book that couldn't be filmed. By the standards of 1934, it was simply too shocking, not because of any particular sex scenes, which could always be disguised, but because of the essential immorality of the whole story. When the unemployed hitchhiker stopped at Cora's roadside diner, he took a job there mainly out of hunger for Cora, and when the two of them decided to murder Cora's middle-aged husband, generally referred to only as "the Greek," they killed him simply to get him out of the way. It was Cora's idea.

"They hang you for that," Frank protested.

"Not if you do it right. . . ."

"He never did anything to me. He's all right."

"The hell he's all right. He stinks, I tell you. He's greasy and he stinks."

So the novel lay untouched in the M-G-M storehouse until Billy Wilder and Raymond Chandler managed to turn Cain's equally unsavory *Double Indemnity* into a hit for Paramount, and then M-G-M dug out *Postman* to see if something couldn't be done with it.* Carey Wilson, the producer of the Andy Hardy series, was put in charge of making it acceptable. Americans had been through a war by now, and perhaps they weren't as innocent as they liked to think they had been. And perhaps if the script put a lot of emphasis on the two murderers being killed at the end, unsatisfied and unhappy in their sinfulness . . . To win the approval of the censors at what was now called the Johnston Office,† Director Tay Garnett said, the studio "raised the tone" of the whole story. "I guess you could say we've lifted it from the gutter up to, well, the sidewalk." Garnett even called for Cora to be dressed entirely in white, on the theory that, as Garnett put it, "dressing Lana in white somehow made everything she did less sensuous."

The Johnston Office hadn't reckoned on Lana Turner, who was then twenty-five and at the height of her luscious beauty. She had already shown, in films like *Ziegfeld Girl* and *Honky Tonk* and *Somewhere I'll Find You,* that she couldn't act very well, and that she didn't need to act very well. She glowed. At this point, she was also personally on the hunt. She had just been through her second divorce, and she liked going out. "The war had just ended, and . . . the men were home," she recalled. "They seemed to catch your eye everywhere you went, like the first greening after a thaw. How I'd love to dress up and go dancing with a handsome dark man. Ciro's was a favorite haunt. . . . Ciro's was designed for dramatic entrances and exits because a long flight of stairs led down to the tables and dance floor. . . . I'd usually be

---

* In the midst of the war, the young Italian director Luchino Visconti solved all these problems by simply stealing Cain's novel, resetting it in a *trattoria* by the marshes along the Po, and retitling it *Ossessione* (1942). M-G-M subsequently barred his film from the U.S.

† Eric Johnston, who replaced Will Hays as head of the Motion Picture Association in 1945, was a cheery enthusiast who had talked his way up from door-to-door vacuum-cleaner salesman to president of the United States Chamber of Commerce. Johnston was an avid delegator of responsibility, so he delegated responsibility for Hollywood's self-censorship to Joseph I. Breen, an ardent Catholic who had played the same role under Hays. Johnston assigned to himself the role of Hollywood's official oracle. He made many speeches in favor of free enterprise. He later organized the Hollywood blacklist.

dressed in something clingy, black or white, sometimes gold, occasionally red.
I'd wear diamonds and a fur of some kind draped over one shoulder. Often
white fur, my favorite. Maybe ermine or silver fox."

The "handsome dark man" in her new film was to be John Garfield, who
had achieved a modest success in modest films like *The Sea Wolf* and now
stood at the brink of bigger things. As part of his success, Garfield felt himself
entitled to proposition virtually every woman he met, and so he greeted his
new co-star by saying, "Hey, Lana, how's about a little quickie?" She answered appropriately, "You bastard!" According to studio gossip, things eventually went further than that, but perhaps that was only studio gossip. It was
standard in those days to make love scenes appear more authentic by spreading
word that the principals continued their romance offscreen. Garfield and Miss
Turner needed no such publicity. Their love scenes, in which, by today's
standards, nothing happened, were among the most erotic ever filmed. The
image of Lana Turner in her white bathing suit on Laguna Beach was one
that nobody who saw it ever forgot.

It almost didn't get filmed at all, however, for Garnett wanted to work on
location as much as possible, and when he took his whole crew on the fifty-
mile trek to Laguna Beach, a fog rolled in. "Each day we'd go down to the
beach and sit there in the dense mist, waiting and hoping," Miss Turner
recalled. "After several hours the production people would give up and send
us back to our lodgings." With the studio managers grumbling about delays,
Garnett nervously decided to move another fifteen miles down the coast to San
Clemente—not yet haunted by the ghost of President Nixon—to try his luck
there. More fog. More complaints from the home office. Garnett desperately
decided to return to Laguna Beach. Still more fog. Still louder criticisms from
the studio. Threats of dismissal. Garnett pleaded for time. Days stretched
into weeks.

"That's when Tay fell off the wagon," Miss Turner said. Garnett was
one of those journeyman directors who satisfied themselves in keeping things
orderly (he eventually made more than a hundred films, very few of distinction). A heavy drinker, he had given up alcohol three years earlier, but now
the fog and the delays and the constant criticism and anxiety were all too
much for him. "Nobody could control him," Miss Turner said. "He was a
roaring, mean, furniture-smashing drunk. The girl friend he'd brought along
stayed for a while, then gave up. The studio sent nurses, but even they
couldn't help."

Nobody at Laguna Beach knew quite what to do. There were rumors
that Garnett would be replaced, that the location shooting would be abandoned, even that the whole film would be canceled. To prevent anything like
that, Garfield and Miss Turner went to visit the drunken director to see what
could be done. Garfield talked his way past the attendant nurses and went on
in alone. He returned shaken.

"It's terrible, Lana," he said. "He didn't know who I was. When I tried to talk to him, he'd say, 'Sure, Johnny boy, whatever you think.' But a moment later he'd start shouting, 'Who the hell are you? Get out of my room.' Then he came at me with the cane he always carries."

"Maybe if I went to see him," Miss Turner offered.

Garfield was skeptical. So were the nurses. They said they first had to quiet Garnett down. They managed to get his cane away from him. Then they let her in.

"What I found was a besotted man who regretted what he'd done . . ." Miss Turner said. "He sniffled and begged my forgiveness. Now he was rational enough to be sent back to Los Angeles for treatment. By the time he returned a week later, the fog had obligingly lifted, and we were able to complete the film."

•   •   •

If there was any writer who disliked Hollywood more than Raymond Chandler, it was William Faulkner. "They worship death here," he once remarked at dinner with a friend. "They don't worship money, they worship death." A small, trim man, his mustache by now gray, Faulkner was in Hollywood because almost nobody bought his books, not even *The Sound and the Fury* (1929), not even *Light in August* (1932). His first four novels had sold an average of two thousand copies, and when he tried to dash off a best-seller, *Sanctuary* (1931), his publisher soon collapsed in bankruptcy. So he came to Hollywood in 1932 and signed a contract with M-G-M at what he considered a princely five hundred dollars per week.

M-G-M's story editor, Sam Marx, asked him to start work on a wrestling story for Wallace Beery. "I want to write for Mickey Mouse," said Faulkner, quasi innocent. When informed that Mickey Mouse belonged to the Disney studio, Faulkner said, "Then what about newsreels? I like cartoons and newsreels." Marx sent Faulkner to a projection room to watch Wallace Beery in *The Champ* and asked an office boy to go along with him to answer any questions. Ten minutes later, the boy returned and told Marx that Faulkner had disappeared after asking only one question: "How do I get out of here?" According to other accounts, Faulkner emerged from the projection room repeatedly saying to himself, "Jesus Christ, it ain't possible!"

M-G-M put the novelist to work at patching and revising various projects, almost none of which were ever filmed, then cut his pay to $250 and finally fired him the following year. He stoically went back to Mississippi and began writing his most majestic novel, *Absalom, Absalom!* (1936). That didn't sell either, so he returned to Hollywood to go to work for Darryl Zanuck at Fox at one thousand dollars a week.

Zanuck assigned Faulkner to a film being produced by Nunnally Johnson, who was both a fellow writer and a fellow southerner and who welcomed Faulkner to his palatial office with a great show of courtliness. Faulkner responded by reaching into his pocket and taking out a pint of whiskey. He started to pick at the heavy tinfoil that covered the cork but had difficulty in unsealing the bottle. Dropping his hat to the floor so that he could attack the bottle with both hands, he cut his finger on the tinfoil. He tried to stop the bleeding by licking the finger with his tongue. When that failed, he looked around for some receptacle but could see nothing except his own hat. According to Roark Bradford, the teller of this tale, Faulkner held his dripping finger over his hat while he "continued to work, methodically and silently, until the bottle was finally uncorked. He then tilted it, drank half its contents, and passed it to Johnson.

" 'Have a drink of whiskey?' he offered.

" 'I don't mind if I do,' said Johnson, finishing off the pint. This, according to the legend, was the beginning of a drunk which ended three weeks later, when studio sleuths found both Faulkner and Johnson in an Okie camp, sobered them up, and got them to work."

In 1937, Faulkner was fired again and returned to Mississippi to write *The Wild Palms* (1939) and *The Hamlet* (1940). By 1942, his royalty statement from Random House credited him with three hundred dollars as his total earnings for that year from whatever novels were still in print (and by the following year, they were all out of print, except for a Modern Library edition of *Sanctuary*). So Faulkner had to return once again to Hollywood, to Warner Bros., which granted him in the summer of 1942 one of its seven-year contracts. It paid him a starting wage of three hundred dollars a week, substantially less than either of his previous jobs. At the end of this seven-year Warners contract, Faulkner would win the Nobel Prize, but now he was working at the pay scale of a "junior writer." He was forty-five.

Hal Wallis, the Warners production chief, summoned Faulkner to his office and said he was interested in having him write a film treatment of a contemporary war memoir titled *God Is My Co-Pilot*.

"Do you want to do it?" he asked.

"No," said Faulkner.

"Have you read the book?"

"No."

"Do you want to read it?"

"No."

"What *do* you want to do?"

"Go home to Mississippi."

"You're under contract and you'll work here," Wallis snapped. And Faulkner did work, at whatever he was told to do. He wrote a full-scale 153-page screenplay for a Washington-inspired epic known only as "De Gaulle Story," which Warners shelved when De Gaulle began irritating his allies. Faulkner was then put to work on "Liberator Story," the saga of an American bomber; and *Northern Pursuit,* an Errol Flynn movie about Nazi spies working their way across Canada; and *Air Force,* another bomber saga, this one directed by Howard Hawks. When asked later how he kept producing twenty-five pages of script every week, Faulkner said, "I just kept saying to myself, they're going to pay me Saturday, they're going to pay me Saturday."

It was perhaps his encounters with people like Hal Wallis that inspired the legend that Faulkner asked permission to work at home and then took that as permission to work in Mississippi. Darryl Zanuck claimed that Faulkner had pulled this trick on him while writing *The Road to Glory* for Howard Hawks in 1936. "I thought home meant where he was living in Beverly Hills!" said Zanuck, who seems not to have realized that Faulkner lived in cheap hotels or roomed with friends far from Beverly Hills. Jack Warner claimed that he was the victim of exactly the same ruse nearly a decade later. "Mr. Faulkner, how could you do this to me?" Warner recalled protesting on the long-distance phone. "How could you leave town without letting me know? You said you'd be working at home." And Faulkner patiently answered, "This is my home. I live in Mississippi." It is theoretically possible that both these events occurred just as the two studio chiefs said they did, but it seems hardly likely.* Faulkner himself told several versions of the legend, including a claim that it was all "a pure lie by some press agent fella."

The one important man in Hollywood who understood and appreciated Faulkner was Howard Hawks. One year older than the novelist, Hawks had spent the previous two decades as a director, and his movies were not only skillful but successful—*The Dawn Patrol, Scarface, Twentieth Century.* His success gave him considerable independence, so his films generally bore a Hawks touch, direct, unpretentious, based on a strong and fast-moving story, usually about men in action. Hawks himself was like that. He loved hunting, flying, auto racing, prowling the wilderness. He rode a motorcycle until he was nearly eighty. He also took a large part in the writing of all his films, and he produced most of them too.

Hawks had discovered Faulkner early. He read his first novel, *Soldier's Pay,* shortly after it appeared in 1926. He bought the film rights to one of Faulkner's war stories, "Turn About," and at a time when, as he put it, "nobody'd ever heard of Faulkner," he began trying to hire him. Faulkner only reluctantly joined in the filming of "Turn About" at M-G-M and got only a partial script credit for the picture that became *Today We Live* (1933), starring Gary Cooper and Joan Crawford. But Hawks and Faulkner became lifelong friends, and Hawks repeatedly found work for him. Faulkner never actually wrote a single finished script for Hawks, so film scholars have tried in vain to determine exactly what he contributed to the director's projects. Hawks liked to improvise on the set; he liked to have Faulkner there as a kind of carpenter, or perhaps he just liked to have him around. "If I wanted a scene or a story, I'd call up Bill and get it," Hawks once said. "He could write almost anything. . . . We seemed to talk the same language. He knew what I

---

* For that matter, Jesse L. Lasky, Jr., a screenwriter during these years, declared that the victim of Faulkner's homesickness was Louis B. Mayer. Norman Zierold wrote in *The Moguls* that it was Harry Cohn.

wanted. Bill drank too much, but when he wasn't drinking he was awful
good."

Hawks liked to take Faulkner on hunting expeditions, and when Clark
Gable heard one day that the director was setting off for the Imperial Valley
early the next morning, he asked to go along. Hawks agreed. The three of
them were driving through Palm Springs, as Hawks later recalled, when the
talk turned to writing. Gable, whose ignorance was almost classic, idly asked
Hawks's gray-haired friend who he thought were good writers. "Thomas
Mann, Willa Cather, John Dos Passos, Ernest Hemingway, and myself,"
Faulkner said. Gable seemed mildly surprised.

"Oh, do you write, Mr. Faulkner?" he asked.

"Yeah," Faulkner admitted. "What do *you* do, Mr. Gable?"

Perhaps that was intended as a sarcastic retort, but Hawks wondered. "I
don't think Gable ever read a book, and I don't think Faulkner ever went to
see a movie," he said. "So they might have been on the level."

If Hawks felt an echoing admiration for the chronicler of Yoknapatawpha
County, he felt even more for Ernest Hemingway, who had both the creative
talent of Faulkner and the money to live like Hawks. The director repeatedly
tried to hire him, but Hemingway kept shrugging off all his efforts.

"I don't want to go out to Hollywood," Hemingway said to Hawks as they
were fishing together off Key West early in 1943. "I don't like it. And I
wouldn't know what to do."

"You wouldn't have to come to Hollywood," Hawks said, according to his
account of the scene. "We can go fishing or hunting. We can meet here, Sun
Valley, Africa, any place you want, and write a story."

Hemingway still balked, so Hawks began taunting him, telling him that
he could make a good movie out of anything.

"I can make a movie out of the worst thing you ever wrote," Hawks said.

"What's the worst thing I ever wrote?" Hemingway immediately demanded.

"That piece of junk called *To Have and Have Not*," Hawks claimed he
said. He also claimed that Hemingway only answered, "I needed money."

To Have and Have Not was by no means junk. Harry Morgan was one of
Hemingway's more realistic heroes, about the only one who lived with a wife
and worked for a living, and the climactic gun battle aboard Morgan's fishing
boat made a very powerful conclusion. But Hawks bought the movie rights to
the novel for a modest ten thousand dollars and then proceeded to tear it to
pieces. "There wasn't *anything* in the picture that was in the book," he later
gloated. To help him at his task, Hawks hired a veteran screenwriter named
Jules Furthman plus his old friend Faulkner, but the transformation of *To
Have and Have Not* was very much the director's own work. He seemed to
think he could make it a kind of sequel to *Casablanca,* and so he moved the
story from Key West in the Depression-ridden 1930's to Martinique in the
wartime 1940's, thus ringing in once again the background conflict between

Vichyites and the Free French. And who could be a more inevitable Harry Morgan than the original Rick, Humphrey Bogart?

Hawks had apparently long dreamed of discovering a beautiful girl whom he could mold like a Galatea into a star of his own creation. He had already discovered one such creature, a model named Nancy Roe Gross, but instead of making her a star, he married her, just a year after getting his divorce from Norma Shearer's sister. The new Mrs. Hawks was twenty-four, her husband forty-five; she called him, for some reason, Steve; he called her Slim. On the cover of *Harper's Bazaar,* she saw a girl who she thought might serve Hawks as the toy he was looking for. A beautiful face, but hard, slightly Slavic, with a wide mouth and wide-set eyes. Hawks was interested. He was then working in partnership with Charlie Feldman, that former agent who had married the girl of Louis B. Mayer's dreams, and though Selznick and Columbia were also interested in the *Harper's Bazaar* cover girl, Feldman persuaded her to come to Hollywood to be tested and signed by Hawks.

Born Betty Perske, she had taken her mother's name of Bacall when she went into modeling. She was now eighteen and ready to conquer the world. Feldman took her to meet Hawks for lunch at the Brown Derby, and she was impressed by the "very tall man with close-cropped gray hair and broad shoulders." Feldman said her teeth would have to be fixed; Hawks said that wouldn't be necessary. He tested her, and she looked good, but he had nothing for her to do. In Miss Bacall's retrospective view, Hawks was a rather frightening figure of authority, who talked grandly about his own triumphs and occasionally unnerved her by making anti-Semitic remarks ("Do you notice how noisy it is in here suddenly? That's because Lee Forbstein just walked in—Jews always make more noise"), at which she paled but discreetly said nothing. Hawks's recollection, on the other hand, was that this attractive girl's voice was so bad, so high and nasal, that he wanted to get rid of her. "I had to tell her that we made pictures about a fairly sophisticated girl, that the kind of girls I like in a movie didn't have little high nasal voices. I said, 'You just can't possibly read any of the lines we write.' Didn't bother her, she said, 'What do I do to change my voice?' "

Hawks told her to go somewhere and practice keeping her voice low, husky. Miss Bacall began driving out Mulholland Drive in her nine-hundred-dollar used Plymouth until she found a quiet spot where she could read aloud, in a low-pitched voice, from a current best-seller about Jesus Christ, Lloyd Douglas's *The Robe.* "If anyone had passed by, they would have found me a candidate for an asylum," she recalled. "Who sat on mountaintops in cars reading books aloud to the canyons? Who did? I did!" Hawks also taught Miss Bacall something more important: how to behave in the way he thought "sophisticated" women should behave. In Hawks's slightly peculiar view, women became more attractive when they played the aggressor, the pursuer. Miss Bacall had those possibilities, but she was young and nervous. When Hawks once asked her why she couldn't get herself a ride home from a party at his house, she said, "I don't do too well with men," and when he suggested that she try insulting one, she did, and thus got a ride home with Clark Gable.

Hawks, in his turn, was impressed. He saw in her "that quality of insolence. That hadn't been seen." After nearly a year of keeping her idle, he decided to make her the heroine of his Hemingway picture. For that, he needed a new test that would win the approval of Jack Warner, so he wrote a bit of dialogue himself, wrote for his young protégée the world-weary lines that she was to make famous: "You know how to whistle, don't you, Steve? You just put your lips together and blow." Hawks showed the test to Warner, who loved it, and to Bogart, who told Miss Bacall, "We'll have lots of fun together." Everybody liked the test so much that Hawks wanted to insert the lines he had written somewhere in the wreckage of Hemingway's novel. "Faulkner was the one who found a place to put it," Hawks recalled. "He said, 'If we put these people in a hotel corridor where nobody else is around, then I think we can make that scene work.' So we did it. I wrote the line, but he wrote the stuff that led up to it."

The only other thing that Betty Bacall needed now was a new first name. Hawks wanted something resonant. He asked her what her grandmother's name was. Sophie, she told him. That wasn't quite what he had in mind. He saw her a few days later and told her that her name would be Lauren, and if anyone asked her about its origins, she was to answer that it was an old family name. And so he had created her, the sassy young Lauren Bacall, but before he could begin to savor the fruits of his invention, she fell in love with the forty-five-year-old Bogart, and he with her. Though Hawks was somewhat jealous at first and tried to break up the romance on his set, he eventually found it a "funny thing" that Bogart had been captivated by "the character she played, so that she had to keep playing it the rest of her life."

To Have and Have Not wasn't a particularly good movie, and yet it became one of the triumphs of 1945. It was a typical Hawks creation, fast-moving, breezy—Hawks's version of Harry Morgan and his wife even called each other, like the Hawkses at home, Steve and Slim—but Bogart and Miss Bacall were so obviously in love with each other that they cast their own romantic glow over the whole film. Jack Warner, who had originally regarded it as Hawks's sequel to Casablanca (complete even to Hoagy Carmichael, replacing Dooley Wilson, at the nightclub piano), now wanted a new movie that would be a sequel to this. As early as the drive back from the preview, he said to Hawks, "We'd better do another picture with these two people. Do you know a story?" Hawks said he did. Warner asked what it was like, and Hawks, knowing how Warner's mind worked, said, "Something like Maltese Falcon." So Warner advanced Hawks $50,000 to buy Raymond Chandler's The Big Sleep, and Hawks artfully bought the novel from Chandler for $5,000, artfully keeping the other $45,000 for himself. Chandler was not free to write the screenplay, since he was under contract to Paramount; Hawks once again hired Faulkner, together with two professionals, Jules Furthman and Leigh Brackett.

Chandler liked the idea of Bogart as his private detective, Philip Marlowe. "Bogart can be tough without a gun," he wrote to a friend in England. "Also he has a sense of humor that contains that grating undertone of contempt. Bogart is the genuine article." There was only one problem. Marlowe didn't really like women and particularly didn't like the two spoiled daughters of his client, old General Sternwood. When the younger one, who eventually turned out to be the murderer, came stealing into Marlowe's bed, he threw her out. When the older one kissed him and invited herself to his apartment, he fended her off with probing questions. "You son of a bitch," said Vivian Sternwood.

That wouldn't do at all for Lauren Bacall, or for Hawks's general admiration for adventurous women. When Chandler's Marlowe went into a bookstore, the woman in charge of the place offered him nothing but a few wisecracks. Hawks's Marlowe suggested a drink, and she put a sign on the door saying CLOSED FOR THE DAY. When Chandler's Marlowe hired a cab to tail someone, the driver was simply "a fresh-faced kid"; Hawks turned the cabbie into a pretty girl and had her ask Marlowe to call on her again, preferably at night, if he ever wanted another "tail job." Chandler's novel ended with Marlowe ordering Vivian Sternwood to have her homicidal younger sister locked up in a mental institution, and then departing to deal with some gangsters who were threatening the Sternwood family. Hawks's film ended, of course, with Bogart and Bacall united. "What's wrong with you?" he says. "Nothing that you can't fix," says she.

Chandler could hardly complain about changes in the plot. His original novel was a tangle of loose ends, and when Hawks's three screenwriters turned in their script, one of them said, "There are a lot of things that don't make sense." Hawks didn't care. "Good," he said. "Let's try it and see whether the audience likes that." So they just started in, and in due time they inevitably came to the question of who murdered Owen Taylor, the Sternwoods' family chauffeur. He was not an important character, and it was not an important murder, but still—there he was, sitting in Vivian Sternwood's black Buick sedan under ten feet of water off a Lido fishing pier. Hawks and the writers pored over Chandler's novel, but Chandler himself, apparently by oversight, had never explained who killed the chauffeur. So Hawks sent him a telegram asking him who had committed the murder. Chandler went back through his book, reflected on the mystery, and then sent a return telegram: "I DON'T KNOW."

Hawks still didn't care. He said later that this incomprehensible story was "the first time I made a picture and just decided I wasn't going to explain things. I was just going to try and make good scenes." The interviewer eliciting these reminiscences, Joseph McBride, seemed to think that Hawks had discovered some avant-garde method. "It's a revolutionary thing you did," said McBride, "because it became the method of modern films that people don't care if the plot makes sense if it's fun." Hawks was happy to agree. "It's just my way of telling a story," he said.

The only ones who argued that the narrative of *The Big Sleep* was supposed to make sense were the censors from the Johnston Office, and they disapproved of Chandler's ending in the original script. They disapproved of the fact that nobody in the Sternwood family was punished, that even the gangsters finally went on about their business. Hawks turned on the censors and challenged them to provide an ending themselves. "I said, 'OK, you write a scene for me,' " Hawks recalled. "And they did, and it was a lot more violent, it was everything I wanted. I made it and was very happy about it."

The basic idea of the new ending, whether or not anyone from the Johnston Office actually proposed it, was that Marlowe returned to the scene of the first murder and was trapped there by the gangsters. At this point, Chandler himself was consulted, and he suggested an interesting outcome. In Chandler's version, Carmen Sternwood, the younger sister, was also trapped in the house with Marlowe. The detective knew that whoever first emerged from the house would probably be shot down, and he knew that Carmen was the murderer, and he knew that if she understood the situation, she would have no qualm about killing him. "He didn't feel like playing God or saving his skin by letting Carmen leave," Chandler later wrote. "Neither did he feel like playing Sir Philip Sidney to save a worthless life. So he put it up to God by tossing a coin. Before he tossed the coin, he prayed out loud, in a sort of way. The gist of his prayer was that he, Marlowe, had done the best he knew how and through no fault of his own was put in a position of making a decision God had no right to force him to make. He wanted that decision made by the authority who allowed all this mess to happen." The coin came down heads, indicating that Marlowe should let the girl go her own way, even to her death. She started toward the door. He started to stop her. She pulled a gun on him and laughed. Then a burst from one of the gangsters' machine guns, fired more or less at random, drilled through the door and killed her. But Hawks didn't use Chandler's ending. Too complicated, perhaps. In the final version, which had no Carmen Sternwood in it, the burst of machine gun fire accidentally cut down the chief gangster, enabling Bogart to walk out of the trap and into his new wife's embrace.

She was not quite his new wife yet. They had agreed to marry as soon as Bogart could get a divorce from the quarrelsome Mayo Methot, but the third Mrs. Bogart did not go quietly. All through the filming of *The Big Sleep*, there were fights and scenes. Bogart decided to leave home. Then friends told him that his wife would kill herself if he left. She promised to stop drinking if he would stay. She had to go to a hospital. He decided she deserved a last chance. Miss Bacall wept. And so on. At one point, when Bogart and Miss Bacall were enjoying themselves aboard his yacht, Mrs. Bogart came back early from a shopping trip. Miss Bacall had to hide in the ship's head until Mrs. Bogart departed again. On another occasion, Miss Bacall picked up a telephone and heard an angry voice shouting, "Listen, you Jewish bitch—who's going to wash his socks? Are *you?*" Early in May, Mrs. Bogart finally gave up and got her divorce. Less than two weeks later, Bogart took a weekend break from some reshooting on *The Big Sleep* and married Miss Bacall on the Ohio farm of the novelist Louis Bromfield.

So everything ended happily, except for William Faulkner, who decided that he could not bear working for Warner Bros. any longer. "I think I have had about all of Hollywood I can stand," he wrote to his agent, Harold Ober. "I feel bad, depressed, dreadful sense of wasting time, I imagine most of the symptoms of some kind of blow-up or collapse. Feeling as I do, I am actually afraid to stay here much longer."

Part of Faulkner's difficulty was a matter of health. He complained of being "not well, physically, have lost weight, etc.," though that was nothing unusual for an alcoholic nearing the age of fifty. Part was desperation about his continuing failure as a novelist. "My books have never sold, are out of print," wrote the author of *The Sound and the Fury* and *Light in August*. "The labor (the creation of my apocryphal country) of my life, even if I have a few things yet to add to it, will never make a living for me." And part was simply a dislike of Los Angeles and everything in it. "Nobody here does anything," he complained to a fellow writer named Paul Wellman as they waited on a street corner for the bus to Burbank. "There's nobody here with any roots. Even the houses are built out of mud and chicken wire. Nothing ever happens and after a while a couple of leaves fall off a tree and then it'll be another year."

Faulkner told Warners in September of 1945 that he wanted to go back to Mississippi and finish a novel. It was to be about a mutiny in France toward the end of World War I, about a Christlike figure who ended as the Unknown Soldier. Faulkner had been fascinated by the idea ever since he first heard it in 1942 from the director Henry Hathaway and a free-lance producer named William Bacher, who had given him a thousand-dollar advance to write it as a novel that they could then buy for filming. Faulkner also told Warners that he owned a mare that was going to foal, and he wanted it to foal in Mississippi, and so he was going to take it there and stay there. The studio offered to grant him a six-months leave without pay to finish his novel, on the understanding that Warners would have first chance at the movie rights. Faulkner naturally had to decline, since he had already sold the movie option to the two men who had told him the idea. Warners said he couldn't take any leave unless he signed the agreement. Faulkner cleared out his desk and left.

Back in Mississippi, the novelist wrote a very deferential personal appeal to Jack Warner, whom he even addressed as Colonel Warner, asking to be released from his contract. This was a contract, it should be remembered, under which Warner Bros. was giving Faulkner nothing—no money, no office, no benefits of any kind. Yet Warners treated him, as it treated its actors, like somebody who had to be confined to the studio for the contractual period of seven years. And while rebellious stars like Olivia de Havilland sued for the right to work for competing studios, Faulkner was asking only the right to stay in Mississippi and write his novel. "I feel that I have made a bust at moving picture writing and therefore have mis-spent and will continue to mis-spend time which at my age I cannot afford," he wrote to Warner. He then recited the thin list of movie work accomplished for Warners. He had done "the best work I knew how" on a half-dozen scripts, but only two were produced, and he had been credited for his work on those "partly through the friendship of Director Howard Hawks." And finally, perhaps a little too cal-culatingly, he appealed to Warner's rather insubstantial sense of honor, to "that same fairness which you have shown before in such situations."

Warner didn't bother to answer. The reply came from R. J. Obringer, of the studio's legal department, demanding that Faulkner sign the leave agree-ment. And just as Warner had blacklisted Miss de Havilland, he now seemed to think that he could exercise similar power over the entire publishing busi-ness. "He has already made vague though dire threats about warning any editor to buy my stuff at his peril, if I don't come back," Faulkner wrote to Malcolm Cowley, who had just put together the Viking *Portable Faulkner,* which was to become an important element in bringing the novelist's best work back into print.

On into 1946, Warners continued its pursuit of the errant Faulkner. Obringer wrote him a stern letter warning him that he had violated his contract. Only when Ober sent Warners the first sixty-four pages of Faulk-ner's new novel (which was then called "Who?") as clear evidence that it was not anything the studio would want to film, and only when Bennett Cerf of Random House made his own personal appeal to Warner to leave Faulkner in peace, only then did Warner agree at least to stop harassing Faulkner until the novel was finished. Before that day came, the Nobel Prize for 1949 would finally reduce the Warners contract to a dead letter. So Faulkner went on writing *A Fable,* mercifully unaware that the unfinished novel he regarded as his *magnum opus* would actually turn out to be one of his worst books, that all his best work was already behind him.

•   •   •

The honking of distant auto horns one August afternoon brought to most Americans their first news that the war had finally come to its inevitable end. First a few horns, then soon more and more of them, then shouts from window to window, and then everybody began parading through the streets under showers of confetti. It was a happy day, but it didn't have that stunning surprise of the war's beginning, that sense that all of life had suddenly become different. The outcome had long been certain, and the main difference that it promised—promised falsely—was that peace would bring a restoration of life as it had once been.

This did not mean a return to the Depression, of course. The era of the breadline and the dole was over, and everybody now expected to prosper. There had been enough talk of sacrifice; it was time to concentrate on making more money, making more and spending more. The American Federation of Labor had pledged to Roosevelt that there would be no strikes for the duration of the war, but well before V-day, the rival Hollywood unions were already getting ready to fight. As early as January of 1945, the first strike vote was taken. It involved a supposedly jurisdictional dispute, one of those internecine quarrels that few outsiders can either understand or judge, yet on each side of the dispute there began to form the ragged coalitions of right and left that would soon tear Hollywood apart.

At the center of the conflict were seventy-seven interior decorators, who had formed their own little union and negotiated a five-year contract with the studios back in 1937. That was the period when Willie Bioff of IATSE was trying to seize control of everything within reach. In 1939, IATSE organized and demanded studio recognition for a new Local 44 that included what it called "set dressers." The studios answered that they already had a contract with the independent decorators. By the time that contract expired in 1942, Bioff and IATSE president George Browne were in prison for racketeering, and IATSE had been inherited by Richard Walsh, a pudgy Brooklyn Irishman who had been one of Browne's vice-presidents. Walsh withdrew IATSE's request to represent the decorators on condition that no other outside group could represent the decorators either. The studios agreed.

Late in 1943, however, the decorators voted to strengthen their little union by affiliating with Local 1421 of the painters' union, a somewhat shaggy organization that also included designers, illustrators, and model builders. Most important, the chief of the painters was Herbert Sorrell, a sturdy ex-boxer who had actually served his apprenticeship with a brush and bucket. He liked to describe himself as "just a dumb painter." After serving as a picket captain in a painters' strike in 1937, Sorrell won election as head of the Hollywood local and helped organize the bitter but successful cartoonists' strike against the Walt Disney studio in 1941.

Sorrell was unusual in another way: He had resisted both the threats and the inducements of Willie Bioff, who once suggested that they could make some money by working together. Sorrell not only rejected Bioff's offer but began organizing an anti-IATSE coalition called the Conference of Studio Unions. The CSU was everything that IATSE was not: militant, leftist, and honest. By 1945, Sorrell's CSU had grown to a total of nine unions, including the painters, carpenters, and machinists, nearly ten thousand workers in all, a serious challenge to IATSE's control of its sixteen thousand members. So when Sorrell requested a new contract for the seventy-seven decoraters, IATSE once again demanded recognition for its own group of "set dressers." IATSE president Walsh warned that all his men would walk out if the studios gave in to Sorrell.

The War Labor Board ruled in favor of Sorrell, but the studios tried to avoid a confrontation. They claimed they were helpless, caught in the middle between two rival unions. There was considerable evidence, though, that the studios by now found IATSE a congenial partner. Bioff's successor as IATSE's Hollywood representative was a beefy professional named Roy Brewer, a man who seemed to understand things. Brewer had been head of the AFL's Nebraska Labor Federation, and he was to become one of the major figures in Hollywood's impending labor wars and in the political struggles that grew out of them. He had just resigned from his wartime job with the War Labor Board in Washington when Walsh recruited him to take charge of the IATSE forces in Hollywood. There he found Sorrell on the attack and the studios anxiously maneuvering to delay the inevitable clash.

On March 12, 1945, Sorrell decided that he would wait no longer. His CSU went out on strike and threw up picket lines around the studios. The IATSE chiefs accepted the challenge. They sent bands of workers bulling through the CSU picket lines. William Green, president of the AFL, to which both rival unions belonged, sent Sorrell a telegram that accused him of violating the labor federation's wartime no-strike pledge. "I officially disavow your strike," Green declared. To California's most fervent right-wingers, Sorrell was simply a Communist, out to make trouble. The state legislature's Jack Tenney, chief propagator of alarms about Reds, declared that Sorrell "has persistently followed the Communist Party line. He subscribed to the Communist Party publication, the *People's World*. . . ." It was true that Sorrell had often supported Communist positions—notably denouncing Roosevelt as a "warmonger" in 1940, the era of the Hitler-Stalin alliance, and then changing to interventionism when the Nazis invaded Russia—but the one issue on which Sorrell and the Communists very markedly differed was the Hollywood strike. *People's World* loyally supported the AFL's no-strike pledge and blamed both Sorrell and the producers for breaking it. Sorrell in turn charged his enemies with conspiracy and corruption. Though IATSE's gangster chiefs were now in jail, Sorrell ridiculed the larger union's claim of having reformed. He later testified before a House committee that IATSE and the studios had conspired against their own workers ever since the 1930's, and "this conspiracy goes on now."

Hollywood divided. The Screen Writers Guild somewhat reluctantly voted to support the CSU picket lines; the Screen Actors Guild somewhat reluctantly voted to cross them. At the actual studio gates, people made their decisions somewhat capriciously. Salka Viertel recalled separate groups of writers and secretaries meeting in the cafeteria just across from Warner Bros. One writer who claimed that he could work only by dictating to his secretary suggested that they all wait to see what the secretaries decided. "We stepped out onto the sidewalk to watch what the 'girls' would do," Mrs. Viertel said. "About thirty of them came out and for a while they stood undecided, watching the slowly moving pickets and the studio police, who were protecting the entrance. Finally an energetic young woman threw back her head, said 'What the hell!' and ran defiantly across the street and through the passive picket line. The others promptly followed. . . ." Mrs. Viertel asked her own secretary what had happened at her meeting, and she said that most of the secretaries at first sympathized with the strikers, "but one girl, who has worked for Ayn Rand, swayed them by insisting that the strikers were just a bunch of Communists and that a decent person had to be against them."

Once the battle lines had been established, the studios summarily fired all the striking decorators, and the CSU refused to accept the dismissals. As the deadlock continued, but failed to shut down the studios, some striking unions gave up (the Screen Publicists Guild, for one), some newcomers joined in (the Screen Cartoonists Guild). The Japanese surrender that August formally ended the AFL's no-strike pledge, so various larger unions began choosing sides in the Hollywood struggle. The AFL's big rival, the CIO, formally voted to support the strike. The Teamsters, then a member of the AFL, strongly opposed it. Lawrence P. Lindeloff, the international head of Sorrell's own union of painters, first denounced the strike, then came out in favor of it.

Though strikes cost employers a lot, they cost workers a lot more (in this case, over eight months, an estimated fifteen million dollars). While the CSU workers walked the picket lines all through that spring and summer, they were unable to keep IATSE workers from pushing their way into the heavily guarded studios. Early in October, Sorrell decided he would have to concentrate his forces, and he picked Warners for the battle. The first forty pickets arrived at the studio at 5 A.M., and soon there were about 750 marching to and fro. When the first IATSE workers appeared at the gate, the pickets overturned three of their cars. The streets glittered with shards of broken glass. The Burbank police and Warners studio guards beat back the picketers with clubs and sprayed them with fire hoses. Jack Warner and his executives watched the battle from the roof of the studio.

More IATSE workers arrived to join the fight. Some of them tried to overturn a CSU sound truck, and the driver slugged one who attacked with a wrench. A striking painter named A. Kieser was stabbed in the nose and forehead by a strikebreaker with a penknife. A picketing secretary named Helen McCall was hit in the eye by a gas bomb. The police arrested Sorrell on suspicion of inciting a riot and held him on fifteen hundred dollars bond.

Sorrell was back on the streets the next day, and this time the picketing seemed to succeed in shutting down Warners. Except for a few chorus girls rehearsing a dance sequence, all work stopped on the three films in production. Warners lawyers were in court, though, to get an injunction against further mass picketing, and the IATSE men went to enforce the injunction the next morning. Several hundred IATSE men formed a column six abreast across the street from the pickets patrolling the Olive Avenue entrance to the Warners studio. At 6 A.M., they marched forward, and the two armies met in a storm of fists, clubs, even flares. This time, nearly eighty people were injured before police from four nearby towns could restore a semblance of order. Eight combatants were arrested, including one twenty-nine-year-old secretary to a Universal producer, who was charged with possession of a blackjack.

The combined power of the police, studio guards, and IATSE was too much for the strikers, who were beaten back from the studio gates and permitted only to stage sitdowns. It was Washington that saved them. At the end of October, the National Labor Relations Board ruled that the decorators were entitled to join the painters. Grudgingly, the studios and IATSE gave way. For Sorrell and his allies, it was a victory, but perhaps a Pyrrhic victory. The cry of Communist influence in Hollywood had sounded once again, and the forces behind it were getting stronger. Their cry would soon reverberate far beyond the impulsive urgings of Ayn Rand's secretary.

•   •   •

At three o'clock in the morning on September 16, 1945, Theodore Dreiser lurched up out of bed at his Spanish stucco house on North Kings Road and began turning on all the lights. He called out for his wife, whom he had married just the previous year after a quarter century of turbulent concubinage.

"Helen!"

Helen Dreiser emerged from her own bedroom to find the seventy-four-year-old novelist roaming through the house and still calling her name. She pattered after him, repeatedly telling him that she was there, all to no avail.

"I said, 'I am Helen,' " she later wrote in some notes on the incident. "First he said, 'Everyone thinks she's Helen.' Then I told him quietly that I could prove it. T.D. then said, 'I'll believe you if you say so.' " Mrs. Dreiser thought she had won that exchange, but a few days later, Dreiser confided to a visitor, "It's odd, a strange woman has been here."

It was because of Helen Patges Richardson that Dreiser had first come to Hollywood, back in 1919. She was young and pretty then, aged twenty-five, a secretary in a New York office, and she wanted to be an actress. She admired the author of *Sister Carrie,* who happened to be her second cousin, aged forty-eight, so she went to pay him a visit, and they became lovers, and headed for Los Angeles. Helen started out as an extra, at $7.50 a day, and then found a few minor parts at twenty dollars. She played in Rudolph Valentino's first film, *The Four Horsemen of the Apocalypse* (1921). Dreiser was not very happy about her fledgling career, even though it helped pay the rent. He himself had received a four-thousand-dollar advance to write a novel, *The Bulwark,* about a Quaker whose yearning to do good led to nothing but trouble. He decided to go back to New York to write it. Helen went with him.

Dreiser's major encounter with Hollywood occurred only after the success of *An American Tragedy* (1925). Paramount bought it but didn't know what to do with it. When Sergei Eisenstein visited Hollywood in 1930, someone at the studio conceived the remarkable idea of assigning him to film

Dreiser's novel. Eisenstein feared that the Hays Office would forbid it, but he was assured that the Hays Office approved, and that the studio had budgeted one million dollars for the project. Eisenstein and Ivor Montagu wrote a script that Dreiser wholeheartedly endorsed, but Paramount's executives began getting nervous. "Your scenario," said Ben Schulberg, "is a monstrous challenge to American society."

Paramount junked the whole project and started over again, with the poet Samuel Hoffenstein as scriptwriter and Josef von Sternberg as director. Dreiser's contract included a clause saying that "the Purchaser agrees that it will use its best endeavors to accept such advice, suggestions and criticisms that the Seller may make in so far as it may, in the judgment of the Purchaser, consistently do so." It was an ambiguous clause, which Dreiser thought gave him some control over the filming of his novel, but which in fact gave Paramount the right, after listening to whatever Dreiser might want to say, to do as it pleased.

Once the contracts were signed, Hoffenstein set to work writing a script, and Dreiser, who had discovered a new girl, set off with her for Cuba, leaving no forwarding address. When Hoffenstein finished his script and wanted to get Dreiser's approval, Dreiser could not be found. Paramount sent out official notices that filming would soon begin. Dreiser reappeared in New Orleans, and denounced all previous correspondence as "the usual Hollywood swill and bunk." He demanded the right to discuss Hoffenstein's script. With some trepidation, Hoffenstein sent his screenplay to New Orleans and asked if he could meet Dreiser there. "IF YOU CAN DISCUSS THIS AMICABLY OTHERWISE NOT," Dreiser wired back. Amicable as could be, Hoffenstein flew to New Orleans, to find at his hotel a note from Dreiser saying that the script was "nothing less than an insult," and that "to avoid saying how deeply I feel this, I am leaving New Orleans now without seeing you. You will understand, I am sure."

Hoffenstein understood. Paramount understood. The studio went ahead and started making the movie. Dreiser publicly denounced it, before filming even started, as "a cheap, tawdry, tabloid confession story." He threatened legal action if Paramount went ahead. Paramount delayed long enough to invite him to state his views and objections, then resumed work on the film. Dreiser denounced all of Hollywood as "Hooeyland" and declared that *An American Tragedy* had been "traduced" into "a Mexican comedy." And he did sue, demanding that Paramount show cause why it should not be restrained from distributing the film. Since such a suit by an artist defending his work against Hollywood adaptation was extremely rare, almost unprecedented, cultural historians tend to see Dreiser as the hero of the trial in White Plains, New York, in 1931, but in fact the Paramount attorneys blackened Dreiser's reputation and the judge rejected his petition.

Nearly ten years later, ten years poorer and wearier, Dreiser moved back to Hollywood, partly to negotiate a movie sale of *Sister Carrie*. He hated the place. "This region is stuffed with hard boiled savage climbers," he wrote to his old friend H. L. Mencken, "the lowest grade of political grafters, quacks not calculable as to number or variety, all grades of God-shouters . . . and loafers, prostitutes, murderers and perverts." To another friend, he offered another objection: "The movies are solidly Jewish. They've dug in, employ only Jews with American names. . . . The dollar sign is the guide—mentally & physically. That America should be led—the mass—by their direction is beyond all believing. In addition they are arrogant, insolent and contemptuous."

But he thought he could sell *Sister Carrie* to Universal, and he wrote the decaying John Barrymore to urge him to "live to present Hurstwood for me." For the sake of "the dollar sign," the once-uncompromising Dreiser was even willing to make compromises with the Johnston Office. To the objection that Carrie's "sins" were never punished, he proposed that this "can be adjusted." He even suggested, about his first and best novel, that "a different ending could be used—a somewhat more optimistic ending—several of which I have in mind." So now that Dreiser was willing to be reasonable, as the phrase goes, a deal could be made. It was not Universal, though, but RKO that rescued Dreiser from deepening poverty in the fall of 1940 by buying *Sister Carrie* for forty thousand dollars.

In his politics, however, Dreiser was anything but reasonable. The only constants, tenuously linked by his sympathy for the downtrodden, were an unreasoning devotion to Stalin's Russia and an equally unreasoning hatred of the British Empire. This led Dreiser into some weird positions. He rather admired not only Stalin but Hitler, and so, almost alone among American radicals, he felt no shame over the Hitler-Stalin pact. "Hasn't anyone ever bothered to tell you the facts of life?" he demanded of one skeptical interviewer. "Don't you realize that France and England were all set to attack Russia?" And of President Roosevelt, who failed to share his fantasies, Dreiser wrote to Mencken: "I begin to suspect that Hitler is correct. The president may be part Jewish."

To organize these views, Dreiser hired for a thousand dollars a young British novelist, Cedric Belfrage, to help him write an antiwar book to be called "Is America Worth Saving?" Belfrage marveled at the great man's obscurity in Hollywood. "I can recall introducing him to movie people whom I knew . . ." he said, "who obviously had never heard of him." He marveled even more at Dreiser's working habits: "Along about noon he would begin to sag with weariness and he and I would stroll along to the drugstore . . . to get a pint of whisky. With this in a paper bag we returned . . . and within a few minutes Dreiser was out of action. . . . Dreiser began to ramble and could not organize his thoughts." Somehow, the dreadful book got patched together, acquired a new title, *America Is Worth Saving,* and then appeared just before Hitler's invasion of Russia made it obsolete. Dreiser sent one autographed copy to Stalin.

It is strange and marvelous how some dying artists are unable to die until they have finished what they feel to be their essential work. Wagner, for example, held himself together until the premiere of *Parsifal* and then journeyed to Venice and died. Dreiser, now past seventy, both physically and mentally infirm, determined to finish *The Bulwark*, that novel about the Quaker for which Horace Liveright had paid him a four-thousand-dollar advance back before the First World War. And he did it. Then he determined to complete the story of Frank Cowperwood, the raging entrepreneur who had not been heard from since the publication of *The Titan* in 1914. *The Stoic,* this last volume was called, and though Dreiser had little strength left, he kept laboring away all that summer. "While he dictated much of the writing which I took down directly on the typewriter," Mrs. Dreiser said, "there was always the necessary discussion about scenes, action, structure, and he tired easily. . . . Day after day, we worked on opposite sides of his long work table, Teddie in his old-fashioned yellow-winged rocking chair and I at the typewriter. . . . It was all he wanted to do."

There was one other thing. Back in 1932, Dreiser had told Earl Browder, the head of the Communist Party, that he wanted to join. Browder, who regarded the novelist as "not . . . quite adult," politely turned him away. But now, in the summer of 1945, Browder was expelled from the party and replaced by Dreiser's old friend William Z. Foster. Dreiser was also getting regular visits now from John Howard Lawson, the screenwriter, who talked about literature and politics and the possibilities of Dreiser's joining the party. And besides, Dreiser's popularity in Russia contrasted sharply with his fading celebrity in America. When the UN was founded in San Francisco that spring, several Soviet delegates came to Los Angeles and paid courtesy calls on Dreiser. And when Dreiser wrote a letter to Stalin to ask why he never earned any royalties from Russia (the Soviets had never signed the Bern Convention and acknowledged no obligation to pay royalties to foreign authors), he soon received a check for $34,600. So there was a certain inevitability in Dreiser's writing to Foster from Hollywood on July 20, 1945, "to tell you of my desire to become a member of the Communist Political Association." There was an inevitability, too, in the fact that Dreiser only corrected and approved the letter of application that was actually written by a party functionary. "Dear Comrade Dreiser . . ." Foster replied. "I . . . extend to you this official welcome into our organization."

Shortly before Christmas, Helen Dreiser had a strange dream. "Teddie and I were operating an open plane of peculiar design," she recalled. "He was sitting in the rear, steering it with a rudder like that of a boat. We were flying over water toward a shore on which there were hundreds of people and I was concerned with the problem of gliding into a safe landing over the heads of the crowd. Glancing back to see if all was well with Teddie, I became terrified when I saw he had fallen over to one side. I went back quickly to where he was sitting and kissed him on the side of his mouth. Then I realized I must rush back to my place or we would crash. We glided to safety on the shore. . . ."

Christmas was not a very happy time. Dreiser sat at the piano beside an old friend and grew tearful as she played "On the Banks of the Wabash" and other songs written by Dreiser's celebrated brother, Paul Dresser. To another woman, he said morosely, "I am the loneliest man in the world." He had finished a draft of *The Stoic* and sent it to a younger colleague, James T. Farrell, and Farrell had just sent back a nine-page commentary, suggesting revisions, particularly in the ending. "I simply stopped writing at the end because I was tired," Dreiser confessed, adding a vow that he would somehow rewrite the last two chapters. He rewrote the next-to-last chapter on December 27, but at five o'clock he had to stop, exhausted. Mrs. Dreiser drove him to the beach at Venice, and they went for a stroll on the boardwalk, admiring a spectacular sunset, which Mrs. Dreiser described as "all blended in neutral shades of grays and blues with streaks of turquoise and cerise."

At three o'clock in the morning, he called out, "*Helen,* I have an *intense* pain." He struggled out of bed and then fell down. Mrs. Dreiser called a doctor, who provided drugs and an oxygen tent. Dreiser survived the night. A friend came the next day and asked him how he felt. Dreiser said only, "Bum." As Mrs. Dreiser sat alone next to the dozing man, she noticed that his hands were cold. Then he suddenly said, "Kiss me, Helen." "I did, *on the side of the mouth,*" she said, recalling her dream, "and then I kissed him again." Dreiser kept sinking, fading, until, at about six o'clock in the morning of December 28, "his breath became shallower and shallower until I felt it stop."

There were some of Dreiser's leftist friends who thought that the old radical wouldn't want to be buried in Forest Lawn, but Helen Dreiser knew better. She remembered that they had been at a funeral in the Whispering Pines section that August, and Dreiser had remarked to her that he had "never seen a more beautiful resting place." So she had the funeral service held at Forest Lawn's Church of the Recessional, and the organist played Bach's "Come, Kindly Death." To an audience of less than a hundred people, John Howard Lawson delivered a eulogy on the forces that had led Dreiser to communism. Charlie Chaplin then recited one of Dreiser's poems, which Mrs. Dreiser later had inscribed on a plaque at the grave:

> Oh, space!
> Change!
> Toward which we run
> So gladly,
> Or from which we retreat
> In terror—
> Yet that promises to bear us
> In itself
> Forever.

Oh, what is this
That knows the road I came?

Then he was buried in an expensive lot in the Whispering Pines section.
It was not far from the grave where Tom Mix lay, still wearing the belt buckle
that spelled out his name in diamonds.

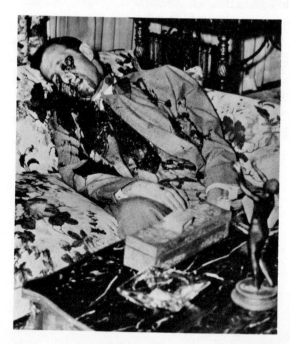

Bugsy Siegel, Hollywood's favorite racketeer, came to a bloody end. *Below,* he enjoyed joking with his friend George Raft.

8

TREACHERY

(1946)

In the summers, the temperatures in the Mojave Desert rise to more than 120 degrees. Along what is now U.S. Route 15, running northeast from Barstow, the creosote bushes and the samphire stand like miniature skeletons in the grayish alkali flats. Everything seems lifeless, lifeless and eternally hot. So the two men who drove here one day in 1945 had loaded cans of extra gasoline and water into the back of their car for the three-hundred-mile trip from Los Angeles, but the bigger of the two kept grumbling about the hardships of the journey to this remote outpost known as Las Vegas. The smaller man, who stood barely five feet four but seemed to be in charge of the expedition, admitted later that Las Vegas was "a dinky, horrible, little oasis town," but he said that the two of them would be pioneers. Here in the middle of nowhere, as he subsequently told an interviewer, here in this baked and parched wasteland, they would build the greatest gambling casino in the world. ("Here we'll have fun . . ." the Widow Begbick had said, "Gin and whiskey/Girls and boys. . . .")

"We decided to . . . call it the Flamingo," said the little man, a Polish-born entrepreneur named Maier Suchowljansky, better known as Meyer Lansky. "We thought up the name one day when we were at Hialeah Race Track, in Florida. There's a pretty little lake there and in the evening you can watch the flocks of pink flamingoes rise in the sky. There's a local legend that flamingoes are a sign of good luck and anyone who shoots the birds will have seven years of misfortune. So because of the good luck connection, Bugsy had the idea of naming our Las Vegas project."

Bugsy was the nickname hated by the man who bore it, Ben Siegel. He and Lansky had grown up in the slums of New York, Lansky on the Lower East Side, Siegel in the Williamsburg section of Brooklyn. According to one hardly credible tale, they first met when Lansky acted as Good Samaritan and rescued the twelve-year-old Siegel from a girl's bedroom, where he was being furiously assaulted by the girl's young lover, Salvatore Lucania, later to become Lucky Luciano. More likely, all three of the future gangsters met in the ordinary course of New York street warfare.

Both Lansky and Siegel came from poor but respectable families. Though neither boy got beyond grammar school, the elder Lanskys found their son a job as a tool and die maker; Siegel's brother Maurice eventually became a successful physician in Los Angeles. New York's East Side provided endless temptations to a pair of ambitious boys, however, particularly when Prohibition brought to organized crime a quasi-legitimacy, even glamour. The New York underworld was roughly divided, during these years of the late 1920's, between the Italian mobsters like Luciano, Frank Costello, and Joey Adonis, and the Jewish gangs headed by Jacob "Gurrah" Shapiro and Louis "Lepke" Buchalter. Lansky and Siegel soon organized their own bootlegging operation, with the help of such future celebrities as Arthur "Dutch Schultz" Flegenheimer and Abner "Longie" Zwillman. They apparently did not control any specific "territory" but simply imported large quantities of high-quality liquor, notably from the Canadian distilleries of Samuel Bronfman, and sold it wherever profits were to be found. By the mid-1920's, Lansky and his partners were estimated to be making, after such expenses as five million dollars per year in graft, an annual profit of four million dollars.

The end of Prohibition in 1934 forced the bootleggers to find new fields of endeavor. Some, like Joseph P. Kennedy, became eminently respectable. Sam Bronfman evolved into the philanthropic patriarch of Seagram's Distilleries, and Lewis Rosenstiel did much the same at Schenley's. Others shifted their efforts into various forms of what is commonly called racketeering. Buchalter, for one, built a substantial commercial empire by simply extorting money from Jewish enterprises, notably clothing and fur stores, butcher shops, groceries, and restaurants. He was all too successful. His notoriety soon made him a prime target for Thomas E. Dewey, who had received a state appointment in 1935 as a special district attorney in charge of racketeering. Lansky was more discreet. He decided to leave New York and to organize a gambling empire in the South. From his new headquarters in Miami, he developed the casinos of Florida's Gold Coast, the luxurious resorts around New Orleans, and the pleasure domes of Fulgencio Batista's Cuba. Lansky always remained in the background, a quiet, polite little man, rarely seen, and never convicted of anything, and yet he played as large a part as anyone in creating the flamboyant social style of what is known today as the Sunbelt.

Lansky's friend Siegel also decided to leave New York at the end of Prohibition, but the place that lured him was Los Angeles, and particularly Hollywood. In contrast to Lansky, Siegel loved display, glitter, celebrity. When he moved west in 1936, he first rented a mansion on McCarthy Drive from the opera singer Lawrence Tibbett. Then he began building a mansion of his own on Delfern Avenue in Holmby Hills. He had red marble walls installed in his bathroom, and a tier of slot machines in his lounge, and secret passages from the sliding bookshelves in his library up to the attic. He enrolled himself in the Hillcrest Country Club and his two daughters at the DuBrock Riding Academy.

In a society that regarded Jack Warner and Harry Cohn as distinguished feudal barons, Siegel fitted quite well. Raymond Chandler, who took note of such things, saw a band of studio executives trooping back from lunch one day and paused to marvel at the sight. "They looked so exactly like a bunch of topflight Chicago gangsters moving in to read the death sentence on the beaten competitor," he wrote to a friend. "It brought home to me in a flash the strange psychological and spiritual kinship between the operations of big money business and the rackets. Same faces, same expressions, same manners. Same way of dressing and same exaggerated leisure of movement."

Siegel seems to have nourished a secret ambition to become a movie star. He was good-looking in a rugged, square-chinned way, certainly as much so as his old friend George Raft, who had once been a New York street-corner tough named Georgie Ranft and who now made four thousand dollars a week. Siegel was vain about his looks; he massaged his face with skin creams and slept with an elastic strip tied under his chin. But it was beneath him to seek work as a mere actor, for he was already rich and successful. He called himself a "sportsman." His sponsor in Hollywood society was a wealthy woman, born Dorothy Taylor, who preened herself on bearing the title of Countess Di Frasso. Her wealth, estimated at between ten and fifteen million dollars, came from her father's leather-goods factory in upstate New York, and her title came from her second husband, a penniless Roman who remained in Rome while his countess gave parties in Beverly Hills. She had just finished a stormy affair with Gary Cooper when she met Siegel at the Santa Anita racetrack and decided that he would do nicely as Cooper's successor.

What Bugsy Siegel really did in Los Angeles remains half hidden in clouds of police speculation, for nobody knows with much precision what actually happens in the underworld. Siegel liked to gamble, and he often bet as much as five thousand dollars a day on horse races, which generally came out as he expected. That, he told the Internal Revenue Service, was the only source of his income, which he claimed was about fifty thousand dollars a year. Any reports that said otherwise were hearsay. To the extent that the eastern gangs did form a national crime syndicate, though, Siegel seems to have been their chief representative in Los Angeles, and to the extent that they dominated all forms of gambling, Siegel controlled a large share in these operations—bookmaking, roulette, crap games, numbers, everything. According to one account, he also explored, like Willie Bioff, the possibilities of organizing a union of movie extras—the kind of union that would be paid by the studios not to strike—but Siegel's real profession was gambling.

In the late 1930's, Siegel was one of the major investors (15 percent) in the S.S. Rex, a luxurious gambling ship that floated just beyond the territorial waters off Santa Monica until Governor Earl Warren's operatives finally seized it. In 1939, when Moses Annenberg abandoned his national monopoly on racing results, the Trans-National, the heirs of Al Capone set up their own news service, Trans-America, with Siegel in charge of bringing all West Coast bookies into the fold. By 1945, that alone was earning Siegel an estimated $25,000 a month. His overall income has been computed at $500,000 a year, roughly ten times the amount on which he paid taxes.

The only crime for which Siegel was actually prosecuted was the shooting in 1940 of Harry "Big Greenie" Greenbaum, a fugitive hoodlum who was suspected of trying to inform New York police about the activities of Louis "Lepke" Buchalter. Lepke sent Siegel two of his killers from the New York organization known as Murder Inc., and the three of them shot down Greenbaum outside a rooming house a few blocks off Hollywood Boulevard. Siegel was actually arrested and indicted for this murder, so he called in the celebrated Jerry Giesler to rescue him. It turned out, providentially, that the Brooklyn authorities were unwilling to permit any of their star witnesses against Lepke to travel to Los Angeles to testify against Siegel, so the indictment had to be dropped. Then, when the Brooklyn authorities mysteriously changed their minds, and Siegel was reindicted, the main witness suddenly fell out a New York hotel window while in police custody, and so the new indictment against Siegel had to be abandoned. It was perhaps only conicidental that the Los Angeles district attorney who finally cleared Siegel was the same John Dockweiler who was later to prove so righteous in the prosecution of Errol Flynn—and that this same Dockweiler had also received a thirty-thousand-dollar campaign contribution from Siegel. Dockweiler loudly declared that he had been unaware of Siegel's donation, and when it became publicly known, he refunded the money to the newly liberated gangster.

The war years brought prosperity to the Los Angeles underworld, just as they did to the expanding city as a whole (Siegel, it later turned out, organized a firm known as the California Metals Company, which somehow accumulated six million dollars' worth of "surplus" materials in a warehouse on Antonio Avenue), but it was the coming of peace that inspired entrepreneurs like Lansky and Siegel with grand visions of the future. Now, finally, there was lots of money around, and people wanted to play. Furthermore, traveling was going to be easy and popular. People wanted not only to play but to play in new places.

Las Vegas might have impressed any ordinary observer as an implausible El Dorado. Flat, hot, dry, it had nothing whatever to recommend it. Spanish explorers had somewhat charitably named it "The Meadows" and then moved on. Mormon settlers from Utah had made a brief effort to establish an outpost in the 1850's but then relinquished it again to the Paiute Indians. The Union Pacific established a stop in 1905, though only as a way station on the line to the coast. Nevada state authorities did whatever they could think of to attract outsiders—legalized gambling, legalized prostitution, quick divorces—but most of the outsiders gravitated to the more established town of Reno, some three hundred miles to the north. Las Vegas, despite a temporary influx of money during the building of the nearby Boulder Dam, remained a ranch town of no more than ten thousand inhabitants. Its handful of modest gambling halls, several of them partly financed by Lansky and Siegel, occupied only about two downtown blocks, near Fremont and Second streets. "For Christ's sake, Ben!" protested one of Siegel's confederates, Morris Sidwertz, alias Little Moe Sedway, when he first saw the proposed site of the legendary Flamingo. "Seven miles out of town. Not a tree in sight, and nothing but bugs and coyotes and heat."

But that was the whole point, the idea itself. "The choice of the desert was deliberate," Lansky said. "Once you got tourists there, after they had eaten and drunk all they could, there was only one thing left—to go gambling." On September 13, 1945, Sedway acquired from a Las Vegas widow a roadside tract of thirty acres surrounding the hulk of a bankrupt motel. Two months later, Sedway transferred this same property to Greg Bautzer, a dashing young Hollywood attorney who was also notable for having deflowered the seventeen-year-old Lana Turner ("I must confess that I didn't enjoy it at all," she said). Bautzer in turn transferred the property to an organization called the Nevada Projects Corp., in which the largest shareholder was Bugsy Siegel. Another substantial partner was Meyer Lansky. Siegel's backers provided him with a total of one million dollars to build the Flamingo. He chose as the builder Del Webb, a Phoenix contractor who was later celebrated as the builder of Sun City, owner of the New York Yankees, and friend to J. Edgar Hoover.

It should have been fairly easy to build a casino for a million dollars, but Siegel was determined to build not just a casino but the greatest casino ever built. The illuminated pillar at its entrance would be visible for miles across the desert, a beacon to the new palace of pleasure, where everything was permitted. In 1946, however, the American economy was still entangled in wartime regulations and wartime shortages. Siegel had to maneuver, partly by paying black market prices, partly by using connections. He called on Nevada's pliable Senator Pat McCarran, a conservative later celebrated for his investigations of alleged subversives, to help provide copper, steel, and other materials that were in short supply. He persuaded movie executives to delve into studio warehouses for lumber, piping, cement. He sent to Mexico and even Italy (what better use for Mafia connections?) to acquire fine marble and rare wood. He wanted a sunken tub in every bathroom, and a porcelain bidet. There were labor shortages too. Siegel flew in carpenters and plasterers, and he paid them as much as fifty dollars a day.

Things kept going wrong. The boiler room turned out to be too small, and the enlargement cost $115,000. Alterations in the kitchen cost $30,000. The novelty known as air conditioning broke down. The heavy curtains for the casino turned out to be highly flammable and had to be taken down and chemically treated. Siegel had ordered a special fourth-floor penthouse suite for himself, and he was dismayed to find his living room ceiling crossed by a steel beam only five feet eight inches from the floor. It cost him $22,500 to have it moved.

Siegel's confederates were surprised and irritated by the dedication with which the mercurial Siegel built his palace, his insistence on supervising every detail, and on maintaining the highest quality, regardless of cost. Many of them attributed Siegel's extravagance to his desire to impress the woman in his penthouse, Virginia Hill. She was a voluptuous creature, by now thirty, plump, red-haired, and she swore like a stevedore. She had been born Onie Hill, one of ten children of a drunken marble-cutter in Alabama, but the FBI ultimately listed twenty other names she used: Virginia Norma Hall, Virginia Herman, Virginia Oney d'Algy, Virginia Gonzalez . . . Gonzalez was actually the name of her second husband, a Mexican dancer, and after she cast him off in her mid-twenties, she gave up marrying. She bought expensive clothes and gave expensive parties and drank expensive whiskey. In Mexican casinos, she was sometimes known by the not very complimentary nickname of "The Flamingo," and perhaps that, too, was an element in the naming of Siegel's palace.

Virginia Hill carried and spent large sums of cash. A Chicago bookmaker named Joe Epstein, who knew her shortly after she left Alabama, periodically sent her mysterious packages of greenbacks for the rest of her life. Joey Adonis, the king of New York gambling, first took her to Hollywood, where she vaguely hoped to become an actress. Bugsy Siegel met her in a nightclub there, and, to the extent that he was capable of such things, he fell in love with her. Siegel's wife, Esta, had quietly accepted all his previous philandering, but his obsession with Virginia Hill was so public that she gave him the traditional ultimatum. Siegel responded by promising her six hundred dollars a week for life, so she went to Reno for a divorce, and then back to New York. Siegel bought Virginia Hill a ruby-and-diamond ring and flew her to Mexico and married her in the fall of 1946.

By now the million-dollar budget for the Flamingo was long forgotten; the costs were rising to two million, then higher, and still Siegel couldn't get the job done. He had to borrow more from Lansky and his friends, people who were not accustomed to waiting long for repayment. Siegel determined to stage the grand opening of the Flamingo casino on December 26, 1946, the day after Christmas, even though the hotel itself was not yet finished. There would be a gala floor show. Siegel signed up Jimmy Durante to star in it, and Georgie Jessel would be master of ceremonies. Billy Wilkerson, the publisher of *The Hollywood Reporter*, who also owned a share in the Flamingo, sent invitations to all the usual Hollywood celebrities.

In late afternoon of that opening night, when Siegel went to inspect the illuminated plastic waterfall at the entrance to the Flamingo, he found the waterfall dry, the lights unlit. A workman told him that a cat had crept into the structure the previous night and given birth to kittens; they would all have to be flushed out. Siegel forbade it. "It's bad luck for a gambler to touch a cat," he said. So the fountain was not turned on for opening night, but Siegel's luck could hardly have been worse. There was a sudden storm in Los Angeles, and the Constellations that Siegel had chartered to ferry movie stars to his opening could not take off. Nobody seemed to want to come to the great event anyway. Jessel and Durante arrived to do their routines, of course, along with Xavier Cugat and his band. George Raft made the trip in his Cadillac, but the only other guests who could be considered Hollywood celebrities provided a distinctly unimpressive gathering: George Sanders, Charles Coburn, Sonny Tufts. There can rarely have been a more cheerless scene than the newly opened casino at the half-empty and half-finished Flamingo, standing alone in the Nevada desert on the night after Christmas.

Even the gambling tables lost money. Siegel couldn't figure out whether his employees were cheating, or whether local gamblers were more skillful than he thought, or whether it was simply a matter of bad luck, but the Flamingo lost $300,000 on gambling alone during its first two weeks of operation. And by now, Siegel's building costs were stupefying. The furnishing of the ninety-two rooms was running to $3,500 each. Overall, the cost of the Flamingo had climbed from the original one million to more than four million dollars. Siegel made a drastic decision: He closed down the whole place until he could get it finished. Virginia Hill, tired of the venture—tired particularly of Siegel's outbursts of bad temper—returned to Beverly Hills. There she rented a mansion on North Linden Drive and began giving parties.

On March 1, 1947, Siegel finally got the furniture installed and the hotel open, but though the spotlights now shone invitingly across the desert, the Flamingo still failed to bring in the fortunes that Siegel had so long expected. The operating loss for the first six months was $774,000, the total cost, six million dollars. Siegel scrambled to raise new funds wherever he could find them, but the gangsters who had originally sponsored the Flamingo were becoming convinced that the disaster was largely Siegel's own fault. Not only did they blame him for mishandling the project, but there were rumors that the losses might not be as great as Siegel said, that Siegel might be hiding some of the money for himself.

In December of 1946, even before the original opening of the Flamingo, there was a remarkable meeting at the Hotel Nacional in Havana. The host was Meyer Lansky, and the guest of honor was Lucky Luciano, Lansky's boyhood friend, whose deportation from New York to Italy had lasted just nine months before he returned to Cuba to look after his interests. Lansky, the original organizer of the Nacional's casino back in 1937, invited Luciano to stay there, and he was pleased to see that the hotel's Christmas attraction would be Frank Sinatra. He invited all the barons to Havana to welcome the return of Luciano—Frank Costello and Joe Adonis from New York, as well as Vito Genovese and Joe Bonnano; Carlos Marcello from New Orleans, Santos Trafficante from Florida; the whole lot.

It was inevitable that the chieftains assembled at the Hotel Nacional should consider Bugsy Siegel's venture in Las Vegas. Just as inevitably, they were appalled to hear the reports that the Flamingo was costing millions more than planned, that some of their money was being spent at the whim of Virginia Hill, and that some of it might be going to Switzerland. "This sort of behavior meant only one thing in the underworld," said one of Lansky's closest associates, Joseph "Doc" Stacher, in an interview shortly before his death in Israel. "Bugsy was going to be hit. Meyer knew that too, but he did all he could to save his friend. He begged the men to be patient. . . . It was the first time I ever heard Meyer become so emotional. . . . He pleaded with everybody there to remember the great services that Bugsy had performed for all of them. They looked at him stony-faced, without saying a word." According to Stacher, Luciano himself later accosted Lansky and said Siegel would have to be punished. "If you don't have the heart to do it, Meyer, I will have to order the execution myself."

Bugsy Siegel had all kinds of troubles. Virginia Hill came back to spend a weekend in the Flamingo penthouse, and Siegel picked a quarrel with her because he found her reading a copy of *Time,* "that crummy magazine." He knocked the magazine out of her hands and then gave her a shove. She hit him over the forehead with her spike-heeled shoe, then hit him several more times and ran out. But after all of Siegel's work and worry, the Flamingo finally seemed to be making money. May was profitable; June would be better. Siegel apologized to Virginia and invited her to take a trip to Paris.

In mid-June, Meyer Lansky himself arrived at the Flamingo to spend a few days. He was not there to gamble; he apparently never left his room. There were some meetings. Nobody really knows what happened. According to Doc Stacher's version, which is presumably Lansky's own version, Lansky did his best to defend Siegel to the end. Other speculations suggest that Lansky himself decided Siegel must be punished, that his last trip to Las Vegas was his version of the kiss of death.

Siegel seemed to have no premonitions about what would happen. He spent his last few days on various secret meetings and negotiations, but he showed no particular sign of anxiety. He flew to Los Angeles just after midnight on June 20 and let himself into Virginia Hill's house with a golden key that she had given him. She herself had gone to Paris, but her brother Chick was staying in the house.

The following evening, Siegel drove to a seafood restaurant named Jack's, in Ocean Park, together with Chick Hill, Chick's girlfriend, Jerri Mason, and a business associate named Allen Smiley. As they emerged from the restaurant shortly after 9 P.M., somebody handed Siegel a copy of the next morning's *Los Angeles Times,* which bore a stamp on the front page that said, "Good night. Sleep well. With the compliments of Jack's." When they got back to the house on Linden Drive, Siegel suddenly sniffed the air suspiciously.

"There's a strong smell of flowers in here," he said to Chick.

"I don't smell anything," Chick said. "There isn't a flower in the house."

"Can't you smell them, Jerri?" Siegel persisted.

"No, I can't," she said.

Siegel shooed Chick and Jerri upstairs so that he could talk business with Smiley. Chick later remembered telling Jerri that his grandmother, Virginia's grandmother, had once told him that "when someone smells flowers and there aren't any in the house, it means they're going to die." Jerri told him, as they retired to the bedroom, that his grandmother's tale was just silly superstition.

Downstairs, where Siegel sat on the sofa with the newspaper open across his lap, he and Smiley were clearly visible through the undrawn curtains on the living room window. Outside in the darkness, a man armed with a .30/30 carbine slowly took aim through some garden latticework. He fired, then fired again, nine times in all. The first bullet through the window smashed Siegel squarely in the face, knocking out his right eye and sending it flying some fifteen feet away onto the tiled floor of the dining room. As Siegel's head sank back against the sofa, the second bullet hit him in the neck. Another bullet tore through Smiley's sleeve as he dove to the floor. Another shattered a small marble figure of Bacchus that stood on Virginia Hill's piano. Another embedded itself in a painting of a nude holding a wineglass.

One of the first reporters to reach the scene was Florabel Muir of the *New York Daily News,* who noted that the living room was filled with the smell of the night-blooming jasmine that grew just outside the window. She lifted the blood-spattered newspaper on Siegel's lap to see what he might have been reading. She also checked the flight of Siegel's eye. "From the jamb of the wide doorway . . ." she recalled, "I picked up the sliver of flesh from which his long eyelashes extended."

Within twenty minutes of the killing, while the police were still arriving at the house in Beverly Hills, and long before any official news reached Las Vegas, three men marched into the lobby of the Flamingo. There were fierce sandstorms tearing through the sky that night, and the casino was half empty. One of the three newcomers was Little Moe Sedway, who had originally bought this property for Siegel but later quarreled with him; the second was Gus Greenbaum, the head of gambling operations in Tucson; the third was Morris Rosen, an ex-burglar from New York who now worked for Lansky. They announced to the casino staff that there had been a change in management. They were taking over. And so it was. Nobody disputed them. And during the first year in which Gus Greenbaum managed the Flamingo, it showed a profit of four million dollars.

In contrast to Hollywood's gangster movies, the killings among real gangsters often don't get solved. Nobody ever discovered who fired nine shots through Bugsy Siegel's window, just as nobody ever discovered who attached the explosives to the accelerator of Willie Bioff's truck. Nobody ever discovered, for that matter, who eventually broke into Gus Greenbaum's house and cut his throat with a butcher knife. But Meyer Lansky, who never learned that crime does not pay, had amassed a fortune estimated at $300 million when he finally died of cancer in 1983 in the fullness of his eighty-second year.

•   •   •

Marriage to the incomparable Rita Hayworth apparently palled on Orson Welles. "Mr. Welles showed no interest in establishing a home," the actress was to testify at the divorce hearing in 1947, just four years after the wedding. "Mr. Welles told me he never should have married in the first place, as it interfered with his freedom in his way of life." Her restless husband might well have corroborated that view. "Women are stupid," he once told a French interviewer. "I 've known some who are less stupid than others, but they're all stupid." Though Welles's "freedom in his way of life" meant a good deal of roistering, it also involved a good deal of hard work. After his debacle in Brazil, he struggled with several ambitious projects—including both *War and Peace* and *Crime and Punishment*—then undertook to show a suspicious Hollywood that he could make a perfectly orthodox film, on time and on budget. Welles directed, starred in, and partly wrote *The Stranger* (1946) for Sam Spiegel (during Spiegel's temporary phase of calling himself S. P. Eagle). Though it was hardly a masterpiece, it was taut and dramatic, a very creditable piece of work.

One of the most interesting (and generally unrecognized) aspects of *The Stranger* was that it was the first Hollywood film to deal explicitly with the Nazi Holocaust, not as mere mistreatment but as mass slaughter. Welles's film argued a somewhat implausible thesis, that a major SS official named Franz Kindler could disguise himself as a history teacher in a small Connecticut village, but in narrating the authorities' efforts to trap Kindler, Welles included some documentary footage considerably stronger than anything that Hollywood's professional liberals had yet brought to the screen. Here is what happened in the Nazi concentration camps, said the pursuer, Edward G. Robinson. Here—look at it. "This is a gas chamber. . . . This is a lime pit . . . ."

Welles himself was a fervent liberal in those days. He campaigned noisily for Roosevelt in the 1944 race and even substituted for the President in a debate with Thomas Dewey at the Astor Hotel in New York. Early in 1945, he began producing a daily editorial column, "Orson Welles's Almanac," in the *New York Post*. It started with chatter and commentary about show business but soon veered into liberal political sermons. Welles attended and applauded the birth of the United Nations in San Francisco. He worried about Washington's apparent inability to organize a stable peace. "We are still building our Bulwarks against Bolshevism," Welles wrote. "The phony fear of Communism is smoke-screening the real menace of renascent Fascism."

But Welles was also an actor who yearned to play Faustus, who might cry, as Faustus did, " 'Tis magic, magic that hath ravished me." He no longer sawed Rita Hayworth in half for the amusement of soldiers at the Hollywood canteen, but he continued to be ravished by the possibilities in a fan of playing cards or a rabbit in a top hat. During one period of domestic difficulties early in 1946, he went east to try his repertoire of magic tricks in a spectacular stage version of Jules Verne's *Around the World in Eighty Days*. For this, he persuaded Cole Porter to write the music, and Mike Todd to provide the financing. During the pre-Broadway tryout in Boston, however, Todd abruptly abandoned the whole project. Welles decided to see what new funds he could raise himself, starting with the fifty thousand dollars needed to pay an overdue bill for costumes. One of the few people he knew who could commit himself to such a sum in one telephone call was Rita Hayworth's boss, Harry Cohn, the despot of Columbia Pictures.

"If you advance me the fifty thousand," Welles supposedly proposed from a backstage telephone in Boston, "I'll make a deal with you to write and direct a picture. I've got a suspense story that can be made inexpensively."

"Yeah?" Cohn grunted. "What is it?"

Welles apparently had nothing in mind more definite than the idea that he could shoot a thriller on the streets of New York, once he got *Around the World* successfully launched there, but to soothe Cohn's suspicions, he began to improvise. According to legend, he spotted a nearby stagehand reading a paperback novel titled *If I Die Before I Wake,* by Sherwood King, and that was enough to inspire Welles to promise mystery, dreams, wild fantasy. "Buy the novel and I'll make the film," he said. Cohn impulsively agreed. "Later," Welles told an interviewer, "I read the book and it was horrible, so I set myself, top speed, to write a story."*

First, though, there was *Around the World in Eighty Days,* which Welles did manage to bring to Broadway in the fall of 1946, where it received what are known as "mixed notices," survived for seventy-four performances, and cost Welles himself the impressive sum of $350,000 in debts. "That will be enough magic for a while, thank you," Welles remarked. And so he returned to Hollywood to submit to the dictates of Harry Cohn. What Cohn now wanted was not a cheap New York thriller but a first-class film for his biggest star, the biggest star in Hollywood, Welles's estranged wife, Rita Hayworth.

Miss Hayworth had reached the height of a success beyond anything that Harry Cohn could understand, beyond anything that the actress herself could understand. To millions of Americans, she had mysteriously become the personification of glamour, of female beauty, of all those intangible and incomprehensible elements that could be filmed, packaged, and sold. When the United States staged its first postwar atomic test at Bikini atoll that July 1—devastating an anchored armada of seventy-five warships manned only by a captive flock of 4,800 goats, pigs, and rats—the nuclear bomb that exploded in their midst was painted with a pinup picture of Rita Hayworth and named the "Gilda."

It was *Gilda,* released just that spring, that elevated Miss Hayworth beyond her triumphs as a dancer in *Cover Girl* and changed her into an international phenomenon, worthy of the nuclear explosion at Bikini. Like most such affairs, this legendary film was largely a series of accidents. The original screenplay was the work of one Marion Parsonnet, but Harry Cohn assigned the job of producing it to Virginia Van Upp, who had not only written *Cover Girl* but shepherded Miss Hayworth through all the problems of the production. And now Miss Van Upp kept rewriting *Gilda,* rewriting only a page or two at a time, often on the night before a scene was scheduled for shooting. "We never knew what was coming next, and we even started the picture without a leading man," said Charles Vidor, the director.

---

* Unfortunately for this tale, *If I Die Before I Wake* was published in 1938, and there was no paperback edition until 1962, so it would not have been easy for Welles to spot a copy in 1946. Actually, Columbia already owned the rights to this thriller, which it had bought as a vehicle for Franchot Tone.

There was a peculiar and perverted quality to *Gilda*. According to one theory, the relationship between the male characters was simply homosexual, at best partly repressed. According to another, the relationships were all sadomasochistic. At one point, the hero, played by Glenn Ford, contemptuously told Gilda that he had been assigned to take charge of her, "like the laundry." Gilda reacted by playing the wanton.

The designer Jean Louis, supposedly inspired by John Singer Sargent's famous portrait of the décolleté Madame X, created for Miss Hayworth a fetishistic black satin strapless gown, with elbow-length gloves, and the dance director Jack Cole devised the strip-tease routine in which she flung those gloves to her audience. The director, Vidor, expected the filming of "Put the blame on Mame" would be difficult, but he was pleasantly surprised the moment Miss Hayworth appeared. "She sauntered on the stage holding her head high, in that magnificent way she does," he said, "stepping along like a sleek young tiger cub, and the whistles that sounded would have shamed a canary's convention. She enjoyed every second of it. Then she did that elaborate difficult 'Mame' number in two takes." Ford ended the dance by slapping her face, which was very much as Hollywood convention said it should be.

At the end, the censors had to be placated, of course, and so Miss Van Upp produced a finale in which it turned out that Gilda had always been faithful and virtuous, and had just pretended otherwise to arouse her tormentor. By now everything about Rita Hayworth had become rather unreal. The trademark, the luxurious red hair, was dyed. The voice that sang was the dubbed-in voice of Anita Ellis. And now that the star was supposed to be an actress, Miss Van Upp provided the rather diffident Miss Hayworth with the false personality of a wanton. If the censors preferred that her wantonness be shown to be false, that was really quite reasonable, since Miss Hayworth's laborious efforts to mimic wantonness depended heavily on the audience's imagination. And yet that audience seemed to want not real sensuality so much as a confirmation of its own suspicions. Gilda descended from a long line of temptresses: Circe, Cleopatra, Lucrezia Borgia, Carmen, Nana—all beautiful, untrustworthy, ultimately malevolent, *belles dames sans merci*. The tradition reached a kind of apotheosis in the outpouring of *film noir* of the 1940's, in the treacherous heroines of Chandler or Cain, as interpreted by Lang or Wilder. Gilda teased her men and then denied them, or so it seemed, and if Glenn Ford slapped Miss Hayworth in the face, wasn't that what she deserved? If she was a "love goddess," as the tabloid newspapers liked to say, she was a goddess feared and mistrusted.

This was the point at which Harry Cohn, who yearned to dominate Miss Hayworth but could never have her, assigned her to work for Orson Welles, who had had her and no longer wanted her. And Welles, who knew that the famous Gilda had very little to do with his own estranged wife, seized on the image that was already on the verge of self-parody and exaggerated it yet a little more. If Gilda was a temptress and a tease, who had sold herself to an aged millionaire, Elsa Bannister would be not only the cold young wife of a paralyzed lawyer but also a woman willing and able to lie, betray, murder. Welles's first step was to order the famous Hayworth hair cut off.

And dyed a completely different color. Welles himself mulled over the many possibilities and then settled on something called "topaz blonde." Columbia's chief hair stylist, Helen Hunt, was summoned back from a honeymoon in New York to shear the studio's most important star. "When I met Rita to do the job Orson and sixteen photographers were there in my department," she recalled. "Orson stood over me and the Press stood on chairs all along the back. I think Orson wanted to take credit for a new Rita. . . . Rita was always being told what to do by her husbands and she did it willingly. Many people wrote for a lock; even a minister from Canada who wrote and said it was against the teachings of the bible to cut hair . . . and could he have some? The hair was finally tossed in the basket."

The Lady from Shanghai was to be a characteristically Wellesian story of greed and deception and violence. Welles cast himself in the heroic but slightly absurd role of a thick-brogued Irish sailor, Michael O'Hara, who shipped out aboard a yacht appropriately named the *Circe,* on which a severely crippled lawyer named Arthur Bannister planned to sail from New York to California. Circe, of course, was the exotic Mrs. Bannister, as played by Miss Hayworth, the lady from Shanghai, who had married the lawyer only because he had blackmailed her into it. Welles cruelly trained his cameras on Bannister's lurching canes, and even more cruelly had O'Hara say of one of his employer's parties that it was "no more like a picnic than Bannister was like a man." Bannister, brilliantly played by Everett Sloane, invariably addressed his blank-eyed wife as "lover," pronouncing it every time with a mixture of hatred and despair.

The filming of *The Lady from Shanghai* was as chaotic as its origins. Welles apparently had imagined something in a quasi-documentary style, a bit like Louis de Rochemont's *March of Time* (which he had once used as a framework for *Citizen Kane*), but his new film had no real locus to be documented, and no very definite script either. After only minimum preparations, under the mistrustful eye of Harry Cohn, whose only strong opinion on the matter was that he hated Rita Hayworth's new hairdo, Welles took his cast to Acapulco, where even a well-organized and disciplined crew would have had difficulties in making a movie. Every outing into the countryside was apt to encounter alligators or poisonous snakes; clouds of insects interfered with the lighting; even a single sunbathing scene required more than two dozen Mexicans to scrape the rocks clear of barnacles. But Welles was never organized or disciplined. He rewrote the dialogue almost every day, quarreled with his actors, then took Miss Hayworth off to Mexico City to see the bullfights. The budget of $1.25 million and sixty days of shooting climbed toward $2 million and ninety days.

Most remarkable of all, Welles never saw any of the daily rushes of the film he had shot. Everything was shipped back to Hollywood, undeveloped, and there a strong-minded Columbia film editor named Viola Lawrence did what she could with it. One of her first surprises was that Welles was shooting a Rita Hayworth movie without a single close-up of his star (this was apparently his private revenge on the studio makeup technicians, who spent hours preparing Miss Hayworth for the camera). Miss Lawrence complained to Harry Cohn; Cohn ordered close-ups; Welles balked; Cohn fumed. There were worse problems. The script that Welles had so blithely hammered together out of various bits and pieces (it included not only the original thriller and his own recollections of Brazil but even a few quasi-Confucian sayings from the works of Lin Yutang) made very little sense. When Harry Cohn saw the first screening of what Miss Lawrence had put together out of the film shipped from Acapulco, he was outraged. He offered a thousand dollars to anyone who could explain the plot to him. Nobody offered; nobody got paid.

To hell with it, Harry Cohn decided. He stored away Welles's erratic but brilliant film as a hopeless failure. More than a year passed before the authorities in the accounting department persuaded him to release a patched-together remnant, in the spring of 1948, to earn whatever it could earn. It earned very little. By then, Orson Welles was through. He had produced his strange *Macbeth*—all filmed in three weeks on rainy moors and leaking caves, with Welles outfitted in furs and growling in a weird Scots accent—and then fled to Europe.

His marriage to Rita Hayworth ended in November of 1947, when she testified that he spent his evenings working. "What do you expect?" said Eduardo Cansino, the eternal father. "Welles is a fine man, but you can't leave a young girl like Rita alone while you sit up all night working." Some persistent reporter presumably asked him to say something like that, and so he said it. Louella Parsons, who had hated Welles ever since *Citizen Kane,* virtually demanded that his wife join in the conventional Hollywood denunciations, but all she could get was a statement—if Miss Hayworth actually said it—that "Orson's a genius and never forgets it. But I don't want to say too much against him because he's the father of my daughter. And I think if you loved a man enough to marry him, the least you could do, if you must part, is to say nothing against him." That was an admirable philosophy—and Rita Hayworth was an admirable woman—but people kept asking her the same questions, and eventually the answers got sharper. "He was tormented, possessive, insecure . . . ." one interviewer quoted her as saying, "a genius, crazy like a horse, and a marvelous man, completely unaware of reality."

She may, of course, never have said any such thing. And even if she said it, that did not necessarily make it true. She herself had by now become so separated from reality that she began to play principally legends: Carmen in 1948, Salome in 1953, and all the usual variations. None of them really amounted to much. After *The Lady from Shanghai*, Rita Hayworth, too, was finished, at the age of thirty. All unaware of her destiny, just as Welles was unaware of his, she sailed off on her first trip to Europe and there she would meet a handsome young man known as Aly Khan, who had been deeply stirred by *Gilda*. "Every man I've known," Miss Hayworth sadly said later to Virginia Van Upp, "has fallen in love with Gilda—and wakened with me."

• • •

Thomas Mann's decision to build himself a house on San Remo Drive in Pacific Palisades was not inspired solely by his love of the southern California climate. According to Janet Flanner, who wrote a *New Yorker* profile of Mann in 1941 under the title of "Goethe in Hollywood," the novelist had other reasons for settling on the Pacific coast. He had begun toying with "the idea of writing a Hollywood novel as a parallel to 'The Magic Mountain' and its special theme of sickness." Miss Flanner offered no details of the prospective plot or characters but reported that Mann "thinks there is a psychological condition peculiar to Hollywood which makes of it an island not unlike his island of Davos, on its Swiss mountaintop."

Since Mann knew and cared little about movies, and since his command of English was limited, it was perhaps all for the best that he abandoned this idea and concentrated on finishing his biblical tetralogy, *Joseph and His Brothers* (1933–44). This work did surprisingly well, and indeed made Mann rich. The final volume, *Joseph the Provider*, was a Book-of-the-Month Club choice in 1944 and sold about two hundred thousand copies. There was even some talk that it might fulfill another of Mann's California ambitions, a Hollywood sale. After all, if Werfel's *Bernadette* could become a successful movie, why not the famous novels of Thomas Mann?

Joseph was actually bought some years later by Louis B. Mayer, who planned it as his first independent production after his departure from M-G-M. Mayer assigned the project to a veteran M-G-M screenwriter, John Lee Mahin, and then sent Mahin's script to David O. Selznick to see if Jennifer Jones might play the role of Potiphar's wife. Selznick agreed, provided that the character could be made less "consistently villainous." He thought that Mahin's script needed "a great deal of work," but that the possibilities in the story of Joseph were grand. "You have working for you that greatest of all showmanship combinations—sex and religion," Selznick declared. "You have father love, mother love, brother love; you have lust and sentiment; you have a faithful husband and you have an unfaithful wife; you have complete blueprints for every conceivable production value, including spectacle, exterior scenes of great beauty, interiors of great pomp and circumstance, magnificent costumes, daring and revealing costumes, boudoir scenes, royalty and panoply, family life—indeed, the whole catalog of elements of mass appeal." Despite all this, the film was never produced.

While Thomas Mann was getting rich, his older brother, Heinrich, was sinking into penury. His hundred-dollar weekly dole as a useless screenwriter at Warner Bros. had stopped at the end of one year, and after that he survived only on Thomas's chilly donations. He remained nonetheless proud. When Alfred Knopf bought his memoirs but wanted to make some editorial changes, he refused to allow it. "He thought he was writer enough to decide *for himself* what HE ought to write," his wife, Nelly, wrote to a friend.

Nelly herself, the ex-barmaid whom Mann had married and brought away with him during the fall of France, was getting increasingly alcoholic and increasingly crazy. Several times, she took overdoses of sleeping pills. "She drank secretly," according to Salka Viertel, "slipping out into the bathroom or kitchen, coyly refusing the drinks offered at parties; then insisted on driving Heinrich home, to which he heroically consented." Herbert Marcuse's brother, Ludwig, reported that he was once invited to dinner at Mann's house and was greeted by Nelly standing naked in the doorway. At dinner, she kept saying, "Oh, I've got such an old husband," until Mann got up and left the table, as did the rest of the embarrassed guests. Yet while Mann labored away on books that nobody published, Nelly had to go out and get a job as a nurse in a hospital. "It overtaxes her and shames me," said Mann, who was by now unemployable at seventy-three. "What can I do?"

Nelly got arrested for drunken driving. She didn't know what to do either. For the fifth time, she swallowed an overdose of sleeping pills. "She had broken a probation for drunken driving," Salka Viertel observed, "and in her panic about appearing in court, she put an end to her constant tussle with the police, her struggle with a language she could never learn, her fear of aging, and her losing battle with liquor." Thomas Mann, who had his own order of priorities, recorded Nelly's end somewhat differently. "Adrian's dialogue with the long-awaited visitor . . . was still in its early stages when a telephone call from my brother Heinrich informed us of the death of her who had shared his life for so many years." Nelly's suicide, in other words, was only a brief interruption in the labor that now obsessed Mann, the writing of *Doctor Faustus.*

The idea had haunted him for nearly half a century, and when he looked back through his journals, as he repeatedly did, he found there "the three-line outline of the Dr. Faust of 1901." As a young man, the novelist had not felt any need to write down the details of what he had in mind, and when the old man tried to evoke his faded vision, he recalled not *Faust* so much as "the Munich days, the never-realized plans for *The Lovers* and *Maya*. . . . Shame and strong sentimentality at remembrance of these youthful sorrows." But that was mere nostalgia. To any German intellectual, *Faust* embodied much of the national legend, and to attempt a variation on Goethe's masterpiece must have seemed as daunting as to attempt a tenth symphony. "Do I still have strength for new conceptions?" Mann worried in his journal. It was March of 1943. Mann went to downtown Los Angeles to hear Horowitz play the Brahms B-flat Concerto. "Gloomy weather: rainy, cold. With a headache, I drew up outlines and notes."

Mann's eponymous Faust was to be a composer, of course, and to go mad, of course. Mann read Nietzsche, and E. T. A. Hoffmann, and Paul Bekker's *Musikgeschichte*, and the letters of Luther, and he listened to radio news reports on the war. "Massive and systematic bombings of Hitler's continent," he noted. "Advances of the Russians in the Crimea." He didn't want to write about Faust; he wanted to write something more cheerful, to complete the long-unfinished *Confessions of Felix Krull, Confidence Man.* "And yet the thorn was in my flesh," Mann later recorded, "the thorn of curiosity about the new and dangerous task." What made it dangerous, perhaps, was that it was beyond his capabilities, for what he planned to write, in the middle of a war between his native country and his land of exile, was "nothing less than the novel of my era, disguised as the story of an artist's life, a terribly imperiled and sinful artist."

One problem in Mann's effort to make his hero a composer was that his own knowledge of music was limited. He had loved and listened to it all his life, but when he tried to write about it, he gasped and gushed (for example, in *Richard Wagner and the Ring*: "What would man be, above all what would an artist be, without admiration, enthusiasm, absorption, devotion to something not himself . . . ?"). To create a composer, Mann needed to learn more about what composers actually did, how they worked, how they thought, and that need kept leading him toward one of his neighbors. "Gathering at the Werfels with the Schönbergs," he recorded in his journal. "Pumped S. a great deal on music and the life of a composer. To my deep pleasure, he himself insists we must all get together more often."

Schoenberg was now on the brink of a crisis. He was about to become seventy, and the rules of the California university system required that he retire from his post as a teacher at UCLA. The prospect drove him to desperation. "My career is not one which is ended by age . . ." he wrote in protest to the office of the university controller in Berkeley. "I do not feel I am an old man, because I am still improving my teaching methods." The university was unmoved. At Schoenberg's seventieth birthday, as his eyesight failed and he learned that he had diabetes, he was inexorably forced into retirement. And since he had only been on the faculty for eight years, his pension was $29.60 per month. He had to live on what he could earn from a dozen or so private pupils. He even applied for a Guggenheim Fellowship, and the Guggenheim authorities, presumably interested mainly in bright young talents, rejected him. "Dining with the Schönbergs in Brentwood," Mann wrote in his journal. "Excellent Viennese coffee. Talking with Sch. at length about music. . . ." And again: "Soirée at the Werfels' with Stravinsky; talked about Schönberg. . . ." Schoenberg sent Mann his textbook on harmony, *Harmonielehre*, which Mann pored over and judged to be "the strangest mingling of piety toward tradition and revolution."

Mann's real teacher, though, was Theodor Adorno, who was apparently trying to promote his own interests and got swallowed up in the far more powerful interests of Thomas Mann. Born Theodor Wiesengrund, Adorno preferred to use the name of his mother, a singer of Corsican origin, and from boyhood he felt a passionate love of music. He studied composition in Vienna with Alban Berg, and piano with Edward Steuermann (Salka Viertel's brother), but there was something lacking in his artistic gifts, something that turned him from music to the theory of music. At twenty-eight, he became a lecturer in philosophy at the University of Frankfurt and a leading figure in that sociological movement known as the Frankfurt School. Driven westward by the Nazis, he ended in Los Angeles, a brilliantly cantankerous thinker in search of an audience. He met Mann, who was already enmeshed in the creation of *Faustus,* and showed him the manuscript of a study much influenced by Schoenberg, "Zur Philosophie der modernen Musik." "The whole thing had the strangest affinity to the idea of my book . . ." Mann wrote. "This was my man."

Like his diabolic hero, Adrian Leverkühn, Mann drained his teacher of knowledge. Adorno came repeatedly to Mann's house and lectured, performed, answered Mann's groping questions. Mann persuaded Adorno to teach him all the intricacies of Schoenberg's twelve-tone method, and even quoted substantially, without credit, from Adorno's own writings on Schoenberg. Adorno loved to be used, though, to be studied, quoted, exploited. Once, when the two of them were discussing parallels between Goethe and Beethoven, Adorno went to the piano and played through Beethoven's last piano sonata, Opus III. Mann made characteristic use of the piece, devoting several pages of his novel to his fervid imaginings about its inner significance.*

Day in, day out, from nine in the morning until noon, Mann kept writing. In the background, Leverkühn's Germany slid to its ruin, and every once in a while Mann noted some new landmark in his journals. In June of 1944, on Mann's sixty-ninth birthday, a friend telephoned him the news of D-day, and he regarded it as "one of the harmonies of my life . . . that the longed-for . . . event was taking place on this day, my day." Bombers raided Berlin; Paris was liberated; Mann kept writing *Doctor Faustus.* "Surviving means victory," he observed when he heard of Hitler's suicide in the spring of 1945. "By continuing to live I had fought and cast mockery and a curse into the faces of those blasphemers of humanity."

The survivor's health was failing, however. He suffered fevers as high as 102 every afternoon. He tried the new wonder drug, penicillin, but nothing worked. His wife put him to bed. "I went over much of Nietzsche again," he wrote, "especially his *Use and Disadvantage of History.*" An X-ray showed a shadow on his lung. He was startled that the disease that had haunted *The Magic Mountain* should strike at him. He was taken to Chicago for more expert diagnosis, and the doctor there decided that it was cancer. Mann seems not to have known this verdict, not to have wanted to know, but he stoically underwent surgery, and survived, and went back to work on *Doctor Faustus.* A bit later, when another illness prevented him from sleeping at night, he wrote in his diary: "Even without sleep I will work."

Schoenberg was even more harshly stricken that same year of 1946. He had a heart attack of such severity that his heart stopped. He was theoretically dead, but a doctor brought him back to life with an injection directly into the heart. "I have risen from real death and now feel very well," he wrote to a

---

* No less characteristically, Mann included some coy pedantry that he considered a compliment to his teacher. He tried to transform the beautiful theme of the Adagio into a series of what he called "poetic little illustrative phrases," which his translator rendered as "Heav-en's blue, lov-ers' pain . . . meadow-land." In German, "meadow-land" is *Wiesengrund,* Adorno's original name, which Mann said he slipped into his novel "by way of showing my gratitude."

friend. He decided to translate his experience into music, a trio for strings, and since he could no longer see well enough to compose on ordinary music paper, he had some specially printed, with the lines of the staves far apart.

At dinner at the Manns', Schoenberg told the novelist about his new trio and "the experiences . . . secretly woven into the composition." It would be difficult for any uninstructed listener to decipher these secret weavings, but Schoenberg described them to Mann in detail. "He had, he said, represented his illness and medical treatment in the music, including even the male nurses and all the other oddities of American hospitals. The work was extremely difficult to play [but] very rewarding because of its extraordinary tonal effects. I worked the association of 'impossible but rewarding' into the chapter on Leverkühn's chamber music."

On January 29, 1947, Mann finally announced to his wife that *Doctor Faustus* was finished. No sooner said than he was off on a lecture tour to deliver his thoughts on Nietzsche. The tour took him to Washington and New York and London, but at the prospect of returning to Germany again, he blanched. It is a little difficult now to recall the ferocity with which Goebbels had condemned Mann's works to the bonfire, or the pain that such a condemnation inflicted on so genteel and straitlaced a writer as Mann. His American riches and success had scarcely assuaged his sense of rejection and exile. And now, from the rubble of conquered Germany, there already arose a babble of voices claiming that Mann had deserted his own people. "It was harder to preserve one's personality here than to broadcast messages to the German people from over there," wrote one of these reemerging accusers. Mann was understandably indignant about any such claims from any such "personality." All books published in Germany during the Hitler years were "worse than worthless," he declared. "A stench of blood and disgrace clings to them."

Mann seems to have believed that his real answer lay in *Doctor Faustus*, and he was dismayed to see, on its appearance in 1948, that its effect was that of a large stone monument newly unveiled in a public park. The Book-of-the-Month Club once again provided its stamp of approval, but the reviews were solemn rather than enthusiastic. Mann, who had originally declared that this was to be "nothing less than the novel of my era," now complained to his daughter Erika that "they all place such dreadful stress on the G-e-r-m-a-n allegory."

The most interesting reaction, though, came from the German exile community in Los Angeles, from the man who saw himself as the model for Mann's "terribly imperiled and sinful artist." It was Alma Mahler Werfel, naturally, who provoked the controversy. She bustled over to see Mann and "praised the beauty of the novel," but added some cluckings of surprise that he had made such extensive use of Schoenberg's theory of atonality.

"So you recognized it?" Mann asked, "slightly put out," according to Mrs. Werfel's account. She answered that "no musician could fail to recognize it." Mann began to worry. "Do you think Schoenberg will mind?" he asked. Mrs. Werfel only "shrugged, not wanting to set off a general discussion," but she then hastened to see Schoenberg and to tell him about Mann's activities. "Schoenberg," she reported, not without satisfaction, "was outraged."

Schoenberg apparently asked Mrs. Werfel to persuade Mann to have a special notice printed in every copy of *Doctor Faustus*, stating that the twelvetone theory attributed to Leverkühn was Schoenberg's invention. Mrs. Werfel said she telephoned Mann's home and got his wife, Katia, who "at first resented the idea." ("She always drank far too many sweet liqueurs and was rather malicious by nature," Mrs. Mann later wrote of Mrs. Werfel. "She loved to start gossip, and it was she who got Arnold Schoenberg going on the business of the twelve-tone system, telling him that Thomas Mann had stolen his theory.") Schoenberg really had no proprietary rights to his theory, of course, any more than André Breton did to surrealism, or, for that matter, Einstein to relativity. But Schoenberg was old and neglected, impoverished and embittered, and the idea that his rich and famous fellow refugee had used their dinner table conversations about his unplayed music in a best-selling novel—and without ever mentioning his name . . . was all too much.

Schoenberg didn't even read *Doctor Faustus*, declaring that his eyes were too weak for such an effort, but he began planning a bizarre response. This took the form of an article, written by Schoenberg under the pseudonym of Hugo Triebsamen, allegedly for the *Encyclopedia Americana* of 1988, in which the misguided Triebsamen falsely attributed the invention of twelve-tone music to Thomas Mann. Schoenberg then sent this macabre creation to Mann with a bitter note explaining that it was intended to demonstrate the potential damage that Mann had done him. Mann was baffled, partly because he actually believed, since his ego was almost as large as that of Schoenberg, that he had made Schoenberg's theory his own. "Within the sphere of the book . . ." he argued, "the idea of the twelve-tone technique assumes a coloration and a character which it does not possess in its own right and which —is this not so?—in a sense make it really my property."

Mann did realize, though, that Schoenberg's "delusions of persecution" derived from "a life suspended between glorification and neglect," and so he finally agreed, after many more phone calls, to give credit to Schoenberg for his theories in all future editions of *Doctor Faustus*. "It is my sincere hope," Mann rather grandly declared, "that he may arise above bitterness and suspicion and that he may find peace in the assurance of his greatness and glory."

•   •   •

The ugly strike of 1945, which had theoretically been settled by the victory of Herb Sorrell's Conference of Studio Unions over the larger and stronger forces of IATSE, remained very much unsettled. Two angrily competitive union coalitions still confronted each other, and Hollywood was still ruled by a coterie of producers who feared and hated both unions as much as the unions feared and hated each other. According to the producers, they and their employees were all quite happy until the unions began making trouble.

"We have never had a dispute with the labor in Hollywood over wages, hours, or working conditions," M-G-M's Eddie Mannix testified—falsely testified—lied—to a House subcommittee investigating the Hollywood strikes. Ben Kahan, a Columbia vice-president who identified himself at these same hearings as the unofficial chairman of the studio executives responsible for labor relations, was more specific. He said the labor wars that broke out in 1945 began "not because of any question as to wages, hours, or working conditions, but solely because of jurisdictional disputes."

What Kahan airily dismissed as a series of jurisdictional disputes, however, was an important struggle for power (as well as the wages, hours, and working conditions that Kahan claimed were not at issue). To both IATSE and the producers, Sorrell and his CSU were a dangerous threat, probably Communist-dominated. That, in any case, was the charge with which they planned to resist Sorrell's challenge. When a new CSU strike appeared imminent early in 1946, IATSE's chief official in Hollywood, Roy Brewer, denounced it as "a last desperate effort to keep Communist control of certain AFL unions in Hollywood." Sorrell, on the other hand, insisted that Brewer and IATSE president Richard Walsh were simply the heirs to the corrupt empire of Willie Bioff and George Browne. Walsh had been one of IATSE's vice-presidents under Browne, after all, and most of the union's other executives remained in the same seats of power. Sorrell described IATSE as "a company-dominated union run by a group of racketeers." He said the IATSE leaders had engaged in a "criminal conspiracy . . . to deprive a lot of workers of their rights."

While both Brewer and Sorrell undoubtedly exaggerated each other's malefactions, Stewart Meacham, the regional director of the National Labor Relations Board, was probably accurate in saying that "the producers and the IATSE . . . did not want peace. They were determined to destroy the Conference of Studio Unions." Brewer was even more accurate in telling an inquiring priest named George H. Dunne that "the IATSE and the Conference cannot exist together in Hollywood. It is war to the finish."

The first step was the prosecution of Sorrell for the whole array of misdemeanors committed during the violent climax of the 1945 strike. On January 9, 1946, the CSU leader was convicted on nine counts of contempt of court for having sent masses of pickets to blockade the gates at Warner Bros. He was sentenced to sixteen days in prison and a fine of seventeen thousand dollars. He paid the fine under protest, and after a month's freedom on a writ of habeas corpus, he served his term in prison. In April, he was taken back to court, along with eight others, on a charge of rioting during the melee outside Warners. A jury acquitted him of that but convicted him on a minor charge of "failure to disperse."

Throughout all this, Sorrell was trying to negotiate a new wage contract for his unions. The studios offered a ridiculous 10 percent wage increase; Sorrell demanded an equally ridiculous 50 percent. Both sides finally agreed to 25 percent, but then the "jurisdictional disputes" once again providentially intervened. This time, the conflict centered on the machinists who had gone out on strike with Sorrell's CSU in 1945 and the rival machinists who had been hired to replace them. These strikebreakers, with IATSE support, insisted on their right to keep their jobs. Sorrell called all his unions out on strike again on July 1. The studios quickly decided to avoid combat. Everyone gathered at a conference and worked out a truce known as the Treaty of Beverly Hills; everyone returned to work while negotiations continued. Sorrell gloated at the prospects after what seemed another victory. "From now on, we dictate," he said.

The most difficult problem involved not the machinists but the carpenters, who traditionally had enjoyed the right to build and install all movie sets. IATSE challenged that right, partly because it represented the "grips" who moved props and furniture around, partly because the carpenters belonged to Sorrell's CSU. When both sides appealed to AFL president William Green, since all these quarreling unions were members of the disorganized coalition that called itself a federation of labor, Green characteristically appointed a three-man committee to consider the problem. These three implausible judges were William C. Doherty, head of the postal workers union, Felix H. Knight of the barbers, and William C. Birthright of the trainmen. Given thirty days to resolve a dispute that had baffled more experienced experts for many years, the three journeyed to Los Angeles, spent several hours touring one studio, Paramount, interviewed a few of the rival combatants, and then retreated to write their report.

That report turned out to be a marvel of ambiguity. "All trim and millwork on the sets and stages" should be done by the carpenters, said the three Solomons, while IATSE men should undertake "the erection of sets on stages." Both sides immediately began arguing about the meaning of the word "erection," whether it meant building sets or simply putting together things already built. IATSE claimed the former, and thus claimed some three hundred jobs held by Sorrell's carpenters. Although IATSE had no unions specifically chartered for such work, it immediately organized a new local designated as "set erectors." The producers, predictably, sided with IATSE and gave its members the work; the carpenters, just as predictably, appealed to AFL headquarters for a "clarification."

Now the carpenters were not just a few handymen who hammered nails in the back lots of Warner Bros. Their commander in chief, Bill Hutcheson, was a crusty old swashbuckler who had risen to the exalted role of an AFL vice-president, a man who, when he asked for a clarification, wanted things clarified very much his own way. The three wise men responded, that August, much as Hutcheson wished. They had never meant, they clarified, to deprive a single Hollywood carpenter of a single job. All carpentry of all sorts, they said, should be done by the carpenters. The IATSE chiefs were furious. Their lawyers argued that the AFL committee had long since completed its work and had no right now to "clarify" its own decision at the expense of the IATSE workers. The studios, as usual, sided with IATSE. They did more.

In a series of secret meetings with IATSE's Roy Brewer, the studio negotiators agreed to confront another strike by Sorrell. Brewer, in turn, promised that his IATSE workers would crash through Sorrell's picket lines and keep the studios open. According to the minutes of a producer's meeting, subsequently read to a congressional hearing, the plan was ruthlessly simple: "By 9 A.M., Monday, clear out all carpenters first, then clear out all painters, following which proceed to take on IA men to do the work."

Whether this represented an unprovoked strike by aggressive leftists in the CSU or a deliberately calculated provocation and lockout by the producers remains arguable to this day. In any case, Sorrell called his ten thousand workers out on strike, and Brewer sent his sixteen thousand workers in to do their jobs. The first major clashes occurred outside Warners, where strikers threw bricks and rocks at IATSE workers trying to get through the gates. Burbank police fired shots into the air. Some two hundred people engaged in another fracas outside the M-G-M studio in Culver City. Stones, shouts, shovings—each side accused the other of using "goon squads." Eight studios in all were involved, eight studios at work on the filming of fifty pictures. Amid all the uproar, IATSE's Roy Brewer soon demonstrated that he could provide the workers to keep the studios open and operating. The studio chiefs were grateful. Work went on.

Then began an elaborate series of efforts at mediation. One of the first and most important of these efforts was led by Ronald Reagan, who had just succeeded Robert Montgomery as president of the Screen Actors Guild, and who reacted to the prevailing spirit of violence by carrying a .32 Smith & Wesson in a shoulder holster. Reagan later condemned Sorrell as a Communist, but at this point he still regarded himself as "a near-hopeless hemophiliac liberal," and he decided, not unreasonably, that the major force behind the strike was Bill Hutcheson of the carpenters union. So he led a delegation of movie actors to the AFL convention in Chicago and asked for a meeting with Hutcheson. Hutcheson gruffly refused. Reagan's group then "wangled," as he put it, a meeting with the three arbitrators who had first ruled for IATSE and then "clarified" their ruling in favor of the carpenters. Under questioning, Reagan said, the three had admitted that their clarification "was a mistake," but they added that "a third clarification would be another mistake." They had acted, they told Reagan, "as a result of . . . months of ceaseless pressure on the part of Hutcheson."

Reagan's committee included some rather celebrated names: Walter Pidgeon, Dick Powell, Gene Kelly, Robert Taylor, George Murphy, Alexis Smith, and Reagan's own wife, Jane Wyman. They all went to AFL president Green, according to Reagan, and blamed the strike on Hutcheson. They threatened to fly movie stars to every major city in the country to denounce Hutcheson. "To our consternation," Reagan recalled, "Green burst into tears. With his cheeks still wet, he said brokenly, 'What can I do? We are a federation of independent unions. I have no power to do anything.'"

Reagan finally arranged a meeting with Hutcheson and found him mired in twenty-year-old conflicts, thirty-year-old conflicts, between his carpenters and other unions. They wrangled over how many carpenters' jobs were jeopardized by the strike, how many carpenters were involved, even how many carpenters there were in Hutcheson's union. But finally Hutcheson told Reagan, according to Reagan, that if the actors could get IATSE to back down on the three hundred disputed jobs, "I'll run Sorrell out of Hollywood and break up the CSU in five minutes."* The actors reflected on this remarkable proposition as they rode down in the elevator from Hutcheson's hotel room, and then in the deserted lobby they met Herb Sorrell. They told him, perhaps naively, perhaps maliciously, what Hutcheson had said. "It doesn't matter a damn what Hutcheson says," Sorrell retorted, according to Reagan. "This thing is going on, no matter what he does! When it ends up, there'll be only one man running labor in Hollywood and that man will be me!"

The membership of the Screen Actors Guild voted overwhelmingly on October 2, 1946, to back Reagan's leadership, denounce the CSU strike as a jurisdictional dispute, and cross the picket lines. The SAG also took the lead in organizing a declaration by twenty-four other Hollywood unions to that effect. The year before, Sorrell had been saved by Washington, by the National Labor Relations Board's ruling in his favor. Now there was no sign of any such rescue. On the contrary, the national elections of 1946, which took place less than two months after Sorrell's unions went out on strike, were ruinous. A nation weary of wartime restrictions voted overwhelmingly for whatever alternatives a renascent Republican party could offer. In their strongest showing since the stock market crash of 1929, the Republicans won most of the governorships, a narrow majority in the Senate, and a large majority in the House.

Important positions changed hands. One of them was the chairmanship of the House Un-American Activities Committee, which had been bumbling along, since the retirement of Martin Dies, under the aegis of Democratic Representative Edward J. Hart of New Jersey. It now acquired the spirited Republican leadership of another New Jerseyan, J. Parnell Thomas, who seemed to believe that the entire New Deal was a nightmare to be exposed, illuminated, and destroyed. One of the newly elected congressmen assigned to help him in his efforts was a young Los Angeles lawyer named Richard Nixon, victor over the hapless liberal Jerry Voorhis. Another newcomer who would soon achieve a considerable celebrity was the freshman senator from Wisconsin, Joe McCarthy. But the national sickness subsequently known as McCarthyism was already being nurtured by President Truman. Just three weeks after the Republican triumph in the election, Truman assigned an interagency committee to start checking the "loyalty" of more than two million government employees.

In the narrow little world of Hollywood, the immediate effect of this

---

* Or so Reagan said in his memoirs. In his appearance before the House Un-American Activities Committee in October of 1947, Reagan testified that Hutcheson had actually said that he "would run this Sorrell and the other Commies out."

conservative shift was that there was no longer any New Deal to help Herb Sorrell and his strikers. They were on their own, without either the numbers or the weapons to defeat the forces that they had committed themselves to challenge. Under a court injunction to limit the number of pickets to no more than eight at any studio gate, Sorrell sent 1,500 to lay siege at Columbia. Police arrested 610 men, including Sorrell, and 69 women. By the end of that November week, the arrests totaled 802, on various charges of assault with deadly weapons, conspiracy to commit extortion, unlawful assembly, and interference with the orderly adminstration of justice. Bail was set at five thousand dollars each.

Sorrell later charged that these prosecutions were all part of a "conspiracy to destroy the CSU," that Warners put policemen from Burbank and Glendale on the studio payroll, that M-G-M paid thirty-two dollars per day for every policeman used at the Culver City studio, and that M-G-M manager Eddie Mannix "told the policemen when and when not to cause trouble with the pickets." The studios seem to have engaged in still more clandestine maneuvers. The efforts of IATSE workers to break through Sorrell's picket lines naturally depended heavily on which side the teamsters union would take. The teamsters local voted to honor the CSU picket lines, but the chief of the local, Joe Touhy, threatened to bring in out-of-state teamsters to support the IATSE strikebreakers "and see that they are carried through."

Touhy naturally would not have attempted such coercion without the approval of the corrupt union's leaders, Dan Tobin and Dave Beck, but what was particularly interesting was Touhy's negotiations with Joe Schenck, who had been pardoned by President Truman for his intrigues with Willie Bioff, released from prison, and reinstalled in the executive offices at 20th Century–Fox. Several months before the strike began, Schenck promised to hire Touhy as "industrial relations director" for National Theaters, a chain of movie houses of which Schenck was an executive officer. Touhy, who had been getting $175 per week from the teamsters, went on Schenck's payroll on January 1, 1947, roughly three months after he helped break the strike, at $400 a week, plus $100 in expenses, on a seven-year contract that escalated to $500 a week for the last three years.

Then there were the more direct methods. Early in March of 1947, Sorrell and his wife were going to a union meeting at a church in Glendale. Shortly after he had dropped off his wife, he was stopped by three men in another car. One of the three was in police uniform and had a police badge and a police gun. "I didn't resist," Sorrell said later, "because I thought I was going to a police station. He put handcuffs on me. When I went to get into the car somebody hit me on the side of the head. . . . They tied me, and every time I moved or tried to get up, they hit me over the head with a gun." Sorrell said he heard the men discussing a reward for killing him, but then they drove away. He was found at the side of the road by a passing motorist, who took him to a nearby hospital. In this case, in contrast to the strikers' picketing outside the movie studios, nobody was ever arrested or prosecuted.

The strike went on. It is virtually impossible, of course, for workers to win a strike unless they can shut down the employer's plants, or else persuade the government to intervene on their side. Since Sorrell and his CSU could do neither of these things, they were doomed to stand on the sidewalks outside the studios and shout insults at the IATSE men going to work every day. Their last remaining hope was that by their persistence they might somehow win over that nebulous force known as public opinion. This was highly un-likely, since the press showed little interest and less sympathy. And Sorrell's opponents kept bringing in the issue of communism.

This question dragged on even longer than the strike. Lawrence P. Lin-deloff, the head of the painters union, testified before a House subcommittee in 1948 that he had talked to Sorrell several times about the matter and concluded that "he may be a radical, but I couldn't accuse him of being a Communist." More impartial corroboration came from Pat Casey, who had served as chairman of the Motion Picture Producers Association Labor Coun-cil for twenty years, and who testified: "I've dealt with Herb Sorrell since 1937 or 1938. In my opinion, he's not a Communist."

By this time, though, the authorities had unearthed a Communist Party membership card made out to Herbert Stewart, Stewart being Sorrell's moth-er's maiden name. A Los Angeles handwriting expert, Clark Sellers, said that the signature on the card was by Sorrell, but Sorrell denied it, denied that he "ever saw a Communist Party card." Republican Congressman Thomas L. Owens of Illinois, a member of the House subcommittee investigating the strike, handed Sorrell the card and asked him if he didn't think the handwrit-ing looked like his.

"I'd say it looks very much like my handwriting, but it is not my hand-writing," Sorrell said. He acknowledged that his mother's name had been Stewart and added, "I suppose that's why they put it on there."

Owens pointed out to him that the second letter in the name on the card looked like both a *t* and an *o*. "It looks like you started to write Sorrell and then wrote Stewart, doesn't it?" Owens asked. "That's the way it looks," Sorrell said.

FBI Director J. Edgar Hoover resolved these contradictions by telling the subcommittee that the Communist Party card had definitely been signed by Sorrell. At that time, such a judgment by Hoover was considered definitive. Now that more is known about his corrupt and capricious rule of the FBI, his testimony seems considerably less authoritative, though it may quite well have been true.

This was all secondary, however, to the painters and carpenters and other pickets parading to and fro outside the gates of Warners or Metro. They had been trapped, as they increasingly realized, in a battle they could not win. They marched, they shouted slogans, but nothing happened. Winters are not hard in Los Angeles, and this was not like a strike in Chicago or Boston, but still, the strikers had to go without pay while they watched the IATSE work-ers ride through the gates to their jobs in the flourishing studios. There seemed to be no end in sight, and scarcely the possibility of an end.

The end came, as it usually does, obliquely, blurred by a smoke screen of lies and equivocations. The painters, Sorrell's own union, voted in October of 1947 that the members of their union were entitled to cross the CSU picket lines if they were suffering personal hardships. And who among them, after a year of striking, was not suffering personal hardships? Sorrell officially supported the move. How could he do otherwise? He could not win. So they all trickled back to work, on whatever terms they could get. The progressive labor movement in Hollywood had been broken, and the studios left it to the machinery of the AFL to settle with Herb Sorrell. The defeated CSU simply disintegrated and faded away, but there were punishments to be inflicted, scores to be settled. The international headquarters of the painters union demanded in 1951 that Sorrell be expelled from the leadership of Hollywood's Local 644 on the ground that he had "willfully and knowingly" associated with "organizations and groups which subscribe to the doctrines of the Communist parties." Sorrell said he would resign if the members of Local 644 asked him to do so. Local 644, numbering perhaps three hundred painters, refused. It voted to support its battered leader. The international headquarters thereupon revoked the local's charter early in 1952, thus depriving it of all authority. Sorrell's paychecks of $255 per week stopped. When he sued the international headquarters on the ground that he had a three-year contract, the suit didn't come to trial until the summer of 1955. By this time, Sorrell claimed that the union owed him $20,670. Sorrell lost.

●   ●   ●

"How could this man so methodically take these women out and cut them up and burn them in his incinerator, and then tend his flowers, with the black smoke coming out of the chimney?" It was almost a rhetorical question that Charlie Chaplin blurted out to his oldest son, in the spring of 1946, as he neared the end of his script for *Monsieur Verdoux*. Charles Chaplin, Jr., by now twenty-one and newly discharged from the army, could offer no answer, but that was hardly expected. "In the next instant," the son recalled, "he would snap out of his brown study and start pantomiming the gruesome episode, turning it into such comedy that I couldn't help laughing." That summer, the same pantomime became one of the opening scenes of *Monsieur Verdoux*: Chaplin pruning his roses, the incinerator gushing smoke in the background, Chaplin nearly stepping on a caterpillar, shuddering at the possibility of such cruelty, tenderly rescuing the caterpillar from harm's way.

Chaplin had found what he thought was a perceptive answer to his question, and that was to portray Verdoux as a simple businessman, who courted rich old women and then killed them for their property. A businessman would do anything for profit, in Chaplin's formulation, and so business logically led to war and the death of millions. "Wars, conflict—it's all business," Verdoux said to a press conference shortly before his execution. "One murder makes a villain; millions a hero. Numbers sanctify!" This quasi-leftist equation of business and war was actually less Marxian than Brechtian, but when Chaplin hopefully showed his script to Bertolt Brecht, he received a bewildering response. "Oh," the playwright commented after thumbing through Chaplin's work, "you write a script Chinese fashion."

Serious critics, of the kind who complain that Brecht's *Mahagonny* is not an accurate representation of contemporary life, naturally objected to both the philosophizing in *Monsieur Verdoux* and the philosophy itself. Perhaps the sharpest of these was Dwight Macdonald, who declared that Chaplin's comparison of murderers to political leaders represented "an irony that was probably first observed by some ur-Montaigne of the time of Belshazzar." More generally, Macdonald went on, "it was a sad day for Chaplin when the intellectuals convinced him that he was the Tragic Clown, the Little Man. . . . The nature of reality, which he understood intuitively as a mime, became opaque to him when he tried to think about it."

This was one of the sad consequences of the coming of sound to films; it required words, which implied thought. Chaplin resisted sound as long as he could. *City Lights* (1931) and *Modern Times* (1936) perpetuated the silent film for nearly a decade after *The Jazz Singer* had doomed it. But to proclaim that the philosophical arguments of *Monsieur Verdoux* are familiar or oversimplified or wrong, or all three, is like objecting to the political reasoning of Picasso's *Guernica*. No matter how much Chaplin may be criticized for pretentiousness, naïveté, sentimentality, and various other intellectual sins, he nonetheless managed, more than any other filmmaker in Hollywood, to grasp the central problems of his time, to make his films as commentaries on them, and to make the right commentaries. To have dramatized the lust for money in 1925 (*The Gold Rush*), the mechanization of life in 1936 (*Modern Times*), the threat of Nazism in 1940 (*The Great Dictator*), and the ambiguities of mass murder in 1946 implies an artistic prescience well beyond the arguing of Chaplin's critics. Perhaps it is precisely because *Monsieur Verdoux* was not about the Holocaust that the image of the incinerator behind the rose garden speaks so tellingly.

None of Chaplin's achievements would have been possible, of course, if he had been required to submit his ideas to Louis B. Mayer or Darryl F. Zanuck or any of their nervous deputies. Chaplin committed to his faith in *Monsieur Verdoux* the astonishing (for 1946) sum of two million dollars. But though he didn't have to subject his idea to the views of any executive producers, he did have to win the approval of the censors at the Johnston Office, and the censors disapproved of almost everything. In a letter to Chaplin, they began by declaring that they were not disputing the political views expressed in *Monsieur Verdoux* but hinted that they might yet return to raise objections on this front. "We pass over those elements which seem to be anti-social in their concept and significance," the letter said. "There are the sections of the story in which Verdoux indicts the 'System' and impugns the present-day social structure." Having brought up this issue only to declare that they were "passing over" it, the censors then turned from mass murder to a more serious concern, "a distasteful flavor of illicit sex, which in our judgment is not good."

The censors listed and explained, as was their profession, all the immoralities that could not be tolerated. When one of Verdoux's wives asked him to "come to bed," for example, the censors asked Chaplin to change it to "go to bed." More difficult was Verdoux's encounter with a young prostitute, whom he planned to poison simply to test the efficacy of a new drug, but then befriended, fed, paid, and sent home. The censors objected to any suggestion that the girl was actually a prostitute. They objected to Verdoux asking her, "How long have you been at this game?" or expressing the view that "an attractive girl like you would have done better." When the girl first reacted to Verdoux's offers of help by saying, "What is this, the Salvation Army?" the censors stiffly declared that "the reference to the Salvation Army is likely, in our opinion, to give offense to that group." Toward the end of the movie, Verdoux once again encountered the girl, now fashionably dressed and riding in a limousine provided by a munitions maker (another touch of Brecht, or perhaps the Shaw of *Major Barbara*). "Please inject into the dialogue some reference to the munitions manufacturer as the girl's fiancé," the censors said, "this to avoid the suggestion that the girl is now a kept woman."

It was quite possible that the Johnston Office saw its work entirely in terms of references to "illicit sex"; it is also quite possible that it really opposed the movie on political grounds but waged the battle on questions of sex because that was its basic mandate from the producers. In any case, Chaplin had to argue about each of the censors' objections. He had his most difficult time with one of Breen's assistants, "a tall, dour young man," according to Chaplin's recollections, who asked, "What have you against the Catholic Church?" Chaplin countered by inquiring, "Why do you ask?" The dour young man slammed the script of *Monsieur Verdoux* onto a table and started thumbing through it to find the penultimate scene, in which a priest visited Verdoux in his death cell. Why did Chaplin make Verdoux address the priest as "my good man"?

"Well, isn't he a good man?" Chaplin parried.

"That's facetious . . ." said the censor. "You don't call a priest 'a good man,' you call him 'Father.' "

"Very well, we'll call him 'Father,' " Chaplin said.

And so on. How could Chaplin have made Verdoux say, "I am at peace with God, my conflict is with man"? How could he have made Verdoux say, "Who knows what sin is, born as it was from Heaven, from God's fallen angel, who knows what mysterious destiny it serves?"

"I believe that sin is just as great a mystery as virtue," Chaplin said.

"That's a lot of pseudo-philosophizing. . ." the censor said. "And this line, 'May the Lord have mercy on your soul.' And Verdoux says, 'Why not? After all it belongs to Him.' "

"What's wrong with that?" Chaplin asked.

" 'Why not?' You don't talk to a priest like that. . . . You impugn society and the whole state."

There it was. Chaplin impugned society and the whole state. But Breen himself, in contrast to his young assistant, was ready to be reasonable. He was tired of all these arguments, always the same. In one pitiful complaint that summed up all his conflicts with Hollywood's more pretentious filmmakers, he said to Chaplin, "Don't make the girl another prostitute. Almost every script in Hollywood has a prostitute."

Chaplin confessed that he "felt embarrassed" that he had indulged in such a cliché. He "promised not to stress the fact." When the film was actually made, in a remarkably brief twelve weeks, and then shown to representatives of the Catholic Legion of Decency and other "religious groups of various denominations," Breen approved, and swept others along in his approval. "It's okay—we can let it go, eh?" Breen said. "All right, Charlie, go ahead." It had been nearly a decade since *The Great Dictator,* which had made a lot of money, and Chaplin thought *Monsieur Verdoux* would do just as well. He gave a private showing of the finished film to some of his most distinguished friends in Hollywood, and Thomas Mann, for one, stood up and applauded.

Chaplin seemed unaware of how rapidly the postwar political winds were changing. While he was editing *Monsieur Verdoux,* a United States marshal telephoned him to announce that he was being summoned to appear before the House Un-American Activities Committee. Chaplin didn't seem to mind, or didn't seem to feel threatened, or didn't admit to feeling threatened. When his summons was mysteriously postponed, and then postponed again, he sent the committee a defiant telegram. "FOR YOUR CONVENIENCE I WILL TELL YOU WHAT I THINK YOU WANT TO KNOW," the telegram said. "I AM NOT A COMMUNIST, NEITHER HAVE I EVER JOINED ANY POLITICAL PARTY OR ORGANIZATION IN MY LIFE. . . ." The committee politely thanked him for his telegram and said it was not interested in questioning him after all. One of the committee's most powerful Democrats, John Rankin of Mississippi, nonetheless attacked him for having allegedly "refused" to become an American citizen, and for making "loathsome pictures" that might corrupt American youth.*

The New York premiere of *Monsieur Verdoux* in April of 1947 filled Chaplin with foreboding. There was "an uneasy atmosphere in the theatre that night, a feeling that the audience had come to prove something," he recalled. Some people laughed, but there were hisses too, and even the laughter seemed to Chaplin like a "challenging laughter against the hissing faction." He sat writhing in his seat, twisting his program to shreds, then whispered to his wife, Oona, that he was going out into the lobby. "I can't take it," he said. He prowled around the lobby for a while, "torn between listening for laughs and getting away from it all." He crept up into the gallery to check the audience there, and everywhere he found the same kind of nervous laughter, joyless laughter.

The next day, Chaplin held a press conference. The publicity staff at

---

* By Rankin's standards, that was fairly mild. On an earlier occasion, he had denounced Chaplin as "perverted" and said he had "become notorious for his forcible seduction of white girls."

United Artists doubted the wisdom of this maneuver, for the press had been fairly hostile ever since the Joan Barry trial, but Chaplin insisted. In the packed ballroom of the Gotham Hotel, Chaplin made the fatal error, at the very beginning, of appearing on the defensive. "Proceed with the butchery . . ." he said with leaden humor. "Fire ahead at this old gray head." After a few skirmishing questions, a woman seated near the front made a blunt demand: "Are you a Communist?"

"I am not a Communist!" Chaplin said.

"A Communist sympathizer was the question," someone else said, though that had not been the question.

"A Communist sympathizer . . . ?" Chaplin echoed. "I don't know what you mean by a 'Communist sympathizer.' I'd say this—that during the war, I sympathized very much with Russia because I believe that she was holding the front . . . that she helped contribute a considerable amount of fighting and dying to bring victory to the Allies."

This opened the gate for James W. Fay, a representative of a publication called *Catholic War Veterans,* who began hectoring Chaplin for his frequent statement that he considered himself a citizen not of any one country but of the world. "Mr. Chaplin," Fay proclaimed, "the men who secured the beachheads, the men who advanced in the face of enemy fire, and the poor fellows who were drafted like myself, and their families and buddies, resent that remark."

Chaplin got flustered. He invoked his own sons—"two of them were on those beachheads." He stammered apologies. "Nevertheless, I—I—I've done my share," he pleaded, "and whatever I said, it is not by any means to be meant derogatory to your Catholic—uh—uh—uh—GI's."

Such apologies only whetted the reporters' appetites, and so there followed a barrage of questions like "What were the things you did do for the war effort?" And did he know Hanns Eisler, and "are you aware of the fact that his brother is the Soviet agent, so attested by—?"

At about this time, there came a rumble of protest from the balcony, and a shaggy-haired film critic rose to ask a shaggy-haired question. "How does it feel to be an artist who has enriched the world with so much happiness and understanding of the little people, and to be derided and held up to hate and scorn by the so-called representatives of the press?"

"I'm sorry, I didn't follow you, you'll have to repeat that question again," Chaplin said, startled and pleased at such an expression of support.

"I don't know if I can," said James Agee, who reviewed movies for *Time,* and for *The Nation,* and for himself. The only transcript of the press conference failed to catch much of Agee's original declaration, and his restatement of it verges on the incoherent: "What are people who care a damn about freedom—who really care for it—think of a country and the people in it, who congratulate themselves upon this country as the finest on earth and as a 'free country,' when so many of the people in this country pry into what a man's citizenship is, try to tell him his business from hour to hour." Chaplin was touched. He could think of nothing to answer except, "No comment, but thank you."

Agee praised *Monsieur Verdoux* in *Time* as "one of the most notable films in years." If it was not the finest of all Chaplin pictures, "it is certainly the most fascinating," and Chaplin's playing of the title role was "one of the most beautiful single performances ever put on film." Agee then wrote a series of three reviews in *The Nation,* not only praising "the great poet and his great poem," but attacking all Chaplin's detractors. The unfavorable reviews, he said, were "of interest . . . chiefly as a definitive measure of the difference between the thing a man of genius puts before the world and the things the world is equipped to see in it."

Well, we must forgive passionate critics their passions. If *Monsieur Verdoux* was unworthy of Agee's enthusiasm, it was still far better than the carping of lesser critics indicated. The carping was nonetheless understandable, for *Monsieur Verdoux* was a very unpleasant film, bitter, sour, cruel. When Chaplin abandoned his beloved tramp in *The Great Dictator,* he preserved a recognizable variant in the little barber, and the barber's impassioned speech at the close provided a happy ending of sorts. But Verdoux, the seducer and murderer of friendless women, was a monster. Prissy, with a prissy little mustache and a prissy little accent, he represented the murderer as pervert. Verdoux loved his real wife and child, to be sure, and loved pets too, but so did the ultimate prissy mass-murderer, Heinrich Himmler.

Yet Chaplin wanted his audience to sympathize with Verdoux, to identify with him, share in his monstrous crimes and his monstrous justifications of those crimes. And though we tend to see Verdoux's killings in the context of the Holocaust, Chaplin went a step further and insisted that Verdoux's killings mirrored not just the massacres of the recent past but the massacres of the imminent future, the atomic bomb, our weapon, and therefore us. No, the critics insisted, that was too much. The only thing worse than Chaplin's accusations was his caprice in ornamenting his accusations with brilliant slapstick. To take the volcanically absurd figure of Martha Raye out into the deep in a rowboat (would Theodore Dreiser have enjoyed the parody created by the man who had been a pallbearer at his funeral?), to creep up on her with a hangman's noose, to retreat at the last moment because of some Swiss yodelers—could such a film be taken seriously? Well, what is serious? Chaplin might have asked. He himself billed *Monsieur Verdoux* as "a comedy of murder."

Monsieur Verdoux did well at the box office for a few weeks, then began to falter. This was probably a consequence of the first viewers disliking the movie and telling their friends to avoid it, but Chaplin put most of the blame on right-wing pressure groups. He recalled a United Artists executive showing him a picture in the *New York Daily News* of the New Jersey Catholic Legion picketing outside a theater with signs saying "Chaplin's a fellow traveler" and "Send Chaplin to Russia." Chaplin said that bookings all over the country were canceled after the American Legion threatened to boycott any theater that showed a Chaplin film. In Denver, Legion threats closed *Monsieur Verdoux* just one night after it opened. After six weeks of this, Chaplin angrily withdrew the film from distribution and didn't show it again in the United States for nearly twenty years. He remained convinced, though, that it was "the cleverest and most brilliant film I have yet made."

• • •

Here is one last note on Bugsy Siegel's Flamingo Hotel in Las Vegas, which is now, perhaps inevitably, the Flamingo Hilton. It is all very up-to-date, with rows of computerized poker games and so on, except for those aspects that are relentlessly anachronistic, like the Gay Nineties bartenders in their red string neckties and the weary waitresses in décolletage and black net stockings. Throughout the windowless casinos that never close, the main sound is the clicking of the gambling machines and the dead voices of the men who tend them.

Las Vegas today is what hell might be like if hell had been planned and built by New York gangsters. It is the kingdom of pleasure, where everything is permitted, then perverted and parodied. Where pleasure is defined (as in *Mahagonny*) in terms of indulgences for sale, gambling, whiskey, prostitution. Where thousands of tourists are herded into a row of garish hotels and encouraged to squander their money in joyless revelry until it is all gone. Pleasure grimly organized and sold, around the clock, mass produced and mass consumed—what could be more hellish than a gangster vision of paradise?

The physical structure of Bugsy Siegel's Flamingo has changed considerably over the course of a half century. A series of photographs on the wall of one obscure corridor document the continual expansions and alterations: pillars appear and disappear, pine trees give way to palms, the roof rises, wings sprout, neon lights keep getting bigger and brighter. The present owners and managers do not advertise the founders of their hotel, but they are not unaware of the Flamingo's origins. Out in the back courtyard, not far from the swimming pool, there is a rather handsome rose garden. A plaque at one edge of the garden suggests in lugubrious tones its special quality.

"Not many people realize," it says, "that besides all of Bugsy Siegel's professional activities, his wheeling and dealing with the underworld, he was also an accomplished gardener. . . . This is the original site of his famous rose garden. Roses have flourished here for over thirty years, and each year they bloom bigger and with a deeper red than the year before. Rumor has it that Bugsy used a secret formula to keep his roses so beautiful and richly red. . . . Remember Filthy Frankie Giannattasio? How about the notorious Big Howie Dennis? Perhaps you recall the scurrilous Mad Dog Neville? They were all associated with Bugsy at one time or another and coincidentally they all vanished into thin air rather suddenly. No trace was ever found of any of them. The rumor also says that if you stand on this spot at midnight under a full moon you can hear three muffled voices saying, 'Bugsy, how do you like the roses, Bugsy?' "

The HUAC Hearings (*from top down*): Dalton Trumbo was a noisily hostile witness, Bertolt Brecht dodged and equivocated, Jack Warner (*right*) did his best to please Chairman J. Parnell Thomas.

9
UN-AMERICANISM
(1947)

Charles Laughton was so nervous during the last preview performances that he kept putting his hands in his pockets and rubbing his genitals. People in the audience could hardly help noticing. Some snickered. Nobody backstage dared tell Laughton the reason for the laughter. Everyone relied on Helene Weigel, Bertolt Brecht's wife, to do something. "Helli got his pants away on the pretext of pressing them," said a young member of the cast, Frances Heflin, the sister of Van Heflin. "She wanted his hands out of his pockets, so she sewed them up." Laughton was frantic when he found the pockets sewn up, and when he learned why, but though he insisted that the stitches be removed, he behaved himself better on opening night.

And it was quite an opening night. Charlie Chaplin was there, and Ingrid Bergman, and Frank Lloyd Wright, Charles Boyer, Billy Wilder, Olivia de Havilland, John Garfield, Igor Stravinsky—all of these were among the people who crowded into the 260-seat Coronet Theater on La Cienega Boulevard for what proved to be, in retrospect, one of the major theatrical events of its time, presenting Laughton in his first stage appearance in nearly fifteen years, the premiere of Brecht's greatest play, *Galileo*. In addition to being a splendid piece of theater, *Galileo* dug into two of the most troubling issues of the day, the responsibility of the scientists who had built the atomic bomb and the responsibility of intellectuals who were summoned for interrogation about their political beliefs. The audience viewed Brecht's probings with misgivings; it remained restless. The newspaper reviews also sounded somewhat dubious. The *New York Times* was reasonably representative in declaring that the play was "barren of climaxes and even sparse in stirring moments." Hearst's *Los Angeles Examiner* called it "a fussy, juvenile harangue."

That ambiguous night at the Coronet Theater had been an extraordinarily long time in coming. Brecht had originally written *Galileo* in Denmark, in one three-week burst of creativity during the autumn of 1938, and there had even been a staging in the wartime isolation of Zurich in 1943. By then, Brecht was enmeshed in the controversies over *Hangmen Also Die*. Despite the bitter end to those quarrels, he stubbornly went on hatching new ideas for movies. With Salka Viertel's son Hans, he discussed the possibilities of a film about Shakespeare's difficulties in getting financial support for the Globe Theater. He professed to see in this many similarities to contemporary Hollywood: "Collective writing, fast writing-on-order, the same motifs used over again. . . ." He wrote an outline entitled "Uncle Sam's Property," which told the story of a bayonet being passed from one owner to another. He wrote a full narrative treatment, "The Crouching Venus," about a museum curator in occupied Marseilles who saved a famous statue from a German official who wanted to acquire it. He wrote an outline for a film version of one of his most moving poems, "Children's Crusade 1939." He discussed a modern version of *Lysistrata*. He worked on more than fifty film projects in all.

His only sale came by accident. During 1942 and '43, he collaborated with Lion Feuchtwanger on an unsuccessful play about a modern Joan of Arc in the French resistance, *The Visions of Simone Machard*. When the two collaborators inevitably quarreled and split, Brecht took all theatrical rights to the project and Feuchtwanger all rights to a prospective novel he planned to write. Sam Goldwyn rejected Brecht's play but bought Feuchtwanger's novel for fifty thousand dollars, hoping to star Teresa Wright as the saintly heroine. Feuchtwanger needlessly but graciously gave Brecht twenty thousand dollars. Goldwyn never produced the film.

Brecht knew perfectly well that all these movie projects were secondary to his vocation in the theater, and after the dispute over *Simone Machard*, he settled down to work on his major new play of these Hollywood years, *The Caucasian Chalk Circle*. But the writing of a play was only the first step in the long series of maneuvers that might or might not lead to a stage production. Brecht already had a whole portfolio of earlier work in various stages of negotiation. He had updated his 1928 version of Hašek's *Good Soldier Schweik* into *Schweyk in the Second World War*, for example, in the hope that Peter Lorre would star in it. He explored the possibility of his old collaborator Kurt Weill setting the play to music. He got Berthold Viertel, Salka's husband, to direct four scenes from *The Private Life of the Master Race* in New York in German in 1942 (a complete English version only very belatedly reached the stage in June of 1945).

The most important of these maneuverings began in Salka Viertel's salon on a Sunday afternoon in March of 1944, when Brecht first encountered the elephantine figure of Charles Laughton. He had seen and admired Laughton's best prewar films—*Rembrandt* and *The Private Life of Henry VIII*—so he was ready to treat the actor seriously, and, of course, to make use of him. Laughton was still earning a star-worthy $100,000 per picture, though several of his recent films had been undistinguished failures (*The Tuttles of Tahiti, Stand By for Action, The Man from Down Under*), and he felt a hunger to be taken seriously, even to be used. Brecht showed Laughton the manuscript of *Schweyk;* Laughton was suitably impressed. They became friends. Brecht even wrote a poem entitled "Laughton's Belly":

> Here it was: not unexpected, but not usual either
> And built of foods which he

At his leisure had selected, for his entertainment.
And to a good plan, excellently carried out.

Laughton's acerbic wife, Elsa Lanchester, was less impressed with
Brecht. "He smoked awful cigars . . ." she observed. "Or perhaps the passing
through Brecht made the smoke come out with the sourest, bitterest
smell. . . . He hadn't many teeth and his mouth opened in a complete circle,
so you'd see one or two little tombstones sticking out of this black hole. A very
unpleasant sight." But Laughton was charmed by his new discovery. "Often
L would come and meet me in the garden," Brecht wrote long afterward,
"running barefoot in shirt and trousers over the damp grass, and would show
me some changes in his flowerbeds, for his garden always occupied him."

Laughton was proud of his garden, overlooking the ocean from the
heights of Pacific Palisades. Brecht wrote a poem praising its giant eucalyptus
trees, its lemon hedge, its ferns and fuchsias and bright anemones and "the
lordly lawn." Laughton was deeply upset that autumn when eight or ten feet
at the edge of his garden suddenly broke away and slid down the hillside.
Brecht ended his poem on that note of dismay: "Alas, the lovely garden . . ./
Is built of crumbling rock . . ./There is not much time left in which to
complete it."

Laughton and Brecht were the most implausible partners, aliens from
two countries at war: one fat, one thin; one rich and famous, the other
penniless and obscure; one a guilt-ridden homosexual, the other a shameless
philanderer; one a connoisseur, indifferent to politics, the other a radical in
all things. What bound them together was *Galileo*, which Brecht was now
determined to rewrite with and for Laughton. Brecht had wanted from the
start to portray Galileo as the father of modern physics, the apostle of a "new
age." Even then, in Denmark, Brecht had known a physicist who worked for
Nils Bohr, so he was fully aware of Bohr's efforts to explain to the world Otto
Hahn's success, late in 1938, in splitting the atom. But the central fact about
Galileo, apart from his great discoveries, was that he had recanted them under
the threat of torture by the Inquisition. Brecht's original idea was apparently
the conventional one, to portray Galileo as the supreme rationalist, who cun-
ningly feigned acquiescence to authority so that he could go on with his life
and his work. It was thus that Galileo survived to write his celebrated *Discorsi*.
As his disciple Andrea later said: "We cried: 'Your hands are stained!' You
say: 'Better stained than empty.' . . . And: 'If there are obstacles, the shortest
line between two points may be the crooked line.' "

There is a theory, most strongly argued by Trotsky's biographer Isaac
Deutscher, that Brecht's account of the struggle between Galileo and the
church was at least partly inspired by the Soviet purge trials of 1936–38, that
Brecht, never the most orthodox of radicals, had "some sympathy with Trot-
skyism," and that "the Galileo of his drama is Zinoviev, or Bukharin or
Rakovsky dressed up in historical costume." There may be some truth in this,

for *Galileo* is a complicated play, with subtext buried beneath subtext, but the idea of saying or doing anything for the sake of survival ran deep in Brecht's work. It was the guiding principle of both Mac the Knife and Jenny, of Mother Courage and Schweyk. In a time of extreme crisis, this hunger for survival can lead to ugly collaborations, but it can also lead to the very reasonable alternative chosen by the refugee, to the folk wisdom implicit in the saying that he who fights and runs away will live to fight another day.

The first thing to do with *Galileo*, though, was to produce a working draft in English. Brecht, who still knew little English, offered Laughton, who knew no German, a literal and rather Germanic translation that he said had been done by "a secretary." Apparently dismayed by that, Laughton hired two young writers he knew at M-G-M, Brainerd Duffield and Emerson Crocker, to produce something readable. These two also knew relatively little German, so the version that they produced in November of 1944 was quite free. Laughton and Brecht both professed to like it, but that was only the beginning. Laughton yearned to write, and Brecht liked to keep rewriting, so they met regularly in Laughton's study to rework the whole play. Laughton had to break off in February of 1945 to film *Captain Kidd,* and again in August to make *Because of Him,* but the work continued. Brecht wrote a poem about that too: "Still your people and mine were tearing each other to pieces when we/Pored over those tattered exercise books, looking/Up words in dictionaries, and time after time/Crossed out our texts . . ./Again and again I turned actor, demonstrating/A character's gestures and tone of voice, and you/Turned writer. Yet neither I nor you/Stepped outside his profession."

Brecht's journal of this period showed no entry concerning either August 6 or August 9, the dates of the American atomic raids on Hiroshima and Nagasaki, but Brecht later claimed that everyone had been appalled. "The day the bomb was dropped will not easily be forgotten by anyone who spent it in the United States . . ." he wrote some years afterward in his preface to the German edition of *Galileo.* "The great city arose that morning to an astonishing display of mourning. I heard bus drivers and women in markets express nothing but horror. It was a victory but it was received with the shame of defeat." Though this was a recollection strongly discolored by both politics and hindsight, Brecht clearly believed that the public view of Galileo would never be the same. "Overnight the biography of the founder of the new system of physics read differently," he wrote. "The infernal effect of the great bomb placed the conflict between Galileo and the authorities of his day in a new and sharper light. . . . Galileo's crime (his abjuration) can be regarded as the 'original sin' of modern natural sciences."

Galileo's crime? Just a few years earlier, Brecht had portrayed it as a shrewd evasion, justified for several good reasons. Now he, Brecht, recanted all that.

"ANDREA: You gained time to write a book that only you could write. Had you burned at the stake in a blaze of glory they would have won.

"GALILEO: They have won. And there is no such thing as a scientific work that only one man can write.

"ANDREA: Then why did you recant, tell me that!

"GALILEO: I recanted because I was afraid of physical pain.

"ANDREA: No!

"GALILEO: They showed me the instruments."

When Andrea still tried to argue that the higher good of science had been served, Brecht forced Galileo to repudiate that too. The only purpose of science is "to ease human existence," according to Galileo, and science for its own sake would lead only to "a progress away from the bulk of humanity" until "some new achievement would be echoed by a universal howl of horror." In his recantation, Galileo insisted: "I have betrayed my profession. Any man who does what I have done must not be tolerated in the ranks of science."

Part of this was Brecht's self-laceration over his own flight from Europe, his sense, as he had written in that poem to Salka Viertel, of self-hatred over his own survival; part of the self-laceration was also slightly self-indulgent, as in the twisted proverb, *Qui s'accuse, s'excuse.* In addition to all these complexities, Brecht, as a matter of principle, never wanted his heroes to be heroic. He declared repeatedly (and in vain) that Mac the Knife was not to be portrayed as romantically attractive, and Mother Courage was not courageous.

But Brecht was not the only creator of *Galileo.* Laughton, who would have to go out on stage and *be* the scientific renegade, had no intention of making himself despicable. So Laughton resisted all Brecht's efforts to condemn Galileo, and if Galileo had to condemn himself, then Laughton would make him heroic in doing so. "Laughton . . . has a kind of devil in his head," Brecht complained in his journal, "that has transformed scorn for himself into empty pride—pride in the greatness of his crime, etc."

At the end of a year's work, the two of them finally agreed on their script. Laughton read it aloud to Orson Welles, who happily agreed to direct it. Contracts were signed early in 1946, Mike Todd was brought in as producer, and rehearsals were scheduled for August. There must be some predictable limit, though, to the length of time four grandiose egos can work together on a project. Welles was the first to go. "Brecht was very, very tiresome today," he wrote to Laughton, "until (I'm sorry to say) I was stern and a trifle shitty. Then he behaved. I hate working like that." As for Todd, when he told Brecht that he planned to acquire some leftover Renaissance furniture and other props from a Hollywood studio, Brecht promptly brought the curtain down on him.

Other angels could always be found. John Houseman had founded an organization called Pelican Productions, and one of his friends had happily discovered what Houseman called "certain underworld elements that . . . were trying to divert some of their Las Vegas profits into Hollywood show business." The producer rented the little Coronet Theater and set out to bring Culture to Los Angeles. He worried about opening with *Galileo,* however, and decided to precede it with Thornton Wilder's *The Skin of Our Teeth*. And finally, it was Laughton who put up $25,000 of his own money, half the production costs, to underwrite a four-week run of *Galileo*. He had a deep emotional commitment to Brecht's play, which was by now partly his play. He had again been forced to interrupt his collaboration with Brecht to make a film, *The Paradine Case,* for Alfred Hitchcock and David Selznick, and then again for that marvelous Kenneth Fearing nightmare about Time Inc., *The Big Clock.* In June of 1947, with Joseph Losey hired as a director who would defer to all of Brecht's wishes, and T. Edward Hambleton recruited as a backer who would pay Brecht's bills, *Galileo* finally went into rehearsals.

Brecht, as usual, was impossible. He insisted on controlling everything and quarreled ferociously with anyone who disagreed. He wanted the costumes just so and the sets just so, and he kept rewriting the script, adding new characters, and then ordering the costumes changed again. Part of all this was perfectionism, part was pure temperament, but the most important reason for all the controversy was that Brecht totally opposed—hated—all the prevailing fashions in the American theater. He hated the idea that the stage represented "reality"; he wanted the theater to remain always a scene of spectacles. He hated the idea that actors should try to "be" the characters they were playing; he wanted them to be themselves, players, performers. In trying to impose his ideas of how he wanted his work produced, he had to deal with people who often couldn't understand what he was talking about. His views contradicted everything they had been taught, everything they by now took for granted. The problem was epitomized in an exchange with Abe Burrows, whom Laughton had recruited to rewrite a song that Brecht had assigned to a wandering street singer. "I kept trying to find out what was to be the tone of the song I was going to write," Burrows recalled. "Our conversation went something like this:

ME: Is this fellow praising Galileo?
BRECHT: No.
ME: Is he knocking him?
BRECHT: No.
ME: Well, Mr. Brecht, how does this fellow feel about Galileo?
BRECHT: He feels nothing.
ME: Well, why does this fellow stand up there and sing a song?
BRECHT: Because I want him to."

That kind of dialogue, repeated over and over again, might have driven anyone to the point of fury, but Brecht, even at the best of times, was rude and domineering. John Houseman had heard "horror stories" about Brecht's behavior, and now he found them all true. "His attitude was consistently objectionable and outrageous," Houseman recalled. "In his determination to impose the precise style and interpretation he wanted . . . he was harsh, intolerant, and, often, brutal and abusive." One of the main victims of this abuse was the choreographer Anna Sokolow, who had ideas of her own about how to stage the street scenes. Brecht told her, in front of the assembled cast, that he would not allow "a lot of Broadway commercial shit." When she didn't quit, he got her fired. The only participant he accepted without arguments was Hanns Eisler, a fellow refugee and fellow leftist, who had written the music for *Hangmen Also Die* and who had now composed for *Galileo* a fascinating accompaniment for harpsichord, small orchestra, and a cappella choir (Stravinsky came to several rehearsals to hear it). But Losey, the director, survived only by doing exactly what Brecht told him. Only once, in fact, was Losey so goaded and provoked that he threw the script at Brecht and went home. He was working in his garden when Laughton telephoned with the inevitable plea that he return to the theater. " 'I will,' I said, 'if Brecht apologizes to me,' " Losey recalled. "Laughton hung up, and after a while he called back saying, 'Brecht says please come back, and he also says you should know Brecht never apologizes.' I went back."

So it was Laughton, the great blubbering baby, famous for driving other directors to fury with his self-indulgent fits of temperament, who, having become involved with someone even more temperamental than he, now had to play the unfamiliar role of diplomat and conciliator. To everyone's pleased surprise, he did. He guided and soothed and encouraged, and all this on the troupe's top salary of forty dollars per week, yet the prospect of his first opening night in more than a decade terrified him. He resorted to the peculiar satisfactions of narcolepsy. "Not catnaps but deep, heavy slumber," Houseman recalled, "into which he would sink at strange and unexpected moments —in the midst of making up, while going over lines and sometimes even between scenes—and from which it became increasingly difficult for our stage managers to arouse him."

Then there came that inevitable moment when he exploded. It happened, as usual, on the pettiest pretext. Ruth Berlau, the Danish actress, translator, collaborator, mistress, who had accompanied Brecht and his family all the way across Russia, now considered herself a photographer, so she was flitting about in the balcony of the Coronet Theater, photographing the last rehearsals for some vague publicity purpose. Click, click, click. Suddenly something in Laughton snapped. "Laughton broke off in the middle of a scene," Houseman recalled, "and came slowly down to the edge of the stage. He glared up at the balcony, his face twisted into a strange grimace that made him look as though he were about to burst into tears. Then he started to howl at her. He accused her of violating him as an artist, of trying to ruin his performance and to destroy him as a man. The more he raged, the wilder he became: he threatened to smash her camera; he said he would kill her if he ever saw her again in the theatre. He was still yelling long after she had fled into La Cienega Boulevard."

Galileo finally opened in the middle of a July heat wave so intense that electric fans had to be installed on both sides of the stage, with buckets of ice in front of them. Though the reviews were "mixed," every seat had already been sold for the four-week run, and Laughton was determined to move the production on to New York. The American National Theater and Academy

(ANTA) offered a limited engagement opening December 7. Maybe, then, there would be more Brecht productions, perhaps even movie sales. By now, however, Brecht was also hearing siren calls from Europe. The Soviet occupation authorities in Berlin were interested in his returning to stage some of his works there. Brecht was characteristically wary, but he began applying for visas to visit Switzerland.

On September 19, just a month after *Galileo* had ended its run in Los Angeles, a seedy and slightly tipsy man appeared at the door of Brecht's house in Santa Monica and handed him a folded pink document that began with the words "By authority of the House of Representatives of the Congress of the United States of America . . ." It went on to summon Brecht to "appear before the Un-American Activities Committee . . . in their chamber in the city of Washington . . . and there testify touching matters of inquiry committed to the said Committee. . . . Herein fail not."

The process server was hardly worthy of such lofty language. He rather resembled a character out of Brecht's plays. Helli Weigel offered him some coffee and he sat there complaining about the hardships of his job, the way people tried to evade him, the way his feet hurt. He seemed to appreciate the Brechts' hospitality. He confided to them that the government paid expenses and per diem compensation for witnesses summoned to Washington, and that if Brecht went by train but claimed reimbursement for auto mileage, he could make a profit on the trip. Brecht was pleased by such revelations. The Good Soldier Schweyk was alive and at work in Hollywood.

• • •

Brecht was not much worried, apparently, for the House committee was summoning witnesses all over Hollywood. *Variety* and *The Hollywood Reporter* published lists (not entirely accurate) of more than forty people who had received subpoenas: Clifford Odets, Donald Ogden Stewart, Ring Lardner, Jr., Dalton Trumbo, John Howard Lawson, Lester Cole. . . . A veteran screenwriter whose credits ranged from a Charlie Chan picture to *The House of Seven Gables,* Cole was getting a haircut in the M-G-M barbershop when the phone rang and he found himself talking to Eddie Mannix.

"Lester?" the studio manager said. "In my outside office there's a U.S. marshal with a subpoena for you. You want to duck while I hold him?"

"Duck?" Cole echoed. "Where to? Tell him I'm in the third seat in the barbershop."

More notable than this clutch of leftist screenwriters were the conservative eminences whom the committee was inviting to testify about the Communist threat: Louis B. Mayer and Jack Warner and Walt Disney, Gary Cooper and Robert Taylor and Ronald Reagan. It promised to be a great show.

Although the HUAC investigations of the movie business have acquired the status of a national legend, Hollywood was never really more than an entertaining diversion in the committee's zigzagging crusade. *Martin Dies' Story,* the memoirs of the committee's founding chairman, never even mentioned Dies's forays into show business in the late 1930's. His targets were

primarily President Roosevelt and the labor unions, secondarily liberals, foreigners, and anyone else who aroused his ire. When Dies retired because of
bad health in 1944, his powers devolved onto John Rankin of Mississippi, who
hopefully announced that an investigation of Hollywood would reveal "the
greatest hotbed of subversive activities in the United States" and perhaps even
"one of the most dangerous plots ever instigated for the overthrow of the
government." Rankin was apparently inspired to these views by the prominence of Jews in Hollywood, but he imagined Jewish threats everywhere. He
once denounced Walter Winchell as "a little slime-mongering kike," and he
even baited a congressional colleague, Emanuel Celler, by referring to him as
"the Jewish gentleman from New York." When Celler protested, the courtly
Mississippian asked, "Does the member from New York object to being called
a Jew or does he object to being called a gentleman?"

Once the 1946 elections had brought the Republicans to power in Congress, the challenge of investigating Hollywood fell to the new HUAC chairman, J. Parnell Thomas. It was a little hard, at the start, for Hollywood to
take this pudgy, jowly figure very seriously. The son of a Jersey City police
commissioner, Thomas had been born John Parnell Feeney, Jr., but after his
father's death, he decided to adopt his mother's maiden name. It is probably
unfair to accuse anyone who calls himself J. Parnell of trying to hide his Irish
origins; on the other hand, the future congressman was quite candid about
why the name Thomas seemed preferable to Feeney. "Your petitioner . . ."
he told the court, "believes that he can get recognition and business under
the name of Thomas that he could not get under the name of Feeney."

Recognition and business, those were the goals to achieve. Feeney/
Thomas went to the Wharton School of Finance for a time, then left to join
the army in World War I, rose to be a captain, worked as a bond salesman in
New York, and began thinking about a career in politics. Since Catholicism
might prove as much a hindrance as the name Feeney, he changed not only
his name but his religion. He made a point of attending the Baptist church,
but occasionally told interviewers he was an Episcopalian, and a Mason as
well. He was elected mayor of Allendale, New Jersey, in 1931, and then a
state assemblyman in 1935. In the legislature, he had an experience that he
later said had changed his life. The governor of New Jersey had proposed a
sales tax to raise money for the relief of the unemployed, and some of these
people on relief invaded the Assembly to lobby for the bill. They ate and slept
there, played mandolins, and generally dismayed people like J. Parnell
Thomas. He began what he called a "quiet" investigation of these troublemakers and discovered that one of them had once been a Communist Party
candidate for governor of Ohio. That was enough for Thomas to demand that
the authorities expel the demonstrators as dangerous revolutionaries. "Or if
they are to be treated as guests of the state," he added, "let's do the job
properly. Feed them caviar. Feed them chocolate eclairs."

These local controversies were still unresolved when Thomas saw a
greater opportunity, in 1936, in the death of the congressman for the Seventh
District. Thomas ran for the seat and won. He had a talent for gestures. One

of the first bills that he proposed called for the public hanging of kidnappers. He saw possibilities in the creation of a committee on un-American activities. He asked for and won appointment as one of the founding members in 1938. The seniority system inexorably brought him to the chairmanship, and by May of 1947, he was able to announce to the press that "hundreds of very prominent film capital people have been named as Communists to us."

Like the new Senator McCarthy's subsequent announcement that he had a list of 205 card-carrying Communists in the State Department, Thomas's talk of "hundreds" of prominent Hollywood Communists was pure fantasy. They didn't exist. The total of Communist Party members in the movie business was never large. After years of interrogations, supported by all the evidence accumulated by the FBI and the movie studios, the House committee issued a list in 1952 of everyone in Hollywood who had ever been identified as (not proved to be) a past or present Communist, and the grand total came to 324 employees or wives of employees of the movie industry. This in a work force of more than thirty thousand.* And even if the term "important" be extended to encompass second-rate directors and mediocre screenwriters, scarcely two or three dozen Communists could be said to have any importance whatsoever. Near the start of the congressional hearings, in fact, when the studio heads held a meeting at the Hillcrest Country Club to discuss the Communist problem, Louis B. Mayer named the young son of a well-known producer as a ringleader of Hollywood radicals. Sam Goldwyn responded with commendable *sang-froid*. "If that snot-nosed baby is the Red boss in Hollywood, then, gentlemen, we've got nothing to fear," Goldwyn said. "Let's go home."

What, then, was the House committee trying to accomplish? The least plausible answer, which nonetheless deserves a moment's consideration, is that the congressmen were genuinely concerned about the possibility of Communist domination of a major medium of information. Recent revelations of Soviet spying were in the air, and the committee was struggling with its first actual piece of legislation, a bill drafted by Rankin to punish by ten years in jail any attempt "in any course of instruction or teaching in any public or private school, college or university to advocate or to express or convey the impression of sympathy with or approval of, Communism or Communist ideology." This was a bit strong even for the Un-American Activities Committee. A majority of the committee members could not bring themselves to recommend Rankin's measure to the full House, but they went on considering various proposals to outlaw communism.

The second least plausible explanation, which both the Hollywood producers and the dissenting radicals professed to believe, was that the House

---

* The official estimates of Communist fund-raising in Hollywood were probably similarly exaggerated. HUAC claimed in 1950 that $926,568.36 had been contributed to eight groups that it said were Communist fronts. Murray Kempton, a reasonably fair-minded observer, has estimated that the Communist Party probably "would have been fortunate to net as much as half a million dollars out of its Hollywood fronts in fifteen years."

committee sought to dominate the movie industry, to tell the producers what movies to make. Jack Warner was reasonably typical, once the HUAC hearings got under way, in decrying government interference in Hollywood. "We can't fight dictatorships by borrowing dictatorial methods," he said, in a prepared statement that sounded like someone else's handiwork. "Nor can we defend freedom by curtailing liberties, but we can attack with a free press and a free screen." John Howard Lawson, the Communist screenwriter who was to play the role of chief demon at these same hearings, sounded equally pious in testifying about the need for a "free screen." "J. Parnell Thomas and the Un-American interests he serves . . . are afraid of the American people," Lawson declared in a statement that Thomas refused to let him read. "They don't want to muzzle me. They want to muzzle public opinion. They want to muzzle the great Voice of democracy. . . ."

The real explanation of the committee's objectives is probably the obvious one: partisan politics. Just as President Truman was more or less continuing Roosevelt's New Deal, so Thomas was continuing to play the harassing role originally performed by Dies. Like Dies, Thomas represented the small-town worrier who couldn't figure things out but suspected that many of his daily problems were the fault of dark forces in distant places, international cartels, giant labor unions, foreign radicals. Dies and Thomas and the committee all represented, in other words, the constituency of the bewildered and the resentful, all those people whom Nathanael West had described as "tired of oranges, even of avocado pears . . . [the] cheated and betrayed."

And then there was the matter of publicity, not as an adjunct to politics but as the essence of it. To say that J. Parnell Thomas was a publicity seeker, which he was, misses the point that publicity is the blood of politics. There are no issues, really, except on rare occasions of war or disaster, only images and competing images. Even before television made this obvious, J. Parnell Thomas sensed that his essentially purposeless investigations of communism might bring him great rewards (what made Tom Dewey a presidential candidate, after all, if not his highly publicized investigations of New York gangsters?). One of Thomas's committee members, young Dick Nixon, saw similar possibilities but had the shrewdness and the patience to bide his time until he encountered the great drama that would make him famous, the clash between Whittaker Chambers and Alger Hiss. The Un-American Activities Committee had long been tempted by Hollywood, and by the publicity that accompanied every suggestion of an investigation of the movies, but Dies's probing tentacles had been rather harshly beaten back in 1941. And the committee had many other fields to explore. (When Congressman Dickstein had been asked back in the 1930's exactly whom his proposed Un-American Activities Committee would be authorized to investigate, he had prophetically answered: "Everybody!") So the committee began the year 1947 by inquiring into the United Auto Workers' role in the continuing strike at Allis-Chalmers, and the United Electrical Workers' role in a strike in Bridgeport, Connecticut, and the Food, Tobacco, and Agricultural Workers' role in a strike at the Reynolds Tobacco Company plant in Winston-Salem. Labor unions, as Hollywood would learn, were a matter of continuing interest to the Un-American Activities Committee.

In its more or less random explorations, the committee had inevitably been struck by the activities of Louis Budenz, a former managing editor of the *Daily Worker,* who had somehow found God and now sought only to condemn and expiate his former sins. He began making radio speeches to denounce the Evil One, an all-powerful agent who he claimed was traveling throughout the United States as the secret representative of the Kremlin. "This man never shows his face," Budenz said. "Communist leaders never see him, but they follow his orders or suggestions implicitly." The Un-American Activities Committee was thrilled. It summoned Budenz to come and tell all he knew about the worldwide Communist conspiracy, and Rankin welcomed him with a burst of his customary rhetoric. "Are you familiar," he demanded, "with the rape of innocent women, the murder of innocent men, the plunder of the peasants and the robbery of the helpless people . . . by the Communist regime?"

Budenz eventually identified the Kremlin master agent, the man who never showed his face, as Gerhart Eisler, an obscure German operative who may quite possibly have been all that Budenz said he was. The committee had no difficulty in demonstrating that Eisler had repeatedly lied to U.S. immigration authorities, used several false names (Edwards, Brown, Berger, Liptzin), and traveled on a forged passport. This and more was detailed in the testimony of Eisler's older sister, Elfriede, who now called herself Ruth Fischer and was writing a denunciation of German communism for the Harvard University Press. She described her brother, whom she had not spoken to for many years, as a Soviet police agent, a murderer, and a "terrorist." She was not a great deal kinder to her other brother, Hanns, the Hollywood composer, whom she described as "a Communist in a philosophical sense."

Gerhart Eisler was already in the custody of the Immigration Service, which wanted to deport him. Brought from Ellis Island to Capitol Hill by two Immigration Service agents, he proved to be a waspishly intractable witness. When the committee's chief investigator, Robert Stripling, asked him to take the stand, he said, "I am not going to take the stand."

"Mr. Eisler, will you raise your right hand?" said Stripling.

"No," said Eisler.

"Mr. Eisler . . ." said Chairman Thomas, "you want to remember that you are a guest of this nation."

"I am not treated as a guest . . ." said Eisler. "I am a political prisoner."

The committee duly cited Eisler for contempt (the resolution to do so represented Congressman Nixon's maiden speech) and moved on to Hanns Eisler, who also offered rich possibilities for the committee's interrogators. When Eisler was trying to get a visa to the United States in 1940, his application was supported by such influential admirers as Dorothy Thompson, Malcolm Cowley, Clifford Odets, and—of all people the committee would like to embarrass—Eleanor Roosevelt. Unlike his truculent brother, Hanns Eisler parried the committee's questions with remarkably sassy wit. When Stripling described him as "the Karl Marx of Communism in the musical field," Eisler said, "I would be flattered."

"Mr. Eisler . . ." Stripling persisted, "haven't you on a number of occasions said, in effect, that music is one of the most powerful weapons for the bringing about of the revolution?"

"Sure," said Eisler. "Napoleon the First said—"

"Never mind Napoleon," Thomas interrupted. "You tell us what you said."

"I consider myself, in this matter, a pupil of Napoleon," the completely unfazed Eisler retorted. "I think in music I can enlighten and help people in distress in their fight for their rights. In Germany we didn't do so well. . . . The truth is, songs cannot destroy Fascism, but they are necessary. . . . It's a matter of musical taste whether you like them. . . . If you don't like them, I am sorry; you can listen to 'Open the Door, Richard.' "

In questioning Eisler about his various compositions, Stripling repeatedly asked him about his collaborations with Brecht. Had he written the music for *Die Massnahme (The Measures Taken)*, Brecht's radical play of 1930; for *Kühle Wampe*, the Berlin film of 1932; for *Hangmen Also Die*? Eisler cheerfully acknowledged them all (though he seemed to think he was protecting his friend by avoiding any mention of Brecht's name). But he would not admit to being a Communist. "I would be a swindler if I called myself a Communist," he said. "I have no right. The Communist underground workers in every country have proven that they are heroes. I am not a hero. I am a composer."

● ● ●

J. Parnell Thomas began his investigation of Hollywood in May of 1947 with a series of interrogations in his suite at the Biltmore Hotel in Los Angeles. These meetings were supposedly closed, private, but after each afternoon's session, Thomas and Stripling told reporters about the wonders they were discovering. Their indirect targets, as usual, were the New Deal and the labor unions. Thomas declared that "the government" had "wielded the iron fist in order to get the companies to put on certain Communist propaganda," and that the main vehicle for this propaganda, the Screen Writers Guild, was "lousy with Communists." As evidence for these charges, Thomas reported that Robert Taylor had testified that government officials had delayed his entry into the navy in 1943 until he had finished filming M-G-M's *Song of Russia*, which Thomas described as "Communist propaganda that favored its ideologies, its institutions and its way of life over the same things in America." The committee's most implausible witness, Ginger Rogers's mother, Lela Rogers, told the investigators that her daughter had bravely refused to speak a typical piece of Communist propaganda, "Share and share alike—that's democracy," which had appeared in Dalton Trumbo's script for *Tender Comrade*.

There were fourteen of what Thomas called "friendly witnesses," and on the basis of their testimony, he announced his conclusions. White House pressure had forced the studios to produce "flagrant Communist propaganda films"; Washington intrigues had helped Communist union leaders to threaten the studios, and Communist writers were subtly infusing Moscow's propaganda into the movies. After this verdict, the trial could begin. All these un-American maneuvers needed to be publicly exposed and publicly condemned and he, J. Parnell Thomas, proposed to do so. The pink subpoenas that circulated through Hollywood that September were proof that he was very much in earnest.

Herbert Biberman, a rather pompous producer and director whose most recent films included *Abilene Town* and *New Orleans,* was one of the first to see the obvious pattern in the subpoenas and to do something about it. He got on the telephone and invited a group of the prospective witnesses to assemble at eight o'clock that same evening in the home of the director Lewis Milestone to discuss with some lawyers how they should defend themselves. The nineteen witnesses were mostly writers: Dalton Trumbo, John Howard Lawson, Lester Cole, Alvah Bessie, Richard Collins, Gordon Kahn, Howard Koch, Ring Lardner, Jr., Albert Maltz, Samuel Ornitz, and Waldo Salt. And Brecht. There were also a few who had graduated from writing into directing and producing: Edward Dmytryk, Irving Pichel, Adrian Scott, Robert Rossen. And one actor, Larry Parks. Most of them were or had recently been members of the Communist Party (as the authorities well knew, since the CP's Los Angeles secretary was an FBI informer). Perhaps by coincidence, only one of the nineteen had done military service during the recent war. Perhaps by coincidence, at least ten were Jews; perhaps by coincidence, but more likely not. *The Hollywood Reporter* was apparently the first to call them "the unfriendly witnesses," but they took pride in the term and applied it freely to themselves. It was left to the malicious Billy Wilder to say, "Only two of them have talent. The rest are just unfriendly."

Biberman had invited to the meeting four prominent defense lawyers, notably Robert Kenny, who, despite the handicap of a withered arm, had succeeded Earl Warren as state attorney general (and fully supported Warren's activities in the incarceration of the Japanese). Almost equally well known was Bartley Crum, a corporation lawyer and a Republican. The other two were militant leftists, Ben Margolis and Charles Katz, charter members of the National Lawyers Guild.

The lawyers reviewed the alternatives. The most extreme course would be a total refusal to answer any questions and a rejection of the committee's right to question anyone about political beliefs. This appealed to some of the more aggressive among the nineteen, but it would prevent them from presenting their case to the public. Equally provocative would be a defiant acknowledgment and defense of Communist Party membership, but though that was theoretically legal, the largely unused Smith Act of 1940 now made it possible to prosecute Communists on charges of advocating the overthrow of the government. As a third possibility, the witnesses could simply deny their Communist Party membership, but that left them open to prosecution for perjury, punishable by five years in jail. The safest course, as subsequent witnesses soon discovered, was to plead the Fifth Amendment against self-incrimination, but the nineteen disliked that because it seemed to imply that they had committed some crime.

They finally decided, at the urging of Trumbo and Lardner, on the First Amendment, which proclaimed that Congress had no right to make any law restricting free speech or peaceable assembly, and therefore presumably had no right to investigate such matters. Supreme Court precedents seemed to support this defense. In an 1880 case known as *Kilbourn* v. *Thompson,* the court had ruled that the government could not compel a citizen to disclose his political views. In a 1943 decision rejecting compulsory salutes to the flag, Justice Robert Jackson had declared that the government could not make anyone profess his loyalty or punish him for refusing to do so.

In retrospect, this decision to rely on the First Amendment still seems the right one. It is quite possible that if the Hollywood witnesses had politely declined to answer any questions and cited the First Amendment as their reason, they might have won their fight. But Kenny apparently convinced them that they would have a stronger case in court if instead of refusing to answer and citing the First Amendment, they evaded and parried all questions and yet denied that they were refusing to answer. When the Supreme Court finally ruled in their favor on any contempt charges, Kenny argued, a splendid constitutional principle would be strongly and very publicly upheld. "Before the Ten actually went off to the pokey, nobody believed anybody was going to jail," Kenny told an interviewer nearly thirty years later. "Even the judges who handed out the sentences thought this was nothing more than a test case. Contempt of Congress—it's just a high-grade misdemeanor anyway— a year and a thousand maximum. Nobody had served time on the charge since the 1920s. That was when Harry Sinclair of Sinclair Oil did thirty days for his behavior during the Congressional investigation of the Teapot Dome affair."

There was a good deal of arguing at Biberman's meeting that night, and at later meetings as well. Bessie, who was a devout Communist and had fought bravely in Spain, wanted to adopt the tactic of proclaiming his party membership and saying he was proud of it. Koch, who was not a Communist, wanted to say so before the committee, but several others shouted him down. Kenny later claimed that the witnesses all decided their course on their own. "It was not a collective decision, though it came after inter-member deliberation," he said. One of the witnesses, Edward Dmytryk, remembered the scene quite differently. He said that those present at the meeting had agreed "that all decisions be made only by unanimous consent, and, once made, must be strictly adhered to. . . . Larry Parks moved the rule (at the instigation, he later told me, of one of the Communist lawyers of the group) and I voted willingly for its adoption." *

The only one who balked at the planned strategy was Brecht. He apologized to the others but pointed out that he was not an American citizen. He had strong misgivings about whether the Bill of Rights' protection of citizens applied to aliens like him. He had recently received the necessary papers to go to Switzerland, and he feared that if he resisted the committee, it might prevent his departure. The others said they understood. "He seemed to have the uncomfortable feeling," Trumbo wrote later, "based, perhaps, on earlier hassles over un-German activities, that all those doctors of humane letters who earned their bread by writing about his plays and describing his genius would forget, somehow, to set the alarm clock on the day he went to jail."

But the nineteen had no intention or expectation of going to jail. "We thought we were winners," Lardner said. "We didn't anticipate that our careers would be wrecked." Nor did they feel isolated or helpless; nor was there much reason why they should. Not long after the subpoenas arrived, John Huston was having lunch at Lucey's restaurant on Melrose Avenue with William Wyler, whose *The Best Years of Our Lives* had won that year's Academy Award, and the writer Philip Dunne, son of Finley Peter Dunne, and the three of them decided to form a Committee for the First Amendment. They called on Ira Gershwin to open his home for the founding meeting, and according to one writer who was there that night, "You could not get into the place. The excitement was intense. The town was full of enthusiasm because they all felt they were going to win. Every star was there."

The committee gathered an impressive collection of supporters: Humphrey Bogart, Rita Hayworth, Katharine Hepburn, Myrna Loy, Groucho Marx, Judy Garland, Frank Sinatra, Gene Kelly, Paulette Goddard, Fredric March, plus a few literary figures like George S. Kaufman and Archibald MacLeish, and even a few of the big producers: Walter Wanger, William Goetz, Jerry Wald. (A certain amount of recruitment was presumably involved in the assembling of this army. Lester Cole later recalled that he had gone to Ronald Reagan's house to ask him to join the First Amendment group. "It was early evening when I arrived and Jane Wyman, then his wife, came to the door. I introduced myself, asked to see him, and she became uneasy. Wyman told me Reagan was lying down, not feeling well, but she'd talk to him. She was back in moments, I thought seemingly embarrassed, asked me to tell Humphrey Bogart and Willie Wyler that he was not well, but was thinking seriously about joining them. He would let them know the next day. He didn't. . . .")

* Or so Dmytryk said in his 1978 memoir, *It's a Hell of a Life But Not a Bad Living.* On the other hand, when he reappeared before the House committee in 1951, after serving a prison term for contempt and then deciding to cooperate with the authorities, he was asked about this same point: "Was there an agreement by all to resort to that general procedure of refusing to testify?" Dmytryk answered: "We were very careful not to discuss this in the group. We felt there was some danger that this might constitute conspiracy."

No less important to the nineteen witnesses was the fact that the studio bosses appeared perfectly willing to keep them at work. Lardner, who had just bought a large house in Santa Monica that summer on the strength of a new contract at two thousand dollars per week with 20th Century–Fox, was soon asked to start another picture. Lester Cole, who had just negotiated a handsome M-G-M contract that would escalate over four years from $1,250 to $2,500 a week, feared that the studio might balk because of the subpoena, but Eddie Mannix summoned him the next day and gruffly asked him to sign. "No half-ass Congressman is going to tell M-G-M how to run its business," Mannix said.

•   •   •

The best technique for fighting a congressional committee had just been brilliantly demonstrated that summer by a man who deserved investigation far more than any Hollywood writer. In contrast to a Dalton Trumbo or a Lester Cole, who might or might not have slipped a few leftist tidbits past the watchful eye of Louis B. Mayer, Howard Hughes had undeniably persuaded the federal government to pay him some sixty million dollars to produce war planes, which Hughes had then failed to produce. Such extravagance could easily be forgotten now that the war was over, but the same 1946 elections that awarded the Republicans the chairmanship of the House Un-American Activities Committee also awarded them the chairmanship of a Senate group generally known as the War Investigating Committee. President Truman, once an obscure senator, had ridden to fame on this committee's inquiries into various wartime financial scandals. Its new chairman was a dour figure from Maine, Senator Owen Brewster, who hungered just as strongly as J. Parnell Thomas to expose the wickednesses of the Roosevelt administration.

Brewster had reasons of his own for concentrating on Hughes, and when committee investigators went to California to riffle through Hughes's corporate papers, they discovered a treasure, the expense accounts of Johnny Meyer. Plump and affable, Meyer was an operator, a hand-shaker and connection-maker. He had started with CBS, then moved to the Cleveland Wheat Exchange, then come to Hollywood and worked for Warner Bros. as a press agent assigned to Errol Flynn. A press agent for Errol Flynn presumably had certain social skills that would also be useful to Hughes, so Hughes hired him. When the Senate investigators unearthed Meyer's expense accounts, they discovered many savory details of Hughes's courtship of Colonel Elliott Roosevelt, who had once been chief of the Mediterranean Allied Photo Reconnaissance Command and had then been sent on a tour of aircraft plants to search for a much-needed new reconnaissance plane. Roosevelt's five-man search team had duly reached Los Angeles in August of 1943, and there they duly encountered Johnny Meyer, who, among other good deeds, introduced Roosevelt to a young actress, Faye Emerson. So now Meyer was brought to Washington in the summer of 1947 and made to testify about expense-account items like these: $1,000 worth of hotel accommodations, liquor, and racetrack tickets for the President's son and his new friend, Miss Emerson, whom he was soon planning to marry; nylon stockings for Miss Emerson, $132; a "loan" to Roosevelt on the eve of his marriage to Miss Emerson, $1,000; wedding party, $850, including $220 worth of champagne; a honeymoon hotel bill at the Beverly Hills Hotel, $576.83.

And more: bills for other Air Corps officers who were friends of Colonel Roosevelt, and for girls who were friends of these friends. The total, Meyer said, came to $5,083.79. Rich stuff, this, rich evidence of wartime sacrifices. Elliott Roosevelt angrily insisted on testifying in his own defense: "I deny with all my heart and soul that Johnny Meyer ever got me a girl!" He even demanded of Meyer: "Were any of these girls there specifically to entertain me?" Meyer parried adroitly: "That is hard to say, because you were quite busy with Miss Emerson."

"Are you stating?" Roosevelt pursued, in defense of his fellow officers, "that those girls were there to entertain them?" Meyer was perfectly willing to explain how these things worked: "They sat around with us and had drinks with us and went to dinner with us, and the girls were probably not with anyone, they just danced with anyone who asked them to."

Roosevelt insisted, however, that he and his team had inspected and admired Hughes's plane, and despite the criticisms of other Air Force officers (who were quite correct, as it turned out, in their predictions that Hughes's plane wouldn't work), they had recommended it on its merits. More generally, Roosevelt swore that Brewster and other Republican leaders had "spent a good portion of their time since my father died trying to smear him." Confronted with Meyer's expense accounts, Roosevelt could only answer that Meyer had falsified them, padded them, lied about them; confronted with Roosevelt's charges, Meyer resorted to ducking and weaving and smiling, always smiling. Hughes was more combative. "They're lying about me, and they're not going to get away with it," he said, according to one account, as he kicked a zebra-skin chair across Cary Grant's living room.

Hughes had good reason to be suspicious. Quite apart from the Republican-run committee's desire to blacken the name of Roosevelt, Senator Brewster was well known to be friendly, as they say, to Pan American Airways, and Pan Am's president, Juan Trippe, was well known to be furious at Hughes's triumph in getting Washington's approval for his TWA to compete with Pan Am on the lucrative transatlantic air routes to Europe. Now Hughes declared in a statement to the press that Brewster's investigation of Hughes's airplane deals was all part of a conspiracy: "I charge specifically that at a lunch in the Mayflower Hotel in Washington, D.C., last February, Senator Brewster in so many words told me that the hearings need not go on if I agreed to merge the TWA airline with Pan American Airways."

To deal with this charge, Brewster formed a subcommittee headed by Senator Homer Ferguson of Michigan, a silver-haired former judge. The first witness in the crowded and floodlit Senate Caucus Room was, of course, Hughes. He looked, according to one contemporary account, like "an enormously rich Huckleberry Finn, tieless and hatless, in a soiled shirt and a rumpled sports jacket borrowed from his butler-valet, his long, thin wrists protruding from sleeves that were inches too short." Repeating his charge against Brewster, Hughes said, "I think Senator Brewster should take the stand. Allow me to cross-examine him and bring in witnesses." Ferguson said he would think about that later, but Brewster responded with senatorial bluster: "It would be inconceivable to anyone that a man so long in the public eye as I have been—in the Maine legislature, governor of Maine, member of the United States House of Representatives and now a United States Senator —could have made so bald a proposition as he describes. It sounds a little more like Hollywood than Washington. No one of any competence or experience could make such a proposition, and I never did." He further charged that Hughes was trying to intimidate him, and "if chairmen of committees are to be intimidated, then Senate investigations may as well cease."

"Do you have any questions?" Ferguson asked Hughes.

"Between two hundred and five hundred questions, just about," Hughes answered. He stayed up all that night, writing out questions for Brewster, and then returned to the committee room in a new gray suit to resume his attack. He called Brewster "one of the greatest trick-shot artists in Washington." Ferguson countercharged that Hughes was "trying to discredit this committee." And then: "The integrity of the United States Senate is at stake." Hughes insisted that Brewster was being evasive. "Senator Brewster's story is a pack of lies," he said, "and I can tear it apart if given the opportunity." The crowd of onlookers burst into applause.

Both sides went on exchanging accusations in the press. Hughes said that his hotel room had been bugged at the behest of Pan Am. Brewster sneered at one of Hughes's planes, the gigantic wooden "Spruce Goose," as a "flying lumberyard" that would never actually fly. Hughes declared that "if the flying boat fails to fly, I will probably exile myself from this country. . . . I mean it." Brewster, by now engaged in a reelection campaign that he was destined to lose, jibed that Hughes was "a young man who found time while others were fighting the war to produce *The Outlaw*."

With the hearings adjourned, Hughes could concentrate on his Spruce Goose. In two days and two nights, at a cost of $55,000, he had the plane's parts carted from Culver City to Long Beach and reassembled there. Then he invited Brewster and his committee to join him in taking the behemoth on its first outing. The senators said they were busy. Hughes then invited the press to come and watch, at his expense. Several dozen reporters showed up, and Hughes took them out into the windswept bay, forcing his gigantic plane through the choppy waters at a speed of about forty miles per hour. Then, after depositing the reporters back on the dock, Hughes said he wanted to make one more run. He opened the throttles until the eight engines reached a speed of ninety miles an hour, and then, shuddering, the plane slowly soared up out of the water. Hughes got it up to about seventy feet and cruised along for a mile or so, then happily brought it back. "It just felt so buoyant and good, I just pulled it up," he said.

The Spruce Goose never flew again. But Hughes could not give it up. He spent about one million dollars a year to keep it in storage for nearly three decades. After his death in 1976, it passed on to others, who opened it up as a tourist attraction, and that it remains to this day.

•   •   •

When the nineteen Hollywood witnesses flew to Washington and established themselves at the Shoreham Hotel, they suddenly felt themselves in enemy territory. Zanuck and Goldwyn were mere names here, and Eddie Mannix's writ did not apply. Howard Koch, for one, was appalled at the general atmosphere of suspicion. "We were in our own capital, yet no foreign city could have been more alien and hostile," he recalled. "All our hotel rooms were bugged. When we . . . wanted to talk with each other or with our attorneys, we had either to keep twirling a metal key to jam the circuit or to go out of doors." Another of the nineteen, Gordon Kahn, said that none of the "unfriendly" witnesses had a single telephone conversation without "strange clickings" on the line. "Waiters hovered too long at tables where these men dined," he reported. Whenever one of the witnesses wanted to meet someone in the lobby, "sauntering figures took nearby chairs and leaned back to listen better."

But the producers were still behind them, or so they thought. On the night of October 19, Kenny, Crum, and the other lawyers went to another suite at the Shoreham Hotel to see Eric Johnston, president of the Motion Picture Association, and two of the producers' attorneys, Paul V. McNutt and Maurice Benjamin. Kenny showed Johnston the papers he had filed to challenge the committee's hearings on constitutional grounds. "We are maintaining that the Thomas Committee aims at censorship of the screen by intimidation," Kenny said.

"We share your feelings, gentlemen," Johnston said. "And we support your position."

But Kenny and his associates were worried about some of the things that Chairman Thomas was saying to the press. "He was quoted," Kenny complained, "as saying that the producers had agreed to establish a blacklist throughout the motion picture industry."

"That report is nonsense!" Johnston answered with a great show of indignation. "As long as I live I will never be a party to anything as un-American as a blacklist, and any statement purporting to quote me as agreeing to a blacklist is a libel upon me as a good American."

"Eric, I knew you were being misquoted," Crum said, shaking Johnston by the hand. "I'd never believe that you'd go along with anything as vicious as a blacklist."

"The witnesses we represent will be more than delighted to have that assurance from you," said Charles Katz.

"Tell the boys not to worry," said Johnston. "There'll never be a blacklist. We're not going to go totalitarian to please this committee."

The committee had its own plans. Two days before the hearings began,

Chairman Thomas had even staged a kind of rehearsal for the benefit of nine newsreel cameras arrayed in the brightly lit Caucus Room of the House's Old Office Building. He marched in, took his seat behind the rostrum, and nearly disappeared from sight. A Washington telephone directory had to be found for him to sit on, with a red silk pillow on top of that. Now, on Monday, October 20, respectably late at twenty minutes past 10 A.M. Thomas once again marched into the crowded Caucus Room and established himself on his pillow. The newsreel cameras whirred; there was even one television camera. Thomas welcomed his audience with a short opening statement on the importance of his crusade. "Over 85 million people attend the movies each week . . ." he said. "It is not unnatural—in fact it is very logical—that subversive and undemocratic forces should attempt to use this medium for un-American purposes. . . ."

No sooner had Thomas signaled for the first witness to be called than Kenny rose to argue a motion that the whole proceeding be stopped on constitutional grounds.

"What is your name, please?" said Thomas, who knew perfectly well who Kenny was. Only after Kenny had formally identified himself did Thomas tell him that his clients would not be questioned until the following week, and that he should submit his petition then. Kenny asked if he could cross-examine the "friendly" witnesses. "You may not ask one more thing at this time," Thomas said. "Please be seated."

The first major witness was Jack Warner. Chroniclers of these hearings have tended to emphasize Thomas's gavel-pounding clashes with the leftist writers who eventually went to prison as the Hollywood Ten, but there was more to be learned from the outpourings of the "friendly" witnesses, particularly this first one. Jack Warner was in many ways Hollywood incarnate. He was vain, ignorant, pretentious, deceitful, greedy, ruthless, and passionately fond of telling bad jokes. (When Field Marshal Montgomery paid a state visit to Hollywood, Sam Goldwyn introduced him at a studio lunch as "my good friend Marshall Field Montgomery," and Warner could not resist correcting his fellow producer: "What Sam meant to say was Marshall Field Montgomery Ward.") While the Warner Bros. studio became notorious for cheap sets and cut-rate productions, and its lawsuits against rebellious stars like Bette Davis and Olivia de Havilland, Jack Warner built up a personal fortune estimated at forty million dollars. Yet by some mysterious alchemy, Warner Bros. produced a fair share of the best movies made during this whole period. *The Maltese Falcon, Sergeant York, Casablanca, Kings Row, Yankee Doodle Dandy*—these were all Warners pictures.

There was also a yellow streak in Jack Warner. He was terrified every time he faced a fight with some blusterer like Errol Flynn. And no sooner had J. Parnell Thomas summoned him to the preliminary committee hearings in Los Angeles that spring than Warner began babbling. He claimed both that Washington had exerted political pressure on him and that Communists had tried to influence the making of Warner Bros. films, but he insisted that he had always done his best in the cause of Americanism. John Huston later recalled asking Warner what kind of questions the committee had put to him. "They wanted to know the names of people I thought might be Communists out here . . ." Warner said nervously. "I told them the names of a few." When Huston expressed disapproval, Warner got still more nervous. "I guess I shouldn't have, should I?" he pleaded. "I guess I'm a squealer, huh?"

In Washington, despite his declarations about defending "a free press and a free screen," Warner offered an opening statement worthy of J. Parnell Thomas himself. "Ideological termites have burrowed into many American industries," Warner said. "I say let us dig them out and get rid of them." And again: "Subversive germs breed in dark corners. Let's get light into those corners." Warner even claimed that his studio would be happy to organize a "pest-removal fund" that would "ship to Russia the people who don't like our American system of government."

Splendid, splendid, but the committee wanted Warner to do his part by naming some of these termites and subversive germs that he had found burrowing in his studio. Warner tried at first to be evasive. "I have never seen a Communist," he said, "and I wouldn't know one if I saw one." Stripling, the chief investigator, reminded Warner that he had done better in his private testimony in Los Angeles. Stripling now read a good deal of that testimony aloud. Warner had been asked whether there had been a time when he noticed an increased Communist influence in Hollywood, and he had said that in 1936 and 1937 he became aware of "that type of writing coming into our scenarios." Now, perhaps under the influence of studio lawyers, he was reluctant to call anyone a Communist, but he did acknowledge that "there are people with un-American leanings who have been writing . . . types of— what I personally term un-American principles, for want of a better name."

And who were these people with un-American leanings? Warner equivocated. "When I say these people are Communists . . . it is from hearsay," he said. But he did keep declaring that he had dismissed them. When Stripling had pressed for names during the Los Angeles hearings, Warner finally began spewing them forth: Bessie and Kahn, Koch, Lardner, Lawson, Maltz, Rossen, Trumbo, Wexley, Guy Endore, Emmet Lavery, Irwin Shaw, Clifford Odets, Sheridan Gibney, Julius and Phil Epstein. Not only were these not all Communists, but not all of them had been fired by Warner either, and now he wanted to make a few amends. "I was naturally carried away at the time . . ." he testified. "I was rather emotional, being in a very emotional business. . . ." Specifically, he wanted to say that Endore, Gibney and the Epsteins had never "written any subversive elements." But it was hard, Warner said, to keep track of what all these writers were doing. "Some of these lines have innuendos and double meanings and things like that," he said, "and you have to take eight or ten Harvard law courses to find out what they mean."

Congressman Richard B. Vail suggested that the Hollywood producers should join forces to expel all Communists from their studios. Warner demurred, perhaps once again recalling advice from his lawyers. "I can't, for the life of me, figure where men could get together and try in any form, shape, or manner to deprive a man of a livelihood because of his political beliefs," he said. "It would be a conspiracy. . . ." He would soon learn otherwise.

Checked, rebuffed by an apparent ally, the committee retaliated by turning to Warner's production of *Mission to Moscow*. In his ghostwritten 1965 memoirs, Warner claimed that he had made this film at the explicit request of President Roosevelt himself—a claim that the committee would have enjoyed exploring—but in his congressional appearance, Warner sounded considerably less certain.

"Were you asked to make *Mission to Moscow?*" Stripling had asked him during the Los Angeles hearings.

"I would say we were, to a degree," Warner answered, adding a few more evasions. "You can put it that way, in one form or another."

"Who asked you to make *Mission to Moscow?*" Stripling persisted.

"I would say former Ambassador Davies," Warner said, thus offering nothing more subversive than an author's desire to have his own book filmed.

But now, in Washington, Warner wasn't even sure of that. He said he couldn't remember whether Davies had approached Harry Warner, president of the corporation, or whether Harry had approached Davies, to buy the screen rights to what was, after all, a best-seller. Stripling was getting a bit tired of Warner's uncertainties. He began reading aloud from a book by Quentin Reynolds, *The Curtain Rises* (1944), in which Reynolds described the amazement of the American correspondents in Moscow at seeing this filmed paean to the accomplishments of Joseph Stalin. Warner sounded flustered as he declared that he had never heard of Reynolds's book.

"Is it your opinion . . . that *Mission to Moscow* was a factually correct picture, and you made it as such?" Stripling asked.

"I can't remember," Warner said.

"Would you consider it a propaganda picture?" Stripling persisted.

"A propaganda picture—" Warner echoed.

"Yes."

"In what sense?"

"In the sense that it portrayed Russia and Communism in an entirely different light from what it actually was?"

"I have never been in Russia," Warner protested. "I don't know what Russia is like . . . so how can I tell you if it was right or wrong?"

Well, couldn't Warner have hired some expert to tell him whether his planned film would be accurate? "There are inaccuracies in everything," Warner said. "I have seen a million books—using a big term—and there have been inaccuracies in the text. There can be inaccuracies in everything, especially in a creative art. . . ."

In a creative art—Warner was beginning to get carried away, to lose his sense of the seriousness of the committee's purpose. Expansively, he acknowledged that leftist writers kept trying to slip bits of radical propaganda into their scripts, but since they knew that he, Jack Warner, would cut out all such propaganda, they persisted in their efforts in what Warner called "a humorous vein."

"Not only humorous," said J. Parnell Thomas, sounding a bit shocked.

"Well, strike the word humorous," said Warner. "I stand corrected."

"You might say in an insidious vein," said Thomas.

"Yes, insidious," Warner agreed.

The producer seemed to sense that he might be in danger. Asked once again about the possibility of blacklisting all Communists, he held up two personnel forms that he said his studio had been imposing on all employees ever since 1936. The main one asked: "Are you affiliated with any organization or group antagonistic to the principles of our American form of government?" Warner claimed that some would-be employees had balked at answering and signing this form, and had thus been discovered—like witches commanded to cross running water—discovered and barred from access to Warner Bros. But though his studio was doing everything it could, Warner insisted, un-Americanism was everywhere. In the theater, for example. (Wouldn't the committee like to turn its investigations toward Broadway?) He had recently seen *All My Sons* by a new playwright named Arthur Miller, which dealt with a manufacturer who produced defective airplanes during the war. "That play disgusted me," Warner said. "I almost got into a fist fight in the lobby. I said, 'How dare they?' " Young Arthur Miller did not seem important enough to pillory, but Warner told the committee that the play's director, Elia Kazan, now engaged in directing a film called *Gentleman's Agreement,* was "one of the mob. I pass him by but won't talk to him."

The committee was pretending to investigate the question of whether it should recommend the outlawing of the Communist Party, so it put this question to Jack Warner, who did his best to avoid answering. "I would advocate it providing it did not take away the rights of a free citizen, a good American to make a livelihood," Warner said, "and also that it would not interfere with the Constitution of the United States as well as the Bill of Rights." J. Parnell Thomas bristled at the suggestion that his activities could violate the Constitution.

"If we passed a law, that would be proper legal procedure, wouldn't it?" he asked.

"I, as an individual citizen, naturally am in favor of anything that is good for Americans," Warner said.

"Are you in favor of outlawing the Communist Party?"

"You mean from the ballot?"

"Yes, making it an illegal organization."

"I am in favor of making it an illegal organization."

The next major witness, who represented Hollywood even more than Jack Warner did, was Louis B. Mayer. He, too, had a ghostwritten opening statement to read, in which he declared that he had "maintained a relentless vigilance against un-American influences." And before the committee even had a chance to ask him whether he favored outlawing the Communist Party,

Mayer piously called on the committee to recommend "legislation establishing a national policy regulating employment of Communists in private industry." As for himself, he added, "it is my belief they should be denied the sanctuary of the freedom they seek to destroy."

Only about a week earlier, according to Lester Cole, Mayer had given a private demonstration of how to deal with Communists. He called Cole to his office and told him that he and Dalton Trumbo were two of M-G-M's best writers. "Your kind don't grow on trees," he said. "I don't want to lose you."

"Maybe you won't," said Cole. "It really looks like we have the law on our side."

"I don't give a shit about the law," Mayer said. "It's them goddamn commies that you're tied up with. Break with them. Stick with us. With me. . . . You'll do what you want. Direct your own pictures? Say so. I believe you'd do great. Dough means nothing. We'll tear up the contract, double your salary. You name it, you can have it. Just make the break."

Cole reported that Mayer's eyes filled with tears, as often happened during his negotiations. Unable to think quite what to answer, Cole only shook his head, whereupon Mayer exploded.

"I know about Communism," he roared. "I know what happens to men like that. Take that Communist Roosevelt! A hero, a man of the people! And what happens five minutes after they shoveled the dirt on his grave? The people pissed on it! That's what you want, Lester? Be with *us*, be smart. You got kids, think of them."

"You're a very generous man," Cole said. "I wish I could go along with you, but I can't."

"You're nuts!" Mayer shouted, rising to his feet, pointing to the door. "Goddamn crazy Commie! Get out! Goddamn it, get out!"

Now that Mayer was on the witness stand, he had to be more diplomatic. "Are there any Communists, to your knowledge, in Metro-Goldwyn-Mayer?" asked one of the committee's investigators, H. A. Smith. "There is no proof about it, except they mark them as Communists," Mayer said, groping, now that he had no statement to read, "and when I look at the pictures they have written for us I can't find once where they have written something like that. . . . I have as much contempt for them as anybody living in this world." But were there any Communists at M-G-M? Mayer fell back on anonymous informants and said that "they have mentioned two or three writers to me several times." Smith insisted on details. "Who are these people they have named?" he asked. Mayer cited Trumbo, Cole, and Donald Ogden Stewart. Why didn't Mayer get rid of them, Smith persisted. "I have asked counsel," Mayer said. "They claim that unless you can prove they are Communists they can hold you for damages."

It was clear that Mayer, like Warner, regarded himself as blameless in all things. If there were Communists at M-G-M—and he was not officially admitting any such thing—there was nothing he could do about it. The committee apparently believed that the M-G-M chief needed further guidance, so it turned to one of his wartime creations, *Song of Russia*, a maudlin romance of an American conductor touring the Soviet Union and becoming enamored of the country, its people, and one of its girls, all to the accompaniment of Tchaikovsky. Robert Taylor, who played the conductor, had roused the committee hounds by testifying in Los Angeles that "White House pressure" by "Roosevelt aides" had forced him to make the movie by delaying his naval commission until he had done so. ("In my own defense," Taylor subsequently testified in Washington, "lest I look a little silly by saying I was ever forced to do the picture, I was not forced.") Now Mayer tried to explain how these things worked in wartime Hollywood. "Taylor mentioned his pending commission in the Navy," Mayer said, "so I telephoned the Secretary of the Navy, Frank Knox, and told him of the situation, recalling the good that had been done by *Mrs. Miniver* and other pictures released during the war period. The secretary called back and said he thought Taylor could be given time to make the film before being called to the service."

But about the movie itself—how had it come to be made in the first place? Some writers had outlined a story, Mayer said, and it "seemed a good medium of entertainment and . . . a pat on the back for our then ally, Russia." Mayer added, as a kind of defense, exactly what the committee wanted to attack: "The Government coordinator . . . agreed with us that it would be a good idea to make the picture." Asked who the writers actually were, Mayer said that he could not remember. Perhaps he considered it wiser not to remember that the screenplay had been credited to Richard Collins, one of the "unfriendly" nineteen now under subpoena, and Paul Jarrico, who was eventually to plead the Fifth Amendment before this committee. In any case, Mayer himself had read the script and demanded revisions. "They had farm collectivism in it and I threw it out," he said. "I will not preach any ideology except American." When the revisions were finished, Mayer said, "the final script of *Song of Russia* was little more than a pleasant musical romance—the story of a boy and girl that, except for the music of Tchaikovsky, might just as well have taken place in Switzerland."

Mayer was perhaps too modest. The *New York Times* had greeted the film on its appearance in early 1944 as "really a honey of a topical musical film, full of rare good humor, rich vitality, and a proper respect for the Russians' fight in this war." Nor was that all. Bosley Crowther, the newspaper's chief film critic, hailed *Song of Russia* as "very close to being the best film on Russia yet made in the popular Hollywood idiom." Such a good review just three years before, and now this committee interrogator wanted to know whether Mayer would admit that "scene after scene . . . grossly misrepresented Russia." Mayer, like Warner, pleaded ignorance. "I never was in Russia," he said, overlooking the fact that he had been born there. Unlike the craven Warner, though, Mayer tried to counterattack. "You tell me," he went on, "how you would make a picture laid in Russia that would do any different than what we did there."

"Don't you feel from what you have read . . ." Smith tried again, "that the scenes did not depict Russia in one iota?"

"We did not attempt to depict Russia," Mayer retorted. "We attempted to show a Russian girl entreating this American conductor to conduct a concert in her village . . . and as it inevitably happens this girl fell in love with the conductor and he with her. Then we showed the attack of the Germans on the Russians and the war disrupted this union."

For a more critical anaylsis of this prize specimen, the committee summoned the bizarre figure of Ayn Rand, who was then working as a Hollywood screenwriter and hoping that Warners would soon produce her script of her own 1943 novel, *The Fountainhead.* Miss Rand had been born in 1904 in what she resolutely insisted on calling St. Petersburg, but she had last seen Russia in 1926, so it was a little hard to imagine why the committee considered her an expert on the subject. Still, by comparison with Warner and Mayer, almost anyone might be considered an expert. Miss Rand had not even seen *Song of Russia* on its first appearance, so the committee staged a special screening for her, and now she was prepared to testify that it was filled with pro-Soviet propaganda.

She scornfully described how Robert Taylor arrived in M-G-M's Russia to conduct concerts. "He meets a little Russian girl from a village. . . . He asks her to show him Moscow. She says she has never seen it. He says, 'I will show it to you.' They see it together. The picture then goes into a scene of Moscow, supposedly. I don't know where the studio got its shots, but I have never seen anything like it in Russia. First you see Moscow buildings—big, prosperous-looking, clean buildings, with something like swans or sailboats in the background. Then you see a Moscow restaurant that just never existed there."

If M-G-M's Moscow was exaggerated, M-G-M's typical Russian village was total fantasy. "You see the happy peasants," Miss Rand relentlessly continued. "You see they are meeting the hero at the station with bands, with beautiful blouses and shoes, such as they never wore anywhere. You see children with operetta costumes on them and with a brass band which they could never afford. You see the manicured starlets driving tractors and the happy women who come from work singing. . . ." Robert Taylor not only conducted Tchaikovsky for these happy villagers, but his concert was broadcast throughout the happy country, even to its far frontiers. "There is a border guard . . . listening to the concert," Miss Rand said. "Then there is a scene inside kind of a guardhouse where the guards are listening to the same concert, the beautiful Tchaikovsky music, and they are playing chess. Suddenly there is a Nazi attack on them." Miss Rand was sufficiently an ideologue to point out that the border station where the Nazis attacked the chess-playing, music-loving guards must have been located in central Poland, where Stalin had established them at the time of his alliance with Hitler.

The M-G-M love story followed its inevitable course, boy first losing girl to her "anti-parachute work," and then getting girl so that they can both spread the good word in America. In describing all this, Miss Rand was particularly indignant about Taylor's manager, played by Robert Benchley, who said to the heroine, "You are a fool, but a lot of fools like you died on the village green at Lexington." Quite apart from the the question of whether such a remark would make any sense to a Russian villager, Miss Rand called it "blasphemy," because the men of Lexington were "fighting for political freedom and individual freedom," and "to compare them to somebody, anybody, fighting for a slave state, I think is dreadful."

Congressman John Wood, a Georgia Democrat, tried to get Miss Rand to admit that the United States had a strategic interest in keeping the Soviets at war against Germany, but she disputed even that. "I think we could have used the lend-lease supplies that we sent there to much better advantage ourselves," she said. She therefore rejected completely the idea that a glib film like *Song of Russia* could serve some worthy political purpose. "If the excuse that has been given here is that we had to produce the picture in wartime, just how can it help the war effort?" she asked. "If it is to deceive the American people . . . then that sort of attitude is nothing but the theory of the Nazi elite, that a choice group of intellectual or other leaders will tell people lies for their own good."

"You paint a very dismal picture of Russia," said John McDowell, a Pennsylvania Republican. "You made a great point about the number of children who were unhappy. Doesn't anybody smile in Russia any more?"

"Well, if you ask me literally, pretty much no," said the unbudging Miss Rand.

"They don't smile?" McDowell repeated.

"Not quite that way, no," said Miss Rand.

What Miss Rand could not seem to understand, what the House committee could not seem to understand, was that *Song of Russia* was rubbish not because of any political purpose, subversive or otherwise, but because M-G-M was in the business of producing rubbish. That was its function, its nature, its mission. It hardly knew that political purposes existed. M-G-M was the home of Andy Hardy, of Judy Garland and Esther Williams, and no Communist ideology could ever penetrate or take root in such a playland. When Louis B. Mayer of Minsk decided to make a movie about Russia, he would inevitably make it the Russia of Andy Hardy, accompanied by Tchaikovsky.

The rest of the committee's friendly witnesses provided a lumpy anthology of conservative opinion. Walt Disney complained bitterly about Herb Sorrell's leadership of a strike at his studio in 1941. As a result, he said, "all of the Commie groups began smear campaigns against me and my pictures." Roy Brewer testified that his IATSE forces had saved Hollywood from communism during the strikes of 1945 and 1946. "There has been a real Communist plot to capture our unions in Hollywood, as part of the Communist plan to control the motion-picture industry . . ." Brewer said. "Sorrell has religiously followed the Communist line. . . . There was some of the most unbelievable amounts of violence that have ever appeared on the scene in the history of the American labor movement."

Sam Wood, the principal founder of the Motion Picture Association for the Preservation of American Ideals, and thus the principal instigator of these committee hearings, testified that the chief sources of Communist influence were the writers. Asked to identify some of the most subversive, he offered the by now familiar names, Lawson, Trumbo, and Stewart. "Is there any question in your mind as to whether Lawson is a Communist?" Stripling asked. "If there is, then I haven't any mind," said Wood.

And so on. Morrie Ryskind, who had helped write some of the great Marx Brothers comedies, like *Animal Crackers* and *A Night at the Opera,* said of another writer that "if he isn't a Communist, I don't think Mahatma Gandhi is an Indian." Still another writer, Fred Niblo, Jr., offered similar testimony: "I can't prove that he is a Communist any more than Custer could prove that the people who were massacring him were Indians." Leo McCarey, who had become rich by producing and directing *Going My Way* (1944), in which Bing Crosby demonstrated that a Catholic priest could play boogie-woogie (and still richer by demonstrating in *The Bells of St. Mary's* that not even a nun's starched wimple could detract from the beauty of Ingrid Bergman), testified that his films had not earned any money in the Soviet Union.

"What is the trouble?" asked Stripling.

"Well, I think I have a character in there they do not like," said McCarey.

"Bing Crosby?" Stripling suggested.

"No, God," said McCarey.

Then there were the actors. Adolphe Menjou, a minor player in various costume dramas, testified that he had read many books about communism and regarded it as "an Oriental tyranny, a Kremlin-dominated conspiracy." Robert Taylor (née Spangler Arlington Brugh) swore to his patriotic reluctance to make *Song of Russia* and then went on to declare that he would never take part in any movie with a Communist. "I would not even have to know that he was a Communist," Taylor said. "This may sound biased. However, if I were even suspicious of a person being a Communist with whom I was scheduled to work, I am afraid it would have to be him or me, because life is a little too short to be around people who annoy me as much as these fellow travelers and Communists do."

Gary Cooper was equally opposed to any involvement with Communists, but he couldn't quite remember when any such involvement had actually threatened him.

"I have turned down quite a few scripts because I thought they were tinged with Communistic ideas," Cooper said.

"Can you name any of those scripts?" asked Smith, the committee investigator.

"No, I can't recall any of those scripts to mind," Cooper said.

"Just a minute," Chairman Thomas intervened. "Mr. Cooper, you haven't got that bad a memory."

"I beg your pardon, sir?" said Cooper.

"You must be able to remember some of those scripts you turned down because you thought they were Communist scripts," Thomas said.

"Well, I can't actually give you a title to any of them . . ." Cooper said.

"Most of the scripts I read at night, and if they don't look good to me, I don't finish them, or if I do finish them I send them back as soon as possible to their author. . . . I could never take any of this pinko mouthing very seriously, because I didn't feel it was on the level."

Ronald Reagan was, by comparison, quite eloquent, almost presidential. Speaking as head of the Screen Actors Guild, he said the union had been afflicted by a "small clique" that he described as "suspected of more or less following the tactics that we associate with the Communist Party." He said he had "no investigative force" to ascertain whether these people actually were Communists, and the committee did not press him to name them.

Reagan's testimony could hardly have surprised the committee, for he apparently told all he knew to the FBI the previous April. According to FBI documents made public in a freedom-of-information request by the *San Jose Mercury-News* in 1985, Reagan was an informant listed by the agency as "T-10." The FBI documents reported that both Reagan and Jane Wyman identified various members of the Screen Actors Guild as pro-Communist, though the FBI deleted all mention of the suspects' names. When Reagan's activity as an FBI informant about his own union membership was made public in 1985, a White House spokesman named Rusty Brashear said that Reagan's role was really "very minor." "I'm not sure that this reference to confidential informant is quite what it sounds like," Brashear said.

Reagan ended his testimony—as befitted his role, or his sense of his role —on a note of windy statesmanship. "Sir, I detest, I abhor their philosophy," he said, "but I detest more than that their tactics, which are those of the fifth column, and are dishonest, but at the same time I never as a citizen want to see our country become urged, by either fear or resentment of this group, that we ever compromise with any of our democratic principles through that fear or resentment. I still think that democracy can do it."

This first week of hearings, in which the committee had presumably put forward its strongest evidence on Communist infiltration of Hollywood, ended with the case far from proven. The press was notably unconvinced. "We do not think the Committee is conducting a fair investigation," said a reasonably typical editorial in the *New York Times*. "We think the course on which it is embarked threatens to lead to greater dangers than those with which it is presently concerned." And Hollywood's liberals still boasted considerable fire-power. That Sunday night, October 26, the Committee for the First Amendment broadcast a nationwide radio program entitled "Hollywood Fights Back," in which various celebrities cried defiance at the congressional inquisitors. One of the most important was Thomas Mann, who professed to see analogies between the congressional hearings and the first oppressive measures undertaken by Hitler. Unlike many Hollywood liberals, who coupled their criticisms of the committee with denunciations of communism, Mann insisted on a solemn defense of Marx and Marxism too. "The ignorant and superstitious persecution of the believers in a political and economic doctrine which is, after all, the creation of great minds and great thinkers—I testify that this persecution is not only degrading for the persecutors themselves but also very harmful to the cultural reputation of this country," Mann declared. "As an American of German birth, I finally testify that I am painfully familiar with certain political trends. Spiritual intolerance, political inquisitions, and declining legal security, and all this in the name of an alleged 'state of emergency'. . . . that is how it started in Germany. What followed was fascism, and what followed fascism was war."

Over the bugged telephone lines from Washington, the nineteen witnesses and their lawyers pleaded with friends in Hollywood for an even more public demonstration of support. In what was after all a publicity battle, a confrontation between conflicting sets of images and reputations, the witnesses in Washington asked for a planeload of Hollywood supporters to come and provide a celebrity audience for the next week's hearings. "I became very emotional about it," Lauren Bacall recalled of a meeting of First Amendment stalwarts at the home of William Wyler. "I was up in arms—fervent. I said to Bogie, 'We must go.' He felt strongly about it too. . . . So it was decided that a group of us would fly to Washington—John Huston, Phil Dunne, Ira Gershwin, Danny Kaye, Gene Kelly, Paul Henreid, John Garfield, June Havoc, Evelyn Keyes. . . ." *

Huston was dining at the Brown Derby when he got a telephone call from Howard Hughes, who, despite his perpetual inaccessibility, always seemed to know what was going on. "John, I understand you are planning a trip to Washington, and I just want you to know that you can use one of my airplanes," the head of TWA told Huston. "Not for nothing, because, by law, I have to charge you something, but you can have it for the minimum rate allowable . . . and it will be all to yourselves."

"So that's what we did . . ." Huston reported. "Our plane stopped a couple of times en route to Washington, and we were met each time by sympathetic reporters. We got the feeling that the country was with us, that the national temper resembled ours—indignant and disapproving of what was going on." Lauren Bacall made some of those airport speeches, as did Bogart, Huston, Kaye, and Kelly. "We were a serious group—reasonably well informed, bright, and we all cared . . ." Miss Bacall remembered. "The airport crowds were large and vociferous—cheers went up—God, it was exciting. I couldn't wait to get to Washington. Wouldn't it be incredible if we really could effect a change—if we could make that Committee stop?"

---

* Congressman Rankin soon provided his own evaluation of the visiting celebrities. "I want to read you some of these names," he declared on the House floor, waving a copy of the list. "One of the names is June Havoc. We found out from the Motion Picture Almanac that her real name is June Hovick. Another one was Danny Kaye, and we found out his real name was David Daniel Kaminsky. Another one here is . . . Eddie Cantor, whose real name is Eddie Iskowitz. There is one who calls himself Edward Robinson. His real name is Emmanuel Goldberg [actually, it was Goldenberg]. There is another one here who calls himself Melvyn Douglas, whose real name is Melvyn Hesselberg. There are others too numerous to mention. They are attacking the committee for doing its duty to protect this country and save the American people from the horrible fate the Communists have meted out to the unfortunate Christian people of Europe."

The First Amendment celebrities had planned a variety of political gestures. They brought with them a petition of protest "for redress of grievances." They talked of staging a march to the Capitol to present their petition to House Speaker Joseph Martin. They hoped to bring it to President Truman. But after the long trip and all the speeches and press conferences, they had to concentrate on their main purpose, to present themselves before the newsreel cameras covering Monday morning's reconvening of the Un-American Activities Committee.

Chairman Thomas, the pudgy bond salesman from New Jersey, soon proved that he understood the publicity game better than all these famous movie stars. He started by ceding them a row of reserved seats at the back of his theater. Then he changed the program. Instead of the scheduled first witness, Eric Johnston, the silver-haired figurehead who represented the commercial respectability of Hollywood, Thomas called to the stand the most openly and noisily Communist of all the subpoenaed witnesses, John Howard Lawson.

Lawson, newly fifty-seven, had once seemed a paragon of radical enthusiasm. John Dos Passos, who had long ago sailed with him to France, where the two of them hoped to serve as volunteer ambulance drivers, remembered him as "an extraordinarily diverting fellow, recently out of Williams, with bright brown eyes, untidy hair and a great beak of a nose that made you think of Cyrano de Bergerac. . . . He was a voluble and comical talker. He had drastic ideas on every subject under the sun. . . . He was already writing plays." Lawson's second Broadway production, *Processional* (1925), brought him success at the age of thirty. Subsequent titles tell a story: *Loud Speaker* (1927), *The International* (1928), *Success Story* (1932). Success lured him west, as it lured so many others, and the Hollywood titles began to tell a different story: *Dream of Love* (1928), *Our Blushing Brides* (1930), *Bachelor Apartment* (1931), *Success at Any Price* (1934), his own script from his own play *Success Story*. The idealist, in other words, had become the former idealist.

All these compromises made Lawson all the more active in Hollywood politics. He was the first president of the Screen Writers Guild, and he made no secret of his ideological views. Writing in *New Theatre* magazine in 1934, he announced that he had joined the Communist Party, and he added, "I do not hesitate to say that it is my aim to present the Communist position." There was something sad about Lawson's efforts to "present the Communist position" on the screen. In 1938, the same year in which he wrote *Algiers* to introduce Hedy Lamarr,* he also wrote *Blockade,* Walter Wanger's account of the Spanish civil war, which somehow failed to say which side was which. "This I accepted because it was the only way in which the picture could be undertaken," Lawson said.

As the unofficial leader of Hollywood's Communists from about 1937 to

---

* Mocking the famous line "Come with me to the Casbah," Murray Kempton observed that this, "next to Odets' 'We could make beautiful music together' (*The General Died at Dawn*), may be considered the most permanent cultural contribution by a left-wing scriptwriter during the entire period."

1950, Lawson was less accommodating to his comrades. When Albert Maltz wrote an article in *New Masses* in early 1946 on the question, "What Shall We Ask of Writers?" he made the mistake of declaring that "the accepted understanding of art as a weapon is not a useful guide, but a straitjacket." That was pure Browderism, and Browder had now been expelled from the party, and his ideas of coalition and compromises had been expelled with him. Maltz was summoned to a "discussion" where Lawson led the chorus that shouted accusations of revisionism, aestheticism, ivory towerism, and, as Michael Gold wrote in the *Daily Worker,* "the phony atmosphere of Hollywood." At a second meeting, a week later, the sinner humbly recanted. "I had to retreat or be expelled . . ." Maltz said long afterward, "and expulsion over *this* matter was completely unacceptable to me. I felt the party was the best hope of mankind." Lawson felt the same way; whatever the party said, Lawson said. "I'm sure," said Paul Jarrico, who took over much of Lawson's authority after Lawson went to prison, "that if Jack were told by the Soviets to criticize them, without missing a beat he'd have said, 'Well, you know, the way the Soviets treat dissidents is really criminal.' "

But now, seated under the bright lights in front of the House Un-American Activities Committee, Lawson savored his moment of glory, false glory. He announced that he wanted to read a statement. "Well, all right," said Chairman Thomas, "let me see your statement." Lawson handed the statement to Thomas, and the chairman began reading silently. "For a week, this Committee has conducted an illegal and indecent trial of American citizens, whom the Committee has selected to be publicly pilloried and smeared. I am not here to defend myself, or to answer the agglomeration of falsehoods that has been heaped upon me. . . ." At some point in the midst of all that rhetoric, Thomas stopped reading.

"I don't care to read any more of the statement," he said. "The statement will not be read. I read the first line."

"You have spent one week vilifying me before the American public—" Lawson began.

"Just a minute—" Thomas cried.

"And you refuse to allow me to make a statement on my rights as an American citizen," Lawson went on.

The only record of these extraordinary confrontations is the official transcript, and whoever made that transcript could hardly do justice to the sound of two angry and arrogant men both talking loudly at the same time (actually three, since Thomas and Stripling alternated in interrogating Lawson; actually four, since Thomas's gavel also had a speaking part). Thus, after the customary stating of name and birth and occupation, the first substantive question dealt with Lawson's leadership of the writers' union. The result was bedlam.

STRIPLING: Are you a member of the Screen Writers Guild?

LAWSON: The raising of any question here in regard to membership, political beliefs or affiliation—

STRIPLING: Mr. Chairman—

LAWSON: —is absolutely beyond the powers of this Committee.

STRIPLING: Mr. Chairman—

LAWSON: But—

(*The Chairman pounding gavel.*)

LAWSON: It is a matter of public record that I am a member of the Screen Writers Guild.

STRIPLING: I ask—

(*Applause*)

THOMAS: I want to caution the people in the audience. . . . I do not care for any applause or any demonstrations of one kind or another.

STRIPLING: Now Mr. Chairman, I am going to request that you instruct the witness to be responsive to the questions.

THOMAS: I think the witness will be more responsive to the questions.

LAWSON: Mr. Chairman, you permitted—

THOMAS (*pounding gavel*): Never mind—

LAWSON: —witnesses in this room to make answers of three or four or five hundred words to questions here.

THOMAS: Mr. Lawson, will you please be responsive to these questions and not continue to try to disrupt these hearings?

LAWSON: I am not on trial here, Mr. Chairman. This Committee is on trial here before the American people. Let us get that straight.

And so on. Thomas, like any congressional committee chairman, felt strongly his right to have his way. Lawson defiantly, almost insolently, refused to accept that right. "The Chair will determine what is in the purview of this Committee," Thomas declared at one point. "My rights as an American citizen are no less than the responsibilities of this Committee of Congress," Lawson fired back. Whenever sufficiently provoked, Thomas resorted to banging his gavel. Thus, after Thomas threatened Lawson with a citation for contempt, the transcript rather inadequately reported:

LAWSON: I am glad you have made it perfectly clear that you are going to threaten and intimidate the witnesses, Mr. Chairman.

(*The Chairman pounding gavel.*)

LAWSON: I am an American and I am not at all easy to intimidate, and don't think I am.

(*The Chairman pounding gavel.*)

STRIPLING: Mr. Lawson, I repeat the question. . . .

Since Stripling could not get Lawson either to answer or refuse to answer —since that was the mysterious strategy the witnesses had agreed on— Thomas finally intervened in full force.

THOMAS (*pounding gavel*): We are going to get the answer to that question if we have to stay here for a week. Are you a member of the Communist Party, or have you ever been a member of the Communist Party?

LAWSON: It is unfortunate and tragic that I have to teach this Committee the basic principles of American—

THOMAS (*pounding gavel*): That is not the question. That is not the question. The question is: Have you ever been a member of the Communist Party?

LAWSON: . . . I have told you that I will offer my beliefs, affiliations and everything else to the American public, and they will know where I stand.

THOMAS: *(pounding gavel)*: Excuse the witness—

LAWSON: As they do from what I have written.

THOMAS *(pounding gavel)*: Stand away from the stand—

LAWSON: . . . I shall continue to fight for the Bill of Rights, which you are trying to destroy.

THOMAS: Officers, take this man away from the stand.

(Applause and boos.)

THOMAS *(pounding gavel)*: There will be no demonstrations.

After a squad of police escorted Lawson from the stand, Stripling swore in one of his investigators to testify that Lawson held Communist Party card number 47275. Stripling then began reading into the record a nine-page listing of Lawson's political activities, from advocating the reelection of President Roosevelt to writing articles in the *Daily Worker*.

It was rather an anticlimax when Eric Johnston finally came to testify that afternoon, and yet he was to play an important role in the crisis. As head of the Motion Picture Producers Association, Johnston believed it was his function to defend the industry as a whole, and so he began with a bristling attack on "sensational testimony about Hollywood . . . scare-head stuff which is grossly unfair to a great American industry." Johnston spoke warmly about the importance of free speech. "You can't make good and honest motion pictures in an atmosphere of fear," he said. "I don't propose that Government shall tell the motion picture industry, directly or by coercion, what kind of pictures it ought to make."

The committee did not appreciate these pronouncements. Stripling rather tartly accused Johnston of "attempting to run" the committee's investigation. To show him what the committee's own investigators could do, Stripling darkly inquired whether Johnston knew that one of his own staff members, Edward Cheyfitz, had been a Communist. Johnston responded by reading testimonials to Cheyfitz's good character. "Knowing Mr. Stripling," Johnston said, to explain the fact that he had the testimonials with him, "I prepared for anything."

Though Johnston seemed to cry defiance at the committee, however, he warmly encouraged its self-proclaimed purpose, the "exposing" of Hollywood's Communists. "I'm heart and soul for it," he said. "An exposed Communist is an unarmed Communist. Expose them, but expose them in the traditional American manner." He did not explain what that traditional manner might be, but he seemed to mean only that the exposing should be limited to authentic party members. "Expose Communism, but don't put any American who isn't a Communist in a concentration camp of suspicion," he said. Johnston seemed to see no contradiction between advocating free speech and limiting that freedom to non-Communists, but this was becoming a popular view, not only among former presidents of the chamber of commerce but among a good number of liberals as well. Johnston would soon help to make it Hollywood's official policy.

The kind of man Johnston wanted to silence appeared on the stand the next day in the dapper form of Dalton Trumbo, who had written a lot of successful scripts—*Kitty Foyle* (1940), *Thirty Seconds Over Tokyo* (1944), *Our Vines Have Tender Grapes* (1945)—and who was now being paid four thousand dollars a week by M-G-M. He ostentatiously brought with him a large box containing twenty of his scripts and even several cans filled with prints of his films. He also brought a statement, which Thomas refused to let him read. Having experienced the tornado of John Howard Lawson, Stripling told Trumbo that the committee wanted its main questions answered with a yes or no. "I shall answer in my own words," Trumbo retorted. "Very many questions can be answered 'Yes' or 'No' only by a moron or a slave."

Trumbo insisted on this kind of posturing. He offered up all his scripts for study, challenging Thomas to point out anything subversive. Thomas declined. "Too many pages," he said. The committee only wanted to know whether Trumbo was a member of the Screen Writers Guild, which, of course, it knew he was. Trumbo declared that such questioning could destroy "the rights of American labor to inviolably secret membership."

"Are you answering the question or are you making another speech?" Thomas inquired. "Can't you answer . . . by saying 'Yes' or 'No' or 'I think so' or 'Maybe' or something like that?"

Trumbo started another speech, accusing the committee of trying to equate Guild membership with communism.

"Excuse the witness," Thomas shouted, banging his gavel once more.

"This is the beginning," Trumbo shouted back as he departed, "of the American concentration camp!"

Blinded by ideology, or perhaps simply by egotism, these truculent witnesses seemed to think that that they were devastating Thomas and his committee with their wit, their defiance, and their devotion to humanitarian principles. The reality was quite different. In their shouting and blustering, they provided their audience, both in the hearing room and beyond, with a rather unappetizing spectacle. By wrangling with Thomas, they put themselves on the same level, and lost many of their trusting supporters. "It was a sorry performance," said John Huston, who had helped to found the Committee for the First Amendment and brought his planeload of supporters to the row of reserved seats at the back of the committee room. "You felt your skin crawl and your stomach turn. I disapproved of what was being done to the Ten, but I also disapproved of their response. They had lost a chance to defend a most important principle. . . . Before this spectacle, the attitude of the press had been extremely sympathetic. Now it changed. . . ."

Paul Henreid recalled a general scattering. He said that Huston summoned all his followers to a meeting in his hotel suite at eleven o'clock at night. He announced, among other things, that there was no prospect of a lunch with President Truman. "I think our mission here is finished," he said. "You all have your return tickets, and you can get back any way you want." So get back any way they did, with the hounds of the right-wing press already baying after them. George Sokolsky, a Hearst columnist, was particularly interested in Bogart, demanding in print why he had joined this misguided crusade. "It was suggested to Bogie," Miss Bacall somewhat guardedly recalled, "that he issue a statement saying he was not a Communist and had no sympathy for Communists, and denouncing the unfriendly witnesses. This he refused to do. . . ." Paul Henreid was more blunt: "Bogart gave an interview to the press in which he attempted to retract what he had said and done. 'I didn't know the people I was with were fellow travelers,' he told the reporters. . . . I felt Bogart's statement was a form of betrayal, and it was the end of our friendship." But Bogart also felt betrayed. When the Hollywood celebrities returned home from Washington, there was another meeting at Ira Gershwin's house, and according to a leftist screenwriter named Abe Polonsky, "Bogart was furious. He was shouting at Danny Kaye, 'You fuckers sold me out,' and he left." A few months later, *Photoplay* magazine published under Bogart's byline an article titled "I'm No Communist." Bogart said he had simply been a "dope."

Others went home in other ways. Ronald Reagan, the president of the Screen Actors Guild, returned to Hollywood to discover that his wife wanted no more of him. "I arrived home from the Washington hearing to be told I was leaving," as Reagan rather oddly put it in his memoirs. "I suppose there had been warning signs, if only I hadn't been so busy, but small-town boys grow up thinking only other people get divorced. . . ." Reagan's account is admirably restrained. Miss Wyman, to her credit, has been even more reticent about her separation from the future President. But there had indeed been "warning signs." Ann Sheridan liked both the Reagans, but she sometimes found Ronnie's self-preoccupation a trial. "Ronnie had heard a baseball game and he gave us a play-by-play account," she said about one dinner at the Reagans' home. "After the fourth inning, Jane said, 'Ronnie, please stop, Annie doesn't care about baseball.' But he went on for all nine innings." If a baseball game could so captivate Reagan, one can imagine the amount of talk that the Actors Guild president devoted to union politics. "Don't ask Ronnie what time it is," June Allyson remembered Miss Wyman saying, "because he will tell you how a watch is made."

"I always thought Jane and Ronnie Reagan were one of the best-balanced, merriest, feet-on-the-ground couples around town," Hedda Hopper gushed in *Modern Screen*. "There are some differences in their temperament, of course. Ronnie's easygoing; Jane's high-strung. But only lately have these things mattered. . . . Last June, Jane's baby was born, three months too soon. She didn't live. Jane should never have started work on any picture as soon as she did after her family tragedy. In *Johnny Belinda,* Jane tackled a job that would test a Bernhardt. . . . By the time she wobbled off the last scene, she looked like a ghost, her eyes large in their sockets."

The implication was that Miss Wyman should have stayed in bed, but her performance as a deaf-mute in *Johnny Belinda* was superb. It also won her an Oscar, which was not overwhelmingly important *sub specie aeternitatis* but had its inevitable effect on a Hollywood household. " 'If this comes to a divorce,' sighed Ronnie, with bitter humor," according to Mrs. Hopper, " 'I think I'll name *Johnny Belinda* co-respondent.' "

Back at the Washington hearings, the Hollywood writers talked on. Albert Maltz, who had worked on *This Gun for Hire, Destination Tokyo,* and *Pride of the Marines,* arrived with a prepared statement, and Thomas, as usual, insisted on reading it in advance. Maltz responded by asking whether Thomas had asked to read a statement by Gerald L. K. Smith, the notorious anti-Semite, before letting him read it. Thomas equivocated, then, surprisingly, let Maltz read. "I am an American," Maltz recited, "and I believe there is no more proud word in the vocabulary of man." And so on. "I would rather die," he concluded, "than be a shabby American, groveling before men whose names are Thomas and Rankin, but who now carry out activities in America like those carried out in Germany by Goebbels and Himmler. The American people are going to have to choose between the Bill of Rights and the Thomas Committee. They cannot have both." When Stripling finally got a chance to ask whether Maltz belonged to the Screen Writers Guild, Maltz answered by saying, "Next you are going to ask me what religious group I belong to." Instead, Thomas next said, "Excuse the witness. No more questions. Typical Communist line."

Alvah Bessie, whose screenwriting credits involved nothing more distinguished than some Errol Flynn epics, *Northern Pursuit* and *Objective Burma,* also arrived with a statement. The committee asked him to read just "the first couple of paragraphs," letting the rest be entered silently into the record. Asked, then, whether he was a Communist, Bessie archly pointed out that General Dwight Eisenhower, who was being courted by both Democrats and Republicans as a presidential candidate, had refused to divulge which party he belonged to, if any. "What is good enough for General Eisenhower is good enough for me," Bessie said. After each of these evasive witnesses had been heard, the committee called on one of its investigators to read aloud all the documentary evidence that had been discovered, ranging from the number of the witness's Communist Party card to his signature on various public appeals and petitions.

Samuel Ornitz, a paunchy man already in his late fifties, and already afflicted with cancer, blamed his summons on anti-Semitism. "I wish to address this committee as a Jew . . ." he announced, in the opening statement that he was not allowed to read. "It may be redundant to repeat that anti-Semitism and anti-Communism were the number one poison weapon used by Hitler—but still terribly relevant, lest we forget."

Herbert Biberman engaged Thomas in another shouting match:

BIBERMAN: It has become very clear to me that the real purpose of this investigation—

THOMAS *(pounding gavel):* That is not an answer to the question—

BIBERMAN: —is to drive a wedge—

THOMAS *(pounding gavel):* That is not the question *(pounding gavel).*

BIBERMAN: —into the component parts—

THOMAS *(pounding gavel):* Not the question—

BIBERMAN: —of the motion picture industry.

THOMAS *(pounding gavel):* Ask him the next question.

Edward Dmytryk and Adrian Scott, who had attracted considerable attention by directing and producing *Crossfire,* one of Hollywood's first movies on anti-Semitism, did their best to lecture the committee on civil liberties. Ring Lardner, Jr., by contrast, tried to introduce a characteristic touch of humor. Asked the inevitable question, he started by saying, "I could answer exactly the way you want, Mr. Chairman—"

THOMAS: It is not a question of our wanting you to answer that. It is a very simple question. Anybody would be proud to answer it—any real American. . . .

LARDNER: It depends on the circumstances. I could answer it, but if I did, I would hate myself in the morning.

THOMAS: Leave the witness chair.

The last of the Hollywood Ten, Lester Cole, proved as evasive and abusive as all the others. "This committee is waging a cold war on democracy," he declared in the statement he was not allowed to read. Then Lardner and Cole, like the others, were cited for contempt of Congress. And then the committee summoned the man who turned out to be its last witness, the eleventh of the Hollywood Ten. "Mr. Brecht," said Stripling, "will you please state your full name and present address for the record, please? Speak into the microphone."

"My name is Bertolt Brecht . . ." said Bertolt Brecht. He was wearing a neat dark suit that had been given to him five years earlier by a Los Angeles tailor named Samuel Bernstein, who had encountered him at a reading of Yiddish poetry (including Yiddish translations of Brecht), and, not realizing that the poet's worn clothes expressed his deliberate efforts to make himself look proletarian, had sent Brecht in the mail his own wedding suit, even offering to make any necessary alterations, at no charge. (Bernstein duly received Brecht's letter of thanks, saying that the suit fit him perfectly.) Brecht always looked a bit like a raccoon, or a fox, sharp-eyed, wary, quick, but never more so than now. He also smoked one of his cheap cigars. "I was born in Augsburg, Germany, February 10, 1898," he said.

The committee seemed strangely unready for him. "What was that date again?" Thomas asked, as though he had missed something important.

"Would you give that date again?" asked Stripling. The date was repeated. Representative John McDowell echoed it: "1898?" Brecht repeated it: "1898." The committee then offered Brecht an interpreter, David Baumgardt, a consultant in philosophy at the Library of Congress, and Stripling resumed his interrogation: "You were born in Augsburg, Bavaria, Germany, on February 10, 1888, is that correct?" Brecht docilely agreed to the misstatement. One of the attorneys, Bartley Crum, intervened to say that it was 1898. Brecht agreed again. "Is it '88 or '98?" Stripling asked once more. "Ninety-eight," Brecht said.

Perhaps he had already realized by now that these interrogators would not be difficult to outwit. One of Brecht's friends later remarked that the whole session resembled a zoologist being cross-examined by apes. But if the apes were notable for their blundering ignorance, the zoologist was no less notable for his dissembling, his mixture of lies and equivocations, his pretense of not understanding English combined with a pretense of desiring to please. Thus:

STRIPLING: Have you attended any Communist Party meetings?

BRECHT: No, I don't think so. . . .

THOMAS: Well, aren't you certain?

BRECHT: No—I am certain, yes.

THOMAS: You are certain you have never been to Communist Party meetings?

BRECHT: Yes, I think so. . . .

THOMAS: You are certain?

BRECHT: I think I am certain.

THOMAS: You think you are certain?

BRECHT: Yes, I have not attended such meetings, in my opinion.

And so on. If Brecht was disingenuous on such simple matters as party meetings, he was Byzantine on the matter of his own works. For some reason, perhaps his interest in the Eislers, Stripling was particularly curious about *The Measures Taken,* an indisputably Communist play that attempted to justify the murder of a party worker who had failed to carry out his assignment. Brecht began by saying that what he had written was just "the adaptation of an old religious Japanese play . . . which shows the devotion for an idea until death." Stripling insisted on what he considered the basic question: "Mr. Brecht, may I interrupt you? Would you consider the play to be pro-Communist or anti-Communist, or would it take a neutral position regarding Communists?" Brecht sidestepped: "No, I would say—you see, literature has the right and the duty to give the public the ideas of the time. Now, in this play —of course, I wrote about twenty plays—but in this play I tried to express the feelings and the ideas of the German workers who then fought against Hitler. I also formulated in an artistic—"

STRIPLING: Fighting against Hitler, did you say?

BRECHT: Yes.

In the midst of this esoteric discussion of the meaning of a play that none of Brecht's interrogators had read, Brecht adopted the bizarre tactic of deliberately confusing *The Measures Taken* with *The Yea-Sayer,* a slightly earlier and considerably less authoritarian version of a similar story. Asked about the plot of one play, he answered by describing the other, reasonably confident that the committee wouldn't know the difference. Rightly so, for Stripling soon veered off into the question of how many times Brecht had been to Moscow. J. Parnell Thomas was beginning to weary of it all. "Mr. Stripling, can we hurry this along?" he said. "We have a very heavy schedule this afternoon."

But Stripling kept floundering. He had found in *The People* a song by

Brecht and Eisler that struck him as subversive: "You must be ready to take over; men on the dole, learn it; men in the prisons, learn it; women in the kitchen, learn it. . . ." Brecht challenged the translation, and the interpreter supported him. *Führung* was the word, and the interpreter claimed that it meant not "you must take over" but "you must take the lead." J. Parnell Thomas was beginning to lose his temper at all these thick Germanic quibblings in thick Germanic accents. "I cannot understand the interpreter any more than I can the witness," he complained.

Brecht's admirers have claimed that the poet defeated the committee by outfoxing it, by leading it into obscure byways and escaping every attempt to trap him. But the fact is that he escaped only by denying himself. Was he a member of the Communist Party? Brecht answered Stripling's inevitable question by saying that he had heard his Hollywood "colleagues" declare such questions "not proper," but he, Brecht, was "a guest in this country," and so he would answer as fully as he could: "I was not a member, or am not a member, of any Communist Party." Maybe that was true, but when Stripling went on to ask Brecht whether his plays had been "based on the philosophy of Marx and Lenin," Brecht denied much of what he had thought and written and argued for at least twenty years. "No, I don't think that is quite correct," he said. He acknowledged only that as a playwright concerned with history, he "had to study Marx's ideas about history." Stripling made one last try: "Have you ever made application to join the Communist Party?" Brecht's denial was worthy of Saint Peter: "No, no, no, no, no, never."

J. Parnell Thomas thanked Brecht as "a good example," and so the hearings adjourned, and Brecht was reprieved. And he felt, once again, ashamed. "In the cab, returning to the hotel," Lester Cole recalled, "Brecht grieved; he wondered whether any of us would ever understand and forgive him. Alone in this country, a foreigner, they could hold him, as they did Gerhart Eisler, under one of the Alien Registration Acts in prison for how long—? He wanted to go home. . . . I put an arm around him. Little comfort. At the hotel he explained. The others did understand."

Brecht also understood that he had not only lied but been a coward, not only been a coward but lied. That was what *The Measures Taken* had been about: what makes a man fail his comrades, and what must be done about it. As a playwright, Brecht had been stern; as a witness, he pleaded for understanding and forgiveness. This was what *Galileo* was about, too. What should a man do when, as Galileo put it, "they showed me the instruments?" They had not even shown Brecht the instruments—in fact, there had not really been any instruments to show—but Brecht had recanted anyway, and confessed whatever needed to be confessed. No, no, no, no, no, never.

Brecht's main concern now was to get out of America. Despite all his willingness to oblige the authorities, he still felt threatened, and besides, he had already bought his tickets. The day of his testimony, he fled from Washington to New York with Joseph Losey and T. Edward Hambleton, who were much involved with the prospective New York production of *Galileo,* but what did Brecht care about that now? On October 31, 1947, his last day in America, Brecht met Laughton, who had grown a beard for his role. Should a Brechtian actor playing the role of a bearded man wear a real beard? Probably not, but the main question on Laughton's mind was whether Brecht's testimony before the Un-American Activities Committee would make it dangerous for Laughton to play Brecht's *Galileo*. Brecht's fawning testimony apparently made it all right. Laughton was relieved. Brecht only wanted to get out. In the evening of October 31, he climbed aboard an Air France plane bound for Paris.

• • •

When J. Parnell Thomas adjourned his hearings that Friday afternoon, he wanted to make it clear that the adjournment was not indefinite, that the committee would "resume hearings as soon as possible." Earlier that week, Thomas had declared that his committee had "not been swayed, intimidated or influenced by either Hollywood glamour, pressure groups, threats, ridicule or high-pressure tactics on the part of high-paid puppets and apologists for the motion picture industry." Now he wanted to proclaim that he knew of seventy-nine "prominent" Hollywood figures who were Communists or "had records of Communist affiliations." The committee had heard eleven, but "there are sixty-eight to go." For some mysterious reason, though, the hearings stopped. Waldo Salt, who was scheduled to be the next witness after Brecht, did not testify until 1951.

The leftist witnesses returned to Hollywood in a state of considerable euphoria. Some five hundred cheering supporters welcomed them at the Los Angeles airport, where Lardner made a brief speech saying that the fight must go on. The leaders of the Committee for the First Amendment announced ten more national radio broadcasts. And since the studios took no action against any of the ten hostile witnesses, they considered themselves secure, well protected. As a first step in their defense, they expected a leftist victory in the imminent elections at the Screen Writers Guild. One of the major issues was the Taft-Hartley Act, which had taken effect that summer and required all union officers to file a non-Communist affidavit. The leftists in the SWG promised to fight against the Taft-Hartley requirements. To their surprise, they were soundly defeated in the guild elections of November 20. Two of the unfriendly witnesses, Lester Cole and Gordon Kahn, lost their places on the executive board.

On the day of the SWG elections, Eric Johnston denounced the hostile witnesses in *The Hollywood Reporter*. He said they had done a "tremendous disservice" to the film industry, and he urged the industry itself to "take positive steps to meet this problem." Johnston himself was already organizing those steps. On November 24, J. Parnell Thomas asked Congress to cite the Ten for contempt, Nixon made one of the main speeches in support of the move, and Congress voted in favor by a lopsided 347 to 17. That same day, Johnston presided over a meeting of about fifty of Hollywood's chief executives and producers in one of the public rooms at the Waldorf-Astoria hotel in New York. They were all there, Mayer and both the Schenck brothers, the Warner brothers, the Cohn brothers, Y. Frank Freeman and Barney Balaban of Paramount, Peter Rathvon of RKO, Sam Goldwyn and Walter Wanger, and, as the industry's new legal adviser, there was the former secretary of state and former Supreme Court justice James F. Byrnes.

The problem, said Johnston, was how the movie business as a whole should deal with Communist employees, specifically with the ten witnesses who were now being cited, this very day, for contempt of Congress. His own answer was that they should all be fired. Already there were scattered boycotts and demonstrations in California and Kansas and North Carolina against pictures that involved the ten. The American Legion was threatening a nationwide boycott. The press had originally seemed critical of the House committee, but now it was turning against Hollywood. Two studios, Fox and RKO, had already decided to fire the three witnesses who worked for them (Lardner at Fox, Dmytryk and Scott at RKO), and now it was time for the studios to act together. "I . . . said that, in my opinion, these men would have to make up their minds . . ." Johnston himself later testified. "They would have to fish or cut bait."

Mayer and a few others offered some rumblings of patriotic support. The only one who spoke up against Johnston's plan was Sam Goldwyn.* Dore Schary, the onetime scriptwriter who was now chief of production at RKO, recalled that Goldwyn "was bold enough to suggest that there was an air of panic in the room. Goldwyn, ramrod straight, bald headed, and with a slightly Oriental slant to his eyes, spoke sarcastically and irritated Johnston, who responded with an angry speech . . . asking us whether we were mice or men." Schary said that he now joined Goldwyn, arguing that nobody had yet been convicted of anything, that there was no law against being a Communist, and that, as he put it, "we would dishonor . . . our industry by an action that would inevitably lead to a blacklist." Goldwyn spoke up again and angrily declared that he "would not be allied to any such nonsense as that proposed by Johnston." Walter Wanger also opposed the dismissal of the ten witnesses, and so did M-G-M's Eddie Mannix, who pointed out that there was a California state law against firing anyone because of his political views.

That provoked a remarkable response from the eminent Jimmy Byrnes. He doubted, he said, that any government official "would argue with the decision of the industry to get rid of 'Reds.' " Besides, the "morals clause" in the standard Hollywood contract, which permitted any studio to fire just about anyone for just about anything, could certainly be invoked against the ten. Johnston responded to Byrnes's cue by angrily throwing his hotel room key down on the table and threatening to resign unless the producers supported his proposals.

"No vote was ever taken," Schary recalled. "It was Johnston's threat plus

* Goldwyn and Mayer had disliked each other for years. According to Gary Carey's history of M-G-M, *All the Stars in Heaven,* "their simmering hostility, dating back to the days when Goldwyn was peddling Lasky–Famous Artists films and Mayer was an exhibitor-distributor, erupted one afternoon in the thirties when they chased each other around in the locker room of the Hillcrest Country Club, swapping insults and swatting towels at each other's bottoms."

Byrnes's argument that had won the decision to discharge those cited."
Schary, Goldwyn, and Wanger opposed the decision to the end, but they were
only three among fifty. The majority chose a committee to concoct the necessary statement to the world, a statement proclaiming that Hollywood believed
passionately in free speech and civil liberties but would banish all Communists, that it was indomitably independent but also eager to please. The committee was nicely balanced: Mayer and the pardonend ex-convict Joseph
Schenck for the establishment, Wanger and Schary for the powerless opposition, with Mendel Silberberg, a longtime attorney for the producers, as chairman. Schary said later that he had balked at this honor, but that Goldwyn
urged him on with a whisper: "Do it—maybe they won't go crazy."

Craziness was hardly the committee's plan. It started by announcing that
the producers "deplored" the behavior of the ten cited witnesses. The producers did not want "to prejudge their legal rights," they said, but their actions
"have been a disservice to their employers and have impaired their usefulness
to the industry." Therefore, without any prejudgments of the witnesses'
rights, they were all being fired. "We will forthwith discharge or suspend
without compensation those in our employ, and we will not re-employ any of
the ten until such time as he is acquitted or has purged himself of contempt
and declares under oath that he is not a Communist," said the document that
came to be known as the Waldorf Statement. "On the broader issue of alleged
subversive and disloyal elements in Hollywood . . . we will not knowingly
employ a Communist or a member of any party or group which advocates the
overthrow of the government of the United States. . . . We are frank to recognize that such a policy involves dangers and risks. There is the danger of
hurting innocent people. There is the risk of creating an atmosphere of fear.
We will guard against this danger, this risk, this fear."

So it was done. M-G-M simply suspended the $1,250 per week contract
that Eddie Mannix had so grandly given Lester Cole scarcely a month earlier.
The studio not only suspended Dalton Trumbo's $3,000 per week but refused
to pay him $60,000 due him for work already completed. (Both Trumbo and
Cole sued M-G-M and eventually won a $125,000 settlement.) At 20th Cen-
tury–Fox, Darryl Zanuck could not bring himself to dismiss Lardner, who
was not only very talented but very likable. The producer announced, as
Lardner recalled, "that he would still respect my contract until commanded
otherwise by his board of directors. His board promptly met in New York and
so commanded." Characteristically, Zanuck avoided telling Lardner himself
and sent a lieutenant. "I was reached," Lardner said, "at a meeting with Otto
[Preminger] in his office and requested to leave the premises, which I did."
(Fox, too, eventually had to pay off to settle Lardner's suit.)

When the RKO board voted for the dismissal of Scott and Dmytryk, who
had recently produced and directed the successful *Crossfire*, Dore Schary did
his best to avoid responsibility. First he argued against the dismissal, then he
asked that his nay vote be recorded in the minutes, then he said that he
"would not execute the order to fire Scott and Dmytryk." Board Chairman

Floyd Odlum "was patient," Schary said. He turned to President Peter Rathvon and "told Rathvon to do the firing." Rathvon obliged. "Rathvon called Scott and me into his office and asked us once more to recant and to purge ourselves," Dmytryk recalled. "With hardly any sense of martyrdom at all, we refused. In that case, he informed us, we were no longer employees of RKO. So much for ironclad contracts. We went back to clean out our respective offices. The next day was Thanksgiving. Even a B writer wouldn't have dared that bit of bathos. . . ."

It is still unclear why the Hollywood executives, who had so recently seemed so impervious to the molestations of the Un-American Activities Committee, should have surrendered so soon and so abjectly. The easy answer, often proposed without much evidence, is that the decision was made by the money men in New York, both the executives at the film corporations' headquarters and the banks and other financial interests that supported them. Studio bosses like Mayer or Zanuck were bosses only in Hollywood. Their own bosses in New York attached less importance to the filmmakers' cherished independence when they weighed it against declining box office receipts and the threats of political boycotts.

Not only were the New York executives a bit remote from the actual filmmaking process but they also had to maintain their standing among still more remote financial allies. Warner Bros. had close connections with J. P. Morgan; 20th Century–Fox with New York Trust, General Foods, and Pan Am; RKO with United Fruit and National Can. Zanuck told Philip Dunne that he had "fought" against firing Lardner, but that "the actual decision had been made on Wall Street, by the money men who bankrolled the movie companies."

This may well be true, but it is also true that anonymous Wall Street forces provide a convenient scapegoat both for liberal commentators and for the timorous Hollywood executives themselves. What would have happened if just one of the studio bosses had refused to accept the punishment of the ten witnesses—or the scores of colleagues who later followed them onto the black-list—remains unknowable. It is quite possible, though, that the Waldorf Statement was produced simply because Eric Johnston was the only man in that roomful of anxious producers who had a definite plan of what should be done and was ready to resign to get his way. It is also quite possible, of course, that Johnston was acting not out of any personal conviction ("I will never be a party to anything as un-American as a blacklist," he had said) but simply as the well-paid representative of those same distant Wall Street interests.

Scarcely a week after the purge of the ten, a Philadelphia organization called the Golden Slipper Square Dance Club staged a dinner to present its annual humanitarian award to the makers of *Crossfire*. Scott and Dmytryk could hardly accept the award since they had just been fired. Schary was invited to receive it, but he couldn't bring himself to go. So it was Eric Johnston who went to be saluted for humanitarianism. On accepting the award, he boldly declared that Hollywood was free from all forms of discrimination. "Hollywood," said the father of the blacklist, "has held the door of opportunity open to every man and woman who could meet its technical and artistic standards. . . . What [our industry] is interested in is his skill or talent, ability to produce pictures for the joy and progress of mankind."

• • •

Once Bert Brecht was back in Europe, he could say anything, and anything he said became Brechtian. Gone and forgotten (except, probably, by Brecht) were all the humiliations of life in Santa Monica, the unanswered telephone calls to M-G-M, the struggles to pay the rent, the rejected scripts, the obligation to obey the curfew on enemy aliens—the obscurity, the terrible obscurity in the capital of celebrity. But now, having capitulated and fled, he could pose as a political martyr. "When they accused me of wanting to steal the Empire State Building," he rather grandly said to Donald Ogden Stewart, himself a political refugee, "I thought it was high time to leave."

Everything called him back to Berlin, but Berlin was now a divided and occupied city, and if Brecht could remember the humiliations of Santa Monica, he could also remember the humiliations of being a refugee in Moscow. He went and established himself in Zurich, a good place to make plans, a good place from which to negotiate. He negotiated a contract to adapt and direct *Antigone,* with his talented wife, Helene Weigel, who had been little more than a cook and housekeeper in Hollywood, as the star. He negotiated himself a lucrative publishing contract with the West German firm of Suhrkamp, and a Swiss bank account in which to store the incoming royalties. He even negotiated himself an Austrian passport, by promising (and then reneging on his promise) to produce a Marxist *Everyman* for the Salzburg Festival. "He was wearing his convict's face again," the Swiss writer Max Frisch observed of those days, "little beady bird's eyes sticking out from a flat face above a too-bare neck. A frightening face. . . . One felt like giving him a muffler for his neck."

It took a year of negotiations before Brecht was ready to go to Berlin, and by then the Russian blockade was under way. He went over to the side of the blockaders to negotiate a production of *Mother Courage* in the Soviet sector, again with Miss Weigel as the star. The following summer, in June of 1949, Brecht returned permanently to Berlin to direct his own theater company, the Berliner Ensemble, in his own theater, the Schiffbauerdamm, where his *Threepenny Opera* had opened back in 1928. There he remained, a willing captive among unwilling captives, and when the workers of East Berlin rose in rebellion, and fought Soviet tanks with rocks, Brecht issued a statement in support of the Stalinist regime. He had his Swiss bank account now, his Austrian passport, and his own theater company. But in a poem dated 1953, the year of the revolt, he wondered about his belated success:

> I sit by the roadside
> The driver changes the wheel.

I do not like the place I have come from.
I do not like the place I am going to.
Why with impatience do I
Watch him changing the wheel?

Louis B. Mayer, nearing the end at M-G-M, married Lorena Danker.

10

PREJUDICE

(1948)

The first time Dore Schary met Louis B. Mayer, shortly before the war, the head of M-G-M impressed the cherubic young writer as a man who "radiated power—physical and psychological." And then there was all that Melvillean whiteness. Mayer's office, as Lillian Ross later described it, had walls of white leather, an enormous white desk with four white telephones, a white bar, a white grand piano, and a white fireplace with white andirons. Behind the great man's desk stood an American flag and a number of photographs of his eminent friends, the most prominent being Herbert Hoover, Cardinal Spellman and J. Edgar Hoover. "He held out a hand, short fingered and well manicured," Schary recalled, "then settled into his chair sideways. . . ."

Schary had been working at M-G-M for seven years, had written several successful films, notably *Boys Town* (1938) and *Young Tom Edison* (1940), and now he wanted to try directing. Mayer raised various objections. Somehow, the talk veered onto the subject of low-budget B pictures, a subject of relatively little concern in Mayer's empire. Schary professed great interest. "I believe that low-cost pictures should dare—should challenge—" he proclaimed, according to his own account. Mayer was so impressed by Schary's heavy-breathing enthusiasm that he summoned him back the next day and took him, without explanation, to the Hollywood Park racetrack, where they watched one of Mayer's horses lose. Then Mayer offered Schary the job of overseeing all of the studio's B pictures, eighteen per year. Schary gasped, went home to consult his wife, and then agreed.

There was just one problem: Harry Rapf. "I'll put Harry Rapf with you to bother about budgets," Mayer said. "He'll have nothing to do with the pictures. He's doing nothing—he'll be grateful." That was a promise of trouble. Rapf was one of M-G-M's embarrassments. A graying man with a long, mournful nose, Rapf had once owned a share of the studio, but he had been squeezed out during the reorganizational power plays of the 1920's. He had then been the studio manager, supervising all the routine pictures that paid for Thalberg's more pretentious extravagances. Demoted once again, to working as one producer among many, Rapf tyrannized over everyone assigned to his projects. He had fired an obscure young writer named Dore Schary not once but twice. Now the reborn Schary went to see him, to tell him that Mayer wanted them to work together, and he found that Mayer had already called. "He got up and said, 'L.B. just told me,' " Schary recalled. "Then he started to cry, the tears tumbling out of his pale blue eyes. He told me how grateful he was to me for accepting this new arrangement, and as he went on my embarrassment permitted only short responses—'It's okay,' 'Don't worry,' 'It's going to be all right,' 'Let's have no tears.' "

Schary soon proved a success on his B pictures, enriching M-G-M from such modest outlays as the $400,000 invested in *Lassie Come Home* (1943). But the grateful Harry Rapf could not resist interfering, first asking about scripts, then offering opinions. During one showing of daily rushes of new film by two of Schary's young discoveries, Jules Dassin and Fred Zinnemann, Rapf buzzed the projectionist to stop the film and then announced, "These rushes are lousy. I wouldn't let these two guys direct traffic."

Schary shooed everyone else out of the projection room, including the criticized directors. "Then I turned to their critic," Schary said, "and asked what the hell and why the hell." Rapf retorted that he "wasn't an office boy" and "used to own part of this studio." Schary snapped back that he, Schary, had been given complete control of all B pictures. "We'll see about that," Rapf said as he walked out.

Schary was dismayed to learn shortly afterward that Rapf had left to spend the weekend with Mayer. What would the embittered old man tell the great overlord? Schary worried. To counteract whatever Rapf might say to Mayer, Schary told his own side of the story to Eddie Mannix. On Monday, when Schary came to work expecting a confrontation, he was amazed to hear from Mayer that Rapf had never mentioned any quarrels during their pleasant weekend. Mannix had already informed Mayer about the row, however, and now Mayer summoned Rapf on the intercom. "Get up here right away, now!" he snarled.

Schary anticipated unpleasantness, but he was unprepared for Mayer's wild explosion. No sooner had Rapf entered the white-on-white office than Mayer began shouting at him.

"Goddammit, Harry, you spent a weekend with me and never breathed a word. Mannix told me all about it. You stupid kike bastard—you ought to kiss this man's shoes—get on your knees."

Schary was horrified. He lurched to his feet, hoping to make peace. ("Through the years I had heard many of the top-drawer Jewish studio executives lose their tempers at meetings or in card games and I was always dismayed when one of the first pejorative terms they used was 'kike'—usually 'dirty kike.' ") Mayer waved him back into his chair. Rapf didn't say a word. He just stood there and took it. Schary began feeling sick. "Mayer kept pummelling Rapf with curses," Schary said, "and then L.B. suddenly pointed a finger at Rapf and declared, 'Get out of here, you're fired, get out of your office. You had your last chance, you son of a bitch.' Rapf turned and hurried out."

Schary also hurried out. He stumbled into the nearest executive wash-room and threw up. Then he began feeling remorse, not about his degradation but about his victory. He told Mayer that he wanted Rapf reinstated, that he himself would resign if Rapf were so harshly expelled. Mayer told him not to be foolish, told him that he had to learn to be tough. "If you have to cut, cut fast, finish it quick," Mayer said. Schary still insisted on Rapf's reinstatement, so Mayer shrugged and acquiesced.

He had bigger problems. War seemed imminent. Then Pearl Harbor was attacked. When Mayer gathered his shoals of executives for a pre-Christmas lunch, he told them that they would all have to rededicate themselves to the national struggle. "Many of our young men will be going to war and some will die," Mayer said. "But we who stay at home must help all we can. Please join now in a toast, to our president—Nicholas Schenck."

In contrast to Mayer's concentration on the M-G-M corporate powers, Schary kept having significant thoughts, geopolitical thoughts. He wanted to make a movie that only he could describe: "I was going to tell the story of Hitler, Churchill, Mussolini, and the United States as an American Western epic. The locale was to be a large Western territory; the shape of the area looked a bit like Europe. The time was a few years after the Civil War. Hitler, Goebbels, and Goering were to be three escaped convicts. . . ." To "work with me" on this prospective disaster, Schary wanted a writer of appropriate celebrity, and he managed to snare Sinclair Lewis. After months of collaboration, the two of them produced a script entitled "Storm in the West." Mayer hated it. Not because it was pretentious and absurd but because, as Schary put it, "there were too many other war movies." So the idea was bucked to New York, to Nicholas Schenck, and Schenck was not interested either.

So Schary walked out. That was characteristic of the man, of his youthful abilities and his youthful confidence in those abilities. Mayer was incredulous. Had anyone in Hollywood ever resigned from a major executive position, from a salary of fifteen hundred dollars a week, at the age of thirty-eight, just because one of his scripts had been rejected? "You've got another job," Mayer said, accusingly. Schary denied it. He just wanted to leave.

David Selznick promptly hired Schary as an autonomous producer, at his hard-won rate of fifteen hundred dollars per week, plus 15 percent of the profits of any pictures he made. Schary's first project was a romance about a shell-shocked soldier home on leave. Selznick sent Schary one of his long memos, denouncing the script, forbidding his autonomous producer to produce it. Schary once again resigned. Selznick consulted his wife, Irene, who said, "Schary is right. You made a bargain—you ought to keep it."

Under the title *I'll Be Seeing You* (1945), Schary's first "independent" project grossed seven million dollars. He followed that with a string of successes: *The Spiral Staircase, The Bachelor and the Bobby-Soxer, The Farmer's Daughter,* the last of which won an Oscar for Loretta Young as the best actress of 1947. Then RKO's production chief, Charles Koerner, suddenly sickened and died of leukemia, and RKO president Peter Rathvon took Schary out to lunch and offered him the job. Schary declined, citing his contract with Selznick, but Selznick ridiculed his scruples. "Don't worry about me," he said. "They'll pay a good price for you—I'll make my deal with them."

One of the first projects confronting Schary at RKO was the script of a novel entitled *The Brick Foxhole,* by Peter Brooks. Edward Dmytryk, the writer-director, later described it as "a loose, rambling story of the frustrations of stateside soldiers at the end of the war," in which one of several subplots "concerned the murder of a homosexual by a sadistic bigot." The whole subject of homosexuality was outlawed by the Johnston Office censors, of course, but Adrian Scott, the producer who had optioned the novel, had what Dmytryk called "an inspiration." What if the homosexual victim was made a heterosexual Jew? This was not an equation of vilified minorities that was likely to occur to any Jew, but Scott and Dmytryk were both Gentiles, and they thought that an attack on anti-Semitism would be a commendable project. "Adrian discussed it with our friend Dore Schary," Dmytryk wrote of the first explorations, when Schary was still working for Selznick, "and Schary advised him against it."

Schary naturally remembered things differently. He said that Rathvon, Koerner, and other RKO executives had all rejected the project, now retitled *Crossfire,* but that he vowed to make it one of his first productions. RKO business executives took polls, which showed that less than 10 percent of a typical audience wanted to see such a film. The influential American Jewish Committee, publishers of *Commentary,* urged the studio to halt the production, or change the Jew to a black. Warner Bros. even announced that the picture would not be shown in any Warners theater. Schary did persist, though. He also helped assemble a good cast, notably Robert Ryan as the psychotic killer. So *Crossfire,* which asserted somewhat heavily that it was wrong to murder an American soldier just because he was a Jew, achieved a small-scale but apparently surprising commercial success.*

Schary had a remarkable knack for making the obvious seem fresh. Quite apart from *Crossfire,* the RKO of 1947 blossomed with films of inspiration and good cheer: *I Remember Mama, Sister Kenny, Mr. Blandings Builds His Dream House.* Schary also committed himself to yet another story of wartime heroism, *Battleground.* "By then," Schary later wrote of this period, "I had also traded Theodore Dreiser's melancholy *Sister Carrie* to William Wyler and Paramount for their priority right to *Ivanhoe.*"

Melancholy was obviously not Schary's style, but despite his cheery successes, RKO kept losing money. The melancholy statistics on 1947 amounted to a loss of nearly $2 million. The chief stockholder, Floyd Odlum, was not a movie man but a rancher and flier, someone who liked to maneuver money. After a series of secret nighttime rendezvous in parked cars and obscure way stations, he agreed to sell the whole of RKO, including the production studio with its 2,000 employees, plus 124 movie theaters, for the sum of exactly $8,825,690 to that dark nemesis Howard Hughes.

---

* One surprising critic was Charlie Chaplin. In a discussion with the blacklisted Alvah Bessie, who was trying in vain to sell him on the idea of filming a modern Don Quixote in Franco Spain, Chaplin referred to *Crossfire* as an anti-Semitic picture. "I asked him why he felt that way," Bessie reported, and he said, 'You remember Sam Levene, the way he played the part'; his face changed; he assumed the stance; and he gestured, 'washing' his hands. Inventing words to illustrate what he felt Levene's interpretation of the role of the Jewish victim implied, he said obsequiously, 'Why're you picking on me? I'm a nice feller; really, I'm a nice feller . . .' It was a shattering performance."

Dore Schary was appalled. He complained to Rathvon about the secret dealings, and Rathvon arranged a meeting in the garden behind his own house. "I hear you want to quit," Hughes said as a greeting. "If I were rich and bought a studio, I'd want to run it," Schary said, according to his own account. "But you don't need me at my price simply to deliver your orders."

"You can run the studio," Hughes said, according to another version. "I haven't got any time."

So Schary, who had quit Mayer and quit Selznick to assert his independence, and then found reasons of high principle not to quit when the RKO board fired Scott and Dmytryk as un-American, now found reasons not to quit when Howard Hughes acquired control. Then he began learning that nothing Hughes said could ever be trusted. "Studio personnel told me that Hughes was coming to the studio late at night to see the daily rushes," Schary recalled. "Scripts were being sent to him; he was examining payrolls. After all, he now owned the entire spread and wanted to know what was doing on the range."

Once Hughes knew what was doing on the range, of course, he wanted to make changes. He started telephoning Schary late at night to give orders. He wanted to halt work on one of Schary's favorite projects, *Battleground.* People were tired of war movies, Hughes said. He also wanted a young actress named Barbara Bel Geddes fired. The storm of phone calls showed Schary his future. So he once again resigned. So did Rathvon. Hughes took over.

Schary almost immediately received a call from Louis B. Mayer. The nation's most highly paid executive was in deep trouble—deeper than he realized—and so was M-G-M, so was the whole movie business. Some experts thought that the audiences had changed since the war. People had become more serious, it was said, more sophisticated, less willing to accept the superficial and essentially mindless pictures that kept rolling off the M-G-M assembly line. (Esther Williams, a handsome swimmer with no talent on dry land, was now the studio's biggest box office attraction.) Other experts thought that people were tired of the movies themselves. They were now free to spend their time and money on travel, clothes, sports, whatever they regarded as the good life.

The most lethal competition, though, came from the new fad called television. At the end of the war, there had been only 6,500 TV sets in existence, mostly in bars, and there was nothing much to see on them. By 1948, the number of sets had climbed past one million; it would quadruple in 1949, then triple in 1950, to more than eleven million. The number of commercial broadcasters increased from seven to seventeen in 1947, and to forty-one in 1948, and the FCC authorized seventy more. Smart operators began combining stations into networks. The availability of TV transmission cables along the East Coast inspired both political parties to hold their 1948 presidential conventions in Philadelphia. Milton Berle became a national celebrity on Tuesday night's Texaco Star Theatre, and then came the Kraft Television Theatre, the Philco Television Playhouse, the Alcoa Theatre, the General Electric Theatre (which would soon feature Ronald Reagan). What was visible on the ten-inch screen was not the "vital, thinking men's blockbusters" that Darryl Zanuck had said the postwar audiences would want, but it was all available in the living room (or bar), and, most important of all, it was free.

Millions of people suddenly stopped going to the movies. Attendance sank from eighty million per week in 1946 to sixty-seven million in 1948 to sixty million in 1950, and it kept sinking. M-G-M, long the biggest and richest studio in Hollywood, suffered grievously from these financial blows. Loew's, Inc., which had earned a gross income of $18 million in the first twelve months after the end of the war, declined to $4 million during the fiscal year from September of 1947 to September of 1948, and that led to a 1947–48 net deficit of $6.5 million. Louis B. Mayer, who was supposed to be the great showman, didn't know what to do, and neither did the company president, Nicholas Schenck. One day in 1948, David Sarnoff of NBC asked to meet Schenck to discuss an alliance, and Schenck politely declined. "I said, 'David, what have you got to offer? We've got the pictures,' " Schenck told Schary some years later, apparently without any realization that he had behaved like a fool. "So the same thing goes today. What have they got to offer?"

One thing Schenck did know was that Mayer could not be left in despotic command of M-G-M. For all his white furniture and his million-dollar salary, Mayer had never actually made a movie, and his lordly dominion over his producers tended to reduce them to subservient creatures whose only aim was to please him. Garson Kanin has provided a telling snapshot of Mayer's vice-presidents and producers assembled in the executive dining room on the top floor of the Thalberg Building. There was one long table, set with expensive linen, silver, china, crystal. "In front of each place was a collection of pill bottles," Kanin recalled. "No executives had less than a dozen. Some had as many as twenty or thirty. Various pills and capsules and drops had to be taken with various types of foods, for all sorts of ailments, some real and some imagined."

Benny Thau, that vice-president who Herman Mankiewicz had said was responsible for informing Mayer of any appearance of the north wind, arrived one day and swept all his pill bottles into a manila envelope. He told the waitress to throw them away, not needed any more. Amid a general buzz of curiosity and concern, Thau ordered knockwurst and sauerkraut, wolfed everything down, then took off his wristwatch and studied it, then interrupted the general conversation by saying, "Excuse me, please." "He unbuttoned his vest, leaned back in his chair," Kanin reported. "Conversation continued. Thau took no part in it. He remained in his strange, withdrawn position for five minutes, then sat up brightly, and said, 'I swear to God, it works.' " When somebody asked what it was that worked, Thau earnestly answered: "This new short-wave radio treatment I'm on. There's this new doctor and I'm on a short-wave with him. After every meal, he sends out these short-waves and they completely digest my food."

But somebody had to get the work done, to produce the movies. The legendary Thalberg, whatever his shortcomings, had actually had ideas about what films should be, which was more than anyone could say of Benny Thau and the other sycophants who clustered around the throne of Louis B. Mayer. Schenck insisted that Mayer discover a new Thalberg, and Mayer, who had secretly hated Thalberg, could only acquiesce. Schenck was the boss, known to many of his underlings as "the general." Mayer started, inevitably, by propositioning his lost son-in-law, Selznick, and Selznick just as inevitably refused. Mayer then tried some even more implausible gambles. He propositioned Walter Wanger, and even Joe Manckiewicz, who had quit M-G-M after the row with Mayer over his affair with Judy Garland. Both of these prospective victims rejected Mayer's advances. Then Mayer (or Schenck) heard that Schary had walked out on Howard Hughes.

Mayer invited Schary to his house and offered him, without any preliminaries, the job of vice-president in charge of production, the same job he himself officially held. Mayer spoke of retiring in a year or two. Then he drifted off, as he usually did, into talking about the old days with Thalberg. "Believe me, [he] was a genius, but he was money mad," Mayer said. "That was his problem. Money—money—that ruined him." Schary had no such problem. All he asked was six thousand dollars a week (this at about the time that Arnold Schoenberg was forced into retirement from UCLA on a pension of $29.60 per month) and complete authority over all the studio's productions. Nick Schenck flew in that weekend, traveling incognito because he was avoiding a summons in some now-forgotten lawsuit, and they sparred a bit over Schary's terms. Mayer later telephoned Schary to tell him not to compromise. "Schenck will give in—he has to—he wants you," Mayer said.

So the deal was made. Schary arrived at M-G-M in June of 1948, bringing along several of his wife's paintings, a bowling trophy, a collection of lead soldiers, and the script of *Battleground,* which he had bought from Hughes. Mayer also disliked *Battleground,* but Schary was in charge now, with Schenck behind him, so he ordered the film into production (and it made a handsome profit). Mayer, playing the role of mentor, warned Schary against Schenck. "Don't trust him," Mayer said. "He'll bring you caviar when you leave New York and flowers in your room when you get back there—but he's only smiles and caviar and roses—and the rest of him is all shit." Mayer also said that he had defended Schary against Westbrook Pegler's view that he was a Communist. "Do you think I'd have a Communist work for me?" he had asked the columnist. "Well, L.B., thanks," Schary answered. "But you know, people get strange ideas. About a month ago, someone I know asked me, 'Dore, how is it that you, a liberal, can work for a fascist?' I put him in his place by defending you."

Well, Schary was a nuisance, but Mayer had other things on his mind. Like romance. There was a Russian-Jewish doctor named Jessie Marmorston who had entered his life in 1942, a specialist in endocrine glands, a dark and handsome and very forceful woman who fascinated him but was not quite what he wanted. He courted a somewhat less forceful dancer, Ann Miller, and a somewhat less forceful singer, Ginny Simms, but neither of them particularly wanted to replace the aging Maggie Mayer, even though the divorce court had certified Mayer's financial vulnerability by ordering him to settle upon his wife the impressive sum of three million dollars. Then, in the midst of selling off all his racehorses, including the one that had thrown him and broken his pelvis, Mayer met a onetime Warner Bros. dancer named Lorena Danker, widow of an advertising man, Danny Danker. Once again, at the age of sixty-three—or was it sixty-six?—he was in love.

In December of 1948, Mayer proposed that they fly to Yuma, Arizona, to be married, all by themselves, away from the Hollywood press. Then came a storm that made all flights impossible, and Mrs. Danker, who was not so demure as some of her predecessors, said, "Now or never." So Mayer and his prospective bride took the train, along with the inevitable Howard Strickling, the publicity man, and Whitey Hendrey, chief of the M-G-M studio police, plus Mrs. Danker's eleven-year-old daughter, Suzanne. They arrived in Yuma at four in the morning, and tried to have breakfast at a motel, and inevitably the reporters and photographers began to assemble. So they finally fled to the office of Sheriff J. A. Beard, where, overlooking the bare yard of the Yuma County Jail, Louis B. Mayer pledged himself to his new wife.

●   ●   ●

"This is a tough one," Dore Schary kept saying on the phone to New York. "But our feeling is to take her out because otherwise you're going to be in a hole—and you won't have a movie."

"Do what you have to do," said Nick Schenck.

What they had to do was solve the problem of Judy Garland, who was practically synonymous with M-G-M's famous musicals—Judy Garland of *The Wizard of Oz* and *Babes in Arms* and *Meet Me in St. Louis.* For that Judy Garland, the studio had bought Irving Berlin's *Annie Get Your Gun,* but the star was by now such a prisoner of her drug addiction and her unreasoning fears that she often could not even get to the studio, and her performances there were nearly worthless. More than one million dollars invested so far, and nothing to show for it. And yet she was still only twenty-six. "Do what you have to do," said Nick Schenck.

By Hollywood standards, M-G-M had been exceptionally sympathetic and understanding. Late in 1946, after the success of *Ziegfeld Follies* and *Till the Clouds Roll By,* the studio had torn up her $3,000 per week contract and promised her a prodigious $5,600 per week for the next five years. And she didn't have to make more than two pictures a year, and she would always be the star. Then the studio had bought her S. N. Behrman's *The Pirate,* with her husband, Vincente Minnelli, as the director. But she had dieted so much that she weighed less than a hundred pounds, and often she didn't show up on the set for two or three days at a time, and when she did, Minnelli had to chauffeur her directly from the studio to her psychiatrist, the eminent Dr. Simmel. Simmel was old and refused to watch over her on the set, so another psychiatrist, Frederick Hacker, was hired to stand by at the studio. None of this really worked. One night, she telephoned the Ira Gershwins and asked if she could spend the night there, then lay on a guest room couch and simply started screaming. After several minutes of screaming, she stopped and said to Mrs. Gershwin, "Do you believe me?"

"Yes," said Lee Gershwin. Then Judy Garland went back to her screaming until she finally passed out.

Soon after that, she made a pretense of attempting suicide. "I'm going to kill myself!" she shouted in the midst of an argument with Minnelli. She ran to the bathroom, locked herself in, broke a water glass, and scratched herself across the wrist. Minnelli broke down the door to rescue her, but a Band-Aid was enough to stop the bleeding. Dr. Simmel recommended the Las Campanas sanitarium in Compton. After a few weeks there, she came home again. Then a new psychiatrist named Herbert Kupper suggested the Riggs Foundation in Stockbridge, Massachusetts. After a few weeks there, she went shakily back to work at M-G-M to do *Easter Parade,* again with Minnelli as director. But in the midst of rehearsals, Dr. Kupper told Arthur Freed, the producer, that it would be bad for Miss Garland to work for her husband, so Minnelli was summarily removed from the project. (As an added plot twist, the leading man, Gene Kelly, broke his ankle playing softball, and that was how Fred Astaire came to be the male star of *Easter Parade.)*

"We are happier apart," Minnelli said in announcing the separation that ended the marriage in that summer of 1948. But *Easter Parade* was such a success that M-G-M paid a record price for *Annie Get Your Gun* and announced that a three-million-dollar production was being designed just for Miss Garland. She couldn't get through it. "We started the picture, we did a couple of scenes, and I knew I wasn't good," she said later. "We made all the prerecordings. But I was in a daze. My head wouldn't stop aching."

She would lie awake all night, telephoning people to ask questions like, "What kind of a day do you think it will be?" She took pills—Nembutal, Seconal, amphetamines, tranquilizers. Her skin broke out in rashes. Her hair began to fall out. Yet another new doctor, Fred Pobirs, put her in a hospital and had her undergo six electric shock treatments.

When she returned to *Annie* in the spring of 1949, she was repeatedly late for work, keeping scores of people standing around idle. Mayer, who had been her boss since childhood, had a fatherly talk with her; Schary, too, tried having a talk with her. She kept saying that she was trying as hard as she could. "Do what you have to do," said Nick Schenck.

On Saturday, May 7, Miss Garland came to the studio late, then walked off the set and simply sat in her dressing room, banging her head against a wall. On Monday, she didn't appear at all. On Tuesday, she arrived late and was welcomed by a warning letter from an M-G-M vice-president named Louis K. Sidney: "You must be aware of the fact that your contract with us requires you to be prompt in complying with our instructions. . . ." If she continued to be late, the letter said, the studio would exercise its rights, "including, but not limited to, the right to remove you from 'ANNIE GET YOUR GUN.' " She started shouting protests to anyone who would listen. "I never lost anybody any money in my life!" she cried, waving the letter around.

Reports from the battlefield soon reached the M-G-M executive offices, and after lunch, an official emissary named Lester Peterson arrived at Miss Garland's dressing room with a new letter from Sidney. "You have refused to comply with our instructions . . ." it said. "This is to notify you that for good and sufficient cause and in accordance with the rights granted to us under the provisions of Paragraph 12 of your contract of employment with us . . . we shall refuse to pay you any compensation commencing as of . . ." And so on.

To Peterson's dismay—he naturally assumed that some important M-G-M executive must have told her the news about her firing, and that he was just bringing the legal confirmation—Miss Garland cried out in amazement and rage, then flung herself onto the floor of her dressing room and rolled around, screaming, "No, no, no!"

Peterson made his escape, and soon Miss Garland was having a drink— "I'm going to have that fucking drink"—with the director, Chuck Walters. "I don't believe it," she kept saying, crying and laughing at the same time. "After the money I made for these sons of bitches! These bastards! These lousy bastards! Goddamn them!"

What protected Dore Schary during all the conflicts of his early days at M-G-M was that he seemed to have a Midas touch. He was just as sentimental as Mayer but more skillful, and younger. Not only did Betty Hutton make a splendid success out of Judy Garland's role in *Annie* but the thirty-eight films that emerged from M-G-M during Schary's first year included *On The Town, The Asphalt Jungle, Father of the Bride,* all good middle-class hits. After a deficit of $6.5 million during the fiscal year before Schary's arrival, the studio halted its decline and made a profit of $300,000; the next year, the profits rose to $3.8 million. Schenck was pleased. He gave Schary a large stock option, without even telling Mayer. Mayer was furious at both Schenck and Schary, whom he rather justifiably imagined to be in league against him. He rallied his underlings to resist the new regime. In mid-1951, rumors of executive disagreements reached the newspapers. Unknown to Schary, Mayer wrote a letter to Schenck declaring that either he or Schary must have full control of M-G-M, and the other must go. Schenck wrote back that if that was the choice, he chose Schary. According to Schary's account, he was in Mayer's office to discuss some production plans when the telephone rang and he heard Mayer talking angrily with Schenck's lawyer in New York.

"You can tell Mr. Nicholas Schenck that he and Dore Schary can take the studio and choke on it," Mayer shouted as he hung up. (Mayer's exact language was probably more pungent than Schary could bring himself to report.)

"What was that all about, L.B.?" Schary inquired.

"Sit down and I'll tell you everything," Mayer snarled, "you little kike. . . ."

•   •   •

The most important event in Hollywood in 1948 attracted remarkably little attention. Nor did it take place in Hollywood. Nor was it actually an event but rather a months-long series of events. The essential fact was that the Justice Department persuaded the Supreme Court that the whole Hollywood system, all those rich and powerful studios and all those highly paid executives who talked of their talents for showmanship—all this was actually a criminal conspiracy.

The controversy dated back almost to the beginning of the movie business. As early as 1921, the Federal Trade Commission was investigating such Hollywood practices as block-booking and blind-selling. The producers, many of whom had started out as light-fingered opponents of the patent holders whom they called the "Trust," now insisted on their own right to protect their interests.

In 1940, the antagonists had agreed to a three-year consent decree, in which the government let the studios keep their theaters, and the studios agreed to buy no more theaters, and to limit block-booking to blocks of five films. At the end of three years, both sides were discontented. The government still wanted to separate the studios from their theaters, and the studios still wanted to be free from government restraints. In 1947, the federal district court in New York ruled that the problem was not who owned the movie theaters but how movies were sold to them. It called for sales by auction— free competition, and all that. The only thing that both the producers and the theater owners agreed on was that auctions wouldn't work. Both sides appealed to the Supreme Court.

In February of 1948, Attorney General Tom Clark appeared before the Supreme Court to argue once again that the studios must give up their theaters. There was no other way, he said, "to effectively pry open to competition the channels of trade in the industry." The Justice Department had already submitted to the Court a petition arguing that its plea was not just a matter of free trade in the movie business but of free trade in ideas. "The content of films, regardless of who produces them or exhibits them, must necessarily be conditioned to some extent by the prejudices and moral attitudes of those who control the channels of distribution," the Justice Department brief said. "Only by assurance that the distribution field is open to all may the fullest diversity of film content be had."

The established studios had proved themselves unwilling or unable to permit such a diversity, the Justice Department said. On the contrary, their past efforts had consisted of "creating and maintaining a control of the film market expressly designed to prevent" any views other than their own. "Such a past," the Justice Department said, "gives little hope that they will in the future encourage production of the wide variety of films needed to satisfy the wide variety of tastes possessed by the potential American film audience, rather than a standardized mass product adapted to profitable exhibition in a controlled market."

There had been independent producers from the start, of course. Cecil B. DeMille, for example, had arrived in Hollywood long before Paramount even existed, and though he used Paramount's studio and its distribution system, he remained very much his own boss. United Artists was created in 1919 as a partnership among the highly independent Charlie Chaplin, Mary Pickford, Douglas Fairbanks, and D. W. Griffith. The two producers who were absolutely unable to work for anyone else, David Selznick and Sam Goldwyn, had been independent so long that they had acquired the aura of studios. And after the war, a whole flock of directors and actors began going independent, partly as a way to assert their independence, partly as a way to escape the 85 percent taxes on their high salaries.

One of the first of these was Colonel Frank Capra, who, even before the war ended, launched Liberty Films in the spring of 1945, with two fellow colonels and fellow directors, William Wyler and George Stevens, as partners. Capra felt strongly that Hollywood's wartime prosperity had turned the big studios into assembly lines of mediocrity, and he ridiculed many so-called independent producers as "war profiteers seeking status, socialites seeking glamour, swishy 'uncles' promoting handsome 'nephews,' big daddies buying star parts for blonde chicks, et cetera ad nauseam." Capra, Wyler, and Stevens were all skilled professionals; they would each put up fifty thousand dollars to make use of RKO's facilities, then pay themselves three thousand a week to make one picture a year.

That was not a very promising budget, but it sounded like fun, and Capra started right in by making his most Capra-ish film. It was an engaging story about a good man (Jimmy Stewart, of course) who became such a failure that he wished he had never been born, whereupon a rather Pickwickian guardian angel appeared and showed him what his town would be like if all his unsung good deeds had not been done. *It's a Wonderful Life* (1946) impressed Capra as not only "the greatest film I had ever made" but "the greatest film *anybody* had ever made," but though it still reappears on television, usually at Christmastime, it was not a great commercial success, not enough to keep Liberty Films afloat.

So Capra tried again, with *State of the Union*, a Pulitzer Prize comedy of politics by Howard Lindsay and Russel Crouse. He got Spencer Tracy and Katharine Hepburn as stars, and even President Truman liked the picture, but by the time it appeared in 1948, Capra had discovered that Liberty Films represented "the fastest and most gentlemanly way of going broke ever invented." And by the time Capra sold out to Paramount, many of his fellow independents were negotiating their own disappearance. Times were getting hard in postwar Hollywood. "At least 76 indie units have dropped from the 'active' production lists . . ." *The Hollywood Reporter* said in the summer of 1949. "The Cary Grant–Alfred Hitchcock unit, Leo McCarey's Rainbow Productions, Bill Dozier–Joan Fontaine, Frank Borzage, Douglas Fairbanks, Jr., Robert Montgomery. . . ."

In the midst of this rather confused situation, the Supreme Court spent three months reflecting on the Justice Department's demand for "the fullest diversity of film content." Then it declared in May of 1948 that the Hollywood system was indeed a conspiracy, and that it would finally order the breakup that Thurman Arnold had requested back before the war. "It is clear, so far as the five majors are concerned, that the aim of the conspiracy was exclusionary, i.e. that it was designed to strengthen their hold on the exhibition field," said the seven-to-one opinion written by Justice William O. Douglas. "In other words, the conspiracy had monopoly in exhibition for one of its goals." Instead of breaking up the monopoly then and there, however, the Court sent the case back to the district court for the Southern District of New York for further consideration.

In October, the Justice Department announced once again that it wanted the five major studios to give up their interests in some fourteen hundred movie theaters. It served notice on Paramount, Loew's, RKO, Warners, and Fox that this would be its position when the New York District Court took up the case. Among all the alleged conspirators, the one who cracked was, of all people, Howard Hughes. RKO told the federal authorities at the end of October that it would give up the battle and sell off its interest in 241 theaters within a year. Ten days later, Loew's also surrendered, and then the others gave up. A consent decree was approved by the Justice Department, the studios, and the court. Though it would take another year for the theaters to be sold, and still longer for the studios to realize the devastating implications of what had happened to them, the golden age that Hollywood had founded on a conspiracy was now coming to an end.

●　　●　　●

In the midst of the humdrum routine of the movie capital—the story conferences, the executive lunches, the Saturday night poker games—there occasionally occurred odd and exotic encounters. The first visit, for example, by W. H. Auden to Igor Stravinsky.

Having recently finished his somber Mass, Stravinsky wanted to write an opera, something light and deliberately old-fashioned, out of its time, both pre-modern and pre-Romantic, something almost Mozartean. In the spring of 1947, he had seen a Hogarth exhibition at the Chicago Art Institute, and that seemed to offer great possibilities. Back in Hollywood, he asked Aldous Huxley to recommend a poet to write a libretto on *The Rake's Progress,* and Huxley warmly recommended Auden. Stravinsky was a very frugal man, but he not only invited the customarily penniless Auden to come and spend a week at his house in Hollywood that November, he even paid the poet's air fare from New

York. He also asked his publisher, Boosey & Hawkes, to send him the orchestral scores of the four main Mozart operas, which he called the "source of inspiration for my future opera."

Auden worried about the proprieties. Should he pack a dinner jacket? Stravinsky worried about the accommodations. Was the couch in his den long enough for Auden? How tall was Auden anyway? Stravinsky, a small man, searched in vain through Auden's poetry for some clue. As soon as the visitor arrived, it was clear that he would not fit into his allotted space. But no matter. After a bountiful dinner with lots of wine, Stravinsky arranged a chair and some pillows as an extension to the couch, and Auden bedded down there amid Stravinsky's softly rustling collection of forty parrots and lovebirds.

The two unlikely collaborators got along surprisingly well. Auden admitted later that he had been "scared stiff" (Stravinsky was, among other things, twenty-five years Auden's senior). "Rumor had it that Stravinsky was a difficult person with whom to work. Rumor had lied. [Stravinsky] was a professional artist concerned not for his personal glory, but solely for the thing-to-be-made." On the other side, Stravinsky equally admired Auden's professionalism, as well as his combination of technical virtuosity and thoughtful lyricism. "He *was* inspired," Stravinsky wrote, "and he inspired me."

They worked hard. Within a week, they had agreed on their central characters, on their plot and their general structure. Auden chain-smoked and drank and refused to go anywhere near the ocean. Almost the only time he ventured out of Stravinsky's house, in fact, was when they went to the parish hall of a Hollywood church to see an obscure production of Mozart's *Così Fan Tutte*.

Back in New York, Auden set to work on a full libretto, and he soon sent the first act out to Hollywood. It was a remarkable venture into pastiche: "Now is the season when the Cyprian Queen/With genial charm translates our mortal scene. . . ." Stravinsky was delighted; this was just the kind of witty anachronism that he himself planned to write. "Having chosen a period-piece subject," Stravinsky said later, "I decided to assume the conventions of the period as well, though respectable (progressive) music had pronounced them long since dead."

Stravinsky worked methodically. He started by writing scansion marks over every word in Auden's libretto. Then he memorized every line, pacing up and down as he did so. After reciting each section, he adopted the odd practice of writing down the exact length of time that the music should last before he actually wrote any of the music itself.

Stravinsky was not happy that Auden had recruited his twenty-seven-year-old lover, Chester Kallman, as a collaborator, and that the manuscript for the first act arrived with both men's names on it. But when Auden finally brought him the third act early in 1948—bringing it personally to Washington, where Stravinsky was conducting—the poet assured him that Kallman "is a better librettist than I am," and that the scenes Kallman had written were "at least as good as mine." So Stravinsky acquiesced. And kept working. "Many pages have already been achieved, but I am not quite through the first scene," he wrote to Boosey & Hawkes that summer. "This work affords me great joy and freshness, and nobody need worry about my losing a moment. The music will be very easy to listen to, but making this easiness is very expensive with my time."

•   •   •

"Kike." Now that the word is rarely used any more, it seems peculiarly brutal, but it was hardly less brutal when Mayer used it on Rapf and Schary. Yet if it is difficult to recall how cruel and how pervasive anti-Semitism was in the America of the 1940's, it is no less difficult to realize that it was a relatively recent phenomenon. Only in 1861 did Congress vote that army chaplains must all be ministers of "some Christian faith" (a measure reversed by the lobbying of the Board of Delegates of American Israelites); only in 1864 did Protestant leaders try to have the Constitution amended to declare the United States a Christian nation (and they were defeated again by the American Israelites); only in 1877 did there occur the scandalous scene in which Joseph Seligman, the New York banker, was publicly refused accommodations for himself and his family at the Grand Union Hotel in Saratoga Springs.

There had always been a certain amount of bias and hostility, of course, for the first Americans all came from Europe and brought Europe's prejudices with them. Nonetheless, the Constitution of 1787 was the first national charter in the world that forbade any distinctions based on religion and thus treated Jews and Christians exactly alike. There were, to be sure, very few Jews. The first census, in 1790, recorded only about two thousand, one tenth of one percent in a population of some two million. Still, it was one of the fundamental principles of the new nation that Jews of whatever national origin were no different from English Quakers or Italian Catholics or French Huguenots or anybody else.

There was probably a certain amount of hypocrisy in this, since the population was overwhelmingly British and overwhelmingly Protestant, and it did nobody any harm to be tolerant toward small minorities. That system and that hypocrisy changed forever during the great migrations that started shortly before the Civil War. Between 1840 and 1870, more than 6.5 million immigrants flooded in, including the first small wave of German Jews like the Seligmans, the Warburgs, Schiffs, Morgenthaus, and Rosenwalds. The United States was so preoccupied with its black slaves and ex-slaves that it only gradually realized how its white population was changing. In the 1870's alone, 2.8 million immigrants arrived; in the 1880's, the total climbed to 5.2 million. The flood reached a record one million a year in 1905, then rose to an all-time high of 1,285,000 in 1907. These were no longer Puritans and settlers but simply the poor, the Poles and Italians and Greeks who were needed to work the mills and mines that American industry was building. Among them came the penniless Jews of Eastern Europe, many driven out by

czarist pogroms and steered westward by other European nations' unwilling-
ness to take them in. At the turn of the century, Britain was receiving only
2,500 Jewish immigrants a year while New York was receiving more than
10,000 a month.

And so the official restrictions began. Not only against the Jews, of
course, but also in the Chinese Exclusion Act of 1882, and in the Jim Crow
laws of the 1890's, and finally in the ethnic quota system embodied in the
Immigration Act of 1924. Unofficial discrimination was worse. A study of
help-wanted ads in Chicago newspapers showed that the phrase "Christians
only" or "Gentiles only" appeared in 0.3 percent of the ads in 1911, then rose
to 4 percent in 1921, 13.3 percent in 1926, and still held at 9.4 percent in
1937. Henry Ford's *Dearborn Independent,* which had a circulation of 700,000
copies, began in 1920 to campaign against what it called "the Jewish problem"
and to republish its campaignings in books with titles like *The International
Jew* and *Aspects of Jewish Power in the United States.*

This was not simply one of Henry Ford's peculiarities. The Philadelphia
Chamber of Commerce issued a bulletin advocating specific restrictions
against "the Hebrew element." A Connecticut chamber of commerce publicly
asked property owners not to sell to Jews. A Milwaukee golf club requested
that eight Jewish charter members resign. The Century Club in New York
rejected the application of Dr. Jacques Loeb, a distinguished scientist at the
Rockefeller Institute.

Harvard's president A. Lawrence Lowell, in his graduation address for
1922, openly advocated quotas to limit Jewish admissions, a suggestion formally rejected by the Harvard trustees but widely practiced in prestigious
universities during the 1920's. By the end of that decade, anti-Semitic discrimination in education, social organizations, jobs, and housing was more
widespread and more open in the United States than in Europe, including
pre-Hitler Germany. "Today it is no secret that Jews have great difficulty in
gaining admission to the institutions of higher learning," said an article in
Harper's in 1933, "and that their opportunities for legal and medical training
are limited to a minimum. It is equally well-known that the professions of
banking, engineering and teaching are closed to all but a few, and the quasi-
public service corporations vigorously exclude them. In the mechanical trades,
the discrimination is almost as widespread as in the professions, and in clerical
work, generally speaking, it is worst of all."

This was the atmosphere in which the Mayers and Warners and Gold-
wyns grew up and learned the realities of American life, and came to Hollywood, and fought, and gouged, and prospered. Their basic attitude throughout
these conflicts, though, was a yearning for assimilation, a belief in the legend
of the "melting pot," a suppression or even a symbolic denial of all Jewishness,
and an invincible faith in the idea that if they could not achieve full assimilation themselves, then they could achieve it for their children. Their insistence
on changing names was, in a way, the simplest and most insignificant of
evasions—even a Julia Turner was renamed Lana, after all—and yet there

was something profoundly degrading in the unwritten rule that no star could have a Jewish name.

Emmanuel Goldenberg, who had come from Romania, left a poignant description of his struggle to deal with the standard view that Goldenberg was "too long, too foreign . . . too Jewish." He thought about translating it into Goldenhill or Goldenmount, or even Montedore, but the results seemed "too pretentious . . . and God knows they were contrived." Then he saw a play in which a butler announced, "Madame, a gentleman to see you—a Mr. Robinson." He liked that, but when he told his friends at the American Academy of Dramatic Arts that he was planning to call himself Emmanuel Robinson, he sensed "something less than enthusiasm." After considering all the first names that began with his own initial—Edgar? Egbert? Ellery? Ethan?—he decided to name himself after the king of England, Edward VIII. "But I could not desert the Goldenberg entirely," Edward G. Robinson recalled. "That became the G, my private treaty with my past. . . . Deep down in my deepest heart, I am, and have always been, Emmanuel Goldenberg."

Julius Garfinkle was a more combative man, and though he changed his name to Jules Garfield for the New York stage, he wanted to keep that name in Hollywood. Jack Warner disapproved. He demanded that the newcomer be called James Fielding. Garfield protested that he had a right to keep his theater name.

"What kind of a name is Garfield anyway?" said Jack Warner. "It doesn't sound American."

Garfield said it had been the name of an American president. Warner proposed a compromise, keeping the Garfield but changing Jules to James. "But that was the president's name," said Garfield. "You wouldn't name a goddamn actor Abraham Lincoln, would you?"

"No, kid, we wouldn't," said one of Warner's executives, "because Abe is a name most people would say is Jewish, and we wouldn't want people to get the wrong idea."

"But I *am* Jewish," said the future John Garfield.

"Of course you are," said the Warners executive. "So are *we* . . . most of us. But a lot of people who buy tickets think they don't like Jews. . . . And Jules is a Jew's name."

Sam Goldwyn was perhaps the most blunt in this view. When he hired Danny Kaye straight from Broadway to star in *Up in Arms* in 1940, he was dismayed by the first screen tests. "He looks too—too—" Goldwyn complained. "Well, he *is* Jewish," said Goldwyn's Gentile second wife, Frances. "But let's face it, Jews are funny-looking," said Goldwyn. After much agonizing, including even the idea of buying back Kaye's contract, Goldwyn finally solved his problem by having Kaye's reddish-brown hair dyed blond, thus, in effect, de-Semitizing him. A few years later, when Goldwyn cast Frank Sinatra in the role that Sam Levene had played in the Broadway production of *Guys and Dolls,* Goldwyn stated his view as a general principle: "You can't have a Jew play a Jew. It wouldn't work on the screen."

The studio bosses, who spared themselves the humiliations they inflicted on their stars, expiated their own sins in their own ways, by raising money. Thus Goldwyn, who succeeded the pardoned Joe Schenck as president of the United Jewish Appeal in 1947, proceeded, through what his biographer called "tireless efforts," to raise $8.8 million for Jewish charities. Alvah Bessie, one of the outcast Hollywood Ten, provided a graphic description of how these things were done at Warner Bros. "Every nominally Jewish writer, actor, director and producer was practically ordered to be present . . ." he recalled. "When we were all assembled . . . [Jack Warner] marched in and—to our astonishment—brandished a rubber truncheon, which had probably been a prop for one of the anti-Nazi pictures we were making. He stood behind his table and smashed the length of rubber hose on the wood, and then he smiled and said, 'I've been looking at the results of the Jewish Appeal drive, and believe you me, it ain't good.' Here he paused for effect and said, 'Everybody's gonna double his contribution here and now—or else!' The rubber truncheon crashed on the table again as everyone present, including John Garfield, Jerry Wald . . . Albert Maltz, and I reached for our checkbooks."

Harry Cohn, as always, had his own views of these matters. "Relief for the Jews?" he said when asked to contribute. "What we need is relief *from* the Jews. All the trouble in the world has been caused by Jews and Irishmen."* Cohn, who was quite accustomed to addressing a writer as "Jew-boy," liked to boast that the only Jewish actors he had under contract at Columbia played Indians. In fact, most of the studio bosses regarded most minorities with no more respect than they accorded to the Jews. Jack Warner, for example, once ordered a scene of two blacks kissing to be not only removed from a movie but destroyed. "It's like watching two animals," he said. "Terrible!" Any black kissing a white was forbidden, of course, by the studios' production code. Louis B. Mayer disliked his own studio's highly praised version of Faulkner's *Intruder in the Dust.* The black hero was "too uppity," he told Schary. "He ought to take off his hat when he talks to a white man." Mayer also disapproved of Schary's producing *Go for Broke,* about the heroism of the Nisei 442nd Infantry Battalion. "He's making pictures about the Japs," Mayer grumbled. "Last week, who went to see the picture? All the Japs! This week, the bottom fell out of his box office."

In all this crudity, the Hollywood executives were expressing not simply their own crude prejudices but their own crude sense of what America thought of itself, a completely homogenized white Gentile society. Yet they kept being reminded that it wasn't true. Hedda Hopper recalled Louis B. Mayer asking her—"begged" was the word she used—"to get his daughters into our most private private school, whose principal was a friend of mine." Mrs. Hopper demurred.

---

* Others felt a need for relief from Harry Cohn. When the Columbia boss billed Rosalind Russell for some studio gowns that she wanted to use on a tour of military bases during the war, she retaliated by charging him for the use of her fur coat in a Columbia film. As she went out the door, ostentatiously fanning herself with Cohn's check for $2,700, Cohn shouted after her: "Jew!"

"Mr. Mayer, they don't accept them," she said.

"But they'll take my daughters," Mayer said. "Can't you tell the head mistress how important I am?"

"It won't do any good . . ." Mrs. Hopper said. "They will not take Jews."

Mayer was certainly the least dedicated of Jews, and he may even have considered the idea of converting to Christianity. He not only kept the portrait of Cardinal Spellman prominently displayed by his desk but donated large sums to the cardinal's favorite charities. And even if one did not actually convert, one could always dissemble, play the game. Mayer's granddaughter, Edie's daughter, Barbara Goetz Windom, told an interviewer not long ago about her family's elaborate Christmas parties and Easter egg hunts and said that she was surprised to hear her mother object to a Christian marriage ceremony. "It was the first time I'd heard of any reference to my being Jewish," said the granddaughter of the onetime junk dealer from Minsk.

The suave Rabbi Edgar Magnin presided over Temple B'nai B'rith in downtown Los Angeles—indeed, he built a glittering new temple on Wilshire Boulevard and remained in charge well into the 1980's—but this was a Reform temple so reformed that it included Sunday school classes for the wealthy children of wealthy Hollywood. Their grandparents, whom Budd Schulberg described as "aged anachronisms in their dark suits and long beards, with Yiddish as their daily speech and Hebrew for their daily prayers," were appalled. Their sons had proudly brought them west from New York and established them in villas with orange trees, but they didn't like all this extravagance. "The old men got together and held a council of religious war," Schulberg recalled. "They wanted a real *shul* like the ones they had left behind." The studio executives were anxious to placate their fathers and their forefathers. The old men rented a bungalow for ninety dollars a month, and then the executives sent studio carpenters and painters to recreate, just as in some set for a dramatization of Sholom Aleichem (which these same producers would never have produced), the spiritual center of the half-remembered *shtetl*.

"The results were astonishing," Schulberg recalled. "From the outside, Grandpa's *shul* looked like any other little white bungalow on the street, complete with small green lawn and the obligatory miniature orange or lemon tree. But once you stepped inside you found yourself walking into an old world steeped in Jewish tradition, where Grandpa Max, and Old Man Mayer and Old Man Warner (those seemed to be their official names) and the rest of the immigrant Talmudists finally felt at home. They sent to New York for a *real* rabbi, a little Moses who would see to it that the Laws of the Torah were upheld. . . . When the rabbi arrived, a young man whose features were appropriately hidden by a bushy black beard, Grandpa and his Orthodox pals were driven down to the Santa Fe station in studio limousines as the reception committee. . . ."

•   •   •

What neither the old men in their *shul* nor their sons in their executive offices seemed to realize, most of them, was that whatever relatives they had left behind were all destined for annihilation. In this, they were not alone, of course. President Roosevelt did not realize it, and did not want to be told about it. The State Department and the War Department did not want to be told either, and when they were told, they did their best to ignore the information, and even to suppress it.*

One of those who heard and told was a rather unpleasantly cocksure writer, Ben Hecht. A onetime Chicago newspaperman who fancied himself a novelist—has anyone ever read *Erik Dorn* (1921) or *Gargoyles* (1922) or *Fantazius Mallare* (1923) or *Count Bruga* (1926)?—Hecht achieved his biggest success by collaborating with Charles MacArthur on the hit play *The Front Page* (1928). Even before the first talking pictures, when Hollywood's need for writers would become desperate, Herman Mankiewicz persuaded Paramount to offer Hecht a contract, and then he sent his famous telegram proclaiming that "millions are to be grabbed out here and your only competition is idiots."

It was true. Hecht soon became the fastest hack in Hollywood, and he was paid accordingly. He spent only a week writing his first script, *Underworld,* and Paramount paid him ten thousand dollars for it. Of the sixty movies he eventually wrote, he once estimated, more than half took less than two weeks. His pay went as high as ten thousand per week. From Howard Hughes, he demanded and got one thousand dollars per day, payable at 6 P.M. of each day he worked. David Selznick, who desperately needed him to rewrite *Gone With the Wind* after filming had already started, paid him three thousand per day to salvage the project.

While Hecht was churning out scripts—he once wrote, with different collaborators, four at the same time—he also wrote a daily column, titled *Thousand and One Afternoons,* for the liberal New York newspaper *PM.* For seventy-five dollars per week. This enabled him, among other things, to trumpet his own sense of Jewishness. He had, as he put it, "turned into a Jew in 1939. I had before then been only related to Jews. In that year I became a Jew and looked on the world with Jewish eyes." This was not a popular viewpoint. "The Americanized Jews who ran newspapers and movie studios," Hecht later recalled, "who wrote plays and novels, who were high in government and powerful in the financial, industrial and even social life of the nation were silent." In one of his 1941 columns, "My Tribe Is Called Israel," Hecht struck back. "My angry critics all write that they are proud of being Americans and of wearing carnations, and that they are sick to death of such efforts as mine to Judaize them and increase generally the Jew-consciousness of the world. Good Jews with carnations, it is not I who am bringing this Jew-consciousness back into the world. It is back on all the radios of the world. I

---

* It is also worth remembering that in the supposedly independent Hollywood of today, nobody made a movie critical of the Vietnam war until after it was all over.

don't advise you to take off your carnation. I only suggest that you don't hide behind them too much. They conceal very little."

This last column brought him a letter from a man named Peter Bergson (he was actually Hillel Kook, nephew of the former chief rabbi of Palestine, but he had changed his name to spare his family embarrassment over his political activities). Bergson wanted Hecht to become the American leader of the organization for which he himself worked, a radical Palestinian underground group that called itself the Irgun Zvai Leumi. "They could have selected no more unqualified and uninformed and un-Palestine-minded man in the entire land . . ." Hecht wrote. "I disliked causes. I disliked public speaking. . . . I never attended meetings of any sort. I had no interest in Palestine." Bergson was not to be denied. Hecht joined the cause.

The Irgun was small and impoverished and strongly opposed by Rabbi Stephen Wise and all the other leaders of Jewish respectability. What Bergson had found in Hecht, however, was what the Irgun most needed in America, a brilliant propagandist. Bergson imagined that Hecht could mobilize Hollywood to raise millions of dollars for a Jewish army to fight the Nazis, but Hecht soon found the most prosperous producers solidly opposed. Mayer refused him; Goldwyn refused him; Harry Warner ordered him out of his office. (None of these magnates happened to mention that they had recently attended a private meeting with Joseph P. Kennedy, onetime cofounder of RKO and most recently U.S. ambassador to London, who had warned this gathering of about fifty leading producers that any Jewish protests against Nazism would only lead to increased anti-Semitism in America.) Hecht next went to see Selznick and asked him to serve as cosponsor of a fund-raising dinner.

"I don't want to have anything to do with your cause," Selznick said, "for the simple reason that it's a Jewish political cause. And I am not interested in Jewish political problems. I'm an American and not a Jew. . . . It would be silly of me to pretend suddenly that I'm a Jew, with some sort of full-blown Jewish psychology."

It was wonderfully characteristic of Selznick, the former analysand, to start talking about "full-blown Jewish psychology," but Hecht countered with an equally characteristic challenge. If Selznick thought he was an American rather than a Jew, would he be willing to make a bet on what other people thought of him? Hecht proposed that Selznick name any three people in Hollywood, and then he, Hecht, would call them up and ask them whether they regarded Selznick "as an American or a Jew." If one single one of them thought that Selznick was what he thought he was, "an American," then Hecht would retire in defeat.

Selznick, an inveterate gambler, couldn't resist. The first name that he chose was Martin Quigley, publisher of *Motion Picture Exhibitors' Herald*. Hecht called him up and asked him the poisoned question. "I'd say David Selznick was a Jew," Quigley said.

The second name was Nunnally Johnson, the eminent screenwriter of such pictures as John Steinbeck's *The Grapes of Wrath* and *The Moon Is Down*.

He "hemmed a few moments," Hecht recalled, "but finally offered the same reply."

The third name was Leland Hayward, the agent.

"For God's sake, what's the matter with David?" says Hayward. "He's a Jew and he knows it."

Be it said to Selznick's credit that just as he paid off his thousands of dollars in gambling debts, he now put his name on Hecht's fund-raising invitation. Suddenly Harry Warner changed his mind and accepted; so did Goldwyn. But when the dignitaries all gathered in the 20th Century–Fox commissary, they were appalled to hear one of the speakers, a British colonel who had commanded the Jewish Legion during World War I, criticize the now-beleaguered British for their policies in Palestine. "Sit down! Sit down!" Goldwyn shouted at him. Selznick squirmed. When the speeches ended, the Jews sat silent; the first donation was a modest offer of $300 from Hedda Hopper. Then came some more pledges, a total of $130,000, but only $9,000 of that pledged money was actually paid.

Hecht would not be silenced. He wrote a historical pageant about the Jews, entitled *We Will Never Die,* to be performed in Madison Square Garden as a memorial to the growing number of victims of what was not yet called the Holocaust. The pageant began with a rabbi in canonicals reading a prayer: "Almighty God, Father of the poor and the weak, Hope of all who dream of goodness and justice . . . we are here to say our prayers because of the two million who have been killed in Europe, because they bear the name of your first children—the Jews." Kurt Weill wrote the music, Billy Rose produced, Moss Hart directed, Paul Muni and Edward G. Robinson served as narrators. A record forty thousand people crowded into Madison Square Garden to see two consecutive performances on a cold night early in 1943, and thousands more waited outside in the hope that it would be repeated a second time. Rose then took the production on a highly successful tour of Washington, Philadelphia, Chicago, Boston, and Hollywood, but the pageant's appeal for a Jewish army aroused strong opposition from more conservative Jewish organizations. Warning phone calls were made, pledges of financial support faded, and the pageant came to an end.

There were more immediate problems. The Romanian government let it be known that it would allow seventy thousand Jews to emigrate if someone would provide a home for them and pay their transportation expenses. The State Department reacted as usual, pretending that the proposal was not serious, and that nothing could be done. Hecht wrote and signed a full-page ad in the *New York Times* that began with a jolting headline:

FOR SALE TO HUMANITY
70,000 JEWS
GUARANTEED HUMAN BEINGS AT $50 APIECE

"Roumania is tired of killing Jews," Hecht's ad went on. "It has killed 100,000 of them in two years. Roumania will now give Jews away practically for nothing." The Jewish establishment angrily denounced the ad as irresponsible, sensational, bordering on fraud, and, of course, nothing was done. The Romanian Jews went to their death. "I saw," Hecht wrote later, "that propaganda was incapable of altering anything around it. It might incubate in time . . . but it could only confuse the present or irritate it, or be lost entirely in all the other word noises of its own day."

Returning to the attack nonetheless, Hecht wrote another powerful ad, entitled "My Uncle Abraham Reports." It was inspired by a conference in Moscow late in 1943, at which the Allies promised punishment for Nazi crimes against various groups—the Czechs, the French, the Serbs—a list that somehow omitted the Jews. "I have an uncle who is a ghost . . ." Hecht's ad began. "He was elected last April by the Two Million Jews who have been murdered by the Germans to be their World Delegate. Wherever there are conferences on how to make the World a Better Place, maybe, my Uncle Abraham appears and sits on the window sill and takes notes. . . . Last night my Uncle Abraham was back in a Certain Place where the Two Million murdered Jews met. . . . 'Dishonored dead,' said my Uncle Abraham. . . ." He made his report, then, on the Moscow conference at which all persecuted victims except the Jews had been promised retribution. Some of the dead protested, but Uncle Abraham was stoical.

" 'Little Children,' my Uncle Abraham spoke: 'Be patient. We will be dead a long time. Yesterday when we were killed we were changed from Nobodies to Nobodies. Today, on our Jewish tomb, there is not the Star of David, there is an asterisk. But, who knows, maybe Tomorrow—!'

"This ended the meeting of the Jewish Underground. My Uncle Abraham has gone to the White House in Washington. He is sitting on the window sill two feet away from Mr. Roosevelt. But he has left his notebook behind. . . ."

Roosevelt was reported to be upset by Hecht's attack, but as usual, nothing was done. All the Jews who could be killed were killed, and when some of the dazed survivors managed to reach Palestine after the war, they were met by British barbed wire. Keep out. The Zionist establishment kept negotiating for the promised homeland in Palestine—successfully, as it turned out—while the Irgun did its part in violence, irresponsibility, warfare. It bombed civilians in the King David Hotel. It executed British soldiers in retaliation for British executions. And who knows what mysterious combination of negotiation and gunfire, high principle and guilt, finally persuaded the British to depart?

● ● ●

"Kike." Representative John Rankin had used the word on the floor of Congress to describe Walter Winchell, "the little kike I was telling you about." *Time* magazine published a story on the incident in its issue of February 14, 1944. "This was a new low in demagoguery, even for John Rankin," said *Time,* "but in the entire House, no one rose to protest." On the contrary, when Rankin came to the end of his speech, according to *Time,* "the House rose and gave him prolonged applause."

The story made a strong impression on Laura Z. Hobson, who tore the page out of the magazine and saved it. Mrs. Hobson was a woman of considerable dash. As an advertising copywriter, she met Henry Luce at a cocktail party, talked her way into a job as a *Time* promotion writer, and soon became director of promotion. She also became the mistress of Ralph Ingersoll, the general manager of Time Inc., and then of Eric Hodgins, the managing editor of *Fortune.* Her first novel, *The Trespassers,* achieved a considerable success in 1943. A script editor at United Artists invited her to try writing a screenplay for William Bendix, on spec, then told her that the result was wonderful but "wouldn't play." Characteristically, Mrs. Hobson decided to go to Hollywood on her own to find out "what *would* play." She borrowed two thousand dollars. She got a job at M-G-M, then lost it. Her debts mounted to eleven thousand dollars before she finally sold an original screenplay called *Threesome* to Columbia for exactly eleven thousand dollars. Columbia also hired her at $750 a week.

By this time, the *Time* story about Rankin calling Winchell a "kike" had become the idea for a novel about anti-Semitism. The only plot Mrs. Hobson could think of, though, involved a Gentile journalist being assigned to write a series of articles about anti-Semitism and finding—what? It all seemed rather familiar, preachy, dull. Then she met Michael Arlen at Romanoff's, and remembered *The Green Hat* as one of the excitements of her adolescence, and that reminded her, for some reason, of an old anecdote in which some London matron supposedly said to him, "You sound so British, Mr. Arlen. Is it true that you really are Armenian?" To which Arlen, born Dikran Kuyumjian, had answered, "Would anybody *say* he was Armenian if he wasn't Armenian?" To which Mrs. Hobson, born Laura Zametkin, daughter of the editor of the *Jewish Daily Forward,* answered, in her autobiography, in italics, *"Would anybody say he was Jewish if he wasn't Jewish?"* And then, like another Newton recalling the apple, she added: "Even now, as I sit here on a snow-quieted winter afternoon nearly forty years later, a thin ghost of that moment's sudden charge runs along my nerves, and prickles my skin. It was the thread I needed, the story line to run through the entire book."

Having stumbled onto the MacGuffin that would become *Gentlemen's Agreement*—what would happen to an ordinary middle-class Gentile if he began masquerading as a Jew?—Mrs. Hobson suddenly began experiencing self-important sensations of guilt and anxiety. "Could I," as she put it, "in good conscience, while we were at war, accuse America of harboring anti-Semitism and largely ignoring it?" She decided to ask some influential friends. She wrote a nine-page outline, "a sort of thematic statement of what my book might be." It included the dreadful first sentence that she was to insist on to the end: "Abrupt as anger, depression plunged through him." And then several key scenes, like the one in which his hero told his girl of his scheme of telling people that he was a Jew, and she immediately said, "But you're *not,* are you?" She immediately added that "it wouldn't make any difference, of course," but the hero felt that "something had come across her eyes . . . the instant, the unnameable thing."

Mrs. Hobson sent this offering to her publisher, Richard Simon of Simon and Schuster. She sent it to Norman Cousins, the editor of *The Saturday Review of Literature,* to Dorothy Thompson, the columnist, to Harry Scherman of the Book-of-the-Month Club. Not for nothing had Mrs. Hobson been a success as an advertising and promotion writer. Cousins was the first to answer, with a telegram that said "SINCERELY THRILLED WONDERFUL IDEA. . . ." The others had doubts. Simon predicted that readers would not believe that a Gentile would pose as a Jew, and Dorothy Thompson fretted that "anti-antisemitism campaigns are very dubious means to overcome intolerance." Mrs. Hobson knew better. "Abrupt as anger, depression plunged through him," she wrote, again. "It was one hell of an assignment . . ." She planned to call her novel "Make the Tree Corrupt."

There were interruptions. She worked on a number of unsuccessful film projects. She joined the American Women's Volunteer Services and spent one day a week driving trucks for the navy. Not until the war was nearly over did she excitedly write in her journal: "Pages 16, 17, 18, 19 The Break-Through? at last ?? Chap I ended. Started Chapter II!!!!!" As in all such books, Mrs. Hobson devoted many pages to her hero's discovery of the obvious. Assigned to write about anti-Semitism for *Smith's Weekly,* Phil Green wondered about how to "find some angle." He didn't even notice when his own sister used the term "trying to Jew us down," and then when he remembered it, he regarded it as a sort of revelation. He read *Time*'s account of Rankin's speech and felt the appropriate indignation: "Shame for the Congress twisted in him . . . 'Jesus, what's happening to this country?' " He even read an unnamed novel that sounded rather like *What Makes Sammy Run?* and wondered why the unnamed Schulberg had felt "some savage necessity to pick a Jew who was . . . a swine in the movie business." Not until the fourth chapter did the earnest Phil finally discover his great idea: " 'Oh, God, I've got it. It's the way. It's the only way. I'll *be* Jewish. I'll just say—nobody knows me—I can just say it. I can live it myself . . . Christ, I've got it.' An elation roared through him. He had it, the idea, the lead, the angle. . . . 'I Was Jewish for Six Months.' That was the title. It leaped at him. There was no doubt."

As the feverish style indicates, many exciting things soon happened to Phil Green. In fact, just about every slight that had ever been inflicted on Mrs. Hobson, every slight she had even heard about, she inflicted on her hero. Casual conversations included obnoxious phrases like "little Jew boy." A drunken soldier said, "I don't like offishers. An' shpecially if they're yids." A more genteel doctor praised a Jewish colleague who was "not given to overcharging . . . the way some do." Green began to encounter the barriers. His reservation at a ski resort got canceled after he asked whether the place was "restricted." His own research assistant confessed that she had changed her name from Walovsky to Wales in order to get her job at this liberal-minded magazine, but she protested against letting in "the kikey ones." Green sternly answered that "words like kike and kikey and coon and nigger just make me kind of sick, no matter who says them." Miss Wales became icy. So did Green's fiancée, Kathy, who didn't want him to mention his Jewishness at her sister's party in Connecticut. They quarreled. Green's son got beaten up in school. "They called me 'dirty Jew' and 'stinky kike. . . .' "

It is a little hard to judge, after nearly half a century, whether *Gentleman's Agreement* provided an accurate portrayal of anti-Semitism in the America of 1946. Despite an unavoidable distortion caused by the compression of many episodes into a relatively brief period of time, it probably did. One might think that the war against Nazi Germany would necessarily have changed Americans' views of the Nazis' most cruelly mistreated victims, but that did not happen, at least not until some years later. On the contrary, it was commonplace during and just after the war to hear that the Jews had been the cause of it all, that they had provoked it, profiteered from it, and avoided fighting in it. "During World War II . . . a change in the quality of anti-Semitism began to appear," wrote Ernst Simmel, the psychoanalyst, in *Anti-Semitism: A Social Disease* (1946). "It has taken on the color of German anti-Semitism. It embraces an ever-widening circle of the American population, and the more it expands, the more irrational becomes the defamation of the Jews." Late in 1947, Elmo Roper took a survey for *Fortune* and asked whether various groups were "getting more economic power than is good for the country." Nearly 40 percent answered that this was true of the Jews. To a similar question on political power, about 20 percent said the Jews had too much of it, as compared to only 4 percent citing the Protestants, who actually did have most of the power.

And the anti-Semitic discrimination went right on. Dr. Ernest M. Hopkins, the president of Dartmouth, not only admitted in 1945 that he maintained a quota system but defended it by saying that Dartmouth was "a Christian college founded for the Christianization of its students." Though most universities were more discreet, one postwar study showed that Princeton, for example, limited its Jewish enrollment to 4 percent, that Colgate admitted only four or five out of more than two hundred Jewish applicants. The same system applied in business. Banking, insurance, steel, coal, oil, chemicals, aviation, shipping—all of these, according to the 1947 *Fortune* survey, remained solidly Gentile. This discrimination was not entirely peaceful either. In one brief period of 1946, nearly twenty cases of anti-Semitic vandalism were reported in Los Angeles, including the desecration of Temple Israel and the destruction of an ancient Torah that a refugee rabbi had brought from Berlin. None of these crimes was punished.

It still seems remarkable, though, that *Gentleman's Agreement* attacked anti-Semitism purely in terms of derogatory phrases and restricted ski resorts, without the slightest mention of the fact that millions of Jews had just been massacred in Europe. It is equally remarkable that such a trivializing and conventional book should have been considered "controversial." Looking back,

Mrs. Hobson herself seemed a little puzzled by the general misjudgment of relative evils. "It seems inconceivable now," she wrote in her memoirs in 1983, "that as late as 1944, the world at large still had only a limited conception of how far Hitler's 'final solution' had gone or would go." This was probably true of "the world at large," and it was probably true of the Hollywood fund-raising that Jack Warner conducted with a truncheon, but it was not really true of everyone. It was not true, for example, in the White House or the State Department, nor was it true for the people who saw Ben Hecht's full-page ads in the New York Times proclaiming "guaranteed human beings at $50 apiece."

Perhaps precisely because Mrs. Hobson did unwittingly trivialize the disaster, reducing the unbearable reality of Auschwitz to the easily criticized vulgarities of social discrimination in Connecticut, Gentleman's Agreement achieved a success that anyone but her own publisher could have foreseen. Richard Simon ordered a first printing of 17,500 copies, and before the book was even officially published, in February of 1947, he had to order an additional 40,000. Hollywood was one of the main reasons. Several studios bid on the galley proofs, and Darryl Zanuck bought the book for $75,000. "Gentleman's Agreement . . . is bound to be one of the most discussed novels of the year," said the New York Times. "In fact, it is already one of the most discussed novels of the year." And the Herald-Tribune: "Mrs. Hobson is subtle but not gentle. . . . Her book . . . achieved a terrific emotional tension. . . . This story gets under your skin. It makes you think furiously about your own code, your own silence. It hurts."

Zanuck announced that Gentleman's Agreement would be his only "personal production" during the year 1947, an indication of the commercial weight he planned to put behind the film. His first and best biographer, Mel Gussow, even described it as "probably . . . the definitive Zanuck movie of the period in terms of subject matter (anti-Semitism), source (a best-selling novel), approach (a social situation studied through a human relationship), timeliness, controversy, and quality packaging. Seen today, it seems outmoded, but. . . ." But maybe it was outmoded in its own time as well. Zanuck, however, was perhaps the most eminent of Gentile producers, and what apparently struck many Jewish filmmakers as a subject to be avoided, dreaded, ignored, struck him as "timely" and "controversial." As James Agee wrote about Hollywood's early efforts to deal with racism, "Few things pay off better in prestige and hard cash . . . than safe fearlessness."

Zanuck naturally wanted to win all possible credit for being so bold as to make Hollywood's first movie condemning anti-Semitism, and it galled him that RKO had already gone into production with a low-cost thriller on the same subject, Crossfire. According to Schary, Zanuck wrote to protest. "We exchanged a few notes—" Schary recalled, "then a phone call during which I was compelled to tell him he had not discovered anti-Semitism, and that it would take far more than two pictures to eradicate it. The conversation ended with both of us not having budged one inch."

Having failed to persuade Schary to get out of his way, Zanuck ordered full steam ahead on his project. He hired Moss Hart to write the screenplay. He hired Elia Kazan, who had just finished filming *A Tree Grows in Brooklyn*, as the director. He hired Gregory Peck, who had already demonstrated in *Spellbound* his remarkable gift for bewildered sincerity, as the sincerely bewildered hero. Kazan, too, subscribed to the idea that Mrs. Hobson's novel was something daring. "Lots of rich Jews in Hollywood didn't want *Gentleman's Agreement*," he said. "Don't stir it up!" Kazan neglected to provide any details on which rich Jews in Hollywood said that "it" should not be stirred up, or what form their opposition took, and it is just possible that his own ambition to make controversial films inspired him to imagine more controversy than actually existed. When Kazan subsequently appeared before the House Un-American Activities Committee and named everyone he had ever seen at a Communist meeting, and even took out full-page advertisements to explain and justify his past and present behavior, he cited *Gentleman's Agreement* as "in a healthy American tradition, for it shows Americans exploring a problem and tackling a solution. . . . It is opposite to the picture which Communists present of Americans." *

But what was the actual effect of *Gentleman's Agreement* on the "healthy American tradition"? A survey by Irwin Rosen, published in the *Journal of Psychology* in 1948, reported that 73 percent of the people who had seen the movie acquired a more favorable attitude toward Jews (or said they did), while a significant 26 percent became increasingly anti-Semitic. These somewhat ambiguous figures were further muddied by a control group in which 47 percent reported themselves favorably affected and 52 percent unfavorably. Despite its celebrity in its own time, *Gentleman's Agreement* probably deserved Nora Sayre's harsh judgment of its message, "that if only people wouldn't *behave* badly, or use rude words, then 'prejudice' could be eliminated—if everyone would learn good manners, there would be no problem." Or, as she paraphrased the reaction of Ring Lardner, Jr., after the original screening, "the movie's moral is that you should never be mean to a Jew, because he might turn out to be a gentile."

Gentleman's Agreement does not appear very often nowadays on television or in the revival theaters, and yet one retains a faint but persistent memory of the very decent Gregory Peck repeatedly saying, at every confrontation with Connecticut country club society, that all good men must unite to defeat this "conspiracy of silence." That was Hollywood's silent commentary on the Holocaust. Uncle Abraham would have been a better witness.

•   •   •

So would Arnold Schoenberg. Sitting there in his little house in Brentwood, he understood very well the message that had come from the Warsaw

* Remember that Jack Warner, in testifying before the committee, had singled out Kazan, who was then in the midst of directing *Gentleman's Agreement*, as a subversive, "one of the mob."

ghetto, the message that Hollywood ignored, the message that Jews must fight for their lives, and that nobody else would help them in that fight. But Schoenberg was very old by now. Nearly sixty when the Nazis had expelled him from Berlin, when he had defiantly decided to reconvert from Christianity to Judaism, he was past seventy when the war ended and the full extent of the horrors at Auschwitz and Treblinka became clear. Still, even in his seventies in Brentwood, he had something that he wanted to say.

"I cannot remember everything," cried the narrator of Schoenberg's "A Survivor from Warsaw." "I must have been unconscious most of the time. I remember only the grandiose moment when they all started to sing . . . the old prayer they had neglected for so many years, the forgotten creed." "A Survivor from Warsaw" was incredibly condensed, compressed, a black hole in cultural space. It began with an orchestral shriek, and then the narrator started his terrible story. He and some other Jews had been hiding in the sewers under the battered ruins of the Warsaw ghetto. Shortly before dawn, the Germans discovered them and ordered them out. They stumbled forth, some of them old and sick. A German sergeant kept shouting at them: *Achtung!* The Germans beat them as they emerged, all the time ordering them to move faster. The narrator, beaten, fell unconscious. Others fell on top of him. "The next thing I knew was a soldier saying, 'They are all dead.' " Lying there under the corpses, the survivor heard other Jews being marched away and then starting to sing, in their half-forgotten Hebrew, the *Shema Yisrael.*

It is a complete drama and a very powerful one—replete with such Schoenbergian violences as a high trombone trill, bursts of snare drumming, bugle calls, and a xylophone tremolo—and yet it lasts only six minutes. Schoenberg wrote both the words and the music at high speed in the summer of 1947, then tried to find someone who would perform it. Not until the following spring was "A Survivor from Warsaw" given its premiere at the University of New Mexico by the Albuquerque Orchestra under Kurt Frederick. At the end of this first performance, the audience sat in shocked silence. Frederick played it all over again, and then the audience burst into loud applause. That spring of 1948, when Schoenberg's account of the Warsaw ghetto was first performed, was also the spring in which *Gentleman's Agreement* won the Academy Award as Hollywood's best picture of the previous year.

• • •

A far more interesting picture, which won the New York Film Critics Award as the best foreign movie of 1948, not only concerned itself with Nazism but actually started being filmed in Rome while the German army was still in the process of evacuating the city. That was late in 1944, and Roberto Rossellini had to make *Open City* without any studio sets, with mostly amateur actors, with bits and pieces of black market film. Until then, his work for Mussolini's state-run movie industry had involved mainly propaganda pictures like *The White Ship* (1941) and *The Return of the Pilot* (1942), but he rose to the challenge of filming the German occupation as a quasi-documentary, rough, grainy, crude, alive.

The lords of Hollywood remained indifferent, for *Open City* lacked what they liked to call "production values." One of the film's most important viewers, however, was deeply impressed. "There was darkness and shadows, and sometimes you couldn't hear, and sometimes you couldn't even see it," said Ingrid Bergman, "but that's the way it is in life . . . you can't always see and hear, but you know that something almost beyond understanding is going on." When Miss Bergman asked friends to tell her more about Rossellini, nobody seemed to know anything. "In 1948, foreign films didn't rate in Hollywood," she recalled.

A few months later, she was wandering along Broadway, alone, when she saw a billboard advertising *Paisan* (1946), Rossellini's sequel to *Open City*. She went in and saw what she considered "another great movie," and yet the theater was nearly empty. She herself was sick of Hollywood's "production values"—the elaborate sets, the hairdos always perfect, the orchestral music surging up in the background. She decided that she wanted to make a movie with Rossellini. Being the kind of woman she was, she simply wrote him a letter: "Dear Mr. Rossellini, I saw your films *Open City* and *Paisan,* and enjoyed them very much. If you need a Swedish actress who speaks English very well, who has not forgotten her German, who is not yet very understandable in French, and who, in Italian knows only 'ti amo' I am ready to come and make a film with you."

Almost any other director in the world would immediately have telephoned to invite her onto the next plane. The beautiful star of *Casablanca* and *For Whom the Bell Tolls* had won an Academy Award in *Gaslight* (1944), and she had given such a glorious performance in Hitchcock's *Notorious* (1946) that her co-star Cary Grant had been moved to declare at the Academy Award ceremonies: "I think the Academy ought to set aside a special award for Bergman every year whether she makes a picture or not." Rossellini, however, had never heard of her.

Her letter happened to arrive at Minerva Films in Rome on the day that the studio burned down. Somebody poking around in the debris found the letter and opened it. Rossellini was then engaged in suing Minerva about something or other, but a sympathetic secretary telephoned him to say that there was "a very funny letter for you." Rossellini said he was not talking to Minerva and hung up. It took several more calls before Rossellini agreed to listen to the message from Hollywood, and several more before he learned what his correspondent's name represented (Money!), and then he cabled her a characteristic answer: "I JUST RECEIVED WITH GREAT EMOTION YOUR LETTER WHICH HAPPENS TO ARRIVE ON THE ANNIVERSARY OF MY BIRTHDAY AS THE MOST PRECIOUS GIFT. . . ." And so on.

Despite her flirtatious remark about "ti amo," Miss Bergman seems not to have had any romantic designs on Rossellini, but she was restless, both professionally and personally. Her supposedly happy marriage to Peter Lindstrom, the Swedish doctor, had been in trouble for some time. Lindstrom managed her career, haggled over her contracts, and generally ordered her around. This was quite customary in that period, but although Miss Bergman rather enjoyed imagining herself in the role of Nora in *A Doll's House,* there were limits. One of Lindstrom's rules was that newspaper photographers were not allowed to come to the house to take pictures. When Miss Bergman found it more convenient on one occasion to be photographed at home rather than at the studio, Lindstrom became furious on seeing the pictures in print.

"All right, I made a mistake again," Miss Bergman said. "But everybody makes mistakes, you make mistakes, I make mistakes. . . ."

"I . . . I make mistakes?" her husband echoed.

"Well, yes, don't you make mistakes?"

"No," said Lindstrom. (In recounting this scene, Miss Bergman added that Lindstrom subsequently denied this denial.) "Why should I? I think carefully before I do something. I weigh it. I ponder it, and then I decide."

This announcement persuaded Miss Bergman that it was time for a change. "I asked if Peter would mind if we had a divorce," she recalled. He would indeed mind. "Why should we get a divorce?" he asked. "We haven't had a fight. We've never had a quarrel." So they didn't get a divorce, not then. "I think I was just waiting," she said later, "for someone to come along and help me out of that marriage."

The man who came along was Bob Capa*, the Hungarian photographer who was then at the height of his celebrity as the all-seeing chronicler of war. (The reason you remember those head-on photographs of GI's wading ashore into the gunfire on Omaha Beach is that Capa had waded in ahead of them and then turned back to record their landing.) Miss Bergman, arriving in Paris just after the war to tour military bases with Jack Benny, had never heard of the two young men who pushed a joint letter under her door at the Ritz to invite her out to dinner. One was Capa, and the other was a GI named Irwin Shaw. She went out with them and was charmed. Capa could be irresistibly charming. She met him again in Berlin, then again back in Paris. "And I suppose," she said later, "that's where I began to fall in love with him." It was very intense, even during their separations, but Capa could not give up his career as one of the roving stars of *Life* magazine, any more than she could give up hers. "He told me, 'I cannot marry you. I cannot tie myself down. If they say "Korea tomorrow," and we're married and we have a child, I won't be able to go to Korea. And that's impossible.' " (It was not too many years later that he went to Vietnam and stepped on the land mine that killed him.)

Miss Bergman went back to work. She had wanted all her life to play Joan of Arc—that impossible combination of heroism, mysticism, and martyr-

* This was Miss Bergman's own account. A recent biographer, Laurence Leamer, charges, without offering much evidence, that she had actually been having a series of rather casual affairs since her first years in Hollywood. Her supposed lovers included Gary Cooper; Victor Fleming, the director; Larry Adler, the harmonica virtuoso; and various unidentified others.

dom—but the role had repeatedly eluded her. When she first sailed for America, Selznick had cabled her to tell the press in New York that she was arriving to play Saint Joan, but a Selznick publicity man went to meet the ship at the pier and warned her, "Don't talk too much about Joan of Arc." Nothing ever came of that project. Then, seven years later, she got a telephone call from Maxwell Anderson, the playwright, who said he was "just wondering [if] maybe one day you might like to come to Broadway to do a play?"

"Yes, of course, I'd like to do that," she said. "Tell me, what is your play all about?"

"Joan of Arc," he said.

She agreed without even reading it. And after she had read it, she went walking with Anderson on the Santa Monica beach and signed the contract, right there on the beach, while Selznick and Lindstrom were still haggling with Anderson's agents about the terms. Then, the week after she left for rehearsals in New York, Selznick announced to the press that he was going to make a film of Joan of Arc, starring Jennifer Jones. Nothing ever came of that project either.

Anderson's *Joan of Lorraine* was not really about Saint Joan but rather about a theatrical company rehearsing a play about Saint Joan. Miss Bergman kept prodding Anderson to write in more about his heroine, and he kept obliging her. What opened on Broadway was something of a hybrid, and a rather pretentious one, but Miss Bergman's performance won high praise. *The New Yorker*, for example, said that it "may be incomparable in the theatre of our day."

Victor Fleming, who had directed Miss Bergman in *Dr. Jekyll and Mr. Hyde* back in 1941, now urged her to join him in filming the play. They formed an independent production company, with Walter Wanger as producer. Though Miss Bergman once again received warm praise for her performance, however, the Anderson script remained a burden. When she subsequently saw this 1948 picture on a television rerun of the 1970's, she realized how artificial it had been. "It had that smooth, glossy quality of Hollywood," she said. "All the battle scenes were done in the studio: the towers of Chinon and the French villages were painted backdrops. I didn't think I looked like a peasant girl at all. I just looked like a movie star playing the part of Joan. Clean face, nice hairdo. . . . I suppose when I look back, this is where my instinctive rebellion and resentment began."

Rossellini followed his first cable to Miss Bergman with a long letter explaining his methods: "I must say that my way of working is extremely personal. I do not prepare a scenario, which I think terribly limits the scope of work. Of course I start out with very precise ideas and a mixture of dialogues and intentions which, as things go on, I select and improve." He also proposed an idea for a film, which he wanted to call "Terra di Dio." Driving in the country near Rome, he had noticed a barbed-wire enclosure for displaced persons, and he had stopped to look at it. A guard had ordered him away. He had noticed a woman standing apart from the others, a blond woman dressed all in black, and she had told him that she was a Latvian. Then the guard had chased him away. "The remembrance of this woman haunted me . . ." Rossellini wrote. "Shall we go together and look for her? Shall we together visualize her life?"

Miss Bergman eagerly accepted Rossellini's offer, but she was committed to make a Hitchcock film, *Under Capricorn*, in London that summer. Perhaps she could take a break and come to Italy to discuss it? They agreed to meet in Amalfi, where Rossellini had gone with his mistress, Anna Magnani, the tempestuous star of *Open City*. Even before he had ever met Miss Bergman, Rossellini took the precaution of telling the head porter at his hotel in Amalfi that any letters or telegrams from London should be given to him privately and discreetly. And even though Miss Magnani had never met Miss Bergman either, she had her suspicions. When the head porter received the telegram from London announcing Miss Bergman's arrival in Amalfi, he apparently thought that no message could be too private for Rossellini's well-known traveling companion to hear, so he went to the dining room, where Rossellini was having lunch, where Miss Magnani was applying seasoning to the spaghetti, and he said in a stage whisper, "You say if you receive a telegram from England, I must give it to you privately. Here it is. . . ."

"Ah, grazie," Rossellini said as casually as he could, slipping the telegram into his pocket unread, as though it were a matter of no importance. Miss Magnani went on stirring seasoning into the spaghetti.

"Now," she finally said, holding forth the bowl. "Is this all right—eh, Roberto?"

"Ah, sì, sì, grazie," said Rossellini, all innocence.

"Good," said Miss Magnani. "Here, you can have it." Then she threw the whole bowlful of spaghetti into his face.

● ● ●

Just as the Holocaust eventually changed every Jew's perception of himself—proving forever that there was no such thing as assimilation, and that to be a Jew meant being perpetually vulnerable and in danger—that self-perception also changed fundamentally on the day the Union Jack finally fluttered down the flagpole over Government House on the Hill of Evil Counsel in Jerusalem. With that act, General Sir Alan Gordon Cunningham, the British governor general of Palestine, abandoned the city. He flew on an RAF plane to the port of Haifa, where bagpipers skirled him aboard the light cruiser *Eurylus*. Exactly at midnight, on May 15, 1948, the *Eurylus* steamed past the three-mile limit and fired a flare to celebrate the end of Britain's mandate over Palestine. Just a few hours earlier, David Ben-Gurion and a dozen of his lieutenants and four hundred of his followers had gathered in the heavily guarded auditorium of the Tel Aviv Museum. There, under the blue-and-white-striped Zionist flag, proudly bearing the Star of David that the Jews of the Holocaust had worn in their degradation, they stood and sang the Zionist anthem "Hatikvah": "The ancient longing will be fulfilled, to return to the land . . . of our fathers." Then Ben-Gurion pounded his fist on the table and began to read a document that proclaimed "the establishment of the Jewish state in Palestine, to be called Israel."

Out in southern California, Dore Schary took these events in his own way, which was, in a sense, the way of post-pioneer Hollywood, corporate Hollywood. Comparing the social-minded Schary style at M-G-M to Louis B. Mayer's social-climbing dedication to racehorses, Groucho Marx once made a cruel joke: "In the old days, to see the head of M-G-M, you had to be dressed like a jockey. Today you have to be carrying a plaque for civic service." Schary's sense of civic service was always very civil. Though he sponsored RKO's production of *Crossfire,* his main contribution to anti-anti-Semitism at M-G-M was to be *Ivanhoe* (1953), which deplored medieval discrimination against a beautiful Jewish girl named Rebecca, who was played by Elizabeth Taylor. Of course. Schary also tried for a time to produce a John Huston metamorphosis of *Quo Vadis* (1951), in which Nero became a quasi-Hitler figure staging a quasi-Holocaust in the Colosseum. Still, Schary was stirred by the birth of Israel, and he commissioned the most commercially grandiloquent novelist he could think of, Leon Uris, to write the great saga for M-G-M.

"You must write a dramatic novel about the birth of Israel," Schary told Uris. M-G-M would pay all the expenses for Uris to go to Israel, talk to lots of people, record the whole great story. Uris went to Israel, talked to lots of people, and then, after two years of work, wrote the best-selling novel *Exodus.* Schary bought the movie rights for $75,000, which was then considered a fairly substantial amount of money. But then, somehow, nothing happened. Apparently, the high command at Loew's worried that a movie extolling the triumph of Zionism would offend the British, and these were difficult times in the movie business, and British markets were important. . . .

Ten years after the founding of Israel—we have now drifted into the late 1950's—Otto Preminger happened to be poking around in the office of his brother Ingo, who was Uris's agent, when he unearthed what he later described as "an untidy pile of cardboard boxes filled with manuscript pages." This was *Exodus,* which Schary had commissioned and bought but never produced. Preminger, who had made a whole career out of spotting opportunities, spotted an opportunity. He telephoned the man who was then president of M-G-M, Joseph Vogel, who had fired Dore Schary two years earlier*, and told him that he, Preminger, was prepared to save M-G-M a lot of money.

"What do you mean?" said Vogel.

"You own a book by Leon Uris about the exodus of the Jews to Israel but you'll never produce it," Preminger said, according to his own account. "I'm here to take it off your hands."

---

* Unlike other dismissed movie producers, Schary went off and wrote a successful play, *Sunrise at Campobello,* about the young Roosevelt.

"That's crazy," said Vogel. "Of course we'll produce it. Everyone tells me it's a great book." Thus admitting that he had never read it.

"It is," Preminger said, "but if you make it the Arab countries will close all M-G-M theaters and ban all M-G-M films. You can't afford an Arab boycott but I can. Since I am an independent producer, they can't hurt me too much."

Vogel said M-G-M had no intention of giving up *Exodus*. But he apparently did mention the matter to his board of directors at the next meeting. A week later, he telephoned Preminger. "If you still want to buy it, we're ready to make a deal," he said. "How much are you offering?"

"It cost you $75,000, so I'll pay you $75,000," Preminger said.

"We commissioned the book," Vogel protested. "It was our idea from the start."

"But you can't produce it," Preminger said.

So M-G-M sold *Exodus* to Preminger for $75,000, and he promptly went to Arthur Krim of United Artists and raised $3.5 million to produce it, and the Israelis were eager to help in any way they could. Preminger began with his usual procedure, trying to "work with" Uris several hours a day to produce a script. Preminger regarded this as a rather unequal collaboration—"Just as I direct the actors . . ." he later wrote, "I consider it my job to direct the writer"—so he and Uris almost inevitably quarreled. Ever frugal, Preminger went to Mexico to attempt a similar collaboration with Albert Maltz, one of the Hollywood Ten, who now survived by writing under a pseudonym at reduced rates. "Maltz was impressive to watch," Preminger said. "Whenever I visited him I found him surrounded by tables piled high with research material he was collecting. But he never got around to writing a line."

Preminger then decided on Dalton Trumbo, also hacking under a pseudonym, who cared relatively little about Israel and still less about the niceties of authorship. "He showed me whatever scene he had just written," Preminger said, "and while I worked on it he wrote another one, then did the suggested revisions on the first scene. Then I studied the second while he worked on a third, and so on. . . ."

And so on indeed. So the story of the birth of Israel—or at least the version that M-G-M had commissioned—finally reached the screen in 1960.

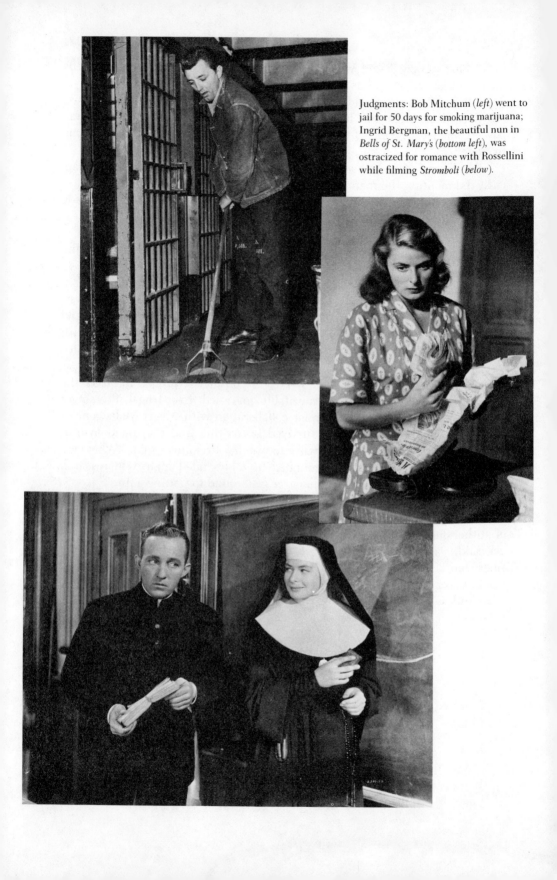

Judgments: Bob Mitchum (*left*) went to jail for 50 days for smoking marijuana; Ingrid Bergman, the beautiful nun in *Bells of St. Mary's* (*bottom left*), was ostracized for romance with Rossellini while filming *Stromboli* (*below*).

11

EXPULSIONS

(1949)

The Naked and the Dead had been one of the big novels of 1948, so there were naturally people in Hollywood who thought that Norman Mailer's saga of the war in the Pacific might be turned into the big movie of 1949. One problem, though, was that the twenty-six-year-old novelist wanted to write the screenplay himself. "We all thought movies were a great art form," his wife Bea said later. "Now Norman had written the great novel, and he wanted to write the great movie." Perhaps even more than that, Mailer wanted to assault the legendary citadel of Hollywood, to confront the great beast, the great Moloch, to be tempted by carnality and corruption, and to survive to tell the tale.

Sam Goldwyn was interested. He wanted Mailer to write an original screenplay for him. Mailer, newly established with his pregnant wife in a two-bedroom house in the hills above Laurel Canyon, called for help. He wrote to Jean Malaquais, a Polish-French novelist who was then teaching at New York University, to come west and collaborate with him. The two of them went to see Goldwyn.

"The living room was huge, lined with dummy books, and Goldwyn met us in his bathrobe," Malaquais recalled. "The agent had told him that we— or rather, I—had a story, so it was up to us to do the talking. Goldwyn stood there making comments, all the while pushing his false teeth back in place, all the while speaking with a lisp. Then he told us to write a two-page outline. I refused, knowing all too well how things are done out there, and a few days later we got a contract for $50,000 to write an original screenplay, with Montgomery Clift and Charles Boyer in view. . . ."

Their "original" idea was a weird adaptation of Nathanael West's *Miss Lonelyhearts*. Instead of a newspaper lovelorn columnist, their hero would be a dispenser of wise counsel over the radio. And there would be heavy philosophical implications. "Our hero, whose sponsor was a coffin manufacturer, gave 'heartfelt' advice to people over the radio, then went out on the sly to actually visit them," Malaquais recalled. "Eventually he publicly denounced the hoax, upon which the audience came and destroyed the radio station. . . ." After a month or so, the two of them had finished about ninety pages. Goldwyn was not pleased. Once again, he called the writers in for a conference. "He came over to me," Malaquais recalled, "and started to preach what a movie is supposed to be, lisping all the while: 'Uth Americanth, ith in

our hearth when we make a movie!' He had grabbed a button on my jacket
and was twisting it, standing there lecturing me, until it suddenly came off.
'But when you Frenthmen make a movie ith dry and intellecthual. Good
thentimenth must be rewarded. Bad thentimenth *mutht* be punithed!' "

The project came to nothing, of course, and *Variety* dutifully announced
that Mailer and Malaquais had broken their contract. The social life continued, however. "As for Norman, who was working on *Barbary Shore,*" Malaquais said, "he was still invited all over the place: he was Norman Mailer."
And he finally sold *The Naked and the Dead,* not to Louis B. Mayer, as he
probably would have liked, but to Norma Productions, a small, new, independent firm run by Burt Lancaster and an agent named Harold Hecht. *"The
Naked and the Dead* was such a strange, difficult book for film that Burt and I
were the only ones in Hollywood interested in doing it," Hecht said later, "so
that's why Mailer wanted to go with us."

To celebrate the deal, Mailer decided to give a party, to invite all of
Hollywood to his hillside cottage to admire him. It was one of the earliest
manifestations of his genius for publicity, more specifically of his genius for
turning social difficulties into publicity triumphs. All of Hollywood accepted
the celebrated novelist's invitation, and all of Hollywood was surprised to find
itself confronting itself. "It was a fiasco of a party," said Shelley Winters, who
arrived with Marlon Brando in the midst of a torrential rainstorm, "because
Norman had invited *everybody* in Hollywood both left and right, and you didn't
do that in 1949. Adolphe Menjou was there snubbing Charlie Chaplin. Bogart
was giving Ginger Rogers the fish eye. Monty and Elizabeth and Marlon were
very uncomfortable."

It was worse than that. John Ford was there too, and Cecil B. DeMille,
eyeing the enemy. Then all the enemies began arguing, and trying to prove
themselves. "Marlon was wearing a borrowed tuxedo because he didn't own a
suit, and it was much too small for him," Miss Winters recalled. "There was
a black bartender there, and Marlon just stood behind the bar and talked to
the bartender in his little suit. I was trying to talk to people, trying to be sexy
and everything, but my dress was soaked. Monty was having a fight with
somebody. . . ."

In the midst of all this, Bea Mailer decided to be the determined hostess.
She started erecting little tables and setting out a typically New York delicatessen buffet. "Big hams and turkeys," Miss Winters recalled, "—stuff like
Norman still serves at his parties—baked beans, potato chips. It was good but
like a picnic, not elegant food like squab and quiche that was usually served
in Hollywood."

Marlon Brando suddenly wanted to go home. There was too much political argument. "This party's making me nervous." he said. Miss Winters
agreed to leave, but in leaving she took Elizabeth Taylor's coat ("We both had
the same blond beaver coats we'd bought wholesale when they were just
coming back in style"). Mailer was dismayed to see Brando departing. "Where
are you going?" he demanded. "You didn't meet anybody." Brando responded

in kind. "What the fuck are you doing here, Mailer?" he asked. "You're not a screenwriter. Why aren't you in Vermont writing your next book?" Mailer's answer evaporated in the general confusion. Not only did Miss Winters wander off in Elizabeth Taylor's beaver coat but Brando took the coat of a young actor named Mickey Knox, whose car was subsequently found to be blocking the driveway. "Nobody could get out," Miss Winters recalled. "Hal Wallis, Mickey's and Burt's boss at Paramount, called me at three A.M. and sent a police car over to retrieve Mickey's keys. I suppose Norman himself had mixed feelings about being in Hollywood. . . ."

Mixed feelings is probably an understatement of the emotional turmoil that eventually produced *The Deer Park,* with all its yearning for Hollywood's riches and celebrity, and all its disgust with that yearning. Mailer saw his own sins as well as he saw the sins of his surroundings. "Out there in Hollywood," he wrote, "I learned what pigs do when they want to appropriate a mystery. They approach in great fear and try to exercise great control. Fear + Control = Corporate Power."

●   ●   ●

The blacklist grew very slowly, almost imperceptibly. At the beginning, in fact, the one thing that everyone seemed to agree on was that there should not be a blacklist. "We are not going to be swayed by hysteria or intimidation from any source," the swayed and intimidated producers had declared after the so-called Waldorf Conference of 1947. "There is the danger of hurting innocent people. There is the risk of creating an atmosphere of fear. . . . We will guard against this danger, this risk, this fear."

In announcing the dismissal of the Hollywood Ten, however, and in promising that "we will not knowingly employ a Communist," the producers left wide open the question of who might be a Communist. And who could provide an authoritative answer to that question, and what to do in cases of doubt. And since Communists did not ordinarily proclaim their party membership, what could there be except cases of doubt?

FBI men kept coming around to ask questions. They couldn't force people to answer, of course, but a refusal to answer became part of the secret record. Investigators for the House Un-American Activities Committee also came around to ask questions, though nobody seemed to know when the committee might call new hearings (not until 1951, as it turned out). Various self-appointed experts offered opinions. American Legion posts offered opinions. So did the Catholic Legion of Decency and newspaper columnists like George Sokolsky and Hedda Hopper.* After a number of opinions had been proclaimed, the object of those opinions came to be known as "controversial." Producers who worried about their financial responsibilities naturally tried to

---

* Mrs. Hopper had a fondness for innuendo. After Dore Schary went to M-G-M in 1948, she observed that "the studio will be known as Metro-Goldwyn-Moscow." Schary immediately threatened to sue both her and the *Los Angeles Times* for $5 million, which prompted the *Times* to kill the item in its later editions, and to apologize.

avoid trouble, and getting involved with controversial people could cause trouble.

But what had anybody actually done? Who could tell? The producers, trying to avoid trouble, hoped that the so-called talent guilds, the unions of actors, writers, and directors, could help by finding some way to screen and purge their own members. Or simply some way to determine who was to be branded and who was not. The guilds themselves were divided. The Hollywood Ten asked the Screen Writers Guild to help finance their ruinously expensive legal appeals, and the Guild refused, but that did not mean that the Guild was ready to punish other writers who might or might not be Communists, or even to find out who actually were Communists.

The age of the loyalty oath was dawning. The Los Angeles authorities imposed such an oath on all city and county employees in 1948, and the University of California imposed one in 1949, requiring the dismissal of anyone who balked. At the urging of the Hollywood studios, some people tried to clear themselves of suspicion not by taking any formal oath but by simply proclaiming their own purity and patriotism. "I am not now and never have been associated with any Communist organization or supporters of communism," said Gregory Peck. "I am not a Communist, never was a Communist, and have no sympathy with Communist activities," said Gene Kelly. "The only line I know how to follow is the American line."

On this matter of loyalty oaths, too, the Hollywood guilds were divided. At the request of Cecil B. DeMille, the board of the Screen Directors Guild passed a bylaw in the fall of 1950 requiring that all members take a loyalty oath. The Guild president, Joseph Mankiewicz, was out of town when De-Mille persuaded the board to act. On Mankiewicz's return, he called a full membership meeting to overrule the board. DeMille did his best to block the meeting, but the members finally assembled and overturned the board. Then, having won his point, Mankiewicz urged all directors to take a "voluntary" loyalty oath.

Protestations of loyalty were often considered insufficient, however, since Communists, like witches, were known to lie about their beliefs. The only real proof of orthodoxy was the ritual of naming other past and present sinners. To avoid that test, some of the guilty and some of the innocent simply departed. Laszlo Löwenstein, who, as Peter Lorre, had graced such films as *The Maltese Falcon* and *Casablanca,* was only a mild Socialist, but he didn't like FBI agents coming to his house to ask him for the names of subversives, so he returned in 1949 to the Germany that he had fled in 1933. Gordon Kahn, a screenwriter who had been one of the original "unfriendly" nineteen summoned by HUAC, responded to rumors of new hearings by fleeing to Mexico. "Life became a nightmare of suspicion and anxiety," said his wife, Barbara. "Letters to Gordon had to be enclosed in envelopes addressed to a Mexican family in order to avoid FBI interference. I had to negotiate the sale of our home and most of our possessions while being hounded by FBI agents."

"Forty-nine, it was forty-nine," said Donald Ogden Stewart, who was probably a Communist but who was also a funny and goodhearted man, the model for Bill in Hemingway's *The Sun Also Rises,* and who now was asked to come and "answer some questions" at the M-G-M offices in New York. "It was suggested that I clear myself . . . and give names and so forth. And that was the end of that beautiful contract."

The blacklist didn't really get well organized until after the 1951 HUAC hearings, when the committee included in its annual report for 1952 an alphabetical list of 324 people who had been named as Communists by cooperative witnesses. Private lists also began circulating. The American Legion drew up a collection of three hundred names, which it admitted had been drawn from "scattered public sources," and which it sent to eight major studios with a request for "such reports to us as you deem proper." Smaller private organizations joined in: Red Channels, Counterattack, Alert.

The compilers of these lists could not punish anyone, for they had no such authority. They left it up to the Hollywood studios to expel or "clear" their own employees. Since the process of "clearing" thus defined the blacklist, the Hollywood authorities naturally wanted to control the process even before the blacklists were formally drawn up and publicized. Among the most assertive of these authorities was Roy Brewer, the triumphant leader of the IATSE unions, who organized in March of 1949 a group called the Motion Picture Industry Council to deal with the "Communist problem." "Communists want to use the movies to soften the minds of the world," Brewer told a reporter. "They shouldn't work in Hollywood because we shouldn't make it possible for them to subvert the free world."

Brewer asked other guilds and unions to send representatives so that his council could identify the subversives and clear the innocent. Among the council's first presidents were Dore Schary and Ronald Reagan. In the fall of 1949, the MPIC joined with the producers and exhibitors to form the Council of Motion Picture Organizations as "a national policy-making authority." The purpose of all this was to convince outsiders that Hollywood needed no policing because it was actively policing itself.

Under Reagan's leadership, the board of the Screen Actors Guild drafted a loyalty oath in 1950, and the following year it openly condoned the blacklist. It claimed that it would "fight against any secret blacklist," but on the other hand, "if any actor . . . has so offended American public opinion that he has made himself unsaleable at the box office, the Guild cannot and would not want to force any employer to hire him."

One of the oddities of the still unacknowledged but increasingly official blacklist was that virtually no top stars were permanently barred. Harassed and intimidated but not banished. People like Howard Da Silva and Gale Sondergaard were blacklisted, along with a number of successful writers and directors, but none of the most glamorous celebrities. One reason was that the studios had to protect their investments in these stars; another was that the stars who found themselves in jeopardy would do almost anything to save their careers.

One of the most notable of these victims was Edward G. Robinson, whom the California Senate Committee on Un-American Activities denounced in 1949 as "frequently involved in Communist fronts and causes." This committee provided a fairly typical list of what had once seemed worthy ventures: "Affiliated with American Committee for Protection of Foreign-Born, a Communist front. Sponsor, American Committee for Yugoslav Relief, a C.P. front. . . . Cited as a supporter, who praised American Youth for Democracy, a Communist youth front. . . . Initiating sponsor, National Congress on Civil Rights. . . . Attended meeting of Communist front, Committee for First Amendment." And so on.

Robinson freely admitted all these activities, but denied ever knowing that the criticized groups were Communist fronts, or denied that they were fronts at all. He then began to experience a certain chill that he vividly described in a series of statements that he attributed to his agent: "Phase 1: 'Hell, Eddie, I've read a lot of scripts submitted for you, and there isn't one that's right for you. Nothing but the best for you, Eddie, baby. You know that.' Phase 2: 'Business in lots of trouble, Eddie, baby. Postwar adjustment and all that crap. I've got something really hot cooking. Believe me, baby.' Phase 3: 'Eddie, it's not so easy at your age. Character parts, you know. After all, you're not exactly a baby, are you, Eddie?' Phase 4: 'There seems to be some opposition to you, Eddie. I'm looking into it. Whatever it is, we'll fight it with every penny we've got. You know that.' Phase 5 (coming from the agent's secretary): 'I'm sorry, Mr. Robinson, but Mr. B. is out of town. I'll give him your message. He'll certainly call you at his earliest convenience.' "

Robinson was not exactly blacklisted. He starred in *All My Sons* for Universal, *Key Largo* for Warners, and *Night Has a Thousand Eyes* for Paramount (1948); *House of Strangers* for Fox and *It's a Great Feeling* for Warners (1949). But the parts offered him were fewer and smaller, and there were other aggravations. Hearst's *Chicago Herald-American* invited him to speak at a ceremony granting citizenship to five hundred new Americans, and then the invitation was withdrawn on the ground that Robinson was "not acceptable." Robinson protested to Hearst himself and got a telegram from an underling, apologizing and reinviting him. Dalton Trumbo asked for a loan for his family, so Robinson sent a check for $2,500, and that somehow became public knowledge and brought scoldings from right-wing Hearst columnists like George Sokolsky and Victor Riesel. Robinson and his accountants drew up an elaborate list of all the contributions he had made to liberal organizations, and he sent the whole bundle to J. Edgar Hoover, who had once sent Robinson praises for his portrayals of FBI agents. Hoover's office sent a form letter of acknowledgment.

"Hear me! Somebody!" Robinson cried out in his recollection of these years. "God in heaven, to whom do I turn? Call me as a witness. Probe me. Ask me questions. Swear me in. I will testify under oath. The House Committee on Un-American Activities refused to call me. There were no accusations against me."

Robinson persisted in his efforts to swear loyalty. With the support of Los Angeles mayor Sam Yorty, he got a chance to appear before HUAC late in 1947, and there he spewed forth his views. "I may not have been as good a husband or father or friend as I should have been," he said, "but I know my Americanism is unblemished and fine and wonderful, and I am proud of it." The committee listened politely and nodded and did nothing. Since the committee had not accused Robinson of anything, what was there for it to do? But the criticisms kept appearing in the press, and the job offers kept declining, and Robinson appealed again to HUAC as what he called "the only tribunal we have in the United States where an American citizen can come and ask for this kind of relief."

It took three years before the committee once again permitted Robinson to tell his tale. "I . . . repeated over and over again that I was not and had never been a member of the Communist Party," he said later. "What the hell good was that . . . ? What they wanted me to say was that I was a dupe, a sucker, a fool, an idiot . . . that I was a tool, an unsuspecting agent of the Communist conspiracy. I didn't say it because I didn't believe it. The third time around, two years later, I said it. My defenses were down and I said it. My judgment was warped and I said it. My heart was sick and I said it."

John Garfield faced a similar persecution and tried in much the same way to save himself. He had never been a Communist, but he had signed on for anything that sounded like a good cause. "You know, I *wanted* to join the Communist party," he told a friend. "I really did . . . I tried. Hell, I'm a *joiner*. But they wouldn't let me in. Can you imagine that? They thought I was too dumb. They said I couldn't be trusted."

Like Robinson, Garfield got fewer parts in the late 1940's, but that was partly because he was choosy, and partly because the films he chose often failed to make money. *We Were Strangers* (1949) had seemed a promising project about Latin American revolutionaries, directed by John Huston and co-starring Jennifer Jones, but it fared badly at the box office. So did *Under My Skin* (Fox, 1950) and *The Breaking Point* (Warners, 1950). So did two worthy efforts to film Hemingway's *My Old Man* and *To Have and Have Not*. The latter actually used Hemingway's real characters and real plot, and failed as notably as Howard Hawks's Bogart-Bacall travesty had succeeded. And then, while playing tennis in the midst of shooting *Under My Skin,* Garfield suffered a heart attack and had to be hospitalized. He was determined to keep his illness secret, and to do his best to ignore it.

He returned to New York to star in Clifford Odets's new play, *The Big Knife,* which was all about Hollywood's commercial pressures on the free spirit. Garfield played an idealistic young movie star much like himself. J. Edward Bromberg played a wicked old producer much like Louis B. Mayer. *The Big Knife* opened in February of 1949 but lasted only three months, and all its principal figures came to bad ends. The ailing Bromberg was summoned by congressional investigators and took the Fifth Amendment, then went to London to appear in Dalton Trumbo's new play, *The Biggest Thief in Town,* then suddenly died of a heart attack. "I, for one, would like to suggest . . . a possible verdict of 'death by political misadventure,' " Odets said in his funeral eulogy for Bromberg. "Men are growing somehow smaller, and life becomes a wearisome and sickening bore when such *unnatural* deaths become a common-place of the day now that citizens of our world are hounded out of home, honor, livelihood and painfully accreted career by the tricks and twists of shameless shabby politicians banded into yapping packs." Well said, in its illiterate fashion, but less than a year later Odets would teach the shameless shabby politicians a lesson in shameless shabbiness. When he testified before HUAC, one of the names he named to clear himself was that of the late Joe Bromberg.

Garfield tried to keep up a brave front. When a former FBI undercover man named John J. Huber claimed that Garfield was among the top ten "drawing cards" used by Communist organizations, the actor answered that the FBI had cleared him for his entertainment tours of military bases during the war. "If they want to string up a man for being liberal," he added, "let them bring on their ropes." But only liberals thought that anybody wanted to string up liberals. The process didn't work that way. As Garfield himself said to the producer Jerry Wald, who had once requested him for a specific part but now had doubts, the whole situation was "like I was a member of your baseball team and you knew I was going to get traded."

Garfield kept pursuing the route to high-minded professional failure. He bought the screen rights to Nelson Algren's *The Man with the Golden Arm* even though he knew that the Production Code forbade movies about drug addiction. He went back on stage to play Ibsen's Peer Gynt, with the predict-able consequences. When he finally got his subpoena from HUAC in March of 1951, he eagerly hoped to disavow any connection with communism and to escape the naming-names trap by professing complete ignorance of everything around him. "They're out to fuck me," he was heard to say just before taking the stand, "but I'm not going to let them."

"I have always hated communism," Garfield had recently told the *New York Times,* and now he reaffirmed it on the witness stand. "It is a tyranny which threatens our country and the peace of the world. . . . I have never been a member of the Communist Party or a sympathizer with any of its doctrines." The interrogators pressed for details. "It appears," said Frank Tavenner, "that you sponsored a dinner at the Ambassador Hotel in Los Angeles on February 4, 1945, under the auspices of the Joint Anti-Fascist Refugee Committee, for the purpose of raising funds."

"I have no knowledge of being a member of that organization," Garfield said, "and I don't have any recollection of sponsoring that dinner."

"Let me ask you," Tavenner persisted, "if you recall at such a meeting that you introduced Paul Robeson?"

"I don't have any recollection," Garfield said.

And so on. Donald Jackson, who had replaced the new Senator Nixon as the Los Angeles representative on the committee, was dissatisfied. "I am still not convinced of the entire accuracy you are giving this committee," he said. "It is your contention that you did not know, during all the . . . years you were in Hollywood . . . a single member of the Communist Party?"

"That is absolutely correct," Garfield said, "because I was not a party member or associated in any shape, way or form."

Garfield thought he had won, but nobody really believed his testimony. HUAC leaked word that it was considering charges of perjury. On the other hand, Garfield's liberal friends (and his assertive wife) criticized him for testifying at all. Garfield found himself in that nebulous world where nothing could be proved or disproved because nothing had been officially charged. He heard that one Hollywood studio was looking for "a John Garfield type," but when he offered himself, his agent was told that "we need a Garfield *type* but we can't use Garfield."

Garfield heard that Arnold Forster, general counsel to the B'nai B'rith Anti-Defamation League, knew how to serve as a mediator between people who were not accused and people who were not accusing them. Forster arranged for *Look* magazine to commission a confessional article by Garfield, which the editors proposed to entitle, in honor of Garfield's roles as a prizefighter in *Body and Soul* and *Golden Boy,* "I Was a Sucker for a Left Hook." Garfield, by now in deep trouble with his wife, moved into a suite at the Warwick Hotel in New York and began to write his confessions. There he heard about Canada Lee.

Leonard Lionel Cornelius Canegata was his real name, but ringside announcers describing his fights as a middleweight boxer found that too complicated, and so he became Canada Lee. He was a man of various talents. "All my life, I've been on the verge of being something," he once said. "I'm almost becoming a concert violinist and I run away to the races. I'm almost a good jockey and I go overweight. I'm almost a champion prizefighter and my eyes go bad."

So he became an actor, a passionate actor at a time when blacks were supposed to be amusing. Some of us remember him reciting the Twenty-Third Psalm in Alfred Hitchcock's *Lifeboat,* and some saw him as Banquo in Orson Welles's all-black *Macbeth,* and some of us saw him in whiteface in *The Duchess of Malfi,* and nobody ever forgot seeing him as the punch-drunk fighter in Garfield's *Body and Soul.* Shortly after that, his name appeared in the mass of hearsay flushed out of the FBI files in the course of the spy trial of Judith Coplon. "The drivel that has come from the so-called secret files of the FBI," Lee called it at a press conference in 1949. "I am not a Communist. . . . I shall continue to speak my mind, I shall continue to help my people gain their rightful place in America."

That's what they all said. The next time Canada Lee came up for a TV role, he was barred by the sponsor, the American Tobacco Company. Over the next three years, he was barred from about forty shows. "How long, how long can a man take this kind of unfair treatment?" he asked the editors of *Variety.* A few months after that, still unemployed and now penniless, he finally attested his patriotism by publicly participating in a denunciation of Paul Robeson. Perhaps as a consequence—who can ever tell?—he was given a role in the filming of Alan Paton's *Cry, the Beloved Country*. It was only a temporary reprieve, and the curtain came down again. "I can't take it any more," Lee told Walter White of the NAACP after a few more months of unemployment. "I'm going to get a shoeshine box and sit outside the Astor Theater. My picture is playing to capacity audiences and, my God, I can't get one day's work." White counseled caution and patience, and Lee, all full of rage and desperation, accepted that counsel. A few months later, he was dead, of high blood pressure, at forty-five.

And John Garfield went on writing his confessions for *Look*. He wrote sixteen pages, then began calling friends, trying to find somebody to talk to. He went to a baseball game with Howard Lindsay, the playwright, and then made a date to come to Lindsay's house for an evening of poker. Oscar Levant was there, and Lindsay's collaborator, Russel Crouse. Garfield drank a lot and lost a lot of money. They talked about Odets's HUAC testimony. Garfield wandered off into the night. He didn't eat or sleep that day or the next.

Hildegard Knef, the young German actress who was returning home after the second of her unsuccessful encounters with Hollywood, accidentally met Garfield in the lobby of her New York hotel, the Plaza. She recalled him as "a chain smoker with a suit like an unmade bed."

"Name's Garfield," he muttered, as she remembered it. "Saw you in *Decision before Dawn*. Liked it." And then, inevitably: "You doing anything? I'd like to talk. Haven't worked for a while. Feel alone."

Miss Knef said that she had to go to a party that Spyros Skouras was giving in her honor at the "21" Club. "He rubbed his stubbled chin," she noted. " 'You're on the way up, eh? How long you have to listen to his bullshit?' "

She invited him to come to Skouras's party, but he demurred. "Me?" he said. "I'd love to see their faces." They agreed to reach each other by telephone—she was scheduled to fly home to Germany the following morning—but when he called her and they brought the telephone to her table, the ceremonies were still going on.

"Can you get away?" Garfield asked. "I feel like the ceiling is coming down around my ears."

Miss Knef said the festivities would go on for another hour or two. Garfield said he would call again. Skouras urged her to invite her friend to join the party, but she only shrugged.

At 1 A.M. Garfield called again, and his voice was thick from liquor. "I have to see you," he said, "gotta talk, walk, speak. Hurry it up."

"Another hour," she said. But when she called him at the end of another hour, there was no answer, and so she boarded the early morning plane for Frankfurt.

Garfield had gone to see a new friend, Iris Whitney, who had an apartment on Gramercy Park. They went out to dinner. They sat in the park. Garfield said he felt sick. Miss Whitney took him home and put him to bed. There later were entirely unsubstantiated rumors that he died in the midst of wild fornications. Perhaps. But the official version is, for once, more plausible —that after three days of anxiety, drinking, sleeplessness, and wandering through the wreckage of his life, John Garfield simply collapsed. Miss Whitney put him to bed with a glass of orange juice on his night table. When she woke up the next morning, she found the orange juice untouched and Garfield dead.

●   ●   ●

The process of expulsion worked in a variety of ways, some political, some nonpolitical, some financial, some moralistic, some a mixture of things. Where, after all, are the dividing lines?

Consider the case of Orson Welles. If the House Un-American Activities Committee had really been trying to extirpate all manifestations of liberalism, as most Hollywood liberals devoutly believed, it would surely have subpoenaed Welles. He had campaigned ardently for Roosevelt, and his newspaper columns and radio shows made him one of Hollywood's most audible supporters of the New Deal heritage, of civil rights for blacks, and peaceful relations with the Soviet Union. Welles had talked of running for Congress and may well have dreamed of bigger possibilities. Frank Fay, an alcoholic vaudevillian who had recently made a comeback in a play called *Harvey*, attracted attention in the fall of 1947 when he told an interviewer that Welles was "red as a firecracker."

The HUAC investigators were not particularly interested in Welles, however. They preferred certifiable Communists who would noisily deny their communism and could then be prosecuted, or else certifiable ex-Communists who would grovel and plead for forgiveness. Welles's complicated finances, on the other hand, seemed to be of considerable interest to the Internal Revenue Service. Welles had deducted as business expenses all the thousands of dollars that he had put into *Around the World in Eighty Days*, and the IRS now challenged those deductions. It is difficult to prove instances of the IRS acting for political reasons, but President Roosevelt had long since inaugurated a policy of asking the Treasury to investigate the taxes of anyone he felt like harassing, a list of victims that ranged from Father Coughlin to Mo Annenberg to the *New York Times*. President Truman's concern for civil liberties was not notably superior to that of his predecessor, and it was remarkable how consistently the tax investigators concentrated their attentions on outspoken liberals. Welles might indeed have tried to evade some of his taxes, and so might Charlie Chaplin, and so might Ronald Reagan, who was then still regarded as a liberal, and so might such free spirits as Preston Sturges and William Saroyan, but while the IRS pursued all these, it seemed considerably less interested in the returns of conservative icons like Walt Disney or Cecil B. DeMille.

Welles did not leave Hollywood in order to escape his tax problems, though the IRS did eventually follow him to Europe and did file liens against all his earnings in the U.S. Nor is there any clear evidence that Hollywood ceased financing Welles's films for political reasons. There were perfectly good business reasons why RKO went to court to claim all rights to *It's All True* for Welles's failure to repay a $200,000 loan, perfectly good reasons why Republic should be furious that Welles left *Macbeth* unfinished for more than a year after he had shot it. By then, by 1948, Europe was exerting its own attractions as a place to make movies. Hollywood producers had discovered that European film crews and locations could be hired cheaply, and European producers had money of their own to offer. Welles negotiated strenuously with Alexander Korda in London to make a film of Rostand's *Cyrano de Bergerac* and another of Wilde's *Salome*. He was less interested, but nonetheless interested, in a proposition from Gregory Ratoff, one of Zanuck's retainers, to come to Rome and star in a film about the eighteenth-century alchemist, magician, and charlatan known as Count Cagliostro.

So although Welles was not literally driven out of Hollywood, and certainly not driven out for political reasons, it just so happened that a number of circumstances in the fall of 1947 made Europe seem considerably more attractive than Hollywood. And so, when William Wyler invited Welles to his home to join in establishing the Committee for the First Amendment in defense of the Hollywood Ten, Welles was wary. He would be happy to support the committee, Welles said, but he had commitments in Europe. His only real commitment was in Hollywood, where *Macbeth* still needed redubbing, not to mention the negotiations over a new score by Jacques Ibert, but Welles seems to have felt an acute need to get away. Since Korda was now being evasive about any specific agreements, Welles signed to play Cagliostro.

He flew off to Rome in such haste that he left behind several "health belts," which were supposed to enable a fat man to sweat off his fat. He also left behind some special makeup and a lot of false noses designed for his performance as Cagliostro. Welles seems to have suffered from a lifelong anxiety about his nose, a feeling that it was too small, too upturned, too cute, not serious. One of his lieutenants wrote to the Excelsior Hotel in Rome that a shipment of false noses was on the way, and that "the noses can be used seven or eight times if Orson is careful in removing them." The lieutenant also sent a shipment of Dexedrine and Proloid.

They were much needed. While Welles spent the first months of 1948 acting in *Cagliostro*, he also devoted his evenings in Rome to re-editing and redubbing *Macbeth*, plus negotiating with Korda on *Cyrano*, plus starting work on what really obsessed him, his own production of *Othello*. Welles had no producer behind him, and consequently no funds for another Shakespeare film. He planned to finance the project with whatever money he could earn as an actor.

Then to Welles's hotel in Rome came a telegram from Rita Hayworth, asking him to come and see her on the Riviera as soon as possible. Their divorce would not become final until that November, and Miss Hayworth was quite openly having an affair with Aly Khan, but apparently she and Welles still cared for each other. "I couldn't get any plane, so I went, stood up, in a cargo plane, to Antibes," Welles said later. "There were candles and champagne ready—and Rita in a marvelous negligée. And the door closed, and she said, 'Here I am.' She . . . asked me to take her back. She said, 'Marry me.'"

Welles returned to Rome the next day and went back to work. Then Korda finally offered Welles an assignment, not to direct but to act in a film to be made by Carol Reed. With some reluctance, and mainly for the money, Welles agreed to play the relatively small part of a megalomaniac black marketer in *The Third Man.* He was more than reluctant. When he arrived on location in Vienna, where Reed planned to start by shooting the fugitive black marketer's flight through the city sewers, Welles shuddered at the smell, complained of having suffered the flu, and said he would have to cancel his whole appearance in the film. It took all of Reed's persuasiveness to cajole him into going to work. Reed even allowed him to rewrite parts of Graham Greene's splendid script, to expand the role of Harry Lime, and to let him proclaim, at the top of the Ferris wheel on the Prater, that richly Wellesian speech about how the age of the Borgias had produced Michelangelo and Leonardo while six centuries of Swiss democracy had produced only the cuckoo clock. The fugitive Welles was never better.

Welles was by now deeply involved in *Othello,* which he planned to start shooting with the $100,000 that he was being paid to act in a 20th Century–Fox epic about Genghis Khan, *The Black Rose.* He persuaded Micheál Mac-Liammóir of the Gate Theatre in Dublin to play Iago for mere promises of a salary, but he kept changing his mind about Desdemona. He started by filming a number of scenes with his current mistress, a minor Italian actress named Lea Padovani, but since she knew no English, her ability to perform Shakespeare was limited. Then he tried a young French actress named Cecile Aubry, who also spoke very little English but had already been hired for *The Black Rose,* so Welles thought she might like to join him in moonlighting on *Othello.* She lasted less than a week. Anatole Litvak, the director, wandered in and urged Welles to try his friend Betsy Blair, who had recently made a brief but striking appearance as a mute psychotic in Litvak's film *The Snake Pit.* As the new Desdemona, she too lasted only a couple of weeks. And now, in the spring of 1949, it was time to go to Morocco to start filming *The Black Rose.*

If Welles's improvisations with *Othello* seem to border on the lunatic, an official Hollywood production like *The Black Rose* was hardly less erratic. This was the beginning of the era in which the Hollywood producers discovered not only that movies could be made more cheaply abroad but that their officially blocked foreign earnings could be spent in no other way. And so, with all the grandiosity with which they had become accustomed to ruling over the plywood-and-papier-mâché sets on their Hollywood back lots, they now invaded the bewildered villages and wildernesses of what had not yet been named the Third World. In the case of *The Black Rose,* which starred Tyrone Power,

Zanuck had assigned the director Henry Hathaway to establish his headquarters in the Moroccan city of Meknès and to start shooting his tale of Genghis Khan in desert sites like the Tinrir Oasis.

The temperatures there reached 120 degrees. And the corporate logistics involved the transportation of not only the movie cameras and 150 tons of cable but also 12,000 arrows, shields, and bows. And four thousand Arab extras had to be prevented from stealing everything in sight while they moved from scene to scene. Orson Welles, as Bayan the Conqueror, wore a costume worthy of his title: a mink-lined Russian leather coat made of three hundred skins hanging from shoulder to foot, and a spiked Saracen helmet with a veil of chain mail. And all this in the sweltering Moroccan desert.

In the midst of all the corporate extravagances, Welles did his best to assemble his own forces. He cajoled MacLiammóir, his Iago, into flying from Dublin to Morocco to start shooting, and when there was no shooting to be done, because Welles was still playing Bayan the Conqueror out in the desert, he cabled MacLiammóir, "I'M SO SORRY BUT . . . WHY DON'T YOU VISIT FEZ? RABAT? MARRAKECH?" At the same time that Welles was assembling his unpaid performers for *Othello,* he was also sending off instructions to a Canadian named Ernest Borneman, whom he had installed in a villa outside Rome, on how to concoct a movie script from Homer's *Odyssey.* He also had to give a deposition in a New York lawsuit by Ferdinand Lundberg accusing him of plagiarizing Lundberg's biography of Hearst in the script for *Citizen Kane.*

Welles finally assembled his penniless players in the Moroccan coastal town of Mogador, where he had found a fifteenth-century Portuguese fortress that struck him as a suitable place in which to recreate Shakespeare's concept of Cyprus. Welles made an attempt to borrow some costumes being used for *The Black Rose,* and when that maneuver failed, he decided to start his filming of *Othello* by shooting the murder of Rodrigo in a steambath, where no costumes would be needed. "We had to go to the public baths and walk in our nightgowns through the streets, and it was heavenly!" Welles dreamily told an interviewer. "I was convinced I was going to die. The wind blew all the time, which seemed to me associated with my death. And things were so terrible, there didn't seem to be any way out of it. And I was absolutely, serenely prepared never to leave Mogador."

The Hollywood realities soon summoned Welles from this Nirvana. Hathaway needed him in London for some additional shooting on *The Black Rose* in the blessed convenience of a studio. Welles sent his Moroccan players —some sixty of them—to a luxury hotel in Venice, to charge their room and board and await further instructions. He had decided, among other things, to hire a new Desdemona, his fourth, Suzanne Cloutier, and to reshoot all the scenes involving her.

And then the money ran out again, totally. Welles was in Rome when he decided to seek salvation in the questionable benevolence of Darryl F. Zanuck, who had after all financed a piece of rubbish like *The Black Rose,* and who was now reported to be investing much of his personal fortune in the high life of the French Riviera. Welles summoned a taxi in Rome and ordered the driver to proceed to France. He arrived at the Hotel du Cap d'Antibes at four in the morning, after a four-hundred-dollar ride, and declared that he would not leave the lobby until Zanuck heard his plea. When Zanuck finally appeared, Welles flung himself on his knees.

"I need $75,000 to finish *Othello*," Welles cried. "You're the only one in the world who can save me!"

"Get up! Get up!" said the embarrassed Zanuck. Remember that Zanuck was tiny, and Welles enormous. Zanuck was accustomed to enjoying scenes like this in the privacy of his office, but what was he to do with this blubbering petitioner on his knees in a hotel lobby? And how could Welles have engaged in such a degrading spectacle, except, of course, for the fact that he was staging and controlling it?

"I'm destitute!" cried Welles, who had thought nothing of taking a taxi from Rome. Zanuck was just as theatrical as Welles but a little more practical. He retired to make a few telephone calls, then ordered a courier to bring $75,000 in hundred-franc bills. He claimed in exchange, almost as a matter of course, 60 percent of any money that Welles's film might earn.

Instead of finishing *Othello* (another three years would pass before the film would actually be edited and released), Welles now decided that he would like to appear on the Paris stage in an oddity called *Time Runs*. This was a combination of an amateurish play that Welles had written about Hollywood, *The Unthinking Lobster*, plus his own condensation of Marlowe's *Doctor Faustus*, featuring himself as Faustus and a young black dancer, Eartha Kitt, as Helen of Troy. There was also music by Duke Ellington. By the time this bedraggled show closed in Paris and lurched off into a tour of the U.S. and British occupation zones of Germany, Welles had dropped *The Unthinking Lobster* and added a fragmentary version of Wilde's *The Importance of Being Earnest* and renamed his production *An Evening with Orson Welles*. By now he was truly a fugitive.

•   •   •

In his later years, when he had become heavy and paunchy, Robert Mitchum liked to tell stories about his lean youth, back in the Depression-ridden 1930's, before he ever came to Hollywood. He had worked as a stevedore then, and a ditchdigger. He rode the rails, got arrested for vagrancy, and even served time on a Georgia chain gang. "Once I was riding a reefer [refrigerator car] into Idaho Falls, eating frozen pears, and it was so cold I had stuffed newspapers under my pants for warmth," he once told an eager interviewer. "Some guy had started a little fire in the car, and when I woke up my pants had burned off. So there I was at 2 A.M. in a cold, strange town, naked. That's always been my challenge. 'So here you are, asshole, find your way out of this.'"

It was a thought that might have occurred to Mitchum in February of 1949 when photographers took pictures of him wearing prison denims and swabbing the floor of the Los Angeles County Jail. He had just been sentenced to sixty days in prison, plus two years probation, on a charge of conspiracy to possess marijuana. That was considered scandalous behavior in those days, but David O. Selznick, part owner of Mitchum's contract, ventured to predict that the young actor would "come out of his trouble a finer man."

Marijuana was such an exotic subject in the 1940's that *Time* magazine felt compelled to include in its story of Mitchum's arrest the previous September a scholarly footnote explaining that "Marijuana, a drug made from Indian hemp, is . . . said to produce a state of exhilaration. . . ." It was not really that exotic, just unpublicized. "Sure, I've been smoking marijuana since I was a kid," Mitchum said at the time of his arrest. But in Hollywood, the whole subject of drugs recalled some of the most disastrous scandals of the 1920's. Olive Thomas, who had been touted as the "Ideal American Girl" in Lewis Selznick's *The Flapper,* jumped out a hotel window in Paris after failing to get the heroin that she needed for her addiction and that of her husband, Jack Pickford, Mary Pickford's brother, who had been the "Ideal American Boy" in *Seventeen.* Events like that had nearly ruined Hollywood, had led to the Hays Office and the Production Code and the Morals Clause, and the banning of virtually all mention of drugs. There was no such thing.

And now here was Bob Mitchum, who had become a star in *The Story of G.I. Joe* (1945), and not only a new star but a new type, cynical, laconic, sexy —here was Mitchum, who earned $3,250 a week, caught trying to snuff out a marijuana cigarette. The circumstances of the arrest were a little peculiar. Two detectives who had been listening outside a three-room cottage in Laurel Canyon tried to open the door and then were let in by a dancer, Vickie Evans. They followed her into the living room, where they found the hostess, a blond movie starlet named Lila Leeds, a real estate man named Robin Ford, and Mitchum. "Well, this is the bitter end of everything—my career, my home, my marriage," Mitchum said.

Time's account a week later was even more apocalyptic: "The most self-conscious city of a self-conscious nation was in for a first-rate scandal, and it hated and feared every whisper of it. . . . Hollywood's laboriously contrived self-portrait was once again in danger of looking like a comic strip—and an ugly one. For years, the world's best pressagents have been plugging the theme that Hollywood is a typical American town, a wholesome little commu-nity. . . . The fact [is] that under the klieg-lit, high-pressure, high-paid strains peculiar to Hollywood, some of its supertense citizens sometimes vola-tilize and take to drink, adultery or dope. . . . Speaking for the whole indus-try, M-G-M's Dore Schary pleaded with the public not to 'indict the entire working personnel of 32,000 well-disciplined and clean-living American citi-zens.' "

Once again, as in the troubles of Errol Flynn and Charlie Chaplin, a cry for help went to Jerry Giesler. The celebrated attorney soon came to the conclusion that Mitchum had been trapped. "His tribulation," Giesler rather mysteriously declared, "was the result of a deliberate design on the part of someone who wished him ill. He had even received warnings, 'Watch your step or something will happen to you.' " At a time when Mitchum's wife was on a visit in the East, according to Giesler's account, the actor had been invited to a party in Laurel Canyon. Soon after he arrived, somebody handed him a reefer. "A split second later the door crashed open," Giesler said. "Mitchum and some of the others at the party were caught with lighted marijuana cigarettes they had just put down. That wasn't all. The place had been bugged; a microphone had been planted on the wall. But the most peculiar thing about the whole affair was that the press had the story before the cops crashed in."

That sounds plausible enough, but neither Giesler nor anyone else ever indicated who might have wanted to trap Mitchum, or why. Ordinarily, somebody would probably have found a way for Mitchum to pay his way out of his troubles, but the publicity surrounding the arrest made that difficult. Giesler decided instead on a go-limp defense of the kind that used to be urged on civil rights demonstrators threatened by deputy sheriffs. Confronted by a grand jury investigation, he counseled Mitchum not to appear. When the grand jury indicted Mitchum, Giesler waived a trial, offered no plea of guilty or not guilty, and asked the trial judge to decide the case entirely on the basis of the evidence that the district attorney had provided to the grand jury.

That was how Giesler managed to snuff out all possibility of a spectacular trial, but at the price of Mitchum's serving sixty days in jail (minus ten days off for good behavior). Nobody has ever disclosed who wanted Mitchum arrested, and the arrest publicized, or who wanted the publicity canceled by a modest jail sentence. Whatever the deal was, in those frightened days of 1949, it was based on the assumption that the American public would be shocked and outraged at the idea that a movie star smoked marijuana. What nobody in Hollywood seemed to realize was that the American public was changing. Letters in defense of Mitchum poured in. RKO, which had been quaking at the possibility of losing its investment in completed Mitchum films, nervously released one of them, *Rachel and the Stranger,* and soon saw to its amazement that the film had become number one at the box office all across the country.

Mitchum, who was supposed to go to prison and suffer, emerged as a kind of folk hero, still cynical, laconic, sexy, and quite unreformed by his incarceration. "I had privacy there," he said. "Nobody envied me, nobody wanted anything from me. Nobody wanted my bars or the bowl of pudding they shoved at me through the slot."

•　•　•

Despite the ordeal of *Monsieur Verdoux,* Charlie Chaplin could not believe that he would ever be ostracized for his political opinions. He could not believe, as he put it, that the American people were "so politically conscious or so humorless as to boycott anyone that could amuse them." He decided, though, that his next movie would be completely nonpolitical, his first such film since *City Lights* back in 1931. This would be a love story, which he described as "something completely opposite to the cynical pessimism of *Monsieur Verdoux*." The idea soon took possession of him. "Under its compulsion I did not give a damn what the outcome would be," he said. "The film had to be made."

Chaplin began writing early in 1948 the story that he originally called "Footlights." He wrote and wrote and wrote. His story took the form of a novel, more than 100,000 words long, most of which he intended only as the background of his two characters. It was a variation on the familiar story of *A Star Is Born*, the theatrical legend of an older man helping a younger woman and then sinking as she rises to stardom. Chaplin's version of the tale was richly autobiographical, combining his memories of his younger self with memories of his alcoholic father and then adding a new sense of what it meant for a professional comedian to lose the heart for comedy. *The Great Dictator* had been slapstick, and even *Monsieur Verdoux* had been subtitled "a comedy of murder," and in both of those films Chaplin had played an essentially clownish character. In *Limelight*, as it came to be called, he played himself for the first time, a white-haired has-been named Calvero who could dress up in funny costumes and do comic turns on the stage but who remained an essentially serious persona, often sentimental, occasionally pretentious.

But what wonders Chaplin could perform in those Edwardian-era comic turns! Like the one in which he cracked a lion tamer's whip as he came marching on stage and then demonstrated in pantomime the high-flying talents of two trained fleas that existed only in the movements of Chaplin's eyes. Or the brilliant finale in which Chaplin tried to play his violin while Buster Keaton sat solemnly at the piano and struggled with the sheet music that kept cascading down into his lap. Chaplin never filmed a funnier scene.

The aging Calvero could only have been played by Chaplin, of course, but his young protégé, Terry, could have been almost anyone. Like most of Chaplin's heroines (and most of his wives), she was supposed to be young and adoring and compliant. And like many of them, like the blind girl in *City Lights* or the crippled wife in *Monsieur Verdoux*, she suffered from a debilitating physical handicap, which enabled Chaplin to work a cure. "I can walk! I can walk! I can walk!" Hollywood was full of pretty girls who could declaim lines like that, but Chaplin was looking for some special quality that he couldn't quite define but thought he could recognize. The playwright Arthur Laurents urged him to consider a beautiful girl he had seen on the London stage in *Ring Around the Moon*, Christopher Fry's adaptation of Jean Anouilh's *L'Invitation au Château*. Her name was Claire Bloom, she was nineteen, and Chaplin asked her to send some photographs. Then he invited her and her mother to New York for a screen test. He recognized her. Only after she had been hired and brought to California and introduced to Chaplin's young wife, Oona, did she see what Chaplin had recognized in her.

Having worked three years on the script, Chaplin now talked obsessively about his graying memories of the London that Miss Bloom had just left. "He reminisced," she recalled, "about the Empire Theatre, the smart music hall of its day, frequented by the smartest courtesans; he talked of his early triumph as a boy actor in a stage adaptation of *Sherlock Holmes*. . . . When we went to his rooms for lunch, he continued with his memories of London and seemed desperate to hear that nothing he had known had changed. In the last few years he had been deeply homesick, he said, but he didn't dare to leave America for fear that the U.S. wouldn't allow him to reenter the country. His family, home, studio, money—everything was in America."

That sounds like paranoia, but the FBI had in fact been maintaining files on Chaplin ever since 1922, when one of the G-men reported that Chaplin had given a reception for a visiting Communist union leader, William Z. Foster, which was attended by many "Parlor Bolsheviki." To this file, which grew to nearly two thousand pages and was finally opened up by one of Chaplin's biographers, David Robinson, the G-men kept adding what Robinson described as "hearsay, rumors, poison-pen letters and cranky unsolicited correspondence, along with the public revelations of Hedda Hopper, Ed Sullivan and other syndicated gossip columnists." At some point, the FBI's operatives discovered a book called *Who's Who in American Jewry*, which claimed that Chaplin's family name was really Thonstein, and so a number of the subsequent reports referred to him as "alias Charlie Chaplin; alias Israel Thonstein."

The FBI secretly played a part in the absurd prosecution of Chaplin on Mann Act charges. J. Edgar Hoover himself assigned his forces to collect evidence against Chaplin. They interviewed scores of witnesses (such as, for example, Hedda Hopper), bugged hotel rooms and telephones, and amassed more than four hundred pages of testimony, all proving nothing whatever except the strange proclivities of the FBI. In 1947, Hoover asked to see a copy of a *Pravda* article in praise of Chaplin, an article that, as it happened, had appeared on the occasion of Chaplin's first film being shown in the Soviet Union in 1923. The FBI subsequently sent this tidbit to Mrs. Hopper, thus using her as an outlet as well as a source of information.

Hoover to Hopper, Hopper to Hoover, this was all gossip, but in November of 1949, the FBI got more serious. Assistant Attorney General Alexander Campbell asked the FBI for the complete Chaplin file for the purposes of a "Security-R investigation." A search through the voluminous collection of papers indicated that gossip was about all there was. "It has been determined," according to an official analysis, "that there are no witnesses available who could offer testimony that Chaplin has been a member of the Communist Party in the past, is now a member, or has contributed funds to the Communist Party."

So Chaplin went on making *Limelight,* true to all the Hollywood traditions of artifice and illusion. To represent the theatrical boardinghouse in the London of his youth, he discovered and used what had originally been built as a row of New York brownstones on the back lot at Paramount. And to show the once-paralyzed Claire Bloom turning into a ballerina, he simply hired Melissa Hayden and then filmed her beautiful dancing from such a distance that nobody could tell the difference. Miss Bloom, who greatly admired Chaplin, almost loved him, found his whole production oddly antiquarian. "I was surprised at how old-fashioned much of what he prescribed seemed," she observed, "—rather theatrical effects that I didn't associate with the modern cinema." *Limelight* is undeniably old-fashioned. It is also incurably sentimental, but Chaplin wanted it just that way. The stylized plot is that of some Tchaikovsky ballet, its philosophizing is that of a Puccini opera. Like them, it is beautiful—pretentious but nonetheless beautiful.

When Chaplin had finished editing *Limelight* early in 1952, he wanted to take a long vacation, to take Oona to England, and to preside over the film's London premiere. The only problem, which should have been a routine matter, was that he needed a reentry permit. The FBI wanted some questions answered. An agent came to Chaplin's door with a stenographer. He wanted to know whether Chaplin was his real name. Chaplin said it was. The agent said, according to Chaplin, " 'Some people say your name is—' (here he mentioned a very foreign name) 'and that you are from Galicia.' " Chaplin denied it. The agent pressed on. "You say you've never been a Communist?" Chaplin denied that too, denied ever belonging to any political organization. And had he ever committed adultery? "What is a healthy man who has lived in this country for thirty-five years supposed to answer?" Chaplin countered. And why had he never become a citizen? "There's no law against that," said Chaplin. "However, I pay my taxes here."

The Internal Revenue Service disputed that, or at least it differed on the amounts due, as it had for many years. In their last battle, shortly after the making of *The Great Dictator,* the IRS had demanded a large supplementary payment, but a court ruled in favor of Chaplin's counterclaim that he had actually overpaid by $24,938. Now, on hearing that Chaplin planned to leave the country, the IRS put in a claim for $200,000 and demanded that he post bond of two million dollars. Chaplin demanded a prompt trial, and the IRS responded with what Chaplin called "a quick settlement for a very nominal sum." So he finally got his reentry permit. But no sooner had Chaplin and Oona reached New York than his lawyer warned him that a former employee of United Artists was suing the studio and might try to subpoena Chaplin, who by now owned half the company. He had to spend most of his last days in New York confined to his room at the Sherry Netherland, then crept aboard the *Queen Elizabeth* at five in the morning and hid in his cabin until the ship sailed.

Two days out at sea, Chaplin had just finished having lunch with Arthur Rubinstein when he heard the news: The Truman administration was announcing that Chaplin's reentry permit had been canceled. If Chaplin tried to return to Hollywood, said Attorney General James McGranery, the Immigration and Naturalization Service would hold him for hearings to "determine whether he is admissible under the laws of the United States." A Justice Department spokesman explained that this involved the U.S. Code of Laws on Aliens and Citizenship, Section 137, Paragraph C, which, with a wonderful blending of condemnations, barred foreigners who might be objectionable on grounds of "morals, health or insanity, or for advocating Communism or associating with Communists or pro-Communist organizations."

Asked for comment by United Press, Chaplin hesitated. "I would like to have told them that the sooner I was rid of that hate-beleaguered atmosphere the better," he later wrote, "that I was fed up with America's insults and moral pomposity, and that the whole subject was damned boring. But everything I possessed was in the States and I was terrified they might find a way of confiscating it. . . . So instead I came out with a pompous statement to the effect that I would return and answer their charges, and that my re-entry permit was . . . a document given to me in good faith by the United States Government—blah, blah, blah." When the *Queen Elizabeth* docked at Southampton, reporters swarmed around Chaplin to hear more. He sounded more pompous than ever. "These are days of turmoil and strife and bitterness," he said. "This is not the day of great artists. This is the day of politics. . . . All I want to do is create a few more films. . . . I've never been political. . . ."

Not everyone supported the Truman adminstration in the banishing of Chaplin. "No political situation, no international menace, can destroy the fact that he is a great artist who has given infinite pleasure to many millions . . ." said the *New York Times*. "Unless there is far more evidence against him than is at the moment visible, the Department of State will not dignify itself or increase the national security if it sends him into exile." Attorney General McGranery really had no evidence, but he huffed and puffed. There had been accusations that Chaplin was a Communist, he said, as well as "grave moral charges." And furthermore, said the attorney general, Chaplin "has been charged with making leering, sneering statements about the country whose gracious hospitality has enriched him." And yet furthermore, said the attorney general, "if what has been said about him is true, he is, in my opinion, an unsavory character."

These somewhat conditional accusations from Washington may seem grossly unfair—indeed, they are grossly unfair—but there were some people who considered the attorney general too gentle. Hedda Hopper, the friend of the FBI, wrote that Chaplin's undeniable talents did not "give him the right to go against our customs, to abhor everything we stand for, to throw our hospitality back in our faces. . . . I abhor what he stands for. . . . Good riddance to bad rubbish." Even such criticisms were not enough for some. "I agree with you that the way the Chaplin case has been handled has been a disgrace for years," wrote one of Mrs. Hopper's readers. "Unfortunately, we aren't able to do much about it when the top decisions are made by the likes

of Acheson and McGranery. You can be sure, however, that I will keep my
eye on the case and possibly after January we will be able to work with an
Administration which will apply the same rules to Chaplin as they do to
ordinary citizens." The letter was signed "Dick Nixon."

Chaplin may have been justified in his fear that all his wealth would be
confiscated. The American Legion had already begun picketing theaters that
were showing *Limelight,* and such major chains as Fox, Loew's, and RKO
refused to show the film. But Chaplin's solution to the threat was so simple
that perhaps nobody in Washington ever thought of it. He sent his twenty-
six-year-old wife back to California to liquidate his entire corporate empire.
She found, to her dismay, that the FBI had been interrogating everyone who
might reveal any past or present scandals—all the household servants, Chaplin's previous wives, employees, relatives, everyone. But nobody had done
anything to prevent Oona from simply going to the bank and emptying Chaplin's safety-deposit box and departing, so that was what she did, all within ten
days. Then the Chaplins bought a fifteen-room villa on thirty-seven acres of
land overlooking the Swiss town of Vevey and the beauties of Lake Geneva,
and there they lived more or less happily forever after. Chaplin created two
more movies, *A King in New York* (1957) and *A Countess from Hong Kong*
(1967), and four more children, Eugene (1953), Jane (1957), Annette (1959),
and Christopher (1962). That made eight by Oona, ten in all. When Chaplin
died in his sleep in 1977, many people all over the world honored him for his
achievements, and very few wondered what ever became of James Mc-
Granery, the onetime attorney general of the United States.

•   •   •

At the 1947 hearings of the House Un-American Activities Committee,
Congressman Nixon asked Jack Warner whether he was making any anti-
Communist movies comparable to the anti-Nazi films of the early war years.
Warner could think of only one, a project entitled *Up Until Now.* That was
obviously not enough to satisfy Nixon. Hollywood has "a positive duty" to
make anti-Communist pictures, he said. J. Parnell Thomas put a similar
question to Louis B. Mayer, and Mayer complimented himself for having
made fun of communism in *Ninotchka* and *Comrade X,* though both pictures
dated back to before the war. The committee's questions made it clear that
Washington expected more from Hollywood.

The trouble was that "message pictures" generally lost money. You want
to send a message, call Western Union, according to the traditional Hollywood
wisdom. This traditional wisdom had been challenged in recent years by a
number of moviemakers who had been influenced by what they had seen and
felt in the armed forces. William Wyler, for example, had won an Academy
Award for *The Best Years of Our Lives* (1946), and Darryl Zanuck achieved
repeated successes with *Gentleman's Agreement* (1947), *The Snake Pit* (1948),
and *Pinky* (1949). But the message in all these pictures was little more than a

high-minded injunction to love thy neighbor, because he is really much like thee. Not only was Gregory Peck not a Jew, as Ring Lardner, Jr., had remarked, but Olivia de Havilland was not really crazy in *The Snake Pit,* and Jeanne Crain was not really black in *Pinky.*

Still, the HUAC hearings, combined with threats of picketing and boycotts by right-wing groups like the American Legion, frightened Hollywood into changing course. According to a detailed study by Dorothy B. Jones in John Cogley's *Report on Blacklisting,* the number of films with what could be described as "social and psychological themes" declined from 28 percent of Hollywood's output in 1947 to 20 percent in 1948 and 18 percent in 1949. At the same time, along with a new emphasis on light entertainment, the production of purposefully anti-Communist pictures rose considerably, from three in 1948 to thirteen in 1952. Some of the now-forgotten titles tell their own story: *The Iron Curtain* (1948); *The Red Menace, The Red Danube,* and *Guilty of Treason* (1949); *I Married a Communist* (1950); *I Was a Communist for the FBI* (1951); *Red Planet Mars* (1952).

Miss Jones, who had served as chief of the film reviewing and analysis section of the Office of War Information, was relentless in her analysis of these films. They were, she said, of three types. "The vast majority were anti-Communist spy thrillers. . . . Except for a change in the identity of the foreign power involved, they were indistinguishable from the Nazi and Japanese spy stories of World War II or from the endless stories about unspecified foreign powers whose spies and secret agents have peopled the Hollywood films of earlier years." The second category of anti-Communist films tried to show how and why the Communist Party had grown in the United States. "American Communist leaders," she wrote, "were characterized in the gangster tradition as tough men who rule with an iron hand and use violence as their primary weapon." The third category "dramatized events of the Cold War which had taken place abroad."

In general, then, Hollywood responded to what Nixon called its "positive duty" by evoking its oldest traditions of melodrama and stereotype. The anti-Communist movies that flowed forth at the end of the 1940's were, in effect, B pictures, the successors to Bulldog Drummond and Boston Blackie. They were cast, designed, and directed accordingly. And though conservatives in both Hollywood and Washington believed that a vast public hungered to see anti-Communist movies, none of them made any money. Perhaps this was because they were so cheaply produced, or perhaps they were cheaply produced because the producers anticipated failure, or perhaps the conventional wisdom was right, that nobody wanted message pictures anyway.

Movies have different ways of conveying messages, however. It is now commonplace, for example, to regard the space-war pictures of the 1950's as an unconscious expression of political paranoia, but a little gem like Don Siegel's *Invasion of the Body Snatchers* (1956) can be interpreted as paranoia either about Communist brainwashing or about conservative conformity. Similarly, Carl Foreman thought when he was writing *High Noon* (1952) that his screenplay about the lone sheriff confronting the outlaw band was a political allegory. Being a leftist (he was subpoenaed by HUAC while the film was in production), Foreman naturally thought of Sheriff Gary Cooper as a courageous liberal standing alone against the gunslingers of the FBI and the American Legion. But *High Noon* turned out to be one of President Eisenhower's favorite films, and he enjoyed showing it to visitors at the White House. *Pravda,* by contrast, criticized it as "a glorification of the individual." Foreman, in a TV interview not long before his death, boasted of Eisenhower's approval. He seemed to take pride in the fact that his supposedly liberal message had appealed to an eminent conservative, and to ignore the inescapable inference that his message had been totally misunderstood.

The most peculiar of all the anti-Communist movies also starred Gary Cooper and also was intended as a paean to individualism, an attack on not only communism but all forms of collectivism, egalitarianism, and even altruism. Its creator, Ayn Rand, was a most peculiar woman even by Hollywood standards of peculiarity. She was rather impressive, though, in the zeal with which she argued her beliefs.

She had been born Alice Rosenbaum in St. Petersburg in 1905, so she was just twelve when the Bolsheviks seized the Winter Palace. Her father was a merchant, and both her parents were nonpracticing Jews. They fled from the Red capital to the White-held Crimea, but the end of the civil war drove them back north again. Ayn studied history at the University of Petrograd, discovered Nietzsche and Dostoyevsky and the film epics being produced in Berlin, Lubitsch's *Madame Du Barry,* Lang's *Siegfried.* When she graduated at nineteen, the only job she could find in the bleak and hunger-ridden Soviet capital was as a guide in a historical museum. This was one of those intermittent periods of renewed contacts between Russia and the West. There came a letter from half-forgotten relatives who had emigrated to Chicago, and Ayn's mother wrote back to see whether Ayn could come for a visit. Granted a temporary passport, Ayn celebrated her twenty-first birthday in Berlin. A few weeks later, she landed in New York with fifty dollars in her pocketbook and ideas for a dozen plays and movies.

Ayn Rand was, of course, an Ayn Rand character. She sat in her relatives' apartment in Chicago and wrote out four original film scenarios. She didn't even know English very well yet, but this was still the age of silent movies. That summer of 1926, she got a Chicago movie distributor to write her a letter of introduction to some official at the Cecil B. DeMille studio, then borrowed a hundred dollars and set off for Hollywood. The day after she arrived, she took a bus to the DeMille studio, presented her letter to the official, and was told there were no jobs available. As she was walking out, she saw an open roadster parked near the studio gate, and in it sat Cecil B. DeMille. She stopped and stared at the great man, then walked on. The roadster promptly followed her.

"Why were you looking at me?" asked Cecil B. DeMille.

Miss Rand explained that she had just come from Russia, and that she had admired his films. DeMille opened the car door and said, "Get in."

As they drove to the set where DeMille was shooting *The King of Kings*, Miss Rand told him about her ambitions to write movies. He invited her to stay and watch how films were actually made. She came every day, watching intensely. At the end of a week, DeMille offered her a job as an extra. She was hardly pretty, with her short hair and piercing eyes, but she had a certain electricity.

She submitted her four scenarios to DeMille, and he rejected all of them. She wrote a fifth, which he liked but also rejected. But he hired her as a junior writer, assigned to produce brief outlines of stories that had already been bought. He paid her twenty-five dollars a week. She considered herself rich. She was an Ayn Rand character, who had come to a land where anything was possible. Unfortunately, the possibilities also included ruin. When DeMille closed his studio and moved to M-G-M, Miss Rand was out on the street. She sold subscriptions to *The Hollywood Reporter*, she worked as a waitress, and finally she got back into the movie business as a filing clerk in the wardrobe department at RKO. She married an actor she had met on the set of *The King of Kings*, Frank O'Connor, and he now worked regularly enough for her to go back to writing.

In 1930, she began a novel about the Soviet Union, *We, the Living*, which she described as "a novel about Man against the State." To finance that, she wrote a movie script set in a Siberian prison camp, "Red Pawn," and after a few rejections, she sold it to Universal for fifteen hundred dollars. She quit her job in the wardrobe department. She wrote a play, *The Night of January 16th*, in which the outcome of a trial was decided by a jury drawn from the audience, different each night. A Broadway producer invited her to New York to help with rehearsals, but when the producer ran out of money, she had to scramble for piecework as a free-lance reader for RKO. When the producer finally began rehearsals, he and Miss Rand quarreled fiercely about revisions. The resulting compromise ran seven months on Broadway but left Miss Rand frustrated and angry. In 1936, her novel finally appeared and received poor reviews, many of them criticizing her anti-Soviet views.

By this time, she was already immersed in a much bigger and more complicated novel, *The Fountainhead*. "The first purpose of this book," she wrote in one of her early notes on it, "is *a defense of egoism in its real meaning.*" Her idea had come partly from the New York skyscrapers that she had first admired in photographs she had seen in Russia. She wanted to write about the men who made them. She was more directly inspired by a woman she knew in Hollywood, an executive who kept scheming and maneuvering in pursuit of success. "Can you tell me what it is that you want?" she had asked her. "What is your goal in life?"

"I'll tell you what I want," the woman had answered. "If nobody had an automobile, then *I* would want to have *one* automobile. If some people have *one*, then *I* want to have *two*."

"I see," said Miss Rand, dismayed at the pointlessness of such a goal. How different from her own view of her own ambitions, a relentless pursuit of truth, regardless of material rewards. In the spirit of the times, she turned these contrasting female dummies into contrasting male dummies. Thus were born Howard Roark, the hard, fierce, uncompromising Randian genius, and Peter Keating, the whining, untalented manipulator. And, of course, the rich and beautiful Dominique, whom Miss Rand described as "myself in a bad mood." Dominique teased and then rejected Keating, who wanted to marry her for social reasons, but when she encountered Howard Roark in a quarry, splitting open walls of rock with his pneumatic drill, she began quivering. "She saw his mouth and the silent contempt in the shape of his mouth," Miss Rand wrote, perhaps with a little quivering of her own, "the planes of his gaunt, hollow cheeks; the cold, pure brilliance of the eyes that had no trace of pity. She knew it was the most beautiful face she would ever see. . . . She felt a convulsion of anger, of protest, of resistance—and of pleasure. . . . She was wondering what he would look like naked." She heard that some of the workmen were ex-convicts, and she wondered whether Roark was one too. "She wondered whether they whipped convicts nowadays. She hoped they did. At the thought of it, she felt a sinking gasp. . . ."

Miss Rand spent three years on planning and research (she even spent several months as an eavesdropping typist in a New York architect's office), and she spent two more years writing and rewriting her opening chapters before she reached that throbbing encounter in the quarry. Her agent urged her to submit the first third to a publisher. It apparently never occurred to her that anyone might have aesthetic objections to both her novel and her hero, whose fearlessly "modern" projects have been described by Nora Sayre as resembling "the Los Angeles airport combined with the visions of the early Uris brothers." Some of the publishers raised political objections, though, to the Rand/Roark tirades against "the rule of the mob," which the publishers euphemistically described as against the spirit of the times, too intellectual, too controversial.

Miss Rand decided that President Roosevelt was leading her new nation toward the same kind of "collectivism" that she had fled. She volunteered her services to the Republican presidential campaign of Wendell Willkie and spent several months writing polemics and addressing street-corner gatherings in New York. Willkie's failure to run an aggressively conservative campaign dismayed her; he lacked that Roarkian refusal to compromise. By now penniless, she returned to the drudgery of reading scripts at Paramount while she labored by night on the novel that nobody seemed to want. Into it she wrote more and more details of the artist rejected. Finally, toward the end of 1941, she found a publisher of somewhat conservative cast, Bobbs-Merrill, and after two more years of hard work, she finished her novel with a characteristically erotic scene of Dominique soaring upward in the elevator of Roark's skyscraper. At the top, she found, "there was only the ocean and the sky and the figure of Howard Roark."

Most of the reviews were again hostile, though a woman named Lorine Pruette hailed Miss Rand in the *New York Times Book Review* as "a writer of great power . . . a subtle and ingenious mind." Sales were slow, but after a few months they mysteriously began to climb, as though Miss Rand had tapped some political or psychological fountainhead that no one else had recognized. Warner Bros. began to inquire about movie rights. Miss Rand demanded a very ambitious $50,000. "One day, the rights to *The Fountainhead* will be worth much more than that," she said. Warners agreed to meet her price. Two years later, when sales of the novel had reached an astonishing 100,000 copies, Paramount would offer Warners $450,000 for the movie rights, and Warners would reject the offer.

Miss Rand, who had left Hollywood in 1934 as an obscure and badly paid scriptwriter, returned nine years later with a new mink coat and a Warners contract to adapt her best-selling novel for the screen. She bought a fourteen-acre ranch in the San Fernando Valley with a steel-and-glass house that might have been designed by Howard Roark but was actually by Richard Neutra. She had always been ultraconservative, of course, but in her new state of prosperity, she was appalled by the extent to which "collectivist" ideas had taken hold in wartime Hollywood. She was one of the earliest members of the Motion Picture Alliance for the Preservation of American Ideals, the organization that Sam Wood had founded in 1944 to lobby for the view that the movie business is "dedicated to the preservation and continuance of the American scene."

She finished her *Fountainhead* screenplay in six months, and Mervyn LeRoy hoped to film it with Humphrey Bogart and Barbara Stanwyck in the lead roles, but Warners decided that this was too big a production to undertake until wartime restrictions ended. Miss Rand found other things to do. Not only did she sign a long-term contract with Warners, but she wrote for the Alliance for the Preservation of American Ideals an interesting tract entitled "Screen Guide for Americans." "The purpose of the Communists in Hollywood," she said, "is *not* the production of movies openly advocating Communism. Their purpose is *to corrupt our moral premises by corrupting nonpolitical movies*—by introducing small, casual bits of propaganda into innocent stories—thus making people absorb the basic principles of collectivism by indirection and implication."

Miss Rand provided a handy set of rules for every patriotic moviemaker to follow:

"Don't Smear the Free Enterprise System.

"Don't Deify the 'Common Man.'

"Don't Glorify Failure.

"Don't Smear Industrialists.

"Don't Smear Success."

"All too often," Miss Rand declared, "industrialists, bankers, and busi-

nessmen are presented on the screen as villains, crooks, chiselers, or ex-
ploiters. It is the *moral* (not just political but *moral*) duty of every decent man
in the motion picture industry to throw into the ashcan, where it belongs,
every story that smears industrialists as such. . . . It is the Communists'
intention to think that personal success is somehow achieved at the expense
of others and that every man has hurt somebody by becoming successful. . . . Don't let yourself be fooled when the Reds tell you that what they
want to destroy are men like Hitler and Mussolini. What they want to destroy
are men like Shakespeare, Chopin and Edison."

No Communist propagandist was ever more hostile to successful businessmen than Miss Rand herself—*The Fountainhead* is full of tirades against
their philistinism—but her credentials as a right-wing polemicist almost inevitably brought her before the HUAC hearings of 1947 as a "friendly" witness. And since sales of *The Fountainhead* had by now reached a prodigious
400,000 hardcover copies, Warners treated it as a "prestige" film when it
finally went into production in 1948. Gary Cooper, who had just signed a six-
picture contract after an unsuccessful attempt at independent production,
selected *The Fountainhead* as his first choice. For Dominique, Warners picked
a young actress whom it hoped to develop into a major star, Patricia Neal. As
director, the studio hired King Vidor, who had worked on large-scale pictures
like M-G-M's *Northwest Passage* and Selznick's *Duel in the Sun.*

To Miss Rand, this was just a new battlefield on which she had to defend
every line in her story. "She was under constant pressure to disguise, dilute
or tone down the philosophical theme of her novel . . ." according to one of
her followers, Barbara Branden. "She argued with studio executives, with the
agents and lawyers of various stars, with the Johnston Office. . . . She won.
Her script was shot exactly as she wrote it. In an unprecedented studio ruling,
the actors were forbidden to improvise on the set." Perhaps that accounts for
the listless quality in this expensively glossy production. Veterans like Cooper
and Raymond Massey looked as though they had difficulty in believing the
rhetoric that Miss Rand had written for them. Her erotic imagery, however,
was just as faithfully preserved. Her heroine first spied Gary Cooper forcing
his pneumatic drill horizontally into a wall of rock. She, on horseback, looked
scornfully down at him; he, clutching his drill, looked scornfully up at her;
she lashed him across the face with her whip. And so on.

If Pat Neal seemed somewhat more credible than the script, that was
because her main function was to be in love with Cooper, and she was. In his
younger days, Cooper had been well known for pursuing any actress within
reach, but since his marriage in 1933 to a wealthy New York girl named
Veronica Balfe, he had made a reasonably conscientious effort to remain
faithful. Pat Neal ended all that. She was twenty-two and beautiful and
talented and in love with him. She wanted to marry him. He was forty-seven,
past the peak of his career, and susceptible. The affair that began on the set
of *The Fountainhead* continued through another film they made together,

Bright Leaf, continued after her departure from Warners in 1950, continued through his comeback in *High Noon.* When Cooper's health began to disintegrate in a series of operations for hernias and ulcers, Miss Neal was at his bedside; his wife sent flowers.

Cooper repeatedly told Miss Neal that he couldn't leave his wife; there were separations and reunions. As Veronica Cooper became aware of the situation, she, too, veered between rejection and acceptance. At one point, she announced: "I am a Catholic and under no circumstances would I consider absolute divorce." At another, she was quoted as saying, "Any time Gary wants a divorce he can have one." Cooper still couldn't decide, and after five years, Miss Neal finally decided to marry the English writer Roald Dahl.

The Fountainhead proved to be another message picture that did not do very well. Even in the Cold War atmosphere of mid-1949, the reviews were tepid, and the box office brought no profits. History has not been kind either. Nora Sayre wrote in *Running Time* that Cooper played his love scenes "with all the sexuality of an ironing board," and that his relationship with the heroine was "a sadomasochistic passion in which rape is more satisfying than 'surrender.' " All in all, she concluded, since "only those who had read [the novel] could have followed the tormented logic of [the] script," the screen version "can be revered as one of the funniest films of any period."

•   •   •

Roberto Rossellini probably didn't have to go to America to sign up Ingrid Bergman for his new film, but in January of 1949 the New York Film Critics chose *Paisan* as the best foreign movie of the previous year and invited Rossellini to come to New York to receive their award. Before he left Rome, according to a correspondent for a Los Angeles newspaper, Rossellini said, "I'm going to put the horns on Mr. Bergman." In New York, he sent Miss Bergman a wire: "I JUST ARRIVE FRIENDLY." She cabled back: "WAITING FOR YOU IN THE WILD WEST."

Rossellini needed no further invitation to take the train for California and register at the Beverly Hills Hotel. Miss Bergman promptly invited him to save money by coming to stay at her house on Benedict Canyon Drive. She also started raising money for his film. Sam Goldwyn had long wanted her to star in one of his pictures, but he had never managed to find the right story. Now she telephoned him and said, "Sam, I have a story I like. Would you like to do this one? It's by an Italian named Roberto Rossellini."

"Sure," said Goldwyn. Only then did he venture to look at the murky outline that Rossellini had sent to Miss Bergman. "Sounds very artistic," he said. Miss Bergman brought the two of them together, and she served as interpreter for Rossellini's version of French and Goldwyn's version of English. Then the press was called in to witness Goldwyn and Rossellini signing contracts. Goldwyn invited various Hollywood grandees to have dinner at his house and see Rossellini's unreleased new film, *Germany, Year Zero,* a bleak quasi-documentary that Rossellini imagined to be the completion of a trilogy begun by *Open City* and *Paisan*. "The picture finished and the lights went on," Miss Bergman recalled. *"And no one said a word.* Not a word. No applause. Complete silence. Twenty people. Not a sound. This freezing cold silence from all these people. Instinctively I stood up and walked to Roberto, threw an arm around him and kissed him on the cheek, to show everybody— something—I didn't know what I wanted to show—but I had to protect him."

Goldwyn understood the signs—not Miss Bergman's kiss for Rossellini but the silence of his dinner guests. He telephoned Miss Bergman and canceled his financial support. "I'm sorry, I can't do the movie," he said. "I can't understand the man. I don't know what he's doing, what he's talking about."

Well, who else was there? Well, there was always Howard Hughes. Like almost everyone else, Hughes had yearned for Miss Bergman. He had even enlisted Cary Grant to arrange a double date for the two of them with Miss Bergman and Irene Selznick. Then, dancing at El Morocco, Hughes had said, "I'm so lonely, I'm so terribly lonely." Miss Bergman told him not to be silly. She found him rather tiresome.

When Hughes acquired RKO, he telephoned Miss Bergman and said, "I've just bought a film studio for you."

"What have you done?" said Miss Bergman, who had been drying her hair when she picked up the phone.

"I've just bought a film studio for you," Hughes repeated. "I've bought RKO. It's yours. It's my present to you. Are you happy now?"

Miss Bergman treated it as a joke, and turned Hughes aside, but now her husband suggested that Hughes would finance Rossellini's film if Miss Bergman just asked him.

"No, I don't want to," she said. "You know I'm afraid of that man."

"I'm sure you can handle him," Dr. Lindstrom said. So she called Hughes at his bungalow at the Beverly Hills Hotel, and he appeared on her doorstep fifteen minutes later in his white tennis clothes and white shoes.

"Sure, okay, I'll do the picture," Hughes said. "How much money do you need?"

"Listen, don't you want to hear the story?" Miss Bergman asked.

"No, I don't want to hear the story," Hughes said. "I'm not interested. I don't care what sort of story it is. Are you beautiful in it? Are you going to have wonderful clothes?"

"No, I'm playing a DP in some horrible camp," Miss Bergman said, laughing. "I'm going to wear the worst and cheapest things you ever saw."

"Too bad," Hughes said. "The next picture you're going to do you'll look great."

With the financing arranged, Rossellini headed back toward Rome at the end of February while the Lindstroms went skiing in Aspen. There had already been items in the gossip columns about Rossellini and Miss Bergman going on drives together, but all three players in the game seem to have agreed tacitly to pretend that nothing was happening. "I knew that he [Rossellini] liked me," Miss Bergman recalled later, but she added, "If people had looked suspicious when I mentioned Italy, I would certainly have said quite indignantly, 'I'm going to make a movie—that's all I'm going for.'"

This guileless masquerade hardly lasted beyond Miss Bergman's arrival in Rome, where she was greeted by a cheering crowd of well-wishers. From the throng emerged Rossellini, who presented her with a large bouquet, kissed her on both cheeks, and whispered, "*Je t'aime.*" Then he escorted her into his red sports car and drove her off to the Excelsior Hotel, where more crowds welcomed them, and friends waited with champagne. "I was simply overwhelmed," Miss Bergman said.

That was just the beginning. Rossellini took his star on a leisurely tour down the coast, to Monte Cassino, Capri, Amalfi. "He knew all about the history and the monuments and the ruins . . . all about the legends," she said. As they climbed hand in hand up a stairway toward one of those round towers guarding the coastal route, a pursuing photographer took their picture, and it appeared on a full page in *Life.* Newspaper editorialists began to cluck with disapproval. Miss Bergman ignored them. From Amalfi, she wrote to Dr. Lindstrom that she was leaving him for Rossellini. "It was not my intention to fall in love and go to Italy forever . . ." she wrote. "But how can I help it or change it?"

Rossellini was determined to shoot his film on Stromboli, the northernmost of the Lipari islands, about fifty miles north of Messina and the Sicilian coast. It had a live volcano that periodically spouted lava from its two-thousand-foot cone, but it had very little else—no running water, no electricity, no telephones, no newspapers. The five hundred or so inhabitants, mostly old people, lived on money sent by relatives on the mainland. A steamer made the fourteen-hour trip from Naples once a week to bring food and mail. Rossellini's preparations for his movie were almost equally primitive. He had no script, and except for Miss Bergman, no cast. He had picked up two fishermen on a beach and planned to use one or the other as the leading man. Then, with some of the local villagers, he would improvise.

"Roberto would give them an idea of what to talk about and they'd chatter away," Miss Bergman recalled, "and I'd stand there like an idiot, because . . . I didn't know what they were saying. . . . So I stood there saying, 'Have you finished yet?' or 'What do I answer to that?' Absolute chaos. So to solve it, Roberto attached a string to one of their big toes inside their shoes. Then he stood there, holding this bunch of strings, and first he'd pull that string and one man spoke, then he'd pull another string and another man spoke. I didn't have a string on my toe, so I didn't know when I was supposed to speak. . . . I thought I was going crazy."

Rossellini apparently thought that the isolation of Stromboli would keep the press away, but the press treated this romance as one of the major events of the year. Nobody seemed to remember that Miss Bergman had played a fallen woman in *Dr. Jekyll and Mr. Hyde* and another one in *Arch of Triumph,* an adulteress in *Casablanca* and another one in *Notorious,* only that she had been the smiling nun in *The Bells of St. Mary's,* and that her most recently released film was *Joan of Arc.* Reporters hired boats and began prowling around Stromboli (one even disguised himself as a monk), questioning the natives about the circumstances of Miss Bergman's life, where her bedroom was, how many toothbrushes were visible in her bathroom. "We have been continually hunted," Miss Bergman wrote to a friend. "The photographers have been everywhere."

As these stories flowed back to the United States, the authorities in Hollywood began worrying that there would be such a public outcry that Miss Bergman's past and present films would all have to be suppressed. Joseph I. Breen, who had been director of the Production Code Administration but now was nervously occupying an executive position at RKO, wrote Miss Bergman to urge her to deny all the stories that she was planning to leave her husband. "Such stories . . ." he warned, "may very well *destroy your career as a motion picture artist.* They may result in the American public becoming so thoroughly enraged that your pictures will be ignored, and your box-office value ruined. . . . [They] constitute a major scandal and may well result in complete disaster personally."

Walter Wanger, who had financed *Saint Joan,* and who liked to consider himself an intellectual producer of bold social concerns, sent a cable that seemed to reflect naked terror: "THE MALICIOUS STORIES ABOUT YOUR BEHAVIOR NEED IMMEDIATE CONTRADICTION FROM YOU. IF YOU ARE NOT CONCERNED ABOUT YOURSELF AND YOUR FAMILY YOU SHOULD REALIZE THAT BECAUSE I BELIEVED IN YOU AND YOUR HONESTY, I HAVE MADE A HUGE INVESTMENT ENDANGERING MY FUTURE AND THAT OF MY FAMILY WHICH YOU ARE JEOPARDIZING. . . . DO NOT FOOL YOURSELF BY THINKING THAT WHAT YOU ARE DOING IS OF SUCH COURAGEOUS PROPORTIONS OR SO ARTISTIC TO EXCUSE WHAT ORDINARY PEOPLE BELIEVE."

The uproar could hardly help forcing a confrontation between Miss Bergman and her husband. Lindstrom, though stunned by her letter from Amalfi, did not want a divorce; he wanted her to return home. She refused; she had to finish *Stromboli.* They finally agreed to meet at a hotel in Messina. Rossellini, who feared that Lindstrom might persuade his wife to return to him, only grudgingly agreed to the meeting.

"I went into Petter's room," Miss Bergman recalled, "and he quickly locked the door. Then Roberto went crazy." Rossellini went to the police and claimed that Miss Bergman was being held behind locked doors against her will. "But Signor Rossellini, she is his wife," one of the police officers said. Rossellini furiously assigned three of his underlings to guard all the entrances to the hotel. Then he leaped into his car and began racing it around the building, as though to catch Lindstrom wherever he might emerge with his kidnap victim. "Roberto was circling around and around every thirty seconds —vroom—vroom—vroom—with me saying, 'Here he comes again . . . here he comes again!' " Miss Bergman recalled. "He never stopped all night long, hour after hour, and I just sat at the window and stared out and listened to Petter talking until the dawn came up. It was a nightmare."

After issuing an ambiguous statement to the effect that she and her husband had met and "clarified our situation," Miss Bergman returned with Rossellini to Stromboli, and to the shambles of their picture. Shooting was far behind schedule, and Rossellini continued improvising. At one point, he kept his entire cast and crew bobbing idly in a flotilla of fishing boats while they waited for an annual tuna run. When the fish finally appeared, Rossellini shot a scene that lasted less than a minute in the final film. RKO sent various emissaries to regain control of the project, a real writer to write real dialogue, a production manager, a publicity adviser, but Rossellini went his own way. The scheduled six weeks of shooting stretched to sixteen. One of the RKO envoys finally threatened to shut down production unless the filming finished the following day. Rossellini sent the studio a long cable, signed by Miss Bergman, pleading illnesses and the weather, charging defamation and violation of contract. RKO backed off, and Rossellini finally brought filming to an end.

Back in Rome three days later, Miss Bergman's publicist, Joseph Henry Steele, called a press conference to announce that Miss Bergman had given up trying to negotiate with Lindstrom. "I have instructed my lawyer to start divorce proceedings immediately," her statement said. "Also, with the conclusion of the picture, it is my intention to retire into private life." From this, the Rome newspaper *Giornale della Sera* drew a daring conclusion and proclaimed that Miss Bergman was pregnant.

That prospect struck the guardians of morality as the final outrage. Divorces were common enough, and adultery could always be denied, but for a married woman to have a baby by a man who was married to someone else— that was too much. But for the time being, Miss Bergman admitted nothing, so the press kept pursuing her. In from Hollywood flew Hedda Hopper, demanding an exclusive interview and all the details of Miss Bergman's private life. Rossellini wanted her barred, but Steele took the usual stand that the press must be accommodated. So Mrs. Hopper was granted an hour-long interview, most of it avoiding the central point.

"One more question, then I'll go, Ingrid," Mrs. Hopper finally said. "What's all this about you being pregnant?"

"Oh, my goodness, Hedda," Miss Bergman said with a lighthearted laugh. "Do I look it?"

"That's all I wanted to know," Mrs. Hopper said. She then cabled her syndicate a long story that said, among other things: "Ingrid declares she will bring suit against the Italian papers which said she was going to have a baby. I don't blame her; there is not a word of truth in it."

Steele, the public relations man, had also left Italy believing that all reports about Miss Bergman's pregnancy were simply lying gossip. He had urged Rossellini to sue *Giornale della Sera* for libel, and Rossellini said he would. Reporters in Hollywood kept asking Steele about Miss Bergman's condition, and when he asked her what he should say, she finally wrote him, late in November, the truth. "This is for your eyes alone . . ." she said. "If again somebody prints that I am pregnant, don't sue them, as you so bravely wanted to do here in Rome, because you will be sure to lose your case. . . . Dearest Joe, maybe you suspected it toward the end. The question was always in your eyes, but I couldn't bring myself to tell you the truth."

Steele was shocked. "It was like having your leg blown off," he recalled, "and having no sensation of it at first, then the feeling that something hit you, but it's dark and you can't see, and your hands go up and down your body trying to find out what happened." He wrote in alarm to Miss Bergman to warn her of the current state of panic in Hollywood. "No major releasing company will be permitted to release or show the picture [*Stromboli*]. Such organizations as the Legion of Decency, women's clubs, church groups, etc., will rise up in all their fury. The press will editorialize, there'll be speeches. . . . The picture will not make a nickel in this country, and you will thus be deprived of the money you need so badly and on which you count so much. Indeed, it is not exaggerating to envision that Roberto's future pictures, with or without you, will also be banned in this country."

Steele urged her to try to keep the baby's birth secret, but Miss Bergman only wrote back cheerful accounts of Rossellini starting a new film about Saint Francis. As Steele worried more and more about Miss Bergman's impending ruin, he decided on a drastic and wholly misguided attempt to save her financial stake in *Stromboli* (she and Rossellini jointly owned 60 percent of the film). He arranged a secret meeting with Howard Hughes in Hughes's bungalow at the Beverly Hills Hotel. He swore Hughes to secrecy, admitted that Miss Bergman would "never forgive me" for talking but said that he was "doing it only for Ingrid," and then told Hughes the secret.

"Ingrid is going to have a baby."

"What did you say?" said Hughes.

"Ingrid is pregnant—she's going to have a baby."

"How do you know?"

"She wrote me."

Hughes's next question was about the expected date. Steele guessed at three months and then pressed on with his explanation for his visit. "If this story gets out in the open, *Stromboli* won't be worth a dime. I think you should rush it out as fast as you can—give it a saturation booking; maybe five hundred theaters—before anybody starts banning it. Give Ingrid a break, Howard."

Hughes agreed, according to Steele, who thereupon went home to bed with what he called "mixed emotions." He woke up the next morning to learn that the *Los Angeles Examiner* was shrieking the news:

INGRID BERGMAN BABY DUE
IN THREE MONTHS AT ROME

Hughes's idea of how to help his film and its star was to call in the press and provide some scandal. Not since he had arranged the banning of *The Outlaw* had he enjoyed such an opportunity. He telephoned Louella Parsons, and Mrs. Parsons rose to the occasion as only she could rise. "Few women in history, or men either, have made the sacrifice the Swedish star has made for love . . ." she wrote. "Mary Queen of Scots gave up her throne because of her love for the Earl of Bothwell. . . . King Edward VIII renounced his throne to marry the woman he loved, Wallis Simpson. . . . Now, the question is, Will Dr. Lindstrom grant her request for a divorce so that her child may be born in wedlock. . . ?"

Knowing that Miss Bergman would be dismayed by the disclosure, as indeed she was, Steele went and protested to Mrs. Parsons. "This is a terribly cruel thing you have done, Louella," he said.

"I had to, honey, I had to," she said. "I've felt awful about it ever since. Just awful. I couldn't sleep last night for thinking about it. I went to church today and prayed. It was big news—you know that—the biggest story I ever got."

Nobody seemed to notice that the cruelest behavior had been that of Howard Hughes, who had given away Miss Bergman's secret solely in the hope that the publicity would make money for him. Having done so, he proceeded to re-edit *Stromboli* (the title was his idea) according to his own tastes. The result was a film that Rossellini denounced and disavowed, and the New York critics were merciless. The *Times* called it "incredibly feeble, inarticulate, uninspiring, and painfully banal." The *Herald Tribune* said: "There is neither sense nor sensation to be found in it. *Stromboli* profits only from notoriety."

Hughes was determined to continue exploiting the notoriety. He promoted *Stromboli* with a series of advertisements featuring a spouting volcano of such obviously erotic design that even Eric Johnston of the ordinarily complaisant Motion Picture Producers Association was moved to protest. Hughes called in Dore Schary, who had apparently impressed him by walking out when Hughes took over at RKO.

"Am I right or wrong about those ads for *Stromboli?*" Hughes asked.

"You're wrong, Howard," Schary answered. "They're obscene."

Hughes withdrew the ads, but the public fulminations went on, and the principal target was not Hughes and not even Rossellini but always Miss Bergman. There was an oddly political undercurrent to all this moralizing about the fall of Saint Joan, as though Miss Bergman had not only betrayed her fans but betrayed the society that had so idealized her. Reporters and photographers besieged the Rome hospital where she finally gave birth, in February of 1950, two weeks before the premiere of *Stromboli*, to a son, whom she named Robertino. There was no way to legitimize the baby except by the legally dubious expedient of a Mexican proxy divorce and a Mexican proxy marriage, which took place the following month.

Senator Edwin C. Johnson of Colorado thereupon reared up in the Senate to denounce Miss Bergman as "a powerful influence for evil," to accuse her of "an assault upon the institution of marriage," to suggest that she might be suffering from "the dreaded mental disease schizophrenia," and to introduce a bill for "the licensing of actresses, producers and films by a division of the Department of Commerce." Senator Johnson placed particular emphasis on the fact that Miss Bergman, like many controversial figures in Hollywood, was a foreigner. (Lindstrom had become a U.S. citizen the previous fall.) "Under our law," said the senator, "no alien guilty of turpitude can set foot on American soil again. Mrs. Petter Lindstrom has deliberately exiled herself from a country which was so good to her."

The American Way, however, would not only survive her exile but benefit from it. "If out of the degradation associated with *Stromboli,* decency and common sense can be established in Hollywood," Senator Johnson declared, "Ingrid Bergman will not have destroyed her career for naught. Out of her ashes may come a better Hollywood."

•   •   •

In his seventy-ninth and last year of life, Heinrich Mann was tempted by the devil. He was penniless and sick, afflicted with the pain of angina, forbidden to climb stairs. His sister-in-law, Katia, who despised him, found him a new apartment near Thomas Mann's estate on San Remo Drive so that she could keep watch over him. Two years earlier, he had finally managed to finish his last novel, *Der Atem* (The Breath), but it had not yet been published in German, and nobody wanted to translate it into English. And then, in the spring of 1949, came the temptation.

The Communist regime in East Germany awarded Mann its German National Prize for Art and Literature and asked him to return to Berlin to serve as president of the German Academy of Arts. It offered him not only a salary and an office but a villa and a chauffeur, all the perquisites that Hollywood reserved for its studio executives. This was not a sudden move, for Mann's works had long been popular in the East. In fact, he was one of only four foreign authors then published in the Soviet Union, and his accumulated royalties would make him rich if only he could return from his destitution in Hollywood to collect the wealth awaiting him in East Berlin. "A millionaire in East-Marks," he sighed to a friend. "Still it's very nice to die a millionaire."

Though Mann considered himself a Socialist, he was quite aware of the evils of Walter Ulbricht, who now ruled as the Soviet Gauleiter of East Germany. He remembered how Ulbricht had criticized Britain and France for rejecting one of Hitler's peace offers in February of 1940, when the Hitler-Stalin pact was still in force. "I can't sit at a table," Mann had once said of

Ulbricht, "with a man who suddenly claims that the table we are sitting at is not a table but a duckpond, and who wants to force me to agree with him." He was also perfectly aware that the Ulbricht regime's invitation to him— coming in the midst of the Berlin blockade—was part of the East Germans' effort to acquire international respectability and legitimacy. Still, Heinrich Mann had readers in the East, an audience, people who took him and his views seriously. In Hollywood, he was nothing. "In fifty years I have not been so completely disregarded as now," he wrote to a friend in the summer of 1949. "If one had no need of dollars, one would laugh. At least let me smile."

Mann was quite unable to decide how to deal with the temptation. He anxiously asked his younger brother Thomas for advice, and Thomas, that strait-laced conservative, offered a surprising answer. Thomas himself had been going through a similar crisis that same spring. He had been under increasing pressure to return to Germany, to confront the critics who attacked him for abandoning the Fatherland during its years of crisis. "Why must I come in person to Germany?" he wrote in anguish to a friend. " 'Where I am is Germany,' and where my books are, there I am too."

But 1949 was the two hundredth anniversary of Goethe's birth, and Germans who wanted to extol Goethe as a symbol of the better things in German history kept inviting Mann to join in the celebrations. "I shall probably have to, and my peace is gone," he said as he ruminated over an invitation to lecture in Munich. After accepting that, he felt no less obligation to lecture in Goethe's own city of Weimar, which lay in Communist East Germany.

He was in England, to lecture on Goethe at Oxford, when he received the news that his son Klaus, tormented by mental illness, oppressed by the shadow of his father's fame, defiant in his open homosexuality, had committed suicide in Cannes. Mann did not go to the funeral of his son; neither did his wife, Katia. The only member of the family who did go was Klaus's younger brother, Michael, on tour with the San Francisco Symphony Orchestra in Germany, who belatedly appeared at the open grave after the service was over and played a largo on his viola.

Mann continued on his stately procession to Sweden, to receive an honorary degree; to Switzerland, for a series of lectures; and then to Germany. Many West Germans were shocked and angered that Mann should venture through the Iron Curtain into the despised East. The East Germans were correspondingly appreciative. Schoolgirls lined the flag-bedecked streets to welcome Mann to Weimar. Mann was flattered, impressed. "I have looked into [their] faces and seen resolute good will and pure idealism," he wrote. To his older brother back in California, fretting over the temptations of East Berlin, Mann urged acceptance. Accept the money, accept the homage and the flattery, abandon Los Angeles and go east.

Heinrich agreed. But in December of 1949, the Czech passport on which Mann had come to America was suddenly canceled in a general recall of all Czech passports. It took until the following spring for Mann to get his papers in order and book passage on the Polish ship *Batory*. A month before the ship sailed, Mann spent a long evening listening to Puccini on the radio, then went to bed and suffered a brain hemorrhage, from which he never awoke. "It was, at bottom, the most merciful solution . . ." Thomas Mann wrote to a friend. "The Temianka-Quartet played a slow and beautiful movement from Debussy. It was how he would have wished it. Then I followed the coffin over the warm grass of the cemetery."

But the accounts were not yet settled. The House Un-American Activities Committee had not forgotten Thomas Mann's support for the Hollywood Ten, or his statement comparing their case to the first days of Nazism in Germany. The United States consulate in Munich had warned him not to go to East Germany. Now, in this same spring in which Heinrich died, Mann was scheduled to deliver an address at the Library of Congress on "The Years of My Life," which was to deal with America's "mindless hysteria" about communism. HUAC charged that the Library of Congress was "infested with Communists," and the library thought it would be best to cancel Mann's speech. If Washington was succumbing to "mindless hysteria," so was California. The Beverly Wilshire Hotel refused to rent a dining room to a political group that was to be addressed by Mann.

Mann's sense of outrage boiled over in his letters. "A good many people here are on their way to becoming martyrs—namely, all those who oppose the destruction of democracy, a process which is in full swing under the guise of protecting that democracy. Doesn't it all strike you as dreadfully familiar . . . ?" And again: "This land of pioneers and liberty is at present supporting the old, worn-out, rotten and corrupt forces throughout the world." And again: "The 'cold war' is bringing physical and moral ruin upon America; that is why I am against it—and not 'against America.' If the Mundt-Nixon Bill should be passed, I shall *flee*—head over heels, together with my seven honorary doctorates."

Congress was not opposed to the idea. Just as Senator Nixon endorsed the expulsion of Charlie Chaplin, just as Senator Johnson endorsed the expulsion of Ingrid Bergman, Representative Donald L. Jackson of Los Angeles inserted into the *Congressional Record* an article in *The New Leader* that described Mann as "one of the world's foremost apologists for Stalin and company." Congressman Jackson added his own view that "our eminent guest within the gates of what we Americans consider to be a land of liberty and justice will do well to lard his obvious sympathies for communism and communists with a few strips of common sense and common gratitude. Mr. Mann should remember that guests who complain about the fare at the table of their hosts are seldom invited to another meal."

Mann was engaged, in these portentous times, in an engagingly frivolous project, the completion of *Confessions of Felix Krull, Confidence Man.* He had put it aside back in 1911 to write *Death in Venice,* and now, after a lapse of more than forty years, he began writing again on the same page that marked the ending of the original manuscript. How much could he have cared about what Congressman Jackson thought was due from "guests . . . at the table of their hosts"? "The sick, tense atmosphere of this country oppresses me," Mann wrote to a friend, and to another he expressed a yearning "to go back to the old earth." This could never be the bloodstained earth of Germany, but Mann needed a home where the language was German. He abandoned Pacific Palisades in the summer of 1952—"I have no desire to rest my bones in this soulless soil, which I owe nothing, and which knows nothing of me"—and flew to his last exile, in Zurich.

The end: Gloria Swanson went gloriously mad in *Sunset Boulevard*.

12

FAREWELLS

(1950)

Gloria Swanson was attending the coronation of King George VI when she got a telegram from Hollywood saying that Harry Cohn wanted her there immediately to sign a contract to appear in something called *The Second Mrs. Draper*. So she hurried back, only to find that Cohn had changed his mind. "I don't want you to play a stepmother, an older woman involved with a young guy," he said. "I want you in a very sympathetic role." Cohn agreed to put Miss Swanson on salary while his lieutenants searched for a new project for her. Somebody suggested a play, which was now owned by David Selznick, that Tallulah Bankhead had recently done on Broadway, and Miss Swanson liked that. It had a great death scene. To make sure of Cohn's support, Miss Swanson insisted on going to his home and reading aloud to him the whole twenty-five-page scenario. She was in tears when she finished, and Cohn said she was wonderful, but he wanted to wait until the next day to telephone her with his final decision.

She stayed home all morning to wait for the call. Then the phone rang.

"It's Harry Cohn, Gloria," said Harry Cohn. "The answer is no."

"But why, Harry?" asked Miss Swanson, who said later that she began to feel like screaming.

"Because if David Selznick wants to sell it," said Cohn, with impeccable Hollywood logic, "that means it can't be any good."

Miss Swanson could not remember exactly what she said next, only that "deep inside me a dam burst." She began shouting curses and denunciations such as Harry Cohn had probably never heard in all his years of despotism. "I flew into the greatest rage of my life," she said. "I told him exactly what I thought of him and all the other vulgar boors in the studios who wouldn't know a good story if it bit them. . . . I screamed and swore and called him everything I could think of. I only stopped, exhausted, when I realized that I had pulled the thirty-foot extension cord out of the wall."

So Miss Swanson canceled her contract with Columbia and moved to New York. The death scene that Harry Cohn had denied her was eventually played by Bette Davis, in the very successful movie *Dark Victory*. Then, as in those traditional shots of calendar pages turning in the wind, a decade passed. Miss Swanson's phone rang in New York. "I suddenly got a call from somebody at Paramount," she told an interviewer, "—my old studio, you know, the one you might say I built—and some nauseating little creep said they wanted me to fly out to the coast at once—*at once,* mind you—and take a screen test for the role in this movie. Test for a part in a picture? Me? Test? I was revolted. Never made a test in my life. Then Mr. Wilder called. I was rude to him. I said what the hell do you have to test me for? You want to see if I'm alive, do you?"

Billy Wilder was used to such things, to the extent that anyone ever gets used to such things. He had last seen Gloria Swanson when she was making a Jerome Kern confection called *Music in the Air* (1934), and he was barely surviving in a cubicle in the Chateau Marmont, with a Murphy bed and a hot plate. *Music in the Air* was being directed by his friend Joe May, and he used to hang around the set, and he finally got a partial screenwriting credit, his first in America. There is no indication that Miss Swanson ever met him, or if she did, ever remembered him.

Billy Wilder, of course, had become very big, considerably more so than Miss Swanson. ("You used to be big," Wilder wrote the casual insult for Bill Holden to throw at her, thus setting up the most famous line she ever spoke: "I am big. It's the pictures that got small.") *Double Indemnity* had proven Wilder's gifts as a director as well as a writer, and it had made enough money to give him a very free hand at Paramount. He had used every bit of that freedom in making one of his most brilliant films, *The Lost Weekend.* Y. Frank Freeman, the head of production, was out of town when Buddy DeSylva authorized the purchase of Charles Jackson's bleak novel about an alcoholic's pursuit of self-destruction. When Freeman returned, he announced the only terms on which he would permit the film: "Over my dead body." But Barney Balaban, the company president in faraway New York, okayed the project, so Wilder went ahead. The idea was important to him. He had recently witnessed, experienced, survived the alcoholism of Raymond Chandler. His regular partner, Charles Brackett, had an even more painful knowledge of the subject: His wife was an alcoholic, and so was his daughter, who died in a drunken fall downstairs. Indeed, the staid and respectable Brackett seemed to attract Hollywood's literary alcoholics. He had nursed Scott Fitzgerald through several binges; he nursed Bob Benchley, and Dorothy Parker, and Dashiell Hammett.

What a grim subject, and how grimly Wilder filmed it, on location in New York: P. J. Clarke's saloon, the shadows under the Third Avenue El, the nighttime fear in the psychiatric ward of Bellevue Hospital. The famous sequence of the unshaven Ray Milland lurching up Third Avenue, trying to hock his typewriter at some pawnshop and not realizing that the pawnshops were all closed for Yom Kippur—that was all filmed on one Sunday, with Milland actually trekking from 55th Street to 110th Street while Wilder's camera followed him from inside a bakery truck. And then the scene of Milland screaming in the terror of delirium tremens as an imaginary bat pursued an imaginary mouse in the darkness of his apartment—had anyone, in all the years of Hollywood's fascination with the macabre, ever filmed a scene of greater horror?

Laughter was what greeted the preview of *The Lost Weekend* in Santa Barbara, laughter and giggles and cards that said the movie was disgusting. Y. Frank Freeman triumphantly decreed that this depressing film should be shelved, abandoned, killed. There was even a report that Frank Costello, the gangster, acting on behalf of the liquor industry, would pay Paramount five million dollars for the negative so that it could be destroyed. But after about six months of delay, Balaban decided that it was a waste of money to make movies and then shelve them, so he ordered *The Lost Weekend* released in the fall of 1945. It got marvelous reviews; it also won Wilder his first Academy Award as director and another as co-screenwriter.

In this time of triumph, Wilder became afflicted with a touch of megalomania. Shooting *The Emperor Waltz* in Canada's Jasper National Park, he decided that the pine trees didn't suit his purposes, so he spent twenty thousand dollars to have pine trees shipped in from California and planted just where he wanted them. Then he had four thousand daisies shipped in and planted just where he wanted them. Then he decided that he didn't like the color of the daisies, so he had them all sprayed with blue paint. While he was at it, he had all the roads in the area repainted ocher. Then he decided that he wanted an island in the middle of Lake Leach, so he had one built out of oil drums, covered with earth and planted with flowers. That island alone cost ninety thousand dollars. *The Emperor Waltz* (1948) earned all the money back and made a handsome profit as well, but it was a dull movie, hardly a Wilder movie at all.

Real Wilder movies were hard and cynical, dedicated to the principle that every man had his price, and every woman too. In his earlier days, Wilder had been greatly influenced by Ernst Lubitsch, though his misanthropy was tempered by Lubitsch's lighthearted romanticism. If Ninotchka lost her austere principles in hedonistic Paris, she lost them to silk stockings and champagne and love. But Lubitsch suffered a severe heart attack in 1944, in the middle of filming *A Royal Scandal,* and that changed him. "The heart attack . . . demoralized him, and he lived in terror of another one," said Otto Preminger, who had taken over and completed *A Royal Scandal.* "One night at a small dinner party in my house he got up after the first course and asked me to take him home at once. 'I'm dying,' he said. 'Please call my doctor.' It turned out to be nothing but a mild indigestion."

One of Lubitsch's great ambitions—it is hard to imagine such a yearning in Billy Wilder—was to film *Der Rosenkavalier.* There were problems about studio financing, about copyrights, about everything, but Lubitsch persisted. Marlene Dietrich, who inevitably became involved in such things, thought she had found him the perfect romantic hero, and she wanted everyone to come and admire her discovery, Gérard Philipe. This was in November of 1947, when Hollywood was writhing in the aftermath of the HUAC hearings in Washington, and so it was a splendid time to think about something else, like Philipe's great performance in a great new French film, *Le Diable au Corps.* All kinds of people came to the special screening for Lubitsch at the home of William Wyler. Miss Dietrich was there, of course, and Billy Wilder,

and Preminger, and even Mike Romanoff, but Lubitsch himself was unac-
countably missing. He had been taking a shower that afternoon, when the
new heart attack that he had been dreading struck him down and killed him.

The other restraining influence on Billy Wilder was Charles Brackett,
who shared Wilder's love of witty dialogue but shared with him almost nothing
else. He disliked, in fact, many of the essential Wilder qualities—the misanthropy, the sense of the macabre, the cruelty, the sheer wildness. Brackett
had disapproved so strongly of *Double Indemnity* that he refused to have anything to do with it, but he knew that his collaborations with Wilder resulted
in scripts better than either of them could have written on his own. And since
Brackett acted as producer while Wilder directed, they enjoyed a freedom
almost unknown in Hollywood. The only people they had to fight were each
other.

It was originally Brackett's idea to write a comedy about an aging star of
the silent movies and her efforts to revive her career, but neither Brackett nor
Wilder could figure out what to do with the idea, how to turn it into a story.
They happened to be talking about the problem one day with a young Time-
Life reporter named D. M. Marshman, and he proposed a solution. "He
suggested a relationship between the silent movie star and a young man,"
Brackett said, "she living in the past, refusing to believe her days as a star are
gone and holing up in one of those run-down, immense mansions. We saw
the young man as a screenwriter, as a nice guy, maybe from the Middle West,
a man who can't make the grade in Hollywood and who is really down on his
luck." Wilder and Brackett liked the idea so much that they recruited Marshman to join them in writing the script. The next key idea was Wilder's.
"Suppose," he said, "the old dame shoots the boy."

There are several ways of interpreting *Sunset Boulevard* as an autobiographical work. Wilder had once been a hired dancer and escort in a Berlin
hotel, so the embarrassments of a gigolo, such as they are, were familiar to
him. On the other hand, he had just divorced his wife and was now involved
with a much younger woman, a singer, so he also knew the torments of being
in love with someone of a very different age. *Sunset Boulevard* is about all of
that: self-consciousness, infatuation, shame, anguish, incongruity, obsession,
absurdity, and love's refusal to accept any of those things. Wilder had also
decided, even before the making of this film, to end his long partnership with
Brackett, and *Sunset Boulevard* is about that too, about irreconcilability and
parting.

But *Sunset Boulevard* is also very much about Hollywood, about Hollywood power and Hollywood imagery, about its worship of youth and its worship of its own past. (Because of this, Wilder insisted on keeping everything
secret. No script was shown to anyone. The project was known only under a
dummy title, "A Can of Beans.") As his main location, Wilder had to find a
ruined Hollywood palace for his movie queen to reign in, and since nothing in
the real Hollywood could be sufficiently palatial, or sufficiently ruined, Wilder
had to create the Frankensteinian castle of his imagining. He found a Renais-

sance-style mansion at the corner of Wilshire and Crenshaw boulevards, which had been built in 1924 by William Jenkins, a former consul in Mexico, for $250,000. Jenkins had abandoned the place after living there for just a year, and it had then stood vacant for eleven years before being bought by J. Paul Getty, the oil man. When Getty was divorced by his second wife, she got the house, and now she was willing to rent it to Paramount, on one condition. Paramount wanted to build a swimming pool, and if Mrs. Getty didn't like it, the studio would have to remove it.

Paramount built the pool (Mrs. Getty liked it), and it built a lot of other things as well. It put stained-glass windows in the front hall and a pipe organ in the living room. It also installed heavy velvet curtains, and palm trees in the conservatory, and dozens of framed portraits of Miss Swanson. The same procedures applied, on a somewhat smaller scale, to the grand automobile that Wilder felt a silent-movie queen should have. The antique Isotta Fraschini limousine that he rented for five hundred dollars a week was a marvel in itself, but he spent several thousand dollars more in having it upholstered in leopard skin and equipped with a gold telephone for his star to talk to her chauffeur. The chauffeur himself was an Isotta Fraschini among actors, and among the directors of Wilder's youth, Erich von Stroheim. "Erich didn't know how to drive, which humiliated him," Miss Swanson remarked of her chauffeur, "but he acted the scene, and the action of driving, so completely that he was exhausted after each take, even though the car was being towed by ropes the whole while."

As so often happened, Wilder seemed to stumble onto his brilliant cast by a series of accidents. Just as *Double Indemnity* had been saved by the fact that George Raft was too stupid to accept the leading role, *Sunset Boulevard* was saved by the fact that Wilder's first choice as his heroine was immensely vain. Mae West professed to be shocked by Wilder's proposition. At fifty-five, she claimed that she was much too young to play a star of silent movies. Wilder then asked Mary Pickford, and she was willing, but she wanted the role greatly enlarged. Wilder ducked out. Then he asked Pola Negri, and she, like Mae West, thought she was too young to play a woman of fifty. George Cukor, the director, was the one who finally suggested Gloria Swanson for the role of Norma Desmond and even persuaded her to do a screen test to get it.

For the role of the young man, Wilder thought he had everything well settled when he signed up Montgomery Clift. He had envisioned Clift in the part while he was writing the screenplay. Two weeks before shooting was scheduled to start, Clift backed out. "I don't think I could be convincing making love to a woman twice my age," he announced through his agent. This was odd, because Clift was much involved witih the singer Libby Holman, who was in fact about twice his age, and who apparently thought that *Sunset Boulevard* was about her. Clift would probably have been great, but Wilder's alternative choices would probably have been disastrous. Fred MacMurray turned him down. Gene Kelly was tied up at M-G-M. Wilder was reduced to looking through the list of Paramount's contract actors, and that was how he settled on a relatively unknown young man named William Holden.

Just as Wilder on his own had picked Mae West as a grotesque Norma Desmond, Wilder on his own tried to create one of the most lugubrious opening scenes ever filmed. It was to be set in the Los Angeles morgue, with all the corpses talking about how they got there. Wilder not only wrote this scene but actually shot it. "The corpse lying next to me asks me how I died and I say I drowned," Holden recalled. "And he asks me how can a young guy like you drown and I say, 'Well, first I was shot in the back,' and then he says, yeah, he was shot also. He was a Chicago gangster killed in Los Angeles. Then a little kid on a slab across from me says, 'I drowned too—swimming with my friend off the Santa Monica pier. I bet him I could hold my breath two minutes.' Some dame is over by the kid and she says he shouldn't be unhappy as his parents will come and take him to a nice place. Then from way down there's this great big Negro corpse and he says, 'Hey, man, did you get the final score on the Dodger game before you got it?' And I say, no, I died before the morning papers came out. . . ."

Brackett hated such things, of course. He said the scene was morbid and disgusting, but Wilder had a Vienna/Berlin sensibility, and he savored the macabre, and he saw Hollywood as a macabre place. That was why he hired Von Stroheim to play Gloria Swanson's chauffeur (and onetime husband), and why he listened to Von Stroheim's even more macabre suggestions (he wanted to be filmed lovingly washing out Norma Desmond's underclothes). And that was how Wilder wandered into the famous exchange with his cameraman, John F. Seitz, who asked how Wilder wanted him to film the funeral of Norma Desmond's pet chimpanzee, thus enabling Wilder to say, "Oh, just your usual monkey funeral shot, Johnny."

Despite the air of frivolity, though, Wilder was completely serious about what he was doing. When Bill Holden made a Brando-style fuss about needing to know more about the character of Joe Gillis, Wilder countered by asking, "Do you know Bill Holden?"

"Of course," said Holden, who actually had very little idea of how little he knew Bill Holden, an innocence that was exactly what Wilder wanted when he said, "Then you know Joe Gillis."

Gloria Swanson was old enough and shrewd enough to see the strategy. "Wilder deliberately left us on our own," she recalled, "made us dig into ourselves, knowing full well that such a script, about Hollywood's excesses and neuroses, was bound to give the Hollywood people acting in it healthy doubts, about the material or about themselves. . . . The more you thought about the film, the more it seemed to be a modern extension of Pirandello, or some sort of living exercise in science fiction."

It was all of that, but it also had a wonderfully Gothic atmosphere, an eeriness, and largely because of Miss Swanson, it had a quality that most Hollywood films lacked: passion. Norma Desmond really had wild feelings about Joe Gillis. When she couldn't keep him, it was as natural to her as it would have been to Medea or Phaedra to kill him and then go mad. She went mad in a purely Hollywood way, of course, descending that stairway under the bright lights and announcing that she was ready for Mr. DeMille to photograph her, but it was all done with such feeling and such style that it was probably the nearest approach to classic tragedy that Hollywood ever achieved.

But there was still that awful beginning in the Los Angeles morgue. To escape the conventional reactions, Paramount decided to try a preview in Evanston, Illinois, not only because corporate statisticians declared this to be the typical American town but because it was the headquarters of the Woman's Christian Temperance Union and therefore could be expected to take a favorable view of the makers of *The Lost Weekend.* That was a mistake. The audience in Evanston laughed and hooted and filled out cards offering a variety of insulting verdicts on Wilder's masterpiece. Wilder told Paramount that Evanston lacked the sophistication to appreciate *Sunset Boulevard.* So the studio tried another preview, in a town that its demographers described as the most sophisticated in the country, which was, of all places, Great Neck, Long Island. They hated *Sunset Boulevard* there too. They not only laughed at it but booed it, hissed it, and razzed it.

Paramount officials reacted by delaying any further showings for six months. Then, by some process of internal revision, Wilder was persuaded, or persuaded himself, to try a new beginning. His new version was quite bizarre too, with the body of Joe Gillis floating in Norma Desmond's swimming pool and then starting to tell the story of how he got there. At least, he was the only talking corpse in the scene, and audiences no longer got the impression that they were about to witness some perverse comedy. Released in the summer of 1950, *Sunset Boulevard* received the excellent reviews that it deserved, and it did well at the box office. The only audience that really disliked it was the collection of movie notables who assembled for its Hollywood premiere. Louis B. Mayer, still the head of M-G-M and thus still the king of Hollywood, not only denounced *Sunset Boulevard* to his entourage of retainers but shouted his hostility at Wilder.

"You bastard," cried Mayer, shaking his fist, "you have disgraced the industry that made you and fed you. You should be tarred and feathered and run out of Hollywood."

Billy Wilder paused for a moment, trying to think what to say, the perfect riposte. Then his instincts provided the answer.

"Fuck you," Billy Wilder said.

●   ●   ●

William Randolph Hearst, who had once seemed so powerful in Orson Welles's portrait of Citizen Kane, now lay dying. He was already well into his eighties when he began suffering from auricular fibrillation, a dangerous heart condition, and his doctors told him he must abandon his mountaintop palace at San Simeon. He wept as he was driven down the hill for the last time, past the zoo with its zebras and camels and its black panther. Hearst and Marion Davies settled into a relatively modest Spanish stucco house in Beverly Hills, with only eight acres of palms and gardens and only two dozen servants to take care of things. They also brought along twelve paintings of Miss Davies in various film roles. Hearst still loved to look at her in private screenings of *The Red Mill* and *Peg o' My Heart* and *When Knighthood Was in Flower.*

Once, when Hearst not only financed all her films but ordered his newspapers to chorus her praises, Miss Davies was generally regarded as his puppet. After all, she was just a stammering seventeen-year-old chorus girl in the Ziegfeld Follies when she met this millionaire publisher nearly forty years her senior. There is a countertheory, though, that Hearst suppressed and destroyed her natural talent for comedy by insisting that she star only in sentimental romances. Still, theirs was a sentimental romance too, and if it was ridiculous for Hearst to fall in love with such a girl, to abandon his wife and children for her, it was hardly less ridiculous for her to love him just as loyally for the next thirty years. She didn't mind absurdities. Making fun of Hearst's magisterial figure, she referred to him as "Droopy drawers." It was true that he gave her jewels and cars and even real estate, anything that he might think she might want, but it was also true that when he was teetering on the edge of bankruptcy in 1937, she hocked everything on which she could raise money and presented him with a totally unexpected check for one million dollars. "I thought: Why have him tortured, for a miserable million dollars . . ." Miss Davies said later. "That was one thing I liked about W.R.—he had no idea of money at all."

Despite Hearst's pretensions, he was the most inept of tycoons. He made millions from mining stocks that he inherited from his father, but he lost millions in his publishing enterprises, his garish combination of sensationalism and jingoism. And though he sounded his trumpets on various crusades like antivivisectionism, his real power was so feeble that he was never able to win any political office, not even as mayor of New York. Droopy drawers indeed. Now, though his hands often shook uncontrollably and his weight had sunk to 125 pounds, he still sat in his wheelchair and dictated memoranda to his embarrassed editors, or told Miss Davies to telephone them in the middle of the night with trivial instructions.

On New Year's Eve of 1950, Anita Loos joined a little delegation to troop over to what she called the "cheerless" Hearst place in Beverly Hills to wish the eighty-seven-year-old chief a happy new year. Along with her came Hearst's Hollywood gossip columnist, Louella Parsons, herself nearly seventy and failing, and Charlie Lederer, who was part of the entourage not because he was a witty scriptwriter but because he was Miss Davies's scapegrace nephew. Before ushering them into "The Presence," Miss Loos said, Miss Davies stammered a warning: "He can't t-t-talk so don't ask h-h-how he is. Just m-m-make conversation as usual—you know, b-b-be idiotic."

"Trying our best to seem nonchalant," Miss Loos recalled, "we filed into a large, sparsely furnished bedroom where W.R. lay inert. But as we spoke those large, liquid eyes shifted to each one of us. Their expression registered mild interest in such items as, 'You're going to love Louella's new porch furniture, Mr. Hearst.' After a few pearls of thought we filed out, vastly shaken. . . ."

●   ●   ●

Up until nearly the end, the Hollywood Ten seemed to be confident that the Supreme Court would overturn their convictions for contempt of Congress. The Court's previous rulings appeared to guarantee that the Ten were entitled to rely on the First Amendment's guarantee of free speech. What ruined these expectations, several of them later said, was the death in 1949 of two liberal New Dealers on the Court, Frank Murphy and Wiley Rutledge, and their replacement by two relatively conservative Truman appointees, Sherman Minton and Attorney General Tom Clark.

In attaching so much importance to the personnel of the Court, the convicted men seemed to be ignoring the whole climate of opinion in the United States. This was a nervous, frightened country, frightened by the Soviets' testing of their first atomic bomb the previous summer, frightened by the Communists' conquest of China that fall. In October of 1949, the eleven leaders of the Communist Party were convicted of advocating the overthrow of the government, an advocacy obviously permitted by the First Amendment but now declared illegal by the Smith Act.

In January of 1950, the most spectacular in a series of spy trials ended with the conviction of Alger Hiss, the former State Department official, on a charge of perjury. The chief beneficiary of the Hiss case was the young California congressman Richard Nixon, who had played a prominent part in Hiss's interrogation before the House Un-American Activities Committee, and who now decided to run for the Senate. His Democratic opponent, the former actress Helen Gahagan Douglas, was an outspokenly liberal congresswoman who had voted to cut off all funds for HUAC. Nixon based his victorious campaign on the implication that Mrs. Douglas was a dangerous leftist. "If she had her way," Nixon said, "the Communist conspiracy would never have been exposed." And again: "Why has she followed the Communist line so many times?"

The Supreme Court decided in April, by a majority of six to two, that there was no reason to review the conviction of the Hollywood Ten. And so, although new appeals were immediately filed, the defendants had to start preparing for the inevitability of actually going to prison: humdrum details like how the mortgage payments would be made, and what should be told to the children.

Dalton Trumbo and John Howard Lawson, whose appeals served as precedents for the other eight, were the first to go to Washington for sentencing. The small crowd at the Los Angeles airport included Trumbo's beautiful wife, Cleo, and their three children, who waved a homemade banner that said: DALTON TRUMBO IS GOING TO JAIL. FREE THE HOLLYWOOD TEN. On June 9,

Trumbo and Lawson were both sentenced to one year in prison and fined a thousand dollars. On June 29, the other defendants received the same sentences.* Whatever sympathy they might have expected on this harsh judgment faded when the Korean War broke out that same week and President Truman promptly ordered U.S. troops to resist the Communist invasion across the thirty-eighth parallel.

To Alvah Bessie, a veteran of the Spanish civil war, the experience of being sentenced to prison in the capital of his own country was a little hard to believe. The Washington court itself, he said, "was impressive, as all American Federal courtrooms are impressive." It was made of oak and marble, and an American flag stood behind the judge, and the court officers were all "soft-spoken, courteous and correct." The white-haired judge, David Pine, "could have been type-cast by Hollywood." The judge listened judiciously to the defense lawyers' arguments for lenience and then judiciously rejected them as irrelevant. He asked Bessie if he had anything to say, and when Bessie said he did, the judge listened judiciously to that too. "Judge Pine smiled several times during the three minutes I spoke and nodded in agreement once or twice," Bessie recalled, "and then he pronounced sentence."

The still incredulous prisoners, none of whom had ever been inside a prison before, none of whom had done anything that could seriously be considered a prisonworthy crime, were then handcuffed and led through marble corridors to an elevator and then down to a municipal jail, quite diferent from the dignified courtroom. "The bullpen was filthy and crowded with men," Bessie recalled. "The paint was peeling off the walls; the open latrine in the corner stank; the men—mostly Negroes—sat on battered wooden benches around the walls, for the most part apathetic, depressed, and disinclined even to ask each other, 'What're *you* in for?' . . . Some Negro prisoners who were being booked shouted through the screening at us, 'Hiya, Hollywood kids!' "

After two weeks in the Washington jail, the Hollywood kids were shipped out to various federal prisons. There were eight minimum-security institutions, and although the prisoners could request a specific one, the government followed its own arcane rules in reaching a final decision. Trumbo, Lawson, and Scott were sent to Ashland, Kentucky; Lardner and Cole to Danbury, Connecticut; Biberman and Bessie to Texarkana, Texas; Maltz and Dmytryk to Millpoint, West Virginia (there they met Clifford Odets, about to leave after completing a three-month term for contempt). Ornitz, already afflicted with cancer, went to the prison hospital in Springfield, Massachusetts.

The prisoners' physical circumstances were not at all bad. "Life here is something like life in a sanitarium," Trumbo wrote to his wife. "The place is airy, immaculate and most attractive, with wide expanse of lawns, and views of green country-side in every direction. The food is good, the attitude is friendly, and the restrictions are not onerous. The regularity of food, sleep

---

* Except for Dmytryk and Biberman, who happened to be brought before a more lenient judge, and who therefore received, for no particular reason, terms of only six months.

[and] work is most relaxing. . . . The sudden shucking off of all responsibility gives one a sense of almost exhilarating relief." The prisoners were given undemanding work. Lardner became a clerk-typist in the parole office; Cole worked in the food warehouse; Dmytryk was a clerk in the prison garage; he also learned how to run a bulldozer, how to build a whiskey still, and how to make a knife. Several of the prisoners took up calisthenics and lost weight. Lardner started to write a novel (which eventually became *The Ecstasy of Owen Muir*). So did Trumbo, though he never finished his. And for every imprisoned writer, this was an opportunity, finally, to read *War and Peace*. Both Trumbo and Cole did so.

The most unusual aspect of the prison lives of the Hollywood Ten, though, was their confrontation with hundreds of men quite unlike anyone they had ever known in Hollywood. "Moving about in the population of the prison," Bessie wrote of Texarkana, "you met inmates who were named Cupcake (short and fat), Bebop (Negro), Turkey (long, red neck), Snake (had one tattooed on his arm . . .), Mother (an old Southern explanation that need not be translated here), Heavy, Slugger, Eleven, Porky, Dimples, Garbage Can (who weighed three hundred pounds and got himself committed regularly so that he could eat free), Muscles, One-Eye, Short-Timer. . . . Kansas City, Double-O (eyeglasses), Tokio, and Buckskin. . . ."

These other prisoners regarded the Hollywood radicals not with the hostility that they might have expected but rather with a kind of disbelief that anyone would go to prison for political reasons. They knew and cared nothing about politics, but they disliked all American authorities. When newsreels were occasionally shown, the prisoners indiscriminately cheered both Stalin and Hitler. Many of these convicts were black—about two thirds in the southern prisons and one third in the North—and both sleeping and eating arrangements were strictly though unofficially segregated. The Hollywood writers, rather guileless in such things, did their best to make friends with the blacks. Occasionally, they succeeded. Cole and Lardner even managed to desegregate the cafeteria in their Connecticut prison.

Dalton Trumbo, once extravagantly well paid for his writing, became an unofficial scrivener for the illiterate and helped a number of imprisoned moonshiners to correspond with their families. He particularly remembered one convict named Cecil, whose letters from his wife, written for her by her daughter, told an endless tale of trying to harvest crops and collecting firewood and tending sick children. "His wife's teeth were very bad," Trumbo reminisced later, "and she'd been to the county two or three times about her teeth. And finally, there came a letter from her that said that although she . . . begged them not to, the county took out all her teeth. She said, 'I haven't got any teeth. . . . All I've got is gums now, and my mouth is all scrunched up. And when you see me you're not going to love me any more because I am so ugly.' In other words, this woman was just heartbroken. . . .

"So I wrote a letter in which Cecil said she wasn't to worry about her teeth, that she would be pretty without her teeth, that as a matter of fact when he first saw her and married her, he never even thought about her teeth and didn't remember whether she had any teeth or not—he didn't give a God-damn about her teeth. She would always be as beautiful as she was because it wasn't her teeth he loved anyhow. A letter came back written by the daughter for the mother. It was a love letter. I can't describe it. Just a complete, total love letter. It was very moving just to read it. . . ."

The most extraordinary encounter of all took place in Danbury, where Lardner and Cole were sternly warned, on their arrival, against any attempts at violence. Cole told the parole officer that he had been "convicted for contempt, not violence," but the parole officer remained suspicious.

"There are rumors already here in advance of your arrival,'" said the parole officer, "that both you and Lardner are prepared for violent revenge if you can get away with it."

"Who the hell could have said that?" Cole wondered.

"Will you swear," the parole officer persisted, "that you are not planning some sort of revenge against J. Parnell Thomas, who is in this institution?"

It was no secret that the crusading congressman had been indicted in 1948 for padding his congressional payroll and taking kickbacks from his employees, that he had delayed the proceedings for nearly a year with claims of bad health, that he had finally pleaded *nolo contendere* and thrown himself on the mercy of the court, which mercifully sentenced him to no more than eighteen months in jail, plus a fine of ten thousand dollars. But Cole and Lardner had not realized that they and their grand inquisitor would be locked up in the same federal prison.

"He must have started the rumor himself," Cole said. "Kill him? My greatest pleasure will be seeing him here with his own kind, petty thieves."

"It's true," the parole officer said. "It was Thomas who suggested it when he learned you were coming here."

Lardner was being given the same warning by another parole officer, and when the two writers next met, they both burst into laughter. "What luck!" said Lardner. "There's got to be a way, a dozen ways, to make the bastard miserable."

When Lardner finally saw the frightened congressman in the prison yard, however, he could not bring himself to speak to him. "He had lost a good deal of weight," Lardner recalled later, "and his face, round and scarlet at our last encounter, was deeply lined and sallow. . . . Neither of us made any social overtures to the other." Cole was more combative. He said that Thomas "scurried at least fifty feet away when he saw us coming," but they finally met at work. Cole had been assigned to cut grass with a sickle, and that brought him near the chicken coops, where Thomas was engaged in scraping up dung with a hoe.

"Hey, Bolshie, I see you still got your sickle," Thomas jeered from behind the chicken fence. "Where's your hammer?"

"And I see just like in Congress, you're still picking up chickenshit," Cole shouted back.

So time passed, month after month, and in the last week of Cole's imprisonment, he encountered a new irony. "That week was torture . . ." he recalled, "because the House Un-American Activities Committee . . . had started new hearings in Hollywood." Every afternoon, at the end of work, the convicts would gather around the radio and listen to the news. Among the first witnesses was Richard Collins, one of the original unfriendly nineteen, who had collaborated with his friend Paul Jarrico in writing the ill-starred *Song of Russia*. Now Collins became, as Cole put it, "the first snitch, stoolie, squealer." He named twenty-six people he had known as Communists, including Jarrico, and Carl Foreman, and Budd Schulberg, which prompted Schulberg to cable the committee that he was ready to "cooperate with you in any way I can." Dmytryk, too, now wanted to testify, after serving his prison term in full, "that the battle for freedom of thought, in which I believed completely, had been twisted into a conspiracy of silence. . . ." The convicts sitting around the radio in the Danbury prison "looked at me and shook their heads," Cole recalled, "some with pity, most with contempt." One of them finally said, "What kind of a horse's ass are you to get into that lousy mob of stool pigeons?"

●　　●　　●

Of all the beautiful girls who flowered in Hollywood during the later 1940's, the most supremely beautiful was Elizabeth Taylor, so her wedding at the age of eighteen was naturally the social event of 1950. She was apparently still a virgin. On her sixteenth birthday, when she had yearned for a date, M-G-M arranged for her to be taken out by Glenn Davis, the All-American football star from West Point. They soon became "engaged to be engaged," as she put it, just before he went off to Korea. When he came back, he gave her a necklace of sixty-nine graduated pearls for her seventeenth birthday. By then, she had become interested in a much richer young man named Bill Pawley. When she and Pawley became engaged, he gave her her first diamond, a 3.5-carat emerald-cut solitaire with two half-carat diamonds on each side. But he wanted her to give up her career, and George Stevens had just hired her to star with Montgomery Clift in *A Place in the Sun*, Stevens's version of Dreiser's *An American Tragedy*. So there were scenes, and the engagement was broken, and Elizabeth Taylor looked very beautiful as the mindless heiress in *A Place in the Sun*.

Conrad Nicholas Hilton, Jr., aged twenty-two, was the son of the chairman of the Hilton Hotel Corporation, an assertive Texan said to be worth about $125 million. The engagement ring that Nicky Hilton gave Miss Taylor bore a five-carat diamond. A few people tried to tell her that Hilton drank too much and had a violent temper, but Miss Taylor's parents approved of him, and so did M-G-M, which scheduled the release of her latest picture, *Father of the Bride*, to appear shortly after her wedding on May 6. The studio also announced that it was providing her with a $3,500 wedding dress, twenty-five yards of shell-white satin sprinkled with seed pearls and bugle beads, plus a train of fifteen yards of satin chiffon, not to mention a veil of silk illusion net, a creation that eventually occupied fifteen M-G-M seamstresses for two months. (What would that cost today, if M-G-M actually had fifteen seamstresses capable of such labors and a star worthy of them?) The studio even provided Miss Taylor with her wedding-night costume, a white satin negligee trimmed with rose-point lace. And almost as a matter of course, it donated the bronze chiffon dress for Miss Taylor's mother and the daffodil-yellow dresses for her seven bridesmaids and her seven attendants.

All kinds of people sent all kinds of presents. A rich uncle named Howard Young provided a $65,000 pearl ring. Conrad Hilton offered a token 100 shares of Hilton hotel stock, then worth only $1,350 but increasing over the next thirty years to more than $150,000. The Gorham Silver Company promised a forty-five-piece silver service, on condition that it could photograph Miss Taylor pouring tea from the Gorham pot; it could. Somebody or other sent a mink coat, and another one for Miss Taylor's mother. "I just love everything about getting married," Miss Taylor said.

It happened at the Church of the Good Shepherd in Beverly Hills, with about six hundred guests crammed into the church and about three thousand admirers pressed against the police barricades outside. Who was actually there? Well, Louella Parsons and Hedda Hopper, of course, and Sheilah Graham too, and Spencer Tracy, Fred Astaire, Ginger Rogers, Esther Williams, June Allyson, Gene Kelly, Debbie Reynolds, Rosalind Russell, Greer Garson, George Murphy, Joan Bennett, and so on. And so on. "Just your usual monkey funeral shot, Johnny," as Billy Wilder had said.

Miss Taylor had seventeen steamer trunks already packed for her honeymoon voyage to the Riviera aboard the *Queen Mary*. The Duke and Duchess of Windsor were also aboard and invited the newlyweds to dinner. Nicky Hilton worried about whether he was supposed to wear evening clothes. (No, he was not.) There were worse contretemps ahead. Screaming crowds gathered everywhere Miss Taylor appeared in Europe, and Miss Taylor, reared and trained in the folkways of the M-G-M lot, spent hours signing autographs. Her husband seethed. Since he was even more spoiled and childish than she, he soon began taking revenge by drinking and gambling and insulting his bride. "I'm so goddamned sick and tired of looking at your face," he shouted on one occasion. On another, he called her "a fucking bore."

The honeymooners returned to Hollywood so that Miss Taylor could resume her career by starring in a movie called *Love Is Better Than Ever,* and after one shrieking argument too many, when Hilton told her to "get the hell out," she did. The celebrated marriage lasted seven months. "My troubles all started," Miss Taylor said in an often-quoted confession to the press, "because I have a woman's body and a child's emotions." No such easy exculpation could be offered by Nicky Hilton, the first of her six husbands. Or by M-G-M, which demanded the return of not only Miss Taylor's wedding dress but those of her bridesmaids. "They didn't even send someone to pick them up," said one of the victims. "We all had to take them back to the studio ourselves."

• • •

"Look at that fat bastard trying to get out of his car," Raymond Chandler remarked to his secretary as they stood waiting in the doorway of Chandler's house in La Jolla. The secretary tried to quiet him by warning him that the fat bastard struggling to emerge from his limousine might be able to hear what he said. "What do I care?" said Chandler.

The reason that the fat bastard had driven all the way to La Jolla to see Chandler was that the novelist's new $2,500-per-week contract with Warner Bros. specified that he could work at home, so anyone who wanted to have a story conference would have to come to La Jolla to do so. Chandler hated such conferences anyway. He described them as "these god-awful jabber sessions which seem to be an inevitable although painful part of the picture business."

The fat bastard didn't greatly enjoy the jabber sessions with Chandler either. "Our collaboration was not very happy," said Alfred Hitchcock, who always insisted on a good deal of collaboration with anyone hired to write one of his pictures. "Sometimes when we were trying to get the idea for a scene, I would offer him a suggestion. Instead of giving it some thought, he would remark to me, very discontentedly, 'If you can go it alone, why the hell do you need me?' "

These were not the best of times for Hitchcock. The last film he had made before breaking away from Selznick, *The Paradine Case* (1948), had not been a success, either artistically or commercially. The two films he had then made on his own, *Rope* (1948) and *Under Capricorn* (1949), had not done well either, and his longtime dream of independent production had ended in failure. Nor had he recovered in his first picture for Warner Bros., *Stage Fright* (1950). Critics now spoke slightingly of his coldness, his affectations and artificiality. But early in 1950, Hitchcock discovered a novel with a captivating idea: Two strangers meet, and one of them proposes an exchange of murders, an exchange of guilt, almost, in a way, an exchange of murderous identities. Each of them would kill someone whom the other wanted dead, and since neither had any motive or any connection to the victim, neither would ever be caught. Hitchcock bought the film rights to *Strangers on a Train* by Patricia Highsmith for a trivial $7,500, then collaborated with a writer named Whitfield Cook on a sixty-five-page "treatment." In trying to develop a full screenplay, though, Hitchcock ran into difficulty. "I couldn't find anyone to work on it with me," he lamented. "They all felt my first draft was so flat and factual that they couldn't see one iota of quality in it."

One of the writers Hitchcock tried to hire was the ruined Dashiell Hammett, but something went wrong in the negotiations, and Hammett faded away. Then, after several more rejections, came the almost equally ruined Chandler, who was to produce for Hitchcock the last movie script he ever wrote. "Why am I doing it?" Chandler wondered aloud. "Partly because I thought I might like Hitch, which I do, and partly because one gets tired of saying no. . . ." The liking did not last long. Chandler wrote a first draft while Hitchcock went scouting locations in the East. When the director returned, he read Chandler's script with some dismay, dictated a lot of changes that he wanted, and then went east again to shoot the tennis matches at Forest Hills (the hero, who had originally been an architect, was now a tennis star, a more photogenic occupation). "Hitchcock . . . directs a film in his head before he knows what the story is," Chandler complained. "You find yourself trying to rationalize the shots he wants to make rather than the story. Every time you get set he jabs you off balance by wanting to do a love scene on top of the Jefferson Memorial or something like that." And again: "He is full of little suggestions and ideas, which have a cramping effect on a writer's initiative. . . . Hitchcock . . . is always ready to sacrifice dramatic logic (insofar as it exists) for the sake of a camera effect or a mood effect. He is aware of this and accepts the handicap. He knows that in almost all his pictures there is some point where the story ceases to make any sense whatever and becomes a chase, but he doesn't mind. This is very hard on a writer, especially on a writer who has any ideas of his own."

When Hitchcock read Chandler's second draft, he decided that Chandler had to be fired. He hoped now to hire Ben Hecht, but all he could get was one of Hecht's assistants, Czenzi Ormonde (though Hecht may have helped too). She wrote a new script with another collaborator, Barbara Keon, and with Hitchcock's wife, Alma, and of course Hitchcock himself. What did such jumbled authorship matter? Chandler had been right—Hitchcock did include the Jefferson Memorial in one scene, and the Washington Monument in another. And he did care primarily for camera effects. For example, the murder of the wife of Guy, the tennis player, whom the psychopathic Bruno strangled even though Guy had never agreed to Bruno's bizarre proposition. Hitchcock built an enormous lens so that he could film the entire murder as a reflection in the eyeglasses dropped by the victim. Or that spectacular ending when the carousel spun wildly out of control. Hitchcock started by filming a toy carousel going faster and faster until it finally exploded. Then he enlarged the film and projected it onto a huge screen and then placed his actors in front of the screen. "This was a most complicated sequence," Hitchcock later explained. "For rear projection shooting there was a screen and behind it an enormous projector lens and the lens of the camera had to be right on that white line. The camera was not photographing the screen and what was on it, it was photographing the light in certain colors; therefore the camera lens had to be level and in line with the projector lens. . . ." And so on.

The only "flaws" in *Strangers on a Train,* as Hitchcock later confided to François Truffaut, were those things that a less cinematic director might have considered essential: "The ineffectiveness of the two main actors and the weakness of the final script." Hitchcock was too critical. Farley Granger was perfectly adequate as Guy, and Robert Walker was quite remarkable as Bruno. Perhaps precisely because he had so often played the role of the nice young man, shyly hungering for affection, the Walker who had emerged from the Menninger Clinic now became almost demonic as the mirror image of his past self, sly, cunning, implicitly homosexual, domineering, and ruthless. And insane. All that most maddens and torments; all that stirs up the lees of things; all truth with malice in it—all this roiled in Robert Walker in the last complete movie he made before he was done to death.

Chandler, of course, could see none of the morbid brilliance in *Strangers on a Train*. "The picture has no guts, no plausibility, no characters and no dialogue," he said. "But of course it's Hitchcock, and a Hitchcock picture always does have something." And to another friend: "I don't know why it's a success, perhaps because Hitchcock succeeded in removing almost every trace of my writing from it."

• • •

Walker's former wife, Jennifer Jones, who had finally married David Selznick in 1949, now had a chance to star with Laurence Olivier in William Wyler's version of *Sister Carrie*, so she didn't tell Wyler that she was pregnant. When her condition became obvious, she admitted to Wyler that she had tried to keep it secret in order not to lose the part. Still, the part was especially difficult now because the fashions of Dreiser's times required tight corsets. Wyler tried, uncharacteristically, to be obliging. "I told her, 'When it's a closeup you don't have to do it, I'll tell you when we see the full figure,' " he recalled. "But she always had herself strapped in. Just watching her made me uncomfortable. She lost the baby after the picture. How much the strapping of her waist had to do with it I don't know."

• • •

Just a few months after the prison gates in Kentucky opened for the release of Trumbo, Lawson, and Scott, they opened again to take in Dashiell Hammett. At the age of fifty-nine, he was a wreck, gaunt, toothless, coughing fitfully. In the food line on his first day in prison, he fainted.

Hammett had not finished a novel for nearly twenty years, though he still made a living from the royalties on his past work. He had recently been trying to write something that he called *December First*, but he never finished that either. His old friend William Wyler invited him out to Hollywood to work on the film adaptation of Sidney Kingsley's play *Detective Story*. He enjoyed going out to dinner with the handsome young Patricia Neal, but he soon realized that he couldn't write the script for Wyler, and he returned the ten-thousand-dollar advance he had received.

Despite all these signs of decrepitude, Hammett's continuing political activities made him an attractive target for the FBI. The agency assigned a man to watch him. This follower reported that Hammett had attended a Communist dinner to denounce the racist Senator Theodore Bilbo of Mississippi, and that he had donated a thousand dollars to the cause. He donated another thousand dollars at a rally in Madison Square Garden to stop the Korean War.

What really aroused the authorities, though, was that when the Supreme Court finally upheld the convictions of the eleven Communist Party leaders in the summer of 1951, four of them jumped bail. This bail of twenty thousand dollars each had been provided by a leftist organization called the Civil Rights Congress, and Hammett was one of four trustees of its bail fund. Federal Judge Sylvester Ryan, in whose court the fugitives had failed to appear for sentencing, not only declared the bail money forfeited but demanded that the four trustees appear before him to tell who had donated the bail money. Hammett, who had no idea who the many donors were, responded to this harassment by pleading the Fifth Amendment against self-incrimination, because, as he told Lillian Hellman, "I don't let cops or judges tell me what I think democracy is." But although the Fifth Amendment is supposed to protect citizens in situations like this, the courts (even the Supreme Court, eventually) held that Hammett was not being asked to incriminate himself since he was being asked only to serve as a witness, and a witness had no right to invoke the Fifth Amendment. Hence, a sentence of six months in Ashland, Kentucky.

The authorities in Ashland took pity on the old man, after their fashion. They assigned him to easy indoor work, like mopping floors and cleaning toilets. He also served on a committee to make sure that all new prisoners knew how to use toilets. One of his fellow committeemen, Frederick Vanderbilt Field, a descendant of Commodore Vanderbilt, and also a fellow trustee of the Civil Rights Congress bail fund, was shocked to discover that there were Americans who didn't know how to use toilets. It dismayed even Hammett, the creator of the tough detective, but prisons usually do provide surprises.

Some newspaper columnists thought it their function to add their insults to Hammett's prison sentence. "Call him Samovar Spade," said Walter Winchell in one of his characteristic efforts at wit. Inside the prison, though, the convicts gathered around the radio every Friday night to hear the broadcast adventures of Sam Spade. Hammett was still involved in litigation with Warner Bros., which claimed that its purchase of *The Maltese Falcon* back in the 1930's gave the studio all rights to the name and persona of Sam Spade forever. For the time being, though, the disembodied radio voice of the tough young Sam Spade was still working in the service of Spade's aged and imprisoned creator.

•   •   •

In the last year of Arnold Schoenberg's life, a former pupil named Dika Newlin went to visit him in Brentwood and found to her amazement that the austere old man "had now discovered TELEVISION!" Schoenberg claimed that he had bought a set just for the children—his younger son was still only nine—but Miss Newlin was not convinced. "No one was more enthralled than he," she observed, "as we sat in front of Hopalong Cassidy with our TV trays in our laps."

•   •   •

Harry Cohn, who ran Columbia, hated his brother Jack, who was the president of the company, and Jack reciprocated his feelings as only a brother could. Jack even tried once to get rid of Harry by going secretly to see A. P. Giannini of the Bank of America, who financed the Cohns and much else besides, to tell him that Harry was wasteful and irresponsible. Giannini smiled understandingly and then called Harry and said, "I think you should know who just visited me." So Harry was not very receptive when Jack suggested to him that Columbia try making a Bible picture.

"Keep your nose out of my end of the business," Harry said.

"I just thought we should make a Bible picture, that's all," said Jack. "There are a lot of good stories in the Bible."

"What the hell do you know about the Bible?" Harry demanded. "I'll bet you don't even know the Lord's Prayer."

"I sure do," said Jack.

"The hell you do!" said Harry. "I'll bet you fifty bucks you can't recite the Lord's Prayer. Come on—put up or shut up."

The brothers both put up fifty dollars.

"Okay, say it," said Harry.

"Now I lay me down to sleep—" Jack began, a little hesitantly.

"That's enough," said Harry, grudgingly surrendering his fifty dollars. "I didn't think you knew it."

Jack was right, though, not about the Lord's Prayer but about the commercial possibilities of the Bible. As the millions who used to go to the movies to watch Blondie or Gene Autry now stayed home and watched much the same sort of thing on the new television set, the Poverty Row studios like Republic and Monogram started going out of business. The soothsayers in the larger studios began to imagine that they could see salvation for themselves in vastness, gigantism. Blockbusters! A cast of thousands! The greatest story ever told!

This was, in a sense, a return to the beginnings, for a French version of the Oberammergau Passion Play was one of the first films that young Louis B. Mayer had shown in his first theater back in 1907. One of the big successes of the following year was Vitagraph's five-reel *Life of Moses*. Hollywood returned once again to religious epics in the early 1920's, after the Fatty Arbuckle scandal of 1921 threatened the fledgling film capital's entire future. Cecil B. DeMille led the process of atonement with his spectacular production of *The Ten Commandments* (1923), which grossed $14 million on an investment of $1.5 million. He followed that with *The King of Kings* (1927) and *The Sign of the Cross* (1932), and lest anyone suspect that he had any commercial motives, he started each day's shooting with a religious service on the set. Indeed, after the filming of the crucifixion in *The King of Kings*, the entire cast had to stand with heads bowed during five minutes of organ music.

Now, in this new time of trial, DeMille once again led the penitential procession back to the half-forgotten gold mine. He wanted to film what he characteristically called "one of the greatest love stories in history or literature, which is also a poignant drama of faith, the story of Samson and Deli-lah." Some other executives apparently expressed skepticism about whether a biblical epic was what the supposedly more sophisticated postwar generation wanted to see, so DeMille had one of his artisans sketch a poster of "a big brawny athlete and, looking at him with an at once seductive and coolly measuring eye, a slim and ravishingly attractive young girl." At a meeting of the skeptics, DeMille recalled, he displayed this picture and said, "That, gentlemen, is *Samson and Delilah.*" Everyone was impressed. DeMille hired as his protagonists the beefy Victor Mature and the aging Hedy Lamarr and produced a thoroughly ludicrous picture, only partially redeemed by the cli-mactic scene in which the blinded Mature pushed against two pillars and brought down a whole temple. Whatever its faults, though, *Samson and Deli-lah* made a lot of money, and that inspired Hollywood's seekers of inspiration.

Quo Vadis was not exactly part of the Bible, but it was sort of biblical. M-G-M had been trying for years to get a usable script out of Henry Sienkie-wicz's turgid novel about the early Christians. With Dore Schary's encourage-ment, John Huston had devised what he regarded as "a modern treatment," in which Nero was portrayed as a prototype for his "fellow madman, Adolf Hitler." Louis B. Mayer was profoundly suspicious. He summoned Huston to his house for a breakfast conference, and since he almost invariably drew all his arguments from the good old days, he began telling Huston how he had taught Jeanette MacDonald to sing "Oh, Sweet Mystery of Life" by singing "Eli, Eli" to her. In Hebrew. She had wept. So Mayer now sang the same dirge to Huston. "Then he said that if I could make *Quo Vadis* into that kind of picture," Huston recalled, "he would crawl to me on his knees and kiss my hands . . . which he then proceeded to do. I sat there and thought, 'This is not happening to me. I've nothing to do with any of this.' "

Huston began casting on a grand scale, Gregory Peck as the hero and Elizabeth Taylor as the heroine, and then he went to Europe and started spending money. About two million dollars had disappeared by the time the differences between Mayer and Huston brought the production to a halt, and Mayer turned everything over to a man he trusted, Mervyn LeRoy.* Gregory Peck had dropped out with an eye infection, and Elizabeth Taylor had other commitments, but what did it matter? LeRoy hired sixty thousand extras and directed them by firing a series of pistol shots from a boom high over Rome's Cinecittà studio. And he acquired more than fifty lions, all that M-G-M scouts could hire in all the circuses of Europe. Since he could never get these

---

* LeRoy had overseen such workmanlike successes as *Little Caesar* (1931) and *The Wizard of Oz* (1939), but he deserves a special kind of fame as a subject of a classic pun. At an executive meeting at M-G-M, Nicholas Schenck was fretting about LeRoy's failure to stay within his budget on *The Wizard of Oz*, and Mayer presented the young Joseph Mankiewicz as an experienced writer and director who could explain such things. When all the executives turned to Mankiewicz for his explanation, Man-kiewicz felt some irresistible impulse to evoke Victor Hugo and blurted out, "I suppose LeRoy s'*amuse*." Schenck said, "What?" Mankiewicz repeated his inspired line. Somebody said, "That's French." Schenck said, "Why are you talking French?" "All I could think of," Mankiewicz said later, "was, 'Why am I here?' "

lions to simulate the desired carnage, he fell back on the oldest Hollywood traditions of fakery. "I wound up having the prop men stuff empty clothing with meat, so it looked like a Christian lying on the ground, and we brought the lions out forcibly and they ate those 'bodies,' " LeRoy recalled. "I augmented that with close-ups of fake lions, which the technicians built, jumping on real people. It worked, although I never did get the scene exactly as I wanted."

But how could he fail? He went to see Pope Pius XII and actually asked the Pope to bless the script of *Quo Vadis*, which he just happened to have brought with him, and the Pope "put his lovely hands on the script, murmured some Latin words, and then said, in English, 'May your film be a successful one.' " It is possible that Pope Pius would have blessed anything at all that was presented to him under the proper auspices, but it soon turned out that he had a special interest in LeRoy's project. "I like the cinema," the Pope said. And there was more. "By the way," the Pope said, "do you remember a movie called *Going My Way?*" How could LeRoy forget the Oscar-winner as the best picture of 1944? And another Oscar for Father Bing Crosby playing a little boogie-woogie and singing "Swinging on a Star"? "I have a print of it," said Pope Pius XII. "Don't you love that scene where the priest takes a little drink?" So *Quo Vadis* eventually cost twelve million dollars but turned into what Huston called "another dreadful spectacle, catering to the audience L.B. thought was there. L.B. was right; the audience *was* there."

And so, in the years of fear and blacklisting, began the age of pious epics: *David and Bathsheba* (1951), *The Robe* (1953), *The Egyptian* (1954), *Land of the Pharaohs* (1955), *Alexander the Great* (1956), *The Ten Commandments* (1956) (by DeMille, again). It was also, of course, the age of sci-fi horrors: *The Thing from Another World* (1950); *The Day the Earth Stood Still* (1951); *Them, The Beast from 20,000 Fathoms, The War of the Worlds, It Came from Outer Space, The Lost Planet, Zombies of the Stratosphere* (all of these in 1953). But never mind—prehistoric monsters and biblical heroes were all pretty much the same, as were prehistoric monsters and Martian invaders of the twenty-first century.

Such films were inspired partly by Hollywood's exploration of large-screen technology as a weapon against the lilliputian television screen. An inventor named Fred Waller devised a system for using three projectors to cast images on a curved screen, and in 1952 he and two partners (Lowell Thomas and Merian C. Cooper) astonished New York with *This Is Cinerama*. In a sense, this, too, was a return to the origins of the cinema. William Friese-Greene had patented a three-dimensional movie process at the turn of the century, and the brothers Louis and Auguste Lumière attracted huge crowds in Paris to their projections of moving film on a fifty-three-by-seventy-foot screen.

Still, reinventing the wheel is the essence of show business. *This Is Cinerama* delighted audiences with a series of spectacles ranging from the triumphal march in *Aïda* at La Scala to a terrifying ride on a roller coaster at

Coney Island. The show ran more than two years in New York and grossed nearly five million dollars. The trouble was that it was expensive to convert ordinary theaters to Cinerama. Once the possibilities of technical novelties became clear, other versions of the wide screen appeared: Paramount's VistaVision, Warnerscope, Todd-AO, Vistarama, Naturama. The search for novelty extended even to 3-D, in which viewers had to don special spectacles to see lions jumping at them in *Bwana Devil*. And even to Smell-O-Vision, in which tubes behind each theater seat provided clues to the solution of a film called *Scent of Mystery*. The most successful of all these experiments was 20th Century–Fox's Cinemascope, which used an anamorphic lens to spread out the projected image to nearly twice the previously standard width, and the first film made by this process was the immensely successful religious epic *The Robe*.

Beyond all such technical questions, though, beyond all commercial questions of the struggle against television (weekly moviegoing continued dropping from about sixty million to forty million during the 1950's), the biblical epics represented a kind of self-portrait of the Hollywood studios in their decline and fall. "The epics were the ideology of the ideology," as Michael Wood has written. "They were Hollywood's own version of *The Last Tycoon*: flights, as Fitzgerald said of his novel, into 'a lavish, romantic past that perhaps will not come again into our time.' . . . Hollywood was Egypt, and Rome, and Jerusalem. The ancient world of the epics was a huge, many-faceted metaphor for Hollywood itself, because . . . these movies are always *about* the creation of such a world in a movie." And having created one of the great cities of the past, the mission of the epic was finally to destroy it. The great idol grandly toppled in *Samson and Delilah;* Rome itself burned in *Quo Vadis*. Though these films professed to acclaim the triumph of Christianity, Wood observed, "doom and apocalypse lurk around these optimistic movies, tokens of catastrophe surround these celebrations of success."

•   •   •

"Hollywood's like Egypt," David Selznick once remarked morosely to Ben Hecht as they walked through the deserted streets at dawn. "Full of crumbling pyramids. . . . It'll just keep on crumbling until finally the wind blows the last studio prop across the sands." First, though, everything must be torn down and rebuilt into something else. The mansion that Billy Wilder found for *Sunset Boulevard* was demolished in 1957 to provide a site for the new Getty headquarters office building. The Spanish hacienda built on Sunset Boulevard by Alla Nazimova in the early 1920's, with a swimming pool in the shape of the Black Sea, gave way in 1927 to the Garden of Allah Hotel, with bungalows occupied by Scott Fitzgerald, Robert Benchley, John O'Hara, and other serious drinkers, and that gave way in 1959 to a bank. The former livery stable that Bette Davis turned into the Hollywood Canteen is now a four-story parking garage. The Mocambo nightclub on Sunset is a parking lot, and all that remains of the nearby Trocadero are the three steps that used to lead to the front door.

On the other hand, the nostalgia business has become very profitable in Hollywood. Musso and Frank's still flourishes on Hollywood Boulevard, and so does Chasen's on Beverly (try the chili, the guidebook says). Nothing typifies the efforts to institutionalize the past better than the migrations of the DeMille barn. A two-story yellow structure, it was originally built in 1895 on the southeast corner of Selma Avenue and Vine Street, and Cecil B. DeMille rented it for Jesse Lasky in 1913 for two hundred dollars a week to make his first spectacle, *The Squaw Man.* Actually, he didn't rent all of it, because the owner, Harry Revier, retained the right to keep his horse and carriage in one corner. When Paramount, the successor to the Lasky company, moved to a twenty-six-acre studio on Melrose Avenue in 1927, the sentimental executives took along the barn, which they used as a company library, then, in a characteristic progression, as a gymnasium, then as a set for the *Bonanza* television series.

In 1979, whether for reasons of nostalgia, publicity, or tax deduction, Paramount bequeathed the increasingly decrepit DeMille barn to the Hollywood Historic Trust, a branch of the Hollywood Chamber of Commerce, and it was moved to a parking lot on Vine Street, just north of Hollywood Boulevard. There, the relic stood unused for three years while various interests argued over its fate. Universal offered to add it to the various props on view to tourists in its back lots, but preservationists opposed that as a desecration. In 1982, the Hollywood Historic Trust finally moved the barn to a "permanent" site across from the Hollywood Bowl and began a $400,000 project to turn it into a movie museum.

●   ●   ●

And what finally happened to all those people, all the characters in the drama of Hollywood in the 1940's? A great many, including all the biggest bosses, went to their downfall and died, as any screenwriter could have predicted, rich and unhappy.

Louis B. Mayer died of leukemia in 1957, shortly after the stockholders of M-G-M voted down the last of his schemes to regain control of the studio. His last words to an associate were: "Nothing matters. Nothing matters." In bed that night, though, he kept asking, "Is she here yet? Is she outside?" Each of his quarreling daughters insisted forever after that she was the one the old man meant.

Darryl F. Zanuck abandoned both his wife and his command of 20th Century–Fox in 1956 so that he could go to Europe with a young Polish adventuress named Bella Darvi. His successors at the studio made such a mess that Zanuck got the stockholders to vote him back into power, with his brash young son, Richard, as chief of production. The two Zanucks then quarreled, and father fired son, but the son and the discarded wife joined dissident stockholders in voting Zanuck into retirement. "I feel tired," said Zanuck, who finally returned to his bed-ridden wife in Palm Springs, then endured five years of lingering illness before his death at the age of seventy-seven.

Jack Warner and Harry Warner didn't speak to each other throughout the whole year before Harry's death in 1958. The reason for the quarrel was that both had agreed to sell their shares of Warner Bros., but Jack reneged, kept control of the studio, and watched the shares rise to three times the price that Harry had received. The last surviving brother, Jack was seventy-five when he finally sold his holdings for $32 million in 1967, but he didn't enjoy his decade of retirement in Palm Springs. "You're nothing if you don't have a studio," he said. "Now I'm just another millionaire."

Harry Cohn was still in charge of everything at Columbia when he died of a heart attack in 1958, at the age of sixty-six. It was raw and rainy on the day of his funeral, but a large crowd gathered to see the last of him, which prompted Red Skelton to remark, "It goes to show that the public will always come if you give them what they want."

Sam Goldwyn suffered a severe stroke in 1969 and spent the next five years bedridden in his home, hugely obese, partly paralyzed, incontinent, staring into space, only intermittently able to speak a few words. At the age of ninety-one, he died in his sleep.

David Selznick kept hoping to make films that would glorify Jennifer Jones. More than ten million dollars in debt, he talked of filming *War and Peace*, then of filming the whole Bible. Then he finally cast Miss Jones in a boring, expensive, and commercially unsuccessful version of Hemingway's *A Farewell to Arms* (1957). Eight years later, haggard and worn at the age of sixty-three, he was talking business in his lawyer's office when he suffered a fatal heart attack.

Jennifer Jones suffered from depressions. Two years after Selznick's death, with her own career in decline, she took a number of pills, telephoned her doctor that she wanted to die, and drove to a four-hundred-foot cliff near Malibu. Searchers found her lying unconscious near shallow surf; they revived her and took her to a hospital. Miss Jones married the millionaire Norton Simon in 1971, and now she is occasionally seen with him at a charity dinner or the opening of an art exhibit.

Many succumbed to cancer, particularly the tough guys. Humphrey Bogart, in 1957, got weaker and weaker until his hands shook as he sipped grape juice through a flexible straw. "Goodbye, Kid," he said to Miss Bacall as she left to run an errand shortly before he slipped into a coma. "Hurry back." And John Wayne, too, and Gary Cooper, and Edward G. Robinson. Also Dalton Trumbo, who had won the 1956 Academy Award under the pseudonym Robert Rich, who had received his first post-imprisonment screenwriting credit from Otto Preminger for *Exodus*—thus beginning the end of the blacklist—though it was not until 1975, just a year before his death at seventy-one, that the Academy actually gave him the Oscar statue that he had won two decades earlier. It was Trumbo who pronounced the epitaph on that ugly era when he said that there had been "no villains or heroes or saints or devils. . . . There were only victims."

And Ingrid Bergman, who survived both the insults of Hollywood and the desertion of Rossellini, who went on stage to play Shaw and Ibsen and O'Neill and won two more Academy Awards, for *Anastasia* in 1956 and *Murder on the Orient Express* in 1974, the same year in which she learned she had cancer. In her last year, 1981, after she finished her last role, in a TV biography of Golda Meir, her right arm began to swell to monstrous size. It weighed almost sixty pounds and had to be covered with a shawl, and she had to hold it up with her left arm. "I am fighting my dragon, my arm," she wrote to a friend. "I cannot get free of it, that is, I cannot have it amputated, thus I fight him. Yet with fun. I call him my dog, I joke with him: 'You are not a dragon, you are a dog, a nasty sick dog. Come on, let's go walking.' Then, carrying him as a sick dog, we go walking together, to see the sun and the trees and the people. While walking, I think: 'Ingrid, it could go worse. You could have gone blind and be incapable of seeing the sun. . . .' " She died in London on her sixty-seventh birthday.

But there are all kinds of survivors too. Who could have imagined that Claudette Colbert, who was already a successful Broadway actress when she appeared in 1927 in a First National silent film, *For the Love of Mike*, would reappear on the New York stage at the age of eighty-one in a 1985 revival of Frederick Lonsdale's half-century-old comedy, *Aren't We All?* Who could have imagined, for that matter, that Lillian Gish, the heroine of *The Birth of a Nation*, would still be rattling around on the lecture circuit in the mid-1980's and showing off the Blackglama mink coat that she received for posing under the slogan "What becomes a legend most?"

The theater has been rather kind to these figures from the past. Mickey Rooney, the onetime Andy Hardy, was thought to be in the last stages of decline when he bounced back to life in *Sugar Babies* (with Ann Miller) and played to sold-out houses for months. Lauren Bacall did much the same in *Cactus Flower*, and even Van Johnson reemerged from obscurity in 1984 to star in *La Cage aux Folles*. Irene Selznick established herself as a producer of such successes as *A Streetcar Named Desire* and *Bell, Book and Candle*, then settled down in the Plaza Hotel to write her memoirs. And Bob Hope, in a kind of vaudeville theater all his own, goes on and on. He is past eighty now, and yet he still spends every Christmas entertaining U.S. troops overseas. If there is no war on, he finds the nearest thing to it—Beirut, Korea, wherever —and turns up with a new collection of pretty girls and those terrible old jokes that have served him so well.

TV has been rather kind, too, at least with its money. The star ratings and the star salaries go to an ever-changing procession of youths, but the networks' insatiable need for material feeds the old as well. It is hard to remember, when watching *Falcon Crest*, that Jane Wyman was once young and beautiful, but she still makes a very good living ($100,000 per episode) as a tyrannical hag. And not too long ago, there was a much-publicized guest appearance on the same show by the reluctantly aging but still resolutely blond Lana Turner. Guest appearances become a way of life, and a guessing game for audiences that have not seen these former stars since they were stars. Was that really Ava Gardner on *Knots Landing?* Yes, and Joan Fontaine on *Dark Mansions,* Ginger Rogers on *Glitter,* Jane Russell on *Yellow Rose,* Olivia de Havilland and June Allyson on *Love Boat.*

John Huston, white-bearded in his late seventies, is probably the most active moviemaker among the veterans of the 1940's. His splendid adaptation of Malcolm Lowry's *Under the Volcano* was a major contender for an Academy Award as the best picture of 1984, and *Prizzi's Honor* won him 1985 nominations for both best picture and best director (though the only Huston who actually won an Oscar was his daughter Anjelica as best supporting actress). But both Hollywood and New York are full of semiretired celebrities who could probably be coaxed out of semiretirement by the right offer. Katharine Hepburn starred in her forty-fifth film, *Grace Quigley,* in 1985. As of mid-1986, Cary Grant still seems a marvel of fitness at eighty-one, and so does Jimmy Stewart at seventy-seven. Marlene Dietrich lives well in Paris at the age of God knows what. These people still appear in evening clothes at testimonial dinners celebrating Hollywood's past, and graduate students come visiting them with tape recorders. The only one who never talks but is occasionally spotted shopping for groceries or simply taking a walk on the Upper East Side of Manhattan is the once-ageless Greta Garbo, now a wrinkled relic of eighty.

•   •   •

As for Ronald Reagan, his prospects at midcentury looked rather bleak. When he returned from filming *The Hasty Heart* in wintry Britain toward the end of 1949, he was infuriated to discover that a Western novel that he had asked Warners to buy for him had been bought and assigned to Errol Flynn, partly because several of Reagan's most recent pictures had not done well. "I'm going to pick my own pictures . . ." Reagan said snappishly in an interview early in 1950. "I could do as good a job of picking as the studio has done. . . . At least I could do no worse." Warners, which was trying like all other studios to cut back on the number of contract actors as it entered the television age, answered Reagan's criticism by negotiating a reduction from two pictures a year to one. Reagan's agent made up the difference by arranging a five-year, five-picture deal with Universal, but no sooner had the contracts been signed than Reagan made a bad slide while playing baseball, broke his right thigh, and had to spend six months in traction.

His divorce had become final the previous summer, and though that restored to him the social possibilities of bachelor life, Reagan at thirty-nine apparently regarded those possibilities with mixed feelings. "I had a comfortable apartment from which, on a clear day, I could see the Mocambo . . ." he rather guardedly said. "My phone was unlisted, but a collection of numbers weren't. Obviously this pattern of living was acceptable if you didn't look more than forty-eight hours ahead."

It was the Hollywood blacklist, strangely enough, that rescued Reagan from some of these uncertainties. He got a telephone call from Mervyn LeRoy, the director, who said that a young actress in his current picture was fretting because her name kept turning up on the membership lists of various Communist front organizations. Could it be that there were two Nancy Davises? Could Reagan, as president of the Screen Actors Guild, find out? And perform a sort of clearing? Reagan checked and said she was clear. She asked if he would like to have dinner. They were married in 1952.

Reagan's career as a movie actor was by now so weather-beaten—"a truly sick industry . . . had virtually ground to a halt," as he put it—that his agents proposed he try a nightclub act in Las Vegas. "You must be kidding," said Reagan. Since he could neither sing nor dance, he could only serve as a sort of master of ceremonies, making a few wry jokes about his inabilities and then introducing other performers. The first offer was to play on Christmas. Reagan declined. The second was to introduce a stripper. Reagan declined. He finally teamed up, early in 1954, with a male singing quartet called The Continentals, who, according to Reagan, "did some sharp comedy material." After "a wonderfully successful two weeks," Reagan was glad enough to get an offer from General Electric to serve as host on a weekly TV series, and to spend ten weeks a year touring GE plants around the country, giving talks, meeting people.

That paid Reagan a starting wage of $125,000 a year, but what finally made him rich was the great land deal. Twentieth Century–Fox paid him $1,931,000 in 1966 for 236 acres of ranchland in the Santa Monica mountains, which he had bought for $85,000 back in 1951. By now, Reagan was running for governor of California, and some people said that he had a promising political future.

NOTES

Chapter 1 Welcome (1939).

Page 1. **To the chamber:** All the obviously firsthand descriptions in this chapter are based on a visit to Hollywood in the summer of 1982.

Page 2. **The waxworks commentary:** Samuel Marx, *Mayer and Thalberg*, p. 199.

Page 2. **Outside the waxworks:** *Newsweek*, Feb. 6, 1984.

Page 3. **A showman:** *New York Times*, March 6, 1950. *Variety*, March 8, 1950. *Time*, March 1, 1943.

Page 4. **Long before Grauman:** Charles Lockwood, *Dream Palaces*, pp. 20–32. See also Kevin Starr, *Inventing the Dream: California Through the Progressive Era*, pp. 283–5.

Page 4. **Back east, winter:** Works Progress Administration, *Los Angeles: A Guide*, pp. 74–5. Starr, *Inventing the Dream*, p. 288.

Page 5. **Many of these pioneers:** Starr, *Inventing the Dream*, pp. 285–7. Michael Conant, *Antitrust in the Motion Picture Industry*, pp. 16–24. Hortense Powdermaker, *Hollywood: The Dream Factory*, p. 89.

Page 6. **Years before Bertolt:** Bertolt Brecht, *Mahagonny*, libretto for CBS recording, pp. 1, 15.

Page 6. **If Brecht's vision:** Lockwood, *Dream Palaces*, p. 36.

Page 6. **Thornton Wilder:** Fred Lawrence Guiles, *Hanging on in Paradise*, p. 38.

Page 6. **The prospect of cataclysm:** Information provided by George C. Page Museum, Los Angeles.

Page 6. **The first Spanish explorers:** John D. Weaver, *Los Angeles: The Enormous Village*, p. 15.

Page 7. **The city that now numbers:** *New York Times*, June 9, 1978; November 17, 1980.

Page 7. **The droning voices:** Joan Didion, *Play It as It Lays*, pp. 103–4.

Page 7. **Miss Didion ascribed:** Joan Didion, *Slouching Towards Bethlehem*, p. 220.

Page 8. **Nathanael West had seen:** Nathanael West, *The Day of the Locust*, p. 78.

Page 8. **West was thirty-five:** Jay Martin, *Nathanael West*, pp. 341, 359.

Page 8. **Like most writers:** In addition to Martin, see Stanley Edgar Hyman, *Nathanael West*, p. 6. Also S. J. Perelman, *The Last Laugh*, p. 163.

Page 8. **Perelman, who first:** Martin, *Nathanael West*, pp. 205, 213. Also S. J. Perelman, *The Most of S. J. Perelman*, p. 47.

Page 9. **West came to Hollywood:** Tom Dardis, *Some Time in the Sun*, p. 140.

Page 9. **West worked hard:** Martin, *Nathanael West*, pp. 213, 262–72.

Page 9. **These were the outcasts:** West, *The Day of the Locust*, p. 12.

Page 10. **The Hollywood that attracted:** Ibid., pp. 96, 100, 104, 156ff.

Page 11. **This city of the inferno:** Martin, *Nathanael West*, pp. 338–40. "Introduction" to *The Day of the Locust*, by Richard Gehman, pp. xii, xi.

Page 11. **Hedy Lamarr. Hedwig:** *New York Times*, Aug. 23, 1970.

Page 11. **Probably it was:** *Time*, Jan. 14, 1935. Hedy Lamarr, *Ecstasy and Me*, p. 29. For the controversy over this book, see *New York Times*, Sept. 27, 1966.

Page 12. **The customs authorities:** *New York Times*, Oct. 27, 1937; Nov. 17, 1940.

Page 12. **By then, of course:** *Time*, July 25, 1938. Also Errol Flynn, *My Wicked, Wicked Ways*, p. 221 (1974).

Page 12. **Frau Mandl's flight:** Lamarr, *Ecstasy and Me*, pp. 41–3. Also Bosley Crowther, *Hollywood Rajah*, p. 220. This is the basic work on Mayer.

Page 13. **This, then, was:** Crowther, *Hollywood Rajah*, pp. 236–41.

Page 13. **That was the most remarkable:** Norman Zierold, *The Moguls*, p. 264.

Page 13n. **The Algiers script:** Larry Swindell, *Charles Boyer,* p. 118.

Page 14. **In 1939, there:** Leo C. Rosten, *Hollywood,* pp. 3–4, 378–9. A pioneering and expertly done sociological study of Hollywood as an industry. See also Conant, *Antitrust,* pp. 25–26. Also Roland Flamini, *Scarlett, Rhett and a Cast of Thousands,* p. 32 (1978).

Page 14. **The creation of fantasy:** Dardis, *Some Time in the Sun,* p. 62. Rosten, *Hollywood,* p. 80. Zierold, *The Moguls,* p. 33.

Page 14. **But the lords:** Crowther, *Hollywood Rajah,* pp. 11–12. Gavin Lambert, *GWTW: The Making of Gone with the Wind,* pp. 4–5. Jack Warner, *My First Hundred Years in Hollywood,* p. 21. Stephen Birmingham, *"The Rest of Us,"* p. 32.

Page 15. **The legend of:** Rosten, *Hollywood,* p. 17.

Page 15. **He spent his boyhood:** Crowther, *Hollywood Rajah,* pp. 28, 221–4, 323. Zierold, *The Moguls,* p. 276. Marx, *Mayer and Thalberg,* pp. 24, 78.

Page 15. **One of the most remarkable:** Zierold, *The Moguls,* p. 21. On Hollywood's misjudgments, see also Powdermaker, *Hollywood: The Dream Factory.*

Page 15. **A Napoleonic lack:** Quoted in Flamini, *Scarlett,* p. 22.

Page 16. **The lords of Hollywood:** Stephen Farber and Marc Green, *Hollywood Dynasties,* p. 19.

Page 16. **Mayer did not read:** Flamini, *Scarlett,* pp. 3–4. Marx, *Mayer and Thalberg,* pp. 17ff.

Page 16. **While Thalberg lived:** Dardis, *Some Time in the Sun,* p. 44. F. Scott Fitzgerald, *The Last Tycoon,* pp. 20, 134.

Page 17. **Thalberg was the:** Marx, *Mayer and Thalberg,* pp. 100, 198.

Page 17. **Mayer and Thalberg:** Flamini, *Scarlett,* pp. 4–5. Lambert, *GWTW,* p. 17.

Page 17. **RKO's Pandro Berman:** Mel Gussow, *Darryl F. Zanuck,* p. 70 (1980).

Page 18. **The Selznicks were:** Zierold, *The Moguls,* pp. 26ff. Irene Mayer Selznick, *A Private View,* p. 107.

Page 18. **Then there was David:** Zierold, *The Moguls,* pp. 43–4. Selznick, *A Private View,* pp. 107–8, 133–7. Hedda Hopper, *The Whole Truth and Nothing But,* p. 114.

Page 19. **Louis B. Mayer warned:** Selznick, *A Private View,* pp. 133–7. Jhan Robbins, *Front Page Marriage: Helen Hayes and Charles MacArthur,* p. 121.

Page 19. **But throughout the:** Lambert, *GWTW,* pp. 32–3, 47–56.

Page 20. **As the beginning:** Flamini, *Scarlett,*

p. 148. Lambert, *GWTW,* p. 51. Ronald Haver, *David O. Selznick's Hollywood,* p. 256.

Page 21. **The flames were:** Flamini, *Scarlett,* p. 154. Also Anne Edwards, *Vivien Leigh,* pp. 88–97.

Page 21. **God never meant:** Work Projects Administration, *Los Angeles,* pp. 52–3. Also William L. Kahrl, *Water and Power,* pp. 20ff.

Page 22. **The new aqueduct:** David Halberstam, *The Powers That Be,* p. 116.

Page 23. **The future of Los Angeles:** Carey McWilliams, *Southern California Country,* p. 195. *New York Times,* July 23, 1935.

Page 23. **By then, the New Deal:** Peter Wiley and Robert Gottlieb, *Empires in the Sun,* pp. 15–19. Joan Didion, *The White Album,* pp. 198–9.

Page 23. **The aqueduct from:** *New York Times,* June 22, 1941. Weaver, *Los Angeles,* p. 127.

Page 23. **Hollywood was not:** *Encyclopaedia Britannica Yearbook,* 1940, p. 460. Flamini, *Scarlett,* p. 327. Edwards, *Vivien Leigh,* pp. 111–13.

Page 24. **War had been inevitable:** Larry Ceplair and Steven Englund, *The Inquisition in Hollywood,* p. 142. This is the most comprehensive (if occasionally murky) book on this complex subject.

Page 24. **The day after:** Nancy Lynn Schwartz, *The Hollywood Writers' Wars,* p. 146ff. Another basic text, though marred by an irritating leftist bias.

Page 24. **Not everyone thought:** William Robert Faith, *Bob Hope,* pp. 136–7.

Page 25. **In France itself:** Arthur Rubinstein, *My Many Years,* p. 460. Pola Negri, *Memoirs of a Star,* p. 390.

Page 25. **The blackouts made:** Salka Viertel, *The Kindness of Strangers,* p. 236. A warmhearted and valuable guide.

Page 25. **Aboard the *Queen Mary:*** Faith, *Bob Hope,* p. 136.

Page 26. **Thanks for the memory:** Bob Hope, *Have Tux, Will Travel,* p. 168.

Page 26. **Ingrid Bergman, after:** Ingrid Bergman and Alan Burgess, *My Story,* p. 106 (1981).

Page 26. **Whether Sweden was safe:** Martin Esslin, *Brecht,* p. 67 (1961). Nigel Hamilton, *The Brothers Mann,* p. 310.

Page 26. **And there in London:** Ernest Jones, *The Life and Work of Sigmund Freud,* vol. 3, p. 245.

Page 26. **Igor Stravinsky, too:** Igor Stravinsky, *Themes and Conclusions,* p. 48. Vera Stravinsky and Robert Craft, *Stravinsky: In Pictures and Documents,* p. 350.

Page 27. **In Hollywood, these events:** Sybille Bedford, *Aldous Huxley,* pp. 381–2.

Page 27. **The origins of:** Charles Chaplin, *My Autobiography*, p. 391. Also David Robinson, *Chaplin*, pp. 493–508. *New York Times*, May 1, 1947. *Time*, May 12, 1947.

Page 27. **Chaplin's political doubts:** Chaplin, *My Autobiography*, pp. 392, 400.

Page 28. **Less rhetorical men:** David Niven, *Bring on the Empty Horses*, p. 101 (1976). Marvelous anecdotes.

Page 28. **On Sunday morning:** Laurence Olivier, *Confessions of an Actor*, p. 110 (1984). A slightly different version appears in Edwards, *Vivien Leigh*, p. 109.

Page 28. **Niven went off:** David Niven, *The Moon's a Balloon*, p. 227 (1973). John Russell Taylor, *Strangers in Paradise*, p. 131.

Page 28. **So Hollywood remained:** Viertel, *Kindness of Strangers*, p. 239. Rosten, *Hollywood*, p. 185.

Chapter 2   Ingatherings (1940).

Page 31. **Proud of his:** H. H. Stuckenschmidt, *Arnold Schoenberg*, pp. 114–15. John Russell Taylor, *Strangers in Paradise*, pp. 49, 384. Hans W. Heinsheimer, *Best Regards to Aida*, pp. 214–16.

Page 32. **Schoenberg was saved:** Arnold Schoenberg, *Letters*, pp. 196–8.

Page 32. **What Schoenberg was doing:** Stuckenschmidt, *Arnold Schoenberg*, p. 117.

Page 32. **Irving Thalberg, the young:** Salka Viertel, *The Kindness of Strangers*, pp. 206–8.

Page 33. **Schoenberg, who was earning:** This is mostly from Viertel, but see also Oscar Levant, *The Memoirs of an Amnesiac*, p. 132.

Page 34. **Schoenberg seemed to think:** Schoenberg, *Letters*, p. 197.

Page 34. **Hollywood's big musical:** Bob Thomas, *Walt Disney*, pp. 151ff.

Page 34. **Disney felt a little:** This is mostly from Thomas, but see also Oliver Daniel, *Stokowski*, pp. 380–5.

Page 35. **Out of such conferences:** Richard Schickel, *The Disney Version*, pp. 242–4.

Page 36. *Sacre de Printemps:* Igor Stravinsky and Robert Craft, *Expositions and Developments*, pp. 159ff.

Page 36. **By this time:** *Time*, Nov. 18, 1940.

Page 36. **Stravinsky had made:** Stravinsky and Craft, *Expositions*, pp. 82, 166.

Page 37. **Stravinsky seemed to:** *Saturday Review*, Jan. 30, 1960.

Page 37. **The week after:** Vera Stravinsky and Robert Craft, *Stravinsky*, p. 354. Alexandre Tansman, *Igor Stravinsky*, pp. 237–8.

Page 37. **Unlike Schoenberg:** Igor Stravinsky, *Themes and Conclusions*, p. 49.

Page 38. **I wonder if:** Bernard Taper, *Balanchine*, p. 191 (1974).

Page 38. **Thus was born:** Igor Stravinsky and Robert Craft, *Memories and Commentaries*, p. 93.

Page 38. **But it was the movies:** *Time*, July 26, 1948.

Page 38. **Stravinsky thereupon stood:** Vera Stravinsky and Craft, *Stravinsky*, p. 357. Also Eric Walter White, *Stravinsky*, p. 376.

Page 39. **Perhaps the most astonishing:** Vera Stravinsky and Craft, *Stravinsky*, p. 364. Also Stravinsky, *Memories*, p. 162.

Page 39. **It was natural:** Mark Evans, *Soundtrack*, p. 69 (1979). Also Ezra Goodman, *The Fifty-Year Decline and Fall of Hollywood*, p. 398. Max Wilk, *The Wit and Wisdom of Hollywood*, p. 197. The story of Tiomkin and Selznick is in Bob Thomas, *Selznick*, pp. 232–5 (1972).

Page 40. **I like it.** Roland Flamini, *Scarlett, Rhett, and a Cast of Thousands*, p. 300. Flamini tells this same story, credited to Thomas, but states the obscenity, whereas Thomas leaves blanks.

Page 40. **On this one occasion:** Hanns Eisler, *A Rebel in Music*, p. 103.

Page 40. **André Previn, who:** Martin Bookspan and Ross Yockey, *André Previn*, p. 48. See also Miklós Rózsa, *Double Life*, who corroborates this absurd story and adds another of his own: "Another [studio head] told the composer that the heroine's music was to be in the major key, the hero's in the minor, and that when the two were together, the music should be in both major and minor!" (p. 98).

Page 41. **Music, major and minor:** Evans, *Soundtrack*, pp. 38ff. Also Taylor, *Strangers in Paradise*, p. 237.

Page 41. **The Hollywood authorities:** Evans, *Soundtrack*, p. 23.

Page 41. **These were the stars:** Bookspan and Yockey, *Previn*, pp. 51, 43.

Page 42. **For the true professionals:** Evans, *Soundtrack*, pp. 30–1.

Page 42. **When these musicians:** *New York Times*, Feb. 28, 1983; Aug. 20, 1976.

Page 42. **These Hollywood musical:** Vera Stravinsky and Craft, *Stravinsky*, p. 359.

Page 42. **The superb RCA:** Arthur Rubinstein, *My Many Years*, p. 494. Also Levant, *Memoirs*, p. 135.

Page 43. **Ben Hecht played:** George Antheil, *Bad Boy of Music*, pp. 308–9.

Pages 43–5. **The rise of Hitler:** Maurice Zolotow, *Billy Wilder in Hollywood*, pp. 19–21, 52, 60, 71, 90. Hardly an inspired work but the best of several books on Wilder. See also Charles Higham, *Bette*, p. 166, and *Sisters*, pp. 122–3.

Page 45. **Fritz Lang, by contrast:** Siegfried Kracauer, *From Caligari to Hitler*, p. 248 (1966).

Page 45. **David Selznick, who:** Taylor, *Strangers*, p. 59.

Page 45. **When David Selznick:** Kenneth L. Geist, *Pictures Will Talk*, pp. 76–8.

Page 46. **Lang did not return:** Peter Bogdanovich, *Fritz Lang in America*, pp. 34–9.

Page 46. **It is remarkable:** Schoenberg, *Letters*, p. 205.

Page 47. **More important, though:** Leo C. Rosten, *Hollywood*, p. 140. Nancy Lynn Schwartz, *The Hollywood Writers' Wars*, p. 83. Bob Thomas, *King Cohn*, p. 102. The basic text on Harry Cohn.

Page 47. **Hollywood's political timidity:** Raymond Chandler, *Selected Letters*, pp. 207–8.

Page 48. **Most Jews of that time:** Ernest Jones, *The Life and Work of Sigmund Freud*, vol. 1, p. 22.

Page 48. **That defense provided:** Author's conversation with someone who asked not to be identified.

Page 48. **Scott Fitzgerald apparently:** Aaron Latham, *Crazy Sundays*, p. 178.

Page 49. **This was the same Mayer:** Ibid., p. 145.

Page 49. **Mayer apparently was:** Geist, *Pictures Will Talk*, p. 91. Latham, *Crazy Sundays*, p. 147. Larry Ceplair and Steven Englund, *The Inquisition in Hollywood*, p. 304.

Page 49. **We're not at war:** Axel Madsen, *William Wyler*, p. 215–17.

Page 49. **Warners had a:** Geist, *Pictures Will Talk*, p. 91.

Page 49. **It also began working:** Hal Wallis and Charles Higham, *Starmaker*, p. 70. Jack Warner, *My First Hundred Years in Hollywood*, p. 262.

Page 50. **Self-dramatization:** Wallis and Higham, *Starmaker*, p. 72.

Page 50. **The Hollywood Production:** Donald Spoto, *The Dark Side of Genius: The Life of Alfred Hitchcock*, pp. 222–36.

Page 50n. **By comparison, Warners':** Colin Shindler, *Hollywood Goes to War*, p. 5.

Page 51. **Such flights of rhetoric:** Michael Korda, *Charmed Lives*, pp. 154–5. Taylor, *Strangers*, pp. 134–5.

Page 51. **Senator Burton Wheeler:** Ceplair and Englund, *The Inquisition*, p. 160. Richard R. Lingeman, *Don't You Know There's a War On?*, p. 172. An excellent account of this whole period.

Page 52. **More ambiguous:** Ceplair and Englund, *The Inquisition*, pp. 156ff. Rosten, *Holly-*

wood, pp. 141–4. Dies's statements come from Martin Dies, "The Reds in Hollywood," *Liberty*, Feb. 17, 1940, and "Is Communism Invading the Movies?" *Liberty*, Feb. 24, 1940.

Page 52. **Dies kept announcing:** Rosten, *Hollywood*, pp. 145–9.

Page 52n. **Though Dies was:** Walter Goodman, *The Committee*, pp. 10–23.

Page 53. **Hollywood's progressives:** Stefan Kanfer, *A Journal of the Plague Years*, p. 27.

Page 53. **None of these political:** Rosten, *Hollywood*, p. 154.

Page 53. **When President Ronald Reagan:** *New York Times*, April 21, 1983. Ronald Reagan and Richard C. Hubler, *Where's the Rest of Me?*, pp. 105–15 (1981). This was written during Reagan's years of obscurity, but the future President is all here. F. Scott Fitzgerald, *The Crack-Up*, p. 66 (1956).

Page 54. **It is easy:** *New York Times*, Oct. 19, 1940.

Page 55. **The message of:** James K. Lyon, *Bertolt Brecht in America*, p. 137.

Page 56. **The refugees kept coming:** Taylor, *Strangers*, pp. 219ff.

Page 56. **Thomas Mann's white-bearded:** Nigel Hamilton, *The Brothers Mann*, p. 313. Taylor, *Strangers*, pp. 143–4.

Page 56. **Franz Werfel:** Alma Mahler Werfel, *And the Bridge Is Love*, pp. 253ff. Karen Monson, *Alma Mahler*, p. 276. Mary Jayne Gold, *Crossroads Marseilles/1940*, p. 184.

Page 56. **Roosevelt's request:** Werfel, *And the Bridge*, p. 265. Varian Fry, *Surrender on Demand*, pp. 57–69. Anthony Heilbut, *Exiled in Paradise*, pp. 40–3. Gold, *Crossroads Marseilles*, pp. 188–91. Monson, *Alma Mahler*, pp. 269ff.

Page 57. **Money and cigarettes:** Werfel, *And the Bridge*, p. 268.

Page 57. **Heinrich Mann contemplated:** Hamilton, *The Brothers Mann*, pp. 314, 320. Taylor, *Strangers*, pp. 145–6.

Page 58. **Werfel was more fortunate:** Werfel, *And the Bridge*, pp. 281, 271.

Page 58. *The Song of Bernadette:* Ibid., p. 272. White, *Stravinsky*, p. 96.

Page 58. **Perhaps, though, the:** Taylor, *Strangers*, p. 163.

Page 58. **And life with Alma:** Vera Stravinsky and Craft, *Stravinsky*, p. 411. S. N. Behrman, *People in a Diary*, p. 171. Werfel, *And the Bridge*, p. 276.

Page 59. **Werfel suffered:** Werfel, *And the Bridge*, pp. 283–4, 292.

Page 59. **The funeral was:** Thomas Mann, *The Story of a Novel: The Genesis of Doctor Faus-*

tus, p. 136. Stravinsky and Craft, *Expositions and Developments*, p. 66.

Chapter 3   Treachery (1941).
Page 61. **Money attracts deals:** Raymond Chandler, *The Little Sister*, p. 181.
Page 61. **Hardly anyone could fit:** *Time*, Nov. 17, 1941. Also Gertrude Jobes, *Motion Picture Empire*, pp. 341–54.
Page 61. **Schenck went to:** *New York Times*, Oct. 10, 1941.
Page 62. **That was the way:** Florabel Muir, *Headline Happy*, p. 91.
Page 62. **His real name:** *New York Herald Tribune*, Nov. 4, 1941; Oct. 28, 1941. *New York Times*, Oct. 28, 1941.
Page 62. **Brought from Russia:** Muir, *Headline Happy*, p. 83. *Time*, Dec. 4, 1939.
Page 62. **As an obscure:** *New York World-Telegram*, Feb. 1, 1949. *New York Times*, Oct. 28, 1941.
Page 62. **John and Barney Balaban:** *New York Times*, Oct. 12, 1943. *New York Mirror*, Oct. 3, 1963.
Page 63. **Bioff began grandly:** *World-Telegram*, Feb. 1, 1949.
Page 63. **So it was:** Bob Thomas, *King Cohn*, p. 199.
Page 64. **My God!:** *Time*, Oct. 18, 1943.
Page 64. **There actually was:** Muir, *Headline Happy*, pp. 88–9.
Page 65. **The antithesis of:** *New York Herald Tribune*, Oct. 28, 1941. Carey McWilliams, *The Education of Carey McWilliams*, p. 89.
Page 65. **The charge that:** *New York Times*, Sept. 8, 1938. Ronald Reagan and Richard C. Hubler, *Where's the Rest of Me?*, p. 185 (1981). *New York Times*, Dec. 2, 1943. John Cogley, *Report on Blacklisting*, vol. 1, pp. 52–3. McWilliams, *Education*, p. 89.
Page 66. **Bioff did win:** Muir, *Headline Happy*, p. 79. *Time*, Sept. 11, 1939.
Page 66. **Many of the actors:** Leo C. Rosten, *Hollywood*, pp. 341, 345.
Page 66. **The Internal Revenue:** *New York Herald Tribune*, Oct. 28, 1941. *New York Times*, Jan. 11, 1940; June 4, 1940; Feb. 20, 1940; Sept. 21, 1940.
Page 67. **The federal prosecutors:** *New York Herald Tribune*, Oct. 23, 1961.
Page 67. **So then Bioff:** *Time*, Oct. 20, 1941.
Page 67. **Bioff described:** *New York Herald Tribune*, Nov. 4, 1943. *Time*, Nov. 17, 1941; Nov. 14, 1955. *New York World-Telegram*, Feb. 1, 1949.
Page 68. **Bioff was a star:** *New York Times*, Oct. 12, 1943. *New York Herald Tribune*, Oct. 23, 1961.
Page 68. **On emerging from prison:** *Time*, Nov. 14, 1955. Westbrook Pegler columns in *New York Journal-American*, March 26–30, 1956. *New York Times*, Nov. 5, 1955. McWilliams, *Education*, p. 91.
Page 68. **Joe Schenck spent:** Anita Loos, *A Girl Like I*, p. 196.
Page 68. **At a meeting:** Budd Schulberg, *What Makes Sammy Run?*, p. 251 (1978). Nancy Lynn Schwartz, *The Hollywood Writers' Wars*, p. 167.
Page 69. **What Makes Sammy Run?** Schulberg, p. 203. Irene Mayer Selznick, *A Private View*, p. 50.
Page 69. **Don't pull that:** Schulberg, *What Makes Sammy Run?*, p. 108.
Page 69. **Jewish anti-Semitism:** Schulberg, *What Makes Sammy Run?*, pp. 215, 232.
Page 69n. **Samuel Goldwyn, after:** Arthur Marx, *Goldwyn*, p. 286.
Page 70. **Hollywood was accustomed:** Budd Schulberg, *Moving Pictures*, pp. 51, 307.
Page 70. **The element that:** Carey McWilliams, *Southern California Country*, pp. 224–9.
Page 70. **The arrival of:** David Halberstam, *The Powers That Be*, pp. 99–111.
Page 71. **In the prosperous 1920's:** Schwartz, *Hollywood Writers' Wars*, pp. 8–9.
Page 72. **The studios were:** Samuel Marx, *Mayer and Thalberg*, pp. 206–7.
Page 72. **The technicians were:** Schwartz, *Hollywood Writers' Wars*, pp. 12, 14.
Page 72n. **Thau was sometimes:** Roland Flamini, *Ava*, p. 18. S. N. Behrman, *People in a Diary*, pp. 157–8.
Pages 73–4. **Early in 1933:** Schwartz, *Hollywood Writers' Wars*, pp. 21, 59, 129, 60, 67.
Page 74. **When the meeting:** Schulberg, *What Makes Sammy Run?*, p. 158.
Page 74. **But that was:** Schwartz, *Hollywood Writers' Wars*, pp. 31, 73–9.
Page 75. **Schulberg published:** Victor S. Navasky, *Naming Names*, pp. 239–40 (1981).
Page 75. **What remains most:** Schulberg, *What Makes Sammy Run?*, p. 250. Schwartz, *Hollywood Writers' Wars*, pp. 99–130, 172–3.
Page 76. **Sheridan Gibney:** Dore Schary, *Heyday*, p. 113 (1981).
Page 77. **Dashiell Hammett knew:** William F. Nolan, *Hammett*, p. 14.
Page 77. **Hammett had become:** Diane Johnson, *Dashiell Hammett, A Life*, pp. 16–27. Richard Layman, *Shadow Man*, pp. 6–10. Hugh Eames, *Sleuths, Inc.*, p. 107. Also Dashiell Ham-

mett, *The Continental Op,* "Introduction" by Steven Marcus.

Page 77. **Hammett apparently enjoyed:** Eames, *Sleuths, Inc.,* p. 104. Also interview by David Fechheimer, quoted in Eames, p. 108.

Page 77. **As part of:** Ibid., p. 107. Lillian Hellman, *Scoundrel Time,* p. 45 (1977).

Page 78. **Miss Hellman's admiring:** Johnson, *Dashiell Hammett,* pp. 96, 100, 106–7, 130, 162–3. Nolan, *Hammett,* pp. 127, 237. Layman, *Shadow Man,* p. 237.

Page 78. **The screenwriter Nunnally Johnson:** *The Letters of Nunnally Johnson,* p. 188.

Page 78. **When Hammett's third:** Nolan, *Hammett,* pp. 110, 113, 90.

Page 79. **The Maltese Falcon was:** Dashiell Hammett, *The Maltese Falcon,* p. 187 (1972).

Page 79. **In a Hollywood:** Nolan, *Hammett,* pp. 117, 156. Hammett, *The Maltese Falcon,* p. 227.

Page 80. **And in 1941:** John Huston, *An Open Book,* p. 88 (1981). Nolan, *Hammett,* p. 179.

Page 80. **Jack Warner grudgingly:** Allen Rivkin and Laura Kerr, *Hello, Hollywood,* pp. 155–6.

Page 80. **The next accident:** Jon Tuska, *The Detective in Hollywood,* pp. 169–72. Also Lewis Yablonsky, *George Raft,* p. 139. Joe Hyams, *Bogie,* p. 68 (1967). Michael Freedland, *The Warner Brothers,* p. 128. Larry Swindell, *Body and Soul,* p. 184.

Page 81. **Now Raft didn't:** Rudy Behlmer, *Inside Warner Bros.,* p. 151. Tuska, *The Detective in Hollywood,* p. 176. Nolan, *Hammett,* p. 180. Huston, *An Open Book,* p. 89.

Page 81. **Much of that success:** Charles Higham and Joel Greenberg, *Hollywood in the Forties,* pp. 20, 36. Charles Higham, *Hollywood at Sunset,* p. 16.

Page 82. **Huston also had:** Hammett, *The Maltese Falcon,* p. 1.

Page 82. **Bogart had not:** Hyams, *Bogie,* pp. 20ff. Louise Brooks, *Lulu in Hollywood,* p. 59.

Pages 83–4. **On late-night television:** Hyams, *Bogie,* pp. 57–63. Raymond Chandler, *The Big Sleep,* p. 72 (1971).

Page 84. **Humor combined:** Hammett, *The Maltese Falcon,* p. 227.

Page 85. **And what financial:** Nolan, *Hammett,* p. 197. Layman, *Shadow Man,* p. 212.

Page 85. **Despite Hollywood's three:** Tony Thomas, *The Films of Ronald Reagan,* pp. 99–132. Reagan and Hubler, *Where's the Rest of Me?,* p. 153. Rosten, *Hollywood,* p. 342.

Page 85. **The year 1941:** Laurence Leamer, *Make-Believe: The Story of Nancy and Ronald Reagan,* pp. 115, 112. Thomas, *The Films of Ronald*

Reagan, p. 122. Reagan and Hubler, *Where's the Rest,* p. 8.

Page 86. **Warners had spent:** Hal Wallis and Charles Higham, *Starmaker,* p. 98. Henry Bellamann, *Kings Row,* p. 3.

Pages 86–7. **Of such burgeoning:** Wallis and Higham, *Starmaker,* pp. 99–100.

Page 86n. **In an interview:** Rex Reed, *Conversations in the Raw,* p. 31.

Page 87. **There was one scene:** Bellamann, *Kings Row,* p. 464.

Pages 88–9. **Ronald Reagan, having:** Reagan and Hubler, *Where's the Rest,* pp. 8–9. Leamer, *Make-Believe,* p. 119.

Page 89. **As in some grotesque:** Pauline Kael, *The Citizen Kane Book,* p. 60. This book (which happily includes the script of the film) was the first major investigation of Mankiewicz's claims to having written *Citizen Kane;* it was strongly attacked by Welles's admirers, notably Peter Bogdanovich (in *Esquire,* October 1972). Richard Meryman, *Mank,* p. 244.

Page 90. **The saga of *Citizen Kane:*** Charles Higham, *The Films of Orson Welles,* pp. 3, 15–16. Charles Higham, *Orson Welles,* pp. 139–42. Higham's second book on Welles is probably the most reliable account of his career. Meryman, *Mank,* pp. 244–5, 133.

Page 90. **Mankiewicz was also:** Kael, *Citizen Kane Book,* pp. 43, 46–47. Meryman, *Mank,* pp. 130, 242. Higham, *Films of Orson Welles,* p. 10.

Page 90n. **As though to test:** Dore Schary, *Heyday,* pp. 54a–75.

Page 91. **Hearst was one:** Joan Didion, *Slouching Towards Bethlehem,* p. xvi. Kael, *Citizen Kane Book,* pp. 50, 101–3.

Page 91. **Welles was pleased:** Ibid., pp. 5–9, 58–67. Higham, *Orson Welles,* pp. 146–59. Barbara Leaming, *Orson Welles.* The Leaming work contains much entertaining detail from her interviews with Welles.

Page 92. **Welles relied:** George Eels, *Malice in Wonderland,* pp. 28, 43–5, 50, 85–6 (1985). *Time,* July 28, 1947.

Page 92n. **She achieved happiness:** Eels, *Malice in Wonderland,* pp. 147–81.

Page 93. **What Mrs. Parsons:** Higham, *Orson Welles,* pp. 168–72. Leaming, *Orson Welles,* pp. 204–11.

Page 94. **It is difficult:** William Shirer, *The Rise and Fall of the Third Reich,* pp. 851–4. Bertolt Brecht, *Seven Plays,* p. 261.

Page 94. **Brecht himself:** Frederic Ewen, *Bertolt Brecht,* pp. 330, 301. Also Martin Esslin, *Brecht. Brecht, Seven Plays,* p. 392.

Page 95. **Brecht never wanted:** James K.

Lyon, *Bertolt Brecht in America*, pp. 23, 27–30. This is the best account of Brecht's Hollywood years, though Bruce Cook's *Brecht in Exile* is also good. Bertolt Brecht, *Mahagonny*, libretto for CBS recording, pp. 16, 20, 22.

Page 96. **But to the Brecht:** Lyon, *Brecht in America*, p. 33. Brecht, *Poems, 1913–1956*, p. 367. Anthony Heilbut, *Exiled in Paradise*, p. 182.

Page 96. **On thinking about Hell:** Brecht, *Poems*, p. 367.

Page 96. **Despite all these:** Bruce Cook, *Brecht in Exile*, pp. 43–54.

Pages 97–8. **In Hollywood, now:** Lyon, *Brecht in America*, pp. 48–51. Cook, *Brecht in Exile*, p. 41.

Page 98. **Again and again:** Brecht, *Poems*, pp. 378–9, 392. Cook, *Brecht in Exile*, p. 104.

Pages 98–9. **By arriving on:** Salka Viertel, *The Kindness of Strangers*, pp. 250–1.

Page 99. **One of the pleasant:** William Robert Faith, *Bob Hope*, pp. 125, 154.

Page 100. **Rubinstein himself recalled:** Arthur Rubinstein, *My Many Years*, p. 486.

Page 100. **Not everyone was:** Lana Turner, *Lana*, p. 75.

Page 100. **The news on the radio:** Ingrid Bergman and Alan Burgess, *My Story*, p. 148 (1981). Beverly Linet, *Ladd*, pp. 63–4 (1980).

Page 101. **John Houseman and:** John Houseman, *Front and Center*, pp. 19–20 (1980).

Page 101. **Maxine Andrews was:** Studs Terkel, *The Good War*, pp. 294–7.

Page 101. **Mary Astor was:** Mary Astor, *My Story*, p. 218.

Page 101. **Gene Tierney and:** Gene Tierney, *Self-Portrait*, p. 21 (1980).

Page 101. **This mixture of:** *New York Times*, Dec. 8, 9, 1941.

Page 102. **None too soon:** Richard R. Lingeman, *Don't You Know There's a War On?*, pp. 24–5.

Page 102. **Los Angeles dreaded:** *New York Times*, Dec. 8, 1941. *Time*, Dec. 22, 1941.

Page 102. **The authorities kept:** Lingeman, *Don't You Know*, p. 28. *New York Times*, Dec. 9, 1941. Peter Irons, *Justice at War*, p. 19.

Page 103. **So Hollywood began:** *Time*, Dec. 22, 1941. Jack Warner, *My First Hundred Years in Hollywood*, p. 282.

Chapter 4   Americanism (1942).
Page 105. **Jimmy Stewart quietly:** Richard R. Lingeman, *Don't You Know There's a War On?*, pp. 170, 179. Hector Arce, *The Secret Life of Tyrone Power*, pp. 155–9 (1980). Henry Fonda, *My Life*, p. 138.

Page 105. **Zanuck, who was:** Mel Gussow, *Darryl F. Zanuck*, pp. 97, 114, 99–100 (1980). Otto Preminger, *Preminger: An Autobiography*, p. 81 (1978).

Page 105. **Each celebrity's call:** Ronald Reagan and Richard C. Hubler, *Where's the Rest of Me?*, p. 122 (1981). Doug McClelland, ed., *Hollywood on Reagan*, p. 32.

Page 106. **By October of 1942:** Lingeman, *Don't You Know*, p. 170.

Page 106. **Women were especially:** Ibid., p. 175. Hedy Lamarr, *Ecstasy and Me*, p. 115. Lana Turner, *Lana*, p. 76. Dorothy Lamour, *My Side of the Road*, p. 115.

Page 106. **It was all:** Lynn Tornabene, *Long Live the King: A Biography of Clark Gable*, pp. 265–6. Garson Kanin, *Hollywood*, p. 55.

Pages 106–7. **Miss Lombard sold:** Tornabene, *Long Live the King*, pp. 267–81.

Page 108. **Los Angeles was:** Whitney Stine, *Mother Goddam*, pp. 175–7 (1975).

Page 108. **Miss Davis also:** Bette Davis, *The Lonely Life*, p. 212.

Page 108. **Bette Davis worked:** Lamarr, *Ecstasy and Me*, pp. 113–14.

Page 108. **Gene Tierney considered:** Gene Tierney, *Self-Portrait*, pp. 98, 12–14, 92 (1980).

Pages 109–10. **Just before she left:** Ibid., pp. 99–100, 108.

Page 110. **These were individual:** Lingeman, *Don't You Know*, pp. 168, 210.

Page 110. **There were problems:** John Huston, *An Open Book*, p. 99 (1981).

Pages 110–12. **The material demands:** Lingeman, *Don't You Know*, pp. 176–81.

Page 111*n*. **Loo, who was born:** *New York Times*, Nov. 22, 1983.

Page 112. **The reason for:** Peter Irons, *Justice at War*, p. 6

Page 112. **This admirable advice:** Allan R. Bosworth, *America's Concentration Camps*, p. 60.

Page 112. **This may seem:** Roy Hoopes, *Americans Remember the Home Front*, pp. 175–6. Hoopes, *Cain*, p. 320.

Page 112. **This was largely:** Bruce Cook, *Brecht in Exile*, p. 72. Bosworth, *America's Concentration Camps*, pp. 63, 211, 68, 59–60. Carey McWilliams, *The Education of Carey McWilliams*, p. 102.

Page 113. **The Japanese who:** Irons, *Justice at War*, pp. 9–13.

Page 114. **The FBI and:** Jeanne Wakatsuki Houston, *Farewell to Manzanar*, p. 7.

Page 114. **The pressure for:** Bosworth, *America's Concentration Camps*, pp. 56, 71. Irons, *Jus-*

tice at War, p. 7. McWilliams, *Education*, p. 104. G. Edward White, *Earl Warren*, pp. 69–75. Cabell Phillips, *The 1940's*, p. 109.

Page 114. **California's other chief:** Bosworth, *America's Concentration Camps*, pp. 61, 100–1, 180. Donald I. Rogers, *Since You Went Away*, p. 82.

Page 115. **DeWitt was no:** Phillips, *The 1940's*, p. 110. Bosworth, *America's Concentration Camps*, pp. 116, 171.

Page 115. **Just as Hollywood:** Hoopes, *Americans Remember*, p. 264. Houston, *Farewell to Manzanar*, pp. 12–13.

Page 116. **Mineta and the rest:** Bosworth, *America's Concentration Camps*, p. 118. Hoopes, *Americans Remember*, pp. 260–1.

Page 116. **"Concentration camp" is:** Houston, *Farewell to Manzanar*, pp. 28, 16.

Page 117. **While Pearl Harbor:** Leo C. Rosten, *Hollywood*, p. 379. Donald L. Barlett and James B. Steele, *Empire*, p. 105. This is the best of many books on Howard Hughes.

Page 117. **Though Glenn Martin:** Christopher Rand, *Los Angeles: The Ultimate City*, pp. 71–2. David Halberstam, *The Powers That Be*, p. 114. John Gunther, *Inside U.S.A.*, p. 27. Peter Wiley and Robert Gottlieb, *Empires in the Sun*, p. 27. Barlett and Steele, *Empire*, p. 75.

Page 117. **Pearl Harbor naturally:** Lingeman, *Don't You Know*, pp. 128, 132. Barlett and Steele, *Empire*, p. 106.

Page 118. **Through no foresight:** Carey McWilliams, *Southern California Country*, p. 339. Wiley and Gottlieb, *Empires in the Sun*, p. 110.

Page 118. **One of the few:** Barlett and Steele, *Empire*, pp. 107, 60–1, 63–7. John Keats, *Howard Hughes*, p. 58.

Pages 119–21. **Hughes was nearly:** Barlett and Steele, *Empire*, pp. 66–8, 73–97. Keats, *Howard Hughes*, p. 9.

Page 119n. **As often happened:** Lester Cole, *Hollywood Red*, p. 94.

Page 121. **On the other hand:** Gussow, *Zanuck*, p. 126. Turner, *Lana*, p. 77. Roland Flamini, *Ava*, p. 69 (1984).

Page 121. **Hughes apparently suffered:** Charles Higham, *Bette*, pp. 123–40 (1982).

Page 122. **This aspect of Hughes:** Veronica Lake, *Veronica*, p. 136.

Page 122. **The disastrous crash:** Barlett and Steele, *Empire*, pp. 106–10. Roland Flamini, *Scarlett, Rhett, and a Cast of Thousands*, p. 88.

Page 122. **The D-2 was:** Barlett and Steele, *Empire*, pp. 113, 115, 117, 156–7. Keats, *Howard Hughes*, pp. 165, 159.

Page 123. **He had other:** Ibid., p. 174. Ben Hecht, *A Child of the Century*, pp. 486–7.

Pages 123–26. **Then came the:** Jane Russell, *My Path and My Detours*, pp. 1–8, 44. Keats, *Howard Hughes*, pp. 174, 182, 148, 151–2, 164, 170–3.

Pages 126–29. **The greatest playwright:** James K. Lyon, *Bertolt Brecht in America*, pp. 45, 53–6, 59–62, 66–9. Cook, *Brecht in Exile*, p. 81. Ronald Hayman, *Brecht*, pp. 256–61, 204–5.

Page 129. **Like Detroit, Hollywood:** John Kobal, *Rita Hayworth*, p. 127. This is the best of several books on Miss Hayworth. Donald Spoto, *The Dark Side of Genius*, p. 252.

Page 130. **George M. Cohan:** James Cagney, *Cagney on Cagney*, p. 105. Patrick McGilligan, *Cagney*, pp. 145–6, 407.

Page 130. **William Cagney was:** Hal Wallis and Charles Higham, *Starmaker*, p. 103. McGilligan, *Cagney*, pp. 149–50. Also Doug Warren, *James Cagney*, pp. 142–7.

Page 131. **Cagney's impression:** *Cagney on Cagney*, pp. 104–7. McGilligan, *Cagney*, pp. 155, 158, 161.

Page 131n. **Miss Leslie was:** Michael Freedland, *The Warner Brothers*, p. 148.

Page 132. **Warners had planned:** McGilligan, *Cagney*, p. 158.

Page 132. **It was typical:** John Russell Taylor, *Strangers in Paradise*, p. 62. *New York Times*, April 12, 1962. Wallis and Higham, *Starmaker*, p. 25.

Page 132. **If Curtiz knew:** David Niven, *Bring on the Empty Horses*, p. 117 (1976). It is worth noting that Michael Korda attributes exactly this same line to his uncle Zoltan Korda (*Charmed Lives*, p. 208).

Page 133. **And there was more:** Wallis and Higham, *Starmaker*, p. 24. *Time*, April 20, 1962. *New York Herald Tribune*, June 16, 1940.

Page 133. **None of this:** *New York Times*, April 12, 1962; Sept. 23, 1943.

Page 133. **Out of somewhere:** Wallis and Higham, *Starmaker*, pp. 83–4. Howard Koch, *As Time Goes By*, p. 77.

Page 134. **Wallis also encountered:** Ingrid Bergman and Alan Burgess, *My Story*, pp. 78–9.

Page 134. **Selznick was perhaps:** Bergman and Burgess, *My Story*, pp. 87–8, 91, 102. Laurence Leamer, *As Time Goes By*, pp. 73, 79, 88, 103, 124.

Page 134n. **The standard Warners:** *New York Times*, Oct. 10, 1985.

Page 134n. **Raft eventually became:** Freedland, *The Warner Brothers*, p. 169.

Page 135. **Miss Bergman went:** Irene Mayer Selznick, *A Private View*, p. 230.

Page 136. **He rented Ingrid:** Wallis and Higham, *Starmaker*, p. 86. Koch, *As Time Goes By*, p. 78. I have altered this scene slightly to conform with an interview with Julius Epstein by Aljean Harmetz in the *New York Times*, Feb. 5, 1984.

Page 136. **The stars were:** Wallis and Higham, *Starmaker*, pp. 87–8. Rudy Behlmer, *Inside Warner Bros.*, p. 199.

Page 136. **And there was:** Koch, *As Time Goes By*, pp. 79–82. Behlmer, *Inside Warner Bros.*, p. 240.

Page 137. **The expensive cast:** Bergman and Burgess, *My Story*, p. 145.

Page 137. **Bogart seemed to:** Joe Hyams, *Bogie*, pp. 76–7 (1967).

Page 138. **In this state:** Paul Henreid, *Ladies' Man*, pp. 128–9.

Page 138. **Casablanca came to:** Bergman and Burgess, *My Story*, p. 145.

Page 138. **Even that ending:** Wallis and Higham, *Starmaker*, pp. 91–2.

Chapter 5   Prejudice (1943).

Page 141. **Just after dark:** *Time*, June 21, 1943. Rodolfo Acuña, *Occupied America: A History of Chicanos*, p. 327.

Page 141. **There was more:** Carey McWilliams, *North from Mexico*, p. 249. John D. Weaver, *Los Angeles*, p. 137.

Page 141. **And more:** Acuña, *Occupied America*, p. 327. *New York Times*, June 9, 10, 1943.

Page 142. **The irony was:** McWilliams, *North from Mexico*, p. 233. Acuña, *Occupied America*, p. 323.

Page 142. **That was because:** Nathanael West, *The Day of the Locust*, p. 137.

Page 142. **The reality was:** Acuña, *Occupied America*, p. 326.

Page 143. **The police attitude:** Ibid., pp. 323, 325. McWilliams, *North from Mexico*, p. 234.

Page 143. **Against that background:** McWilliams, *North from Mexico*, pp. 244–5. Julian Samora and Patricia Vandel Simon, *A History of the Mexican-American People*, p. 117.

Pages 143–44. **The next night:** Acuña, *Occupied America*, p. 327. McWilliams, *North from Mexico*, pp. 246–8. *New York Times*, June 7, 1943.

Page 144. **The Los Angeles police:** Samora and Simon, *A History*, pp. 327–9. *New York Times*, June 10, 12, 1943.

Page 145. **The anti-Mexican riots:** McWilliams, *North from Mexico*, p. 256.

Page 145. **Washington was eager:** Charles Higham, *The Films of Orson Welles*, pp. 85, 87.

Page 145. **The only movie:** Henry Fonda, *My Life*, p. 178.

Page 146. **Hollywood's final verdict:** John Kobal, *Rita Hayworth*, pp. 18–20. I have relied mainly on Kobal's thorough work for the details of the young Rita Hayworth.

Pages 146–47. **Young Margarita:** Ibid., pp. 28–9, 36, 43–50, 174, 181.

Page 147. **Middle-aged men:** Ibid., pp. 50–1. Bob Thomas, *King Cohn*, p. 169.

Page 147. **Sheehan shortened:** Kobal, *Rita Hayworth*, pp. 52, 63, 70–4. Joe Morella and Edward Z. Epstein, *Rita*, p. 253.

Page 148. **Then along came:** Charles Higham, *Orson Welles*, p. 210.

Pages 148–50. **But Judson:** Thomas, *King Cohn*, pp. 72, 170–2. Kobal, *Rita Hayworth*, pp. 76, 80–2, 95, 102, 113, 123.

Page 150. **Once Miss Hayworth:** *Time*, Nov. 10, 1941. Morella and Epstein, *Rita*, p. 257.

Page 150. **It was apparently:** Kobal, *Rita Hayworth*, pp. 154, 159, 161.

Page 150. *Cover Girl:* Author's notes on TV showing.

Pages 151–52. **The purpose of:** Kobal, *Rita Hayworth*, pp. 157, 161–3, 142–4.

Page 152. **Love is eternal:** Joseph McBride, *Orson Welles*, p. 11. Anne Baxter, *Intermission*, p. 119 (1978). André Bazin, *Orson Welles*, pp. 30, 40.

Page 153. **The trip to:** Charles Higham, *The Films of Orson Welles*, pp. 91–2, 95. Bazin, *Orson Welles*, p. 86.

Page 153. **But in 1943:** McBride, *Orson Welles*, p. 42.

Page 153. **Of the Hollywood figures:** Frank Capra, *The Name Above the Title*, pp. 360–3.

Page 154. **Major William Wyler:** Axel Madsen, *William Wyler*, pp. 220–40. John Huston, *An Open Book*, pp. 99ff.

Page 154. **Jack Warner:** Jack Warner, *My First Hundred Years in Hollywood*, p. 283. Michael Freedland, *The Warner Brothers*, pp. 153–5. Rudy Behlmer, *Inside Warner Bros.*, p. 161.

Page 154. **Before that unfortunate:** Warner, *First Hundred Years*, pp. 290ff. Freedland, *The Warner Brothers*, p. 150.

Page 154. **White House officials:** Freedland, *The Warner Brothers*, p. 189. Colin Shindler, *Hollywood Goes to War*, pp. 58–9. Warner, *First Hundred Years*, p. 293. Howard Koch, *As Time Goes By*, pp. 101ff.

Page 155. **Warner's other big:** Freedland, *The Warner Brothers*, pp. 155–6.

Page 155. **Reagan had managed:** Ronald Reagan and Richard C. Hubler, *Where's the Rest of Me?*, pp. 124–5, 127–8, 130.

Page 155. **The Army Air Corps:** Reagan and Hubler, *Where's the Rest*, pp. 132–3. Huston, *An Open Book*, 108.

Page 155n. **In her witty book:** Nora Sayre, *Running Time*, p. 6.

Page 156. **Lieutenant Reagan apparently:** Laurence Leamer, *Make-Believe*, pp. 122–3.

Page 156. **Reagan was always:** Reagan and Hubler, *Where's the Rest*, p. 134.

Pages 156–57. **There was equally:** Gottfried Reinhardt, *The Genius: A Memoir of Max Reinhardt*, pp. 10, 20, 24–5.

Page 158. **In one reasonably:** *Time*, Sept. 20, 1943. James Naremore, *The Magic World of Orson Welles*, p. 137. William Robert Faith, *Bob Hope*, pp. 32–3.

Page 158. **Hope began simply:** Faith, *Bob Hope*, pp. 161–4. Bob Hope, *Have Tux, Will Travel*, p. 189.

Page 158. **A friend urged:** Faith, *Bob Hope*, pp. 173–6. Bob Hope, *I Never Left Home*, p. 48.

Pages 159–60. **By now, the Allies:** Bob Hope, *I Never Left Home*, pp. 3, 8–9, 161–2, 178.

Page 160. **Billy Wilder, who:** Maurice Zolotow, *Billy Wilder in Hollywood*, p. 35.

Page 160. **This *Double Indemnity*:** Roy Hoopes, *Cain*, p. 258. Gay Talese, *The Kingdom and the Power*, p. 22 (1970).

Page 161. **Cain, who had:** Hoopes, *Cain*, pp. 268, 331–2.

Page 161. **At that point:** Zolotow, *Billy Wilder*, p. 108.

Page 162. **Paramount bought *Double*:** Ibid., p. 111. Hoopes, *Cain*, pp. 332–3.

Page 162. **Chandler was a:** Frank MacShane, *The Life of Raymond Chandler*, pp. 35–40 (1978). S. J. Perelman, *The Most of S. J. Perelman*, p. 17.

Page 162. **Summoned to Paramount:** Zolotow, *Billy Wilder*, pp. 113–14.

Page 163. **It was a kind:** MacShane, *Raymond Chandler*, pp. 107, 101. Zolotow, *Billy Wilder*, p. 121.

Page 163. **So the struggles:** Zolotow, *Billy Wilder*, pp. 114–16. MacShane, *Raymond Chandler*, pp. 108–9. Tom Wood, *The Bright Side of Billy Wilder, Primarily*, p. 20.

Pages 164–66. **I don't read:** Zolotow, *Billy Wilder*, pp. 117–19, 123. Hoopes, *Cain*, p. 335. Wood, *Billy Wilder*, p. 84.

Page 166. **It was never:** Gene D. Phillips, *Hemingway and Film*, p. 41. Ingrid Bergman and Alan Burgess, *My Story*, pp. 125, 128. David O. Selznick, *Memo from David O. Selznick*, p. 333.

Page 166. **Hemingway had turned:** Ernest Hemingway, *Selected Letters, 1917–1961*, pp. 577, 540.

Page 166. **Ingrid Bergman was:** Paul Henreid, *Ladies' Man*, p. 130.

Page 167. **The day after:** Bergman and Burgess, *My Story*, pp. 148–9.

Page 167. **Dialogue was one:** Richard Corliss, ed., *Talking Pictures*, pp. 225ff. Nancy Lynn Schwartz, *The Hollywood Writer's Wars*, p. 53. Carlos Baker, *Ernest Hemingway*, p. 371. Hemingway, *Letters*, p. 540.

Page 167. **But even then:** Phillips, *Hemingway and Film*, p. 43. Larry Ceplair and Steven Englund, *The Inquisition in Hollywood*, pp. 210–11.

Page 167. **Wood was by no means:** Ceplair and Englund, *The Inquisition*, p. 211.

Page 168. **After that heroic:** Maurice Zolotow, *Shooting Star: A Biography of John Wayne*, pp.249–53 (1975).

Page 168. **By this time:** Ceplair and Englund, *The Inquisition*, p. 209.

Page 168. **But all this:** Phillips, *Hemingway and Film*, p. 42.

Page 169. **Miss Bergman was:** Bergman and Burgess, *My Story*, pp. 151, 153.

Page 169. **One major Hollywood:** David Niven, *Bring on the Empty Horses*, p. 127. Charles Higham, *Errol Flynn*, pp. 140ff. Michael Freedland, *The Two Lives of Errol Flynn*, p. 164.

Page 169. **To Warner Bros.:** Errol Flynn, *My Wicked, Wicked Ways*, pp. 253–4 (1974). Alvah Bessie, *Inquisition in Eden*, p. 80.

Page 169. **Flynn's search:** Flynn, *Wicked Ways*, p. 239.

Page 170. **Among the many:** Freedland, *The Two Lives*, p. 95.

Page 170. **It was to this:** Flynn, *Wicked Ways*, pp. 239–40. Walsh acknowledged in his own memoirs that he had done the deed. He said that he had done it alone, that no money had changed hands, and that he was a friend of the undertakers, whom he identified as the Malloy Brothers. Raoul Walsh, *Each Man in His Time*, pp. 331–3.

Page 171. **Betty Hansen was:** Jerry Giesler, *The Jerry Giesler Story*, pp. 94–8.

Page 171. **As charges of rape:** Florabel Muir, *Headline Happy*, p. 137. Kenneth Anger, *Hollywood Babylon*, pp. 296, 363–4.

Page 172. **Florabel Muir:** Muir, *Headline Happy*, pp. 136–7, Higham, *Errol Flynn*, p. 185.

Pages 172–75. **Betty Hansen claimed:** I have taken all this verbatim testimony from Giesler, pp. 95, 104, 107, 100, 110–11, 113, 115, 116, 123–5, 130–1, 133, 136, 141.

Page 175. **Two of the three:** Higham, *Errol Flynn*, p. 213.

Page 175. **If Bertolt Brecht:** Luis Buñuel, *My Last Sigh*, p. 189.

Chapter 6   Reunions (1944).

Page 177. **The Hollywood people:** John Huston, *An Open Book*, pp. 109–10.

Page 178–79. **Darryl F. Zanuck:** Mel Gussow, *Darryl F. Zanuck*, pp. 58–9, 105, 75, 109. Leonard Mosley, *Zanuck*, pp. 197, 200–1, 169. Stephen Farber and Marc Green, *Hollywood Dynasties*, pp. 66–7, 93.

Page 180. **Zanuck did produce:** Colin Shindler, *Hollywood Goes to War*, p. 86. Mosley, *Zanuck*, pp. 203–5.

Page 180. **Another one of:** Otto Preminger, *Preminger*, pp. 1, 13.

Pages 181–82. **Then Zanuck handed him:** Preminger, *Preminger*, pp. 21–5, 73, 82. Willi Frischauer, *Behind the Scenes of Otto Preminger*, p. 85.

Page 182. **One of the remarkable:** Preminger, *Preminger*, pp. 85–6.

Page 183. ***Laura* was all:** Gene Tierney, *Self-Portrait*, p. 119.

Pages 183–85. **Zanuck read the script:** Preminger, *Preminger*, pp. 86–9, 92–3. Tierney, *Self-Portrait*, pp. 121–2.

Pages 185–86. **After the emotional:** Charles Chaplin, *My Autobiography*, pp. 396–7, 414–15, 418–19. Also David Robinson, *Chaplin*, pp. 512–28.

Page 186. **For most of his life:** John McCabe, *Charlie Chaplin*, pp. 201, 209. Chaplin, *My Autobiography*, pp. 229–30, 240.

Pages 186–87. **Lillita McMurray was:** McCabe, *Charlie Chaplin*, pp. 141, 143, 160–3.

Pages 187–89. **Paulette Goddard, née:** Chaplin, *My Autobiography*, pp. 400, 407–9, 413–15, 417. Charles Chaplin, Jr., *My Father, Charlie Chaplin*, pp. 258–9.

Page 189. **Warner himself later:** Jack Warner, *My First Hundred Years in Hollywood*, pp. 295–6.

Page 189. **Chaplin insisted that:** Chaplin, *My Autobiography*, p. 407. Warner, *First Hundred Years*, p. 297.

Page 190. **Chaplin went to:** Chaplin, *My Autobiography*, p. 416. McCabe, *Charlie Chaplin*, p. 204.

Page 190. **With the three hundred:** Jerry Giesler, *The Jerry Giesler Story*, p. 187.

Pages 190–92. **A week later:** Chaplin, *My Autobiography*, pp. 419–22. Giesler, *Story*, pp. 183–90. McCabe, *Charlie Chaplin*, pp. 204–8. Hedda Hopper, *From Under My Hat*, pp. 149–53.

Page 192. **One of the cornerstones:** Charles Higham, *Sisters*, p. 145. Also Larry Swindell, *Charles Boyer*, p. 168.

Page 193. **They were frightened:** Lana Turner, *Lana*, p. 17. Daniel Fuchs, *West of the Rockies*, p. 84.

Page 193. **In addition to:** Roland Flamini, *Ava*, pp. 17–18 (1984).

Page 193. **If an actor:** Hortense Powdermaker, *Hollywood: The Dream Factory*, pp. 34–5, 85.

Page 194. **The first rebel:** Charles Higham, *Bette*, pp. 109–21. Bette Davis, *The Lonely Life*, pp. 194–208. Warner, *First Hundred Years*, pp. 248–50.

Page 194. **Still, holdouts and:** Larry Swindell, *Body and Soul, John Garfield*, p. 157. Warner, *First Hundred Years*, p. 234. Joseph Blotner, *Faulkner*, pp. 1121, 1154.

Page 194. **The one star:** Higham, *Sisters*, pp. 135ff., 144–5. Ronald Reagan and Richard C. Hubler, *Where's the Rest of Me?*, p. 123.

Page 195. **What happened was:** Tony Thomas, *The Films of Olivia de Havilland*, pp. 35–7. Higham, *Sisters*, pp. 146, 148.

Page 196. **There was another:** Garth Jowett, *Film: The Democratic Art*, p. 276.

Page 196. **The long and complicated:** Charles Higham, *Hollywood at Sunset*, pp. 22–3.

Page 196. **The suit served:** Jowett, *Film*, pp. 277–8. Higham, *Sisters*, pp. 24–7.

Page 197. **Thunder and lightning:** Author's notes on a TV broadcast.

Page 198. **It is Boris:** Dennis Gifford, *Karloff*, pp. 267–8.

Page 198. **Absurdity:** John Brosnan, *The Horror People*, p. 253. Stephen King, *Stephen King's Danse Macabre*, p. 155.

Page 199. **It is hard to tell:** Cynthia Lindsay, *Dear Boris*, pp. 47–52. Gifford, *Karloff*, p. 37.

Pages 200–1. **Then along came:** Brosnan, *Horror People*, pp. 69, 43. Gifford, *Karloff*, pp. 37–43, 47. Lindsay, *Dear Boris*, p. 54.

Page 201. **It was an enormous:** Gifford, *Karloff*, pp. 190–230, 44, 57. Brosnan, *The Horror People*, pp. 73, 287. Carlos Clarens, *An Illustrated History of the Horror Film*, pp. 73ff.

Page 201. **Karloff, who appeared:** Gifford, *Karloff*, p. 58.

Pages 202–4. **The one man:** Brosnan, *Horror People*, pp. 73–6. Gifford, *Karloff*, p. 269.

Page 204. **One last question:** Brosnan, *Horror People*, p. 287. Clarens, *Illustrated History*, pp. 63–69.

Pages 205–9. **The Hays Office:** James Curtis, *Between Flops: A Biography of Preston Sturges*, p. 180. I have relied on Curtis's splendid biography for most of the details on Sturges's life. See pp. 189, 8–9, 11, 17–19, 21, 26, 29, 50, 55, 62, 67, 58, 66–7, 74, 77, 79, 82–3, 88, 303–9, 116, 125, 128, 131, 135, 119, 109, 175.

Page 209. **At Paramount, though:** André Bazin, *The Cinema of Cruelty*, p. 42.

Pages 209–10. **More important, Sturges:** Charles Lockwood, *The Guide to Hollywood and Beverly Hills*, p. 14. Curtis, *Between Flops*, pp. 118, 120, 137–8, 151, 312–16, 178.

Page 210. **A movie about:** Jowett, *Film*, p. 311.

Pages 210–12. **Like any good:** Richard R. Lingeman, *Don't You Know There's a War On?*, pp. 183, 185–8, 193, 181. Jowett, *Film*, p. 312. Curtis, *Between Flops*, p. 181.

Page 212. **While DeSylva dithered:** Curtis, *Between Flops*, pp. 185–91, 198–9.

Page 213. **Hughes had in fact:** Donald L. Barlett and James B. Steele, *Empire*, pp. 132–4.

Page 213. **Hughes recovered:** Curtis, *Between Flops*, pp. 216–18.

Chapter 7   Breakdowns (1945).
Page 215. **When David Selznick:** Bob Thomas, *Selznick*, p. 224 (1972).

Page 215. **Now, one night:** Irene Mayer Selznick, *A Private View*, pp. 265, 267.

Page 215. **Phyllis Walker had:** David O. Selznick, *Memo from David O. Selznick*, pp. 311, 313, 317.

Page 216. **She had been born:** Thomas, *Selznick*, pp. 198–9.

Page 216. **The Walkers had:** Hedda Hopper, *The Whole Truth and Nothing But*, pp. 177–8. June Allyson, *June Allyson*, p. 53.

Page 216. **It had been several:** Thomas, *Selznick*, pp. 194–7, 209. Selznick, *Memo*, p. 317. Stephen Farber and Marc Green, *Hollywood Dynasties*, p. 69.

Page 217. **This girl is:** Thomas, *Selznick*, pp. 212–13. Ingrid Bergman and Alan Burgess, *My Story*, p. 197.

Page 217. **There was also:** Thomas, *Selznick*, pp. 217–18, 222.

Page 217. **Walker never recovered:** Allyson, *June Allyson*, pp. 53–4. Hopper, *The Whole Truth*, pp. 180–1, 183.

Page 218. **That was in 1951:** Bosley Crowther, *Hollywood Rajah*, pp. 23–4.

Page 218. **It was a psychological:** Selznick, *Memo*, p. 262. Samuel Marx, *Mayer and Thalberg*, pp. 224–5.

Pages 219–20. **Mayer explained:** Crowther, *Hollywood Rajah*, p. 263. Marx, *Mayer and Thalberg*, pp. 226, 228–31.

Page 220. **Then began Mayer's:** Crowther, *Hollywood Rajah*, pp. 262, 267. Gary Carey, *All the Stars in Heaven*, p. 264.

Page 221. **Before she decided:** Selznick, *Memo*, pp. 235–6. Thomas, *Selznick*, p. 207. Paul Roazen, *Freud and His Followers*, p. 507.

Page 221. **It is a little hard:** Marie Jahoda, "The Migration of Psychoanalysis: Its Impact on American Psychology," in Donald Fleming and Bernard Bailyn, eds., *The Intellectual Migration, Europe and America, 1930–1960*, pp. 423–5. Russell Jacoby, *The Repression of Psychoanalysis: Otto Fenichel and the Political Freudians*, p. 3.

Page 222. **The psychoanalysts driven:** Jacoby, *The Repression*, pp. 8, 27, 64, 122, 128. Anthony Heilbut, *Exiled in Paradise*, p. 167.

Page 222. **What attracted the:** Crowther, *Hollywood Rajah*, p. 245.

Page 222. **Artie Shaw, who spent:** Artie Shaw, *The Trouble with Cinderella*, p. 92. Roland Flamini, *Ava*, p. 82.

Page 223. **One unfortunate victim:** Jacoby, *The Repression*, pp. 122–3, 132.

Page 224. **But Hollywood found:** Selznick, *Memo*, p. 236.

Page 224. **One predictable outcome:** Donald Spoto, *The Dark Side of Genius: The Life of Alfred Hitchcock*, pp. 286–7.

Page 224. **Hitchcock's customary method:** Ben Hecht, *A Child of the Century*, p. 482.

Page 224. **It involved a:** John Russell Taylor, *Hitch*, p. 175.

Page 225. **Selznick had grandiose:** Thomas, *Selznick*, p. 225. Spoto, *The Dark Side*, pp. 288, 291.

Page 225. **The most striking:** Ibid., p. 292. Ronald Haver, *David O. Selznick's Hollywood*, pp. 346–8.

Page 225n. **"MacGuffin" was Hitchcock's:** Spoto, *The Dark Side*, pp. 159–60.

Page 226. **But what happened:** Taylor, *Hitch*, p. 177.

Page 226. **Selznick did his best:** Spoto, *The Dark Side*, p. 289.

Page 226. **When Selznick originally:** Thomas, *Selznick*, pp. 225–8. Selznick, *Memo*, p. 360.

Page 226. **The main reason:** Selznick, *Memo*, p. 368.

Pages 227–8. **This constant interference:**

Thomas, *Selznick*, pp. 228–30, 239–40. Taylor, *Hitch*, p. 177. Selznick, *Memo*, p. 292.

Pages 228–30. **After a lifetime:** Frank Mac-Shane, *The Life of Raymond Chandler*, p. 110. But this is really John Houseman's tale. John Houseman, *Front and Center*, pp. 135, 132, 112, 137–41.

Page 230. **This may sound:** John Houseman, "Lost Fortnight," originally published in *Harper's* in August 1965, republished as an Introduction to paperback edition of Raymond Chandler, *The Blue Dahlia*, p. 14. Also Houseman, *Front and Center*, pp. 142–3.

Page 230. **A. Two Cadillac:** Houseman, *Front and Center*, pp. 143–4.

Page 231. **Houseman, who dropped:** Chandler, *The Blue Dahlia*, p. 207. Beverly Linet, *Ladd*, p. 106 (1980).

Page 231. **The film was:** Houseman, *Front and Center*, p. 146. Linet, *Ladd*, pp. 86, 106. *New York Times*, Aug. 17, 1944. Houseman letter to author, Aug. 6, 1984.

Page 231. **Another problem:** MacShane, *Raymond Chandler*, p. 114.

Page 232. **In a strange:** Linet, *Ladd*, pp. 76, 84.

Page 233. **Chandler had prepared:** Chandler, *The Blue Dahlia*, p. 32.

Page 233. **This idea of:** MacShane, *Raymond Chandler*, p. 117.

Pages 233–34. **Chandler grumblingly accepted:** Houseman, *Front and Center*, p. 113. Passages from *The Little Sister* quoted from *The Midnight Chandler*, ed. Joan Kahn, pp. 304–6.

Page 234. **James M. Cain:** Roy Hoopes, *Cain*, p. 238.

Page 234. *The Postman Always:* Ibid., pp. 247, 352, 378.

Page 235. **They hang you:** James M. Cain, *The Postman Always Rings Twice*, p. 14 (1978).

Page 235. **The Johnston Office:** Lana Turner, *Lana*, pp. 83–5.

Page 235n. **In the midst:** Arthur Knight, *The Liveliest Art*, p. 239.

Page 235n. **Eric Johnston:** "More Trouble in Paradise," *Fortune*, Nov. 1946. Larry Ceplair and Steven Englund, *The Inquisition in Hollywood*, p. 247.

Page 236. **The "handsome dark man":** Larry Swindell, *Body and Soul*, p. 202.

Page 236. **It almost didn't:** Turner, *Lana*, pp. 86–7. Also Tay Garnett, *Light Your Torches and Pull Up Your Tights.*

Page 237. **If there was:** Joseph Blotner, *Faulkner*, p. 1162. Tom Dardis, *Some Time in the Sun*, pp. 77, 80.

Pages 237–38. **M-G-M's story editor:** Samuel

Marx, *Mayer and Thalberg*, p. 176. Dardis, *Some Time*, pp. 81, 93–4, 104, 107.

Page 238. **Hal Wallis, the:** Blotner, *Faulkner*, pp. 1155–56, 1129–39. Dardis, *Some Time*, p. 120. *The DeGaulle Story*, a compilation of drafts, outlines and scripts, was published by the University of Mississippi Press in December 1984.

Page 239. **It was perhaps:** Mel Gussow, *Darryl F. Zanuck*, p. 74. Jack Warner, *My First Hundred Years in Hollywood*, pp. 309–10. Dardis, *Some Time*, p. 87.

Page 239. **The one important man:** Gerald Mast, *Howard Hawks, Storyteller*, pp. 7–11.

Pages 239–41. **Hawks had discovered:** Joseph McBride, *Hawks on Hawks*, pp. 56–7, 94–5. Mast, *Howard Hawks*, p. 250.

Page 239n. **For that matter:** Jesse Lasky, Jr., *Whatever Happened to Hollywood?*, p. 229. Norman Zierold, *The Moguls*, p. 158.

Pages 241–42. **Hawks had apparently:** Lauren Bacall, *By Myself*, pp. 71, 77, 95, 86, 93. McBride, *Hawks*, pp. 100–2, 78. 104. Mast, *Howard Hawks*, p. 269.

Page 243. **Chandler liked the idea:** MacShane, *Raymond Chandler*, p. 126. Raymond Chandler, *The Big Sleep*, p. 141 (1971).

Page 243. **That wouldn't do:** McBride, *Hawks*, p. 103. Chandler, *The Big Sleep*, pp. 48, 213. Mast, *Howard Hawks*, p. 271.

Pages 243–44. **Chandler could hardly:** MacShane, *Raymond Chandler*, pp. 126, 125. McBride, *Hawks*, pp. 104–5.

Page 244. **She was not:** Bacall, *By Myself*, pp. 112, 122, 141–3.

Pages 245–46. **So everything ended:** Blotner, *Faulkner*, pp. 1188–9, 1149, 1191, 1197, 1211, 1217.

Page 247. **At the center:** Ronald Reagan and Richard C. Hubler, *Where's the Rest of Me?*, pp. 154–5. "More Trouble in Paradise," *Fortune*, November 1946.

Page 247. **Late in 1943:** Nancy Lynn Schwartz, *The Hollywood Writers' Wars*, p. 221. *Time*, Oct. 7, 1946.

Pages 247–48. **The War Labor Board:** Reagan and Hubler, *Where's the Rest*, p. 157. John Cogley, *Report on Blacklisting*, vol. 1, pp. 55, 61–7. Ceplair and Englund, *The Inquisition*, p. 218. *New York Times*, March 5, 1948.

Page 248. **Hollywood divided:** Salka Viertel, *The Kindness of Strangers*, p. 296.

Page 249. **Once the battle:** Reagan and Hubler, *Where's the Rest*, pp. 158–9. Ceplair and Englund, *The Inquisition*, p. 217. Cogley, *Report*, 1, p. 64. *New York Times*, Oct. 6, 1945.

Page 249. **Sorrell was back:** *New York Times,* Oct. 7, 8, 1945.

Page 250. **At three o'clock:** W. A. Swanberg, *Dreiser,* p. 518. I have relied heavily on Swanberg's solid biography.

Pages 250–52. **It was because:** Ibid., pp. 241–9, 369–77, 463–4, 470–5.

Pages 253–55. **It is strange:** Helen Dreiser, *My Life with Dreiser,* p. 307.

Page 253. **There was one:** Swanberg, *Dreiser,* pp. 393, 510, 513–15.

Page 253. **Shortly before Christmas:** Dreiser, *My Life with Dreiser,* pp. 310–12. Swanberg, *Dreiser,* pp. 520–1, 315–16.

Page 254. **"Oh, Space!"** The quotation here is taken from Swanberg, *Dreiser,* p. 525, who is quoting in turn from Dreiser's *Moods, Philosophical and Emotional* (New York: Simon & Schuster, 1935), but Helen Dreiser's memoirs include a photo of the plaque, on p. 285, with several short lines combined into longer ones.

Chapter 8   Treachery (1946).

Page 257. **In the summers:** Dean Jennings, *We Only Kill Each Other: The Life and Bad Times of Bugsy Siegel,* p. 148. This is somewhat slapdash, but still the basic biography. Peter Wiley and Robert Gottlieb, *Empires in the Sun,* p. 191. Albert Fried, *The Rise and Fall of the Jewish Gangster in America,* p. 230. Dennis Eisenberg, Uri Dan, and Eli Landau, *Meyer Lansky,* p. 226. A remarkable book because Lansky, after a lifetime of silence, seems to have accepted these Israeli journalists as friends—or rather as compatriots—and to have talked quite freely for the first time.

Page 257. **We decided to:** Ibid., p. 226.

Page 257. **Bugsy was the nickname:** Hank Messick, *Lansky,* p. 19. Eisenberg, Dan, and Landau, *Meyer Lansky,* p. 51ff.

Page 257. **Both Lansky and Siegel:** Jennings, *We Only Kill,* p. 25. Eisenberg, Dan, and Landau, *Meyer Lansky,* p. 57. Stephen Birmingham, *"The Rest of Us": The Rise of America's Eastern European Jews,* pp. 153, 201.

Page 258. **The end of Prohibition:** Eisenberg, Dan, and Landau, *Meyer Lansky,* pp. 79–80. Fried, *Jewish Gangster,* pp. 193–6, 234–8. Birmingham, *"The Rest of Us,"* p. 148.

Page 258. **Lansky's friend Siegel:** Jennings, *We Only Kill,* pp. 38, 47–8.

Page 258. **In a society:** Frank MacShane, *The Life of Raymond Chandler,* p. 121 (1978).

Page 259. **Siegel seems to:** Jennings, *We Only Kill,* pp. 23, 39. Larry Swindell, *The Last Hero: A Biography of Gary Cooper,* p. 131.

Page 259. **What Bugsy Siegel:** Jennings, *We Only Kill,* pp. 45, 115. John Roeburt, *"Get Me Giesler,"* pp. 95–6.

Page 259. **In the late 1930's:** Jennings, *We Only Kill,* pp. 44, 142. Fried, *Jewish Gangster,* pp. 48, 258, 249.

Page 259. **The only crime:** Jennings, *We Only Kill,* pp. 83–4, 120–1, 141. Florabel Muir, *Headline Happy,* p. 80.

Page 260. **The war years:** Jennings, *We Only Kill,* p. 139.

Page 260. **Las Vegas might:** Wiley and Gottlieb, *Empires in the Sun,* pp. 191–2. Jennings, *We Only Kill,* pp. 148–50.

Page 261. **But that was:** Jennings, *We Only Kill,* p. 150. Lana Turner, *Lana,* p. 38. Wiley and Gottlieb, *Empires in the Sun,* pp. 162, 184, 207.

Pages 261–63. **It should have:** Jennings, *We Only Kill,* pp. 152–3, 86, 131, 112, 151–5, 159, 161–2. Birmingham, *"The Rest of Us,"* p. 287. (Birmingham identifies Mrs. Siegel as "the former Esther Krakauer.") Eisenberg, Dan, and Landau, *Meyer Lansky,* p. 239.

Pages 263–64. **Even the gambling:** Jennings, *We Only Kill,* pp. 165, 172–3. Eisenberg, Dan, and Landau, *Meyer Lansky,* pp. 232–3, 240.

Pages 264–65. **Siegel seemed to:** Jennings, *We Only Kill,* pp. 199–203. Clinton H. Anderson, *Beverly Hills Is My Beat,* p. 145.

Page 265. **One of the first:** Muir, *Headline Happy,* pp. 197–8.

Page 265. **Within twenty minutes:** Jennings, *We Only Kill,* p. 205. Eisenberg, Dan, and Landau, *Meyer Lansky,* p. 240.

Page 265. **In contrast to:** Jennings, *We Only Kill,* p. 227. *New York Times,* Jan. 16, 1983.

Page 265. **Marriage to the:** John Kobal, *Rita Hayworth,* pp. 219–20. Peter Cowie, *The Cinema of Orson Welles,* p. 242 (1983).

Page 266. **Welles himself was:** James Naremore, *The Magic World of Orson Welles,* pp. 136–41.

Page 267. **But Welles was:** Naremore, *Orson Welles,* p. 151. Bob Thomas, *King Cohn,* p. 221.

Page 267. **Welles apparently had:** Joseph McBride, *Orson Welles,* p. 50.

Page 267. **First, though, there:** Kobal, *Rita Hayworth,* p. 210. Naremore, *Orson Welles,* p. 207. Joe Morella and Edward Z. Epstein, *Rita,* p. 97.

Page 267. **Miss Hayworth had:** Michael Wood, *America in the Movies,* p. 51.

Page 267. **It was *Gilda*:** Kobal, *Rita Hayworth,* pp. 159–60, 200. Morella and Epstein, *Rita,* p. 258.

Page 267n. **Unfortunately for this:** Charles Higham, *Orson Welles*, p. 229.

Pages 268–69. **There was a peculiar:** Kobal, *Rita Hayworth*, pp. 192–213.

Pages 269–70. *The Lady from Shanghai:* Charles Higham, *The Films of Orson Welles*, pp. 111–17. Kobal, *Rita Hayworth*, pp. 215, 219. Naremore, *Orson Welles*, p. 152.

Page 270. **His marriage to:** Morella and Epstein, *Rita*, pp. 102–4. Kobal, *Rita Hayworth*, p. 222.

Page 271. **Thomas Mann's decision:** *The New Yorker*, Dec. 13, 1941.

Page 271. **Since Mann knew:** Nigel Hamilton, *The Brothers Mann*, p. 328.

Page 271. *Joseph* **was actually:** Samuel Marx, *Mayer and Thalberg*, p. 168. David O. Selznick, *Memo from David O. Selznick*, pp. 416, 419.

Page 271. **While Thomas Mann:** Hamilton, *The Brothers Mann*, pp. 321, 328–9.

Page 272. **Nelly got arrested:** Salka Viertel, *The Kindness of Strangers*, p. 279. Thomas Mann, *The Story of a Novel: The Genesis of Doctor Faustus*, p. 105.

Page 272. **The idea had:** Mann, *Story of a Novel*, pp. 17–19.

Page 273. **One problem in:** Thomas Mann, *Essays of Three Decades*, p. 353. Mann, *Story of a Novel*, p. 29.

Page 273. **Schoenberg was now:** Arnold Schoenberg, *Letters*, pp. 213, 254. Mann, *Story of a Novel*, pp. 51–2.

Page 273. **Mann's real teacher:** Mann, *Story of a Novel*, pp. 42–3, 48, 81, 117, 164–5.

Page 274. **Schoenberg was even:** H. H. Stuckenschmidt, *Arnold Schoenberg*, p. 131.

Page 275. **At dinner at:** Mann, *Story of a Novel*, p. 217.

Page 275. **On January 29:** Hamilton, *The Brothers Mann*, pp. 335, 349.

Page 275. **The most interesting:** Alma Mahler Werfel, *And the Bridge Is Love*, pp. 300–1.

Page 276. **Schoenberg apparently asked:** Katia Mann, *Unwritten Memories*, pp. 123–4.

Page 276. **Schoenberg didn't even:** Hamilton, *The Brothers Mann*, pp. 350–5. Mann, *The Story of a Novel*, p. 36.

Page 276. **The ugly strike:** *Hearings before a Special Subcommittee on Education and Labor*, pp. 44, 4.

Page 277. **What Kahan airily:** *New York Times*, Feb. 17, 1946. *Christian Science Monitor*, July 19, 1947. *New York Times*, March 5, 1948.

Page 277. **While both Brewer:** George H. Dunne, *Hollywood Labor Dispute*, pp. 26–7.

Page 277. **The first step:** *PM*, Jan. 9, 1946. *New York Times*, Feb. 21, 1946; April 29, 1946.

Page 277. **Throughout all this:** *New York Times*, July 2, 1946. *Hearings*, pp. 20–1. *Time*, July 15, 1946.

Page 278. **The most difficult:** Dunne, *Hollywood Labor Dispute*, p. 28.

Page 278. **That report turned:** Ibid., p. 29.

Page 278. **Now the carpenters:** Ibid., p. 34.

Page 279. **Whether this represented:** *New York Times*, Feb. 17, 1946; Sept. 27, 1946.

Page 279. **Then began an:** Ronald Reagan and Richard C. Hubler, *Where's the Rest of Me?*, pp. 160, 170–1, 185, 200, 203.

Page 279. **Reagan's committee included:** Ibid., pp. 170, 175.

Page 280. **The membership of:** Lou Cannon, *Reagan*, p. 76. Walter Goodman, *The Committee: The Extraordinary Career of the House Committee on Un-American Activities*, p. 180. A compendious and admirable work.

Page 280. **Important positions changed:** Ibid., pp. 169, 186. Cabell Phillips, *The Truman Presidency*, p. 360.

Page 280. **In the narrow:** *New York Times*, Nov. 16, 1946.

Page 281. **Sorrel later charged:** *New York Times*, March 6, 1948.

Page 281. **Touhy naturally would:** Dunne, *Hollywood Labor Dispute*, p. 35.

Page 281. **Then there were:** *New York Times*, March 4, 1947. *PM*, March 5, 1947.

Page 282. **This question dragged:** *New York Times*, Feb. 27, 1948.

Page 282. **By this time:** *New York Times*, Feb. 27, 1948; March 6, 1948.

Page 283. **The end came:** *New York Times*, Oct. 28, 1947.

Page 283. **So they all trickled:** *New York Times*, April 1, 1951; Jan. 22, 1952; July 23, 1955.

Page 283. **How could this man:** Charles Chaplin, Jr., *My Father, Charlie Chaplin*, p. 312. John McCabe, *Charlie Chaplin*, p. 210.

Page 283. **Chaplin had found:** McCabe, *Charlie Chaplin*, p. 212. Charles Chaplin, *My Autobiography*, p. 471.

Page 284. **Serious critics:** Dwight Macdonald, *On Movies*, p. 118 (1981).

Page 284. **None of Chaplin's:** Roger Manvell, *Chaplin*, p. 204. Chaplin, *My Autobiography*, p. 473.

Page 284. **The censors listed:** Chaplin, *My Autobiography*, pp. 474, 479, 481–4.

Page 286. **The New York premiere:** Chaplin, *My Autobiography*, p. 489.

Pages 286–87. **The next day:** *Film Comment,* Winter 1969. The transcript of the entire press conference appears on pp. 34ff. Chaplin's very inaccurate account is in his autobiography, pp. 486ff.

Page 286*n.* **By Rankin's standards:** Goodman, *The Committee,* p. 173.

Page 288. **Agee praised:** James Agee, *Agee on Film,* vol. 1, pp.371–2, 252–3.

Page 288. *Monsieur Verdoux* **did well:** Chaplin, *My Autobiography,* pp. 490–1.

Page 289. **Here is one last note:** Author's notes on a visit to Las Vegas.

Chapter 9 Un-Americanism (1947).

Page 291. **Charles Laughton was:** Bruce Cook, *Brecht in Exile,* p. 174.

Page 291. **And it was quite:** James K. Lyon, *Bertolt Brecht in America,* p. 196. John Houseman, *Front and Center,* pp. 240–1.

Page 291. **That ambiguous night:** Klaus Völcker, *Brecht Chronicle,* p. 87. Lyon, *Brecht in America,* pp. 72–5.

Page 292. **His only sale:** Lyon, *Brecht in America,* pp. 104–5, 78, 102, 112.

Page 292. **The most important:** Ibid., pp. 107ff. Cook, *Brecht in Exile,* pp. 165ff. Charles Higham, *Charles Laughton,* pp. 118–25.

Pages 292–93. **Here it was:** Bertolt Brecht, *Poems, 1913–1956,* p. 393.

Page 293. **Laughton's acerbic wife:** Elsa Lanchester, *Elsa Lanchester Herself,* p. 193. John Willett, ed., *Brecht on Theatre,* p. 166.

Page 293. **Laughton was proud:** Brecht, *Poems,* p. 397.

Page 293. **Laughton and Brecht:** Bertolt Brecht, *Seven Plays,* p. 398.

Page 293. **There is a theory:** Frederic Ewen, *Bertolt Brecht,* pp. 340–1 (1969).

Page 294. **The first thing:** Lyon, *Brecht in America,* pp. 171, 173–4. Brecht, *Poems,* p. 405.

Page 294. **Brecht's journal:** Houseman, *Front and Center,* p. 230.

Pages 294–95. **Galileo's crime?:** Brecht, *Seven Plays,* pp. 398–400.

Page 295. **But Brecht was:** Lyon, *Brecht in America,* pp. 176, 178–9, 184–5. Houseman, *Front and Center,* pp. 218ff.

Page 296. **Brecht, as usual:** Abe Burrows, *Honest Abe,* p. 75.

Page 296. **That kind of dialogue:** Lyon, *Brecht in America,* p. 186. Houseman, *Front and Center,* pp. 235-6, 238–9.

Page 297. *Galileo* **finally opened:** Houseman, *Front and Center,* p. 237. Cook, *Brecht in Exile,* p. 180. Lyon, *Brecht in America,* p. 312.

Page 298. **On September 19:** Cook, *Brecht in Exile,* p. 183. Gordon Kahn, *Hollywood on Trial,* p. 1. The most detailed account of the Hollywood hearings, but highly partisan.

Page 298. **The process server:** Lyon, *Brecht in America,* p. 315.

Page 298. **Brecht was not much:** Lyon, *Brecht in America,* pp. 317–18. Larry Ceplair and Steven Englund, *The Inquisition in Hollywood,* p. 439. Lester Cole, *Hollywood Red,* p. 265. No one has ever explained the discrepancies between the obviously leaked lists and the list of those who were actually summoned. Both lists are given in Ceplair and Englund, pp. 439–40.

Page 298. **Although the HUAC:** Walter Goodman, *The Committee,* pp. 42, 172–4.

Page 298. **Once the 1946:** *New York Times,* Nov. 20, 1970. *St. Louis Post-Dispatch,* Dec. 1, 1948.

Page 299. **These local controversies:** Ceplair and Englund, *The Inquisition,* p. 256.

Page 300. **Like the new:** Thomas C. Reeves, *The Life and Times of Joe McCarthy,* p. 224. Murray Kempton, *Part of Our Time,* p. 208. Arthur Marx, *Goldwyn,* p. 339.

Page 300. **What, then, was:** Goodman, *The Committee,* p. 196.

Page 300. **The second least:** Kahn, *Hollywood on Trial,* pp. 19, 76.

Page 300*n.* **The official estimates:** Kempton, *Part of Our Time,* p. 198.

Pages 301–2. **The Un-American:** Goodman, *The Committee,* pp. 14, 199, 184, 191. Eric Bentley, ed., *Thirty Years of Treason: Excerpts from Hearings Before the House Committee on Un-American Activities, 1938–1968,* pp. 59–73. A highly selective but convenient anthology of the HUAC testimony.

Pages 302–3. **Gerhart Eisler:** Ibid., pp. 57, 59, 84–6, 94–6. Goodman, *The Committee,* p. 191.

Page 303. **J. Parnell Thomas:** Goodman, *The Committee,* p. 203.

Page 304. **Herbert Biberman:** Lester Cole, *Hollywood Red,* p. 266. Nancy Lynn Schwartz, *The Hollywood Writers' Wars,* p. 302. Cook, *Brecht in Exile,* p. 190. Bruce Cook, *Dalton Trumbo,* p. 149. Ceplair and Englund, *The Inquisition,* says ten were Jews (p. 262). Alvah Bessie, who was one of them, says thirteen were Jews (*Inquisition in Eden,* p. 191). Tom Wood, *The Bright Side of Billy Wilder, Primarily,* p. 4.

Page 304. **Biberman had invited:** Ceplair and Englund, *The Inquisition,* p. 263. Stefan Kanfer, *A Journal of the Plague Years,* p. 41.

Page 304. **The lawyers reviewed:** Ceplair and Englund, *The Inquisition*, pp. 264–5.

Page 304. **They finally decided:** Ring Lardner, Jr., *The Lardners*, p. 320. Victor S. Navasky, *Naming Names*, p. 82 (1981). Ceplair and Englund, *The Inquisition*, p. 269.

Page 305. **In retrospect, this:** Ceplair and Englund, *The Inquisition*, p. 270. Cook, *Trumbo*, p. 187.

Page 305. **There was a:** Ceplair and Englund, *The Inquisition*, p. 265. Cook, *Trumbo*, p. 186. Edward Dmytryk, *It's a Hell of a Life but Not a Bad Living*, p. 95.

Page 306. **The only one:** Dalton Trumbo, *The Time of the Toad*, pp. 137–8. Cook, *Trumbo*, p. 191.

Page 306. **But the nineteen:** Lardner, *The Lardners*, p. 325. Ceplair and Englund, *The Inquisition*, p. 275.

Page 306. **The committee gathered:** Cole, *Hollywood Red*, pp. 269–70.

Page 306n. **Or so Dmytryk said:** Bentley, *Thirty Years*, p. 394.

Page 307. **No less important:** Bentley, *Thirty Years*, p. 192. Cole, *Hollywood Red*, p. 269.

Page 307. **The best technique:** John Keats, *Howard Hughes*, pp. 200ff. Donald L. Barlett and James B. Steele, *Empire*, pp. 145ff.

Pages 307–8, **Brewster had reasons:** Keats, *Howard Hughes*, pp. 202–5. Barlett and Steele, *Empire*, p. 145.

Pages 308–9. **To deal with this:** Keats, *Howard Hughes*, pp. 205–8, 209–13, 216–21.

Page 309. **The Spruce Goose:** Barlett and Steele, *Empire*, p. 158.

Page 310. **When the nineteen:** Howard Koch, *As Time Goes By*, p. 167. Kahn, *Hollywood on Trial*, p. 62.

Page 310. **But the producers:** Kahn, *Hollywood on Trial*, pp. 5–6. Kanfer, *Journal of the Plague Years*, p. 41.

Page 310. **The committee had:** Kahn, *Hollywood on Trial*, p. 6. Goodman, *The Committee*, p. 207. *Hearings Regarding the Communist Infiltration of the Motion Picture Industry*, p. 1. The basic text.

Page 311. **No sooner had:** Kahn, *Hollywood on Trial*, p. 63. Norman Zierold, *The Moguls*, p. 235.

Page 311. **There was also:** John Huston, *An Open Book*, p. 147. *HUAC Hearings*, pp. 10–11.

Pages 312–14. **Splendid, splendid, but:** *HUAC Hearings*, pp. 12, 15–16, 19, 53, 33–5, 38–9, 44. Kahn, *Hollywood on Trial*, pp. 17, 23, 53.

Pages 314–15. **The next major:** *HUAC Hear-*

ings, pp. 70–3. Cole, *Hollywood Red*, p. 272. Kahn, *Hollywood on Trial*, p. 29.

Pages 315–16. **It was clear:** *HUAC Hearings*, pp. 71, 75. Kahn, *Hollywood on Trial*, pp. 28, 53.

Pages 316–17. **Mayer was perhaps:** *New York Times*, Feb. 11, 1944. *HUAC Hearings*, p. 74. Kahn, *Hollywood on Trial*, p. 31.

Pages 317–18. **For a more critical:** Bentley, *Thirty Years*, p. 111. Nora Sayre, *Running Time*, p. 68.

Pages 318–19. **The rest of:** *HUAC Hearings*, pp. 283, 352–6.

Pages 319–20. **And so on:** Kahn, *Hollywood on Trial*, pp. 35–6, 140. Bentley, *Thirty Years*, pp. 122, 139, 144–9. *New York Daily News*, Aug. 26, 1985.

Page 320. **This first week:** Ceplair and Englund, *The Inquisition*, pp. 281–2. Alvah Bessie, *Inquisition in Eden*, p. 222.

Page 321. **Over the bugged:** Lauren Bacall, *By Myself*, p. 159.

Page 321. **Huston was dining:** Huston, *An Open Book*, p. 148.

Page 321n. **Congressman Rankin soon:** Kanfer, *Journal of the Plague Years*, p. 73.

Page 322. **The First Amendment:** Lauren Bacall, p. 160.

Page 322. **Chairman Thomas:** Evelyn Keyes, *Scarlett O'Hara's Younger Sister*, p. 121 (1978).

Page 322. **Lawson, newly:** Ceplair and Englund, *The Inquisition*, pp. 87, 307, 233–5. Schwartz, *Hollywood Writers' Wars*, pp. 59, 311, 152, 235.

Page 322n. **Mocking the famous:** Murray Kempton, *Part of Our Time*, pp. 193–4.

Pages 323–25. **But now, seated:** Bentley, *Thirty Years*, pp. 153–61.

Page 325. **It was rather:** *HUAC Hearings*, pp. 306, 315, 307–8.

Page 326. **The kind of man:** Schwartz, *Hollywood Writers' Wars*, p. 319. Kahn, *Hollywood on Trial*, pp. 78–81. Huston, *An Open Book*, p. 150.

Page 326. **Paul Henreid recalled:** Paul Henreid, *Ladies' Man*, pp. 184–5. Lauren Bacall, p. 163. Schwartz, *Hollywood Writers' Wars*, p. 281. Ceplair and Englund, *The Inquisition*, p. 291.

Page 327. **Others went home:** Ronald Reagan and Richard C. Hubler, *Where's the Rest of Me?*, p. 229. Doug McClelland, *Hollywood on Ronald Reagan*, pp. 76, 74.

Page 327. **Ann Sheridan liked:** Joe Morella and Edward Z. Epstein, *Jane Wyman*, p. 71. June Allyson, *June Allyson*, p. 96.

Pages 328–29. **Back at the:** Schwartz, *Hollywood Writers' Wars*, pp. 312, 301, 314, 272.

Kahn, *Hollywood on Trial*, pp. 87, 90, 94, 98, 100.

Page 329. **Edward Dmytryk:** Bentley, *Thirty Years*, pp. 187, 207.

Page 329. **My name is:** Lyon, *Brecht in America*, pp. 329, 207. Bentley, *Thirty Years*, pp. 207–8.

Page 329. **Perhaps he had:** Martin Esslin, *Brecht*, p. 79.

Pages 330–31. **Stripling: Have you:** Bentley, *Thirty Years*, pp. 214, 211–12, 217–18, 209, 220. Cole, *Hollywood Red*, p. 285.

Page 331. **Brecht's main concern:** Lyon, *Brecht in America*, p. 337. Cook, *Brecht in Exile*, p. 201.

Page 332. **When J. Parnell Thomas:** Kahn, *Hollywood on Trial*, p. 132. Goodman, *The Committee*, p. 220.

Page 332. **The leftist witnesses:** Ceplair and Englund, *The Inquisition*, pp. 288, 295. Schwartz, *Hollywood Writers' Wars*, pp. 263, 265.

Page 332. **On the day:** Ceplair and Englund, *The Inquisition*, p. 326. Goodman, *The Committee*, pp. 218, 222. Schwartz, *Hollywood Writers' Wars*, pp. 278, 167.

Page 333. **The problem, said:** Ceplair and Englund, *The Inquisition*, p. 329. Trumbo, *The Time of the Toad*, p. 21.

Page 333. **Mayer and a few:** Dore Schary, *Heyday*, pp. 167–8.

Page 333. **No vote was:** Schary, *Heyday*, p. 169. Ceplair and Englund, *The Inquisition*, p. 329.

Page 333*n.* **Goldwyn and Mayer:** Gary Carey, *All the Stars in Heaven*, p. 276.

Page 334. **Craziness was hardly:** Schary, *Heyday*, p. 365.

Page 334. **So it was done:** Cole, *Hollywood Red*, pp. 265, 301–3. Dalton Trumbo, *Additional Dialogue, Letters of Dalton Trumbo, 1942–1962*, p. 85. Lardner, *The Lardners*, pp. 325–6. Axel Madsen, *Billy Wilder*, p. 285.

Page 334. **When the RKO:** Schary, *Heyday*, p. 170. Dmytryk, *Hell of a Life*, p.103.

Page 335. **Not only were:** Kanfer, *Journal of the Plague Years*, p. 77. Schwartz, *Hollywood Writers' Wars*, p. 285. Philip Dunne, *Take Two*, p. 212.

Page 335. **Scarcely a week:** Cole, *Hollywood Red*, p. 292. Bessie, *Inquisition in Eden*, p. 226. Kanfer, *Journal of the Plague Years*, p.81.

Page 336. **Once Bert Brecht:** Lyon, *Brecht in America*, p. 335.

Page 336. **Everything called him:** Cook, *Brecht in Exile*, pp. 202–7.

Pages 336–37. **I sit by the:** Bertolt Brecht, *Poems*, p. 439 (quoted in Cook, *Brecht in Exile*, p. 207).

Chapter 10   Prejudice (*1948*).

Page 339. **The first time:** Dore Schary, *Heyday*, p. 118. "Picture" included in Lillian Ross, *Reporting*, p. 240.

Pages 339–41. **There was just:** Budd Schulberg, *Moving Pictures*, pp. 149, 2–6. Schary, *Heyday*, pp. 80, 123, 126–8, 131–4.

Page 341. **So Schary walked out:** Bosley Crowther, *Hollywood Rajah*, p. 278. Schary, *Heyday*, pp. 139, 153.

Page 341. **One of the first:** Schary, *Heyday*, p. 158. Edward Dmytryk, *It's a Hell of a Life but Not a Bad Living*, p. 89. Patricia Erens, *The Jew in American Cinema*, p. 175.

Page 342. **Schary had a:** Schary, *Heyday*, pp. 269, 160, 173. John Keats, *Howard Hughes*, pp. 228–30.

Page 342*n.* **One surprising critic:** Alvah Bessie, *Inquisition in Eden*, p. 241.

Page 343. **So Schary, who:** Schary, *Heyday*, p. 173. Keats, *Howard Hughes*, p. 230.

Pages 343–44. **Schary almost immediately:** Crowther, *Hollywood Rajah*, pp. 273–5. Garth Jowett, *Film: The Democratic Art*, pp. 347–8. Michael Conant, *Antitrust in the Motion Picture Industry*, pp. 4, 13. Martin Mayer, *About Television*, p. 26. Schary, *Heyday*, p. 237.

Page 344. **One thing Schenck:** Garson Kanin, *Hollywood*, pp. 282–3.

Page 345. **Mayer invited Schary:** Schary, *Heyday*, pp. 177–203.

Pages 345–46. **Well, Schary was:** Crowther, *Hollywood Rajah*, pp. 270–2.

Pages 346–48. **This is a:** Gerold Frank, *Judy*, pp. 251, 224, 227–8, 230–1, 244–52.

Page 348. **What protected Dore Schary:** Schary, *Heyday*, pp. 208, 230. Crowther, *Hollywood Rajah*, p. 285.

Page 349. **The controversy dated:** Jowett, *Film*, pp. 201, 276–8.

Pages 349–50. **In 1940, the:** *New York Times*, Feb. 8, 10, 1948.

Page 350. **One of the first:** Frank Capra, *The Name Above the Title*, pp. 412–13, 422, 424, 443.

Page 351. **In the midst:** *New York Times*, May 3, 1948; Oct. 2, 1948; Nov. 2, 9, 10, 1948.

Page 351. **Having recently finished:** Robert Craft, "The Poet and the Rake," in *W. H. Auden, A Tribute*, ed. Stephen Spender, pp. 149–55.

Page 352. **Auden worried about:** Nancy Caldwell Sorel, "First Encounters," *Atlantic Monthly,* January 1985.

Page 352. **The two unlikely:** Vera Stravinsky and Robert Craft, *Stravinsky,* p. 397. Igor Stravinsky, *Themes and Conclusions,* p. 77.

Page 352. **Back in New York:** Libretto and notes for CBS recording of *The Rake's Progress,* p. 11. Stravinsky, *Themes and Conclusions,* p. 54.

Page 352. **Stravinsky worked methodically:** Stravinsky and Craft, *Stravinsky,* pp. 361, 398.

Page 353. **"Kike." Now that:** Carey McWilliams, *A Mask for Privilege: Anti-Semitism in America,* p. 3. McWilliams's evaluation is primarily economic. For a contemporary psychiatric analysis of the subject, see *Anti-Semitism: A Social Disease,* ed. Ernst Simmel, which includes contributions by Simmel, Otto Fenichel, Max Horkheimer, T. W. Adorno, and others.

Pages 353–54. **There had always:** McWilliams, *A Mask,* pp. 18–19.

Page 354. **Harper's:** Article by Johan Smertenko, quoted in McWilliams, *A Mask,* pp. 40–1.

Page 355. **Emmanuel Goldenberg:** Edward G. Robinson, *All My Yesterdays,* pp. 1–2.

Page 355. **Julius Garfinkle:** Larry Swindell, *Body and Soul,* p. 111.

Page 355. **Sam Goldwyn:** Stephen Birmingham, *"The Rest of Us,"* p. 259. Hedda Hopper, *The Whole Truth and Nothing But,* p. 96.

Page 356. **The studio bosses:** Arthur Marx, *Goldwyn,* p. 338. Bessie, *Inquisition in Eden,* p. 64. Stephen Farber and Marc Green, *Hollywood Dynasties,* p. 25.

Page 356. **Harry Cohn, as:** Norman Zierold, *The Moguls,* p. 190. Farber and Green, *Hollywood Dynasties,* p. 24. Michael Freedland, *The Warner Brothers,* p. 200. Nora Sayre, *Running Time,* p. 43. Schary, *Heyday,* pp. 210, 224. Ross, *Reporting,* p. 385.

Page 356. **In all this crudity:** Hopper, *The Whole Truth,* p. 93.

Page 356n. **Others felt a:** Bob Thomas, *King Cohn,* p. 295.

Page 357. **Mayer was certainly:** Farber and Green, *Hollywood Dynasties,* p. 26.

Page 357. **The suave Rabbi:** Schulberg, *Moving Pictures,* pp. 191–2.

Page 358. **One of those:** Ben Hecht, *A Child of the Century,* p. 460. Richard Meryman, *Mank,* p. 133.

Page 358. **It was true:** Hecht, *A Child,* pp. 476, 485, 488.

Page 358. **While Hecht was:** Ibid., pp. 516, 519–21.

Page 359. **This last column:** David S. Wyman, *The Abandonment of the Jews,* p. 85. An excellent and revealing study of this painful subject.

Page 359. **The Irgun was:** Birmingham, *"The Rest of Us,"* pp. 247, 243.

Page 359. **I don't want:** Hecht, *A Child,* pp. 539–40.

Page 360. **Be it said:** Birmingham, *"The Rest of Us,"* pp. 249–51.

Page 360. **Hecht would not:** Hecht, *A Child,* p. 443. Wyman, *Abandonment,* pp. 90–2.

Page 360. **There were more:** Wyman, *Abandonment,* pp. 82, 86. Hecht, *A Child,* p. 587.

Page 361. **Returning to the:** Wyman, *Abandonment,* p. 154.

Pages 361–63. **"Kike." Representative John:** Laura Z. Hobson, *Laura Z.,* pp. 322, 324, 331, 345–9, 351, 363, 365.

Pages 363–64. **There were interruptions:** Laura Z. Hobson, *Gentleman's Agreement,* pp. 1, 9, 52–3, 55, 63, 109, 138, 96, 154, 188.

Page 364. **It is a little:** Simmel, *Anti-Semitism,* p. xvii. McWilliams, *A Mask,* pp. 110–11, 134, 136, 144, 254.

Pages 364–65. **It still seems:** Hobson, *Laura Z.,* pp. 340, 382, 393, 396, 398, 400.

Page 365. **Zanuck announced:** Mel Gussow, *Darryl F. Zanuck,* p. 149. Sayre, *Running Time,* p. 40.

Page 365. **Zanuck naturally wanted:** Schary, *Heyday,* p. 159.

Page 366. **Having failed:** Gussow, *Zanuck,* p. 150. Victor S. Navasky, *Naming Names,* p. 203.

Page 366. **But what was:** Jowett, *Film,* p. 371. Sayre, *Running Time,* pp. 39–40.

Page 367. **I cannot remember:** CBS recording of *The Music of Arnold Schoenberg,* vol. 1, recorded by Robert Craft.

Page 367. **It is a complete:** Craft notes to CBS recording of *The Music of Arnold Schoenberg.* H. H. Stuckenschmidt, *Arnold Schoenberg,* p. 141.

Page 367. **A far more interesting:** Arthur Knight, *The Liveliest Art,* p. 238.

Page 368. **The lords of Hollywood:** Ingrid Bergman and Alan Burgess, *My Story,* pp. 13–15 (1981). This is, of course, the basic source.

Pages 368–71. **A few months later:** Bergman and Burgess, *My Story,* pp. 16–17, 18–20, 180–1, 186, 190, 206, 108, 200, 202, 207, 213, 215, 226, 20–1, 236. John Russell Taylor, *Ingrid Bergman,* p. 80. Laurence Leamer, *As Time Goes By,* pp. 73, 79, 88, 103, 124.

Page 371. **Just as the Holocaust:** *Time,* May 24, 1948.

Page 372. **Out in southern:** Ezra Goodman, *The Fifty-Year Decline and Fall of Hollywood,* p. 186. (Goodman says "civil service," which is presumably a typographical error.) Gary Carey, *All the Stars in Heaven,* p. 287.

Page 372. **You must write:** Willi Frischauer, *Behind the Scenes of Otto Preminger,* pp. 179–80.

Page 372. **Ten years after:** Otto Preminger, *Preminger,* pp. 196–9.

Chapter 11   Expulsions (1949).

Page 375. **The Naked and the Dead:** Hilary Mills, *Mailer,* p. 117.

Page 375. **The living room:** Peter Manso, *Mailer: His Life and Times,* pp. 138, 146–7.

Page 376. **To celebrate:** Patricia Bosworth, *Montgomery Clift,* p. 188 (1979).

Page 376. **It was worse:** Manso, *Mailer,* p. 149.

Page 377. **Mixed feelings is:** Mills, *Mailer,* p. 119.

Page 377. **The blacklist grew:** Dore Schary, *Heyday,* p. 365.

Page 377n. **Mrs. Hopper had:** Schary, *Heyday,* p. 206.

Page 378. **The age of:** Larry Ceplair and Steven Englund, *The Inquisition in Hollywood,* p. 362. Stefan Kanfer, *A Journal of the Plague Years,* pp. 94–5.

Page 378. **On this matter:** Ceplair and Englund, *The Inquisition,* pp. 368–9.

Page 378. **Protestations of loyalty:** *Village Voice,* Aug. 7, 1984.

Page 378. **Forty-nine:** Ceplair and Englund, *The Inquisition,* pp. 363–4.

Page 379. **The blacklist didn't:** John Cogley, *Report on Blacklisting,* vol. 1, pp. 97, 125, 133, 82. Ceplair and Englund, *The Inquisition,* p. 359.

Page 379. **Under Reagan's leadership:** Ronald Reagan and Richard C. Hubler, *Where's the Rest of Me?,* p. 182. Cogley, *Blacklisting,* p. 163, and Ceplair and Englund, *The Inquisition,* p. 367.

Pages 379–81. **One of the oddities:** Edward G. Robinson, *All My Yesterdays,* pp. 212, 243–5, 322, 250, 261, 263.

Page 381. **John Garfield faced:** Larry Swindell, *Body and Soul,* pp. 238, 223, 227–9.

Page 381. **He returned to:** Kanfer, *Journal of the Plague Years,* pp. 156–7.

Pages 382–84. **Garfield tried:** Swindell, *Body and Soul,* pp. 229–40, 243–52, 255–64. Kanfer, *Journal of the Plague Years,* pp. 179–80.

Pages 384–85. **Hildegard Knef:** Hildegard Knef, *The Gift Horse,* pp. 266–7 (1972).

Page 385. **The process of:** Charles Higham, *Orson Welles,* p. 247.

Page 385. **The HUAC investigators:** Barbara Leaming, *Orson Welles,* p. 326. Ted Morgan, *FDR,* p. 621.

Page 386. **Welles did not:** Higham, *Orson Welles,* p. 219. Leaming, *Orson Welles,* p. 348.

Page 386. **So although Welles:** Higham, *Orson Welles,* pp. 247–8.

Page 386. **Then to Welles's:** Leaming, *Orson Welles,* p. 369.

Page 387. **Welles returned to Rome:** Higham, *Orson Welles,* p. 250.

Page 387. **Welles was by now:** Charles Higham, *The Films of Orson Welles,* p. 136.

Pages 387–89. **If Welles's improvisations:** Higham, *Orson Welles,* pp. 136, 260, 263, 270–3. Leaming, *Orson Welles,* pp. 370–1.

Page 389. **In his later years:** *People,* Feb. 14, 1983.

Page 390. **It was a thought:** *Time,* Feb. 21, 1949.

Page 390. **Marijuana was such:** *Time,* Sept. 13, 1948. Kenneth Anger, *Hollywood Babylon,* pp. 20–4.

Page 390. **Time's account:** *Time,* Sept. 13, 1948.

Pages 390–91. **Once again, as:** Jerry Giesler, *The Jerry Giesler Story,* p. 246.

Page 391. **That was how:** *Time,* Oct. 11, 1948.

Page 391. **Mitchum, who was:** *Time,* April 11, 1949.

Pages 391–92. **Despite the ordeal:** Charles Chaplin, *My Autobiography,* p. 493.

Page 392. **Chaplin began writing:** David Robinson, *Chaplin,* p. 550.

Page 392. **The aging Calvero:** Ibid., p. 559.

Page 393. **Having worked three:** Claire Bloom, *Limelight and After,* p. 88 (1983).

Page 393. **That sounds like:** Robinson, *Chaplin,* pp. 750, 752, 754.

Page 394. **So Chaplin went on:** Ibid., p. 564. Bloom, *Limelight,* pp. 89–90.

Page 394. **When Chaplin had:** Chaplin, *My Autobiography,* pp. 496–7. Robinson, *Chaplin,* p. 548. Chaplin and his authorized biographer differ on many details of Chaplin's legal difficulties.

Page 394. **The Internal Revenue:** Chaplin, *My Autobiography,* pp. 495–9. Robinson, *Chaplin,* pp. 511, 570–1.

Pages 394–95. **Two days out:** Robinson, *Chaplin,* p. 572. Chaplin, *My Autobiography,* pp. 501–2.

Pages 395–96. **Not everyone supported:** Robinson, *Chaplin,* pp. 575–0, 579, 581, 673–6.

Page 396. **At the 1947 hearings:** *Hearings Regarding the Communist Infiltration of the Motion Picture Industry*, p. 29. Nora Sayre, *Running Time*, p. 79.

Page 396. **The trouble was:** Sayre, *Running Time*, p. 40.

Page 397. **Still, the HUAC:** John Cogley, *Report on Blacklisting*, vol. 1, pp. 218–20, 215–17. Sayre, *Running Time*, p. 78.

Page 397. **Movies have different:** Sayre, *Running Time*, pp. 178, 199.

Pages 398–99. **The most peculiar:** Nathaniel Branden, *Who Is Ayn Rand?*, pp. 150 73.

Pages 399–400. **She submitted her:** Ibid., pp. 175–82, 190, 192–3.

Page 400. **"I see," said:** Ibid., p. 195. Ayn Rand, *The Fountainhead*, p. 198 (1952).

Page 400. **Miss Rand spent:** Sayre, *Running Time*, p. 74. Branden, *Who Is Ayn Rand?*, pp. 198–9. Rand, *The Fountainhead*, p. 687.

Page 401. **Most of the reviews:** Branden, *Who Is Ayn Rand?*, pp. 204, 207.

Page 401. **She finished her:** Mervyn LeRoy, *Take One*, p. 153. Branden, *Who Is Ayn Rand?*, p. 211. Kanfer, *Journal of the Plague Years*, p. 82.

Page 401. **Miss Rand provided:** Cogley, *Report on Blacklisting*, pp. 1–11.

Page 402. **No Communist propagandist:** Larry Swindell, *The Last Hero: A Biography of Gary Cooper*, p. 264.

Page 402. **To Miss Rand:** Branden, *Who Is Ayn Rand?*, p. 213. Swindell, *The Last Hero*, pp. 267–73.

Page 403. **Cooper repeatedly told:** Swindell, *The Last Hero*, pp. 282–3.

Page 403. **The Fountainhead proved:** Sayre, *Running Time*, pp. 74–8.

Page 403. **Roberto Rossellini probably:** Joseph Henry Steele, *Ingrid Bergman*, p. 168. Ingrid Bergman and Alan Burgess, *My Story*, p. 240.

Pages 403–5. **Rossellini needed no:** Bergman and Burgess, *My Story*, pp. 241–3, 245–7, 249, 257, 259, 264.

Page 405. **Rossellini was determined:** Steele, *Ingrid Bergman*, p. 197.

Page 405. **Roberto would give:** Bergman and Burgess, *My Story*, p. 281.

Pages 405–6. **Rossellini apparently thought:** Steele, *Ingrid Bergman*, pp. 173, 204. Bergman and Burgess, *My Story*, pp. 269, 287–8.

Pages 406–7. **I went into:** Steele, *Ingrid Bergman*, pp. 183–4, 186, 205, 224, 226. Bergman and Burgess, *My Story*, 298, 310, 312.

Pages 407–9. **Steele, the public:** Steele, *Ingrid Bergman*, pp. 254–62. Bergman and Burgess, *My Story*, p. 343.

Page 409. **Hughes was determined:** Dore Schary, *Heyday*, p. 246.

Page 410. **Senator Edwin C. Johnson:** Bergman and Burgess, *My Story*, pp. 331–2.

Pages 410–11. **In his seventy-ninth:** Nigel Hamilton, *The Brothers Mann*, pp. 347–51, 356–7, 352–4. Anthony Heilbut, *Exiled in Paradise*, p. 301.

Page 411. **Heinrich agreed:** Hamilton, *The Brothers Mann*, pp. 357–8, 360–4. Heilbut, *Exiled in Paradise*, pp. 309–10.

Chapter 12 Farewells (1950).

Page 415. **Gloria Swanson was:** Gloria Swanson, *Swanson on Swanson*, p. 465 (1981).

Page 415. **So Miss Swanson:** Maurice Zolotow, *Billy Wilder in Hollywood*, pp. 161, 57.

Page 416. **Billy Wilder, of course:** Ibid., pp. 126–8, 131, 133, 151.

Page 417. **Real Wilder movies:** Otto Preminger, *Preminger: An Autobiography*, p. 108. Charles Higham, *Marlene*, p. 237.

Page 418. **It was originally:** Zolotow, *Billy Wilder*, p. 159. Bob Thomas, *Golden Boy: The Untold Story of William Holden*, p. 70 (1984).

Page 418. **There are several:** Tom Wood, *The Bright Side of Billy Wilder, Primarily*, p. 98.

Page 418. **But Sunset Boulevard:** Ibid., p. 99. Zolotow, *Billy Wilder*, p. 165. Swanson, *Swanson*, p. 500.

Page 419. **As so often happened:** Zolotow, *Billy Wilder*, pp. 159–60.

Page 419. **For the role:** Patricia Bosworth, *Montgomery Clift*, pp. 160, 176. Thomas, *Golden Boy*, pp. 68, 71. Zolotow, *Billy Wilder*, p. 162.

Page 420. **Brackett hated:** Thomas, *Golden Boy*, p. 71. Zolotow, *Billy Wilder*, p. 166.

Page 420. **Gloria Swanson was:** Swanson, *Swanson*, p. 498.

Page 421. **But there was:** Zolotow, *Billy Wilder*, pp. 166–8.

Page 421. **William Randolph Hearst:** W. A. Swanberg, *Citizen Hearst*, pp. 511–16. Anita Loos, *Kiss Hollywood Good-by*, p. 141 (1975).

Page 422. **Once, when Hearst:** Swanberg, *Citizen Hearst*, pp. 305, 489. Marion Davies, *The Times We Had*, pp. 268–9 (1977). Loos, *Kiss Hollywood Good-by*, p. 145.

Page 422. **Despite Hearst's pretensions:** Swanberg, *Citizen Hearst*, pp. 515, 518.

Page 422. **On New Year's Eve:** Loos, *Kiss Hollywood Good-by*, p. 146.

Page 423. **In attaching:** Helen Gahagan Douglas, *A Full Life*, pp. 299, 314. David Halberstam, *The Powers That Be*, p. 260ff.

Page 423. **The Supreme Court:** Edward Dmytryk, *It's a Hell of a Life but Not a Bad Living*, p. 127.

Page 423. **Dalton Trumbo and:** Bruce Cook, *Dalton Trumbo*, p. 208.

Page 424. **To Alvah Bessie:** Alvah Bessie, *Inquisition in Eden*, pp. 23, 250, 253.

Page 424. **After two weeks:** Cook, *Dalton Trumbo*, p. 209. Dmytryk, *Hell of a Life*, p. 135.

Page 424. **The prisoners' physical:** Cook, *Dalton Trumbo*, pp. 214–15. Dmytryk, *Hell of a Life*, p. 135. Lester Cole, *Hollywood Red*, pp. 314, 319. Ring Lardner, Jr., *The Lardners*, p. 328.

Page 425. **The most unusual:** Bessie, *Inquisition in Eden*, p. 58. Cole, *Hollywood Red*, p. 321.

Page 425. **Dalton Trumbo, once:** Cook, *Dalton Trumbo*, pp. 217–18.

Page 426. **The most extraordinary:** Cole, *Hollywood Red*, p. 316.

Page 426. **It was no secret:** *New York Times*, Nov. 20, 1970. Cole, *Hollywood Red*, pp. 317, 209. Lardner, *The Lardners*, p. 322.

Page 427. **So time passed:** Cole, *Hollywood Red*, p. 340. Victor S. Navasky, *Naming Names*, pp. 225–35. Kanfer, *A Journal of the Plague Years*, p. 132.

Pages 427–28. **Of all the beautiful:** Kitty Kelly, *Elizabeth Taylor: The Last Star*, pp. 37–41, 62–7, 70–4.

Page 429. **Look at that:** Frank MacShane, *The Life of Raymond Chandler*, p. 171.

Page 429. **The fat bastard:** Donald Spoto, *The Dark Side of Genius: The Life of Alfred Hitchcock*, pp. 341–3. John Russell Taylor, *Hitch*, p. 192.

Page 429. **One of the writers:** Raymond Chandler, *Raymond Chandler Speaking*, p. 132, quoted in William Luhr, *Raymond Chandler and Film*, p. 82. MacShane, *Raymond Chandler*, p. 175.

Page 430. **When Hitchcock read:** Spoto, *Dark Side*, pp. 344, 352.

Page 430. **The only "flaws":** François Truffaut, *Hitchcock*, p. 146.

Page 431. **Chandler, of course:** MacShane, *Raymond Chandler*, p. 177.

Page 431. **Walker's former wife:** Axel Madsen, *William Wyler*, p. 301.

Page 431. **Just a few months:** Diane Johnson, *Dashiell Hammett*, pp. 3–5, 228–30.

Page 431. **Despite all these:** Ibid., pp. 227, 239–40, 243. Lillian Hellman, *An Unfinished Woman*, p. 229 (1970).

Page 432. **The authorities in:** Johnson, *Dashiell Hammett*, pp. 3–4, 9.

Page 432. **In the last year:** Dika Newlin, *Schoenberg Remembered*, p. 337.

Page 433. **Harry Cohn, who:** Bob Thomas,

King Cohn, pp. 78, 243. Perhaps it is worth noting that this identical anecdote is told about a 19th-century Scottish industrialist named John Tennant in Angela Lambert, *Unquiet Souls*, p. 18.

Page 433. **This was, in a sense:** Kevin Starr, *Inventing the Dream: California Through the Progressive Era*, pp. 330–2.

Page 433. **Now, in this new time:** Cecil B. DeMille, *Autobiography*, pp. 398–9.

Page 434. ***Quo Vadis* was:** Gary Carey, *All the Stars in Heaven*, p. 286. John Huston, *An Open Book*, p. 198.

Page 434. **Huston began casting:** Mervyn LeRoy, *Take One*, pp. 170–2.

Page 434n. **LeRoy had overseen:** Kenneth L. Geist, *Pictures Will Talk: The Life and Films of Joseph L. Mankiewicz*, p. 98.

Page 435. **But how could:** LeRoy, *Take One*, pp. 174–5. Huston, *An Open Book*, p. 199.

Page 435. **And so, in the years:** Daniel Blum, *A New Pictorial History of the Talkies*, rev. by John Kobal, p. 213. Michel Laclos, *Le Fantastique au Cinéma*, p. 196.

Page 435. **Such films were:** Garth Jowett, *Film: The Democratic Art*, pp. 356–7.

Page 436. **Beyond all such:** Michael Wood, *America in the Movies*, pp. 169–78.

Page 436. **Hollywood's like Egypt:** Ben Hecht, *A Child of the Century*, p. 467. Charles Lockwood, *The Guide to Hollywood and Beverly Hills*, pp. 14ff. Ken Schessler, *This is Hollywood*, pp. 21ff.

Page 437. **On the other hand:** Starr, *Inventing the Dream*, p. 295. Dale Pollock, "Born in a Barn: How Hollywood Finally Got a Movie Museum," *PSA magazine*, February 1984.

Page 437. **Louis B. Mayer:** Bosley Crowther, *Hollywood Rajah*, p. 326. Stephen Farber and Marc Green, *Hollywood Dynasties*, pp. 75–6.

Page 437. **Darryl F. Zanuck:** Leonard Mosley, *Zanuck*, pp. 346–60. Farber and Green, *Hollywood Dynasties*, pp. 86–116.

Page 438. **Jack Warner:** Farber and Green, *Hollywood Dynasties*, pp. 38–40.

Page 438. **Sam Goldwyn:** Arthur Marx, *Goldwyn*, pp. 358–9. Stephen Birmingham, *"The Rest of Us,"* pp. 366–7.

Page 438. **David Selznick:** Bob Thomas, *Selznick*, pp. 278–305. Farber and Green, *Hollywood Dynasties*, pp. 79–81.

Page 438. **Jennifer Jones:** Farber and Green, *Hollywood Dynasties*, p. 81. *New York Times*, Nov. 11, 1967.

Page 438. **Many succumbed:** *Lauren Bacall,*

By Myself, pp. 253–5. Larry Ceplair and Steven Englund, *The Inquisition in Hollywood,* p. 419. Victor S. Navasky, *Naming Names,* p. 371.

Page 438. **And Ingrid Bergman:** *New York Times,* Aug. 31, 1982. Oriana Fallaci, "Ingrid, A Study in Courage," *Washington Post,* Sept. 5, 1982.

Page 439. **But there are:** *New York Times,* Dec. 31, 1982.

Page 439. **TV has been:** *Village Voice,* May 21, 1985.

Page 440. **As for Ronald Reagan:** Lou Cannon, *Reagan,* p. 66.

Page 440. **His divorce had:** Ronald Reagan and Richard C. Hubler, *Where's the Rest of Me?,* pp. 265, 280–6. Cannon, *Reagan,* p. 92.

Page 441. **That paid Reagan:** Cannon, *Reagan,* pp. 353–5.

BIBLIOGRAPHY

Acuña, Rodolfo. *Occupied America: A History of Chicanos.* New York: Harper & Row, 1981.

Agee, James. *Agee on Film.* 2 vols. New York: Grosset & Dunlap/Universal Library, 1969.*

Aherne, Brian. *A Dreadful Man.* Assisted by George Sanders and Benita Hulme. New York: Simon & Schuster, 1979.

Alexander, Franz, Samuel Eisenstein, and Martin Grotjahn. *Psychoanalytic Pioneers.* New York: Basic Books, 1966.

Allen, Fred. *Treadmill to Oblivion.* Boston: Atlantic/Little, Brown, 1954.

Allyson, June. *June Allyson.* With Frances Spatz Leighton. New York: Putnam, 1982.

Anderson, Clinton H. *Beverly Hills Is My Beat.* Englewood Cliffs, N.J.: Prentice-Hall, 1960.

Anger, Kenneth. *Kenneth Anger's Hollywood Babylon.* San Francisco: Straight Arrow, 1975; New York: Dell, 1981.

————. *Kenneth Anger's Hollywood Babylon II.* New York: Dutton, 1984; New York: NAL/Plume, 1985.

Antheil, George. *Bad Boy of Music.* Garden City, N.Y.: Doubleday, 1945.

Arce, Hector. *The Secret Life of Tyrone Power.* New York: Morrow, 1979; New York: Bantam, 1980.

Astor, Mary. *A Life on Film.* New York: Delacorte, 1971.

————. *My Story: An Autobiography.* Garden City, N.Y.: Doubleday, 1959.

Bacall, Lauren. *Lauren Bacall, By Myself.* New York: Knopf, 1979.

Bailyn, Bernard. *See* Fleming, Donald.

Baker, Carlos. *Ernest Hemingway: A Life Story.* New York: Scribner, 1969.

Baldwin, James. *The Devil Finds Work: An Essay.* New York: Dial, 1976.

Barlett, Donald L., and James B. Steele. *Empire: The Life, Legend, and Madness of Howard Hughes.* New York: Norton, 1979.

Barnett, Lincoln. *Writing for Life.* Sixteen profiles including Jerry Giesler and Billy Wilder. New York: Sloan Associates, 1951.

Barrymore, Diana, and Gerold Frank. *Too Much, Too Soon.* New York: Holt, 1957.

Barrymore, Lionel. *We Barrymores.* As told to Cameron Shipp. New York: Grosset & Dunlap, 1951.

Baxter, Anne. *Intermission: A True Story.* New York: Putnam, 1976; New York: Ballantine, 1978.

Baxter, John. *The Hollywood Exiles.* New York: Taplinger, 1976.

Bazin, André. *The Cinema of Cruelty, from Buñuel to Hitchcock.* Edited and introduced by François Truffaut. Translated by Sabine d'Estrée and Tiffany Fliss. New York: Seaver, 1972.

————. *Orson Welles: A Critical View.* Foreword by François Truffaut. Profile by Jean Cocteau. Translated by Jonathan Rosenbaum. New York: Harper & Row, 1978.

Beck, Calvin Thomas. *Scream Queens: Heroines of the Horrors.* New York: Macmillan, 1978.

Bedford, Sybille. *Aldous Huxley: A Biography.* New York: Knopf, 1974.

Behlmer, Rudy. *Inside Warner Bros. (1935–1951).* Selected, edited, and annotated by Rudy Behlmer. New York: Viking, 1985.

Behrman, S. N. *People in a Diary: A Memoir.* Boston: Little, Brown, 1972.

Bellamann, Henry. *Kings Row.* New York: Simon & Schuster, 1940.

Benchley, Nathaniel. *Humphrey Bogart.* Boston: Little, Brown, 1975.

————. *Robert Benchley: A Biography.* New York: McGraw-Hill, 1955.

Bentley, Eric, ed. *Thirty Years of Treason: Ex-*

* I list paperback reprints only when those are the editions that I used.

cerpts from Hearings Before the House Committee on Un-American Activities, 1938–1968. New York: Viking, 1971.

Bentley, Eric. See Brecht, Bertolt.

Bergen, Candice. Knock Wood. New York: Simon & Schuster/Linden, 1984.

Bergman, Ingrid, and Alan Burgess. Ingrid Bergman: My Story. New York: Delacorte, 1980; New York: Dell, 1981.

Berman, Susan. Easy Street. New York: Dial, 1981.

Bessie, Alvah. Inquisition in Eden. New York: Macmillan, 1965.

Bessy, Maurice. Charlie Chaplin. Translated by Jane Brenton. New York: Harper & Row, 1985.

Birmingham, Stephen. California Rich. New York: Simon & Schuster, 1980.

———. "The Rest of Us": The Rise of America's Eastern European Jews. Boston: Little, Brown, 1984.

Bishop, Jim. The Mark Hellinger Story: A Biography of Broadway. New York: Appleton-Century-Crofts, 1952.

Biskind, Peter. Seeing Is Believing: How Hollywood Taught Us to Stop Worrying and Love the Fifties. New York: Pantheon, 1983.

Bloom, Claire. Limelight and After: The Education of an Actress. New York: Harper & Row, 1982; New York: Penguin, 1983.

Blotner, Joseph. Faulkner: A Biography. 2 vols. New York: Random House, 1974.

Bluestone, George. Novels into Film. Baltimore: Johns Hopkins Press, 1957; Los Angeles and Berkeley: University of California Press, n.d.

Blum, Daniel. See Kobal, John.

Bogdanovich, Peter. Fritz Lang in America. New York: Praeger, 1969.

———. Pieces of Time. New York: Arbor House/Esquire, n.d.

Bookspan, Martin, and Ross Yockey. André Previn: A Biography. Garden City, N.Y.: Doubleday, 1981.

Borie, Marcia. See Wilkerson, Tichi.

Borsten, Orin. See Wilde, Meta Carpenter.

Bosworth, Allan R. America's Concentration Camps. New York: Norton, 1967.

Bosworth, Patricia. Montgomery Clift. New York: Harcourt Brace Jovanovich, 1978; New York: Bantam, 1979.

Branden, Nathaniel. Who Is Ayn Rand? An Analysis of the Novels of Ayn Rand. With a Biographical Essay by Barbara Branden. New York: Random House, 1962.

Brecht, Bertolt. Poems, 1913–1956. Edited by John Willett and Ralph Manheim. New York: Methuen, 1976.

———. Seven Plays by Bertolt Brecht. Edited by Eric Bentley. New York: Grove, 1961.

———. Short Stories, 1921–1946. Edited by John Willett and Ralph Manheim. Translated by Yvonne Kapp, Hugh Rorrison, Anthony Tatlow. London and New York: Methuen, 1983.

Brenner, Marie. Going Hollywood. New York: Delacorte, 1978.

Brodsly, David. L.A. Freeway: An Appreciative Essay. Berkeley and Los Angeles: University of California Press, 1981.

Brooks, Louise. Lulu in Hollywood. New York: Knopf, 1982.

Brosnan, John. The Horror People. New York: St. Martin's Press, 1976; New York: Plume, 1977.

Brossard, Chandler, ed. The Scene Before You: A New Approach to American Culture. New York: Rinehart, 1955.

Brough, James. See Hopper, Hedda.

Brownlow, Kevin. The Parade's Gone By. New York: Knopf, 1968; Berkeley and Los Angeles: University of California Press, n.d.

Buñuel, Luis. My Last Sigh. Translated by Abigail Israel. New York: Knopf, 1983.

Bürgin, Hans, and Hans-Otto Mayer. Thomas Mann: A Chronicle of His Life. Translated by Eugene Dobson. Birmingham: University of Alabama Press, 1969.

Burrows, Abe. Honest Abe. Boston: Atlantic/Little, Brown, 1980.

Cagney, James. Cagney by Cagney. Garden City, N.Y.: Doubleday, 1976.

Cain, James M. The Postman Always Rings Twice. New York: Knopf, 1934; New York: Vintage, 1978.

Cannon, Lou. Reagan. New York: Putnam, 1982.

Capra, Frank. The Name Above the Title: An Autobiography. New York: Macmillan, 1971; New York: Belvedere, 1982.

Carey, Gary. All the Stars in Heaven: Louis B. Mayer's M-G-M. New York: Dutton, 1981.

———. Judy Holliday: An Intimate Life Story. New York: Seaview, 1982.

———. More About All About Eve: A Colloquy by Gary Carey with Joseph L. Mankiewicz, Together with His Screenplay, All About Eve. New York: Random House, 1972.

Carpenter, Humphrey. W. H. Auden: A Biography. Boston: Houghton Mifflin, 1981.

Carringer, Robert L. The Making of Citizen Kane. Berkeley and Los Angeles: University of California Press, 1985.

Castro, Tony. Chicano Power: The Emergence of Mexican America. New York: Saturday Review Press, 1974.

Caute, David. *The Great Fear: The Anti-Communist Purge Under Truman and Eisenhower.* New York: Simon & Schuster, 1978.

Cavell, Stanley. *The World Viewed: Reflections on the Ontology of Film.* Cambridge, Mass.: Harvard University Press, 1979.

Ceplair, Larry, and Steven Englund. *The Inquisition in Hollywood: Politics in the Film Community, 1930–1960.* Garden City, N.Y.: Doubleday/Anchor, 1980.

Chandler, Raymond. *The Big Sleep.* New York: Knopf, 1939; New York: Ballantine, 1971.

———. *The Blue Dahlia.* Includes "Lost Fortnight: A Memoir," by John Houseman. Carbondale: University of Southern Illinois Press, 1976; New York: Popular Library, n.d.

———. *Farewell, My Lovely.* New York: Knopf, 1940; New York: Penguin, 1949.

———. *The Little Sister.* Boston: Houghton Mifflin, 1949.

———. *Raymond Chandler Speaking.* Edited by Dorothy Gardiner and Katherine Sorley Walker. Boston: Houghton Mifflin, 1962.

———. *Selected Letters of Raymond Chandler.* Edited by Frank MacShane. New York: Columbia University Press, 1981.

Chaplin, Charles. *My Autobiography.* New York: Simon & Schuster, 1964.

Chaplin, Charles, Jr. *My Father, Charlie Chaplin.* With N. and M. Rau. New York: Random House, 1960.

Cimen, Michel. *Kazan on Kazan.* New York: Viking, 1974.

Clarens, Carlos. *An Illustrated History of the Horror Film.* New York: Capricorn, 1967.

Cogley, John. *Report on Blacklisting.* 2 vols. New York: Fund for the Republic, 1956.

Cole, Lester. *Hollywood Red: The Autobiography of Lester Cole.* Palo Alto, Cal.: Ramparts Press, 1981.

Conant, Michael. *Antitrust in the Motion Picture Industry: Economic and Legal Analysis.* Berkeley and Los Angeles: University of California Press, 1960.

Cook, Bruce. *Brecht in Exile.* New York: Holt, Rinehart & Winston, 1982.

———. *Dalton Trumbo.* New York: Scribner, 1977.

Cook, Fred J. *The Secret Rulers: Criminal Syndicates and How They Control the U.S. Underworld.* New York: Duell, Sloan & Pearce, 1966.

Cooper, Jackie. *Please Don't Shoot My Dog: The Autobiography of Jackie Cooper.* With Dick Kleiner. New York: Morrow, 1981; New York: Berkley, 1982.

Copland, Aaron, and Vivian Perlis. *Copland.* New York: St. Martin's/Marek, 1984.

Corliss, Richard, ed. *The Hollywood Screen Writers.* New York: Avon, 1972.

———. *Talking Pictures: Screenwriters in the American Cinema.* Woodstock, N.Y.: Overlook, 1974.

Cowie, Peter. *A Ribbon of Dreams: The Cinema of Orson Welles.* South Brunswick, N.J.: A. S. Barnes, 1973; (retitled *The Cinema of Orson Welles*), New York: Da Capo, 1983.

Craft, Robert. *See* Stravinsky, Igor.

Crawford, Christina. *Mommie Dearest.* New York: Morrow, 1978; New York: Berkley, 1979.

Crowther, Bosley. *Hollywood Rajah: The Life and Times of Louis B. Mayer.* New York: Holt, Rinehart & Winston, 1960.

Culhane, John. *Walt Disney's Fantasia.* New York: Harry N. Abrams, 1983.

Curtis, James. *Between Flops: A Biography of Preston Sturges.* New York: Harcourt Brace, 1982; New York: Limelight, 1984.

Dali, Salvador. *The Secret Life of Salvador Dali.* Translated by Haakon Chevalier. New York: Dial, 1942.

———. *The Unspeakable Confessions of Salvador Dali.* As told to André Parinaud. Translated by Harold J. Salemson. New York: Morrow, 1976.

Dan, Uri. *See* Eisenberg, Dennis.

Daniel, Oliver. *Stokowski, A Counterpoint of View.* New York: Dodd, Mead, 1982.

Dardis, Tom. *Some Time in the Sun.* New York: Scribner, 1976.

Darvi, Andrea. *Pretty Babies: An Insider's Look at the World of the Hollywood Child Star.* New York: McGraw-Hill, 1983.

Davies, Marion. *The Times We Had: Life with William Randolph Hearst.* Foreword by Orson Welles. Indianapolis and New York: Bobbs-Merrill, 1975; New York: Ballantine, 1977.

Davis, Bette. *The Lonely Life: An Autobiography.* New York: Putnam, 1962.

Demetz, Peter, ed. *Brecht: A Collection of Critical Essays.* Englewood Cliffs, N.J.: Prentice-Hall, 1962.

De Havilland, Olivia. *Every Frenchman Has One.* New York: Random House, 1962.

DeMille, Cecil B. *Autobiography.* Edited by Donald Hayne. Englewood Cliffs, N.J.: Prentice-Hall, 1959.

Dickens, Homer. *The Films of Marlene Dietrich.* Secaucus, N.J.: Citadel, 1968.

Didion, Joan. *Play It as It Lays.* New York: Farrar, Straus & Giroux, 1970.

———. *Slouching Towards Bethlehem.* New York: Farrar, Straus & Giroux, 1968.

———. *The White Album.* New York: Simon & Schuster, 1979.

Dies, Martin. *Martin Dies' Story*. New York: Bookmailer, 1963.

DiOrio, Al. *Barbara Stanwyck: A Biography*. New York: Coward, McCann, 1984; New York: Berkley, 1985.

Dmytryk, Edward. *It's a Hell of a Life but Not a Bad Living: A Hollywood Memoir*. New York: Times Books, 1978.

Douglas, Helen Gahagan. *A Full Life*. Garden City, N.Y.: Doubleday, 1982.

Dreiser, Helen. *My Life with Dreiser*. Cleveland and New York: World, 1951.

Dunne, Father George H. *Hollywood Labor Dispute: A Study in Immorality*. Los Angeles: Conference Publishing Co., undated.

Dunne, Philip. *Take Two: A Life in Movies and Politics*. New York: McGraw-Hill, 1980.

Eames, Hugh. *Sleuths, Inc.: Studies of Problem Solvers*. Philadelphia: Lippincott, 1976.

Edwards, Anne. *Vivien Leigh: A Biography*. New York: Simon & Schuster, 1977.

Eells, George. *Hedda and Louella*. New York: Putnam, 1972; (retitled *Malice in Wonderland*), New York: Critic's Choice, 1985.

Eisenberg, Dennis, Uri Dan, and Eli Landau. *Meyer Lansky: Mogul of the Mob*. New York and London: Paddington, 1979.

Eisenstein, Samuel. *See* Alexander, Franz.

Eisler, Hanns. *Composing for the Films*. New York: Oxford University Press, 1979.

———. *Hanns Eisler, A Rebel in Music: Selected Writings*. Edited by Manfred Grabs. Translated by Marjorie Meyer. New York: International Publishers, 1978.

Ephron, Henry. *We Thought We Could Do Anything: The Life of Screenwriters Phoebe and Henry Ephron*. New York: Norton, 1977.

Epstein, Edward Z. *See* Morella, Joe.

Erens, Patricia. *The Jew in American Cinema*. Bloomington: Indiana University Press, 1984.

Esslin, Martin. *Brecht: The Man and His Work*. Garden City, N.Y.: Doubleday, 1960; New York: Anchor, 1961.

Evans, Mark. *Soundtrack: The Music of the Movies*. New York: Hopkinson & Blake, 1975; New York: Da Capo, 1979.

Ewen, Frederic. *Bertolt Brecht: His Life, His Art, and His Times*. New York: Citadel, 1967; 1969.

Faith, William Robert. *Bob Hope: A Life in Comedy*. New York: Putnam, 1982.

Farber, Stephen, and Marc Green. *Hollywood Dynasties*. New York: Putnam/Delilah, 1984.

Farrell, Barry. *Pat and Roald*. New York: Random House, 1969.

Fast, Julius. *See* Henreid, Paul.

Faulkner, William. *Collected Stories*. Contains Faulkner's only Hollywood story, "Golden Land." New York: Random House, 1950.

Fitzgerald, F. Scott. *Afternoon of an Author: A Selection of Uncollected Stories and Essays*. New York: Scribner, 1957.

———. *The Crack-Up: With Other Uncollected Pieces, Note-Books and Unpublished Letters*. Edited by Edmund Wilson. New York: New Directions, 1945; 1956.

———. *The Last Tycoon*. New York: Scribner, 1941.

Flamini, Roland. *Ava: A Biography*. New York: Coward, McCann, 1983; New York: Berkley, 1984.

———. *Scarlett, Rhett, and a Cast of Thousands: The Filming of Gone with the Wind*. New York: Macmillan, 1975; New York: Collier, 1978.

Fleming, Donald, and Bernard Bailyn, eds. *The Intellectual Migration: Europe and America, 1930–1960*. Cambridge, Mass.: Harvard University Press, 1969.

Flynn, Errol. *My Wicked, Wicked Ways*. New York: Putnam, 1959; New York: Berkley, 1974.

Fonda, Henry. *Fonda: My Life*. As told to Howard Teichmann. New York: New American Library, 1981.

Fontaine, Joan. *No Bed of Roses: An Autobiography*. New York: Morrow, 1978.

Fowler, Gene. *Good Night, Sweet Prince: The Life and Times of John Barrymore*. New York: Viking, 1944.

Fraenkel, Heinrich. *See* Manvell, Roger.

Francisco, Charles. *Gentleman: The William Powell Story*. New York: St. Martin's Press, 1985.

Frank, Gerold. *Judy*. New York: Harper & Row, 1975.

———. *See* Barrymore, Diana.

———. *See* Graham, Sheilah.

Freedland, Michael. *The Two Lives of Errol Flynn*. New York: Morrow, 1979; New York: Bantam, 1980.

———. *The Warner Brothers*. New York: St. Martin's Press, 1983.

Fried, Albert. *The Rise and Fall of the Jewish Gangster in America*. New York: Holt, Rinehart & Winston, 1980.

Frischauer, Willi. *Behind the Scenes of Otto Preminger*. New York: Morrow, 1973.

Fry, Varian. *Surrender on Demand*. New York: Random House, 1945.

Fryer, Jonathan. *Isherwood: A Biography*. Garden City, N.Y.: Doubleday, 1978.

Fuchs, Daniel. *West of the Rockies.* New York: Knopf, 1971.

Gader, June Rose. *L.A. Live: Profiles of a City.* New York: St. Martin's Press, 1980.

Garnett, Tay. *Light Your Torches and Pull Up Your Tights.* With Fredda Dudley Balling. New Rochelle, N.Y.: Arlington House, 1973.

Geduld, Harry M., ed. *Authors on Film.* Bloomington: Indiana University Press, 1972.

Geist, Kenneth L. *Pictures Will Talk: The Life and Films of Joseph L. Mankiewicz.* New York: Scribner, 1978.

Gellerman, William. *Martin Dies.* New York: John Day, 1944.

Giesler, Jerry. *The Jerry Giesler Story.* As told to Pete Martin. New York: Simon & Schuster, 1960.

Gifford, Dennis. *Karloff: The Man, the Monster, the Movies.* New York: Curtis, 1973.

Gold, Mary Jayne. *Crossroads Marseilles/1940: A Memoir.* Garden City, N.Y.: Doubleday, 1980.

Goodman, Ezra. *The Fifty-Year Decline and Fall of Hollywood.* New York: Simon & Schuster, 1961.

Goodman, Walter. *The Committee: The Extraordinary Career of the House Committee on Un-American Activities.* New York: Farrar, Straus & Giroux, 1968.

Gottlieb, Robert. *See* Wiley, Peter.

Graham, Sheilah. *Confessions of a Hollywood Columnist.* New York: Morrow, 1969.

———, and Gerold Frank. *Beloved Infidel: The Education of a Woman.* New York: Henry Holt, 1958.

Green, Marc. *See* Farber, Stephen.

Greenberg, Joel. *See* Higham, Charles.

Grotjahn, Martin. *See* Alexander, Franz.

Guiles, Fred Lawrence. *Hanging on in Paradise.* New York: McGraw-Hill, 1975.

———. *Tyrone Power, The Last Idol.* Garden City, N.Y.: Doubleday, 1979; New York: Berkley, 1980.

Gunther, John. *Inside U.S.A.* New York: Harper & Brothers, 1947.

Gussow, Mel. *Don't Say Yes Until I Finish Talking: A Biography of Darryl F. Zanuck.* Garden City, N.Y.: Doubleday, 1971; New York: Da Capo, 1980 (retitled *Darryl F. Zanuck: Don't Say Yes Until I Finish Talking*).

Halberstam, David. *The Powers That Be.* New York: Knopf, 1979.

Hamilton, Nigel. *The Brothers Mann.* New Haven, Conn.: Yale University Press, 1979.

Hammett, Dashiell. *Five Complete Novels: Red Harvest, The Dain Curse, The Maltese Falcon,* *The Glass Key, The Thin Man.* New York: Avenel Books, 1980.

———. *The Continental Op.* Edited by Steven Marcus. New York: Vintage, 1975.

———. *The Maltese Falcon.* New York: Knopf, 1930; New York: Vintage, 1972.

Haun, Harry, ed. *The Movie Quote Book.* New York: Lippincott & Crowell, 1980.

Haver, Ronald. *David O. Selznick's Hollywood.* New York: Knopf, 1980.

Havoc, June. *More Havoc.* New York: Harper & Row, 1980.

Hayes, Helen. *A Gift of Joy.* With Lewis Funke. New York: Evans, 1965.

Hayman, Ronald. *Brecht: A Biography.* New York: Oxford University Press, 1983.

Hayward, Brooke. *Haywire.* New York: Knopf, 1977; New York: Bantam, 1978.

Hecht, Ben. *A Child of the Century.* New York: Simon & Schuster, 1954.

Heilbut, Anthony. *Exiled in Paradise: German Refugee Artists and Intellectuals in America from the 1930's to the Present.* New York: Viking, 1983.

Heinsheimer, Hans W. *Best Regards to Aida: The Defeats and Victories of a Music Man on Two Continents.* New York: Knopf, 1968.

Hellman, Lillian. *An Unfinished Woman: A Memoir.* Boston: Little, Brown, 1969; New York: Bantam, 1970.

———. *Pentimento.* Boston: Little, Brown, 1973; New York: Signet, 1974.

———. *Scoundrel Time.* Boston: Little, Brown, 1976; New York: Bantam, 1977.

Hemingway, Ernest. *Selected Letters, 1917–1961.* Edited by Carlos Baker. New York: Scribner, 1981.

Henreid, Paul. *Ladies' Man: An Autobiography.* With Julius Fast. New York: St. Martin's Press, 1984.

Higham, Charles. *Bette: The Life of Bette Davis.* New York: Macmillan, 1981; New York: Dell, 1982.

———. *Celebrity Circus.* New York: Delacorte, 1979.

———. *Charles Laughton: An Intimate Biography.* Garden City, N.Y.: Doubleday, 1976.

———. *Errol Flynn: The Untold Story.* Garden City, N.Y.: Doubleday, 1980.

———. *The Films of Orson Welles.* Berkeley and Los Angeles: University of California Press, 1970.

———. *Hollywood at Sunset.* New York: Saturday Review Press, 1972.

———. *Kate: The Life of Katharine Hepburn.* New York: Norton, 1975.

———. *Marlene: The Life of Marlene Dietrich*. New York: Norton, 1977.

———. *Orson Welles: The Rise and Fall of an American Genius*. New York: St. Martin's Press, 1985.

———. *Sisters: The Story of Olivia de Havilland and Joan Fontaine*. New York: Coward, McCann, 1984.

———. *Warner Brothers*. New York: Scribner, 1975.

———, and Joel Greenberg. *Hollywood in the Forties*. New York: A. S. Barnes, 1968.

Hill, James. *Rita Hayworth: A Memoir*. New York: Simon & Schuster, 1983.

Hirsch, Foster. *Film Noir: The Dark Side of the Screen*. San Diego: A. S. Barnes, 1981; New York: Da Capo, 1983.

Hirschhorn, Clive. *Gene Kelly: A Biography*. Chicago: Regnery, 1974.

Hobson, Laura Z. *Gentleman's Agreement*. New York: Simon & Schuster, 1947.

———. *Laura Z.: A Life*. New York: Arbor House, 1983.

Hoopes, Roy. *Americans Remember the Home Front: An Oral Narrative*. New York: Hawthorn, 1977.

———. *Cain: The Biography of James M. Cain*. New York: Holt, Rinehart & Winston, 1982.

Hope, Bob. *Have Tux, Will Travel: Bob Hope's Own Story*. As told to Pete Martin. New York: Simon & Schuster, 1954.

———. *I Never Left Home*. New York: Simon & Schuster, 1944.

———. *The Road to Hollywood: My 40-Year Love Affair with the Movies*. With Bob Thomas. Garden City, N.Y.: Doubleday, 1977.

Hopper, Hedda. *From Under My Hat*. Garden City, N.Y.: Doubleday, 1952.

———, and James Brough. *The Whole Truth and Nothing But*. Garden City, N.Y.: Doubleday, 1963.

House Committee on Education and Labor. *Hearings Before a Special Subcommittee on Education and Labor, House of Representatives, 80th Congress, Pursuant to H. Res. 111*. Washington, D.C.: U.S. Printing Office, 1948.

House Committee on Un-American Activities. *Hearings Regarding the Communist Infiltration of the Motion Picture Industry . . . Before the Committee on Un-American Activities, House of Representatives, 80th Congress*. Washington, D.C.: U.S. Printing Office, 1947.

Houseman, John. *Final Dress*. New York: Simon & Schuster, 1983.

———. *Front and Center: A Memoir, 1942–1955*. New York: Simon & Schuster, 1979; New York: Touchstone, 1980.

———. *Run-Through*. New York: Simon & Schuster, 1972.

Houston, James D. *See* Houston, Jeanne Wakatsuki.

Houston, Jeanne Wakatsuki, and James D. Houston. *Farewell to Manzanar*. Boston: Houghton Mifflin, 1973.

Hubler, Richard C. *See* Reagan, Ronald.

Huston, John. *An Open Book*. New York: Knopf, 1980; New York: Ballantine, 1981.

Hyams, Joe. *Bogie: The Biography of Humphrey Bogart*. New York: New American Library, 1966; New York: Signet, 1967.

Hyman, Stanley Edgar. *Nathanael West*. Minneapolis: University of Minnesota Press, 1962.

Insdorf, Annette. *Indelible Shadows: Film and the Holocaust*. New York: Vintage, 1983.

Irons, Peter. *Justice at War: The Story of the Japanese American Internment Cases*. New York: Oxford University Press, 1983.

Isherwood, Christopher. *My Guru and His Disciple*. New York: Farrar, Straus & Giroux, 1980; New York: Penguin, 1981.

Jacoby, Russell. *The Repression of Psychoanalysis: Otto Fenichel and the Political Freudians*. New York: Basic Books, 1983.

Jay, Martin. *Adorno*. Cambridge, Mass.: Harvard University Press, 1984.

Jennings, Dean. *We Only Kill Each Other: The Life and Bad Times of Bugsy Siegel*. Englewood Cliffs, N.J.: Prentice-Hall, 1967.

Jobes, Gertrude. *Motion Picture Empire*. Hamden, Conn.: Archon Books, 1966.

Johnson, Diane. *Dashiell Hammett: A Life*. New York: Random House, 1983.

Johnson, Nunnally. *The Letters of Nunnally Johnson*. Edited by Dorris Johnson and Ellen Leventhal. New York: Knopf, 1981.

Jones, Ernest. *The Life and Work of Sigmund Freud*. 3 vols. New York: Basic Books, 1953–57.

Jowett, Garth. *Film: The Democratic Art*. Boston: Little, Brown, 1976.

Kael, Pauline. *The Citizen Kane Book*. Includes the shooting script of the film. Boston: Little, Brown, 1971; New York: Limelight, 1984.

———. *Kiss Kiss Bang Bang*. Boston: Atlantic/Little, Brown, 1968.

Kahn, Gordon. *Hollywood on Trial: The Story of the Ten Who Were Indicted*. New York: Boni & Gaer, 1948.

Kahrl, William L. *Water and Power: The Conflict over Los Angeles' Water Supply in the Owens Valley*. Berkeley and Los Angeles: University of California Press, 1982.

Kaminsky, Stuart. *Coop: The Life and Legend of Gary Cooper.* New York: St. Martin's Press, 1980.

——. *John Huston: Maker of Magic.* Boston: Houghton Mifflin, 1978.

Kanfer, Stefan. *A Journal of the Plague Years.* New York: Atheneum, 1973.

Kanin, Garson. *Hollywood: Stars and Starlets, Tycoons and Flesh-Peddlers, Moviemakers and Moneymakers, Frauds and Geniuses, Hopefuls and Has-Beens, Great Lovers and Sex Symbols.* New York: Viking, 1974.

——. *Movieola.* New York: Simon & Schuster, 1979.

Keats, John. *Howard Hughes: A Biography.* New York: Random House, 1966.

——. *You Might As Well Live: The Life and Times of Dorothy Parker.* New York: Simon & Schuster, 1970.

Kelly, Kitty. *Elizabeth Taylor: The Last Star.* New York: Simon & Schuster, 1981.

Kempton, Murray. *America Comes of Middle Age: Columns 1950–1962.* Boston: Little, Brown, 1963.

——. *Part of Our Time: Some Monuments and Ruins of the Thirties.* New York: Delta, 1955.

Kerr, Laura. *See* Rivkin, Allen.

Keyes, Evelyn. *Scarlett O'Hara's Younger Sister.* New York: Lyle Stuart, 1977; New York: Fawcett Crest, 1978.

King, Stephen. *Stephen King's Danse Macabre.* New York: Everest House, 1981.

Kirkpatrick, Sidney D. *A Cast of Killers.* New York: Dutton, 1986.

Knef, Hildegard. *The Gift Horse: Report on a Life.* Translated by David Anthony Palastanga. New York: McGraw-Hill, 1971; New York: Dell, 1972.

Knight, Arthur. *The Liveliest Art: A Panoramic History of the Movies.* New York: Macmillan, 1957.

Kobal, John. *Rita Hayworth: The Time, the Place, and the Woman.* New York: Norton, 1977.

——, ed. *A New Pictorial History of the Talkies.* By Daniel Blum; revised and enlarged by John Kobal. New York: Putnam, 1958; New York: Perigee, 1982 (revised).

Koch, Howard. *As Time Goes By: Memoirs of a Writer.* New York: Harcourt Brace Jovanovich, 1979.

——, et al. *Casablanca: Script and Legend.* Woodstock, New York: Overlook, 1973.

Korda, Michael. *Charmed Lives: A Family Romance.* New York: Random House, 1979.

Kracauer, Siegfried. *From Caligari to Hitler: A Psychological History of German Film.* Princeton, N.J.: Princeton University Press, 1947; 1966.

Laclos, Michel. *Le Fantastique au Cinéma.* Paris: Pauvert, 1958.

Lake, Veronica. *Veronica.* With Donald Bain. New York: Citadel, 1971.

Lamarr, Hedy. *Ecstasy and Me: My Life as a Woman.* New York: Bartholomew House, 1966.

Lambert, Gavin. *GWTW: The Making of Gone with the Wind.* Boston: Atlantic/Little, Brown, 1973.

Lamour, Dorothy. *My Side of the Road.* As told to Dick McInnes. Englewood Cliffs, N.J.: Prentice-Hall, 1980.

Lanchester, Elsa. *Elsa Lanchester Herself.* New York: St. Martin's Press, 1983.

Landau, Eli. *See* Eisenberg, Dennis.

Lardner, Ring, Jr. *The Lardners: My Family Reconsidered.* New York: Harper & Row, 1976.

Lasky, Jesse, Jr. *Whatever Happened to Hollywood?* New York: Funk & Wagnalls, 1975.

Lasky, Jesse L. *I Blow My Own Horn.* With Don Weldon. Garden City, N.Y.: Doubleday, 1957.

Latham, Aaron. *Crazy Sundays: F. Scott Fitzgerald in Hollywood.* New York: Viking, 1971.

Lawson, John Howard. *Film: The Creative Process: The Search for an Audio-Visual Language and Structure.* New York: Hill & Wang, 1964.

Layman, Richard. *The Shadow Man: A Documentary Life of Dashiell Hammett.* New York: Harcourt Brace Jovanovich, 1981.

Leamer, Laurence. *As Time Goes By: The Life of Ingrid Bergman.* New York: Harper & Row, 1986.

——. *Make-Believe: The Story of Nancy and Ronald Reagan.* New York: Harper & Row, 1983.

Leaming, Barbara. *Orson Welles: A Biography.* New York: Viking, 1985.

Leigh, Janet. *There Really Was a Hollywood.* Garden City, N.Y.: Doubleday, 1984.

Leites, Nathan. *See* Wolfenstein, Martha.

LeRoy, Mervyn. *Take One.* As told to Dick Kleiner. New York: Hawthorn, 1974.

Levant, Oscar. *The Memoirs of an Amnesiac.* New York: Putnam, 1965.

——. *A Smattering of Ignorance.* Garden City, N.Y.: Doubleday, 1940.

Light, James F. *Nathanael West: An Interpretive Study.* Evanston, Ill.: Northwestern University Press, n.d.

Lindsay, Cynthia. *Dear Boris: The Life of William Henry Pratt, a.k.a. Boris Karloff.* New York: Knopf, 1975.

Linet, Beverly. *Ladd: The Life, the Legend, the*

Legacy of Alan Ladd. New York: Arbor House, 1979; (retitled *Ladd: A Hollywood Tragedy*), New York: Berkley, 1980.

———. *Susan Hayward: Portrait of a Survivor*. New York: Atheneum, 1980; New York: Berkley, 1981.

Lingeman, Richard R. *Don't You Know There's a War On? The American Home Front, 1941–1945*. New York: Putnam, 1970.

Lockwood, Charles. *Dream Palaces: Hollywood at Home*. New York: Viking, 1981.

———. *The Guide to Hollywood and Beverly Hills*. New York: Crown, 1984.

Loos, Anita. *A Girl Like I*. New York: Viking, 1966.

———. *Kiss Hollywood Good-by*. New York: Viking, 1974; New York: Ballantine, 1975.

Luhr, William. *Raymond Chandler and Film*. New York: Ungar, 1982.

Lyon, James K. *Bertolt Brecht in America*. Princeton, N.J.: Princeton University Press, 1980.

McBride, Joseph. *Hawks on Hawks*. Berkeley and Los Angeles: University of California Press, 1982.

———. *Orson Welles, Actor and Director*. New York: Harvest/HBJ, 1977.

McCabe, John. *Charlie Chaplin*. Garden City, N.Y.: Doubleday, 1978.

McClelland, Doug, ed. *Hollywood on Ronald Reagan: Friends and Enemies Discuss Our President, the Actor*. Winchester, Mass.: Faber & Faber, 1983.

Macdonald, Dwight. *On Movies*. Englewood Cliffs, N.J.: Prentice-Hall, 1969; New York: Da Capo, 1981.

McGilligan, Patrick. *Cagney: The Actor as Auteur*. San Diego: A. S. Barnes, 1982.

MacShane, Frank. *The Life of Raymond Chandler*. New York: Dutton, 1976; New York: Penguin, 1978.

McWilliams, Carey. *The Education of Carey McWilliams*. New York: Simon & Schuster, 1979.

———. *A Mask for Privilege: Anti-Semitism in America*. Boston: Little, Brown, 1948.

———. *North from Mexico: The Spanish-Speaking People of the United States*. Philadelphia: Lippincott, 1949.

———. *Southern California Country: An Island on the Land*. New York: Duell, Sloan & Pearce, 1946.

———. *Witch Hunt: The Revival of Heresy*. Boston: Little, Brown, 1950.

Madsen, Axel. *Billy Wilder*. Bloomington: Indiana University Press, 1969.

———. *William Wyler: The Authorized Biography*. New York: Crowell, 1973.

Mailer, Norman. *The Deer Park*. New York: Putnam, 1955; New York: Perigee, 1981.

Malin, Irving. *Nathanael West's Novels*. Carbondale: Southern Illinois University Press, 1972.

Mann, Katia. *Unwritten Memories*. Edited by Elisabeth Von Plessen and Michael Mann. Translated by Hunter and Hildegarde Hannum. New York: Knopf, 1975.

Mann, Thomas. *Doctor Faustus: The Life of the German Composer Adrian Leverkühn as Told to a Friend*. Translated by H. T. Lowe-Porter. New York: Knopf, 1948.

———. *Essays of Three Decades*. Translated by H. T. Lowe-Porter. New York: Knopf, 1947.

———. *The Story of a Novel: The Genesis of Doctor Faustus*. Translated by Richard and Clara Winston. New York: Knopf, 1961.

Manso, Peter. *Mailer: His Life and Times*. New York: Simon & Schuster, 1985.

Manvell, Roger. *Chaplin*. Boston: Little, Brown, 1974.

———, and Heinrich Fraenkel. *The German Cinema*. New York: Praeger, 1971.

Martin, Jay. *Nathanael West: The Art of His Life*. New York: Farrar, Straus & Giroux, 1970.

———, ed. *Nathanael West: A Collection of Critical Essays*. Englewood Cliffs, N.J.: Prentice-Hall, 1971.

Marx, Arthur. *Goldwyn: A Biography of the Man Behind the Myth*. New York: Norton, 1976.

Marx, Samuel. *Mayer and Thalberg: The Make-Believe Saints*. New York: Random House, 1975.

Massey, Raymond. *A Hundred Different Lives: An Autobiography*. Boston: Little, Brown, 1979.

Mast, Gerald. *Howard Hawks, Storyteller*. New York: Oxford University Press, 1982.

———. *The Movies in Our Midst: Documents in the Cultural History of Films in America*. Chicago: University of Chicago Press, 1982.

Mayer, Hans-Otto. *See* Bürgin, Hans.

Mayer, Martin. *About Television*. New York: Harper & Row, 1972.

Meryman, Richard. *Mank: The Wit, World, and Life of Herman Mankiewicz*. New York: Morrow, 1978.

Messick, Hank. *Lansky*. New York: Putnam, 1971.

Mills, Hilary. *Mailer: A Biography*. New York: Empire Books, 1982.

Minter, David. *William Faulkner: His Life and Work*. Baltimore: Johns Hopkins Press, 1980.

Mizener, Arthur. *The Far Side of Paradise: A Biography of F. Scott Fitzgerald*. Boston: Houghton Mifflin, 1951.

Moley, Raymond. *The Hays Office*. Indianapolis and New York: Bobbs-Merrill, 1945.

Monson, Karen. *Alma Mahler: Muse to Genius*. Boston: Houghton Mifflin, 1983.

Moore, Terry. *The Beauty and the Billionaire*. New York: Pocket Books, 1984.

Mordden, Ethan. *Movie Star: A Look at the Women Who Made Hollywood*. New York: St. Martin, 1983.

Morella, Joe, and Edward Z. Epstein. *Jane Wyman: A Biography*. New York: Delacorte, 1985.

———. *Rita: The Life of Rita Hayworth*. New York: Delacorte, 1983.

Morgan, Ted. *FDR: A Biography*. New York: Simon & Schuster, 1985.

Mosley, Leonard. *Zanuck: The Rise and Fall of Hollywood's Last Tycoon*. Boston: Little, Brown, 1984.

Muir, Florabel. *Headline Happy*. New York: Henry Holt, 1950.

Murphy, George. *"Say . . . Didn't You Used to Be George Murphy?"* With Victor Lasky. New York: Bartholomew House, 1970.

Nabokov, Nicholas. *Old Friends and New Music*. Boston: Atlantic/Little, Brown, 1951.

Naremore, James. *The Magic World of Orson Welles*. New York: Oxford University Press, 1978.

Navasky, Victor S. *Naming Names*. New York: Viking, 1980; New York: Penguin, 1981.

Negri, Pola. *Memoirs of a Star*. Garden City, N.Y.: Doubleday, 1970.

Newlin, Dika. *Schoenberg Remembered: Diaries and Recollections, 1938–1976*. New York: Pendragon, 1980.

Newquist, Roy. *Conversations with Joan Crawford*. Secaucus, N.J.: Citadel, 1980.

Niven, David. *Bring on the Empty Horses*. New York: Putnam, 1975; New York: Dell, 1976.

———. *The Moon's a Balloon*. New York: Putnam, 1972; New York: Dell, 1973.

Nolan, William F. *Hammett: A Life at the Edge*. New York: Congdon & Weed, 1983.

———. *John Huston: King Rebel*. Los Angeles: Sherbourne Press, 1965.

Olivier, Laurence. *Confessions of an Actor*. New York: Simon & Schuster, 1982; New York: Penguin, 1984.

Palmer, Lilli. *Change Lobsters and Dance: An Autobiography*. New York: Macmillan, 1975.

Parsons, Louella O. *The Gay Illiterate*. Garden City, N.Y.: Doubleday, 1944.

———. *Tell it to Louella*. New York: Putnam, 1961.

Payne, Robert. *The Great God Pan: A Biography of the Tramp Played by Charles Chaplin*. New York: Hermitage House, 1952.

Percy, Walker. *The Moviegoer*. New York: Knopf, 1961; New York: Avon, 1980.

Perelman, S. J. *The Last Laugh*. Includes an autobiographical fragment, "The Hindsight Saga." New York: Simon & Schuster, 1981.

———. *The Most of S. J. Perelman*. Includes much of *Crazy Like a Fox, Keep It Crisp, The Road to Miltown,* and other early works that are difficult to find. New York: Simon & Schuster, 1957.

Perlis, Vivian. *See* Copland, Aaron.

Pettit, Arthur G. *Images of the Mexican American in Fiction and Film*. College Station: Texas A & M Press, 1980.

Phillips, Cabell. *The 1940's: Decade of Triumph and Trouble*. New York: Macmillan, 1975.

———. *The Truman Presidency: The History of a Triumphant Succession*. New York: Macmillan, 1966.

Phillips, Gene D. *Hemingway and Film*. New York: Ungar, 1980.

Powdermaker, Hortense. *Hollywood: The Dream Factory*. Boston: Little, Brown, 1950.

Pratley, Gerald. *The Cinema of Otto Preminger*. New York: A. S. Barnes, 1971.

Preminger, Marion Hill. *All I Want Is Everything*. New York: Funk & Wagnalls, 1957.

Preminger, Otto. *Preminger: An Autobiography*. Garden City, N.Y.: Doubleday, 1977; New York: Bantam, 1978.

Price, Vincent, and V. B. Price. *Monsters*. New York: Grosset & Dunlap, 1981.

Purdy, Jim. *See* Roffman, Peter.

Quinn, Anthony. *The Original Sin: A Self-Portrait*. Boston: Little, Brown, 1972.

Rand, Ayn. *The Fountainhead*. Indianapolis and New York: Bobbs-Merrill, 1943; New York: Signet, 1952.

Rand, Christopher. *Los Angeles: The Ultimate City*. New York: Oxford University Press, 1967.

Reagan, Nancy. *Nancy*. With Bill Libby. New York: Morrow, 1980.

Reagan, Ronald, and Richard C. Hubler. *Where's the Rest of Me?* New York: Hawthorn, 1965; New York: Dell, 1981.

Reed, Rex. *Conversations in the Raw: Dialogues, Monologues, and Selected Short Subjects*. Cleveland and New York: World, 1969.

Reeves, Thomas C. *The Life and Times of Joe McCarthy: A Biography*. New York: Stein & Day, 1982.

Reinhardt, Gottfried. *The Genius: A Memoir of Max Reinhardt.* New York: Knopf, 1979.

Reit, Seymour. *Masquerade: The Amazing Camouflage Deceptions of World War II.* New York: Hawthorn, 1978.

Rivkin, Allen, and Laura Kerr. *Hello, Hollywood.* Garden City, N.Y.: Doubleday, 1962.

Roazen, Paul. *Freud and His Followers.* New York: Alfred A. Knopf, 1975.

Robbins, Jhan. *Front Page Marriage: Helen Hayes and Charles MacArthur.* New York: Putnam, 1982.

Robinson, David. *Chaplin: His Life and Art.* New York: McGraw-Hill, 1985.

Robinson, Edward G. *All My Yesterdays: An Autobiography.* With Leonard Spiegelgass. New York: Hawthorn, 1973.

Robinson, Edward G., Jr. *My Father, My Son.* With William Dufty. New York: Frederick Fell, 1958.

Robinson, Jill. *Bed/Time/Story.* New York: Random House, 1974; New York: Fawcett, n.d.

Roeburt, John. *"Get Me Giesler."* New York: Belmont, 1962.

Roffman, Peter, and Jim Purdy. *The Hollywood Social Problem Film: Madness, Despair, and Politics from the Depression to the Fifties.* Bloomington: Indiana University Press, 1981.

Rogers, Donald I. *Since You Went Away: From Rosie the Riveter to Bond Drives, World War II at Home.* New Rochelle, N.Y.: Arlington House, 1973.

Rollins, Peter C., ed. *Hollywood as Historian: American Film in a Cultural Context.* Lexington: University of Kentucky Press, 1983.

Rooney, Mickey. *I.E.: An Autobiography.* New York: Putnam, 1965.

Rosen, Charles. *Arnold Schoenberg.* New York: Viking, 1975.

Rosen, Marjorie. *Popcorn Venus: Women, Movies and the American Dream.* New York: Coward, McCann, 1973.

Rosenberg, Bernard, and David Manning White, eds. *Mass Culture: The Popular Arts in America.* Glencoe, Ill.: The Free Press, 1957.

Ross, Lillian. *Reporting.* Includes "Picture." New York: Simon & Schuster, 1969.

Rosten, Leo C. *Hollywood: The Movie Colony, The Movie Makers.* New York: Harcourt, Brace, 1941.

Rothman, William. *Hitchcock: The Murderous Gaze.* Cambridge, Mass.: Harvard University Press, 1982.

Rózsa, Miklós. *Double Life: The Autobiography of Miklós Rózsa.* New York: Hippocrene, 1983.

Rubinstein, Arthur. *My Many Years.* New York: Knopf, 1980.

Russell, Jane. *My Path and My Detours: An Autobiography.* New York: Franklin Watts, 1985.

Sale, Kirkpatrick. *Power Shift: The Rise of the Southern Rim and Its Challenge to the Eastern Establishment.* New York: Random House, 1975.

Samora, Julian, and Patricia Vandel Simon. *A History of the Mexican-American People.* Notre Dame, Ind.: Notre Dame University Press, 1977.

Sanders, George. *Memoirs of a Professional Cad.* New York: Putnam, 1960.

Sayre, Nora. *Running Time: Films of the Cold War.* New York: Dial, 1982.

Schary, Dore. *Heyday.* Boston: Little, Brown, 1979; New York: Berkley, 1981.

Schessler, Ken. *This Is Hollywood: An Unusual Movieland Guide.* La Verne, Cal.: Ken Schessler Productions, 1984.

Schickel, Richard. *D. W. Griffith: An American Life.* New York: Simon & Schuster, 1984.

———. *The Disney Version: The Life, Times, Art and Commerce of Walt Disney.* New York: Simon & Schuster, 1968.

———. *The Men Who Made the Movies: Interviews with Frank Capra, George Cukor, Howard Hawks, Alfred Hitchcock, Vincente Minnelli, King Vidor, Raoul Walsh, and William A. Wellman.* New York: Atheneum, 1975.

Schoenberg, Arnold. *Letters.* Edited by Erwin Stein. Translated by Eithne Wilkins and Ernst Kaiser. New York: St. Martin's Press, 1965.

Schulberg, Budd. *The Four Seasons of Success.* Garden City, N.Y.: Doubleday, 1972.

———. *Moving Pictures: Memories of a Hollywood Prince.* New York: Stein & Day, 1981.

———. *What Makes Sammy Run?* New York: Random House, 1941; New York: Viking, 1978.

Schumach, Murray. *The Face on the Cutting Room Floor: The Story of Movie and TV Censorship.* New York: Morrow, 1964.

Schwartz, Nancy Lynn. *The Hollywood Writers' Wars.* New York: Knopf, 1982.

Segal, Hyman R. *They Called Him Champ: The Story of Champ Segal and His Fabulous Era.* New York: Citadel, 1959.

Selznick, David O. *Memo from David O. Selznick.* Edited by Rudy Behlmer. New York: Viking, 1972.

Selznick, Irene Mayer. *A Private View.* New York: Knopf, 1983.

Shaw, Artie. *The Trouble with Cinderella: An Outline of Identity.* New York: Farrar, Straus & Young, 1952; New York: Da Capo, 1979.

Shepherd, Donald, and Robert F. Slatzer. *Bing Crosby: The Hollow Man*. New York: St. Martin's Press, 1981; New York: Pinnacle, 1982.

Shindler, Colin. *Hollywood Goes to War: Films and American Society, 1939–52*. Boston: Routledge & Kegan Paul, 1979.

Simmel, Ernst, ed. *Anti-Semitism: A Social Disease*. New York: International Universities Press, 1946.

Simon, Patricia Vandel. *See* Samora, Julian.

Sklar, Robert. *Movie-made America: A Cultural History of American Movies*. New York: Random House, 1975.

Skolsky, Sidney. *Don't Get Me Wrong—I Love Hollywood*. New York: Putnam, 1975.

Slatzer, Robert F. *See* Shepherd, Donald.

Slezak, Walter. *My Stomach Goes Travelling: An Irreverent Approach to the Holy Art of Cooking*. Garden City, N.Y.: Doubleday, 1979.

Smith, Jane S. *Elsie de Wolfe: A Life in the High Style*. New York: Atheneum, 1982.

Smith, Julia. *Aaron Copland: His Work and Contribution to American Music*. New York: Dutton, 1955.

Sontag, Susan. *Against Interpretation, and Other Essays*. New York: Farrar, Straus & Giroux, 1966.

———. *On Photography*. New York: Farrar, Straus & Giroux, 1977.

Sorrell, Herbert. *You Don't Choose Your Friends: The Memoirs of Herbert Knott Sorrell*. Interviewed by Elizabeth I. Dixon. Los Angeles: UCLA Oral History Project, 1963.

Sorrell, Walter. *Three Women: Lives of Sex and Genius*. Indianapolis and New York: Bobbs-Merrill, 1975.

Spender, Stephen, ed. *W. H. Auden: A Tribute*. Includes "The Poet and the Rake," by Robert Craft. New York: Macmillan, 1975.

Spoto, Donald. *The Dark Side of Genius: The Life of Alfred Hitchcock*. Boston: Little, Brown, 1983; New York: Ballantine, 1984.

Starr, Kevin. *Inventing the Dream: California Through the Progressive Era*. New York: Oxford University Press, 1985.

Steele, James B. *See* Barlett, Donald L.

Steele, Joseph Henry. *Ingrid Bergman: An Intimate Portrait*. New York: David McKay, 1959.

Stewart, Donald Ogden. *By a Stroke of Luck: An Autobiography*. New York and London: Paddington Press, 1975.

Stine, Whitney. *Mother Goddam: The Story of the Career of Bette Davis, With a Running Commentary by Bette Davis*. New York: Hawthorn, 1974; New York: Berkley, 1975.

Strait, Raymond. *Hollywood's Children*. New York: St. Martin's Press, 1982.

Strasberg, Susan. *Bittersweet*. New York: Putnam, 1980.

Strauss, Helen M. *A Talent for Luck: An Autobiography*. New York: Random House, 1979.

Stravinsky, Igor. *Poetics of Music: In the Form of Six Lessons*. Translated by Arthur Knodel and Ingolf Dahl. Cambridge, Mass.: Harvard University Press, 1947.

———. *Themes and Conclusions*. Berkeley and Los Angeles: University of California Press, 1982.

Stravinsky, Igor, and Robert Craft. *Conversations with Igor Stravinsky*. Berkeley and Los Angeles: University of California Press, 1980.

———. *Dialogues*. Garden City, N.Y.: Doubleday, n.d.; Berkeley and Los Angeles: University of California Press, 1982.

———. *Expositions and Developments*. Garden City, N.Y.: Doubleday, 1962.

———. *Memories and Commentaries*. Berkeley and Los Angeles: University of California Press, 1981.

Stravinsky, Vera, and Robert Craft. *Stravinsky: In Pictures and Documents*. New York: Simon & Schuster, 1978.

Stuckenschmidt, H. H. *Arnold Schoenberg*. Translated by Edith Temple Roberts and Humphrey Searle. New York: Grove, 1959.

Swan, Howard. *Music in the Southwest, 1825–1950*. San Marino, Cal.: The Huntington Library, 1952.

Swanberg, W. A. *Citizen Hearst: A Biography of William Randolph Hearst*. New York: Scribner, 1961.

———. *Dreiser*. New York: Scribner, 1965.

Swanson, Gloria. *Swanson on Swanson: An Autobiography*. New York: Random House, 1980; New York: Pocket Books, 1981.

Swindell, Larry. *Body and Soul: The Story of John Garfield*. New York: Morrow, 1975.

———. *Charles Boyer: The Reluctant Lover*. Garden City, N.Y.: Doubleday, 1983.

———. *The Last Hero: A Biography of Gary Cooper*. Garden City, N.Y.: Doubleday, 1980.

———. *Spencer Tracy: A Biography*. Cleveland and New York: World, 1969.

Szigeti, Joseph. *With Strings Attached: Reminiscences and Reflections*. New York: Knopf, 1947.

Talese, Gay. *The Kingdom and the Power*. Cleveland and New York: World, 1969.

Tansman, Alexandre. *Igor Stravinsky: The Man and His Music*. Translated by Thérèse and Charles Bleefield. New York: Putnam, 1949.

Taper, Bernard. *Balanchine: A Biography.* New York: Macmillan, 1973; New York: Collier, 1974.

Tateishi, John. *And Justice for All: An Oral History of the Japanese American Detention Camps.* New York: Random House, 1984.

Taylor, John Russell. *Hitch: The Life and Times of Alfred Hitchcock.* New York: Pantheon, 1978.

————. *Ingrid Bergman.* New York: St. Martin's Press, 1983.

————. *Strangers in Paradise: The Hollywood Émigrés, 1933–1950.* New York: Holt, Rinehart & Winston, 1983.

Terkel, Studs. *"The Good War."* New York: Pantheon, 1984.

Thomas, Bob. *Golden Boy: The Untold Story of William Holden.* New York: St. Martin's Press, 1983; New York: Berkley, 1984.

————. *Joan Crawford: A Biography.* New York: Simon & Schuster, 1978; New York, Bantam, 1979.

————. *King Cohn: The Life and Times of Harry Cohn.* New York: Putnam, 1967.

————. *Selznick.* Garden City, N.Y.: Doubleday, 1970; New York: Pocket Books, 1972.

————. *Walt Disney: An American Original.* New York: Simon & Schuster, 1976.

————. *See* Hope, Bob.

Thomas, Tony. *The Films of Olivia de Havilland.* Secaucus, N.J.: Citadel, 1983.

————. *The Films of Ronald Reagan.* Secaucus, N.J.: Citadel, 1980.

Thompson, Verita. *Bogie and Me: A Love Story.* With Donald Shepherd. New York: St. Martin's Press, 1982.

Thomson, David. *America in the Dark: The Impact of Hollywood Films on American Culture.* New York: Morrow, 1977.

Thomson, Virgil. *American Music Since 1910.* New York: Holt, Rinehart & Winston, 1971.

Tierney, Gene. *Self-Portrait.* With Mickey Herskowitz. New York: Wyden, 1979; New York: Berkley, 1980.

Tornabene, Lynn. *Long Live the King: A Biography of Clark Gable.* New York: Putnam, 1976.

Truffaut, François. *Hitchcock.* Originally *Le Cinéma Selon Hitchcock,* 1966. With the collaboration of Helen G. Scott. New York: Touchstone, 1967.

Trumbo, Dalton. *Additional Dialogue: Letters of Dalton Trumbo, 1942–1962.* Edited by Helen Manfull. New York: Evans, 1970.

————. *Johnny Got His Gun.* Philadelphia: Lippincott, 1939; New York: Bantam, 1967.

————. *The Time of the Toad: A Study of In-quisition in America and Two Related Pamphlets.* 1949. Reprint. New York: Harper & Row, 1972.

Turner, Lana. *Lana: The Lady, The Legend, The Truth.* New York: Dutton, 1982; New York: Pocket Books, 1983.

Tuska, John. *The Detective in Hollywood.* Garden City, N.Y.: Doubleday, 1978.

Tyler, Parker. *The Hollywood Hallucination.* New York: Simon & Schuster, 1944.

Ursini, James. *The Fabulous Life and Times of Preston Sturges, An American Dreamer.* New York: Curtis, 1973.

Viertel, Salka. *The Kindness of Strangers.* New York: Holt, Rinehart & Winston, 1969.

Völker, Klaus. *Brecht Chronicle.* Translated by Fred Wieck. New York: Seabury/Continuum, 1975.

Wallis, Hal, and Charles Higham. *Starmaker: The Autobiography of Hal Wallis.* Introduction by Katharine Hepburn. New York: Macmillan, 1980.

Walsh, Raoul. *Each Man in His Time.* New York: Farrar, Straus & Giroux, 1974.

Wansell, Geoffrey. *Haunted Idol: The Story of the Real Cary Grant.* New York: Morrow, 1984; New York: Ballantine, 1985.

Warner, Jack. *My First Hundred Years in Hollywood: An Autobiography.* With Dean Jennings. New York: Random House, 1965.

Warren, Doug. *James Cagney: The Authorized Biography.* New York: St. Martin's Press, 1983.

Warshow, Robert. *The Immediate Experience: Movies, Comics, Theatre, and Other Aspects of Popular Culture.* Garden City, N.Y.: Doubleday, 1962.

Weaver, John D. *Los Angeles: The Enormous Village, 1781–1981.* Santa Barbara, Cal.: Capra Press, 1980.

Weglyn, Michi. *Years of Infamy: The Untold Story of America's Concentration Camps.* New York: Morrow, 1976.

Weinberg, Herman. *The Lubitsch Touch.* New York: Dutton, 1968.

Werfel, Alma Mahler. *And the Bridge Is Love.* In collaboration with E. B. Ashton. New York: Harcourt, Brace, 1958.

West, Nathanael. *The Complete Works of Nathanael West.* New York: Farrar, Straus & Cudahy, 1957.

————. *The Day of the Locust.* 1939. Reprint. New York: New Directions, 1950.

————. *Miss Lonelyhearts.* 1933. Reprint. New York: New Directions, n.d.

White, David Manning. *See* Rosenberg, Bernard.

White, Eric Walter. *Igor Stravinsky: The Com-*

poser and His Works. Berkeley and Los Angeles: University of California Press, 1966.

White, G. Edward. *Earl Warren: A Public Life.* New York: Oxford University Press, 1982.

Wilde, Meta Carpenter, and Orin Borsten. *A Loving Gentleman: The Love Story of William Faulkner and Meta Carpenter.* New York: Simon & Schuster, 1976.

Wiley, Peter, and Robert Gottlieb. *Empires in the Sun: The Rise of the New American West.* New York: Putnam, 1982.

Wilk, Max. *The Wit and Wisdom of Hollywood.* New York: Atheneum, 1971.

Wilkerson, Tichi, and Marcia Borie. *The Hollywood Reporter: The Golden Years.* New York: Coward, McCann, 1984.

Willett, John, ed. *Brecht on Theatre: The Development of an Aesthetic.* Translated by John Willett. Hill & Wang, 1964.

Winston, Richard. *Thomas Mann: The Making of an Artist, 1875–1911.* New York: Knopf, 1981.

Winters, Shelley. *Shelley, Also Known as Shirley.* New York: Morrow, 1980.

Wodehouse, P. G. *The World of Mr. Mulliner.* New York: Taplinger, 1972.

Wolfenstein, Martha, and Nathan Leites. *Movies: A Psychological Study.* Glencoe, Ill.: The Free Press, 1950.

Wood, Michael. *America in the Movies: or, "Santa Maria, It Had Slipped My Mind."* New York: Basic Books, 1975.

Wood, Tom. *The Bright Side of Billy Wilder, Primarily.* Garden City, N.Y.: Doubleday, 1970.

Works Progress Administration. *Los Angeles: A Guide to the City and Its Environs.* Compiled by workers of the Writers Program of the Work Projects Administration in Southern California. Los Angeles: WPA, 1941. Revised edition. New York: Hastings House, 1951.

Works Progress Administration. *The WPA Guide to California.* Original title: *California: A Guide to the Golden State.* New York: WPA, 1939; New York: Pantheon, 1984.

Wyman, David S. *The Abandonment of the Jews: America and the Holocaust, 1941–1945.* New York: Pantheon, 1984.

Yablonsky, Lewis. *George Raft.* New York: McGraw-Hill, 1974.

Yockey, Ross. *See* Bookspan, Martin.

Zierold, Norman. *The Moguls.* New York: Coward, McCann, 1969.

Zolotow, Maurice. *Billy Wilder in Hollywood.* New York: Putnam, 1977.

———. *Shooting Star: A Biography of John Wayne.* New York: Simon & Schuster, 1974; New York: Pocket Books, 1975.

Zuckmayer, Carl. *A Part of Myself: Portrait of an Epoch.* Translated by Richard and Clara Winston. New York: Harcourt Brace Jovanovich, 1970.

Zukor, Adolph. *The Public Is Never Wrong: The Autobiography of Adolph Zukor.* With Dale Kramer. New York: Putnam, 1953.

INDEX